AF413429

# Maurizio CATT

Pirelli HangarBicocca

Marsilio Arte

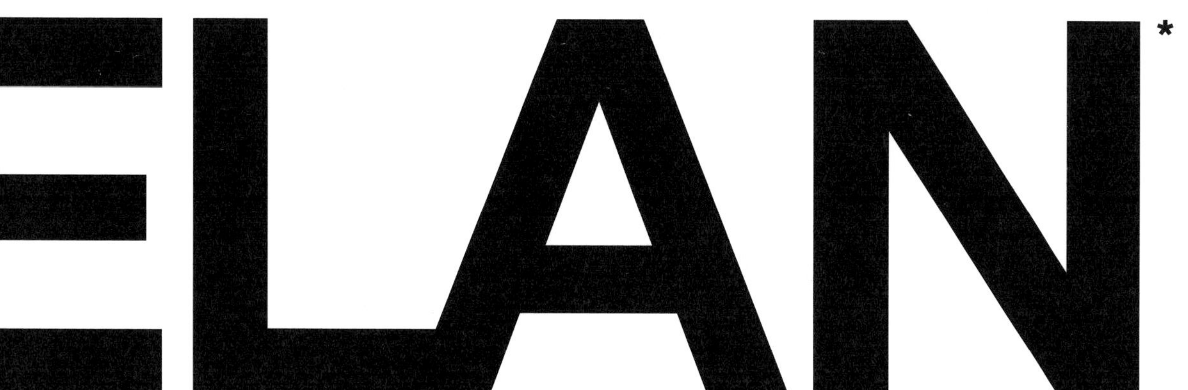

# ELAN*

* [Beware of Yourself]

edited by Roberta Tenconi and Vicente Todolí
with Tatiana Palenzona

*Beware of Yourself* is Pirelli HangarBicocca's third volume devoted to the work of Maurizio Cattelan, one of the most internationally renowned living Italian artists. The editorial project took shape following his solo show "Maurizio Cattelan. Breath Ghosts Blind," inaugurated in 2021 in the Navate space, marking his significant return to a Milanese institution after more than a decade—a city with which the artist has establi- shed  a deep and ongoing dialogue. On that occasion, two volumes had already been published: one dedicated to the exhibition and a second, *INDEX*, bringing together for the first time all the interviews conducted by Cattelan over twenty years.

*Beware of Yourself* is a further step forward on this research journey into the artist's work, offering a broad and multifaceted vision of Cattelan's development from the 1980s until the present. The volume gathers all his works, exhibitions, and projects, providing an organic and comprehensive narrative of his practice, recounted in an unprecedented way through his own voice.

This publication also testifies to the active and ongoing commitment of Pirelli HangarBicocca in supporting contemporary artistic research, by developing long-term projects that ex- tend well beyond the exhibition moment. *Beware of Yourself* is a concrete example of this: a way to offer the public and the artistic community a complex portrait of one of the most influential Italian creative figures of our time.

Marco Tronchetti Provera
*Chairman*
*Pirelli HangarBicocca*

This book is a journey into Maurizio Cattelan's thoughts, an immersion in the reflections that have fueled almost forty years of artistic practice, from his earliest experiments in the second half of the eighties until the present. Through his works, exhibitions, collaborative projects, and writings, the volume recomposes a speculative constellation in which each element becomes a reason to question reality, subvert conventions, and explore the deeper mechanisms of identity and systems of power. Defying any traditional definitions or categories—neither a *catalogue raisonné*, monograph, autobiography, personal diary, nor sourcebook, but all these together—the book is shaped as a fluid organism, a mental map narrated in the first person, in which it is the artist's voice alone that speaks.

Like a stream of consciousness, with no clearly defined beginning or end, the book invites to move freely through the contents, organized around thematic reflections in which Cattelan expresses himself on concepts, processes, biographical episodes, and ironic and radical visions. The structure of the volume reflects a tension between order and disorder: each of the texts deals in depth, but avoiding any hierarchical order, with concepts recurrent in his investigations, followed as their possible development by a selection of works, exhibitions or special projects, presented chronologically and again through the artist's own words. The book also brings together Cattelan's writings between 1987 and the present that have appeared in various publications, recomposed, together with his speeches at the conferral of honorary degrees, in a narrative that renews their significance.

Like an exploration venturing along new paths, the book invites to move freely following the directions suggested by the works and the insights they elicit. The perspective shifts continually, tracing Cattelan's artistic and human development in ever-changing ways.

A rich apparatus completes the volume. Alongside a detailed list of Maurizio Cattelan's works and solo exhibitions, and a chronology that for the first time orders the dates and salient episodes in the artist's life, the book includes the bibliography of his writings and interviews. Many of the words that make up texts in this book originate from the answers given in these conversations—over three hundred in more than thirty-five years—often conducted with or through the voices of friends, collaborators or ghostwriters, along with new insights collected specifically for this publication. Deconstructed and recom-

posed into new writings, his statements form an intellectual self-portrait while reflecting on the collective culture, history, and society of the last forty years.
This volume, born in close collaboration with the Maurizio Cattelan's Archive and Marsilio Arte, is not only the record and sharing of an artistic journey, but a critical device. It invites to question the human condition and what lies hidden behind images, roles, and masks. As in the interplay between mirrors, even the title, *Beware of Yourself*, is a warning that evokes the most profound significance of Cattelan's work, an exhortation to look within while looking outward.

Roberta Tenconi
Vicente Todolí
*with* Tatiana Palenzona

[Table of Contents]

[Note to the Reader]

With very few exceptions, limited editions are excluded
from the analytical presentation of the artist's production.
Apart from some experiments from the 1980s, each piece
is presented with its essential technical data and an image
of its first exhibition appearance; in significant cases,
subsequent installations are also included.
Captions and technical details (including measurements
with decimal numbers) follow the catalogue of the
exhibition at the Solomon R. Guggenheim Museum
in New York (*Maurizio Cattelan: All* [New York: Solomon
R. Guggenheim Museum, 2016]). In some cases, however,
the technical data have been refined and updated
through constant consultation with the Maurizio
Cattelan's Archive.
Current locations of the works are indicated only
in the case of public and private museum collections.
The artist's writings that cite the source at the end
of each text have been republished in their entirety;
in the absence of an official English-language edition,
they were translated specially for this volume.

There's a saying of Marcello's that goes more or less like this:    13
"There's no solution because there's no problem."

It was almost four o'clock, and with the other kids in kindergarten I was looking forward to going home. A curious adult inquired, amused: "What do you want to be when you grow up?" I clearly recall the tiny benches where we sat, and the emotion and discomfort I felt at such an important decision. Roberto answered confidently: "A teacher." I mulled over the question for a moment and mumbled: "A waiter." Unconsciously I had reviewed various occupations without any logical thread, without any purpose, being only interested in getting it over with as soon as I could. It was a period when at any rate I knew "what I was doing." But needs are like fruit, they take time to ripen. At a certain point a beast grew inside me. It had no name and it led me into galleries to ask strange questions. Later I started doodling and now, when people ask me what I do, I feel terribly abashed, not knowing what to say. Legitimate doubt? Trying to find reassurance, I asked around in artistic circles, but there they work too hard to ask such idiotic questions. Slowly, one insight at a time, I build up my project, I realize what I want, ask myself questions, make checks, and cultivate doubt. The project as the statute of life and not of form. The written word and its articulation in subjects, predicates, and object complements has always obsessed me, often making me unhappy. I have always preferred to think out loud to myself, to start a thought and let it expand without control or grammatical restraints, until it becomes nothing, and there just remains the idea of an inexplicable and incomprehensible idea. And sometimes it separates out and materializes in front of me.
And now the automatic project.
It's useless for me to see and even less to use language, unless some sort of thought of the kinds of things or processes I might encounter has been inserted into my system.
Seeing, thinking, elaborating, smoothing, reorganizing, synthesizing, absorbing, and expelling: voiding oneself be able to fill oneself again. The will has never rendered good services to anyone.
What I have written is completely made up from beginning to end, but it matches the truth.

["Pensieri molesti," text published in *Gran Bazaar Harper's Italia*, no. 68 (June–July 1989): 96]

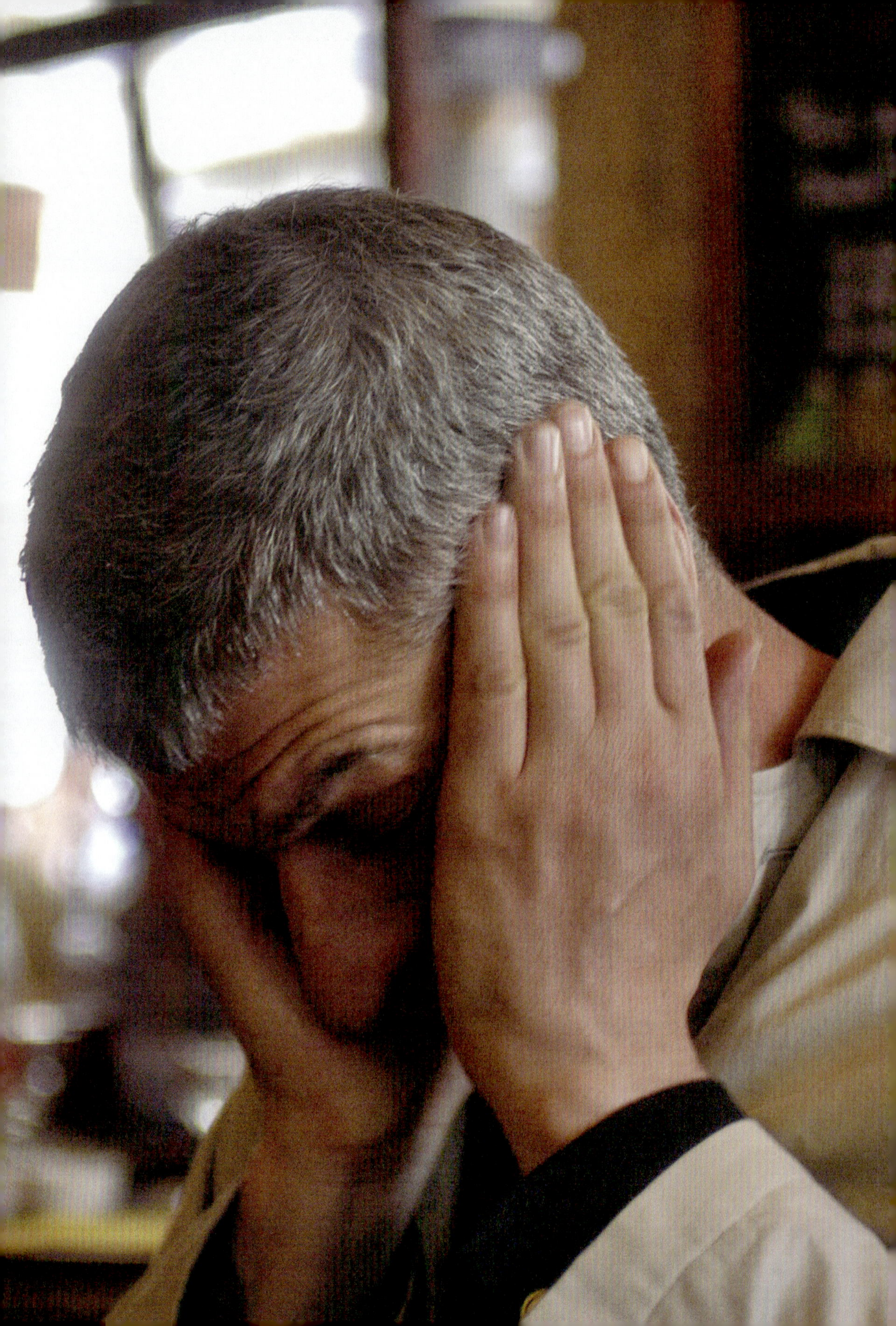

The age we live in makes everybody very well informed and, as a consequence, very emotionally moved by whatever happens, whether they're good or evil things. Art is about forgetting all these feelings, good and bad, and trying to understand what will last longest, which symbols will remain in history. I think art should be critical and the most intense expression of its time. To understand history, we look at artworks, and we'll go on doing this also in the future.

What matters in art is the possibility of permanence, the ability to impress other people's minds. In a way it's like possessing them. I believe that every artist is obsessed with this thought and that art has the task above all of being significant for as long as possible. The work of artists is increasingly about the power of the images they produce: if they're effective, they can last for centuries.

Essentially, what an effective artwork or a successful exhibition does is to treat the familiar as unfamiliar in a very straightforward way. This enables us as artists to draw out the absurdity of our world. What has been concealed by normality is exposed, bringing surprises, and surprise mixed with absurdity usually results in humor. I feel it's extremely important for people to see below and beyond the surface and the appearances of my work. To work well, an image has to be pointed, and in some cases even shocking. But at the same time, very good works—and I'm not necessarily including my own—have a lot more to offer than meets the eye. In that space of discomfort between the surface and the depths lies the secret of a masterpiece.

Good taste and morals are not the right yardstick to apply to art. Wherever the limit is, the first goal of art has to be to move it a little further away, just one centimeter at a time. The best works never make moral judgments, they don't take sides. They exist to convey the tragic complexity of the banal. Art doesn't have a direct and unique purpose, otherwise it's a problem already solved, and there's nothing interesting about it. I've always believed that if a work can be reduced to a clear and crystalline message, it's artistically dead. Art, unlike advertising, mustn't sell anything, but—and this is even more important—it mustn't mean anything either. It's a way of getting away from a one-sided vision. It's a series of unanswered questions condensed into a physical manifestation. If you can raise questions through a work, you can consider yourself an artist.

Art chases the unknown. In art, the themes aren't really important. What counts is the ability to strike other people's imagination, so that they can all find their own meaning in the work before them. Where one person sees death, another sees life, due to the simple fact that each of us has different background experiences by which we interpret reality. The beauty of art is precisely this: the reflections made to arrive at a final form do not count, it only matters if that form is so independent of the thought that created it that it is rich in meanings for others. Independent of thought, but not this alone, because art is a marriage of the conscious with the unconscious. A work of art is a symbolic action. It always combines rational thought and unconscious matter; in fact underlying it is the urgent need to face the darkest parts of oneself, whatever the consequences.

Art is also a way to get rid of your problems by giving them to others in the form of works. In its uselessness, it embodies a thaumaturgical power, for both whoever makes it and whoever observes it. Besides, the moment a work exists in the world, it no longer belongs to the artist, but becomes public property. An artwork is never just the artist's individual experience. It's an object present in the world. It has a moral, social, and practical identity, and is an entity recognized by others and relating to others. So it is not just a physical object, but also a social one. And the greater its significance to others apart from the artist, the more significant it is. In fact, I think that works of art have a lot in common with relics. Regardless of all reasonableness, we are willing to see in them a power that goes beyond their physical presence. Like relics, art requires an act of faith. Both work like magic objects.

So art cannot be closed in on itself. Instead it has to be a magnetic field that attracts the energies of artists into space, and perhaps into cities, enabling them to circulate. It's that sort of magnetism that I'm looking for; it's like a chemical reaction. At the same time, I believe it's important to always keep open a discussion about what art is, what it should do and its ethical value, much more than its economic value. My hope is that for every person who thinks that art is bullshit, there will be another who can explain to the first person where its real value lies.

Art is many things. All contradictory yet all true. Engaging, provocative, exclusive, documentary, participatory, incomprehensible. But I have no idea what art is, after all. I'm an electrician who attended evening school, and in the end, by sitting in the back row of the classroom and copying, I actually managed to get a piece of paper saying I'd qualified.

16

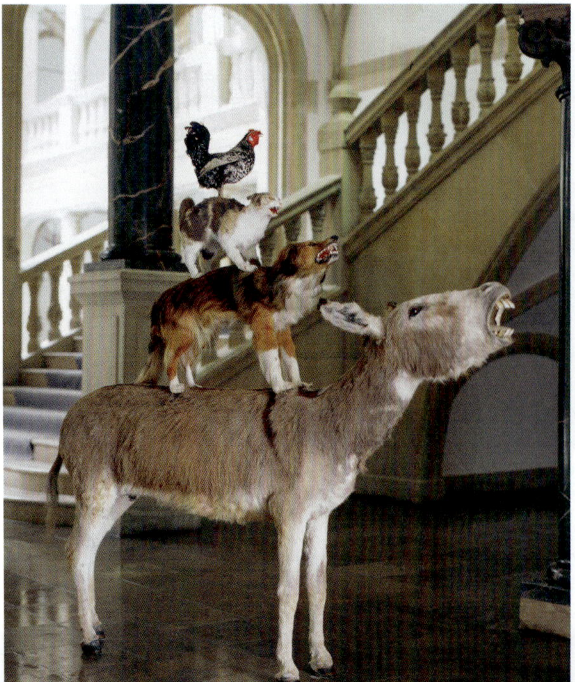

[1] *Love Saves Life*, 1995
Taxidermied donkey, dog, cat and rooster
190 × 120 × 60 cm

This work, with four stuffed animals (a rooster, a cat, a dog, and a donkey), is based on a fairy-tale by the Brothers Grimm, *The Musicians of Bremen*. Each of the creatures runs away from its master, who threatens to kill it because it has grown old and useless. They band together and travel to the town to become musicians. Along the way they trick some thieves out of their hideaway and take over their home to live in it in freedom. I thought that this tale pointed up a socialist moral about how we can put together creativity and friendship and win all our battles.

[1.1] *Love Saves Life*, 1995
"Skulptur. Projekte in Münster 1997," curated by Kasper König, Münster, June 22–September 28, 1997 (group show), installation at the Westfälisches Landesmuseum für Kunst und Kulturgeschichte

[1.2] *Love Saves Life*, 1995
"Una collezione trasversale. Da Duchamp a Nino Calos, da Cattelan a Entang Wiharso," curated by Fabio Cavallucci, ALT Arte Lavoro Territorio, Alzano Lombardo, June 27, 2009–January 10, 2010 (group show)

[1.1]

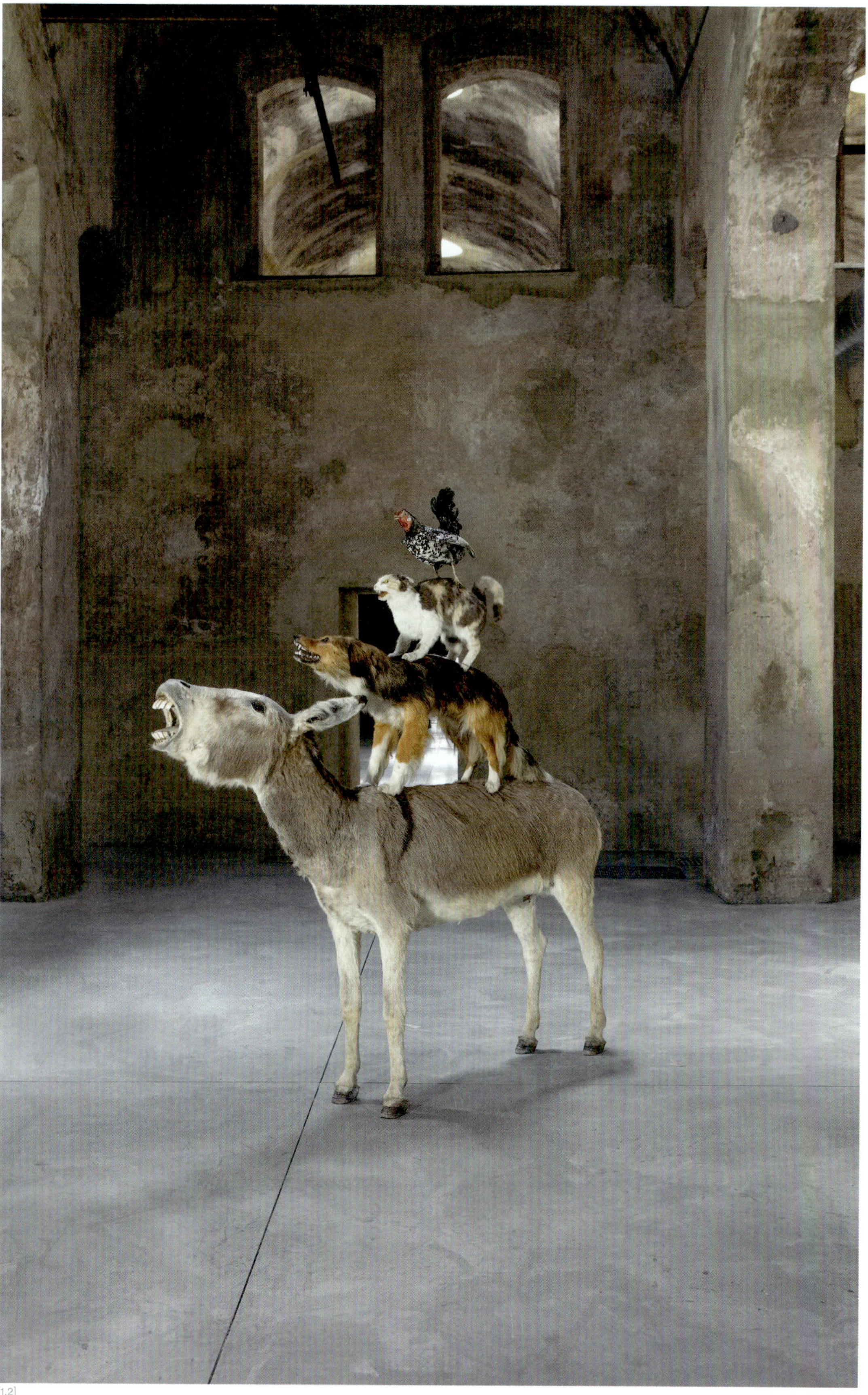

[1.2]

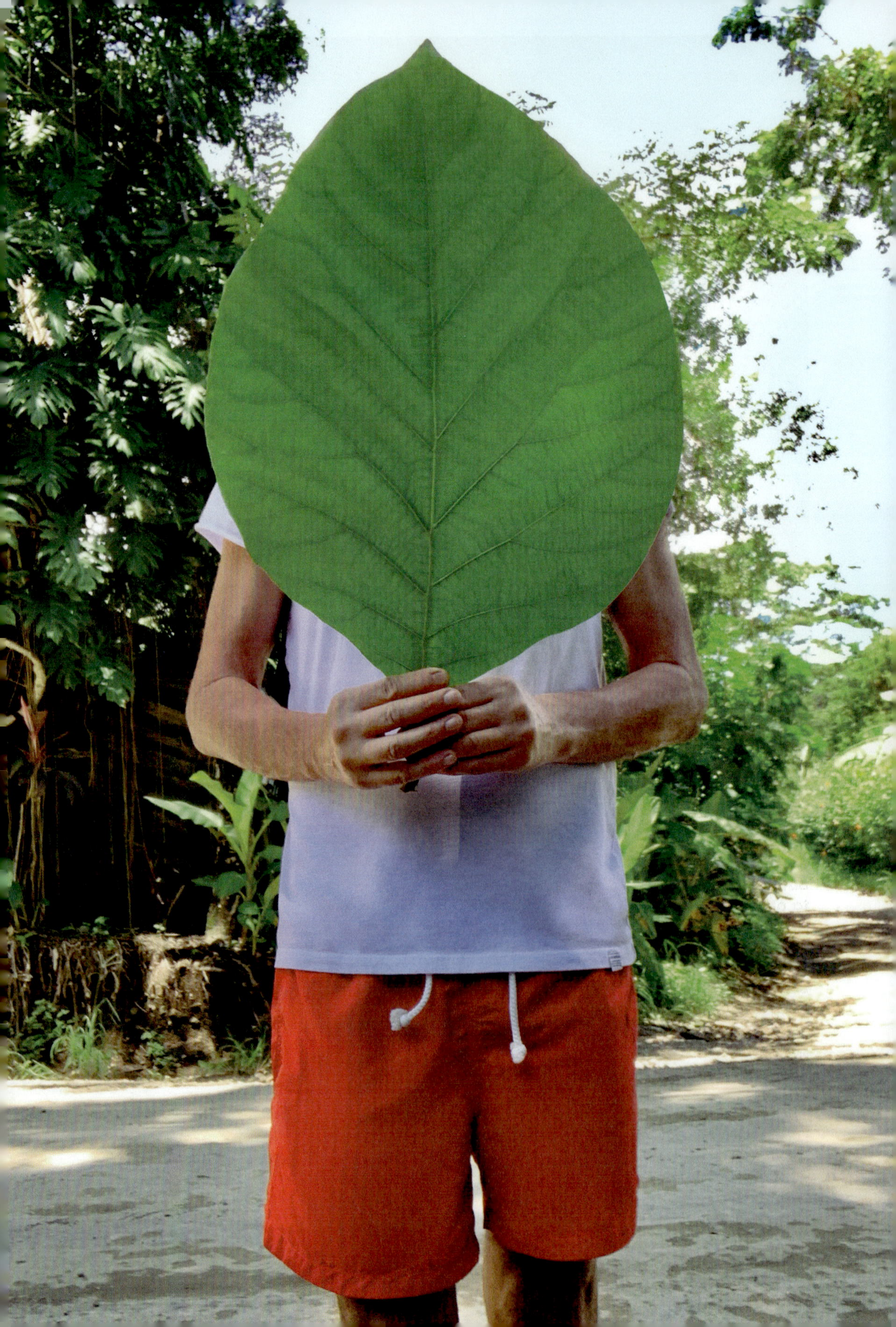

I've always suffered from the feeling of being in the wrong place. Once it was at school, at home, at work, while now it often happens to me even when I'm in a bar. If someone brings a microphone or a camera close to me, then I feel total panic. Over the years I had to invent something to survive. I simply didn't show up whenever my absence was more functional than my presence. I'm also affected by a very serious form of prizophobia. I can't bear to look someone in the face if they're presenting me with a prize, let alone the public. I've always found it more courteous, instead of refusing, to send someone else to collect the prizes for me and try to learn how to do it.

In fact, I do all I can to discourage interviews. It's not that I have anything against them, but I don't think I have anything interesting to say. And then I'm more curious about other people's opinions. In the end, without others, without other people's ideas, without stories, you don't exist, and your work doesn't exist either. So you have to listen to others, not yourself. The same goes for the stunt doubles I use when I'm invited to speak in public. I always find other people more interesting than me. I've even used other people's interviews as my own. Once I copied one out completely. People would stop me and say: "Oh, I didn't know you were born in Corsica and were a student of Bataille." It was the artist Ange Leccia.

When I was a kid, I used to play hide and seek. One day I hid so well my sisters couldn't find me. I got very scared. I thought my family had forgotten about me. After a while as an adult I must have had the same fear that the art world would forget about me if I kept on hiding. Anyway, I don't like the idea of having a public image. In the end you have an image that becomes the reality, whether it is or not. That's the tragedy of many great actors like Peter Falk, who was known only as Columbo. He was great, but a slave to the success of his character. My tragedy was that I was trapped inside myself. I was my character. I was lucky to figure it out in time. Why give up the only thing you have, yourself? Anyway, it's truly dramatic to see how what are called powerful images are in my case perhaps among the few moments when I'm trying not to hide anything.

I'm not a public figure or a famous person. The fact that artists, curators, and people in the art world know you doesn't make you famous. The world out there is much bigger than you can imagine. Then I've never done anything but work. I've never climbed to the top of the Colosseum to attract the TV reporters in helicopters. There are spaces that in any case I like to keep hidden, leaving them to the imagination. My home, for example. Even though in reality there's nothing to imagine and nothing to see. Four walls and the carpeting, no furniture and no paintings on the walls.

It's so hard to tell the truth. Sometimes it takes fiction to make it plausible. And I find the truth terribly boring. Verisimilitude is much more interesting. Also journalists and politicians have realized this. The news stories, electoral campaigns, the posts on social media all feed us with stories and images of *a* reality, plausible but not true. Basically, I'm deeply convinced that a known mistake is better than an unknown truth. The truth isn't out there. It's just the moment when you claim something as your own: this is my truth, that's yours. There are as many truths as there are people who believe in them. The more believers there are, the more universal a truth becomes. As human beings we depend on creating fiction and believing in it. We can call it religion, myth, conspiracy theories, fake news or publicity. Humanity has always based its survival on the ability to imagine things that are untrue, and in some cases to persuade whole populations to believe them. It's the motive force that took us to the moon, but also led us to exterminate millions of people in the concentration camps, unfortunately. It's not clear who first said, "If you repeat a lie long enough, it becomes truth," but it's true. Especially in a world where if you choose the right channels you can make a lie go viral, credibility is more a matter of repetition than rarity.

I often change my mind. I'm usually not much in agreement with what I say. But I'm not sure whether I change my mind or whether I lie a lot. It's somewhere in between. People always reproach me for things I've said and I answer that I didn't mean anything. You can't stand still on the same spot your whole life. You see, you can make fun of yourself—that's the art of the comedian. But being called an impostor implies that you built your life on a lie, to hurt people, to screw people over. Which is not fair in my case. That doesn't mean I've never lied in my work: it was not with the aim of deceiving people, but to search for a certain level of confidence in the work itself and in myself. Some artworks come with a story, and you never know if the story is true or false. I always tell this story that my pope (*La Nona Ora*, 1999) wasn't conceived as a sculpture of him lying on the ground. He was supposed to be standing up, and it was a last-minute decision to change his position and throw in the meteorite. I don't even know whether this was exactly spread as a rumour. It has much more to do with misinformation. I like to publicize artworks with an enormous amount of fake information, and the upshot is that in the end there is no truth.

[2]   *Spermini*, 1997
Painted latex masks
C. 17.3 × 8.4 × 9.8 cm each

In the movie *Face/Off* with John Travolta and Nicolas Cage, the terrorist and the FBI agent who hunts him take each other's faces. The bad guy with the face of the good guy goes back home to the good guy's wife and she starts liking him more than her real husband, without knowing that he isn't her actual husband. It was almost the same with me. At some point I started fearing that people would like my "face" more than the inner me, the artist behind the face. I felt the need, the urgency, to put my real face on my work. Exactly because I didn't want to be called an impostor, someone who never shows his real self.

I made *Spermini* immediately after the 1997 Venice Biennale, directed by Germano Celant, for a solo exhibition at Galleria Massimo Minini in Brescia. Just my face in all its flavors covering an entire wall of the gallery.

At the beginning it started simply as a way not to take myself too seriously—to punish myself as much as I was mocking others. Then it had a different purpose. On the one hand, I like to use myself to disappear. It's strange, but for some reason the more you appear the less they see you: you become a mask, a face that anyone can wear. On the other hand, I wanted my face to work as a prop capable of triggering a sense of closeness to the viewer. I think it's easier to identify with a face than an object. A face is something you share your pain with.

I don't think you can say that in being an artist I'm creating a performance, though I wear many masks, like actors in the past. Besides, it's what we all do every day. We can be father and son at the same time, someone's good friend and another's enemy. We're never one single thing, we're many things at the same time, many masks on top of one another. And I'm interested in the possibility of changing masks and roles to see what happens.

[2]   *Spermini*, 1997 (detail)
"Maurizio Cattelan," Galleria Massimo Minini, Brescia, October 9–November 20, 1997 (solo show)

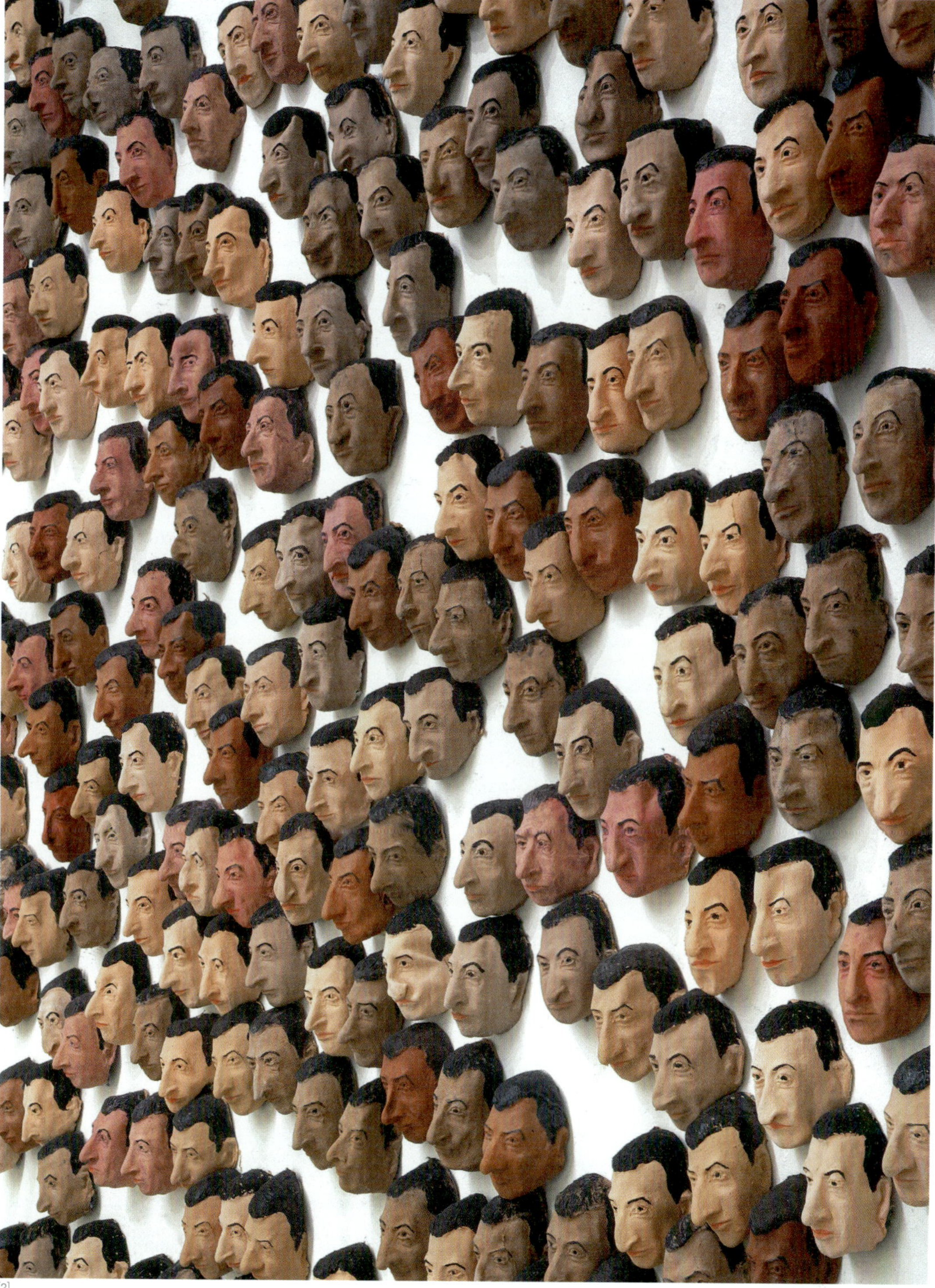

[2]

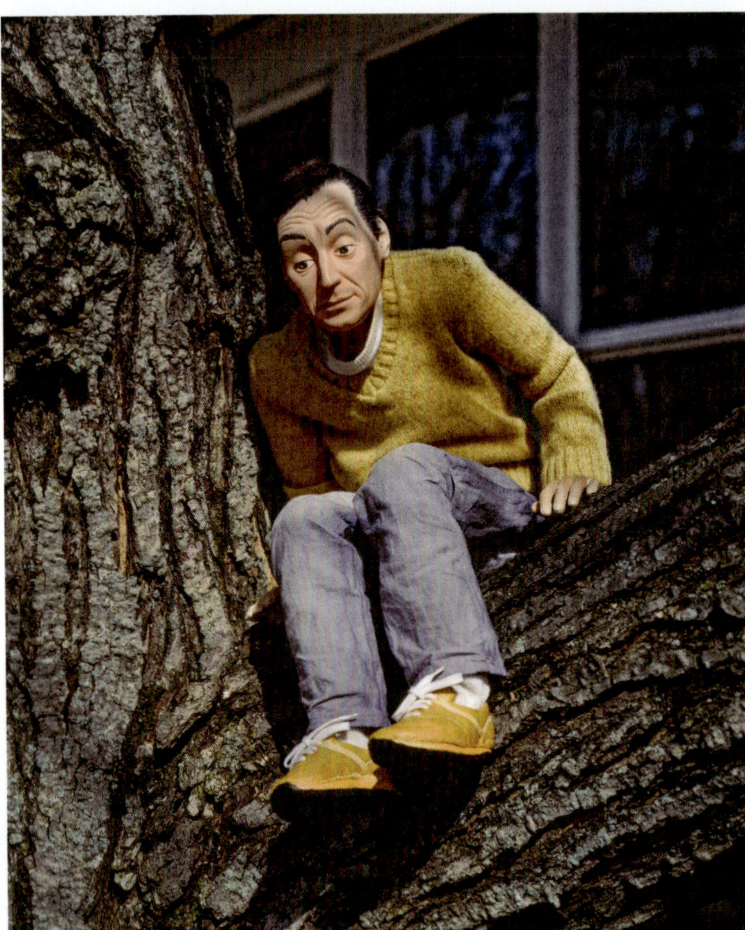



[3.1]  *Mini-me,* 1999
Private house, Cincinnati

[3.2]  *Mini-me,* 1999, and
*Others,* 2011 (detail) [239]
"Not Afraid of Love," curated
by Chiara Parisi, Monnaie de
Paris, October 21, 2016–January
8, 2017 (solo show)

[3.3]  *Mini-me,* 1999

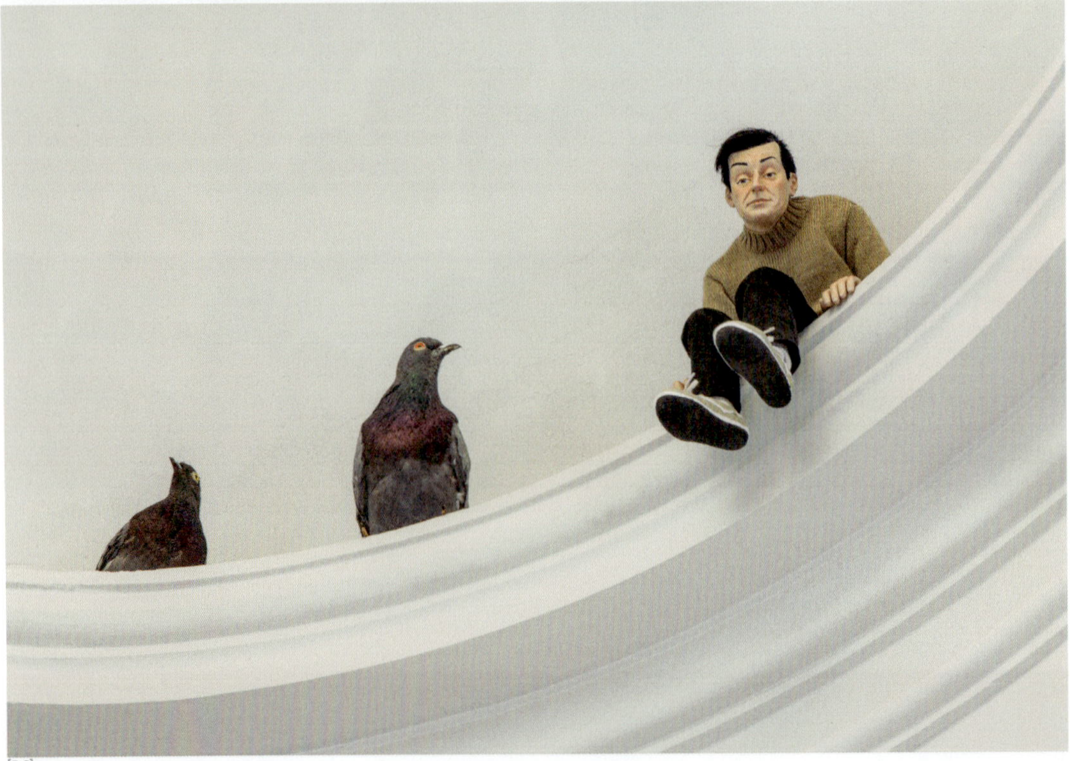

[3]  ***Mini-me*, 1999**
Resin, rubber, paint, synthetic hair,
clothing
45 × 20 × 23 cm

A collector from Cincinnati, Andy Stillpass, a smart guy, approached the artists in an exhibition at CAPC in Bordeaux in 1996, which I took part in, and commissioned them to create some works for his home. I thought of a miniature me to be perched on a tree branch. Then the work ended up inside the house, on a shelf in a bookcase. This is the first version of the work, which was later presented in various exhibitions and became an edition. Each model has its own clothes, different from the others but similar, since the model has always remained those four rags I wore.

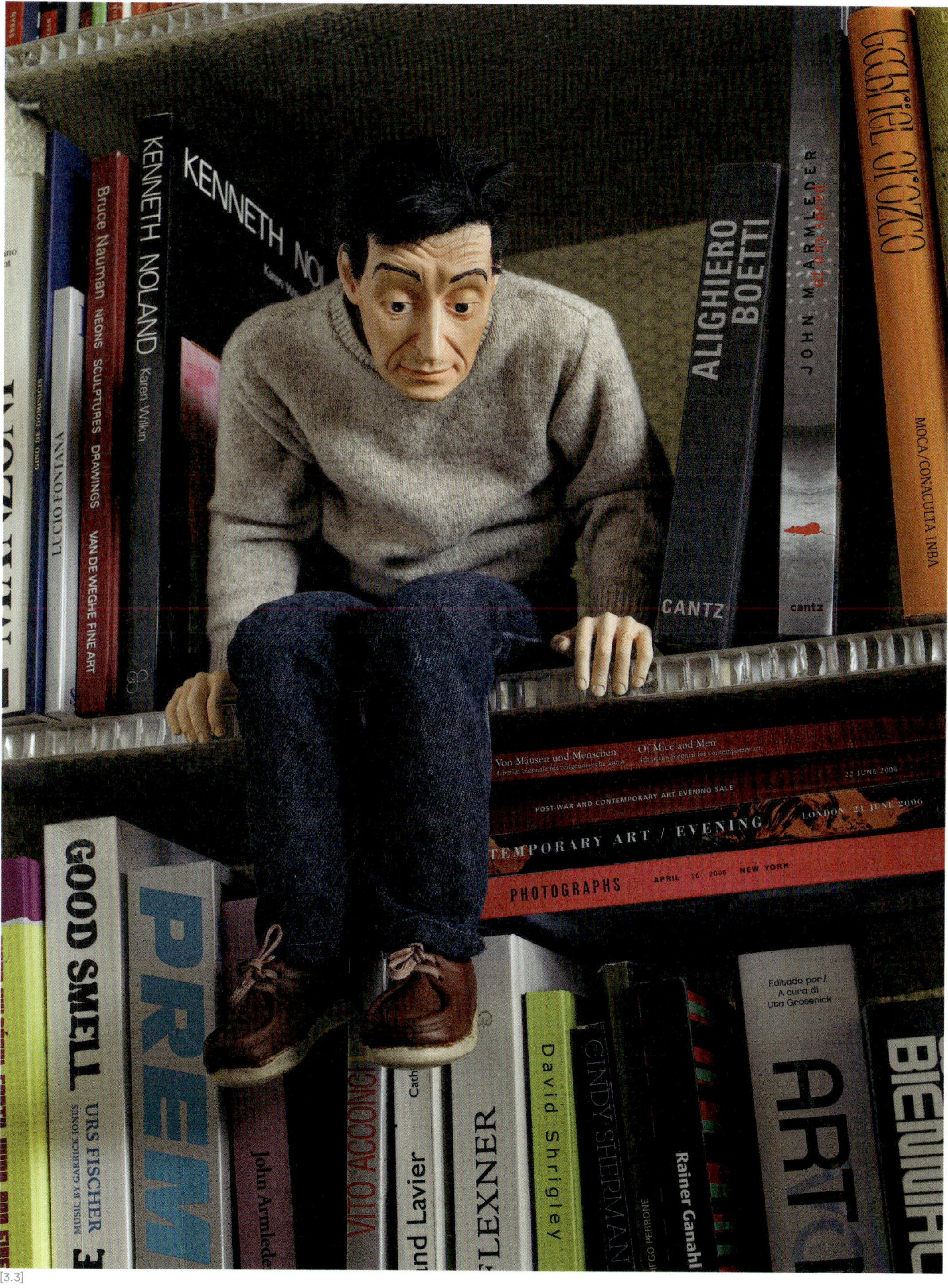

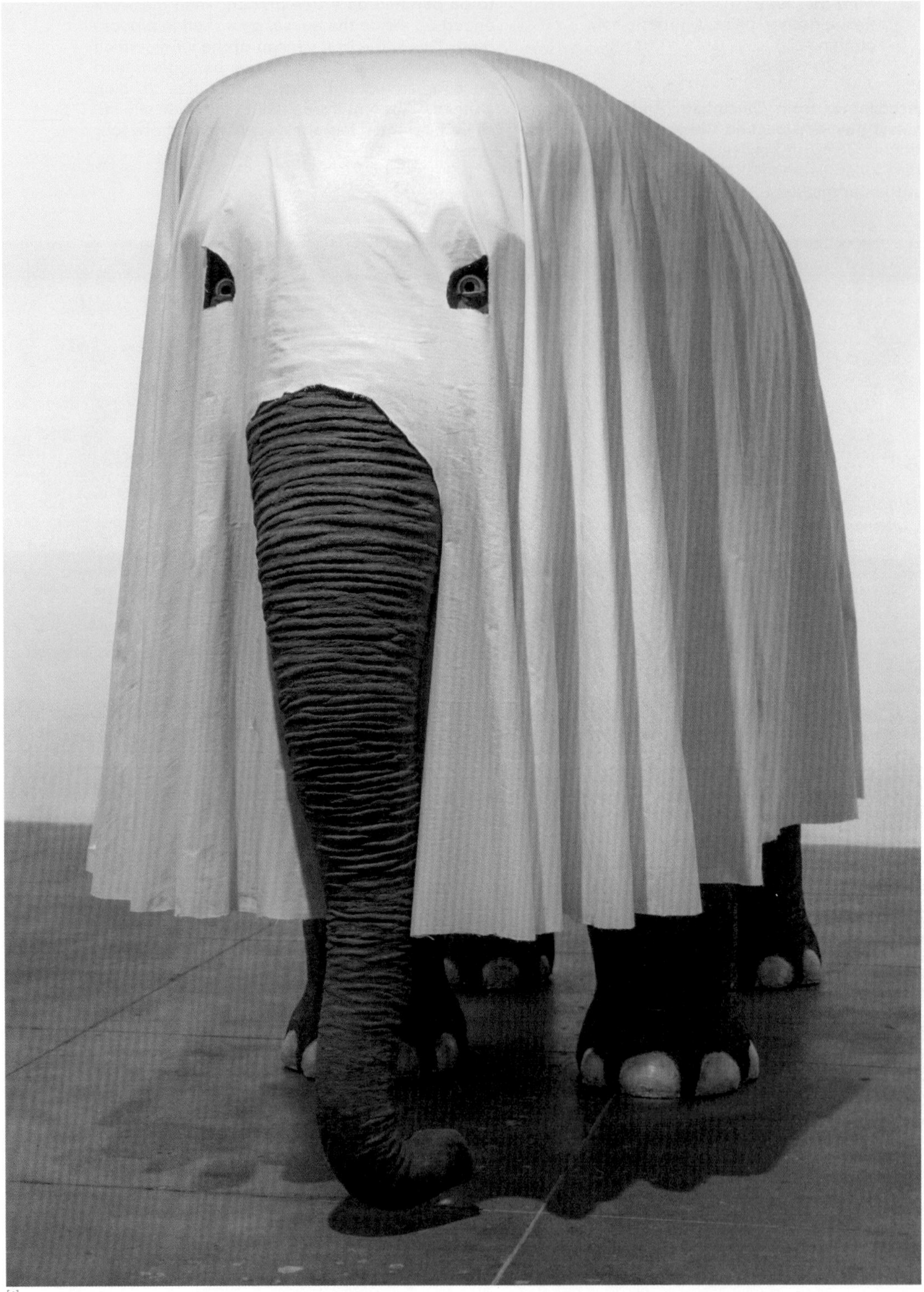

[4]



[4]   *Not Afraid of Love*, 2000
"Maurizio Cattelan," Marian Goodman Gallery, New York,
February 22–March 25, 2000 (solo show)

[5.1]   *Untitled*, 2007
Placard of 3rd Contemporary Art Day in Italy, promoted by
AMACI – Associazione Musei Arte Contemporanea Italiani,
October 6, 2007

[5.2]   *Untitled*, 2007

[4] ***Not Afraid of Love*, 2000**
Styrene, polyester resin, paint, hair, fabric
205.7 × 312.4 × 137.4 cm

*Not Afraid of Love* is a work that escapes from the centre, stands hidden in space and looks at you from a corner. It's the position I like best: you can be marginal, and still in control.
I literally found the title by chance. In New York one day I was strolling in Central Park and I met someone walking around with that phrase, "Not Afraid of Love," written on a sign or his T-shirt. The rest of the work developed during a kind of vacation with Elizabeth Peyton. She worked all the time, I kept thinking about an exhibition but nothing came of it. Then, one day when I had that phrase and an elephant in mind, it came to me, a bit doleful, in a Ku Klux Klan hood, but even then people were laughing less and less.

[5] ***Untitled*, 2007**
Poster
70 × 100 cm

This is a sort of variant of *Not Afraid of Love* (2000): not an elephant hiding but a donkey.
I took the photo for the third edition of the Contemporary Art Day in Italy, but never marketed it.

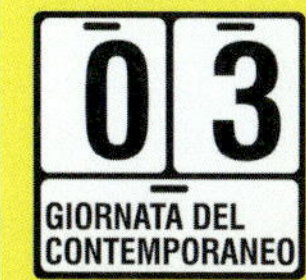


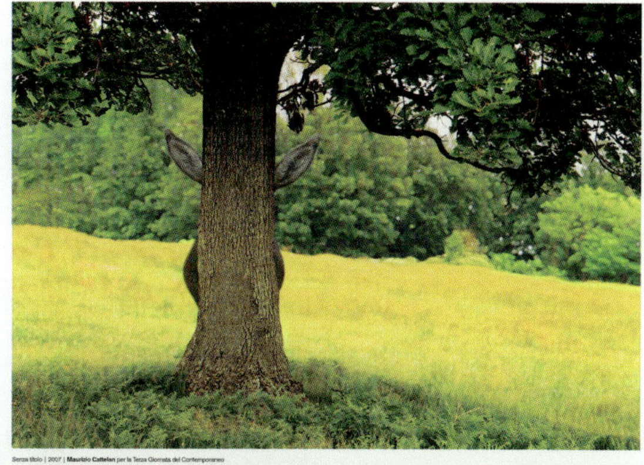


[5.1]

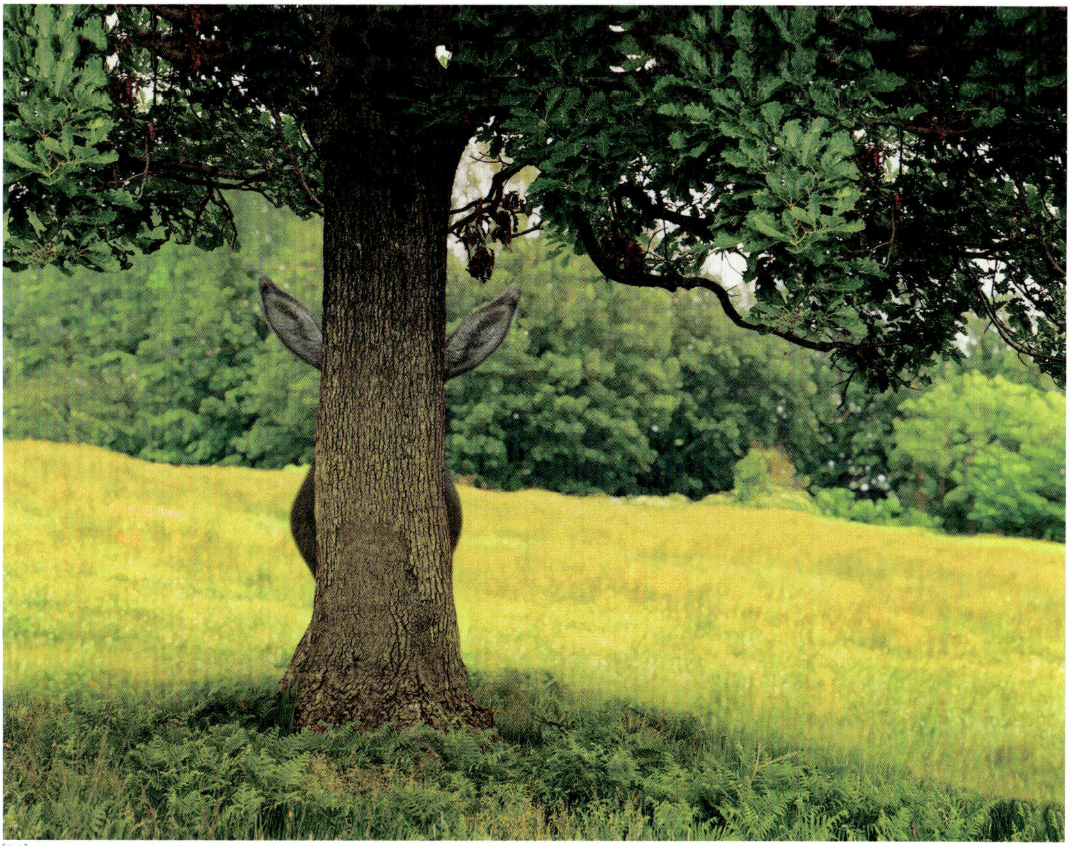

[5.2]

[6]  *Untitled*, **2000**
Gelatin silver print
41.3 × 33 cm
Edition of 60 copies realized
for *Parkett* 59, 2000

The work is an edition for the magazine *Parkett*.
I asked Armin Linke to take the photo. I liked the
idea of the cork in the guy's mouth, as a way to
shut up anyone who talks too much.

[6]  *Untitled*, 2000

[7]  *Untitled*, **2001**
Silicon rubber, epoxy fiberglass,
natural hair, fabric
Figure: 150 × 60 × 40 cm

For the Boijmans Van Beuningen, I liked the idea
of sneaking a disruption into the galleries, as if a
thief or just some curious person had got inside
the museum in his own way. At first I thought of
a work that could be seen through a window, but
after a while I said to myself: "Why stay outside?
Let's bring it inside." This gave me the idea of
making a hole in the floor of a room. It was fantastic. Clearly someone always has to back you
up. In this case the institution had to perform an
act of faith. The piece was also effective because

26

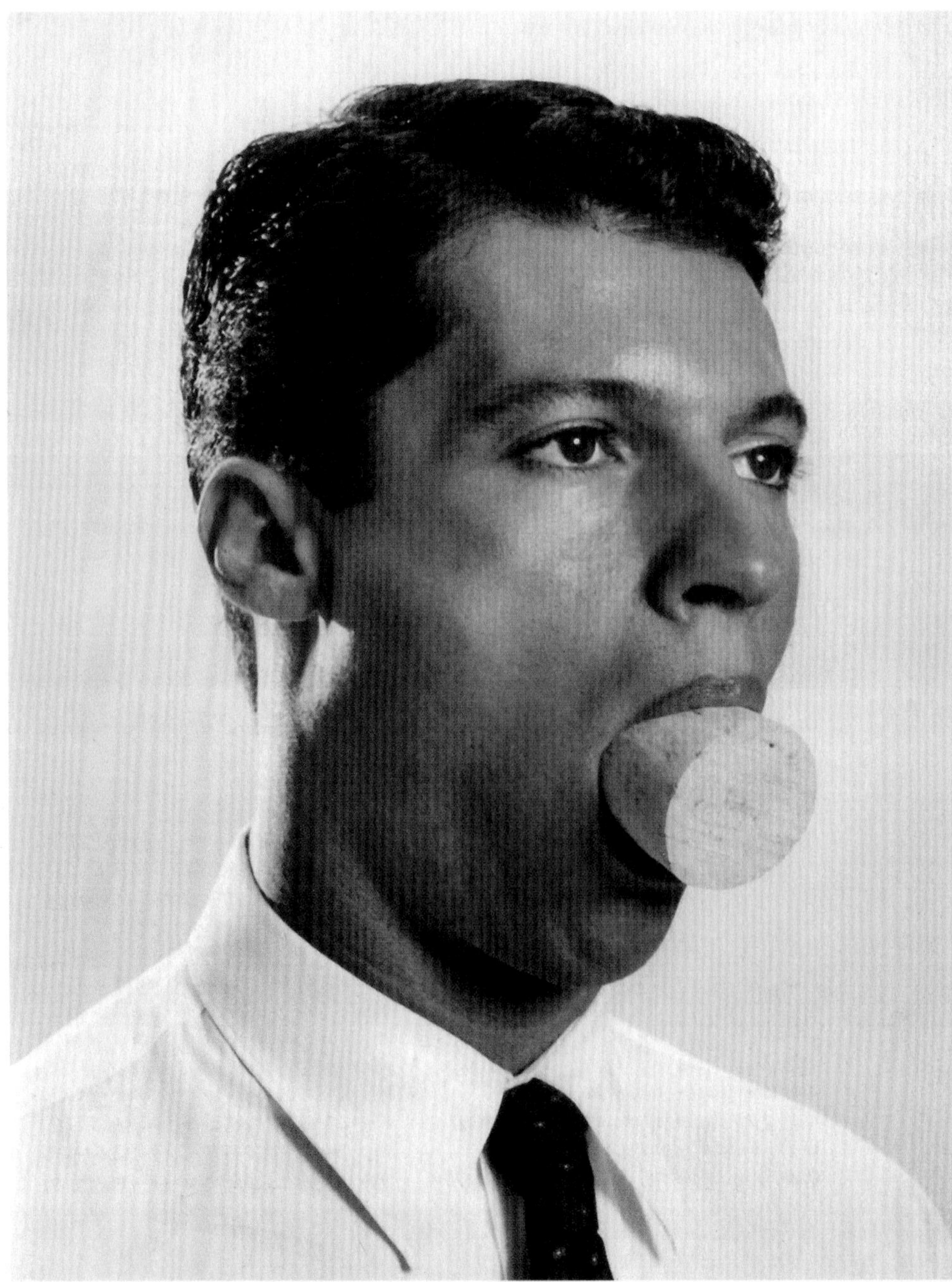

[6]

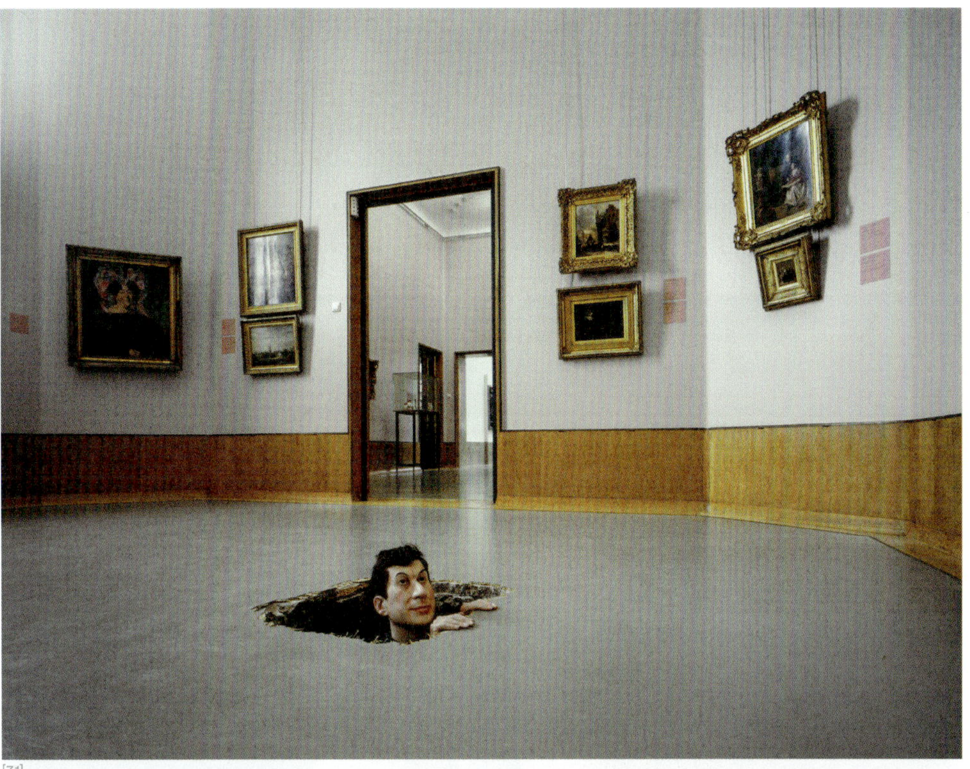

[7.1]

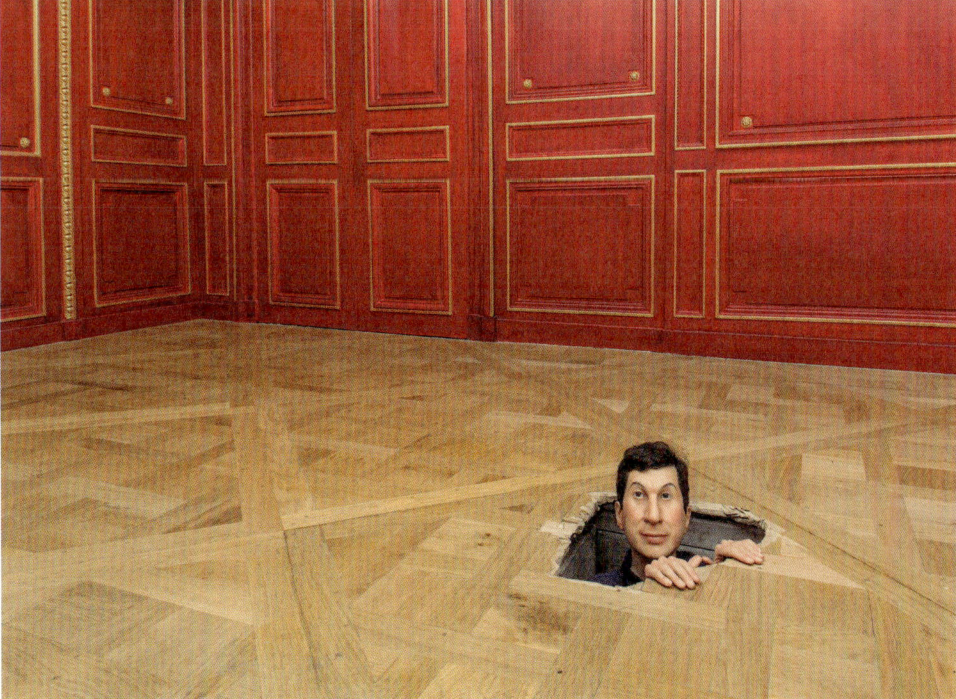

[7.2]



[7.1]  *Untitled*, 2001
Polyester resin, wax, pigment, natural hair, fabric
Figure: 150 × 60 × 40 cm
"Out of Senses. Seven Exhibitions where Artists Use the Museum as a Laboratory," curated by Rein Wolfs *et al.*, Museum Boijmans Van Beuningen, Rotterdam, February 25–April 21, 2002 (group show)

[7.2]  *Untitled*, 2001
Polyester resin, wax, pigment, natural hair, fabric
Figure: 150 × 60 × 40 cm
"Not Afraid of Love," curated by Chiara Parisi, Monnaie de Paris, Octotber 21, 2016–January 8, 2017 (solo show)

28

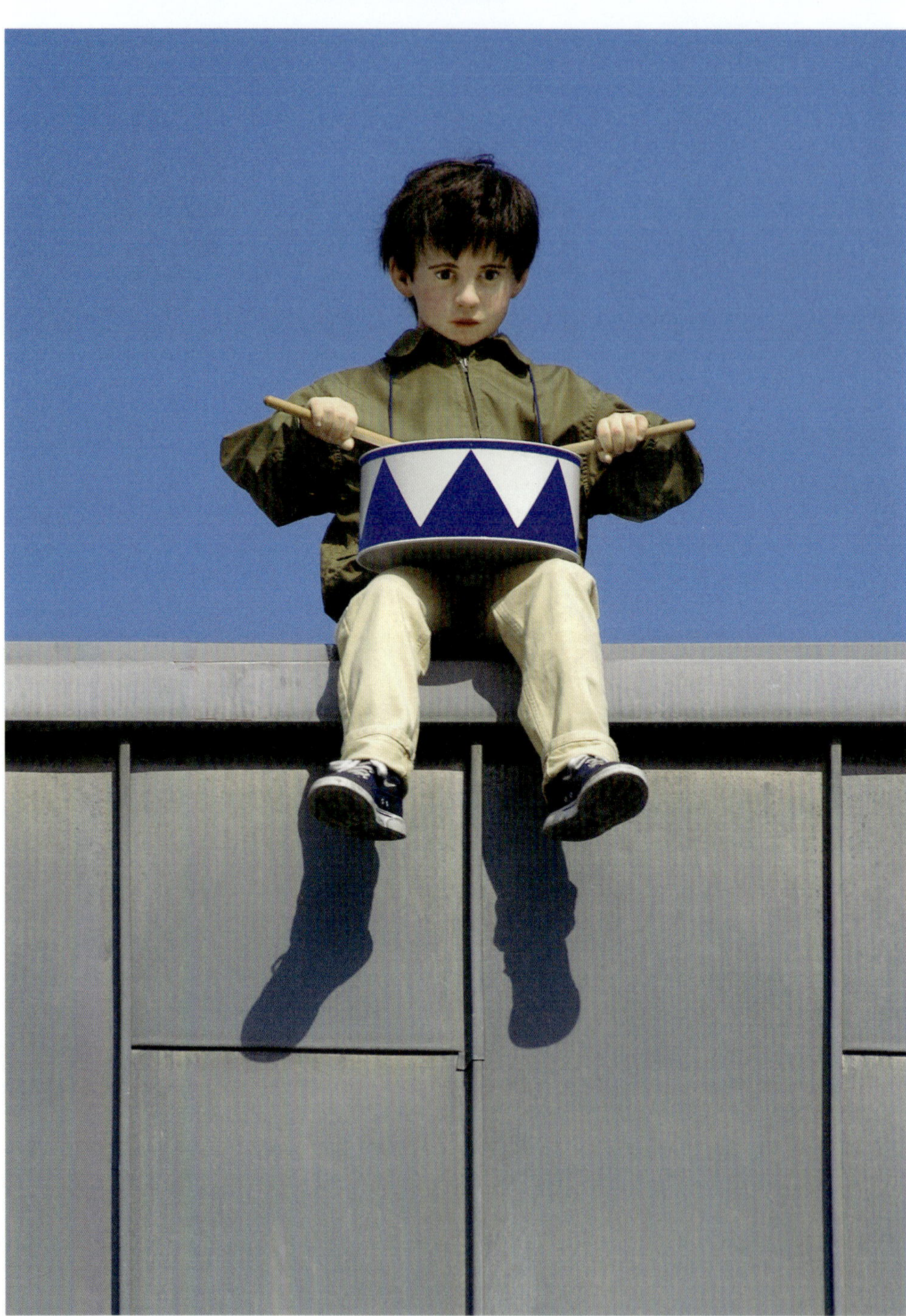

[8.1]

[8.1]   *Untitled*, 2003
"Maurizio Cattelan," Museum Ludwig, Cologne, May 16–
September 2003 (solo show)

[8.2-3]   *Untitled*, 2003
"Contrepoint. L'Art contemporain au Louvre," curated
by Marie-Laure Bernadac, Musée du Louvre, Paris,
November 12, 2004–February 10, 2005 (group show),
installation on the Terrasse Mollien, Cour Napoléon

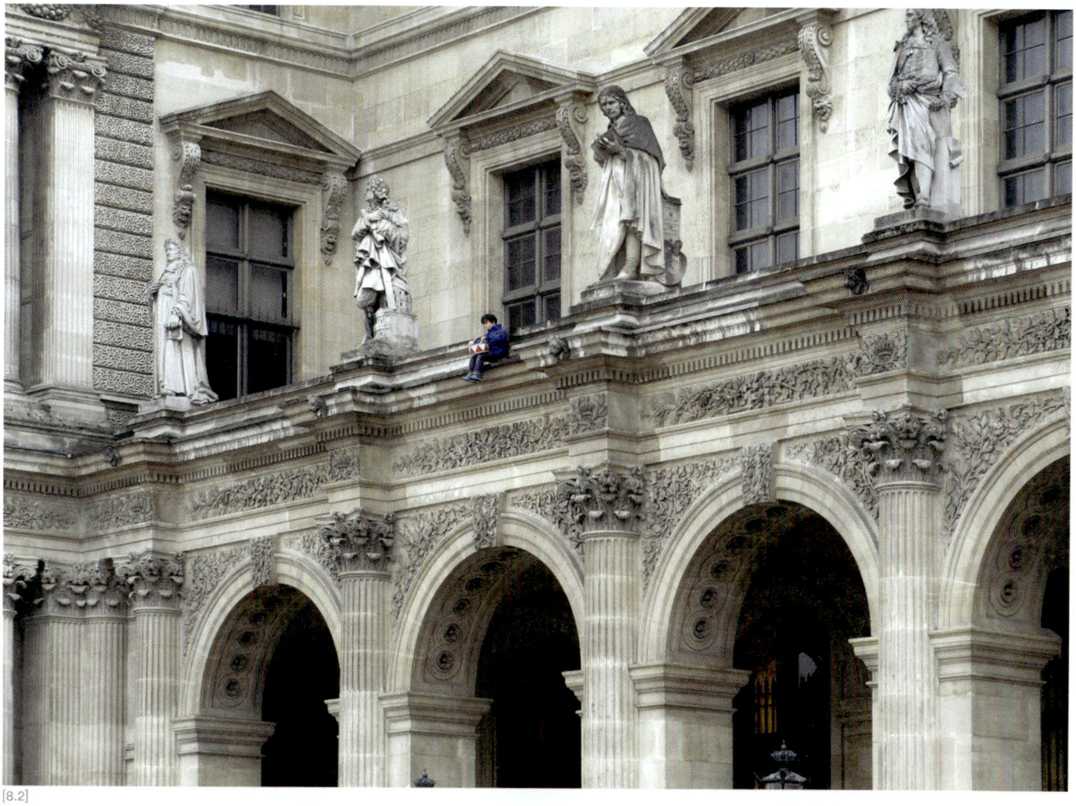

it really was an intruder who had got into the collection of Old Masters.

The installation was later recreated in other exhibition venues. It doesn't bother me if a work conceived for one place is then transferred elsewhere. Works can even escape from the artist's control, sometimes, but they will never escape from the judgment and comments of the public. If a work is good, it should be able to survive elsewhere.

[8]   ***Untitled*, 2003**
Resin, paint, synthetic hair, clothing,
shoes, electronic device, steel drum
80 × 85 × 55.9 cm

I've never had any problems with the classics, even though I skipped art history. When I exhibited the work for the first time, at the Museum Ludwig in Cologne, the child playing the drum might have seemed like an allusion to Günter Grass's novel *The Tin Drum*, where the hero plays a drum to evoke his memories. Then, in 2004, I installed it sitting seraphically at a great height on a facade of the Louvre. The public queuing to enter the museum was more alarmed by fear that the boy might fall than it was excited at the works of art they would be seeing inside.

The work has many references. It was certainly born from a rib of the one shown at the Boijmans Van Beuningen (*Untitled*, 2001), a little me popping up from the floor and looking up at the world from below.

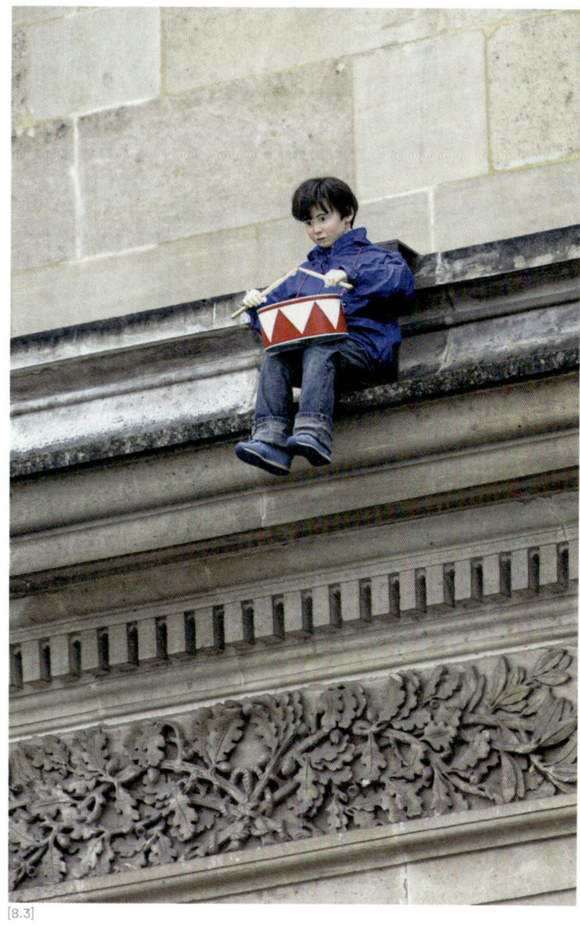

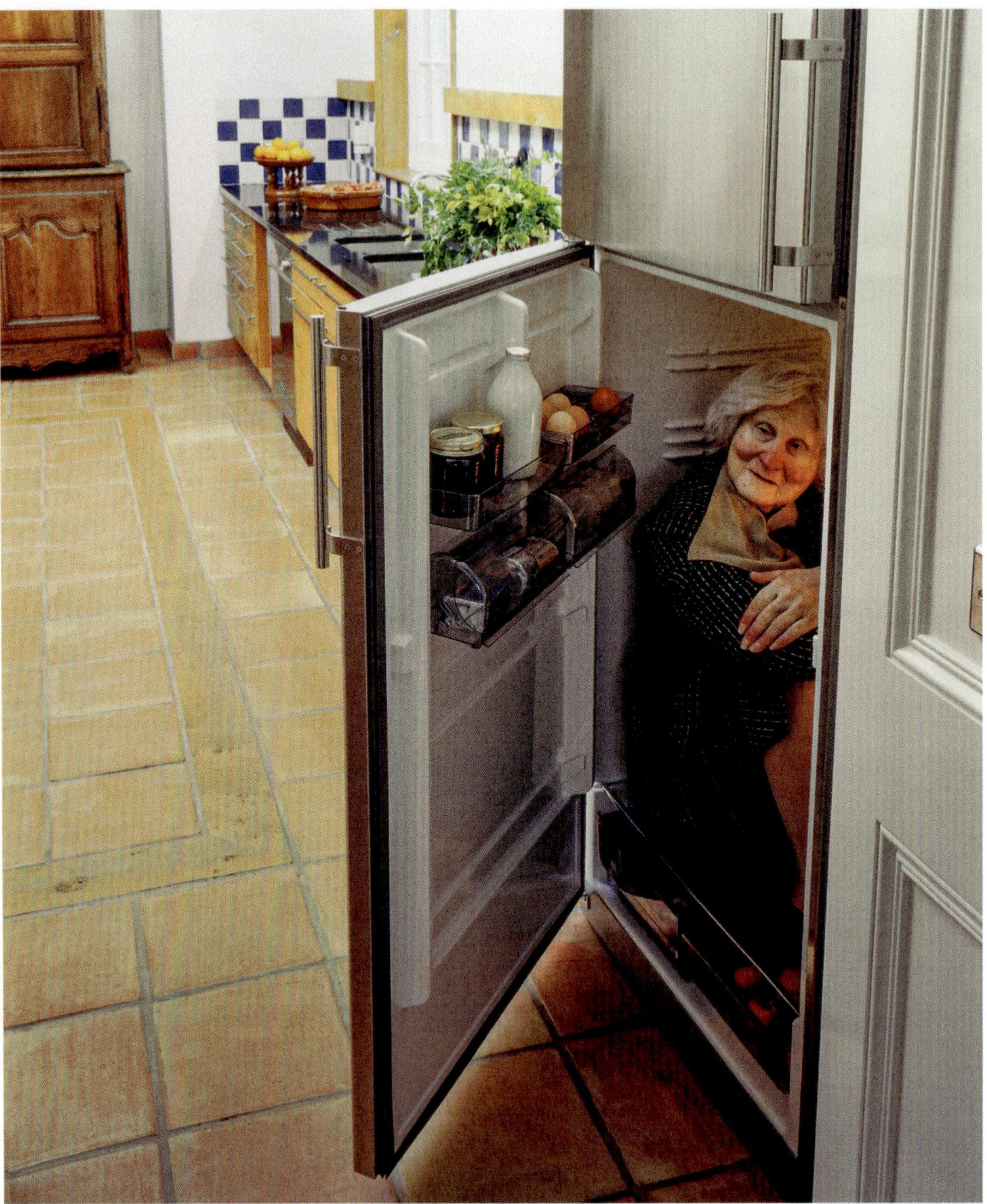

[9]



[9]  *Betsy*, 2002
Polyester resin, wax, pigment, natural hair,
clothing, refrigerator
188 × 75 × 66 cm

This British collector, let's say a Mr. Brown, said
to me in 1999: "Why don't you come to the countryside the next time you're in London? Why don't
we do something together?" And then a day came
when I think it would be nice to do two or three
different works for two or three collectors—a kind
of new dimension outside the routine of galleries.
So this was the first. I never went to his house in
the countryside, but he sent me photos—his kids,
the living room, the garden. In one of these photos
there's a lady in the garden in a hat, and her position already makes her an artwork. So I called the
collector and asked: "Who's that person?" "Oh, it's
my grandmother," he replies. I say: "I want to do
something with her." And he replies: "She's really old, she might die at any moment, so perhaps
it's not the right thing to ask... It would be such a
shock to my parents if she passed away." In the
end we got all the okays, and they accepted the
idea of doing a sculpture of her to keep at home in
the fridge. The lady came to Paris to do the work.
She hadn't traveled for years, so for her it was a
big deal. They told me she was happy about the
trip. So we went to work. Meanwhile I had other
pieces to do, so this one was left a bit to one side.

Before it was finished she died and the work was installed as a memorial. I think it's a good story.

At one point I thought of arranging it so that the door of the refrigerator opened on the other side. So you could see the back of Betsy first and to have an experience that would unfold moment by moment. In the end I didn't, because the work is perfect like this, but the idea of showing a figure first from behind and not making it clear what's happening to it or what it's doing is also in *Charlie Don't Surf* (1997), *Him* (2001), *Breath* (2021), and recently in *November* (2024).

**[10]  *We*, 2010**
Polyester resin, polyurethane, rubber, paint, synthetic hair, fabric, clothing, shoes, wood
68 × 148 × 79 cm

Sometimes I feel like I'm two people, and this is the theme of *We*. I'd been trying to do something about other people but it wasn't as powerful as using my own image. Doing a self-portrait is a device to write your own diary and talk about your feelings.

What often impels me to adopt a given approach is convenience in terms of simplicity of thought. A self-portrait is something truly straightforward, as easy as looking in the mirror in the morning. But in the balance between simplicity and inwardness, the image becomes uncanny. It's extremely familiar to us but also terribly alien. Adopting your own image is the result of obsessive introspection, rather than an excessive desire to place yourself at the center of the gaze, and I think this is true of all self-portraits in the history of art. After all, a double self-portrait conceals confessions, not always conscious, about your inner self.



[9]  *Betsy*, 2002
Private house, Newbury, United Kingdom

[10.1]  *We*, 2010
"Is There Life Before Death?," curated by Franklin Sirmans, The Menil Collection, Houston, February 12–August 15, 2010 (solo show)

[10.2]  *We*, 2010
"Maurizio Cattelan," DESTE Foundation Project Space, Slaughterhouse, Hydra, June 16–September 30, 2010 (solo show)

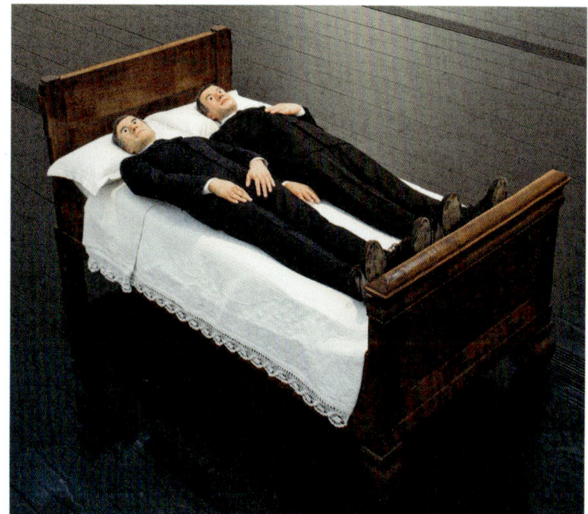

[10.1]

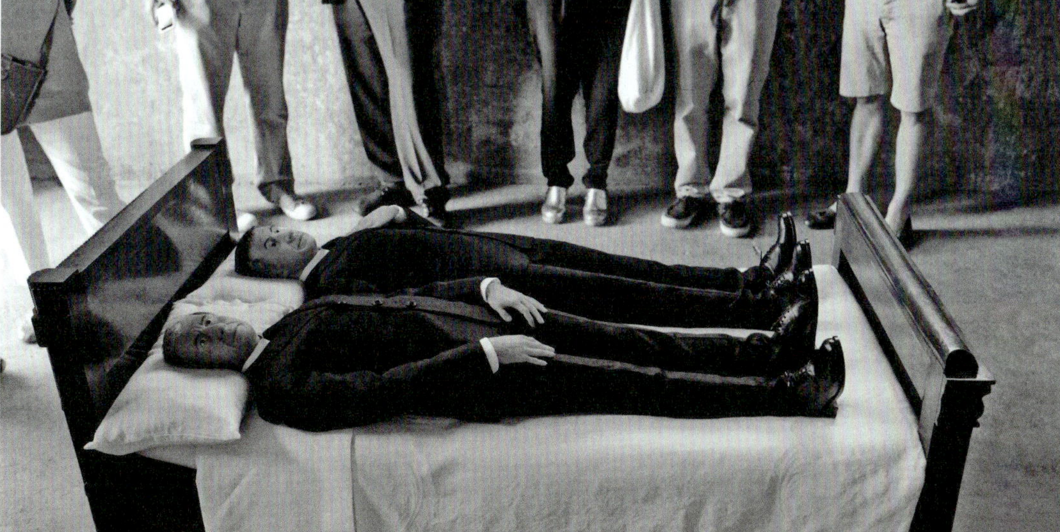

[10.2]

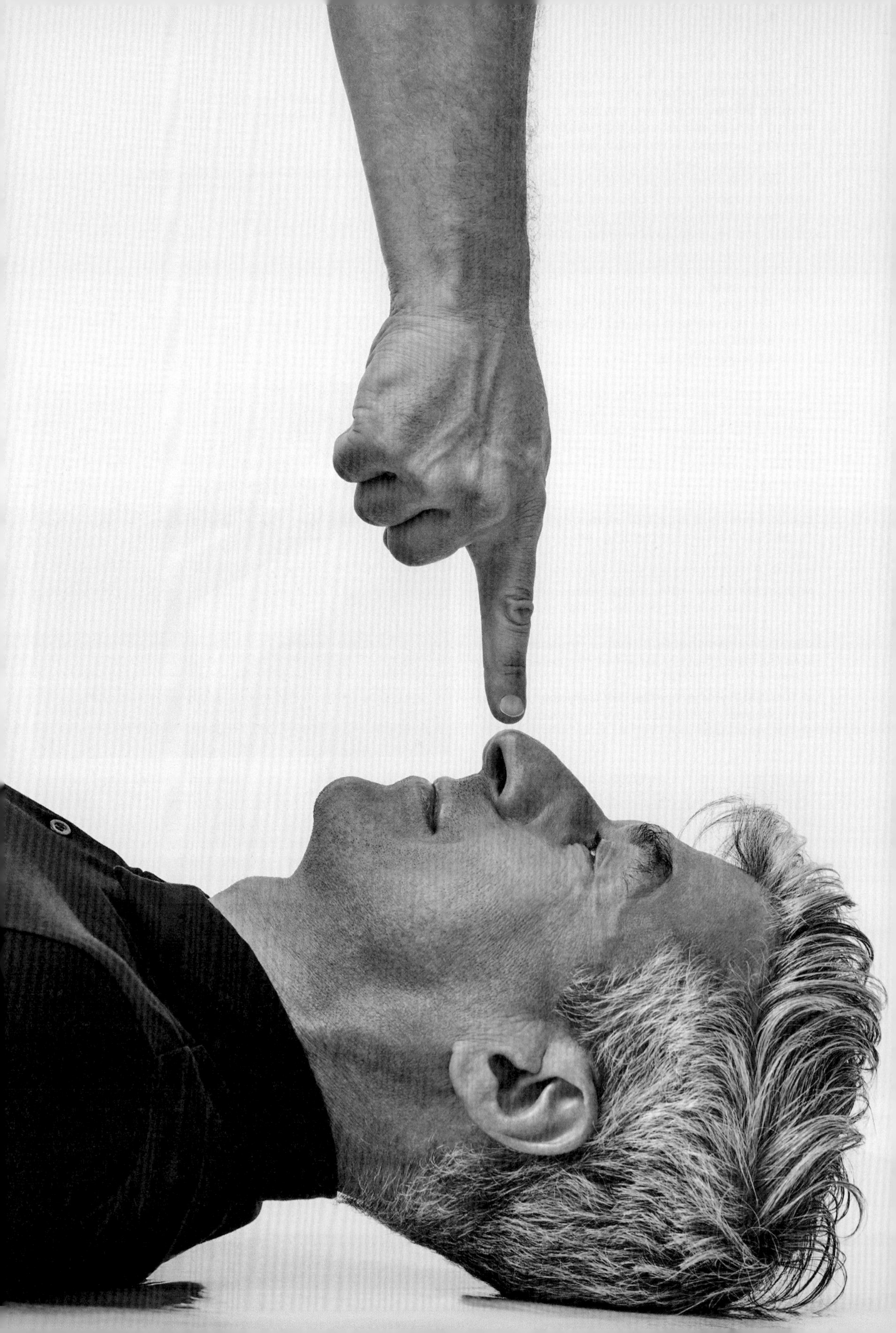

I hate to admit it, because I'm not a great salesman for my things, but some people call my work scandalous, superficial like a wisecrack, clever. My work consists of wondering what we're doing in the world. It consists of getting the attention of adults. It's still a struggle, and it's very painful to continue to see that look of distrust towards my works in the eyes of many critics and curators. I still often struggle to be taken seriously. It took me years to get rid of the stigma of being a prankster as an artist, or even be seen as an artist. I don't know if I'm a serious artist, but I'm a serious person, even a deadly dull one. I won't pretend I'm misunderstood, but it's easy to laugh, to reduce my work to a joke. I won't even pretend to doubt my appreciation, but in the past I've done the same things in areas other than art and I've been treated like an idiot. In the field of art—I don't know why—I do the same things and they're appreciated. On the other hand, as long as people say "Here the idiot counts," why change what I do?

When you start working you care a lot about labels and what people call you—an artist, a genius, a photographer, a prankster, a designer—and everything sounds like its misrepresenting your intentions. Over the years, I've come to the conclusion that any label can fit me, as I'm changing and questioning myself every day. People can see in my works whatever they want; there are countless possible interpretations. The very essence of things lies in what you get out of them.

What allowed me to enter the arena were irreverence and shyness, two sides of the same coin. One is the shield of the other. Irreverence was a stratagem, a ploy that enabled me to be accepted. The problem came later, when everyone started expecting that kind of character and I let them label me with it. There came a time when maybe I should have resisted it, pushed back against that sticky label, but I didn't become aware of it until too late. I think that with time every work will be able to redefine itself, to be performed at a distance from me. When that happens every work will be understood for what it really is, away from my shadow.

My work can be divided into different categories. One is my early work, which was really about the impossibility of doing anything. This is a threat that still gives shape to many of my actions and works. I guess it was really about my insecurity, about failure. Let's say that I just transformed something like failure into a work of art. A second

category speaks about loss, about absence, about death. Another category is humor, a great way to bring anger to the surface by depriving it of violence.
In reality, I've never been interested in defining myself a priori, or making commitments that I couldn't keep, just as I'm not interested in giving definitions in general. For example, I've always been fascinated by the artists who were outside Arte Povera, because they weren't labeled, like Alighiero Boetti and Gino de Dominicis. I don't really care for categories, and I find words terribly dangerous.

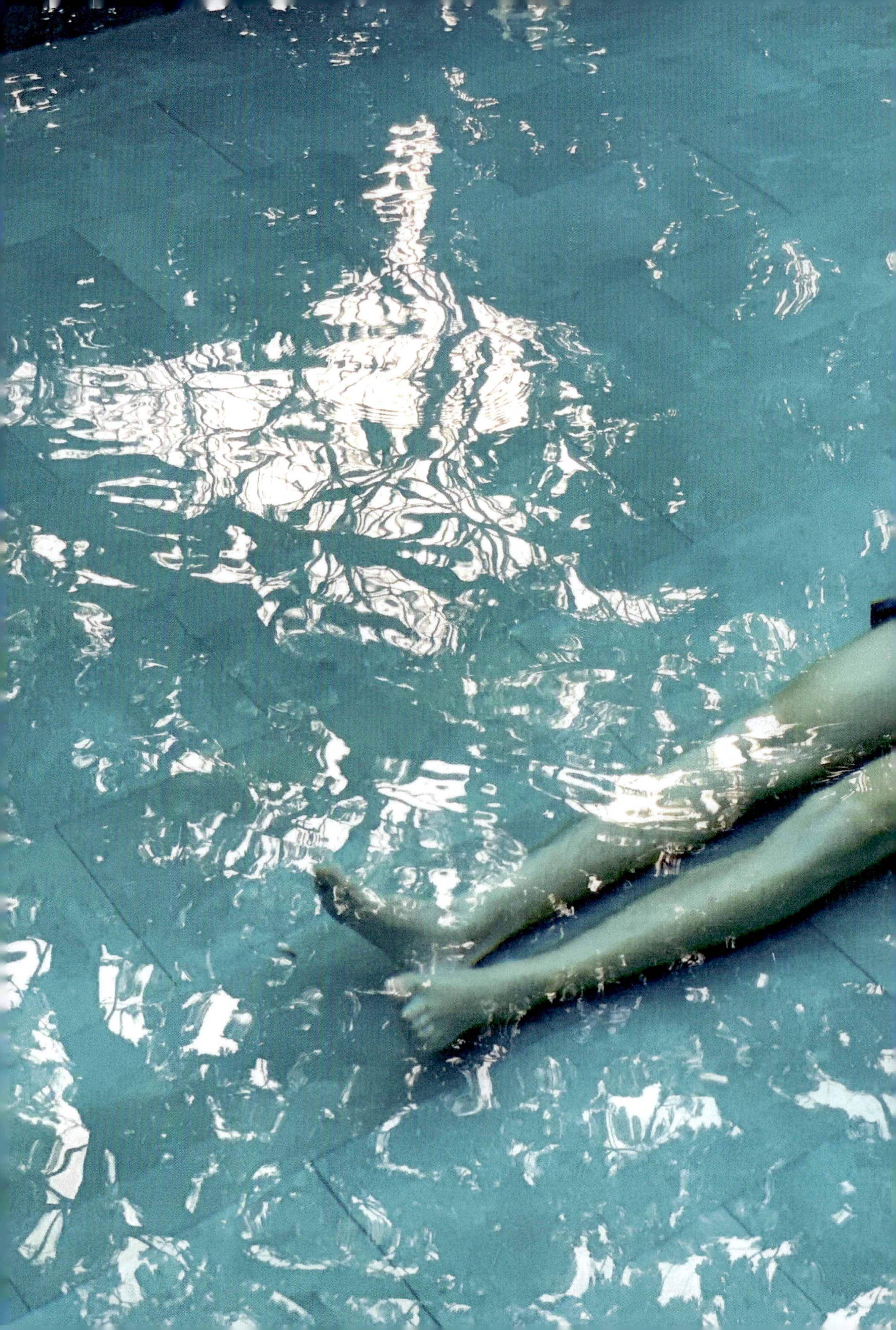

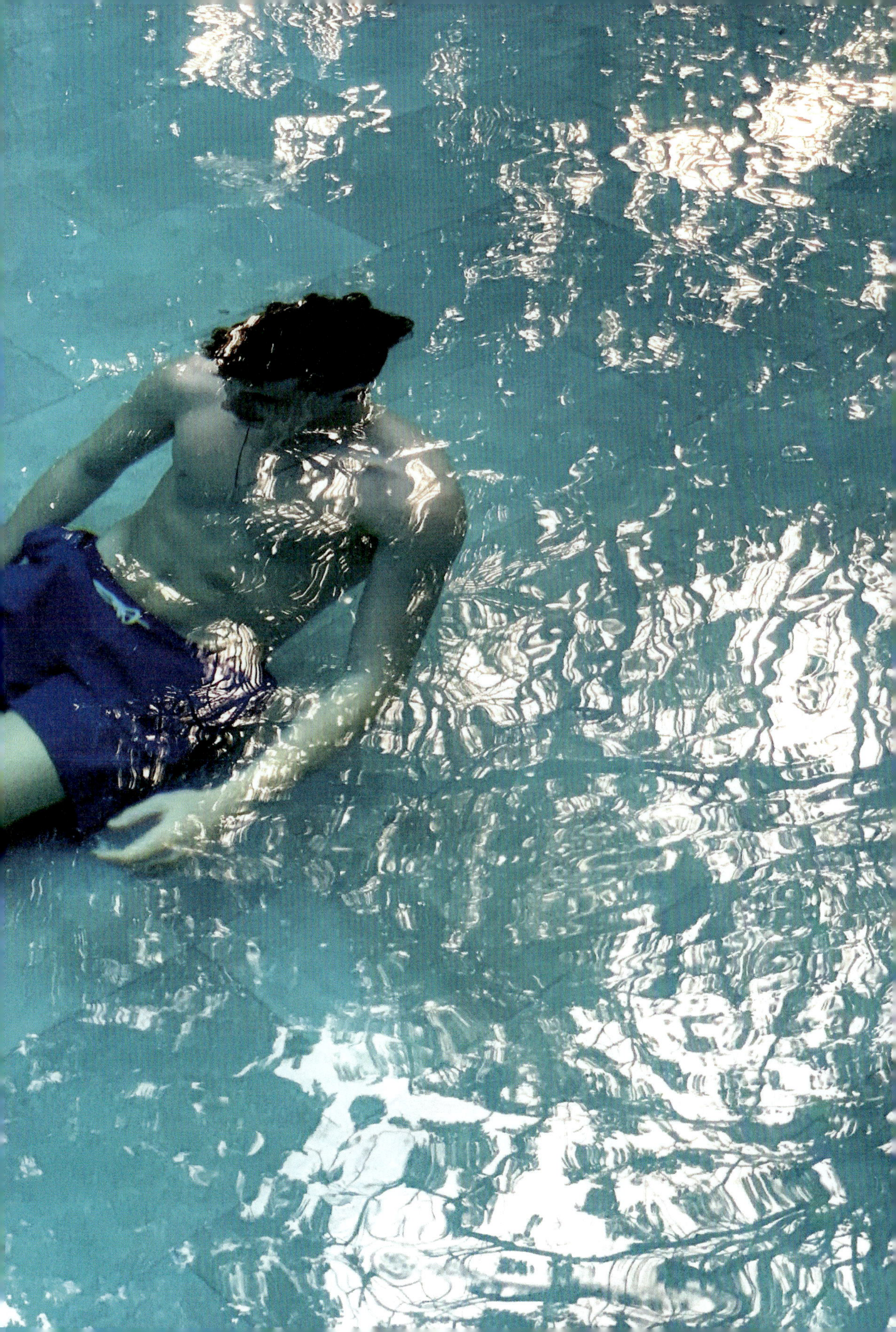

38

I'm interested in every kind of emotion that can enter my work. Some of my pieces are very depressing, though they may look funny on the surface. But if you scratch the surface you see sadness, desolation. You see everything except happiness. On the other hand, humor works exactly like a good work of art: both are meant to make you think twice. A laugh can have two souls. It can be an escape from an embarrassing situation or a moment of clarity. In this way, humor is critical for cognitive reasons, and that's why it interests me so much. But I'm interested in it as a means, never as an end. It has to be a way to avoid a one-sided vision, a key to open the viewer to the ambiguity of the judgment of what is represented. Everything can be said in at least two ways: one that is *really* meant and the another, much more interesting and sometimes comical, which reminds us that the world is much more complicated and contradictory. I see these two ways as phases that are neither separate nor separable. It's as if we had to make a list of all the muscles that we use to breathe. It's a physiological and fluid mechanism, one that can't be dissected. If you start thinking about it, you can't breathe anymore. So the form of every idea can be different; sometimes they're dark ideas undercover, but their playful appearance is really a disguise. Like light for insects, it's a trap, and you end up getting burnt.

As I see it, humor and irony are tragedy in disguise, two sides of the same coin. Laughter is a Trojan horse. It makes direct contact with the unconscious, affecting the imagination and triggering visceral reactions. Then humor is a good way of presenting awkward truths to people who might not want to see them. Every kingdom once needed its court jester, as the person who told truth to the king. Today this role is probably assigned to artists. I don't feel invested with such an important role, yet I admit that sometimes I like to think I'm like a stone in someone's shoe. But I'd be very happy not to be remembered as a court jester. At first that was more of a mask for me to conceal my shyness, but I'm afraid the only result was to turn the spotlights even more on me.

Comedy is a typical human experience. I suspect it's related to the fact that we're the only animals who know we're going to die. Other animals don't know it beforehand, they only understand it there and then, at the moment of dying. They can't express anything like the statement "All men are mortal." But we understand this principle, which is probably why religions and rituals exist. I think comedy is the quintessential human reaction to the fear of death.

Like many of my other works, my stuffed animals are sad and scary, humorous and tragic. The Greeks knew of the strange brotherhood among living things and morphed a lot of luckless mortals into animals. I call my animals puppets, not dolls, because I see them as active, like puppets that come to life in the theater. I relate them to street performances. Animals are a constant, an alarm. But the scariest thing is that I've always spoken only of human beings. Animals make great amplifiers, since we like to think ourselves superior... until the laughter sticks in our throat.

[11] *Bidibidobidiboo*, 1996
Taxidermied squirrel, ceramic, formica, wood, steel, paint
45 × 60 × 58 cm

In this work I struck a good balance between failure and what sculpture is always looking for, a kind of idealistic object. As usual I had to do an exhibition. I had to do something I didn't want to do. I began to think about putting together two different worlds: the human world and the cartoon world. I just thought that the squirrel is a cute animal, and it reminded me of the two from Disney, Chip and Dale, who are always making fun of Donald Duck. I wanted to put the squirrel into a kitchen, but I didn't know what kind. I thought of something very shabby and the first image that came to mind was my family's kitchen. The squirrel's kitchen is my parents' kitchen.

The work is also a kind of self-portrait, although nobody in my family committed suicide. But I grew up with this fucking yellow table! There's a nice story about it. Once my mother was ironing on the dining table and forgot she had left the iron on. It had been left face down on the Formica counter top. So the surface had an iron mark burnt into it. My father was upset with her. How were we going to repair the table? He decided to cut off the part of the table with the burn mark, reducing it by about 15 centimeters. So from that time on our family served all their meals on this shrunken table. That image has stayed with me forever. For the title, I thought

39

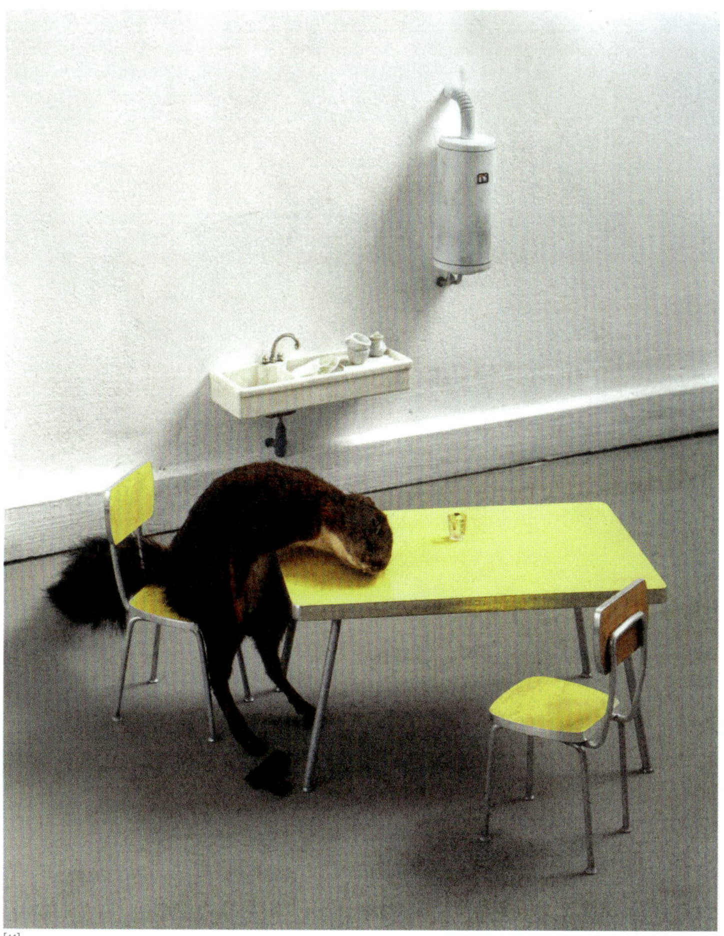

[11]  *Bidibidobidiboo*, 1996
"Maurizio Cattelan," Laure Genillard Gallery, London, February 7–March 23, 1996 (solo show)

[11]

about magic words like "Bibbidi-bobbidi-boo," which could transform something, make something better. That time, however, the magic didn't work.

I showed the piece in London at Laure Genillard's first gallery space, which was small and intimate. I really liked the idea of placing it on the floor in the room. I also liked the idea of seeing the piece while bending or kneeling on the floor. It added a kind of spirituality to the piece. You had to look at it as if you were praying.

I'd say that *Bidibidobidiboo* offers an Italian ending to a sort of Disney story, where the actual magic doesn't happen but you're left with reality. The story shows us that even something as cute and adorable as a tiny squirrel can suffer the same way as everybody else.

[12]  ***Georgia on My Mind*, 1997**
*Papier mâché*, paint, clothing, cigar
Performance with mask during the
opening of "TRUCE. Echoes of Art in an
Age of Endless Conclusions," curated by
Francesco Bonami, SITE Santa Fe, July 18–
October 12, 1997 (group show)

*Georgia on My Mind* was based on the same concept of the Disneyfication of the museum that I would explore the following year with a Picasso impersonator at the MoMA (*Untitled*, 1998). In this case, with the figure of Georgia O'Keeffe, it was a much smaller project—a teaser, in a way. Today this kind of thing is normal, but it wasn't then, there were no mascots. However, this work wasn't perfect. The head was made in the carnival tradition, and it was meant to be playful, but in Santa Fe, a city associated with the memory of O'Keeffe, the figure ended up becoming a ghost.

[13.1]  ***Untitled*, 1998**
Polystyrene, resin, cotton, leather
217.2 × 139.7 × 59.7 cm
Performance with mask during "Projects
65. Maurizio Cattelan," curated by Laura
Hoptman, MoMA – The Museum of
Modern Art, New York, November 6–
December 4, 1998 (solo show)

[13.2]  ***Untitled*, 1998**
Chromogenic print
182.9 × 228.6 cm
Performance with mask during "Projects
65. Maurizio Cattelan," curated by Laura
Hoptman, MoMA – The Museum of
Modern Art, New York, November 6–
December 4, 1998 (solo show)

I like friction and contradictions, which are all I see around me. That's why I don't like the word "criticism," and why the Picasso project I did at the MoMA looks as much like a marketing campaign as it does a comment on the Disneyfication of museums.

At the MoMA, I felt there was simply something missing. I didn't understand why they didn't embrace a more visible means of promotion. There was no reason to be ashamed about it. I thought new strategies will become ever more common in the years ahead. What does it mean to be a cultural institution? Didn't they want more visitors? Or did they just want to be boring? In any

40

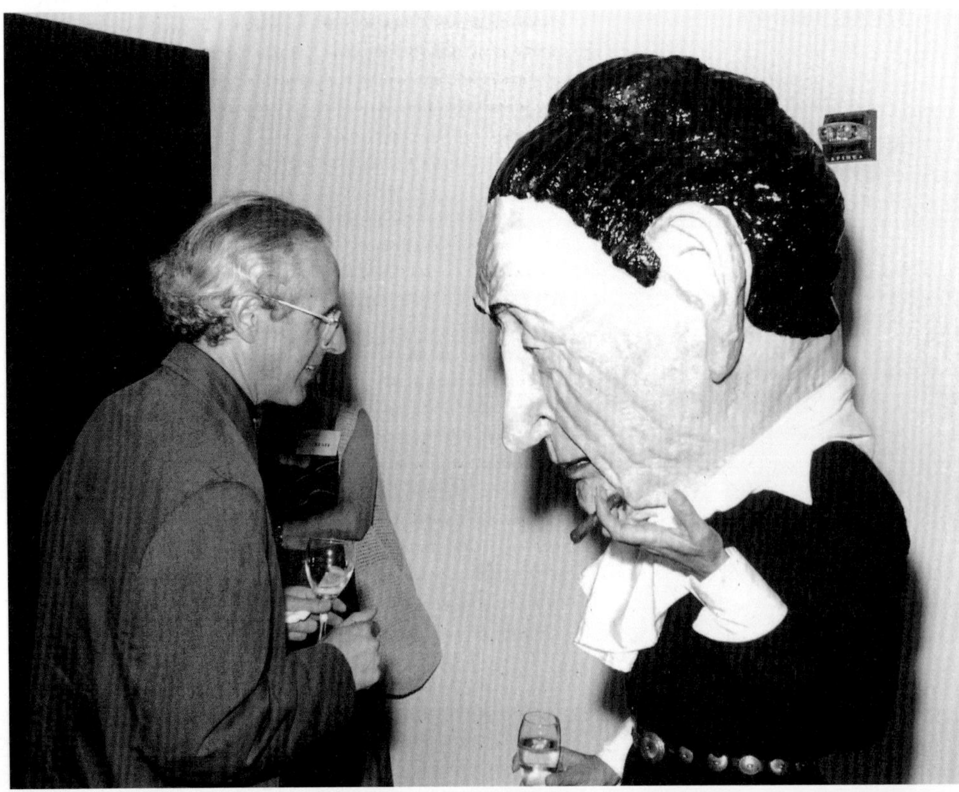

[12]

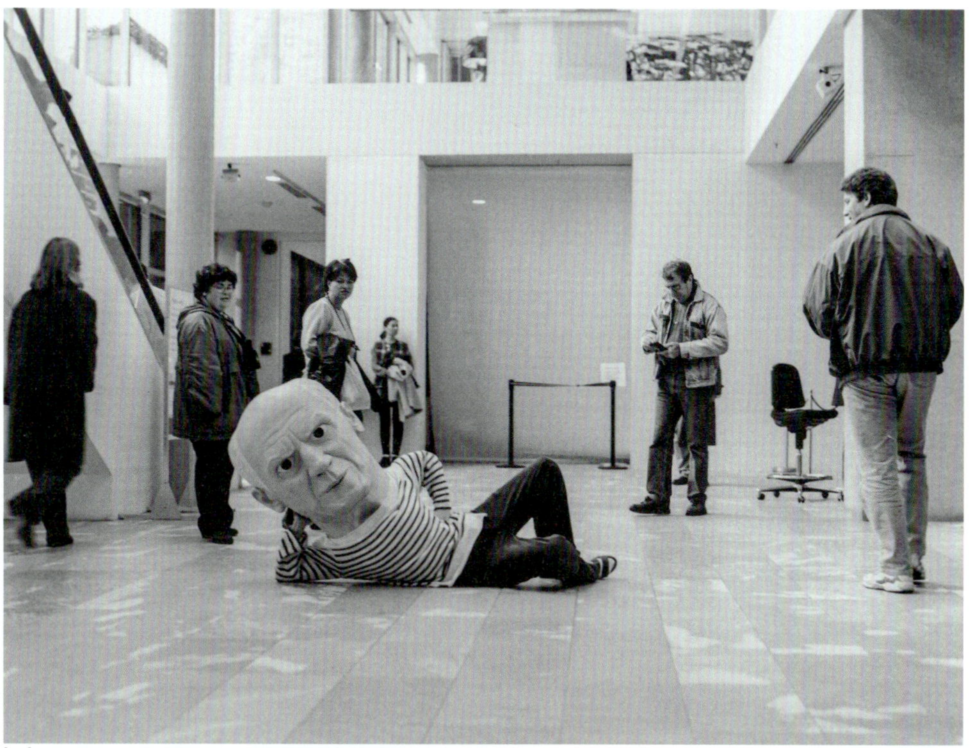

[13.1]

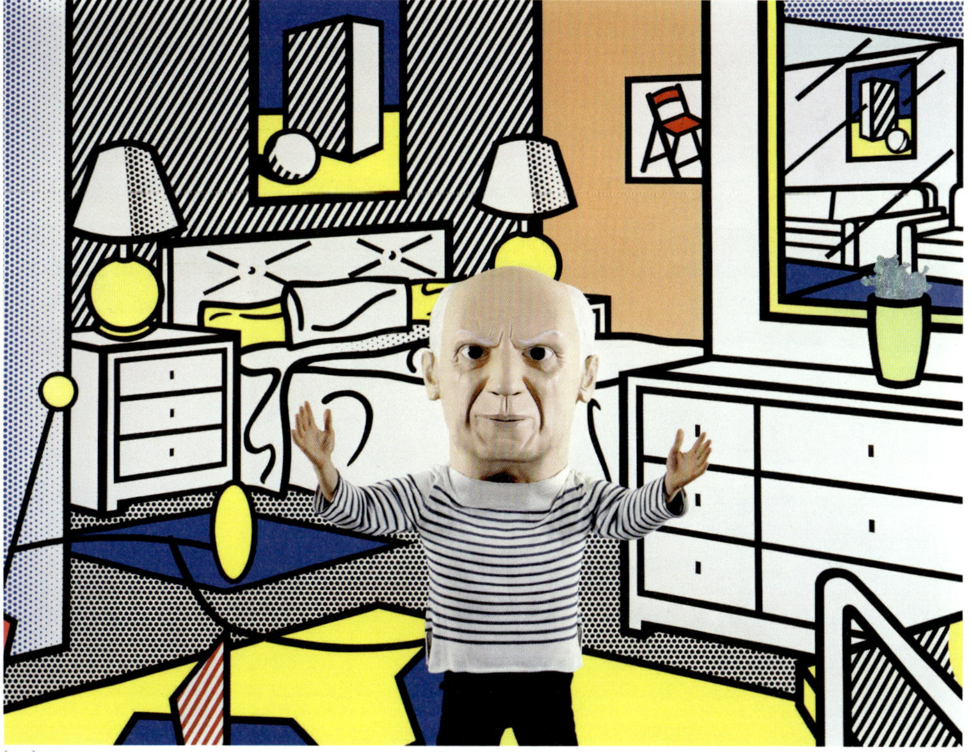

[13.2]



[13.1]  *Untitled*, 1998

[12]  *Georgia on My Mind*, 1997

[13.2]  *Untitled*, 1998

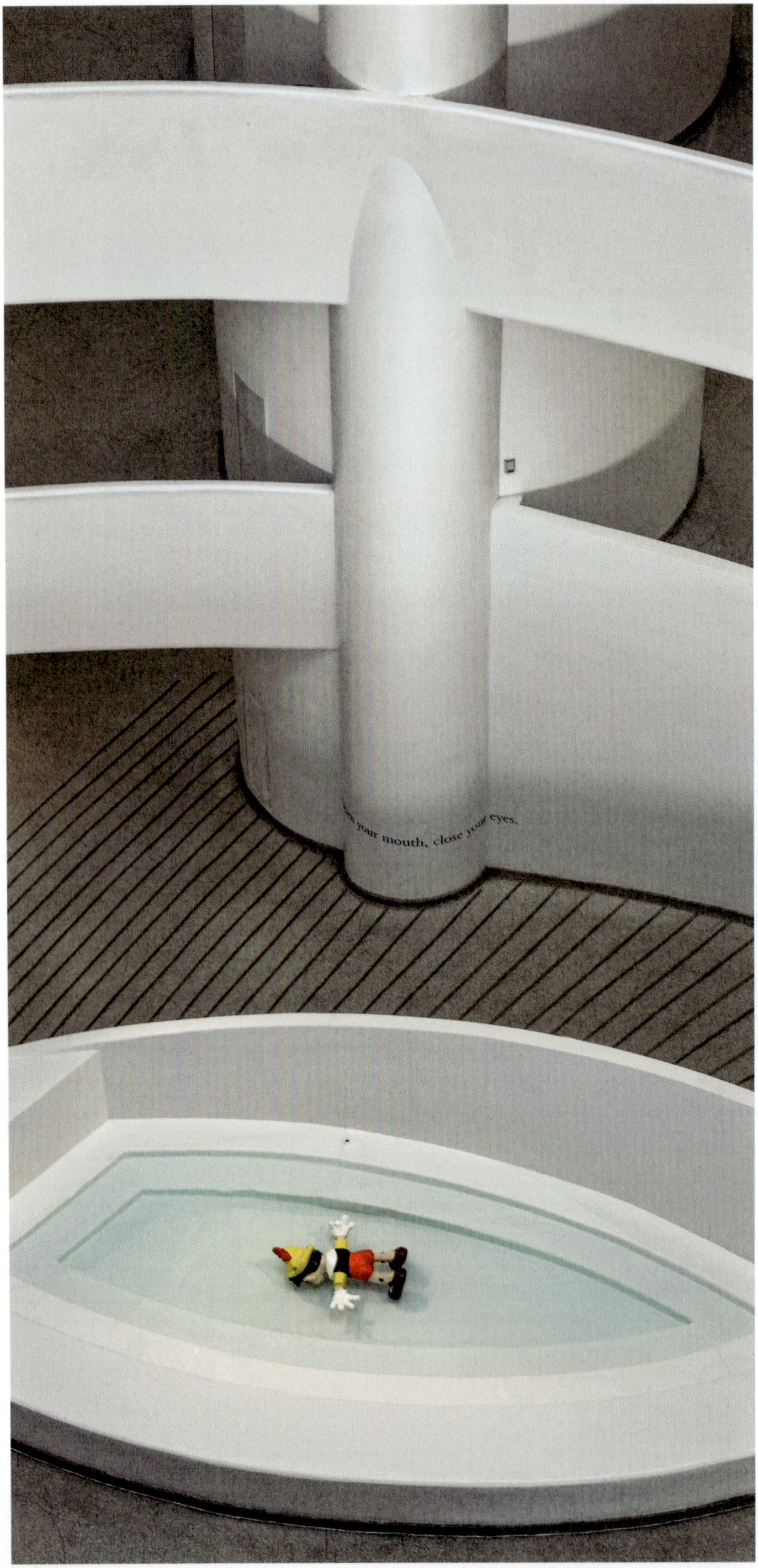

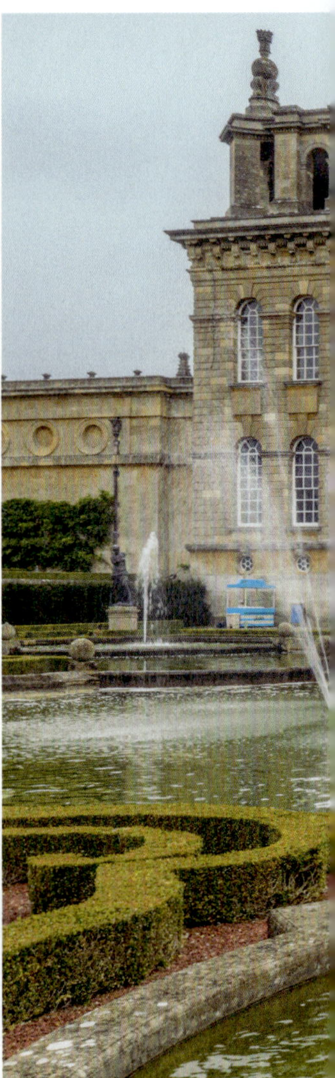

[14.1]

[14.2]

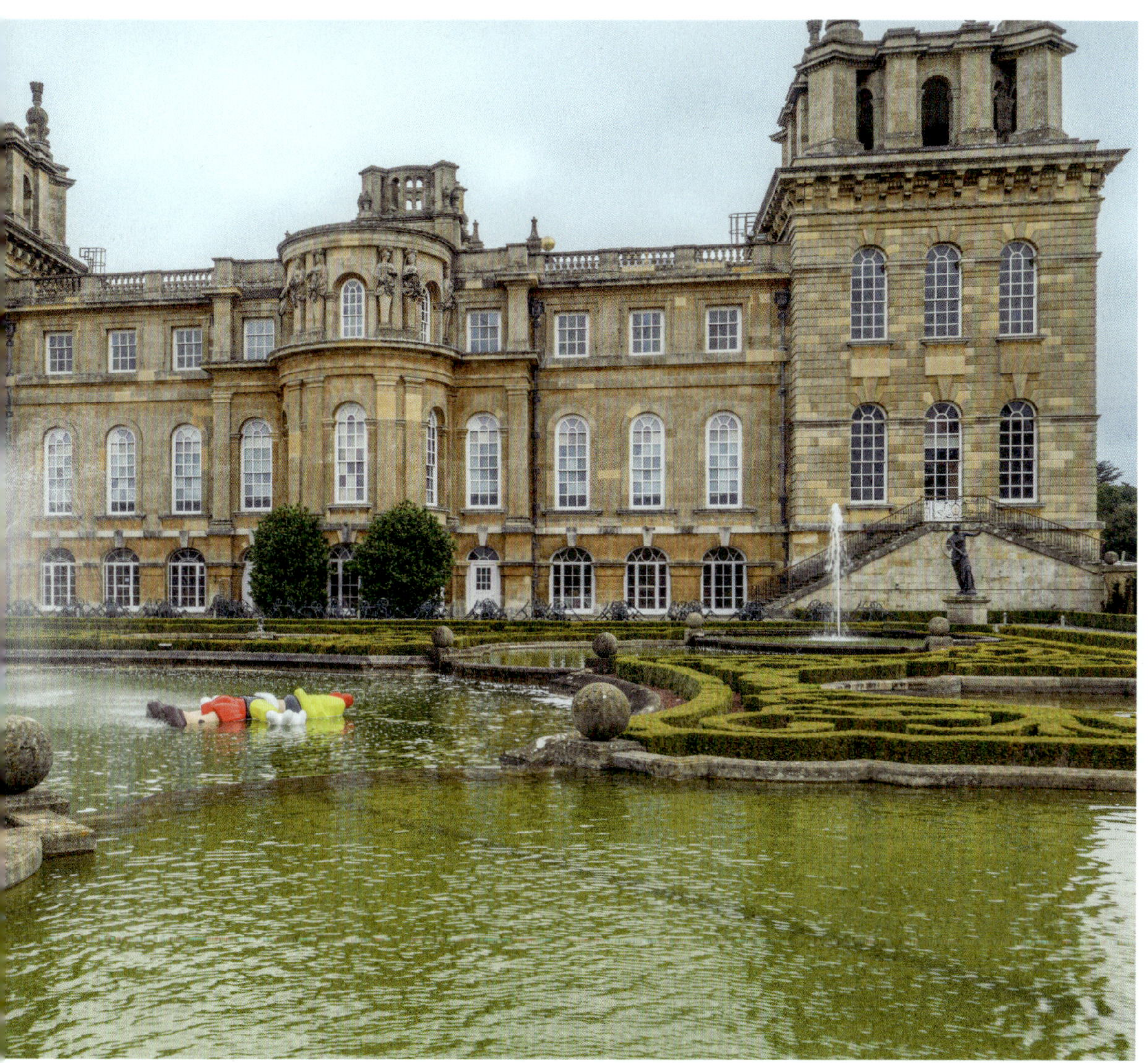

case, they were already selling coffee mugs, T-shirts, calendars, and posters. I don't think it's such a sin.

The Picasso figure was very popular. Lots of people took selfies with him, like the photos next to Mickey Mouse at Disneyland. So I tried not to interfere with whatever happened spontaneously. I used professional actors; I didn't give them any instructions, but I wanted them to do the same things Mickey Mouse does. After a while it was the visitors who directed almost everything. People were crazy to have their picture taken with him. It also showed that people wanted a different kind of memory of that place, a more personal one. If that Picasso did anything, it promoted the museum as a friendly place.

[14]   ***Daddy, Daddy*, 2008**
Polyurethane resin, steel, epoxy paint
37.5 × 97.8 × 87.6 cm

*Daddy, Daddy* is just an image taken from the Disney film *Pinocchio*. In the story, the son sacrifices himself to save his father, enabling him to change from a puppet into a child. Pinocchio is transformed by his feelings, his bond with Geppetto. Goodness knows what would have emerged if Collodi had been in analysis.

[14.1]   *Daddy, Daddy*, 2008
"theanyspacewhatever," curated by Nancy Spector, Solomon R. Guggenheim Museum, New York, October 24, 2008–January 7, 2009 (group show)

[14.2]   *Daddy, Daddy*, 2008
Polyurethane resin, steel, epoxy paint
272 × 123 × 300 cm
"Victory Is Not An Option," curated by Michael Frahm, Blenheim Palace, Woodstock, United Kingdom, September 12–October 27, 2019 (solo show)

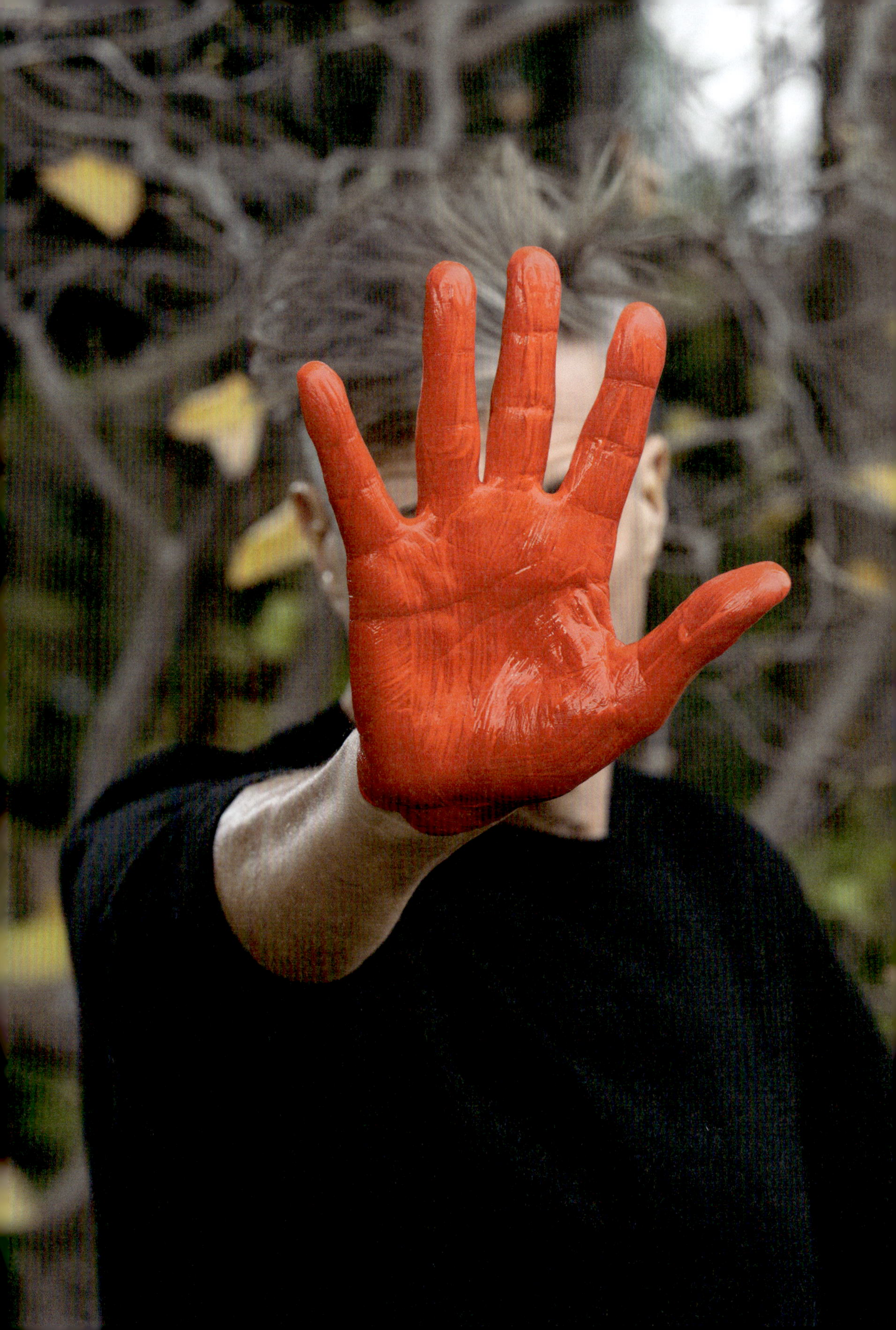

I come from a world that had nothing to do with art. I got lost along the way, entered a gallery and found myself being an artist. It was 1981 and I can recall the exact day. I was on the road between home and the hospital where I worked. There was an art gallery displaying Pistoletto's mirrors in the window. They impressed me so much that I plucked up my courage and went inside to get a better understanding of them. Ever since that day, art has been working its way into my head like a woodworm, small, immovable and voracious. It's like falling in love. The moment you see it, you know your life will never be the same again. It's that idea capable of taking over your mind, and you can't get rid of it. The experience of an artwork is something that marks you forever, as much as love at first sight.

In Padua, together with two other guys—we'd met by affinity and founded a group called Attrazioni Magnetiche [Magnetic Attractions]—I processed images using special equipment, a system that we'd developed starting from a gadget one of them used at the TV network where he worked. Our experiments strayed into comics. It was 1983 and we were also contributing to *Frigidaire*. At the same time we were experimenting with videos, but they weren't real artworks. In 1985 I went to New York. A friend suggested that we take the photos by Attrazioni Magnetiche to a gallery. They liked them, but nothing came of it. After a while, again in 1985, there was, at least on my part, the urge to move on to something else. I felt a manual skill growing in me, and I started making artifacts.

From Padua I settled in a building in the center of Forlì called "Palazzo del Diavolo" [Devil's Palace]. I emptied my apartment of junk and made it my workshop. It was the place of my first experiments. In Forlì I met a group of artists. What they did was very academic, so they weren't a role model for me and I wasn't a threat to them, since I didn't know how to do anything. Their life wasn't very different from mine, but they had style. There was something that attracted me, that excited me. Thanks to a friend who had a workshop, I refurbished my skills with a welder's torch, doing welding and working with materials. Everything turned on my domestic needs, or else I would produce something for my friends. Once I built a table, at another time a lamp, and then a chair. I took a metal sheet and cut it, I mixed other substances and experimented. The days in Forlì were wonderful for the continual discoveries I was making.

I decided to let people know what I was doing. Helped by my girlfriend at the time I took four photos, gave a name to the works, wrote a terrible cover letter in laughable English, and mailed a thousand copies to as many galleries, mostly in New York. It was the place I wanted to move to, my dream. I got three replies, all from Italy. Two of them thanked me and declined the offer, and there was only one, from Bologna, proposing that I should join a group exhibition at the Galleria Neon, which was reopening. That was the first time I set foot in the art world. I knew nothing about it. It was a fantasy. A dream. I made a pact with myself: "If I can support myself within two years, then I'll go on, otherwise I'll change again." My nightmare was to end up making a bad replica of my family. And I couldn't afford to find myself in a situation where I was completely broke and had to ask someone for help. I had no safety net.

Between late 1989 and early 1990 I moved to Milan. I got the yellow pages, copied out the addresses of the specialist magazines, and knocked on all the doors of the publishers' offices. Someone published photos of the lamp I had built, someone else began to sell it. For a year I slept in the same shop that marketed it, Dilmos, in Brera. The lights would be switched off, the shutter was pulled down, and for the night that shop became my home. It was so big that every night I could choose to fall asleep on a different bed.

But after a while, when they asked me to do something more substantial, I realized I wasn't interested. My head was somewhere else. I was thinking about art. There I was, in my late twenties, with no artistic training, desperately trying to come up with something clever, without making a complete fool of myself. I was so afraid of making mistakes that I ended up spending a lot of time alone. The city of art has rules and codes that you have to know and respect to be accepted. The first thing I did was to learn that language and those codes. The result was that many of my projects were seen as a critique of the art world, when in reality they were just my attempt at defining its parameters. Anyway, I remember the fear of doing something, of being judged and compared with others. As long as you decide not to measure yourself against anyone, everything is allowed, but when you confront the art community using the language of the period, everything becomes more complicated. All the same, it's true that comparing yourself with others can be inhibiting, but it can also help you grow.

It was an experience that formed my character. But I wouldn't say that I ever suffered. I always thought that being able to get where I wanted would depend only on my determination. I acted accordingly. I directed all my efforts and attention to being independent, and now I find myself here. They accepted me, with my doubts and fears, and I think that made all the difference, although I was always surprised there were people who found what I was doing interesting enough to buy it, or even just show it. It has been a wonderful adventure so far, and I see myself as privileged. The question that keeps nagging me is when will it end?

In Milan, anyway, some time passed before I could buy a house in Viale Bligny, sixteen square meters in all. I made my first real money in the mid-2000s. Before, even though I already had my own quotation, it was the auction houses that made the money. It was expensive to set up my projects, and I always finished without a penny left in my pocket. But it wasn't all that important. In the New York period, for example, I was able to live quietly on five dollars a day. And when I started to see the light financially, the only thing that really changed was being able to sit down in a restaurant without worrying about the prices. Before that I couldn't really go to a restaurant.

If I could forget where I came from, I would do it at once. I've always been fascinated by the idea of not coming from anywhere, of having no origins, in the style of *The Bourne Identity*. I find an unknown past much more interesting than a miserable one. This has certainly influenced my way of life and my work. Someone once said that a couple of misfortunes in the family are more than enough to make you not feel the need for a master. I think that's why I instinctively felt attracted to the art world. From the outside it looked like a place where no one would tell you to do or not do something, a place where you could experiment and discover things.

## [15]  Homeschooling. The Years at Palazzo del Diavolo: Forlì, 1986–89

[Maurizio Cattelan considers his years at Palazzo del Diavolo in Forlì a formative period, a form of self-schooling. The experiments conducted in that phase were a training ground for his artistic development and led to mature works in the following years]

From the mid-1980s I was living in Forlì. It was a period of experiments. I lived in a large building, nicknamed the "Palazzo del Diavolo." Here I created transitional objects, things that no one could really say what they were. I was also interested in understanding how a house worked, a fixation that hasn't really left me. For instance, one day I would make a hole in a wall, another day I would change the standard position of the switches. Instead of leaving them at the entrance to a room on the right, I would move them all to above the doors. Or, with the project that I called *Passaggio segreto*, I tried to trace domesticity by paths, or to trace life paths in domesticity, through signals that would record an experience. It's a set of works that no longer interests me today. To attain awareness at the time I used energy, instead of attaining it with reflection.

As for objects, what interested me was to shift the point of view. By reinterpreting it, or rather by its semantic refoundation, an object made for one function can become something else, regenerated and capable of amazing. For me the really important point was that the object had its own personality and, depending on the context, could be read as one thing or another. It was a fairly simple idea of reversals of meanings and signifiers, bound up with a sort of recovery of existing things. The continuous reworking of experience, which coincided with the research that I was then carrying out in my life, remained central.

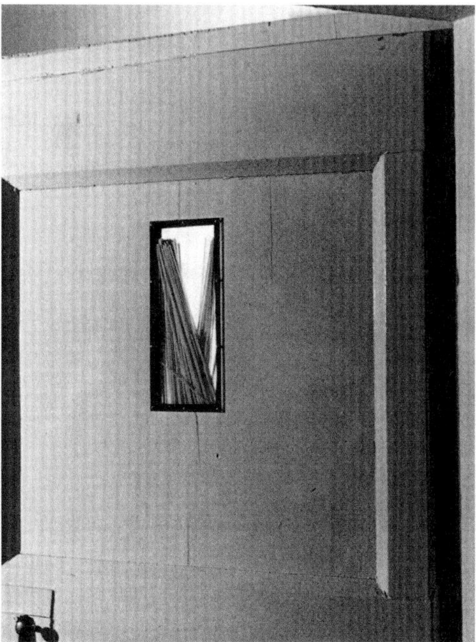

[15.1]

I started by designing tables and chairs. For example, I wanted to make a table that would be unusable, and I created one with more than a thousand legs, a "centipede table." From the functional, the works slowly moved towards something else. *Punto di vista mobile*, on the other hand, was a squat toilet. I liked the object. Instead of squatting you had to climb onto it, using it as a pedestal. I turned other found objects into ready-mades, which came to life after I'd kept them in the house for a while. One of them was the red chair of *Il dubbio di Mongo*, picked up in a flea market. Sometimes I assembled different objects inside a plexiglas structure, such

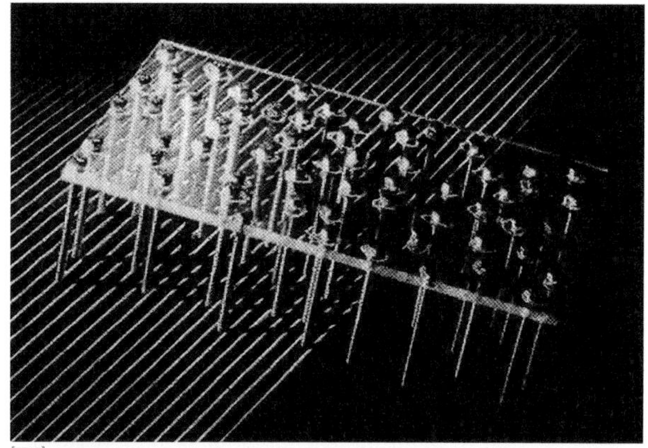

[15.2]

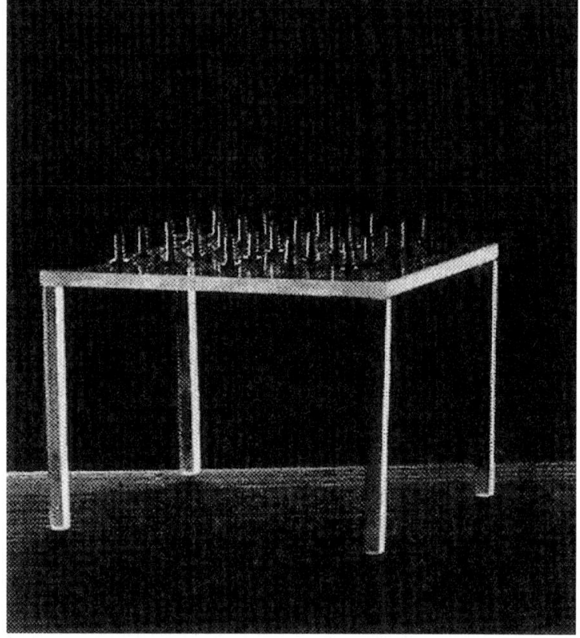

[15.3]

[15.1]  *Passaggio segreto*, 1988
Wood, plexiglas, spaghetti, screws
190 × 80 × 5 cm

[15.2]  *La marcia dei girasoli*, 1986
Milled plexiglas, bolts
7 × 25 × 15 cm

[15.3]  *Il tavolo dei ripensamenti*, 1986
Milled plexiglas, screws
11 × 14 × 12 cm

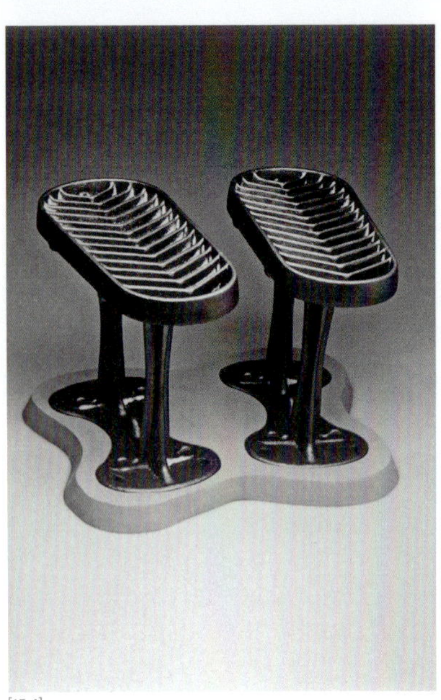

[15.4]

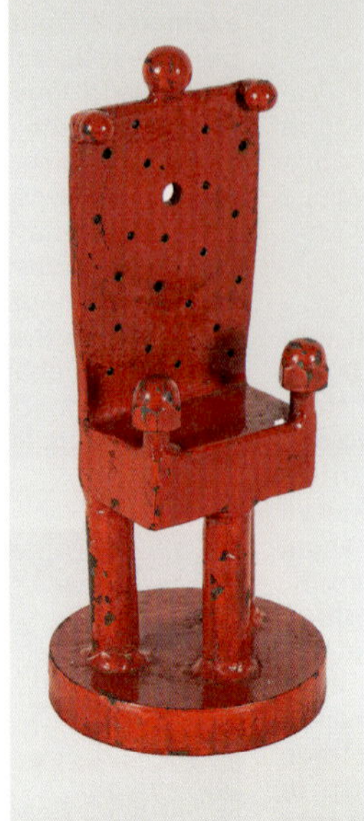

[15.5]

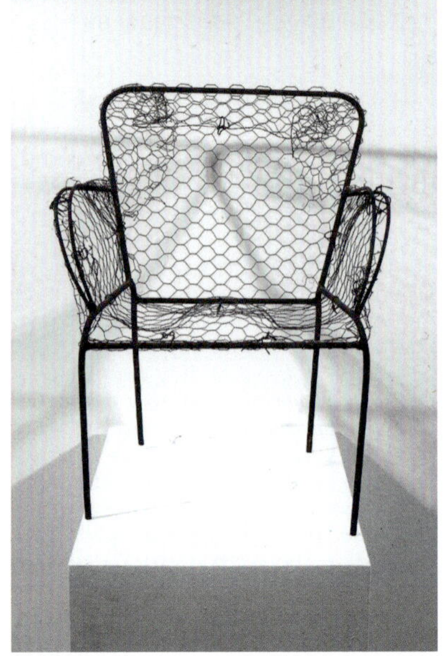

[15.6]



as bicycle parts to recreate a human form (*Untitled*, 1987). Or, more interestingly, I made a human-sculpture lamp out of it. I even had shoes made for *Il ripetente*, a work that exists in various editions. What interested me was the depiction of anthropomorphic imagery. I did various drawings and also made a kind of small being with a stomach out of waste paper.

*Trifidi* was a lamp I produced in an edition, and it kept me going. I presented it at the Neon gallery in Bologna, and then it was distributed by Dilmos, a store in the Brera quarter of Milan. It also went on display in Amsterdam, together with the tables, including *Cerberino*. The tables, too, when viewed from the heights of design, aren't very functional. They had problems of fabrication that a factory would never be bothered with. (They would have done for a product run of ten pieces at most.) In general, I've never bothered to call myself a designer or an artist. I think I'm a skulker in all my activities.

For *Giustificatore* I took a sentence and framed it. It's that Chinese story of the artist who's commissioned by the emperor to make the most beautiful drawing ever seen of a crab. For ten years he does nothing, then in the end, in an instant, before the emperor, he picks up the brush and paints the most perfect crab.

I approached *Angolo dei Ricordi* by thinking about European and Oriental architecture and the fact that there are gray areas in the home as well as in life. But I also wanted to find a solution for the continuous flow of incoming mail. Today I'd toss it all out, but then it was the opposite. I just didn't know what to do with it. I thought that by putting everything in a corner I would solve the problem, but now I don't know if I would do the work again with that mailbox. At the time it was what it should have been, a sort of graveyard for the mail.

The 1988 series *Untitled* was an experiment that grew out of the fact that at the time I collected scraps of paper that I found lying around the town, like shopping lists or slips bearing notes. Since I was also very attentive to what other artists were doing, and everyone was doing screen prints, I thought of doing them too, starting from those pieces of paper. At that time you went to a printer, left the original, came back two days later and they gave you the film. Then you had the stencil made somewhere else, in the format you wanted. The work could even be quite large.

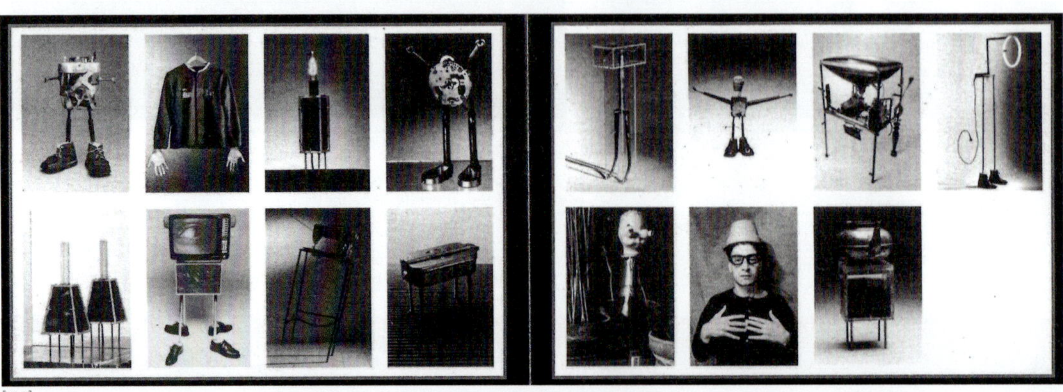

[15.7]

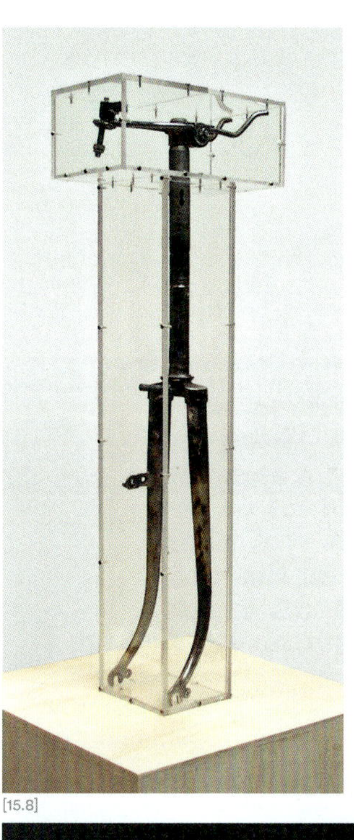

[15.8]

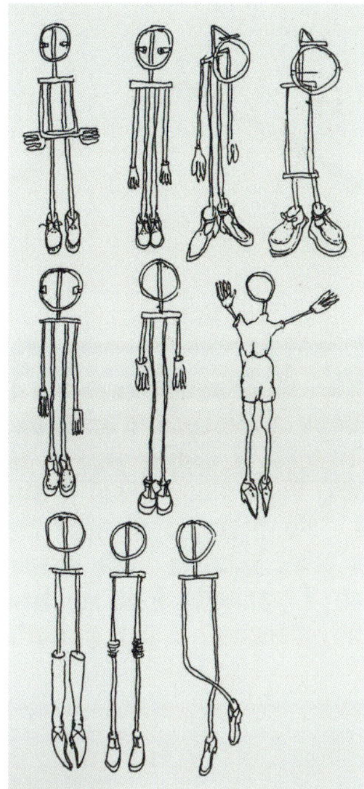

[15.9]

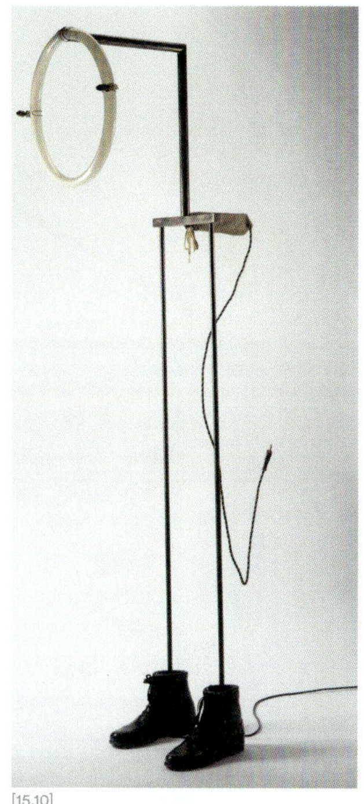

[15.10]

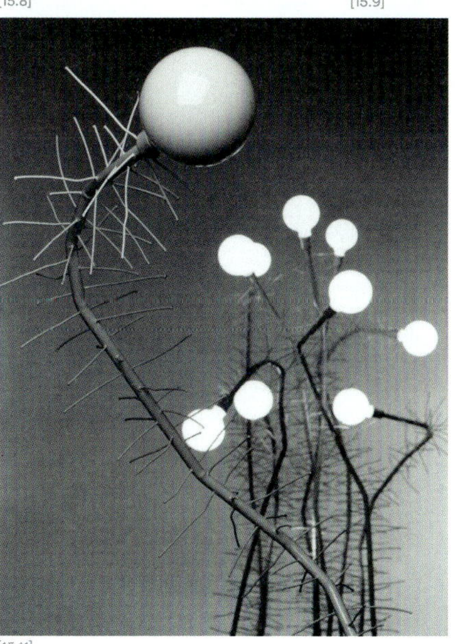

[15.11]

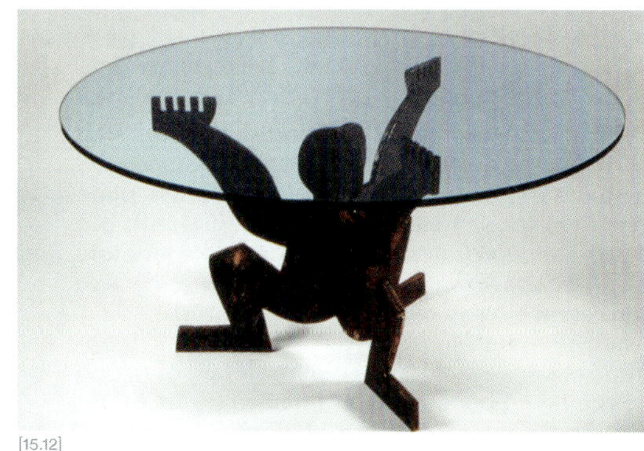

[15.12]



[15.4]  *Punto di vista mobile*, 1989
Cast iron, lacquered wood
40 × 33 × 30 cm

[15.5]  *Il dubbio di Mongo*, 1987–88
Enamelled iron
27 × Ø 13 cm

[15.6]  *Re per un giorno*, 1988
Found metal armchair frame, chicken wire
40 × 50 × 40 cm

[15.7]  Objects realized in 1986–87 illustrated on the
leporello *Le edizioni / The Publishing*, an appendix
to the publication *Gli anni del Diavolo 1985-1991*
(n.p.: Palazzo del Diavolo Edizioni, n.d.)

[15.8]  *Untitled*, 1987
Plexiglas, iron
74.5 × 25 × 14 cm

[15.9]  Drawings published beside *Il ripetente*, in *Maurizio
Cattelan: Personale* (n.p.: Palazzo del Diavolo
Edizioni, 1987)

[15.10]  *Il ripetente*, 1987
Metal, electric wire, neon, shoes
Height 188 cm

[15.11]  *Trifidi*, 1987
Lamps in galvanized iron
200 × 30 × 30 cm

[15.12]  *Cerberino*, 1989
Table with flame-cut raw iron base and crystal top
73.7 cm, Ø between 120 and 160 cm
Produced by Dilmos, Milan

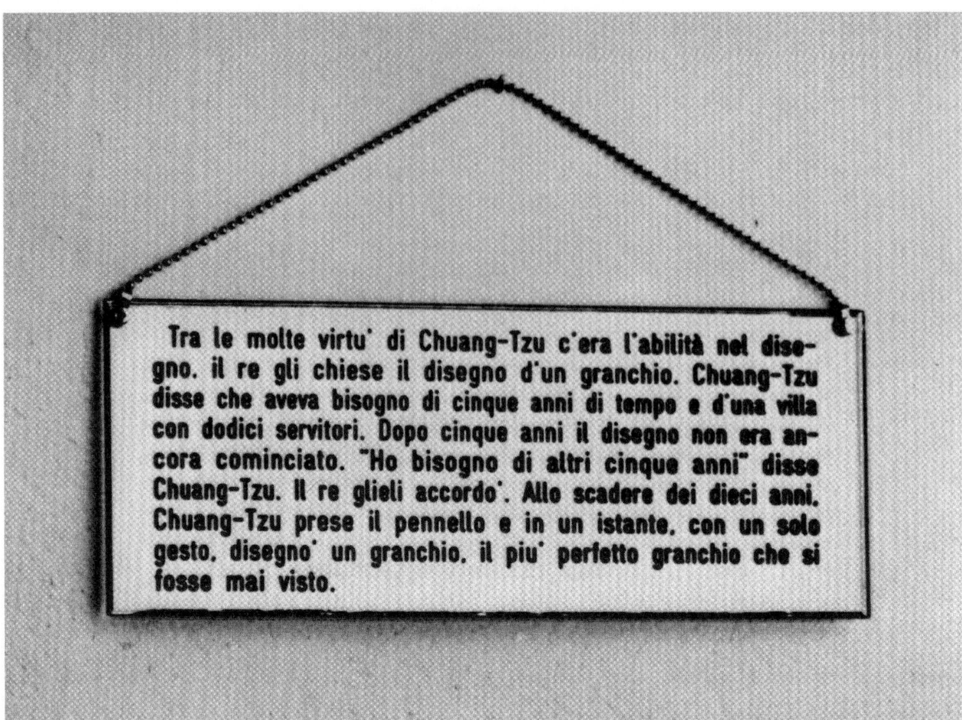



[15.13]

50

I actually made one with a piece of paper that I'd found posted in my building that said: "Non si accettano testimoni di Geova" [No Jehovah's Witnesses]. I had it engraved on a brass plate and then I put it together with other plates I'd got from various professional offices, like doctors and lawyers. I was interested in how a form of intolerance could easily be standardized.

Then I created lists of words for myself: "concentration, discipline..." I did a painting of it, one of the few. Sooner or later I had to try painting, but the experience was short-lived. *Untitled* from 1991 is one of my few canvases. It's connected with the period of the lists at Palazzo del Diavolo.

Then I was interested in the idea of sitting in an armchair and watching someone else paint for me. I even thought I could delegate my work to machinery, computers or biology. But computer science was still primitive, and I also wanted to free myself from electricity. *Cerniere* developed around an idea of nature, but a "cowardly" nature, seen synthetically with a futuristic language and thanks to a coincidence. I had some double glazing and the work materialized accordingly, in continuity with the ones made of plexiglas, in which there is always transparency between the container and the content. I wanted to make a sculpture that would age and I got plants to grow in soil inserted in the double glazing. At first the idea was to hang them on the wall like paintings. (Just as the painter puts paints on the canvas, I'd put the plants.) But then I attached them with zippers. The plants began to take root. I'd never had a great feeling for biology, but caring for the plants gave me another rhythm, right from the morning, when I had to water them. *Cactus vigliacco* is an earlier work, in fiberglass, with heads spurting water.

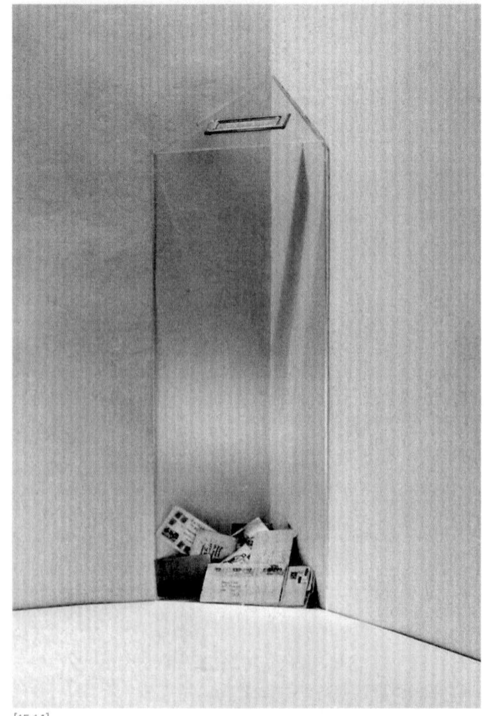

[15.14]

[15.13]  *Giustificatore*, 1989
Milled and painted plexiglas
12 × 30 cm

[15.14]  *Angolo dei Ricordi*, 1989
Plexiglas, brass, correspondence
145 × 45 × 37 cm
"Metessi. Tracce, passaggi, scritture, gesti, impronte d'arte contemporanea," curated by Gabriele Perretta, Galleria Lidia Carrieri, Rome, December 5, 1989–January 15, 1990 (group show)

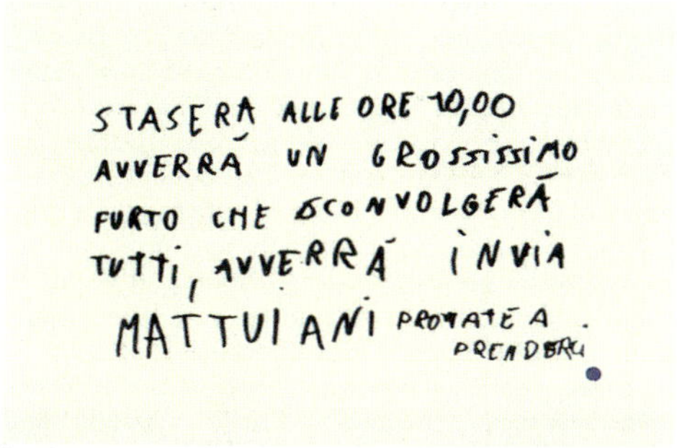

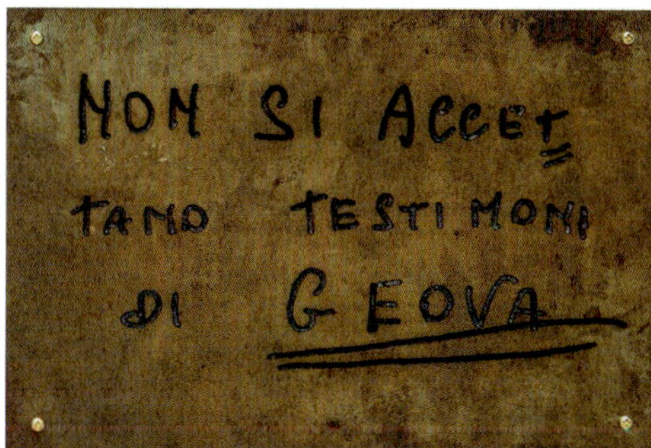


[15.15]

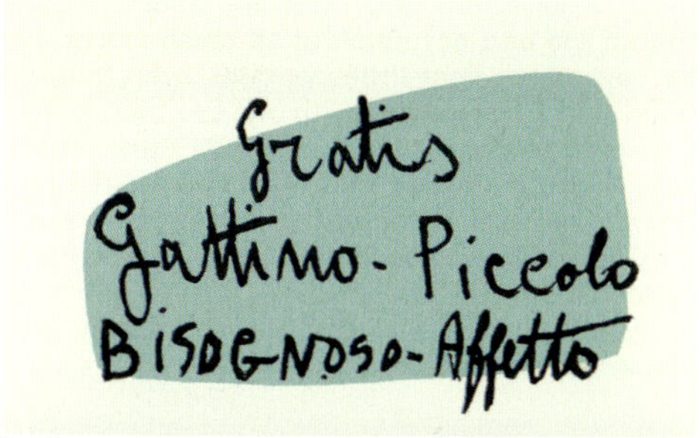

[15.16]



[15.17]

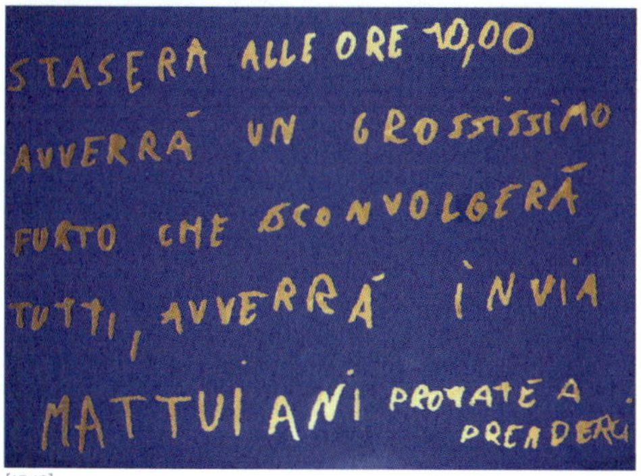

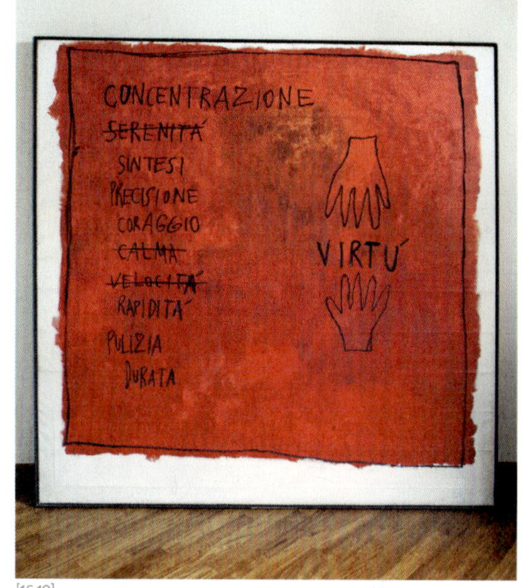


[15.19]

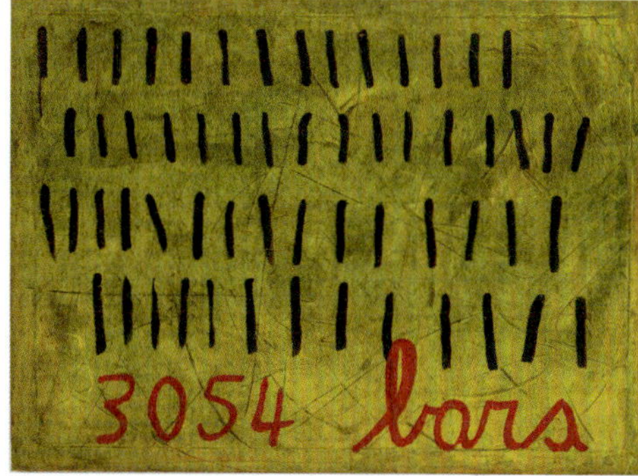


[15.20]



[15.18]

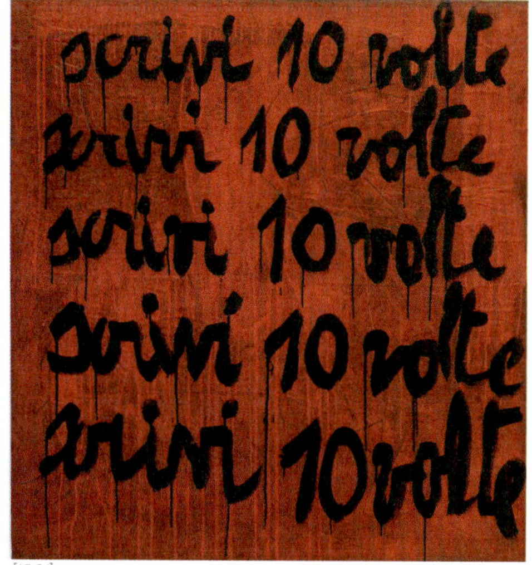


[15.21]

51

[15.15]   *Untitled*, 1988
Silkscreen on paper
60 × 80 cm

[15.16]   *Untitled*, 1988
Silkscreen on paper
60 × 80 cm

[15.17]   *Non si accettano testimoni di Geova*, 1989
6 plates in engraved brass
Variable dimensions

[15.18]   *Stasera alle ore 10,00*, 1986
Acrylic on aluminum
140 × 190 cm

[15.19]   *Untitled*, 1991
Mixed media on canvas
200 × 200 × 4 cm

[15.20]   *Untitled*, 1997
Mixed media on canvas
78 × 103.5 × 3 cm

[15.21]   *Untitled*, 1997
Mixed media on canvas
120 × 110 × 3 cm

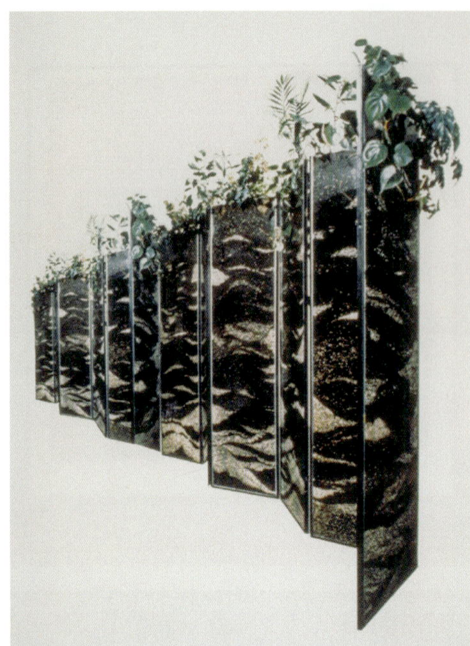

[15.22]

*Rulò* strikes me as epitomizing those years of semantic inversions. This armchair can also be considered an object that simply makes an appearance, because its function of enabling people to sit down is impossible. I did a series of drawings of the ways it could be used. You could piss on it, you could cook on it, it could become the center of a situation, of a happening... From an old ironworker I bought a lathe-worker's or welder's tube, but its only use would be as a grave vase, because of its absurd four handles.

In three years I threw out a lot of stuff. Then, after a while, I stopped and asked myself: "And now what will I do with them?" So I began to make a selection and refashion them. I think that in the end not much of all these works can be saved, but that little contains everything. *Il quadrupede*, a creature with one eye that moves, thanks to a video recorder, and with a furry stomach, is one of the few that were shown. The rest are all works that I published but it didn't seem right to exhibit. Even then it was time to move beyond them. All those works have a patina of irony, but some, if you look at them closely, also display great sadness.

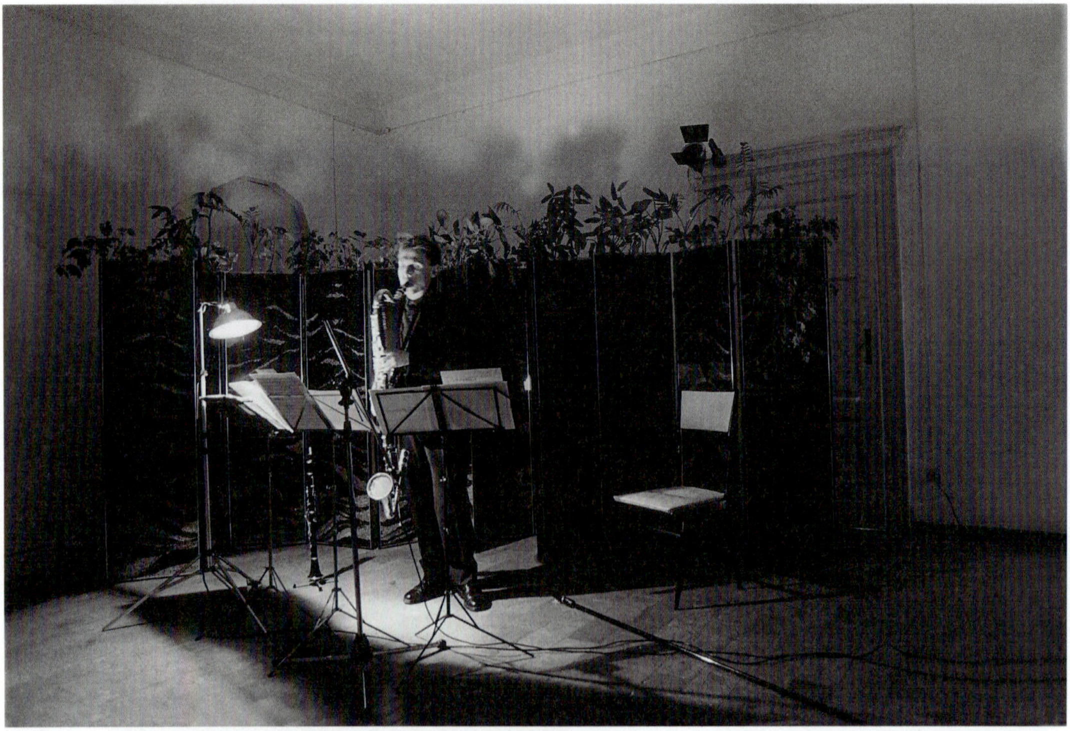

[15.23]

[15.24]   *Cactus vigliacco*, 1987
Portable fountain, iron, fiberglass, water,
hydraulic circuit, plexiglas
220 × Ø 80 cm

[15.22]   *Cerniere*, 1989
Steel, glass, silicon, soil, water, plants
180 × 2000 × 1 cm (extended)

[15.25]   *Rulò*, 1989
Seat in wood and padded velvet
55 × Ø 80 cm
Produced by Dilmos, Milan

[15.23]   *Cerniere*, 1989
"Paesaggi interni," Palazzo del Diavolo, Forlì, 1989,
installation with musical intervention by Roberto Paci Dalò

[15.26]   *Il quadrupede*, 1987
Shoes, hair, TV

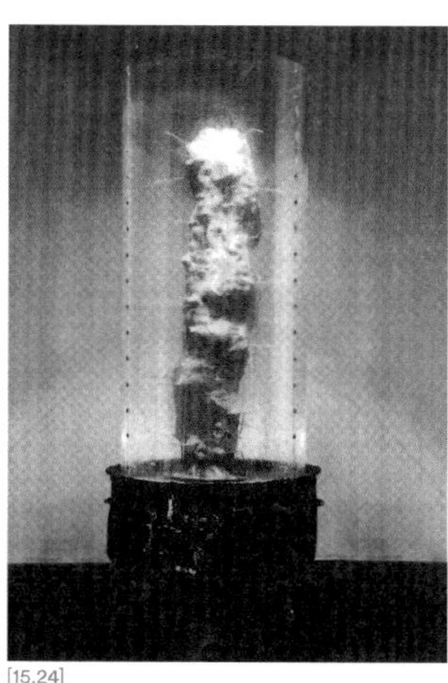
[15.24]

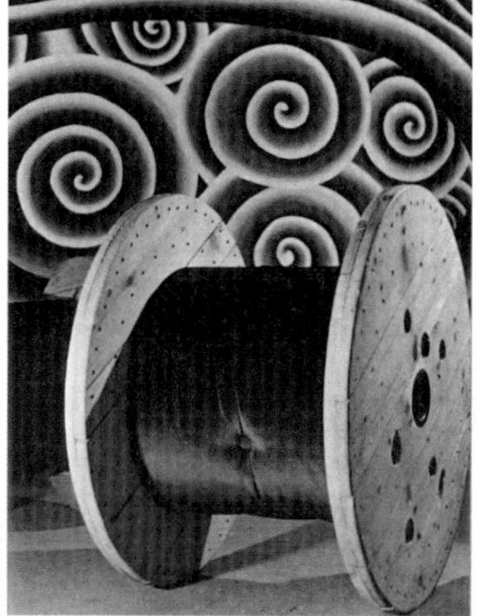
[15.25]

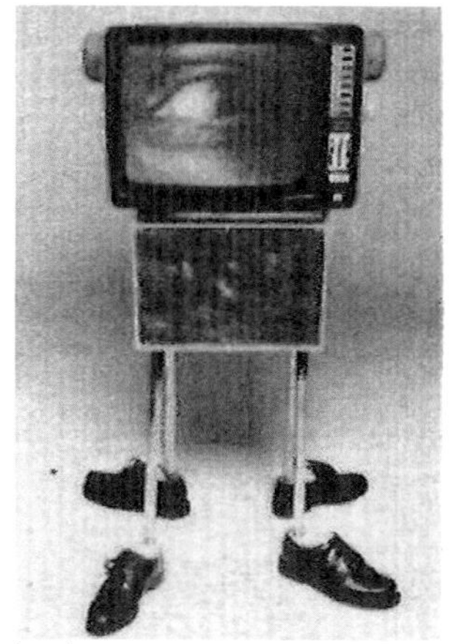
[15.26]

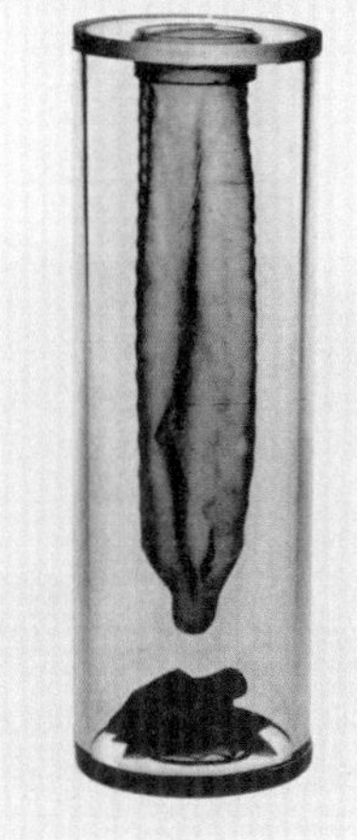
[15.27]

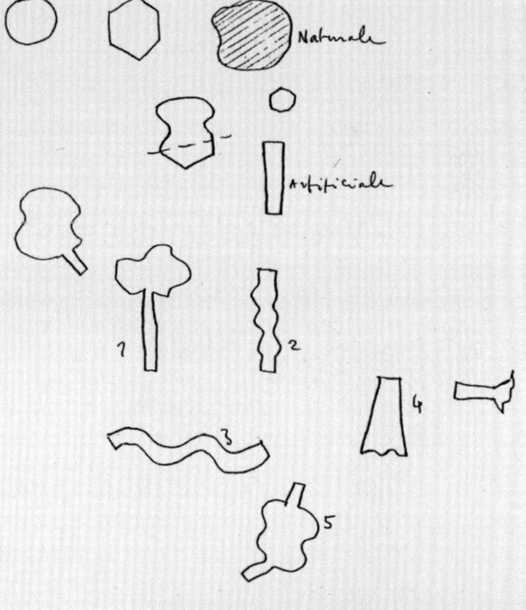

[15.28]

53

[15.27]   *Clessidra*, 1988
Plexiglas, condoms
27 × Ø 8 cm

[15.28]   Synoptic table of possible symbols
for cataloging one's own work, 1989
Pencil on paper
30 × 21 cm

[15.29]   Decorative objects made from glass flasks filled
with water and connected to a pump through
tubes that produce a sound, support in mirror,
c. 1986–89

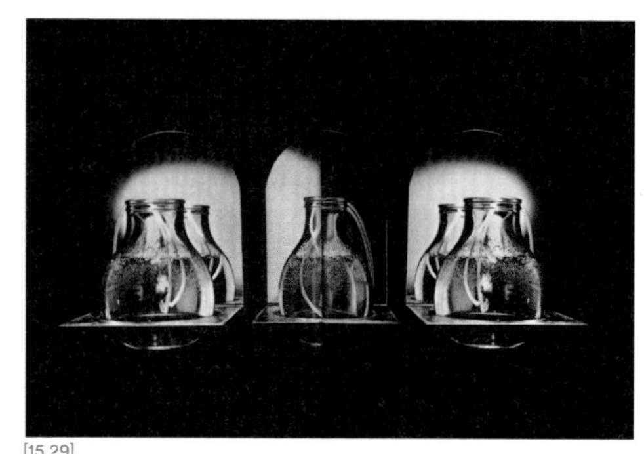
[15.29]

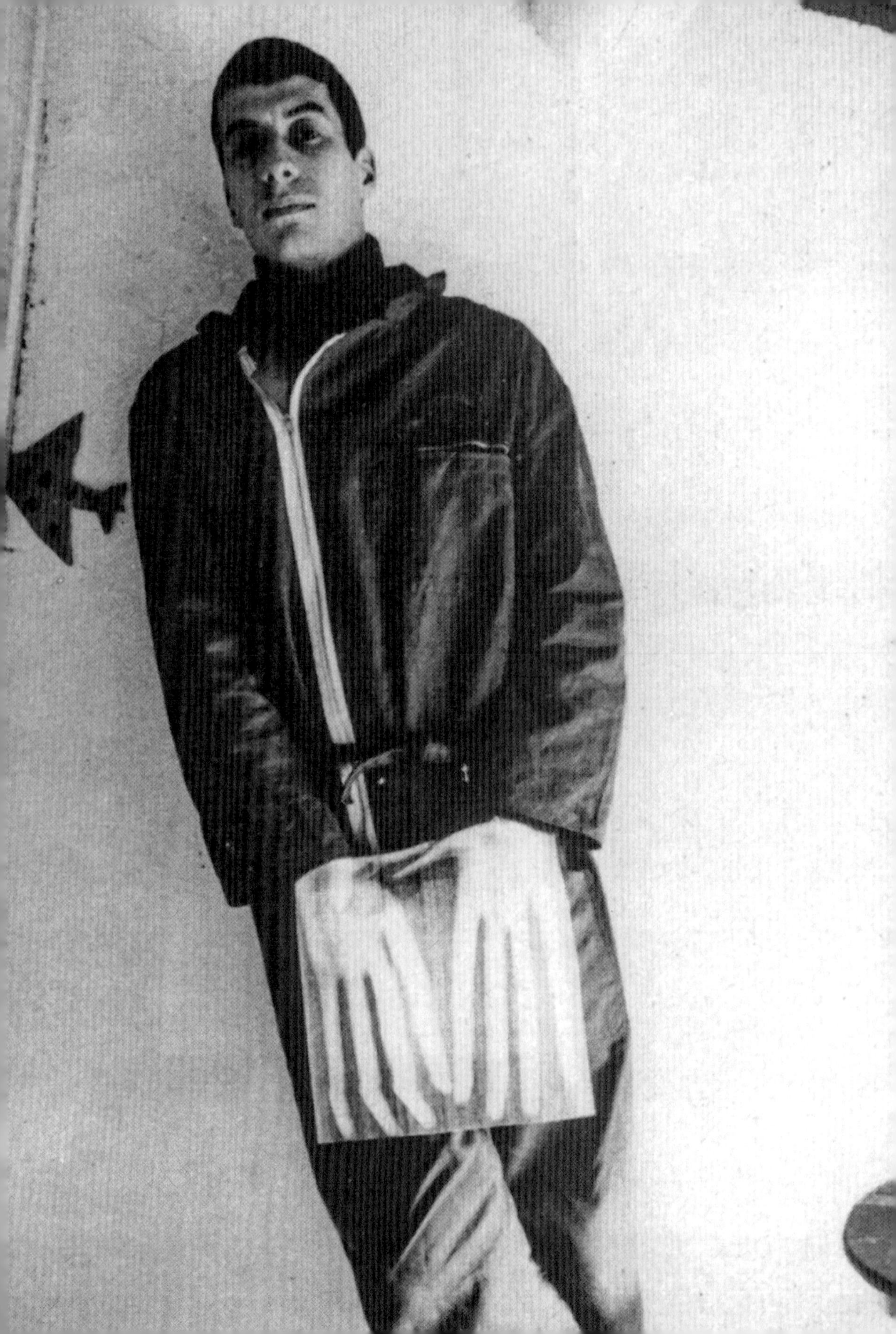

**[Untitled]**

←   Maurizio Cattelan, c. 1987. Photograph published in *Maurizio Cattelan: Personale* (n.p.: Palazzo del Diavolo Edizioni, 1987)

I've always had a good relationship with my body. It was difficult for me to take an interest in just some part of the body or in some bodily organs, even though sincerely my stomach caught all my attention for a while. I still remember the words said during a talk by a person whose face I can't remember: "Your hands are enormous. They could be the hands of a person certainly twice your size." The echoes of these words are still buzzing like mosquitos around me. It was inevitable, my attention first as a foreigner, then as a scientist, every day, very instant, every time my glance fell on them with simulated indifference, they always spitefully appeared a little bigger. How could I have been believing and seeing their normality for such a long time? Nevertheless his voice goes on buzzing. Perhaps I could thank him or, like a virile man, wind myself around him like a boa constrictor and crush him.

It was unthinkable to live as before with a half-size body, unable to endure this disproportion. The temptation to watch them, to get that obsessive phrase out of my head is turning into an obsession.

Sometimes I resolve to stop, forcing myself, yes, from today on I won't look at them anymore, and in the meantime while I'm thinking this, my traitorous eyes settle on them.

The horizon has lowered to the level of my hands. Always in my manifestations something includes or remembers them. Maybe the eyes of a stranger haven't the necessary cunning to catch the connection or the allusions; the only justification is that his hands are exactly the right size for his body.

It's difficult to say when my passion for painting started; I have always desired to portray through the image of the human being its soul or its nature.

Just now, rich in a new revelation on my body, I have become aware that I have been painting bodies for ages; bodies like this, without realizing my fundamental incapacity to express the inmost character of their souls in their big-eyed glances and in their jutting thoraxes. Like the equation where the product remains invariable, so was the result if I was looking at hands.

The walls around me are certainly less appetizing than any butcher's shop, but what a primitive feeling compared to this crowd of hands deprived of their bodies and dangling, victims of a dirty increase and with the only extenuating circumstance being that these bodies were incapable of expressing their souls.

1234 5678 90, 1234 567890 123 4567 890 1234 5678 90. 12345 67 89 0, 12 3456 7890 12 34 5678 90 1234567890. 1 2345, 6789, 0 1234 56789 0, 123456 7890 123 345 6789 0 1234 567 890. 123 45678 90 1234, 5678 90 1234, 5678 90 1234 5678 90, 1234, 567 890 12 3456 7890 1234. 5678 901 234 5678 9012 345 6789 0123456, 78901 2345 678 9012, 34567, 8901. 23456, 78901 234 5678 901 234 56789 01 2. 345 6789 0123, 4567 8901 234 5678 90 1234 567 890 1234, 56789 01234 5678, 90123 4567 890123 4567. 8901 2345 67890, 12345 6789 0123 45678 901.

Rashness went side-by-side my lonely existence for long time. I was almost a man when I encountered the sufferings which afflict the human being: responsibility, and like every true man I could be proud of it. I didn't even cry the day someone told me: "You must be strong. They were two great people. You're sure to be like them." That day I didn't cry, but today I'm very sad, or rather unhappy; when I went downstairs and I saw it wasn't there anymore a voice inside me said: "They have stolen it." People in need of course, a bike whose color is difficult to define—is "stagnant water" a color?—but surely by ripping some-one off they would have got two meals at the canteen, but at what a price! I'm very tired, I always remember everything by halves, sometimes approximately. I'm nearly sure when I say I was three years old when I was riding around the streets in town: a better feeling than being carried about. I'm sure that then I became aware of what is called pleasure. If I've got to choose between flying and walking I much prefer pedaling. Then my ninth birthday came, three gears on the back wheel, a necessary distinction, like the difference between a nag and a thoroughbred. Yes, okay, only three, but true equilibrium must not be confused. This is how I spent my first nine years. I too am caught up in the gears of development and the roar is the noise of our time. An ace of hearts and a wooden peg were enough. I keep escaping and reappearing, timing myself and strengthened by the new voice which said: ppprrrrrr. Today, even without that cunning, I whiz along the asphalt like then, always with the wind behind me, my calves hardening and my feet pushing: poetry isn't an invention, it already exists. Pain is a beginning for a lot of people, others prefer to reach it, but the bike is painful for everyone, a very difficult concept to absorb. I've never brought the symbol of some perverse faith into the question, but I'm as certain that I've seen workers become machinery. Of course I'm not a reformer, apart from some normal repairs. I've spent all my birthdays with this bike, whose colors fade with the years, an indisputable trace of time, with the repetition, each time I get on it, of the first feeling which made me a cyclist. Today life has gained a new face. I've lost a bike.

[Text published in *Maurizio Cattelan: Personale* (n.p.: Palazzo del Diavolo Edizioni, 1987), n.p.]

# Dedicated to Home: Designing the Process

I approached the sphere of design spontaneously, but I see myself more as following a line of expression that strays into art. I come from various experiences of work that have been episodic in nature, and they've helped me understand some of the mechanisms and balances of life, and to develop a method of inquiry. At present I'm busy with some works for an exhibition entitled "Biologia delle passioni" to be held in May at certain galleries: sculpture-objects that arise from everyday life in the home understood as the micro-architecture of life. I have no great long-term desires or even projects in my drawer. I don't even know whether this research will ever lead me to conclusions or to "understanding." I only hope I'll have the strength one day to close the garage door and forget the key in the pocket of some garment. I'm happy to have taken part in a round table with such an enigmatic title for one reason in particular: in this "being" of mine I have many doubts, many questions, and these often provide the outline that I work on and develop. This event has enabled me to realize I'm not alone in this state of mind, and that a sense of uncertainty also pervades other experiences. Probably this is our unconscious strength. I'm not attracted to industry, in fact it rather scares me, so I don't feel I need to appeal to it in any way. The only thing I want to know is whether it's true that the project can be honest and have its own dignity, or whether it's just a means for keeping the profit machine ticking over. Can the thinking project that has consciousness exist, without polluting our nerve endings, or is this just some stupid virginal idealism?

["Dedicato all'abitare: Progettare il processo," text published in *GAP Casa*, no. 58 (June 1989): 105, collected in the context of the round table "Dedicato a… chi produce e a chi vende," curated by Clara Mantica and Luciana Cuomo, at the Dilmos showroom in Milan]

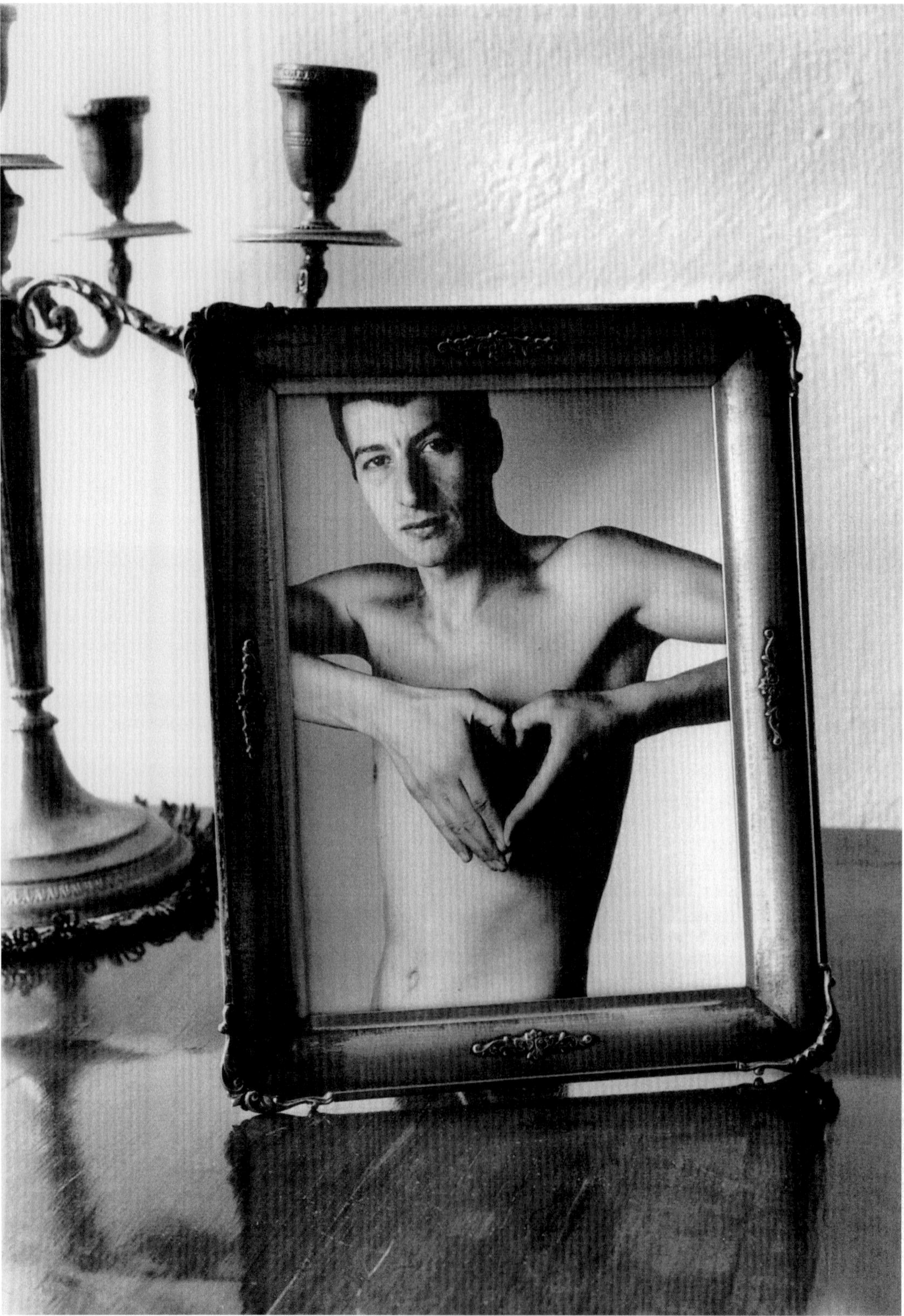



[16.1] *Lessico familiare*, 1989
Oratorio di San Sebastiano, Forlì, 1989 (group show)

[16.2] *Lessico familiare*, 1989
"Not Afraid of Love," curated by Chiara Parisi, Monnaie
de Paris, October 21, 2016–January 8, 2017 (solo show)

[16] ***Lessico familiare**, 1989*
Black-and-white photography,
silver frame
19.7 × 15.2 cm

This was a gift to my fiancée. The sign I make with my hands is inflated now, but it wasn't popular at the time. I had an obsession with hands, and two or three things came out of it that I then interpreted in a couple of photos. It was also my version of the classic portrait put in a silver frame to commemorate some special event. Usually it's a family portrait, but I was alone here. I did the work for an exhibition at the Oratorio di San Sebastiano in Forlì. There wasn't just the frame. At the time a wooden console, complete with candlesticks and a marble decoration, were also part of the work. But there weren't any candles. The truth is that I needed a base for it. I didn't have one, so I took a table from my bedroom. Everything framed the photo, creating a short circuit between the middle-class setting and my bare-chested image, and you couldn't understand how it could have ended up there. Then I realized the photo had to stand on its own. This is the work.

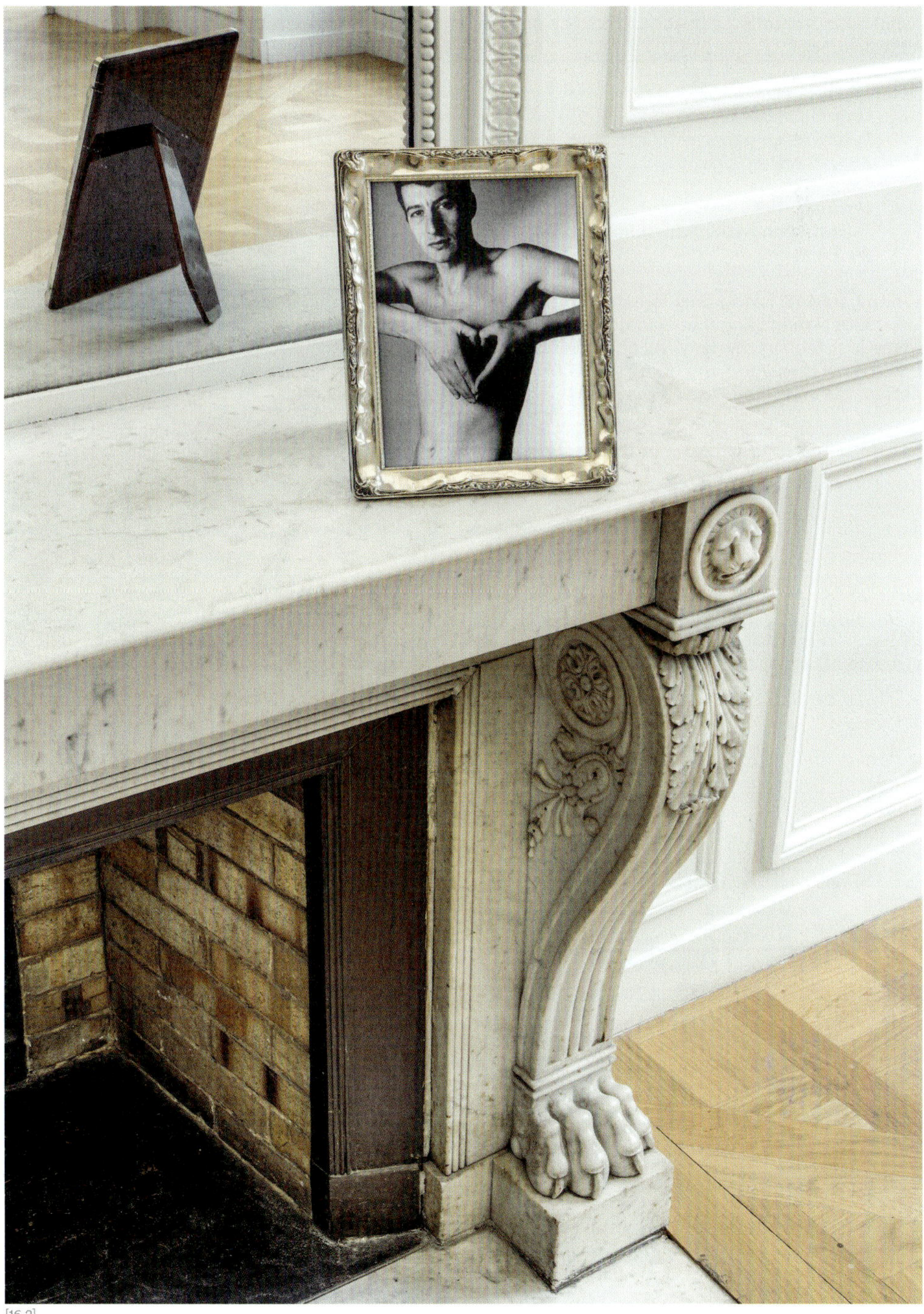

[16.2]

[17] *Grammatica quotidiana*, 1989
Offset lithography on letterpress-printed
board and paper
29.2 × 21 × 5.1 cm

It's a calendar of the kind there used to be in every home. I got this one from a bakery, the Modernissimo in Forlì, where I used to buy bread. I like the idea that every day is the same. It's a perpetual calendar: today, today, today... At the time I knew nothing about conceptual art, but seeing this work again I realize that unconsciously it was perhaps also my answer to the doubts raised at the time about the conception of time and the idea of its linear progression. After all, it was also a calendar promoting a bakery, in other words an advertisement.

[18] *Untitled*, 1989
Typewritten paper with additions in ink
35 × 22 cm

[19] *Untitled*, 1991
Typewritten paper with additions in ink
29.2 × 21 cm

When I started taking part in exhibitions, in the late 1980s, I didn't know how to go about it at all. I was just feeling my way. At any given show I could have presented any of my works from that period, but I felt they weren't the right things. For the group show "Briefing" at the Galleria Luciano Inga-Pin in Milan, until the last minute I tried to come up with something suitable. In the end, the day before, I was desperate, so I said that I did have a work but someone had stolen it from me. A colossal excuse! I invented a story that seemed plausible and then went to the police station in Forlì and told them that I had to show my work in an exhibition, I had put it in the car, and the next morning, when I went out, there was nothing there. Describing it was the most difficult part, because it was impossible to predict how the police would react, especially when it was time to specify that the work was invisible. My statement, recorded on the form, reads verbatim: "Yesterday evening, 21.3.1991, I parked the car of my girlfriend Giambi Patrizia on Via P. Maroncelli, at 8:30 p.m. It was not locked. The car with license plate FO 453979 is a Golf VW. Inside the car was a package containing an 'INVISIBLE' work. It is of sentimental value and was meant to be presented in a show in Milan." The policeman looked at me a bit strangely, but in the end he wrote all this down and stamped it. I sent the police report to the gallery to be exhibited.
Two years earlier I'd done more or less the same thing. I didn't know what to do for a show in the Loggetta Lombardesca in Ravenna, which no one came to. It was just me and the caretaker, and I asked the doctor to write me a note to get out of it, just like I did when I was working and wanted a day off.

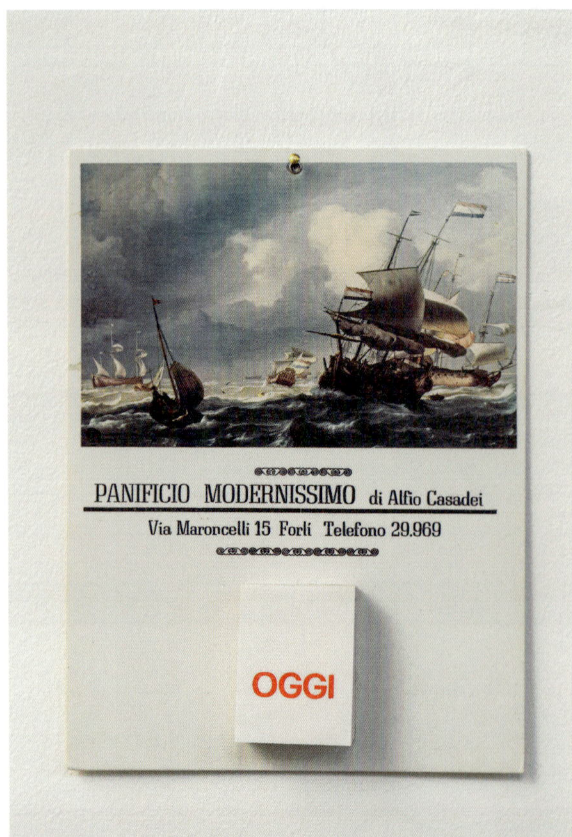


[17.1]

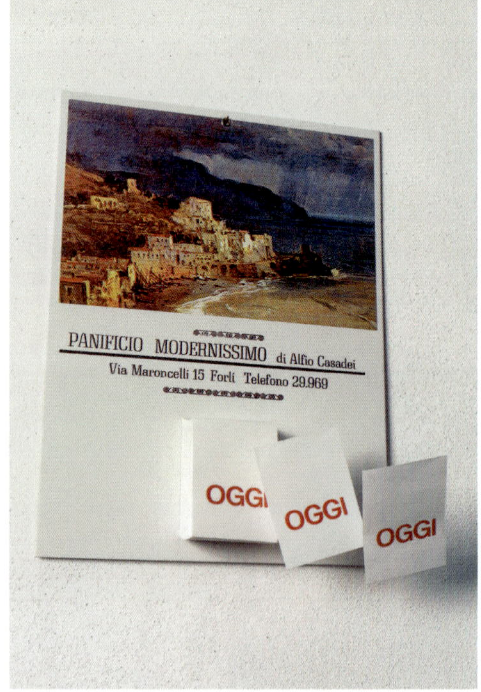


[17.2]

[17.1-2]  *Grammatica quotidiana*, 1989

61

**A** Da consegnare o trasmettere a mezzo Raccomandata A.R. a cura del lavoratore, al datore di lavoro entro due giorni dalla data del rilascio (art. 15 legge 23.4.1981, n. 155).

### REGIONE EMILIA-ROMAGNA

N. ______

#### ATTESTATO DI MALATTIA

Cattelan Maurizio       RO 0620083
(cognome e nome) (1)          (numero libretto)

Prognosi clinica fino al _26.11.88_

Dichiara di essere ammalato dal _12.11.88_

• ☒ inizio malattia   • ☐ continuazione   Ricaduta di malattia precedente? ☐ SI ☒ M

Data _12.11.88_

Dott. Raffaele Di Pal
Medico Chirurgo 13025
V.le Fulcieri 119 medtel. 68263
47100 FORLI'

#### AVVERTENZE PER IL LAVORATORE

1) L'attestato A, a cura del lavoratore (anche se sospeso da non oltre 60 giorni) deve essere recapitato o trasmesso, a mezzo raccomandata con avviso di ricevimento al datore di lavoro entro due giorni dal rilascio.

2) Il certificato B, a cura del lavoratore avente diritto all'indennità giornaliera di malattia a carico dell'INPS (anche se disoccupato o sospeso da non oltre 60 giorni), deve essere recapitato, entro due giorni dal rilascio, alla struttura INPS o USL localmente designata nella cui circoscrizione risiede il lavoratore interessato durante la malattia.

3) L'indennità, a carico dell'INPS, spetta per la durata della malattia (prognosi) indicata dal medico. Il lavoratore, in caso di prosecuzione della malattia, deve comprovare tempestivamente la circostanza mediante nuova documentazione sanitaria (certificato ed attestato) da far pervenire alla struttura INPS o USL localmente designata ed al datore di lavoro con le modalità e nei termini in precedenza indicati.

4) Il ritardo nell'invio o nella presentazione della documentazione sanitaria comporta la perdita del diritto all'indennità giornaliera di malattia per i giorni di ritardo.

5) La visita medica a domicilio, se richiesta entro le ore 10, sarà eseguita di norma nel corso dello stesso giorno: se richiesta invece dopo le ore 10 sarà effettuata entro le ore 12 del giorno successivo.

6) Si raccomanda al lavoratore avete diritto all'indennità di malattia l'esatta compilazione, possibilmente in stampatello, del riquadro a lui riservato sul certificato B, in quanto i dati richiesti sono essenziali per il sollecito adempimento dei compiti dell'INPS, ivi compreso il pagamento diretto dell'indennità di malattia nei casi previsti. L'omissione, ovvero l'inesatta o incompleta indicazione dell'indirizzo sarà considerata quale assenza a visita medica di controllo. Si sottolinea altresì la necessità di compilare l'ultima parte del riquadro nel caso in cui lo stato di malattia sia stato causato da terzi (incidente stradale, ecc.).

• Contrassegnare la casella che interessa.

NOTA: 1) Per le donne coniugate indicare il cognome da nubile.

GASA - 1.000.000 - 1/87

**B** Da recapitare o trasmettere a mezzo Raccomandata A.R. a cura del lavoratore alla struttura INPS o USL localmente designata competente per territorio, presso cui il lavoratore risiede durante la malattia, entro due giorni dalla data del rilascio.

### REGIONE EMILIA-ROMAGNA

N. ______

#### CERTIFICATO DI DIAGNOSI

(da compilarsi a cura del medico - art. 2 DL 30.12.1979, n. 663 e legge conversione 29.2.1980, n. 33, modificato art. 15 legge 23.4.1981, n. 155)

______ (cognome e nome) (1)       ______ (numero libretto)

Prognosi clinica fino al ______

Dichiara di essere ammalato dal ______

• ☐ inizio malattia   • ☐ continuazione   Ricaduta di malattia precedente? ☐ SI ☒ M

Data ______

Dott. Raffaele Di Pal
Medico Chirurgo 13025
V.le Fulcieri 119 medtel. 68263
47100 FORLI'

#### DIAGNOSI

_Astenia psico fisica_

#### VISTO DI RISPONDENZA (da compilarsi a cura della USL)

______ (numero nosologico)

Data ______          (timbro e firma del sanitario USL)

RIQUADRO DA COMPILARSI A CURA DEL LAVORATORE AVENTE DIRITTO ALL'INDENNITÀ DI MALATTIA (in carattere 1° foglio)

#### DICHIARAZIONE DI RESPONSABILITÀ

Il sottoscritto ______ (cognome)   ______ (nome)   ______ (sesso)   ______ (data di nascita)

______ (luogo di nascita)   ______ (indirizzo di residenza: via, n. civico)   ______ (comune)   ______ (C.A.P.)

______ (n. USL)   ______ (presso) (2)   ______ (indirizzo durante la malattia) (3)

______ (presso) (2)   ______ (codice lav. INPS)   ______ (codice fiscale)

dichiara sotto la propria responsabilità

di avere diritto all'indennità di malattia a carico dell'INPS mediante corresponsione

• ☐ a cura del datore di lavoro col sistema del conguaglio

• ☐ diretta a cura dell'INPS in quanto appartenente ad una delle seguenti categorie:

• ☐ operaio agricolo a tempo determinato      ☐ operaio agricolo a tempo indeterminato
• ☐ lavoratore stagionale                      ☐ lav. sospeso senza integrazione salariale ovvero disoccupato.
• ☐ lavoratore a tempo determinato con meno di 30 gg. lavorati negli ultimi 12 mesi.
• ☐ lavoratore settore spettacolo disoccupato, saltuario o a tempo determinato.

LOGGETTA della Pinacoteca Comunale - Ravenna
(denominazione e indirizzo del datore di lavoro) (4)

dichiara di avere n. ______ familiari a carico

Lo stato di malattia è stato causato da terzi ☐   o da infortunio sul lavoro ☐

Data ______       Firma del lavoratore _Maurizio Cattelan_

• contrassegnare la casella che interessa

NOTE: 1) Per le donne coniugate indicare il cognome da nubile; 2) qualora all'indirizzo segnalato dal lavoratore sia reperibile un diverso nominativo ad esempio quello del coniuge, anche quest'ultimo deve essere indicato; 3) da indicare solo se diverso dall'indirizzo abituale; 4) nel caso di lavoratore disoccupato indicare l'ultimo datore di lavoro.

GASA - 1.000.000 - 1/87

[18]

# QUESTURA DI FORLI'

OGGETTO: Verbale di denuncia di patito furto sporta da:
**CATTELAN** Maurizio, nato a Padova il 21.9.1960 ivi residente in via U. Foscolo al civico 22/A, domiciliato in Forlì in via Maroncelli al civico nr; 15 tel. 0543/23865.-

L'anno 1991, addì 22 del mese di Marzo alle ore 08.25, negli Uffici della Squadra Mobile della Questura di Forlì. Innanzi a Noi sottoscritti Ufficiali ed Agenti di P.G., appartenenti alla suidicata Squadra Mobile, diamo atto che é presente **CATTELAN Maurizio**, in oggetto meglio generalizzato, il quale per ogni effetto di legge denuncia quanto segue: Ieri sera 21.3.91, parcheggiavo l'auto della mia ragazza **GIAMBI** Patrizia, in questa via P. Maroncelli, alle ore 20.30, la stessa non era chiusa a chiave. L'auto targata FO 453979 e una GOLF WV. All'interno dell'autovettura si trovava un pacco nel cui interno c'era un'opera "**INVISIBILE**" la stessa ha un valore affettivo e doveva partecipare ad una mostra a Milano. A.D.R.: L'auto, non é assicurata. A.D.R.: Non ho sospetti su alcuno.

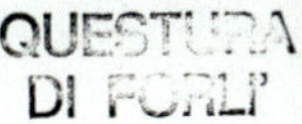

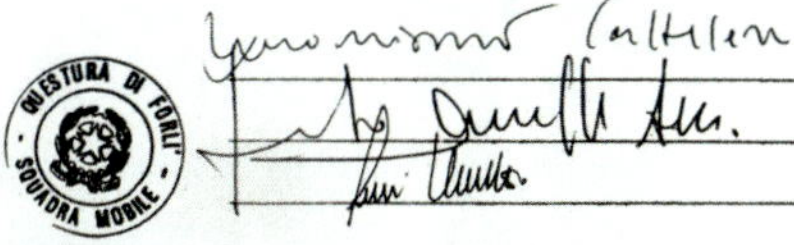

A richiesta dell'interessato e per i soli usi consentiti dalla legge si rilascia copia del presente atto.

COMUNE DI FORLI
______ copia, composta di fogli n. 1
è conforme all'originale.
Forlì ______ 0 2 APR. 1991
IL FUNZIONARIO INCARICATO

[19]

[18]  *Untitled*, 1989
      (recto and verso)

[19]  *Untitled*, 1991

**[20]** *Strategie*, **1990**

> [20.1] *Strategie*, 1990
> 77 copies of *Flash Art*,
> stickers, aluminum supports
> 173 × 161.3 × 20.3 cm
>
> [20.2] *Strategie*, 1990
> 26 copies of *Flash Art*,
> stickers, aluminum supports
>
> [20.3] *Strategie*, 1990
> 15 copies of *Flash Art*,
> stickers, aluminum supports
> 76 × 71 × 20.5 cm
>
> [20.4] *Strategie*, 1990
> Issue of *Flash Art Italia*
> (no. 155, April–May 1990),
> with modified cover
> 27 × 20.5 × 1 cm

I was just beginning to work in the art world, and I liked the idea of having a cover of *Flash Art* devoted to my work. But I was also interested in studying the mechanisms that could lead to that result. It was about leaving certain stages behind, sidestepping the customs that rule the art world, unwritten customs as strict as any other law. Under those rules it was clear that they wouldn't put me on the cover, so I thought I might as well do it myself. I contacted the publisher to get some old copies and made a sculpture in the shape of a house of cards. I did it in three different sizes, combining a different number of magazines. But I didn't stop there. It was also an act of self-legitimization. I went to the printer who worked for *Flash Art* and bought a thousand copies that still hadn't been bound. Then in Ravenna I had my cover printed with the image of the magazine sculpture I'd made and then I presented the magazines in three galleries, because they had to be seen in multiple places, as if it was a real issue and I had actually appeared on a *Flash Art* cover. The galleries were Studio Oggetto in Milan, Studio Leonardi in Genoa, and Neon in Bologna. It was a project with a precise structure.

[20.1]  *Strategie*, 1990

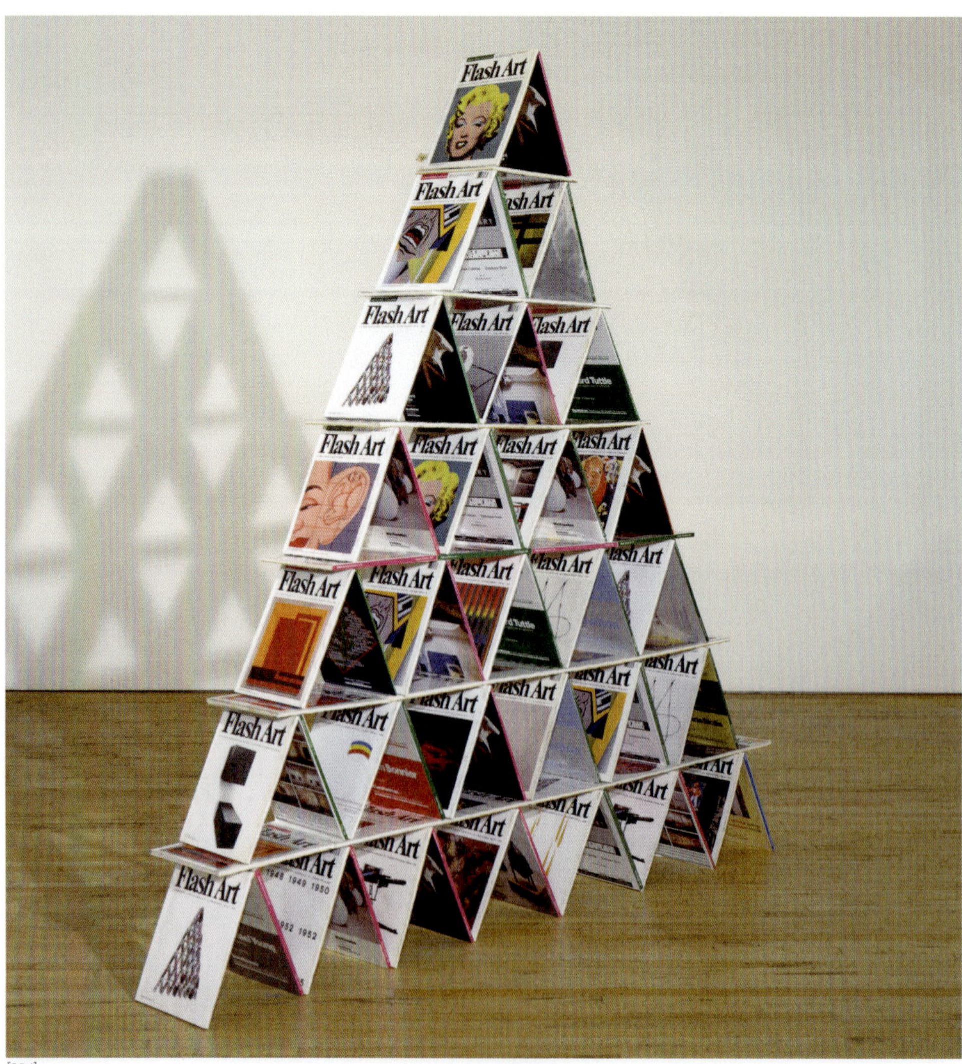


[20.1]

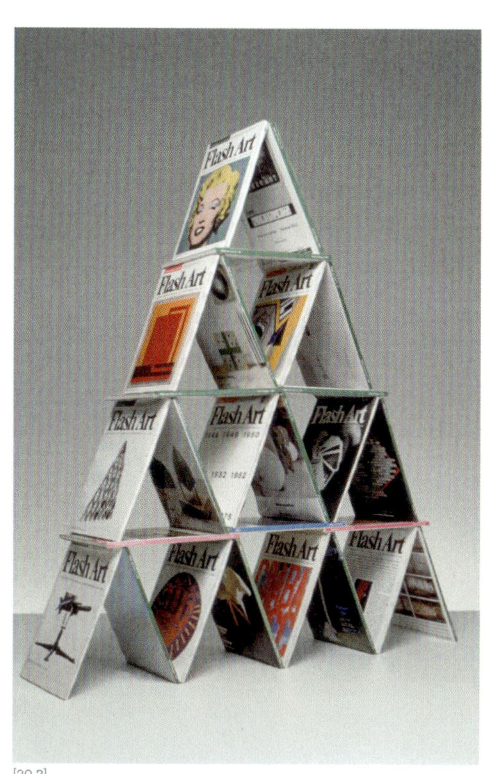

[20.2]

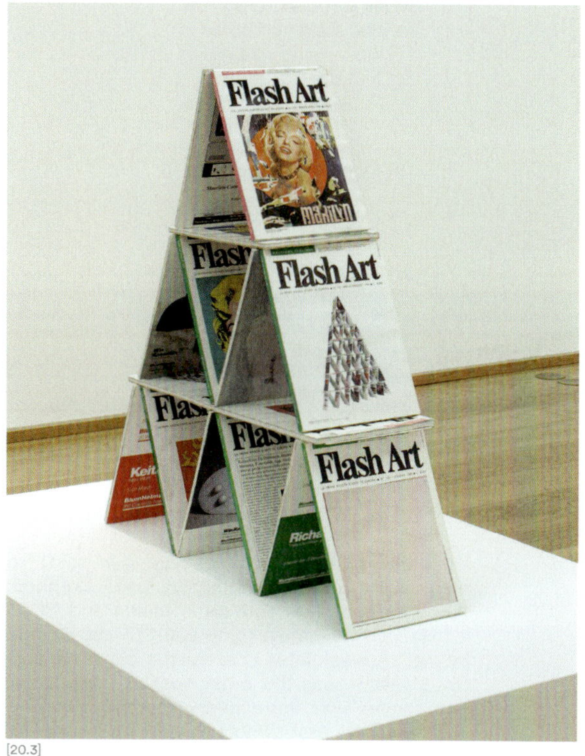

[20.3]

63

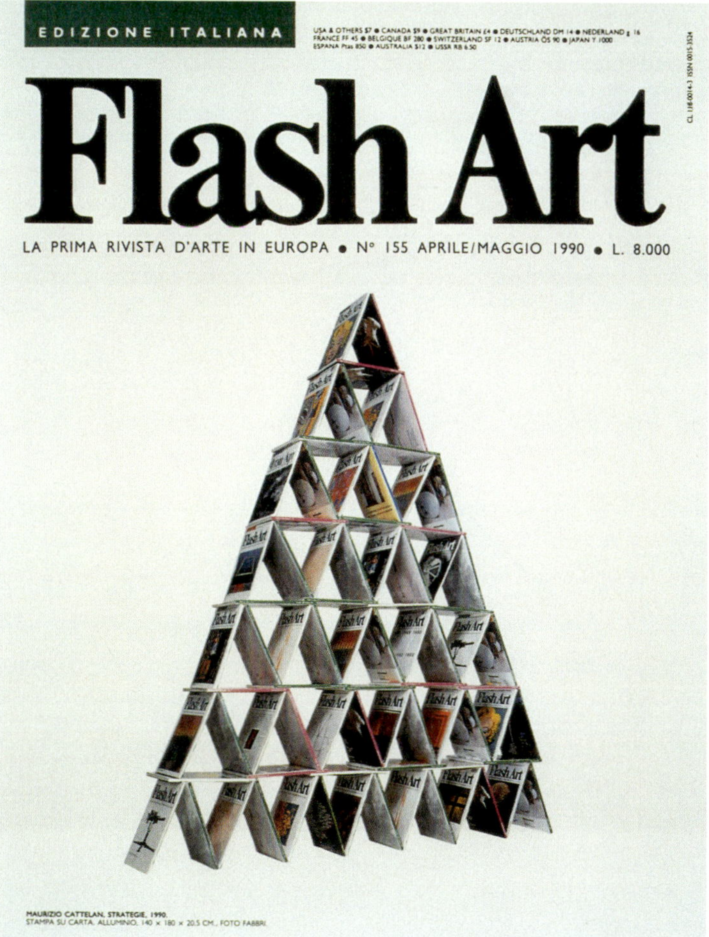


[20.4]

[20.2] *Strategie*, 1990

[20.3] *Strategie*, 1990

[20.4] *Strategie*, 1990

**[21] Series *Untitled*, 1993–99**
Various sizes and color

    [21.1] *Untitled*, 1999
Acrylic on canvas
71 × 71 cm

    [21.2] *Untitled*, 1999
Acrylic on canvas
100 × 120 cm

    [21.3] *Untitled*, 1999
Acrylic on canvas
110 × 110 cm

    [21.4] *Untitled*, 1999
Acrylic on canvas
110 × 110 cm

    [21.5] *Untitled*, 1999
Acrylic on canvas
110 × 110 cm

[21.1]  *Untitled*, 1999

[21.2]  *Untitled*, 1999

[21.3]  *Untitled*, 1999

[21.4]  *Untitled*, 1999

[21.5]  *Untitled*, 1999

I was talking to a collector once, and he said: "I'd really like to have a painting by you." I replied: "Send me a canvas and some paints and I'll do it." He said: "Whatever you want to do, it's fine by me." A week later I received a blank canvas. For a year it was the most horrible nightmare. The canvas was there every morning. Waking up, it was the first thing I saw. Then I gave up. But painting is something you have to try your hand every now and then, so I tried again and decided to cut the Z of Zorro on the canvas. But rather than feeling like a masked character, I felt like an unmasker. All I do is reveal fears, my own and other people's.

64

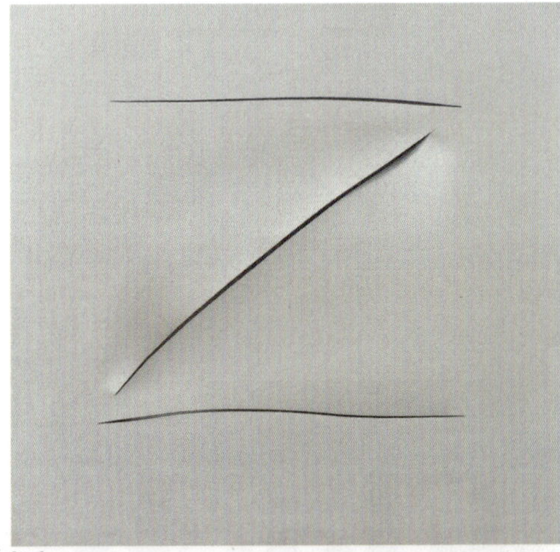

[21.1]

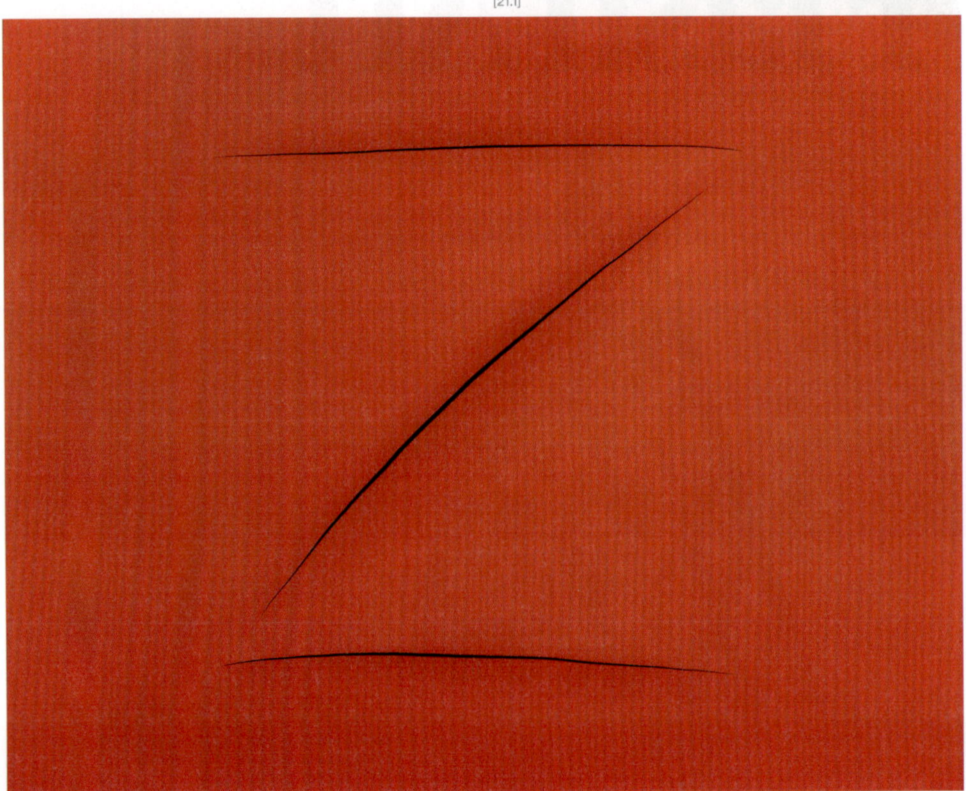

[21.2]

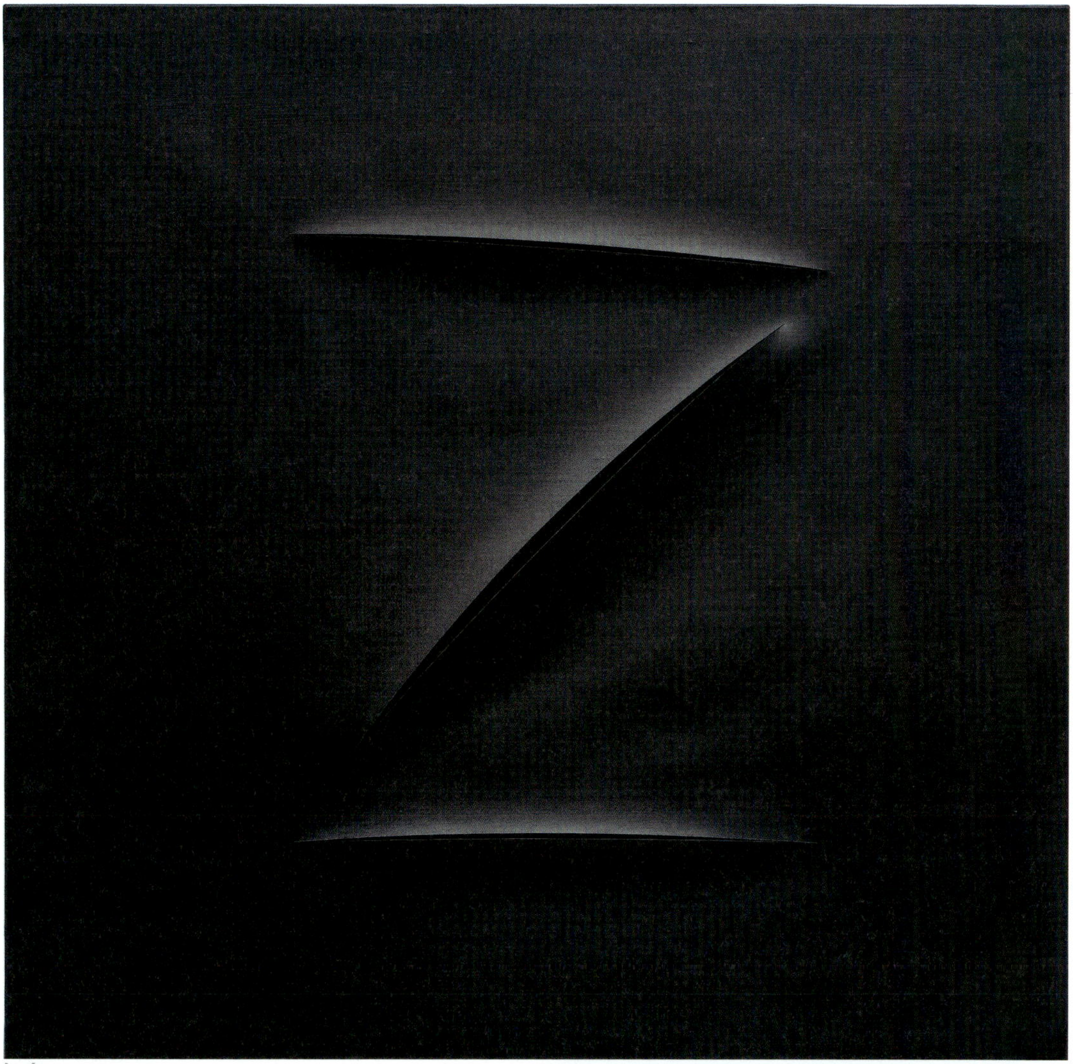

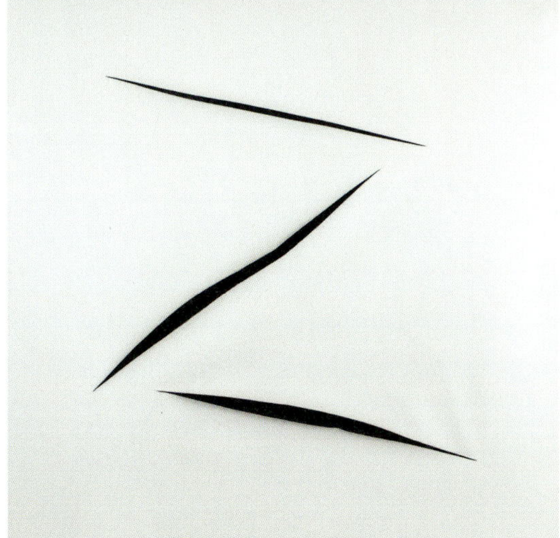

[21.4]

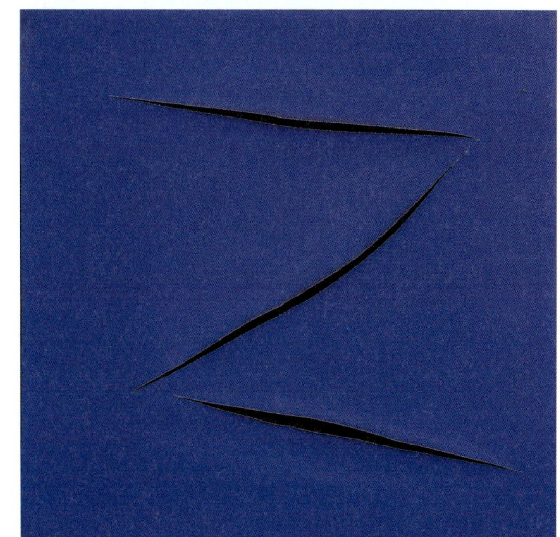

[21.5]

[21.3]

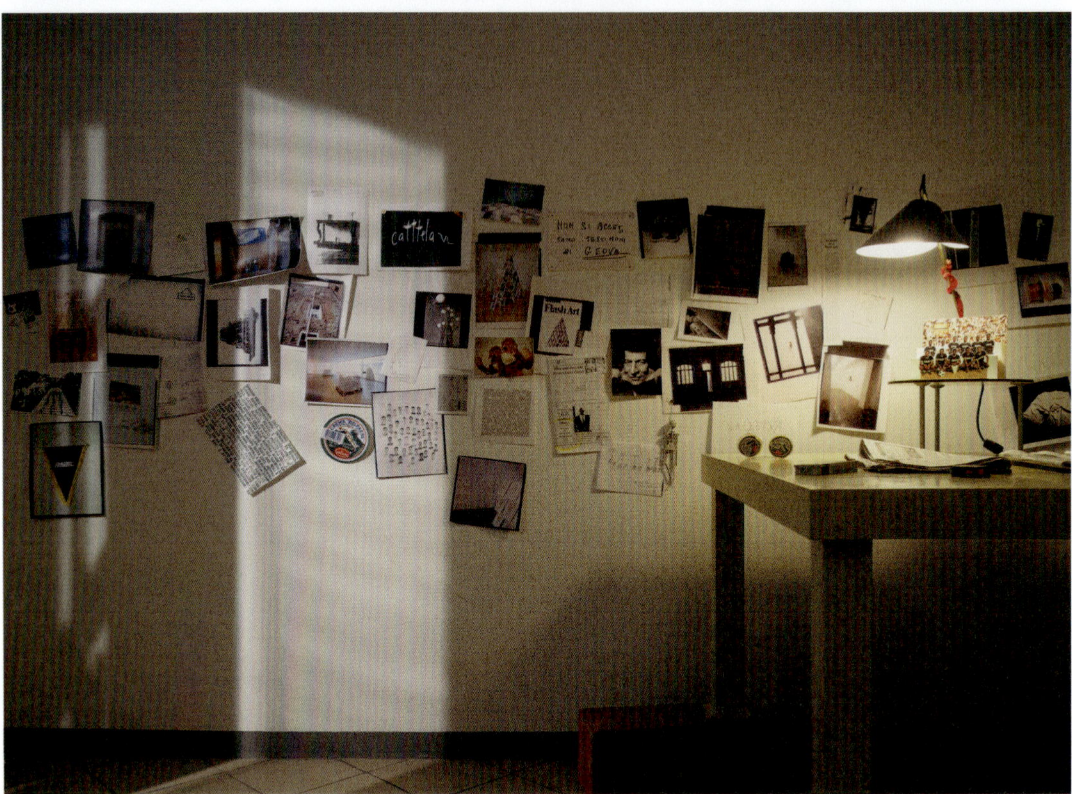



[22]



[22]  *Untitled*, **1994**
Color photograph, face mounted to acrylic
25 × 58 cm

[23]  *Untitled*, **1994–95**
Envelopes, fake postage stamps, ink
10 × 15 cm each

Thinking of a way to show my works, I photographed them all and hung the images on a wall. Then I photographed the installation and made a brochure out of it. This operation led to another project. The following year, I cut out the works from the brochure and used them instead of stamps to send envelopes to myself. In every case I was the person who sent them and received them at my home address in Milan, a cycle without any real purpose. Inexplicably, the post office never noticed that the stamps were fake and all the letters were delivered.
In both cases they were works of promotion, of propaganda. I had sold the photo of the wall with the images to finance the printing of that kind of catalogue, a catalogue without an exhibition.

[22]  *Untitled*, 1994

[23.1-10]  *Untitled*, 1994–95

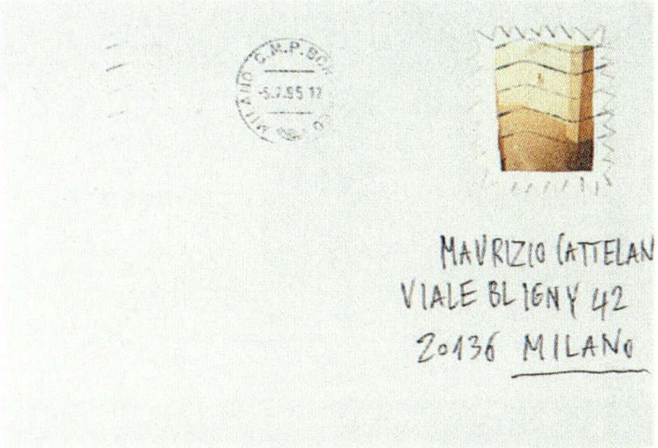

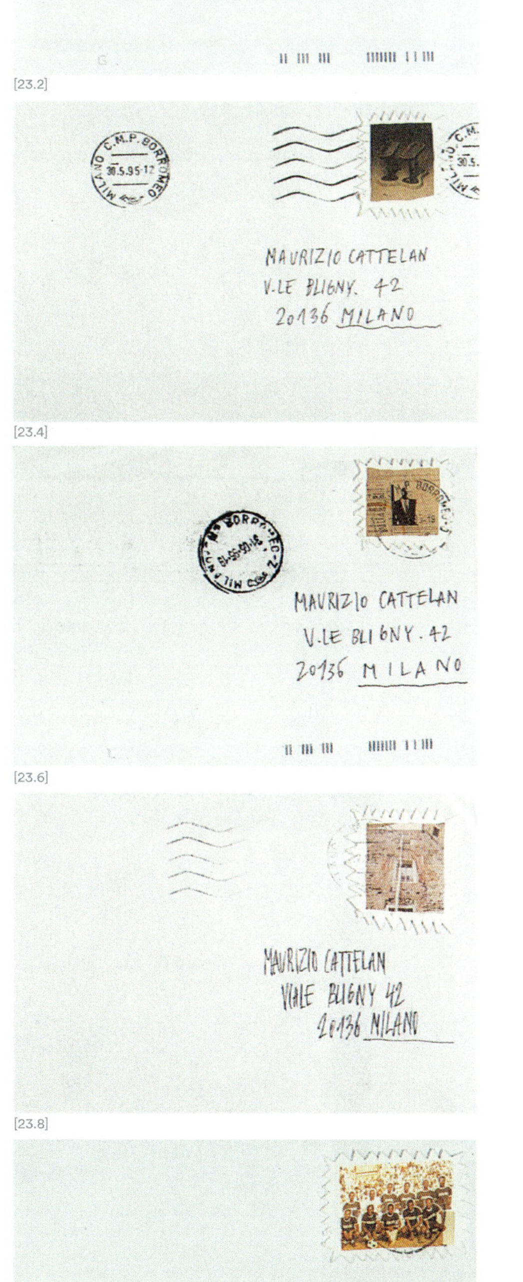


[23.1]

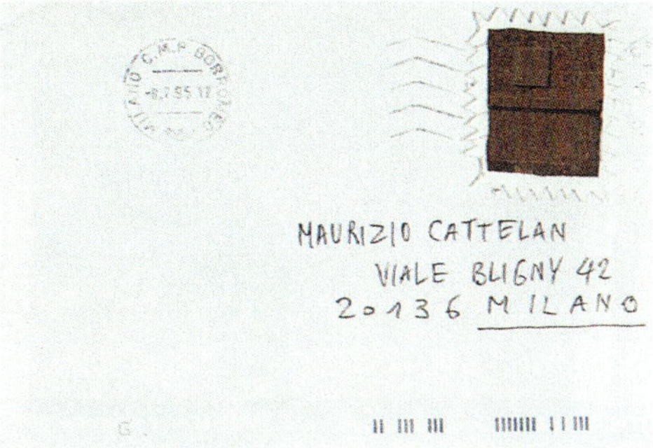

[23.2]

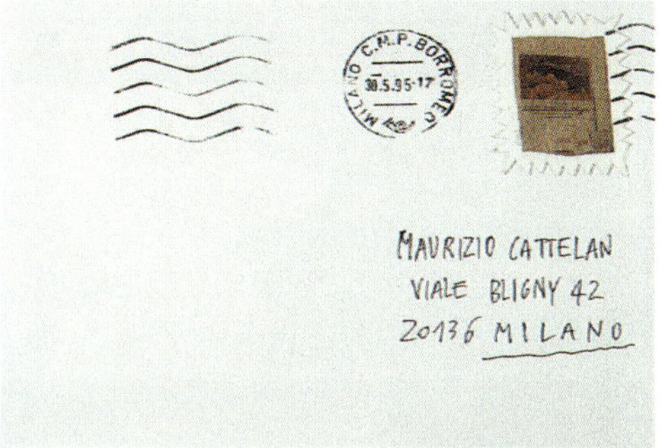

[23.3]



[23.4]

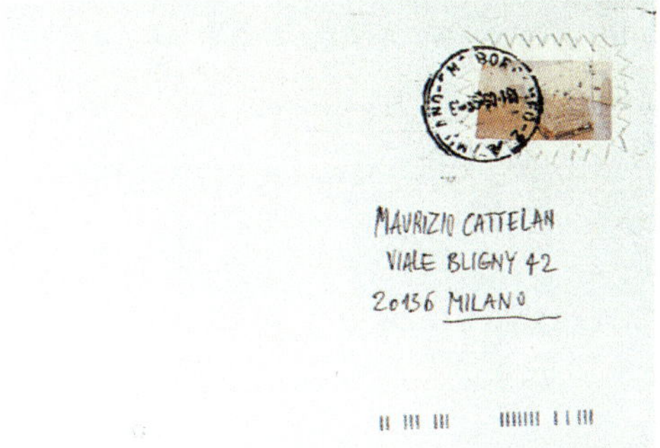

[23.5]



[23.6]

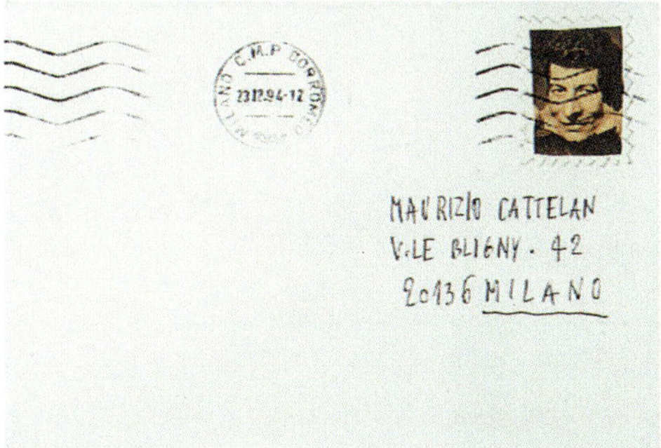

[23.7]



[23.8]

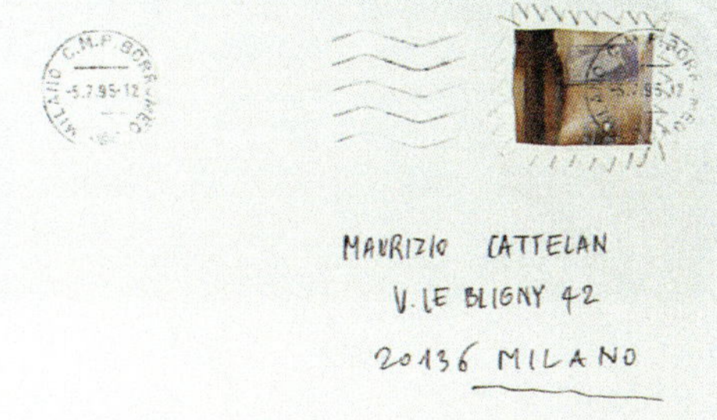


[23.9]



[23.10]

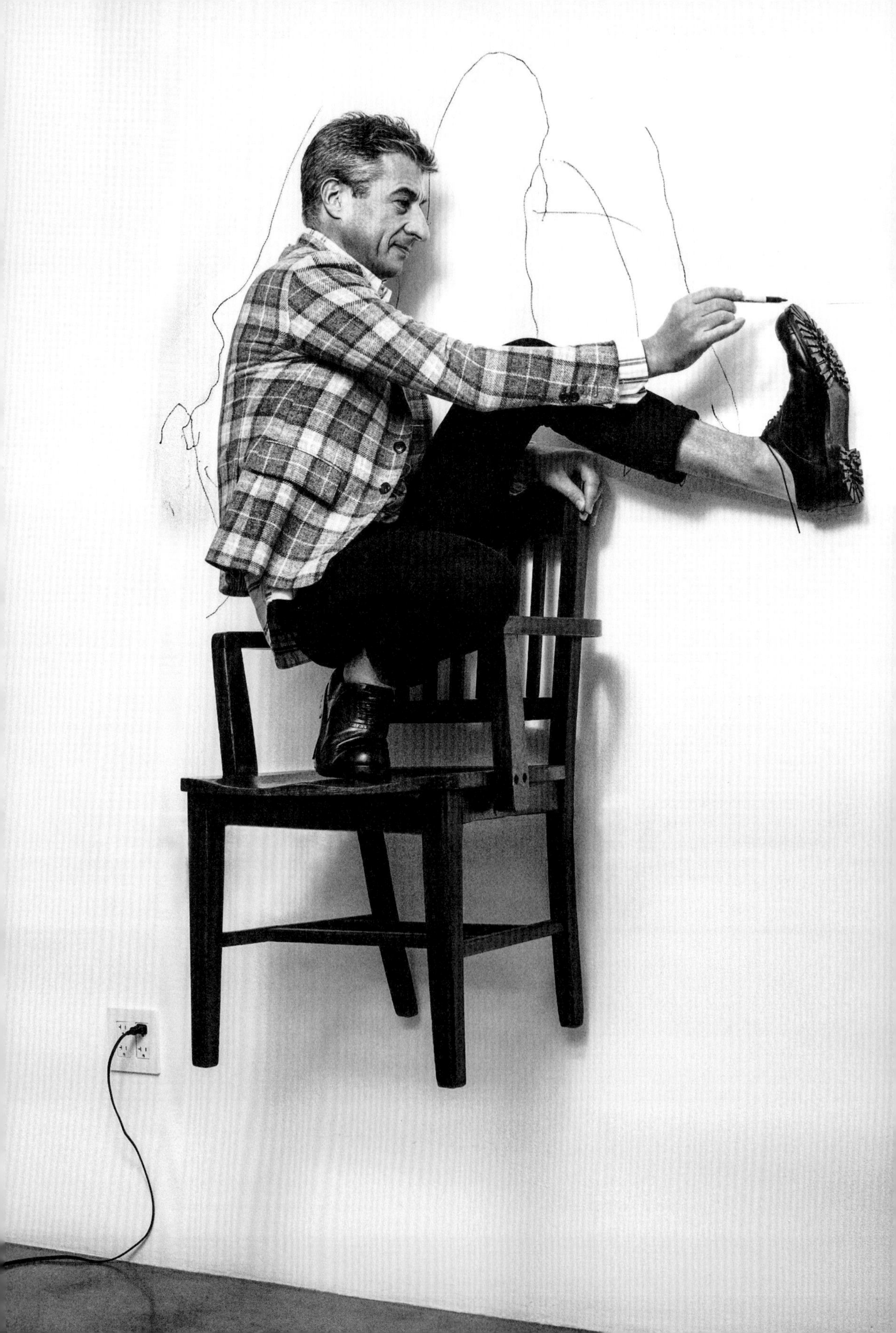

**Things I'll Never Do Again:
The Truth Is Not Out There**





I will not do that thing with my tongue.
I will not fake seizures.
I will not eat things for money.
I will not reincarnate as Sammy Davis, Jr.
I will not instigate revolution.
I will not draw naked ladies.
I will not see Elvis.
I will not encourage others to fly.
I will not be a thirty-two-year-old woman.
I will not cut corners.
I will not sell land in Florida.
I will not do anything bad ever again.
I will not show off.
I will not be a dentist.
I will not torment the emotionally frail.
I will not carve gods.
I will not aim for the head.
I will not send lard through the mail.
I will not dissect things unless instructed.
I will not get very far with this attitude.
I will finish what I sta

[Text published in *Maurizio Cattelan*, eds. Francesco Bonami, Nancy Spector, and Barbara Vanderlinden (London: Phaidon,
2000), 124]

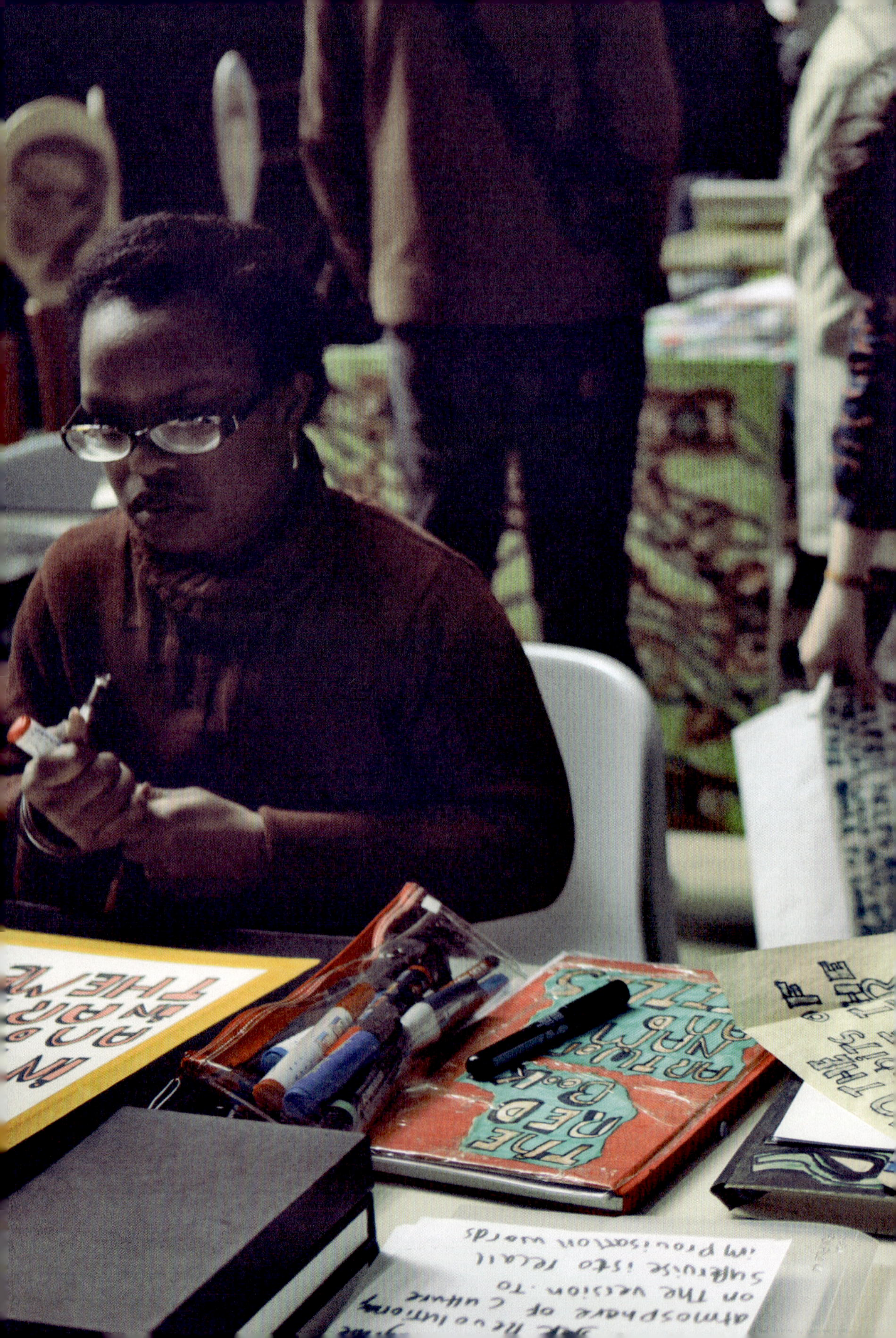
THE RED Book

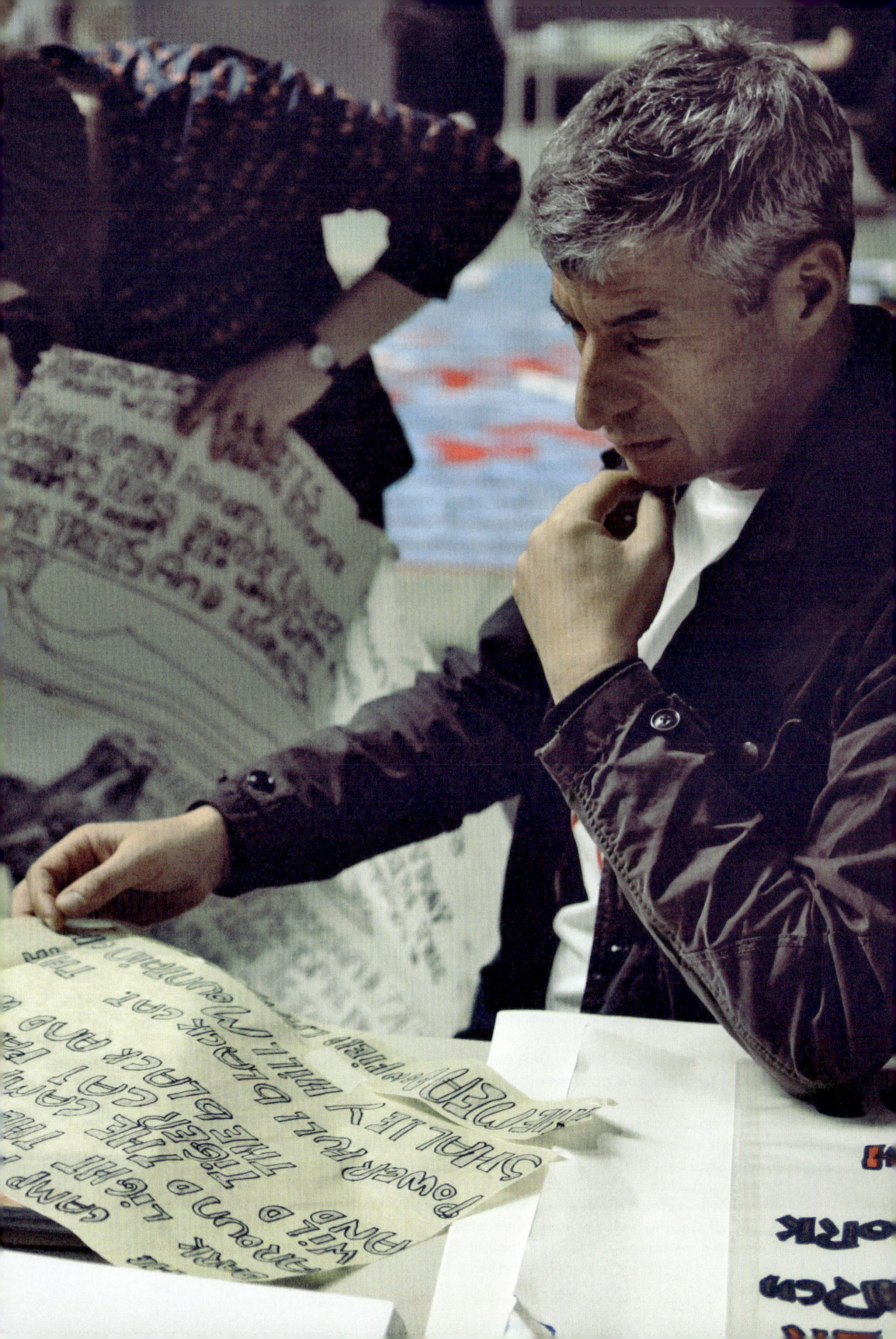

I don't think there are any secret recipes for being creative, and neither are there readymade formulas that can be learned in school or academia. It's like a board game accompanied by a manual of very complicated rules. We all know it's much easier to understand something by starting to play than wasting the whole evening learning the instructions by heart. Learning the ways things are done and not done, learning the rules of the game, can only be useful if you've internalized the freedom to subvert them at the same time.

I never attended the academy. It was enough for me to hang out with the people who did. Fortunately, it's not always true that you have to study at the most expensive schools to find fulfilment in what you do. Exchanging ideas and having good listening skills are worth more than any school. And I don't think a rigid mindset is a part of education, as the strictest education can give birth to the most rebellious minds. I believe mediocrity is more about conforming, one of the most deceptive diseases of our time. More than anything else, everybody desires to be part of a community, to be accepted by it and celebrated. It's a big issue, because the desire for acceptance doesn't allow us to dare to take risks. Having courage is like water for living beings. If there's no risk, there's no art. Education and experience are not the sources of my creativity. I try my best to draw a clear line between me and all my previous works, so that I'm not bound by the past.

I think it's important that young people have the freedom to reinvent their lives with original formats and contents. They should incinerate us, destroy us and then rebuild us. If I think about my career, the best thing to do at the beginning is to stay away from institutions. Often conveying research and experimentation is not their first interest, although a patron can do this. Some people fall in love with artists and, depending on their resources, they might support them all through their careers. And artists have to be stimulated to act boldly, on the very edge of reasonableness.

Apparently some companies periodically swap their various departments around as a way of finding solutions to their problems. Every six months the workers have to start over, without ever really specializing. You see, I try to adopt the same principle. I don't want to die an expert in anything, I want to keep learning. The grave will be my diploma.

**[24]** *Edizioni dell'Obbligo*, **1991**
Notebooks, plexiglas, iron
Notebooks: 29.7 × 21 cm each

I took this work to the Castello di Belgioioso in 1991, at a fair for small publishers, introducing myself as a publisher, the owner of Edizioni dell'Obbligo. A friend who taught in an elementary school let me have her pupils' copybooks, which were in A4 format. I imitated some of the series published by Einaudi. The covers were perfectly printed, but as soon as you turned them over you found elementary school copybooks. I left the name of each kid who had done the cover drawing and given the copybook its title. Leafing through them, you could see what each of those kids would become when they grew up: a teacher, a failure, an entrepreneur, even an addict. The child's psychology was very clear. The titles, like *Scrivere non è il mio lavoro* [Writing is not my job] or *Squaderno della sfelicità* [Uncopybook of unhappiness], were a great clue.
In a way it was my first editorial project. Many others grew out of this work, such as *Lavorare è un brutto mestiere* (1993).

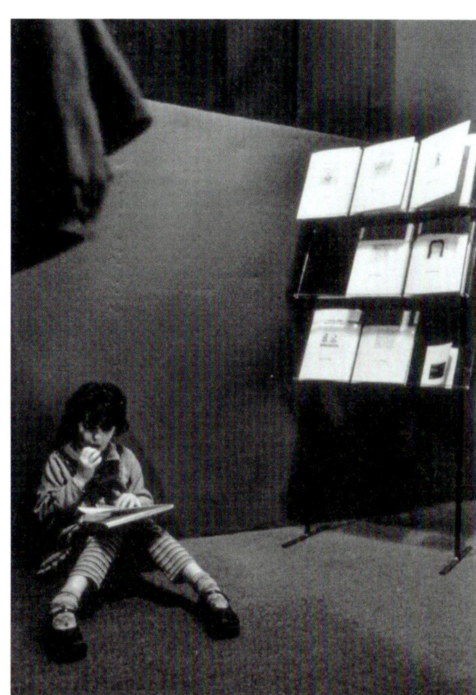

[24.1]

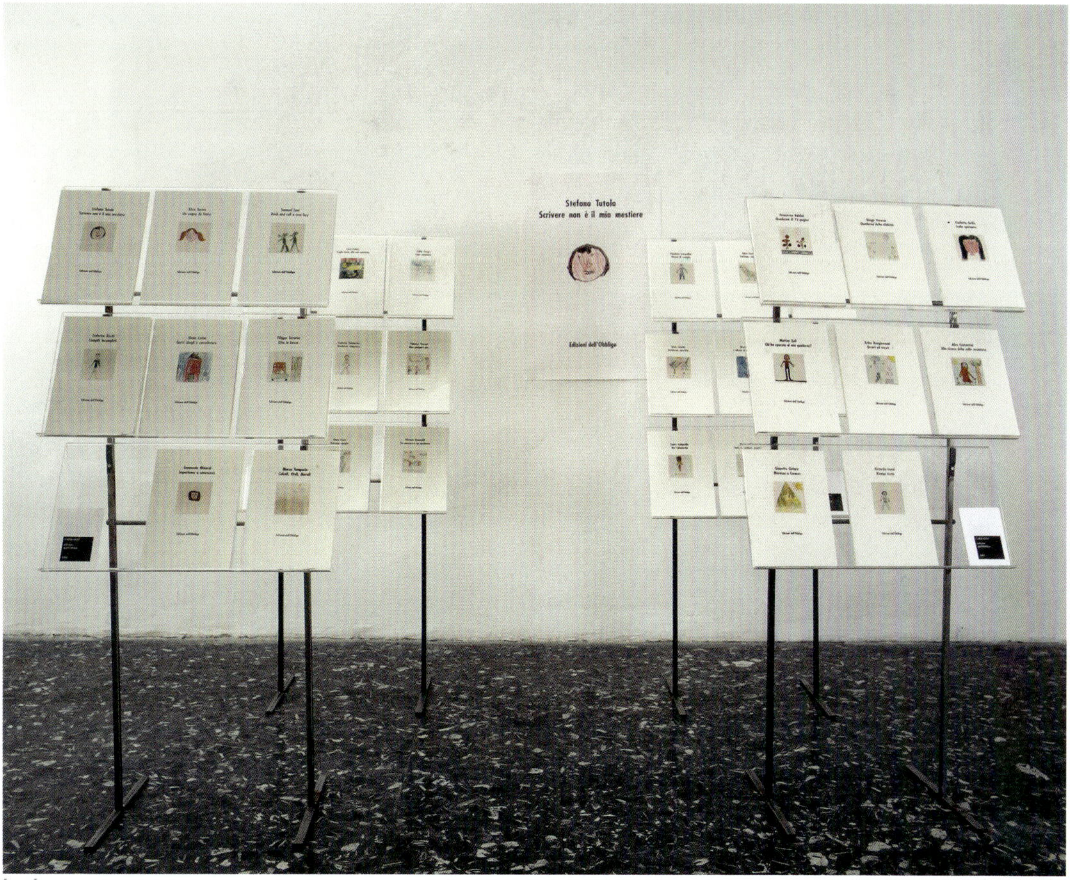

[24.2]

[24.1] *Edizioni dell'Obbligo*, 1991
"Parole nel tempo," Castello di Belgioioso,
May 4–5, 1991 (publishing fair)

[24.2] *Edizioni dell'Obbligo*, 1991
"Edizioni dell'Obbligo," Spazio Juliet, Trieste, February
6–28, 1992 (solo show)

[25] ***Untitled***, 1991
[Initially titled: *Repetita Iuvant*]
29 sheets, ballpoint pen ink
30 × 21 cm each

Like *Edizioni dell'Obbligo* (1991), again for this work I started from real exercises done at school, the ones where kids are made to write lines as a punishment. But I converted these sheets into the class struggle. The children had been forced to write, "Fare la lotta in classe è pericoloso" [Fighting in class is dangerous], and I corrected this in red ink so that all the sentences read, "Fare la lotta di classe è pericoloso" [Class struggle is dangerous].

[26] ***Untitled***, 1994
3 used school notebooks, sound
19.5 × 13.5 cm each (closed)

This work is like *Edizioni dell'Obbligo* (1991). Here I used the pages from some very cute copybooks belonging to children or adolescents that I found. I added music to them, so making them music notebooks, with a tune that played as soon as they were opened.

[25]     *Untitled*, 1991 (detail)

[26.1-5]   *Untitled*, 1994

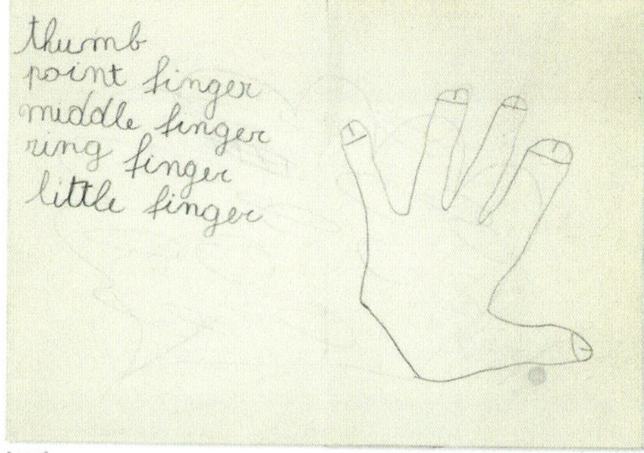


[26.1]

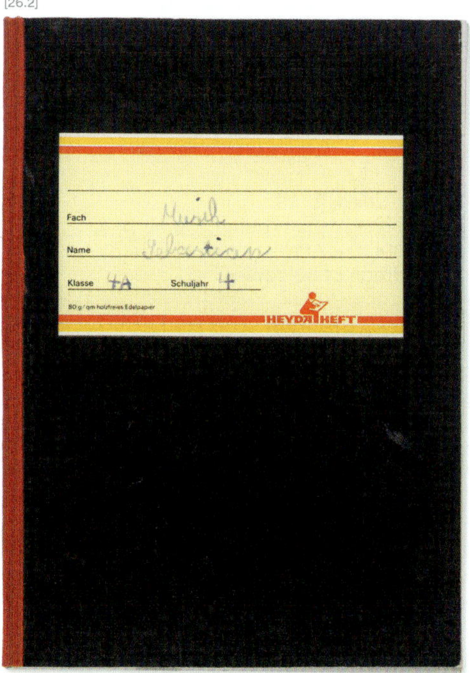


[26.2]



[26.3]

[26.4]

[26.5]

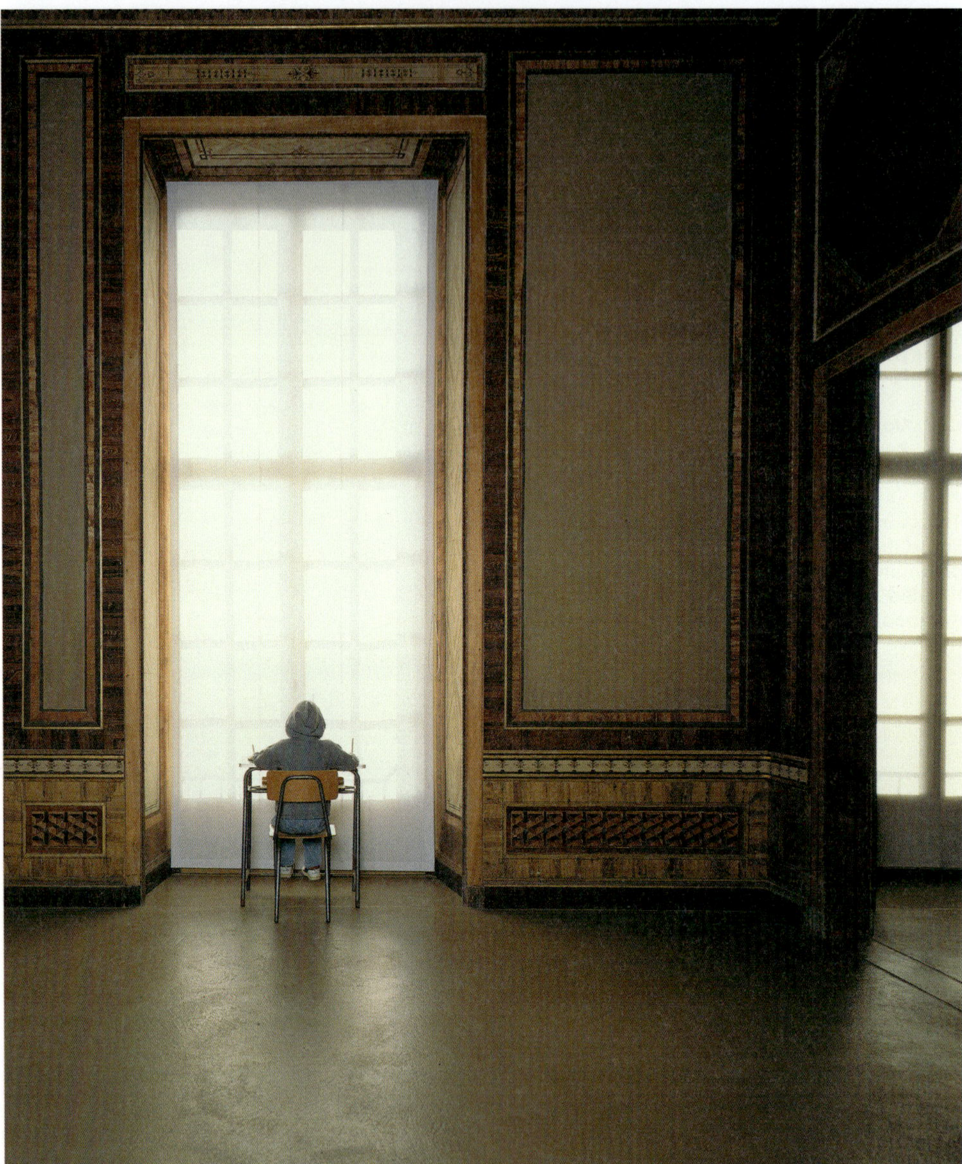

[27.1]



[27] ***Charlie Don't Surf*, 1997**
Latex mannequin, clothing, shoes, pencils,
school desk, chair
112 × 71 × 70 cm

Charlie is me and anyone who suffered like me
at school. If you take a closer look, everything
seems normal, but as soon as you do, you realize this child can't escape. The hands skewered
to the desk also represent me as an adult, and I
wonder which hurts more: a pencil stuck in your
hand or being flunked in third grade.

[28] ***Untitled*, 1997**
Polyurethanic rubber, pigment, pencil
18 × 27 × 10 cm

Charlie's hands have become images in their own
right. I think I've done two or three.

[29] ***Untitled*, 2009**
Polyurethanic rubber, pigment
20 × 10 × 7 cm
Edition of 80 copies

The hand is recurrent in my work, and for a while
it was an obsession. In addition to Charlie's hand,
there are the hands making the heart sign (*Lessico familiare*, 1989), or the ones forming a star
(*Untitled*, 1996); there's the hand with fir trees
growing from it (*Christmas '96*, 1996); there's the
hand alone of *L.O.V.E.* (2010), and then there's the
rubber hand pointing down.

[27.1]   *Charlie Don't Surf*, 1997
"Maurizio Cattelan. Tre installazioni per il Castello,"
curated by Giorgio Verzotti, Castello di Rivoli Museo d'Arte
Contemporanea, Rivoli-Turin, September 25, 1997–January
18, 1988 (solo show)

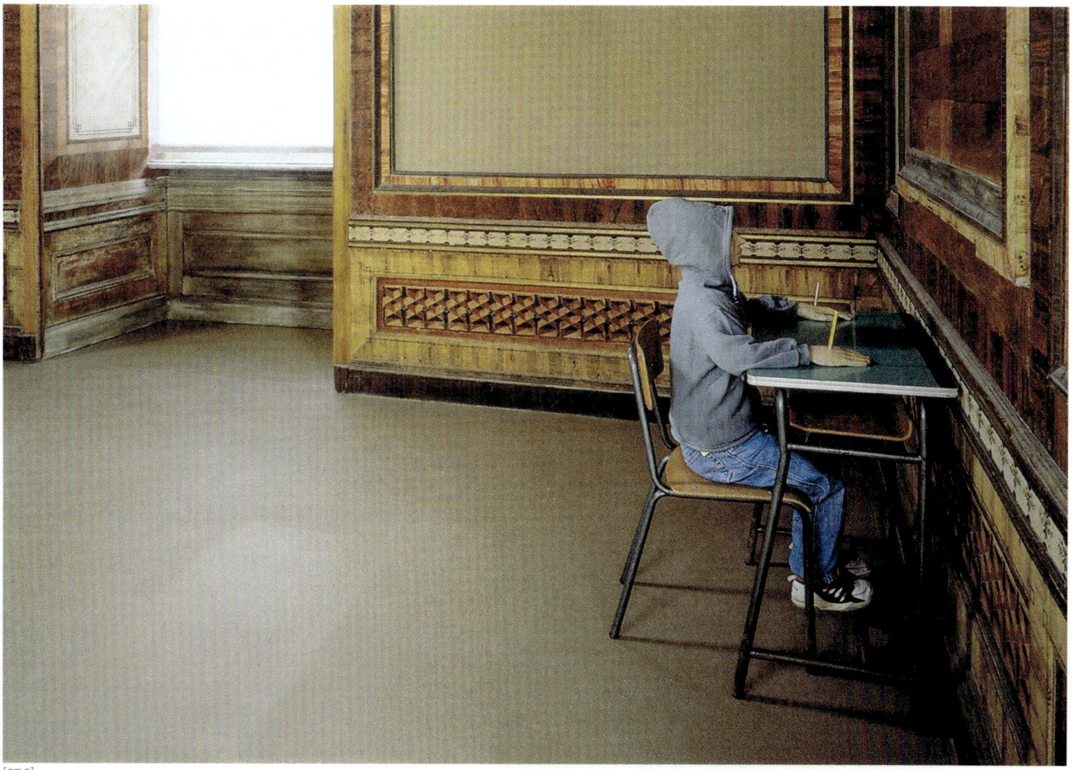

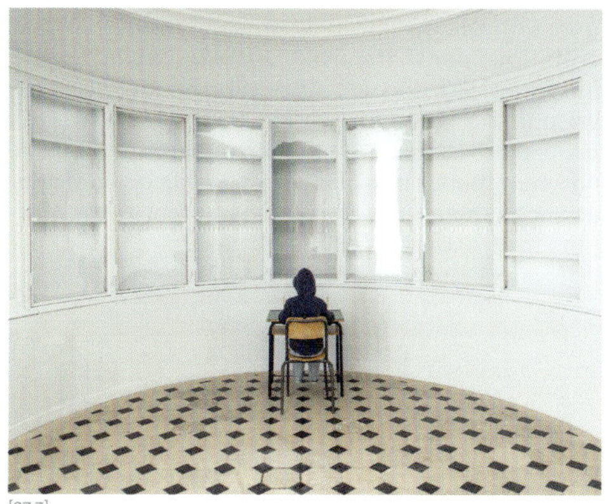

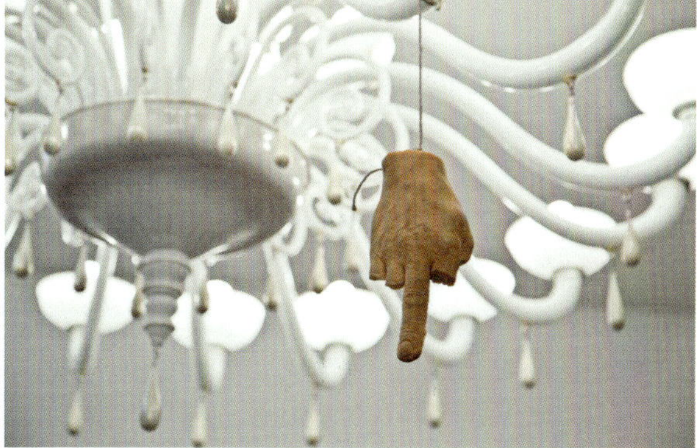

[27.2]  *Charlie Don't Surf*, 1997
Castello di Rivoli Museo d'Arte Contemporanea,
Rivoli-Turin

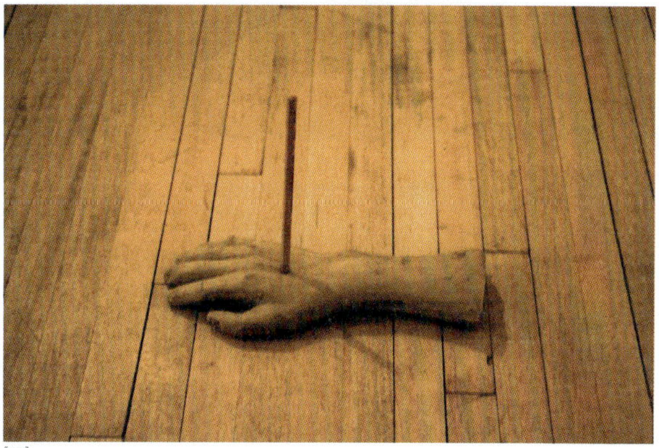

[27.3]  *Charlie Don't Surf*, 1997
"Not Afraid of Love," curated by Chiara Parisi, Monnaie
de Paris, Octotber 21, 2016–January 18, 2017 (solo show)

[28]  *Untitled*, 1997

[29]  *Untitled*, 2009

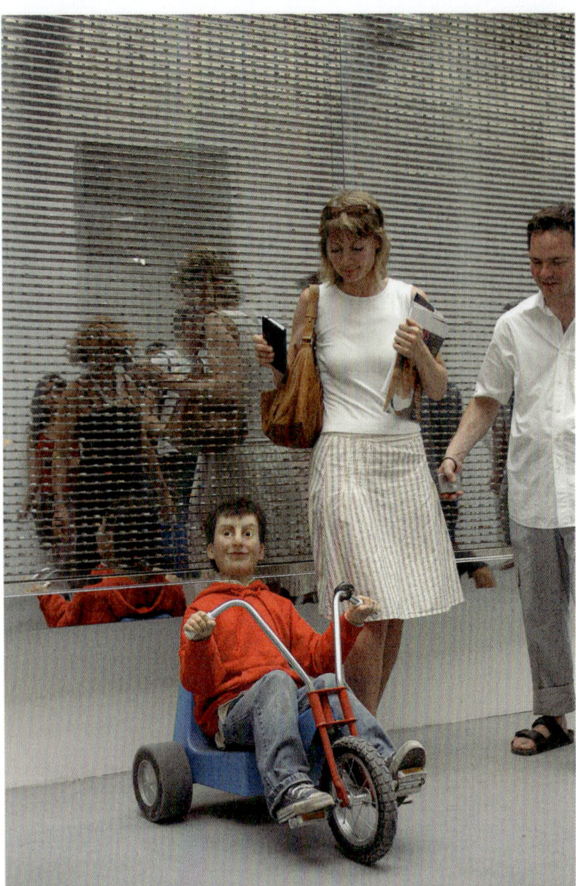

[30.1]

**[30]**  *Charlie*, **2003**
Tricycle, steel, varnish, rubber, resin, silicone, natural hair, paint, clothing, shoes
82 × 92 × 56 cm

I was interested in creating a character and letting him run free in the exhibition space. The kid is mechanical simply because I thought it would occupy the space in a more interesting way. But it's not a comment on mechanization or anything like that.

Maybe he's only taking some exercise! Or maybe we're doing him a favor, training him early for the hardships of life! Joking aside, I like my work to take both sides. I don't like to stand up for any particular point of view: that's the viewers' job. Depending on how you look at it, what I do can appear either generous or exploitative. So, is the kid playing or is he working? Either interpretation is okay by me. I like the ambiguity. Besides, even if he is playing, he has been forced to play. His freedom's been taken away so it doesn't make much difference.

The face though, is hilarious… it's a little bit idiotic. Everything is worked by a remote control—the face, the eyes, the wheels.

This probably goes back to the idea of childhood as a period of confusion. When you're a child, authority seems very warm and protective, even appealing. Authority can make you feel safe and protected. On the other hand, as a kid you're too unruly just to sit still and keep quiet.

I wasn't trying to overthrow the institution or question the structure of power. I'm neither that ambitious nor that naive. I was only trying to find a degree of freedom. After all, the museum is a welcoming place for the kid on the tricycle. He's protected there. He can have fun and nobody will hurt him. I'm not against order or authority as such; I just think that you can create new margins for freedom in every context.

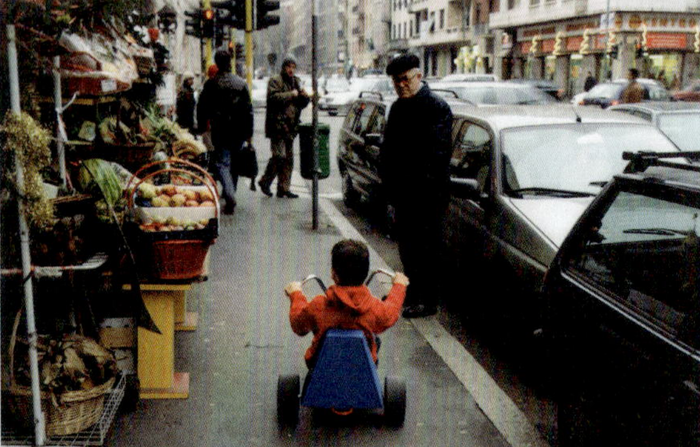

[30.2]

[30.1]  *Charlie*, 2003
"Dreams and Conflicts. The Dictatorship of the Viewer,"
50th Venice Biennale, curated by Francesco Bonami,
June 15–November 2, 2003 (group show)

[30.2-3] *Charlie*, 2003
First test, Milan, 2003

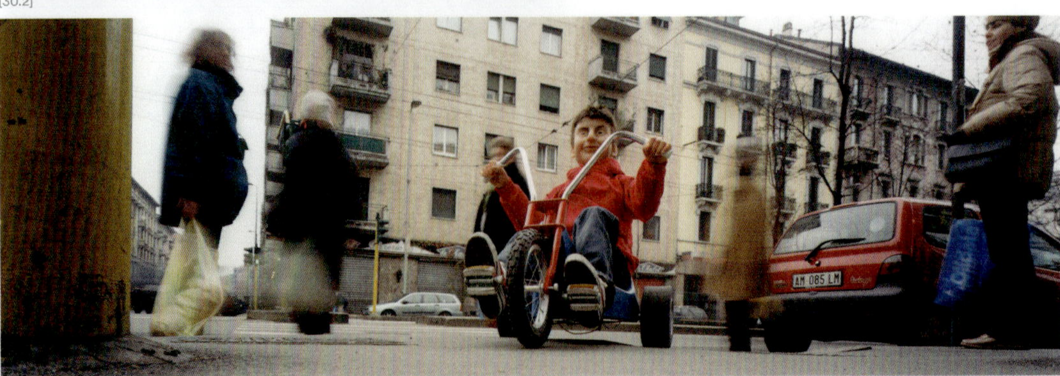

[30.3]

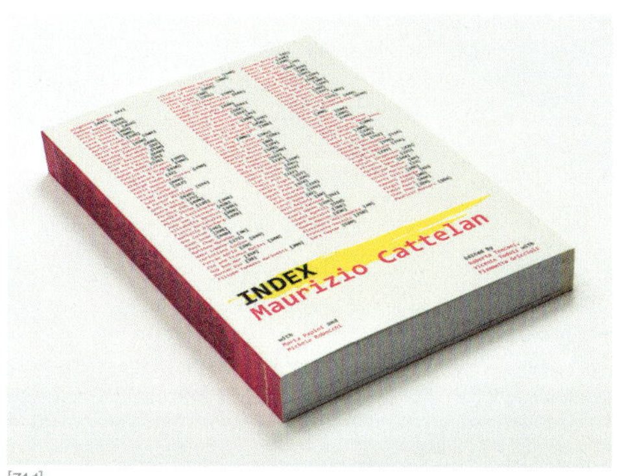

[31.1]

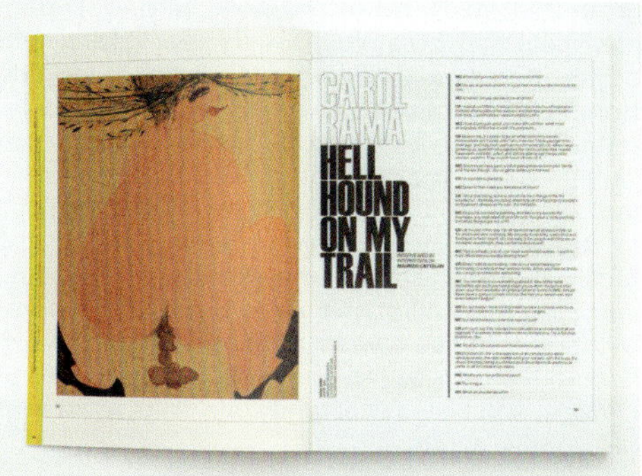

[31.2]

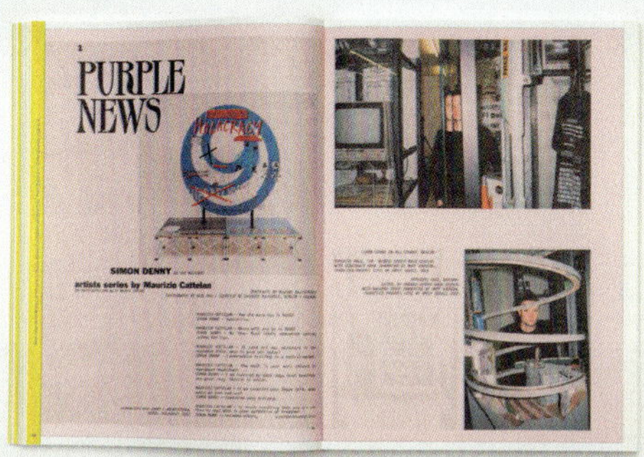

[31.3]

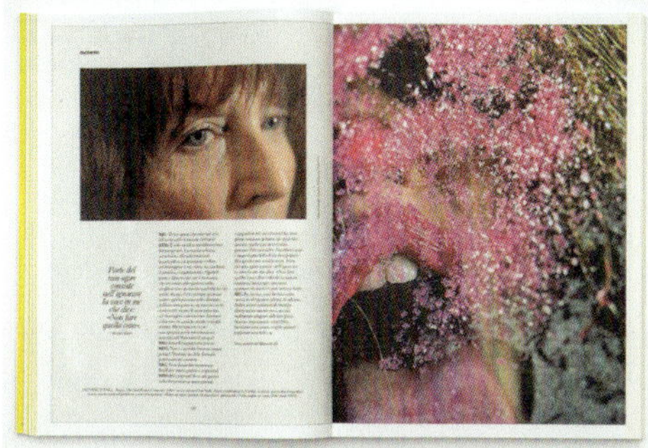

[31.4]

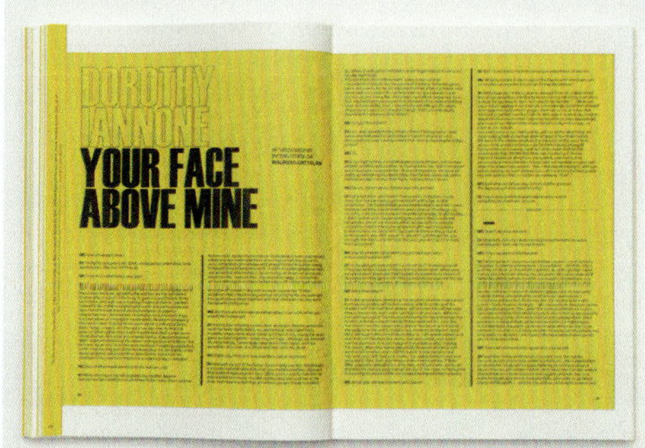

[31.5]

[31.6]

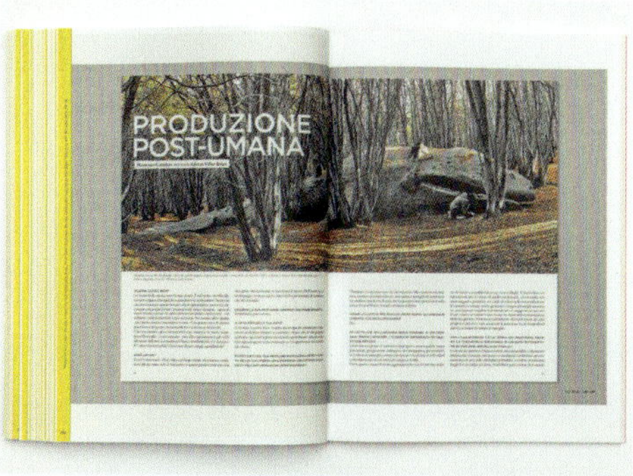

**[31]** ***INDEX*, 2021**
Maurizio Cattelan with Marta Papini
and Michele Robecchi
Book edited by Roberta Tenconi and
Vicente Todolí, with Fiammetta Griccioli;
published by Pirelli HangarBicocca, Milan,
and Marsilio, Venice
21 × 29 cm, 672 pages

Is it better to question or be questioned? I experience every interview I have to give as an interrogation in which I will certainly be found guilty, even if I've done nothing. So it's better to be on the other side. I interview other artists and creatives mainly out of curiosity. I like to hear them talk about themselves and their work, their creative processes, how they develop a concept and turn it into a work, what they read and what they watch. It's like exploring a parallel universe, where everything is slightly different but also familiar. And then I've always learned more from other people's answers than my own.

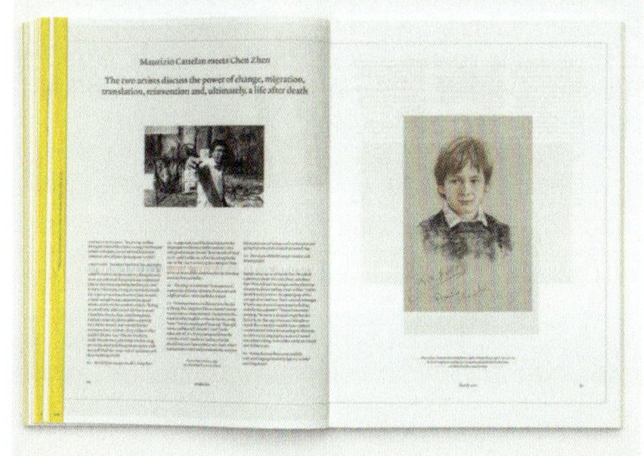

[31.7]

[31.1-7]  *INDEX*, 2021

From 2001 to 2021 I interviewed some 130 people, including creatives, artists, designers, and other figures, some living, others dead, ranging from Alighiero Boetti to Martine Syms. The interviews are collected in this volume. One conversation that really made a deep impression on me was with Virgil Abloh. I remember he had incredible clarity about what he was doing and for what goal. He struck me as generous, modest and ambitious all at the same time, a rare combination that I've always appreciated and I wish I could learn to be like that. We live in an age of change, and he was certainly one of its most representative symbols.

[The book was published on the occasion of the solo exhibition "Maurizio Cattelan. Breath Ghosts Blind," held in 2021–22 at Pirelli HangarBicocca in Milan. The dialogues originally appeared in newspapers and magazines, including *Flash Art*, *Purple Magazine*, *Vogue*, and *il manifesto*, as well as in monographs and exhibition catalogues. In *INDEX* they are republished in facsimile]

[32]  *IT*, **2023**
Belgian black marble
37 × 19 × 41.5 cm

This work could fall into a category to be called "Punishments," along with *Charlie Don't Surf* (1997), the work with just his nailed hand (*Untitled*, 1997), and the ones with stuffed donkeys (*If a Tree Falls in the Forest and There Is No One Around, Does It Make a Sound?*, 1998; *Untitled*, 2002; *Untitled*, 2004).



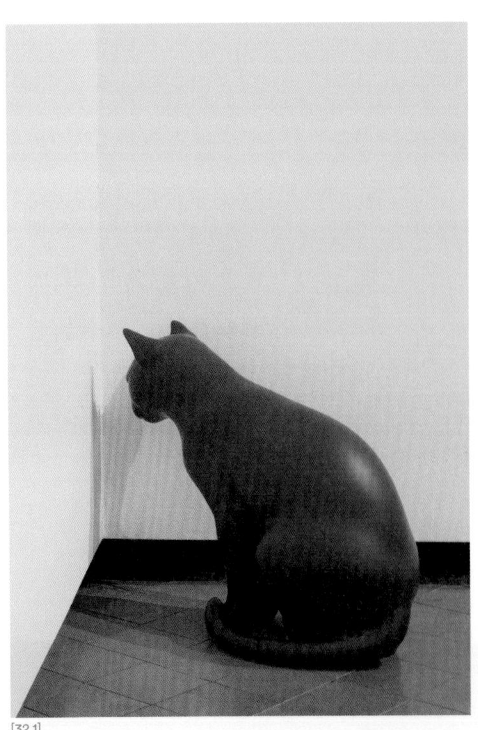

[32.1]

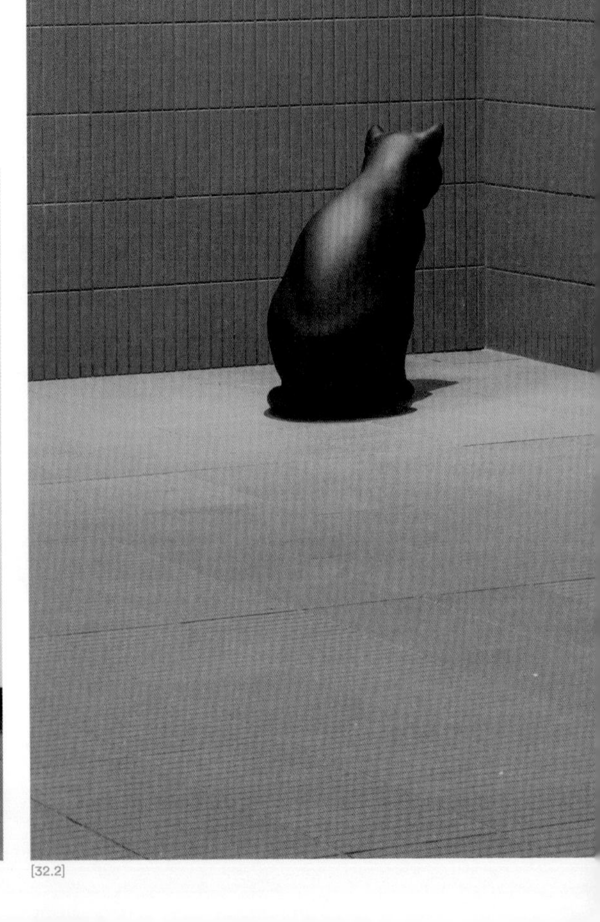

[32.2]

[32.1] *IT*, 2023
"WE," curated by Sungwon Kim, Leeum Museum of Art, Seoul, January 31–July 16, 2023 (solo show)

[32.2] *IT*, 2023
"Maurizio Cattelan. BECAUSE," project for Mutina for Art curated by Sarah Cosulich, with a display by Michael Anastassiades, Arte Fiera, Bologna, February 2–4, 2024 (solo show)

81

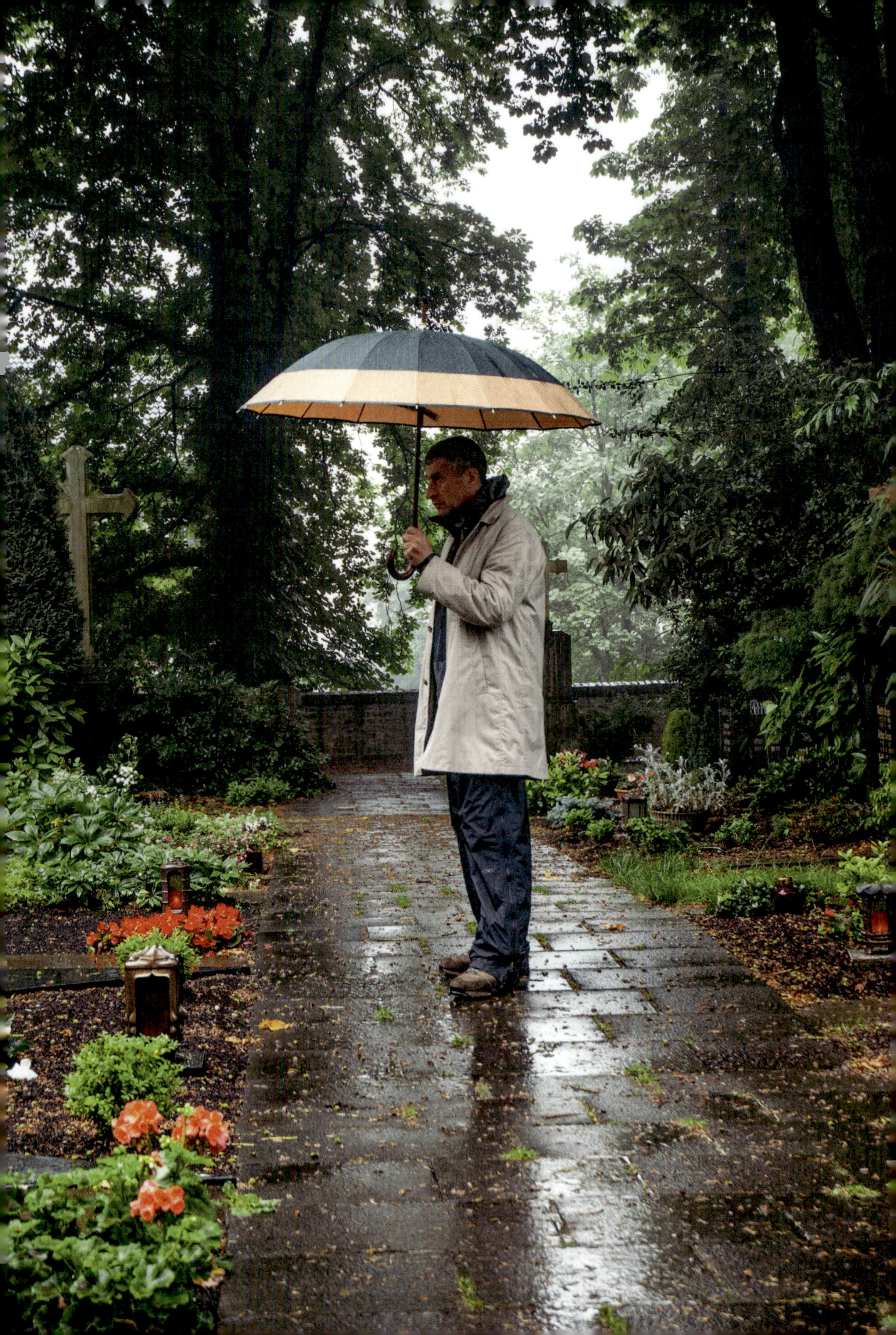

← Maurizio Cattelan portrayed by Zeno Zotti in Stommeln, May 31, 2008, in the graveyard around the St. Martin's Church, where he is installing *Untitled* (2007)



Failure is an ideology underpinning the school system in which we grew up. Instead of handing out grades, low marks, and flunking kids, they ought to teach us how to learn from our mistakes. Then many kids wouldn't think in terms of success and failure. I ended up believing I was a failure starting from elementary school, and I think I stopped only when I was sure of what I was doing. If the dichotomies wrong/right and failure/success hadn't been instilled in me from childhood, everything would have been simpler. I think this is true of many people, who think of themselves as dunces. Today I see failure as the other side of the coin of success.

Someone once said: "Either we make ourselves unhappy or we make ourselves strong. The amount of work is the same." Like everyone, I always work hard so as not to fail, but it's not up to me to decide if I'm successful or not. If I get up in the morning and go to bed at night doing what I want in between, it's normally considered a successful life. For me, satisfaction amounts to failure. I want to keep improving myself. Such improvement can be achieved only from an urgency that has nothing to do with satisfaction. I feel my best when I change my mind, tackle new challenges and fail.

I've always thought that situations where we fail teach us a lot more than situations where we win. The ambition of every artist is to become eternal through their work and everyone has to deal with both sides of the coin: a sense of omnipotence and a sense of failure. It's a rollercoaster of exhilarating climbs and very steep descents. Painful as it is, the second part is also the most significant. My newsvendor often says that failure is the condiment that gives success its flavor, and I couldn't agree more.

So, it has always seemed easier and more honest towards myself to celebrate failures instead of successes. It's curious, because success interests me as a goal, to never say I'm satisfied with what I've achieved, but I find it very difficult to pay the consequences. Being the center of attention makes me very uncomfortable. It's like being with your relatives at Christmas. You want to be nice to your uncles so they'll give you a gift, but you don't want to suffer from their attention. I always feel like I have trouble being understood wherever I go, and even today I'm surprised when they talk to me about things like success and appreciation. It's a position that I've always struggled to accept, regardless of my so-called cultural background or where I am. Warhol said that everyone would have fifteen minutes of fame. If he were alive today, he would consider success fifteen minutes of anonymity.

Fame is a strange beast. And as with all beasts, you're the prey, not the predator. As an artist, gaining recognition and being collected by a museum is fine, but it can also spell the end of you. There's always something terrifying about being part of a museum collection or being invited to work in an institutional setting. Even though it's a celebration of your work, it also frames you. You're trapped. Being accepted can be more dangerous than being rejected, so sometimes I use those opportunities to show off my weaknesses or sneak away. Anyway, all names in the art world are written in pencil.

In my work, the possibilities of a project going one way or another coexist until the work is out there. The method I follow in my practice is really simple. First, I try to develop a kind of poetry, which I can't do. Second, I recognize my failure. This is very important. By recognizing failure, you can find a solution that makes you feel better. The third part is to turn failure into something positive, to fulfill the commitment.

I've been told that mine is an aesthetic of failure. I don't know if that's true. I'm interested in finding the breaking point, the moment when the subject falters and fails. It's there that the humanity and inadequacy of the person show themselves in a crystalline way. And it's with that moment that everyone can identify themselves. Everyone can see themselves in that failure. It happened for centuries with the image of the crucifixion. Perhaps my works are attempts to revive that icon.

If I look back I know I've made a lot of mistakes. I'd like to say that I learned something in making them and recognizing them, but I'm not sure that's really true. Meanwhile, I'm still amazed when they talk to me about success. And in any case, if success has a secret, it's better for it to remain like that. Besides, I come from nothing. My family had nothing, they were very poor. When you come from nothing, your whole life is about running away from nothing. But nothing is more powerful than fame, and will keep chasing you until it has caught you again and swallowed you.

84

[33]  *A.C. Forniture Sud*, 1991

    [33.1]  *Cesena 47 - A.C. Forniture Sud 12*, 1991
Black and white photographic print
120 × 190 cm

    [33.2]  *Cesena 47 - A.C. Forniture Sud 12 (2° tempo)*, 1991
Black and white photographic print on aluminum
125 × 195 cm

    [33.3]  *A.C. Forniture Sud*, 1991
Photographic collage
77 × 100 cm

    [33.4]  *A.C. Forniture Sud*, 1991
Plexiglas, silkscreened and die-cut card, whistle
Edition
18 × 23 × 17.5 cm

Right after the cover of *Flash Art* (*Strategie*, 1990) I did *A.C. Forniture Sud*, a soccer team made up of immigrants. I thought of the most popular thing in Italy, and through a very simple principle I used soccer to represent the emerging phenomenon of immigration from outside the EU. I had the team play matches in which I was the coach and the president of the team. It was a mixture of performance, sculpture, and social commentary. The team was sponsored by a mythical company I called Rauss, a name that recalled the word used in German to say "Out!" It was at the time when the Northern League political party was becoming big.

The best way to promote my team of immigrants was to act on the xenophobia of contemporary society, meaning to become an interloper. The idea for the "illegal" stand I used to present the team at Arte Fiera in Bologna was already inherent in the product promoted. It was an approach common to all the works I was developing at that time: to sneak through the gaps in the meshes that exist in every system, not provocatively and visibly, but mimetically, using its own means. What I wanted to represent in that way was the struggle between the need to be free and an increasingly strong schematism.

It was a project closely related to the concept of privilege. I liked the idea of owning a soccer team, just like the tycoons of finance. That was the sparkle, in the years of Berlusconi and Gullit, but also the ships full of migrants seeking a better future in Italy. Using soccer as a means to get my ideas across was a way to communicate with as many people as possible, to reach a wider public than just the art world. This project did in fact get some coverage in the papers, that normally do not touch contemporary art.

If I could, I would have made *A.C. Forniture Sud* a permanent installation. Of course, the players would have to change every time one of them got their residence permit, replacing them with new immigrants. And, of course, nowadays I would invite [the Lega party's secretary] Matteo Salvini to play a game.

I devised the work in Bologna. The air in the city was electric. You felt the charge in every cre-

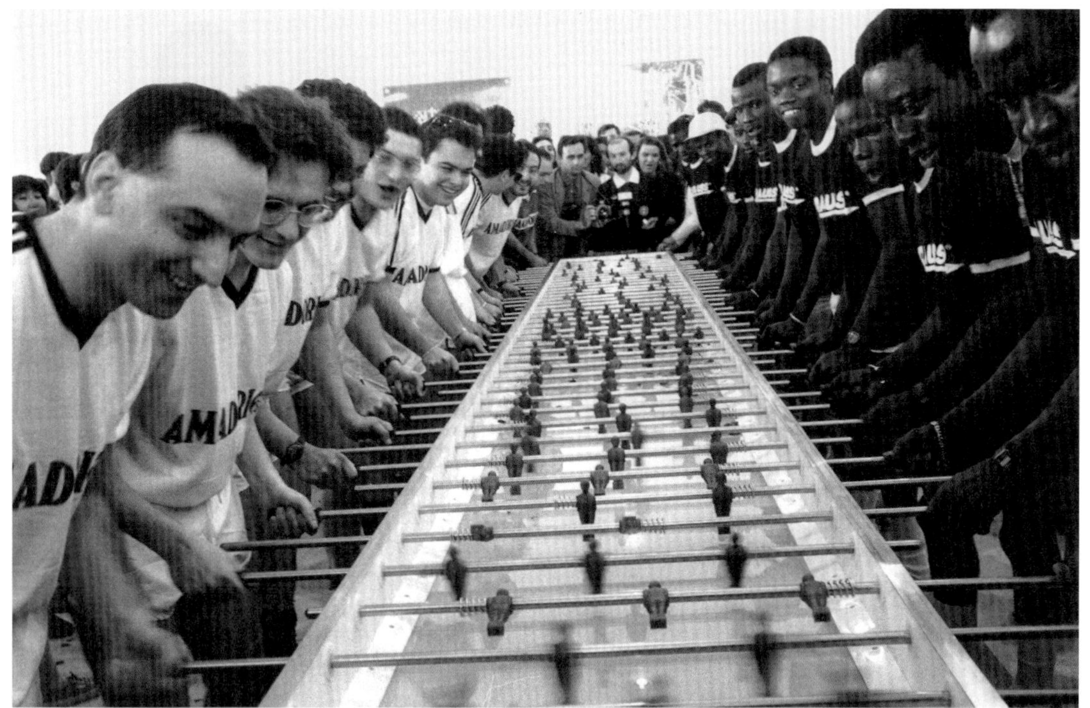



[33.1]

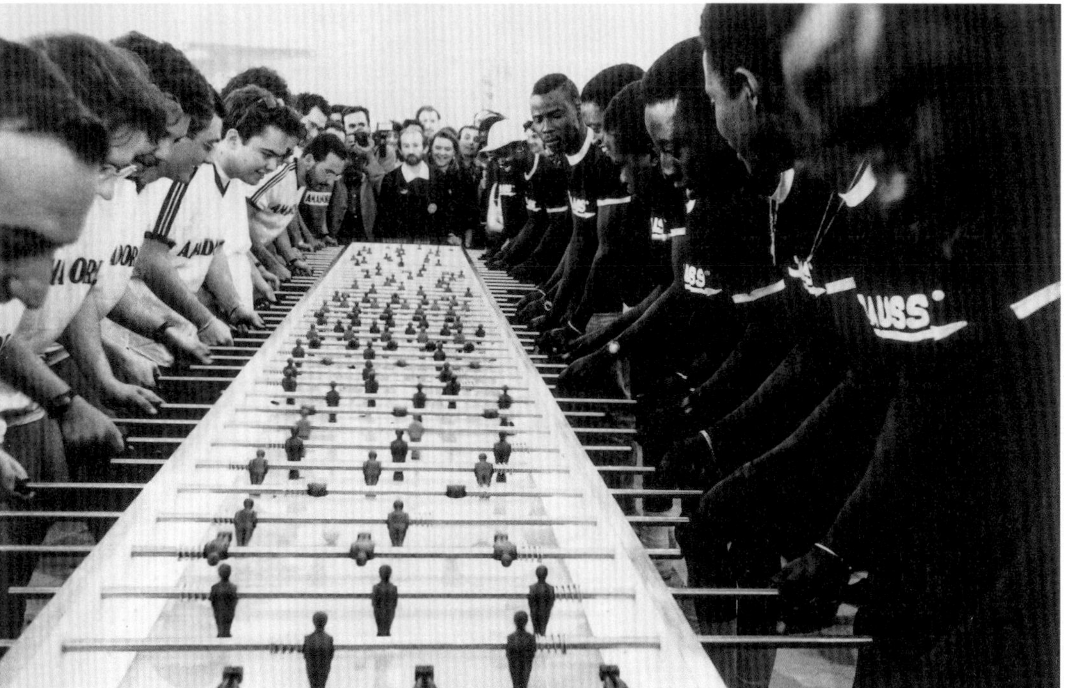



[33.2]

[33.1]  *Cesena 47 - A.C. Forniture Sud 12*, 1991      [33.2]  *Cesena 47 - A.C. Forniture Sud 12 (2° tempo)*, 1991

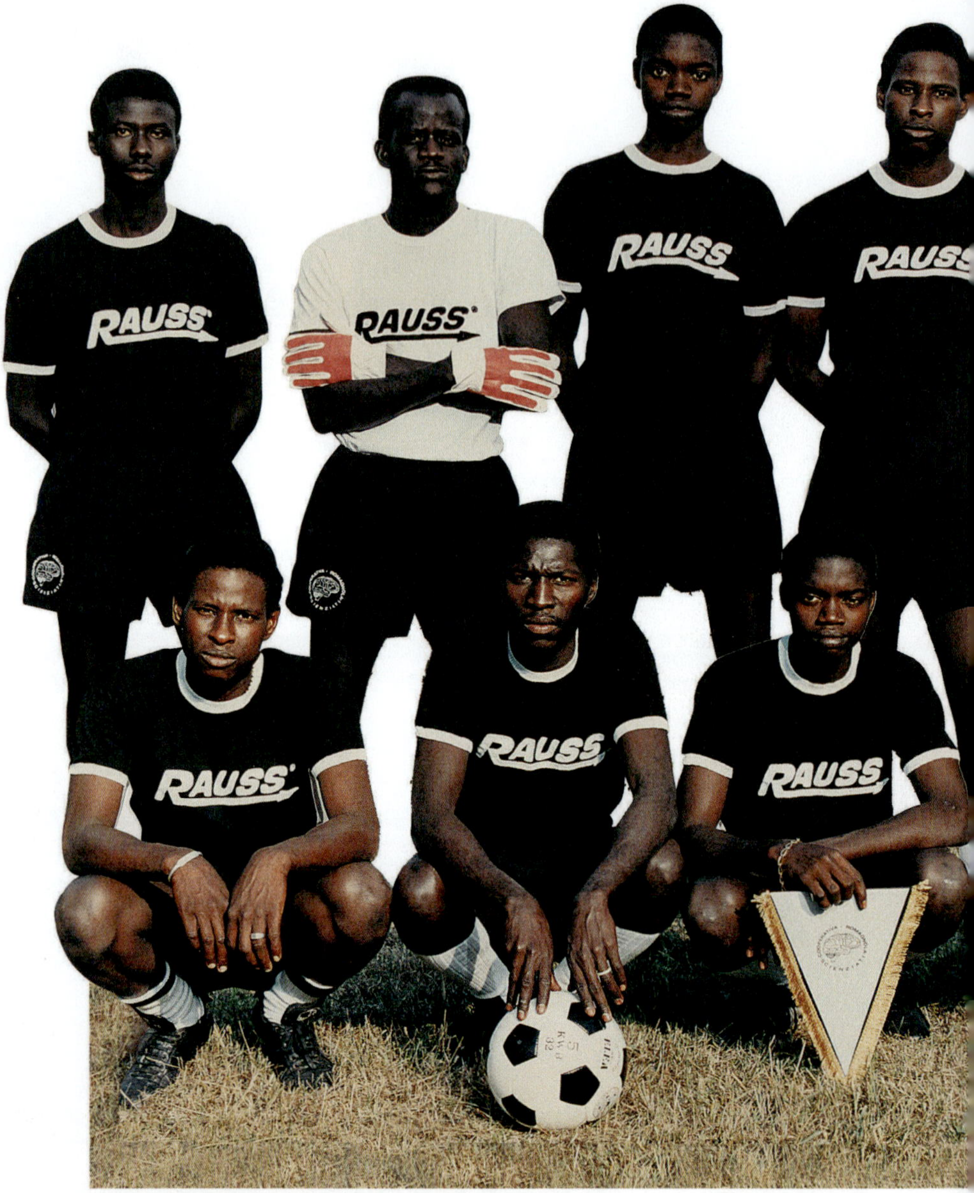

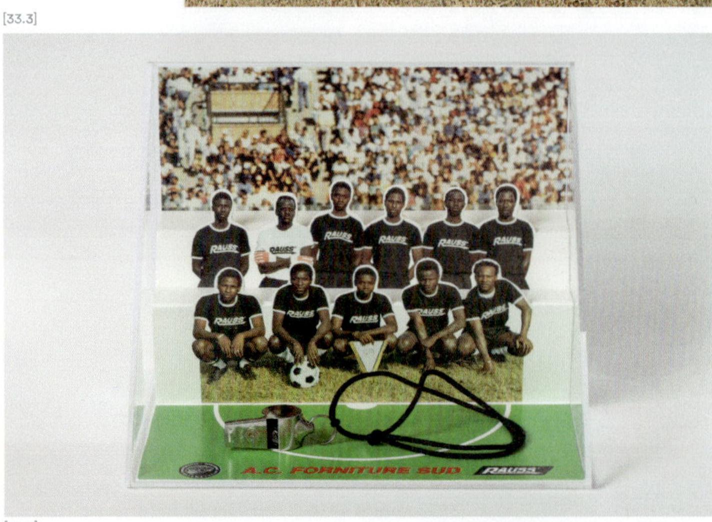

[33.3]

[33.4]

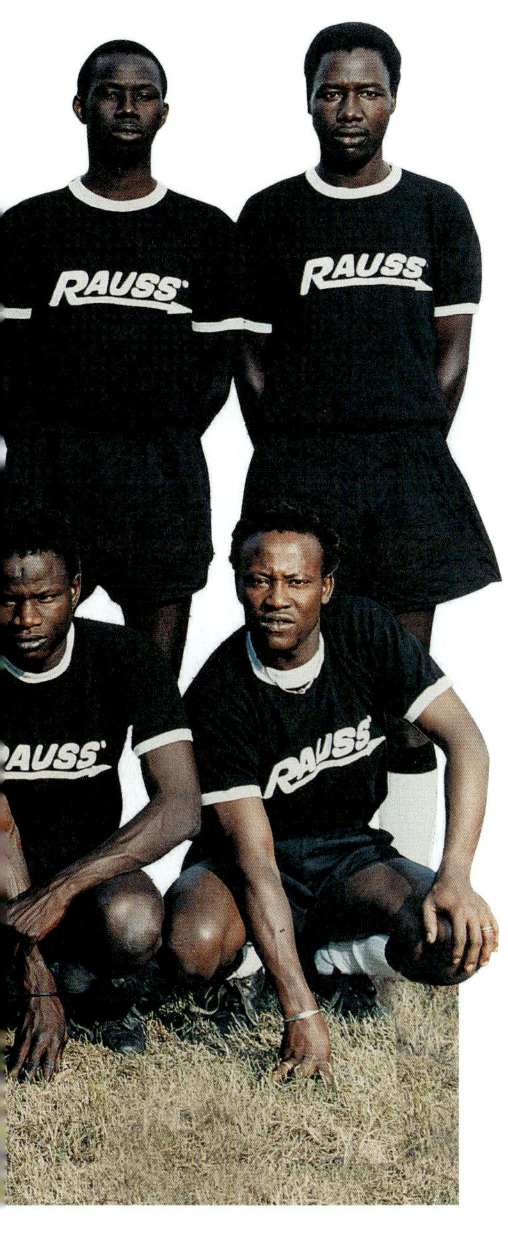

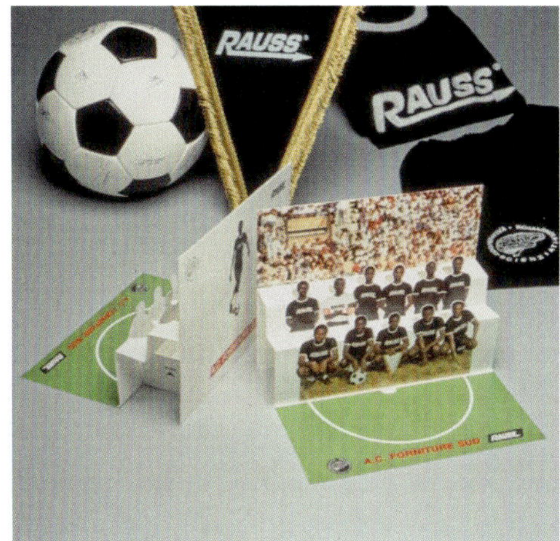
[33.5]

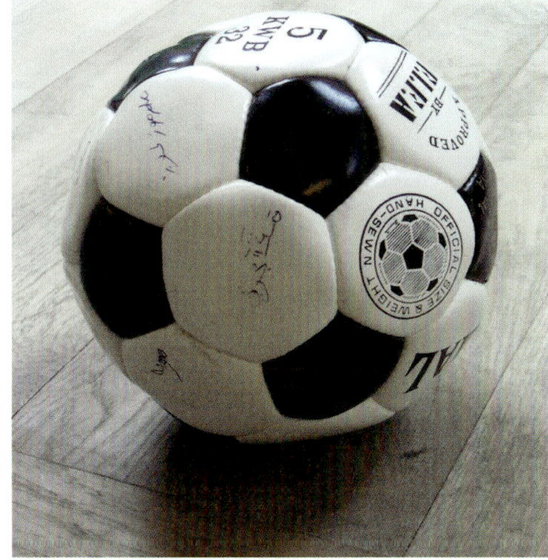
[33.6]



ative discipline, without distinction, like a new Italian renaissance. It was inevitable to gravitate around it. Every city I've lived in has marked a period of my life. Bologna was an excellent starting point. Today, like the rest of the world, it has changed, or perhaps I've changed. When I started going there, Bologna seemed like a metropolis to me, compared to Padua. Then, seen from New York, everything looked very small, but in the end it is always and only a matter of perspective.

[33.3]   *A.C. Forniture Sud*, 1991

[33.4]   *A.C. Forniture Sud*, 1991

[33.5-7]  Promotional material for the soccer team A.C. Forniture Sud, 1991

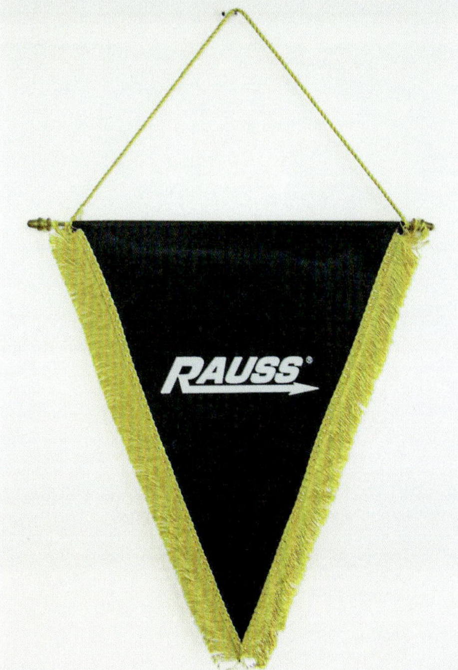
[33.7]

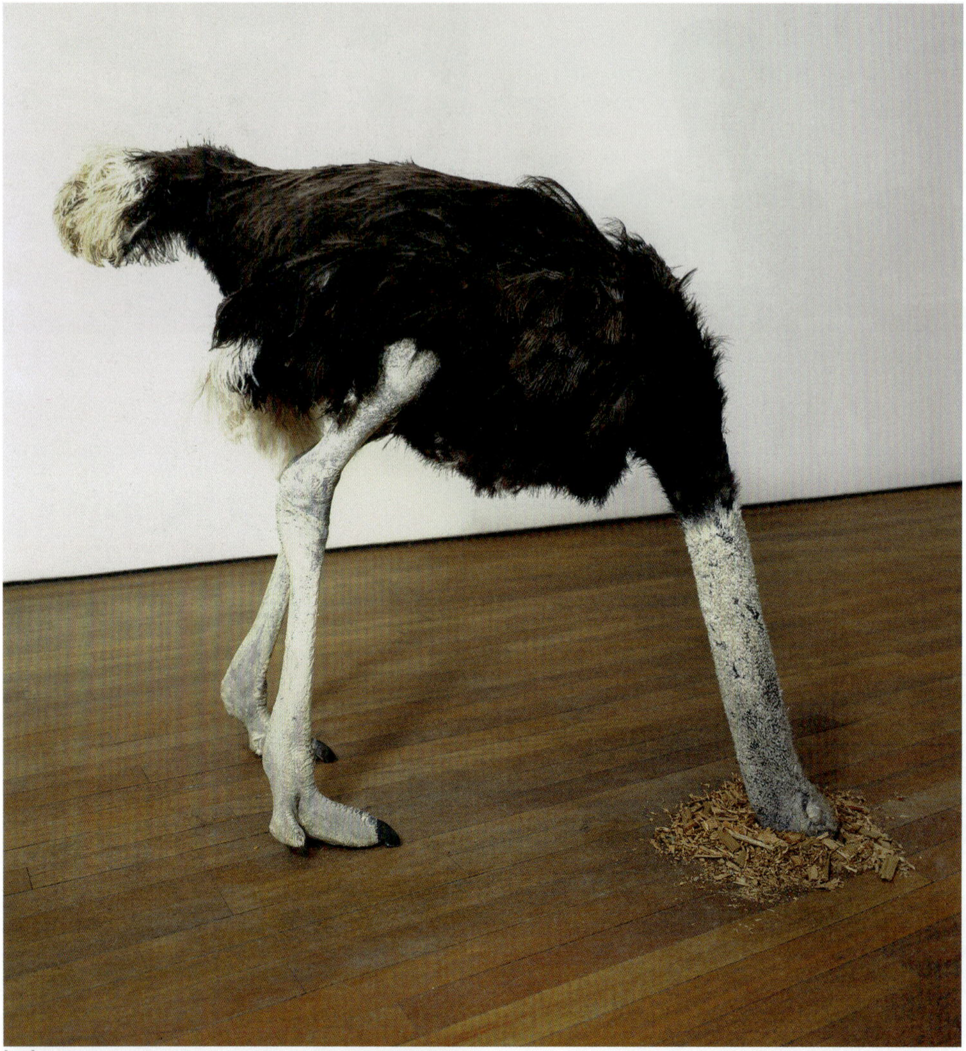

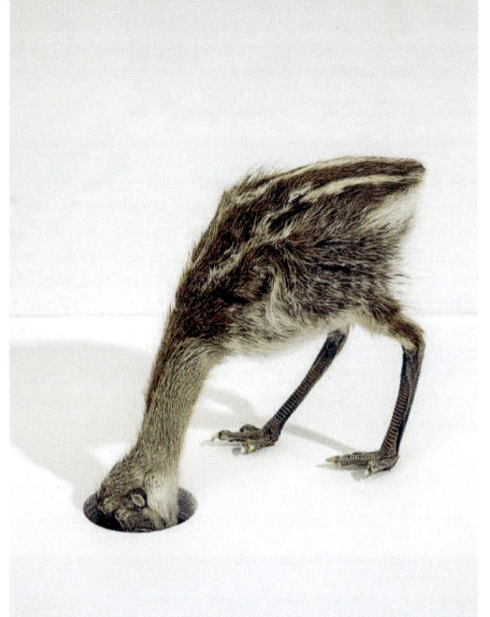

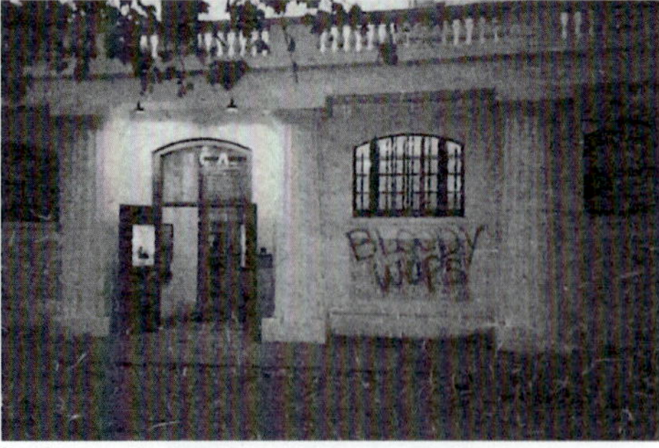



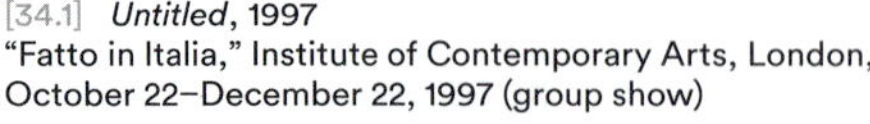

88

[34.1]  *Untitled*, 1997
"Fatto in Italia," Institute of Contemporary Arts, London,
October 22–December 22, 1997 (group show)

[34.2]  The words "Bloody Wops" spray painted on the
external wall of the Institute of Contemporary Arts,
London, 1997

[34.3]  *Untitled*, 1999
Taxidermied baby ostrich
17.8 × 12.7 × 16.5 cm

**[34]** *Untitled*, 1997
Taxidermied ostrich, wood chips
124.5 × 134.6 × 50.8 cm

For the exhibition "Fatto in Italia" at the Institute of Contemporary Arts in London in 1997 I installed an ostrich with its head buried in the gallery floor. He was hiding from the exhibition itself. It was a sort of exercise—I was taking part in a show while trying to keep a distance from it, just like an ostrich, with his head buried in the ground and his ass sticking out. The show was okay, but it opened at the same time as that big "Sensation" exhibition of the Young British Artists at the Royal Academy. The differences in strategy between the British and Italian artists and curators were very noticeable. I felt as if we were the poor relations. We were forced into this stereotype of Italian art, and I couldn't really deal with it. So I did the ostrich, but I also sneaked out and spray-painted a new exhibition on the outside of the building: I wrote "Bloody Wops" across the wall. I was trying to play with the role of the Italian immigrant, but more importantly I was making a point about curators and the absurdity of these kinds of shows, telling them more or less to wake up.

**[35]** *Untitled*, 1999
Hand-carved granite, medium-density fiberboard, steel
219.4 × 277.3 × 33.8 cm

For my exhibition at the Anthony d'Offay Gallery in London in 1999 I created an untitled black granite wall, like Maya Lin's Vietnam Veterans Memorial in Washington D.C. Carved into it are the defeats suffered by the England national soccer team: from the start of its history until that moment it had played 700 games but had lost only 160.
I think it's a work about pride, defeat, missed opportunities and, as a memorial, even about death, in a certain way. Anyway, it's fundamentally about England and the English national soccer team, which for many years taught football to everyone. Italy lost many games against England. But I'm afraid some people got upset. First, because I'm Italian; second, because soccer is one of the two or three subjects you can't touch, and last but not least because they thought it was a stupid idea. People want artists to come up with brilliant ideas, and the wall is not that brilliant. It's a monument to my failure as well.

[35] *Untitled*, 1999
"Maurizio Cattelan," Anthony d'Offay Gallery, London,
April 30–June 16, 1999 (solo show)





[35]

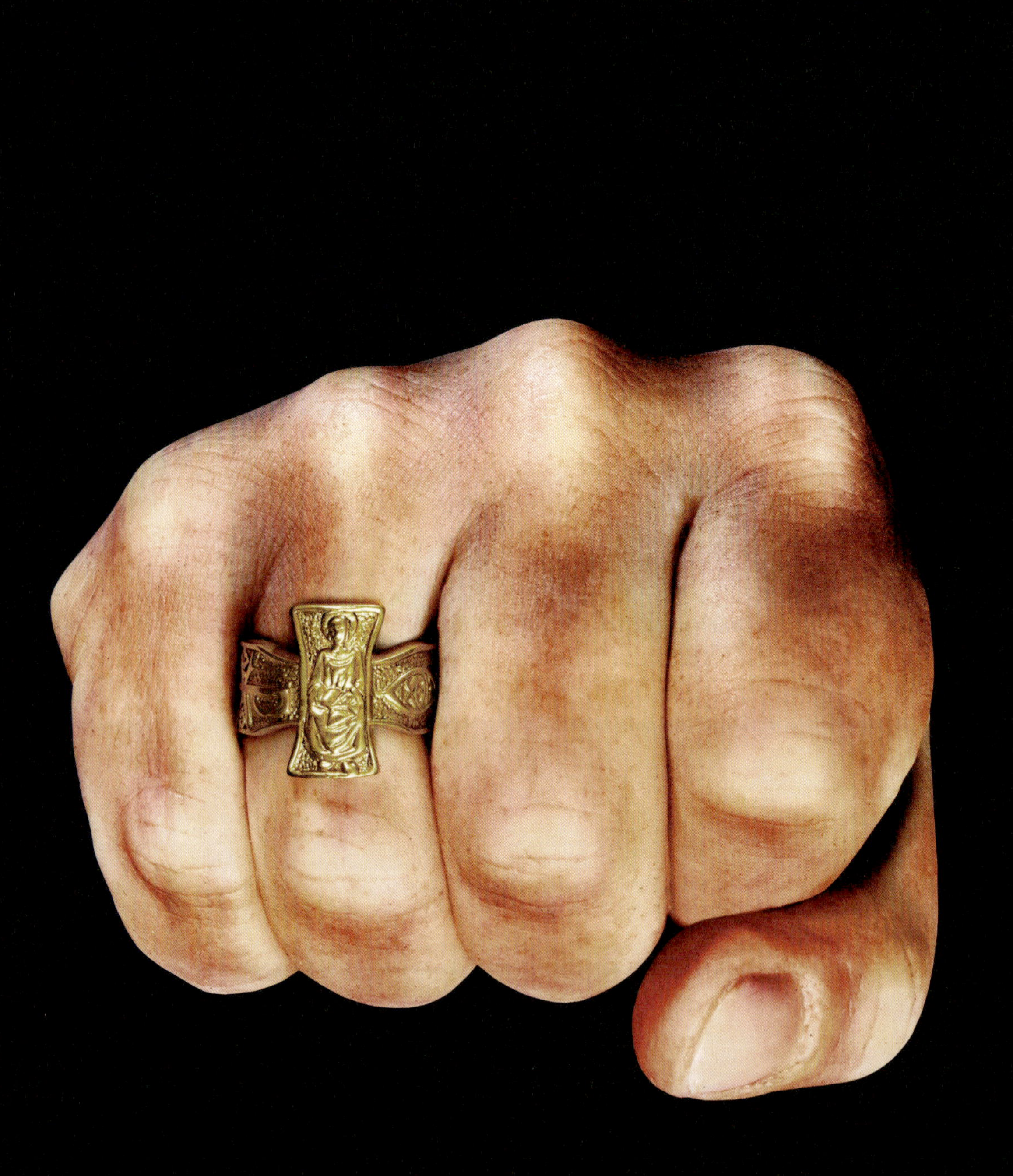

Italy is many things in contradiction with each other. This is its upside and its downside. While we formerly exported both the form of government and the lifestyle, today we have to do the opposite, learning other lifestyles and accepting suggestions from abroad on how to govern better. All the same, we're still a factor in the collective imagination, in a truly global sense, as the place where beauty, love, and the good life are always honored. Couples in love come to us to celebrate their illusion. When they can't come here, they settle for surrogates in Las Vegas or Macau. In short, no country has such a clear brand. I don't mean "Made in Italy," a hackneyed concept, and also a bit shabby. I'm talking about Italy. Anyway, just like all other brands, it should be put in the hands of somebody who knows how to exploit it properly. Italy is a luxury brand, so it should be turned over to the people who know how to make the most of luxury.

In any case, we shouldn't forget that if the image of Italy—a collective and to some extent illusory image—is what it is, we owe it to the fact that in the past, first with the Romans, then with emigration, we spread all over. In America they don't even have a word for the herb we call *rucola*. They used the word our immigrants called it, who spoke only their dialect: *arugula*. Today it's not uncommon for people with four degrees and wealthy people in America to ask me to comment, being Italian, on the pizza or tiramisu they've brought me to eat. No one asks my opinion on a deconstructed dish by Carlo Cracco or on Massimo Bottura's memory of gorgonzola. Why? Because in the end, I fear, it is we ourselves who give others the impression of being largely and above all pizza eaters much more than innovators.

We have perhaps become less elastic, less flexible, older. We're terrified of tomorrow, which we see as an eternal crisis where everything will disappear. We've deluded ourselves with globalization, but what prevails are individualism and regionalism, the only mental protections against an invisible and perhaps non-existent enemy who is threatening to invade us and wipe us out. Everybody's afraid, and Italy more so than others. Because, perhaps, she's more attached to her identity than others.

All the same, Italy continues to remind me of Miloš Forman's film *The Firemen's Ball*, where there's a village festival where a series of unspeakable disasters happen, and yet in the end everyone has fun. Or *The Party* with Peter Sellers. We're a group people,

**unlike, for example, the Americans, who are for one man standing alone against everybody. A Rocky Balboa doesn't go down well here. The Italian cinema duo Bud Spencer and Terence Hill seem to appeal to us more, and maybe they still do: big fistfights where no one really gets hurt.**

[36] *Campagna elettorale*, 1989
Newspaper advertisement

A long time ago, during an election campaign, I bought some advertising space in the Bologna edition of *la Repubblica*. There was no name, only the logo of my fictitious Cooperativa Scienziati Romagnoli and the statement: "Your vote is precious: keep it." Supporting a reflection on the vote with an anonymous electoral advertisement was almost the same thing as supporting a candidate, hoping to get people to reflect on the repetitive, almost unconscious way we take part in a collective social ritual. It wasn't cynical, it was a stance. Elections are a public event where you express your opinion, and I felt I expressed my position like that, especially in the case of the Italian elections. All votes are precious, because they all mean something, even the ones not cast. I don't like it when the vote is seen as confirmation of the previous system and not as a push to change it, make it better, fairer and more inclusive. Abstention can be a form of protest, the sign of a malaise that needs to be reckoned with, not ignored as normal. It's not an anti-political attitude, but an attitude in favor of a politics of excellence.
At that time it was right before the "Clean Hands" investigation, and the ad was a way of protesting, of rebelling against corrupt power. Today, in the era of Cambridge Analytica and fake reviews, it should be updated to "Your like is precious, keep it."

[37] **Cooperativa Scienziati Romagnoli, 1989**

I set up the Cooperativa Scienziati Romagnoli for a critical purpose, ironizing on the monopoly of the cooperative system in the Romagna region. It arose from both my fascination with brands and the urge to express a personal opinion about what was going on around me. It became my alter ego, a screen for doing things without exposing myself personally. A phantom cooperative of scientists who had decided to have their say about politics. I used it for an ad in the newspaper in 1989.

[37] Promotional T-shirt printed for the Cooperativa Scienziati Romagnoli, 1989

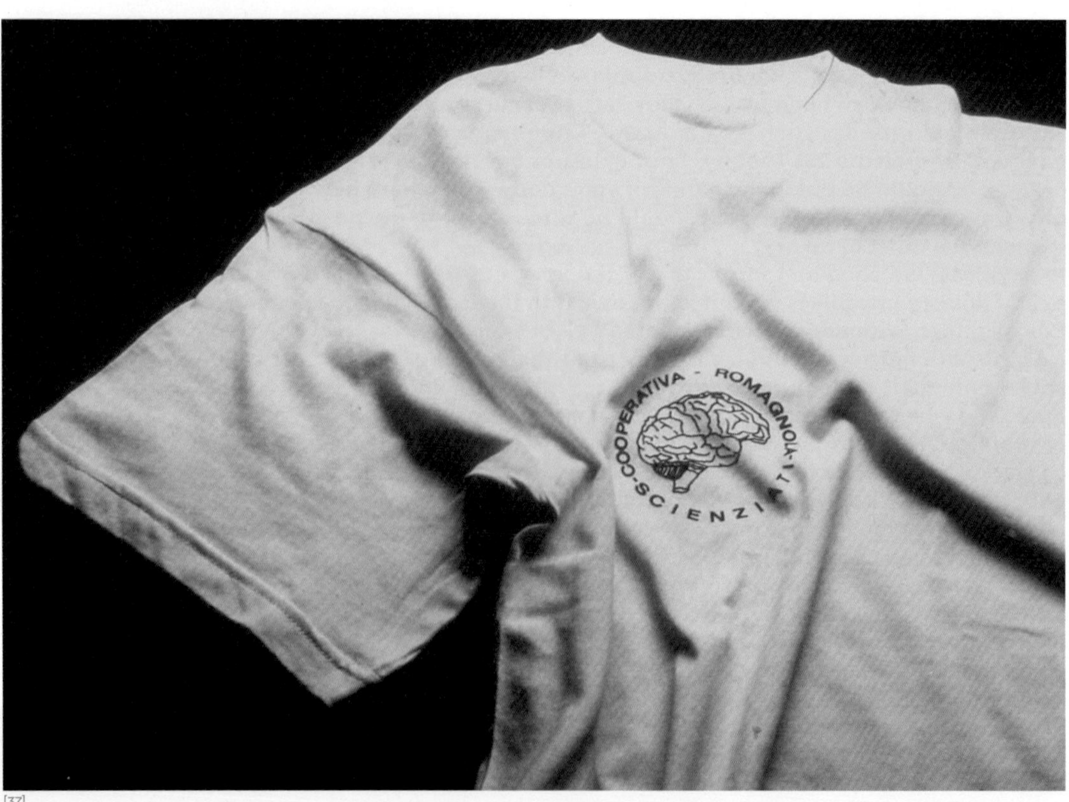

## Nuova retata sui viali e sui colli. Tutti accusati di atti osceni in luogo pubblico

# Blitz anti-lucciole denunciati i clienti

di LUIGI SPEZIA

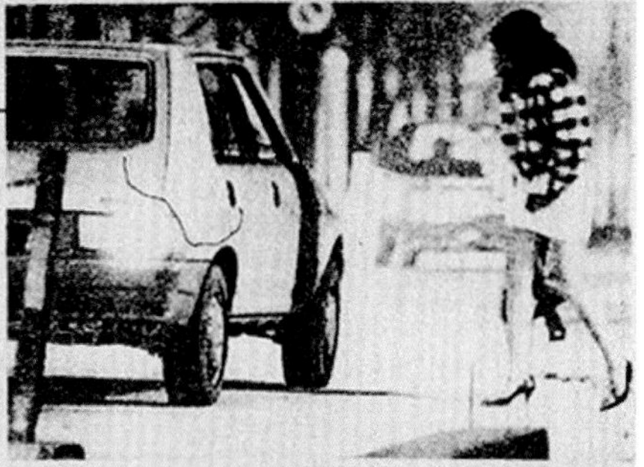

QUESTA volta non è un'escort a girare intorno alle coppiette in intimità. In via Codivilla e nelle vie limitrofe, proprio sopra «Sexstrasse», è il maresciallo che bussa al finestrino dell'auto posteggiata al buio. Paletta bianco-rossa in mano, un pò imbarazzato di trovarsi davanti a uomini di 50 o 60 anni sorpresi con una prostituta, dice soltanto «Scusate, dovete venire in caserma». Le alcove dell'amore a pagamento scoperte. Dieci «belle di notte» africane denunciate per atti osceni. Ma non solo loro. Questa volta è toccato anche ai «clienti»: dieci partner improvvisati delle donne nigeriane sono stati denunciati anch'essi per atti osceni.

### I controlli
### continueranno

Dopo la retata in «Sexstrasse», i controlli che continuano sui viali, i Carabinieri hanno messo in pratica un'altra mossa per scongiurare il mercato del sesso africano. Hanno fatto cadere nella rete i patiti delle bellezze esotiche.

In via di Codivilla, le «gazzelle» del Nucleo radiomobile e i militari del Nucleo Operativo, hanno scoperto anche un minorenne. Un ragazzo di Porretta che era a bordo dell'auto di un amico, insieme ad una prostituta di colore. Il ragazzino è arrossito quando ha visto i militari. Stessa vergogna sulle facce di due suoi amici, anch'essi minorenni, che stavano aspettando il proprio turno e facevano la ronda attorno all'auto: erano venuti in gruppo da Porretta Terme. Dalla caserma hanno chiamato i genitori. Hanno raccontato al padre dove e come avevano trovato il ragazzo e per tutta risposta hanno ricevuto una risata. Chissà, forse per questo genitore è un vanto che suo figlio sia stato con una prostituta.

Fortuna per tutti che il nuovo codice non prevede l'arresto in flagranza per il reato di atti osceni. Già tre anni fa i Carabinieri avevano fatto un paio di retate in centro, avevano arrestato dei medici «clienti» (tra cui un avvocato bolognese) insieme alle lucciole italiane che avevano preso l'abitudine di «appartarsi» sotto le finestre dei condomini. Questa volta i «clienti» pescati dai Carabinieri hanno perduto soltanto qualche ora per le formalità. Non hanno dovuto inventare scuse inverosimili per giustificare la notte dietro le sbarre. «Siamo uomini», hanno detto in molti cercando comprensione. Sono sfilati muti e imbarazzati davanti ai sottufficiali che chiedevano nomi e cognomi. Molti sono padri di famiglia. Le prostitute, invece, accolte nell'ampio atrio della caserma, hanno messo in scena un lamento funebre. Si sono inginocchiate tutte assieme e hanno iniziato a intonare una nenia. Un modo tutto loro di fare resistenza passiva. I carabinieri sono rimasti interdetti: non avevano mai visto né sentito una cosa del genere. Soltanto dopo dieci minuti sono riusciti a convincerle ad alzarsi e a mettersi a sedere. Ora «Sexstrasse» è stata liberata. Le proteste del Comitato di viale Aldini hanno mobilitato una nuova ora le forze dell'ordine. Dopo le retate dei mesi scorsi il mercato del sesso africano ha ripreso l'attività. Ora tutti si domandano se questa volta la cacciata delle «nere» sarà davvero definitiva. L'altra notte un centinaio di abitanti dei viali ha fatto una fiaccolata di protesta a porta San Mamolo.

### La fiaccolata
### di protesta

Ad un certo punto sono passate le pattuglie dei Carabinieri e si è aperta una discussione. Gli abitanti di viale Aldini hanno chiesto che cosa stanno facendo le forze dell'ordine. I militari hanno risposto che la legge non permette di fare più dei controlli e delle denunce di questi giorni.

---

## Sviluppi nell'inchiesta sui falsari

# Per la truffa utilizzavano il nome Armani

VOLEVANO sfruttare il nome dello stilista Giorgio Armani i falsari scoperti la settimana scorsa con il maxiblitz della Squadra mobile. Tra gli assegni sequestrati, alcuni, oltre ad essere intestati «New York City Bank», avevano anche l'intestazione «Jimmy Canola, General Manager Armani Boutiques». Tutto inventato. Nella casa di moda milanese non esiste nessun dirigente con quel nome.

Secondo gli investigatori, questi assegni con doppia intestazione (si chiamano «pubblicitarie» o «personalizzati») sarebbero stati spesi sulle piazze estere. Il nome di Jimmy Canola non avrebbe persuaso nessuno, ma quello di Armani, noto in tutta Europa, sarebbe stata una garanzia più che sufficiente di fronte ad eventuali resistenze ad accettare i titoli di credito da parte delle banche estere.

Per spendere i falsi assegni «personalizzati» sequestrati nella tipografia «Nuova Stampa Estense» erano pochi, ma è stato trovato anche il cliché pronto all'uso: i falsari denunciati dalla Mobile non avrebbero però avuto tante difficoltà. C'è il sospetto che i falsi assegni avrebbero preso la strada di società finanziarie di comodo o consenzienti, o sarebbero arrivati nelle mani di operatori finanziari complici dei falsari che avrebbero avuto molti problemi a piazzarli all'estero, naturalmente dopo averli «riempiti» e magari dopo aver depositato in garanzia titoli di valore inferiore. Gli operatori delle banche estere, di fronte ad un assegno sul quale figura il nome di Armani, presentato da un signore munito di «Rolls» e valigetta 24 ore, avrebbero pagato senza molte esitazioni. Gli assegni, insomma, sarebbero entrati in un giro internazionale gestito da personaggi insospettabili che manovrano con disinvoltura titoli veri e falsi.

I tipografi Secondo Trentini e Silvio Bruschi, stando all'accusa «manovali» dell'organizzazione, fermati e già agli arresti domiciliari, di fronte alle contestazioni si sono difesi dicendo che quel tal signor Canola si era presentato in tipografia e aveva chiesto di stampare alcuni «buoni» della Armani, da regalare ai clienti da spendere nelle boutiques convenzionate. Se questa versione fosse vera, vorrebbe dire che le due, accusate con altre venti persone di associazione per delinquere finalizzata alla truffa, si sono lasciate ingannare da un altro truffatore.

Durante l'operazione, diretta dal capo della Mobile Salvatore Surace e dal responsabile della sezione truffe Giuseppe Preziosa, è stato scoperto anche un secondo tipo di titoli siglati «New York City Bank». Sono «traveller's cheques» che secondo gli investigatori erano probabilmente destinati al mercato interno. Titoli come questi sono generalmente presentati nelle banche italiane per il pagamento dei compensi degli italiani che lavorano negli Stati Uniti.

---


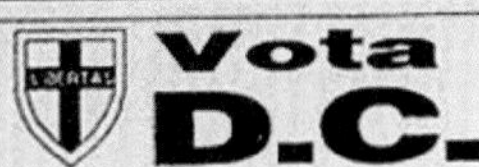


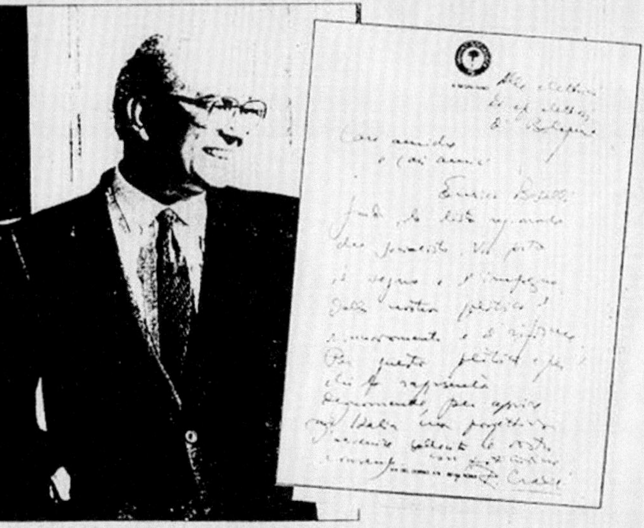


●● Care amiche e cari amici, Enrico Boselli guida la lista regionale dei socialisti. Vi porta il segno e l'impegno della nostra politica di rinnovamento e di riforme. Per questa politica e per chi la rappresenta degnamente, per aprire in Italia una prospettiva d'avvenire, sollecito il vostro consenso. Con gratitudine, Bettino Craxi ●●

Per eleggere Enrico Boselli alla Regione Emilia Romagna è indispensabile scrivere, sulla scheda verde, BOSELLI o 1 accanto al simbolo PSI.

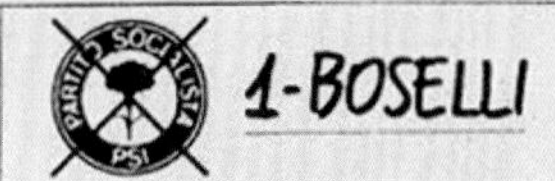





[36]   *Campagna elettorale*, 1989

[38]  *Il Bel Paese*, 1994
Tufted wool carpet
Ø 300 cm

When I was first in New York, in the early 1990s, I felt like a tourist, and naturally I thought about the stereotyped ideas of a country. And so I did *Il Bel Paese*. It didn't need much. The tray of an intercontinental meal in economy class while flying over the Atlantic did it. The occasion was the exhibition "SoggettoSoggetto" at the Castello di Rivoli. I made it into a carpet, round like the label and the wheel of cheese. People could walk over it and actually wipe their shoes on it.

[39]  *I Found My Love in Portofino*, 1994
Bel Paese cheese, rats, plexiglas
160 × 150 × 60 cm

[40]  *Perita*, 1992
Glass jar, eggs
Height 20 cm, Ø 12 cm

[41]  *13-11-1998: My Last Kiss*, 1998
Bread
Length c. 200 cm

I presented *I Found My Love in Portofino* for the first time at P.S.1 in a group show in fall 1994. In a display case on a plinth I placed a wheel of Bel Paese cheese and three live mice. The top of the plinth was pitted, so the rats' droppings fell underneath. It sucked. I think it's the most horrible thing ever set up in that space. The work was live, and a documentary video was made.
Later I installed the work at the Galerie Daniel Buchholz in Cologne, adding a blow-up of the newspaper *Avvenire* when it published the first photo of Aldo Moro detained by the Red Brigades (*Untitled*, 1994). It was Christmas. They were two postcards from Italy, which subverted the picturesque and stereotyped image of the *bel paese*.
I had already done an experiment with food in 1992, by putting eggs in a jar to make a gift (*Perita*), and I thought about it again a few years later, when I made a pair of skis out of bread. I've never skied, but at that time I was reading the story of an explorer who tried to live outside society, relying only on nature and unfortunately failing. For the title I used the date and the words of the last entry in his diary.

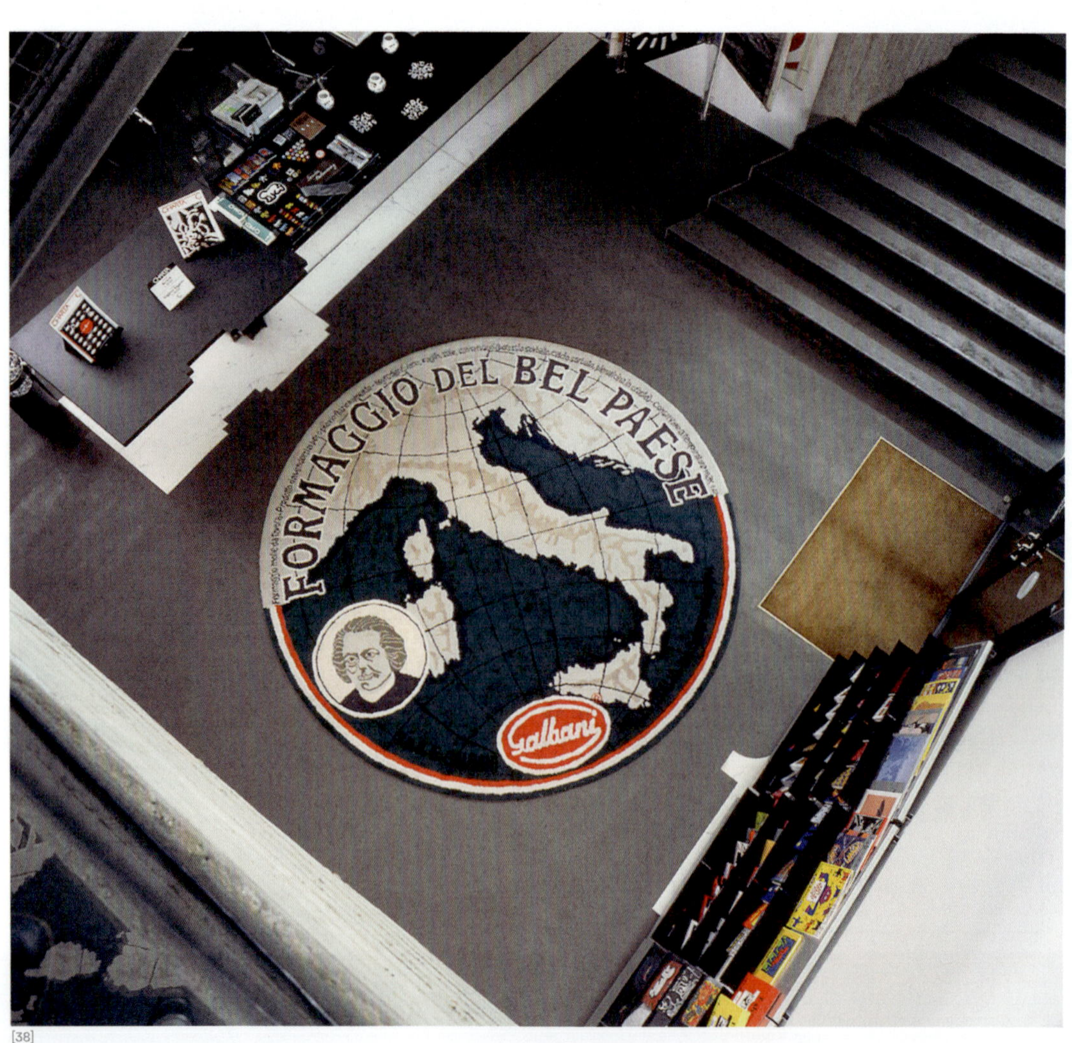

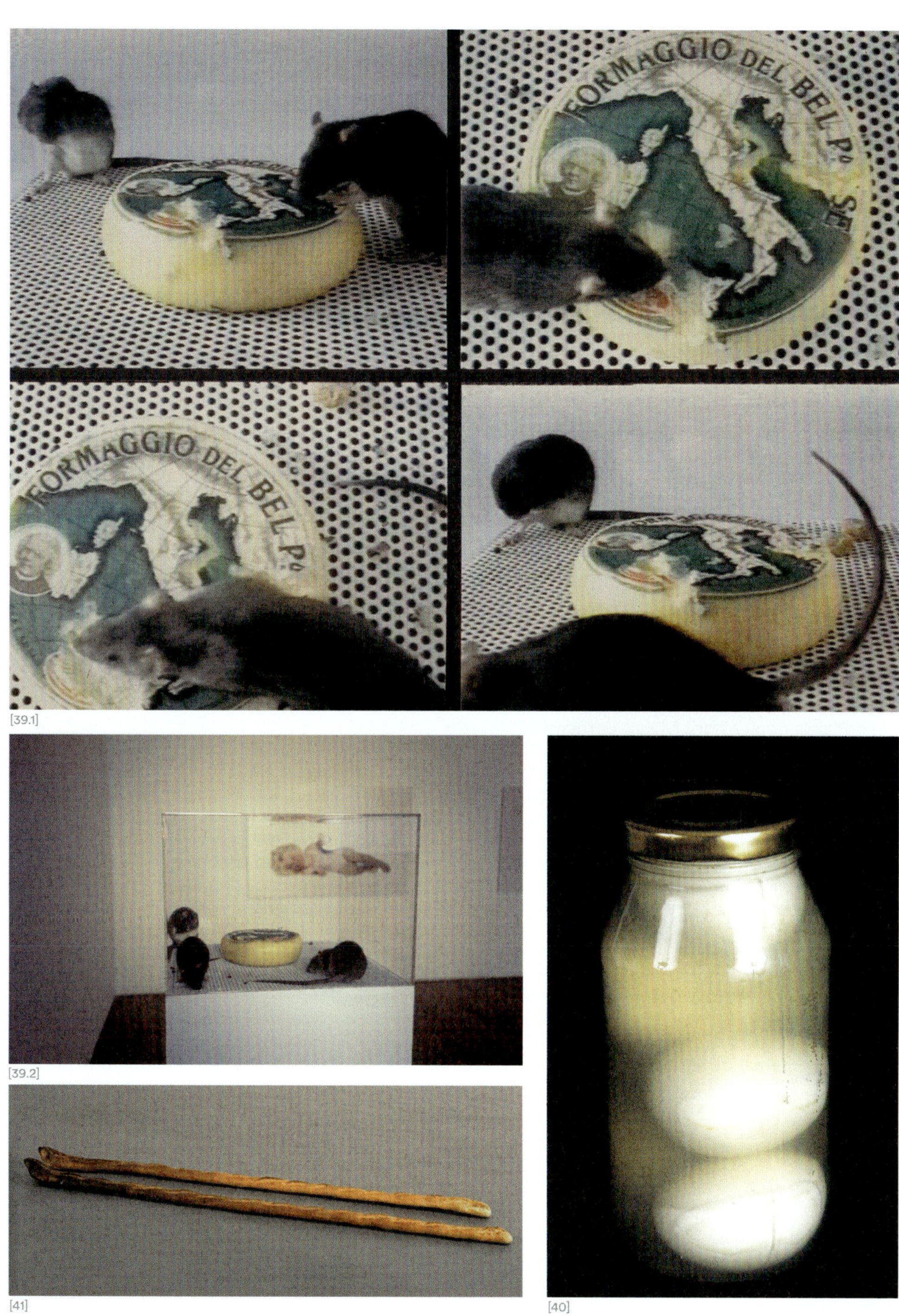

95



[39.1]

[39.2]

[41]

[40]

[39.1]  *I Found My Love in Portofino*, 1994
Documentary video stills

[39.2]  *I Found My Love in Portofino*, 1994
"The Winter of Love (L'Hiver de l'Amour)," curated by
Olivier Zahm and Elein Fleiss, P.S.1 Contemporary Art
Center, New York, October 9, 1994–January 8, 1995
(group show)

[40]  *Perita*, 1992

[41]  *13-11-1998: My Last Kiss*, 1998

[38]  *Il Bel Paese*, 1994
"SoggettoSoggetto. Una nuova relazione nell'arte di oggi,"
curated by Francesca Pasini and Giorgio Verzotti, Castello
di Rivoli Museo d'Arte Contemporanea, Rivoli-Turin, June
24–August 28, 1994 (group show)

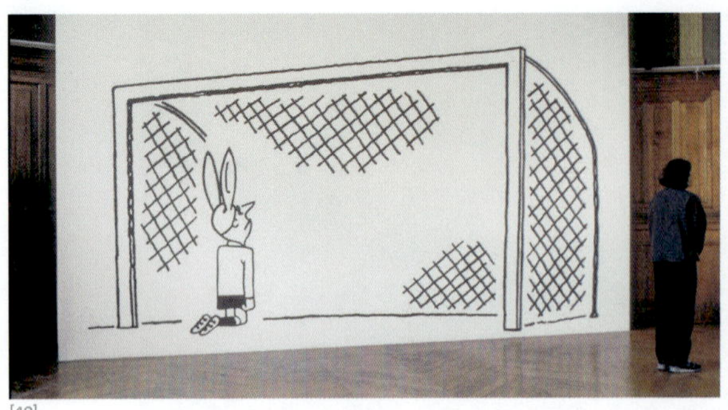
[42]

[42] *Untitled*, 1997
Print, wall posting
Environmental dimensions

Soccer is a religion in Italy. A few years after *A.C. Forniture Sud* and *Stadium* (1991), I returned to the subject and printed a wall-sized drawing with a rabbit goalkeeper kneeling in front of the goal. It looks funny, but it's about failure: a goalkeeper who has let in a goal by committing a blunder.

[43] *L.O.V.E.*, 2010
Carrara marble, Roman travertine
Hand: 470 × 220 × 72 cm;
base: 630 × 470 × 470 cm
Piazza degli Affari, Milan, permanent
installation since September 25, 2010

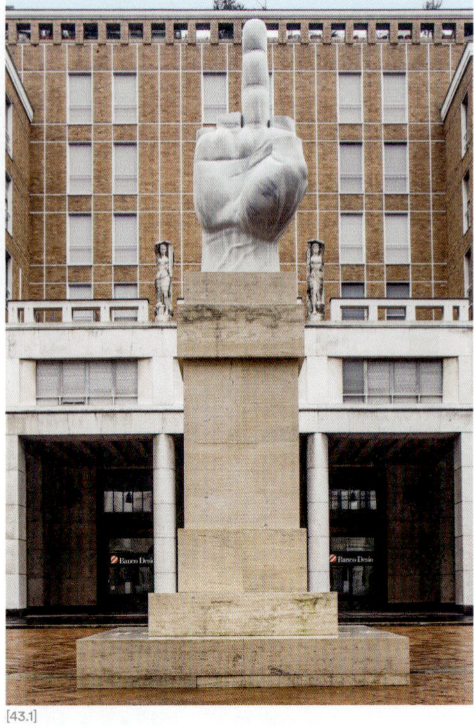
[43.1]

While I was working on the exhibition in Milan that would become "Contro le ideologie," I was also busy with the project for a work in a city square. Actually, even then I didn't know what to do. I had one of the hands in *Ave Maria* (2007), whose fingers I had already chopped off. I put it in my pocket and went to a meeting with the municipal councilor for Culture, who at the time was Massimiliano Finazzer Flory, and suggested installing it in the open. He approved the work, and supported it warmly. It was cooled by the mayor Letizia Moratti, and endorsed by Stefano Boeri, the councilor for Culture in the subsequent administration. Given my previous experiences in Milan, I believe the city council tried to shield itself from possible criticism, but that just triggered controversy.

The hand has a long history in sculpture, and mine essentially derives from a classical image: the colossal marble hand of Constantine in the Capitoline Museums in Rome. Everyone can interpret my work the way they like. To me it was above all important to relate it to a public space. However, since the piazza where it was installed, Piazza degli Affari, is a parking lot, *L.O.V.E.* is more a roundabout than a monument.

If you try to imagine it with all your fingers, you will understand that there is no more perfect



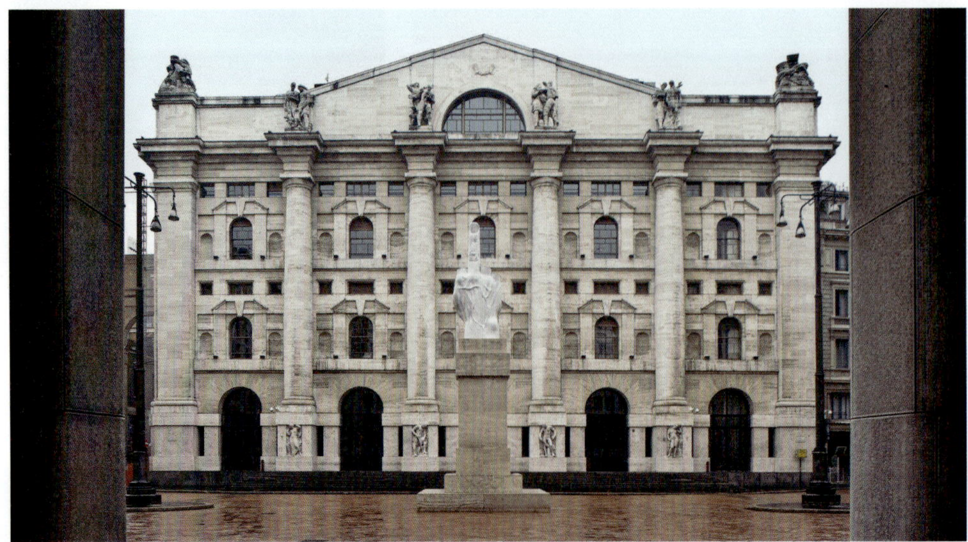
[43.2]

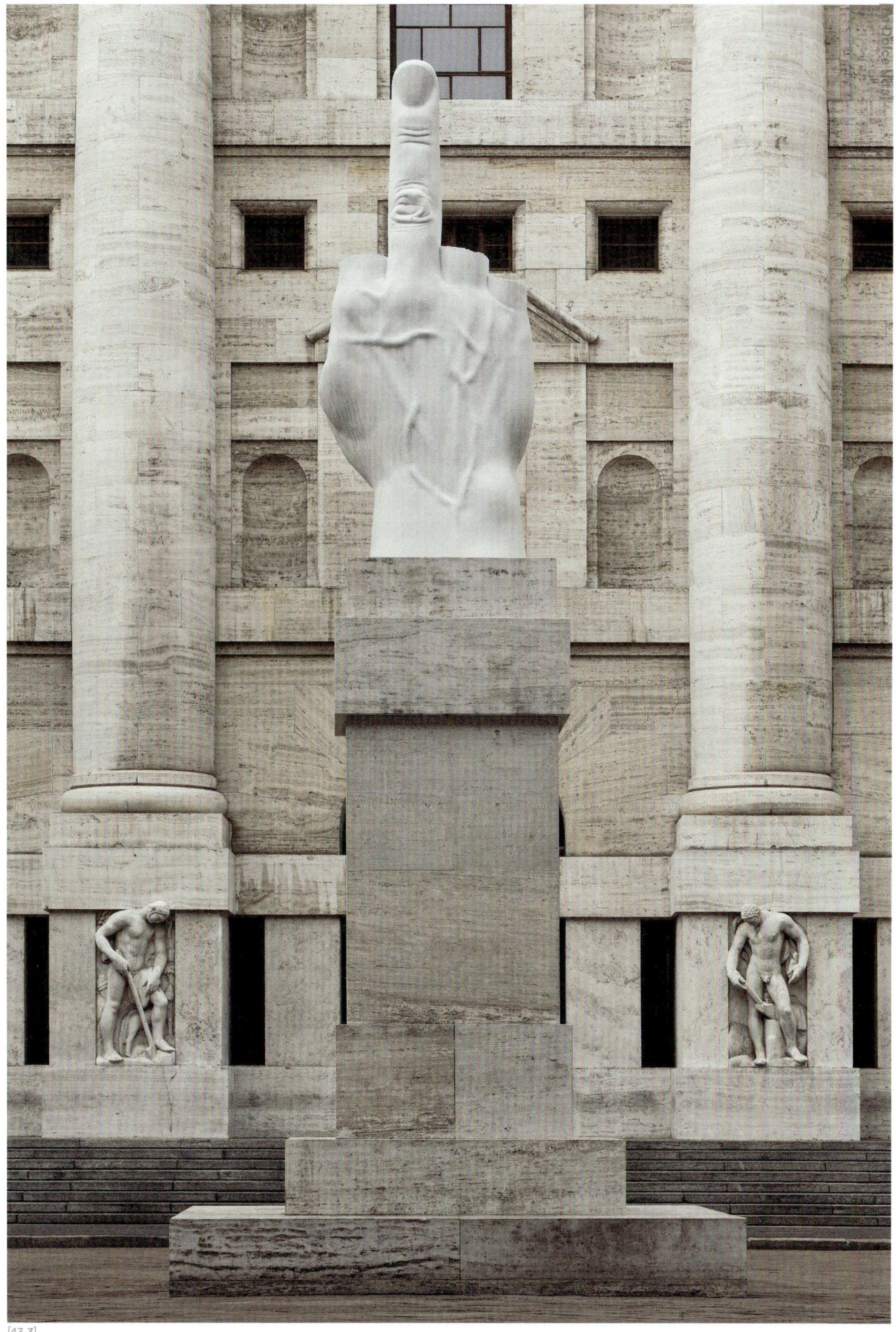

[43.3]

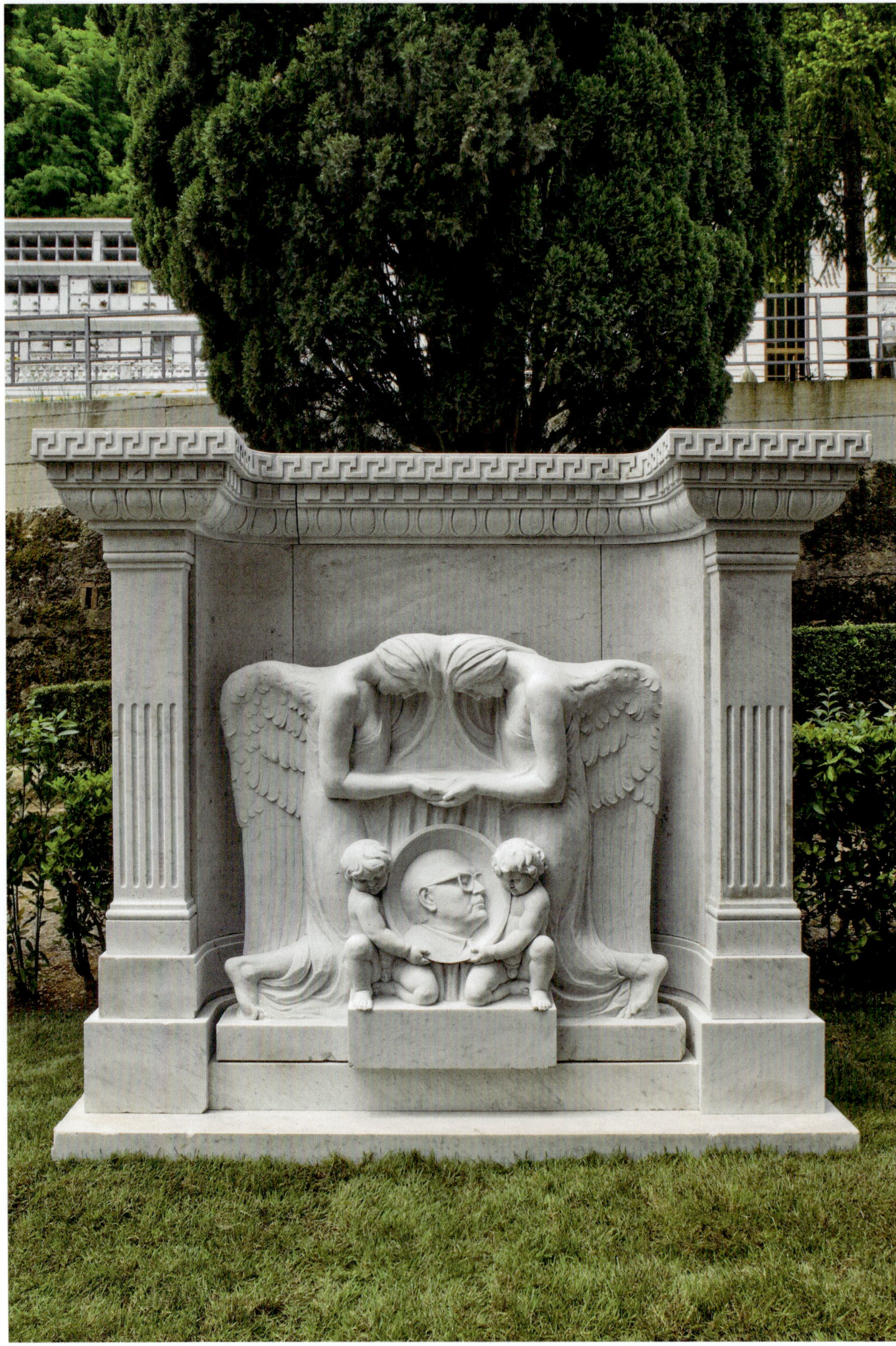

place for my work than that piazza, a splendid example of the identitarian aesthetics of a past regime. The fingers have been amputated, the virile arrogance has become ridiculous. It's a postcard with the words: "A warm greeting to all regimes." But the beauty of art is that there's no single definitive way of seeing it. I always try to focus on several topics at the same time, rather than sending a clear political message that's immediately obvious. In this case, I was intrigued by the conflict with the concept of authority. I wouldn't be surprised if one day a mob pulled down my monument *L.O.V.E.* (Libertà [Freedom] Odio [Hate] Vendetta [Revenge] Eternità [Eternity]). You never see hedge fund guys taking to the street to protest. If for once they had the guts to do so, I think they'd be the ones to pull down the sculpture.

Obviously there is no shortage of other easy reminders. In Italian politics, how many times have we seen Bossi, Santanchè or Berlusconi giving the finger? When politicians become clowns we're all amused, because they make us feel like we're in a big bar that's not even called Bar Italia, but Bar Centrale. So I fell in with the spirit of Bar Centrale. I went inside it too.

I believe that every artwork acquires a different meaning depending on the time it becomes a symbol of. I never expected I would able to predict the political future of the *bel paese* in 2010 with a single image, the hand of a Roman salute with only the middle finger not sawn off. Even in my most perverse fantasies, I never imagined we would ever see fascists and the [leftist] organizers of V-day united in the government of the country. It just shows that art goes far beyond the artist's thought.

In September 2012 the work was officially donated to the Municipality of Milan. *L.O.V.E.* will remind us for decades to come what has happened since the 2008 crisis. A man climbs a mountain because it's there. An artist creates a work because it's not there. Celebratory monuments are torn down at the end of a dictatorship, and perhaps one day the finger will no longer have any reason to exist. It will mean that we'll have passed this phase of our history, and we'll need new images. I hope they'll represent us better than this one.

[44]  *Untitled*, 2010
Carrara marble
155 × 140 × 40 cm

At the Carrara Sculpture Biennale in 2010, my main concern was to encourage reflection, not be provocative. I'm sorry the town council didn't approve of my plan to erect a temporary monument to Bettino Craxi in a piazza in the historic center of the town, replacing the one to Mazzini. If a sculpture is truly a monument, it should still be one even when it gets down from its pedestal. The starting point, anyhow, is the defect of permanence. Permanence translates into perennial availability, reducing our attention threshold.

Mazzini is mysterious. Everybody knows he made a crucial contribution to the unification of Italy, but no one remembers exactly how. So we could have started from him and the part he played, so eliciting a broad reflection on the vulnerability of history. And all the more so when we were just about to celebrate the 150th anniversary of the unification of Italy. Then some of Mazzini's ideas, like those of a republican Italy or a politically united Europe, have proved extraordinarily relevant over time. So Mazzini was the figure to work on, much more than Garibaldi, who's all too popular and also has a monument in Carrara. I liked the idea that Mazzini's temporary absence would turn him into a living person, and then the debate that followed would bring him back into the present. While transforming Craxi, a controversial political figure, into a monument, would have entrusted him to history, just when his role was being discussed again.

In the end I did a funeral monument to Craxi in Carrara's monumental cemetery.

99

[44]  *Untitled*, 2010
"Postmonument," 14th International Sculpture Biennale, Carrara, curated by Fabio Cavallucci, June 26–October 31, 2010 (group show), installation in the monumental cemetery of Marcognano

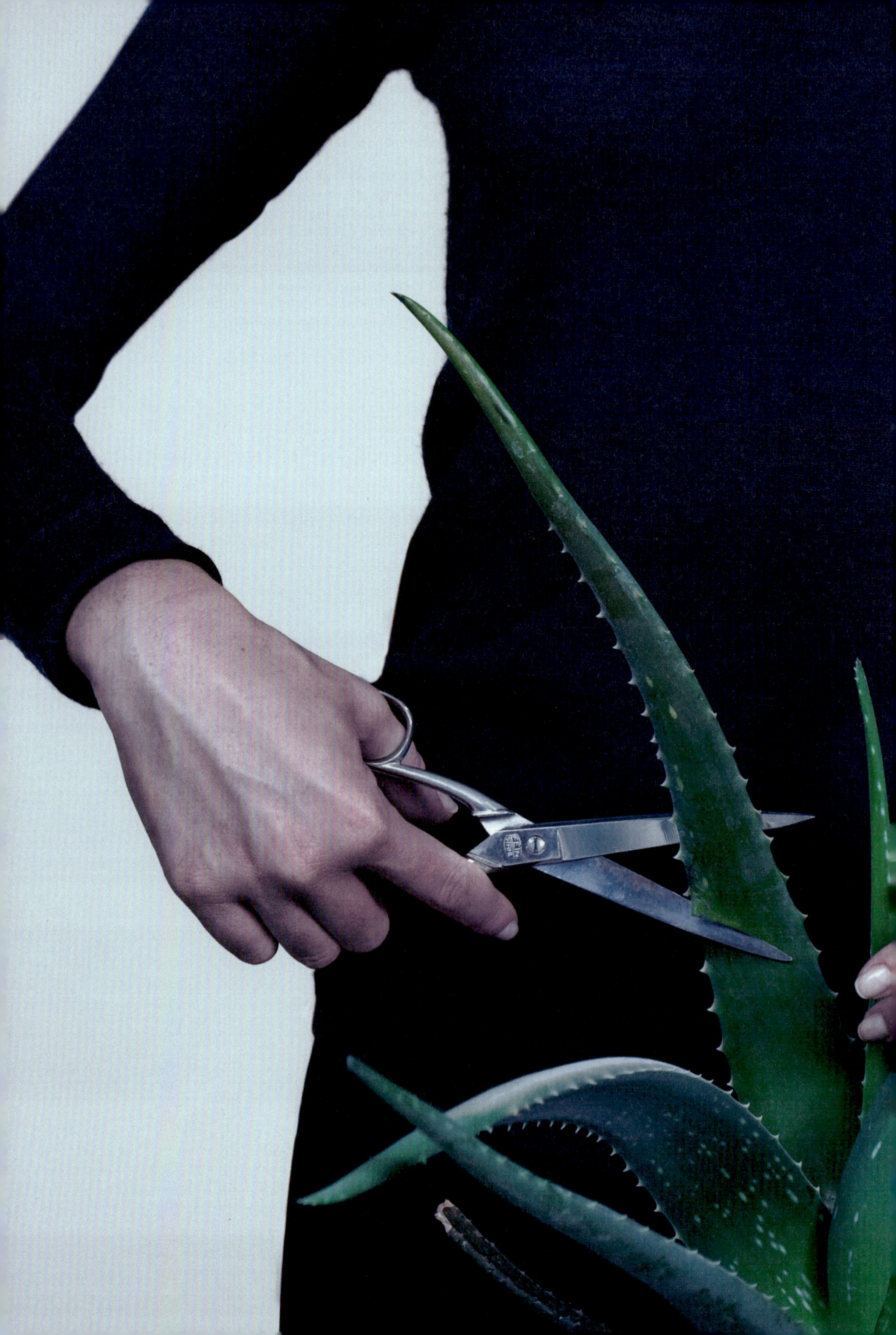

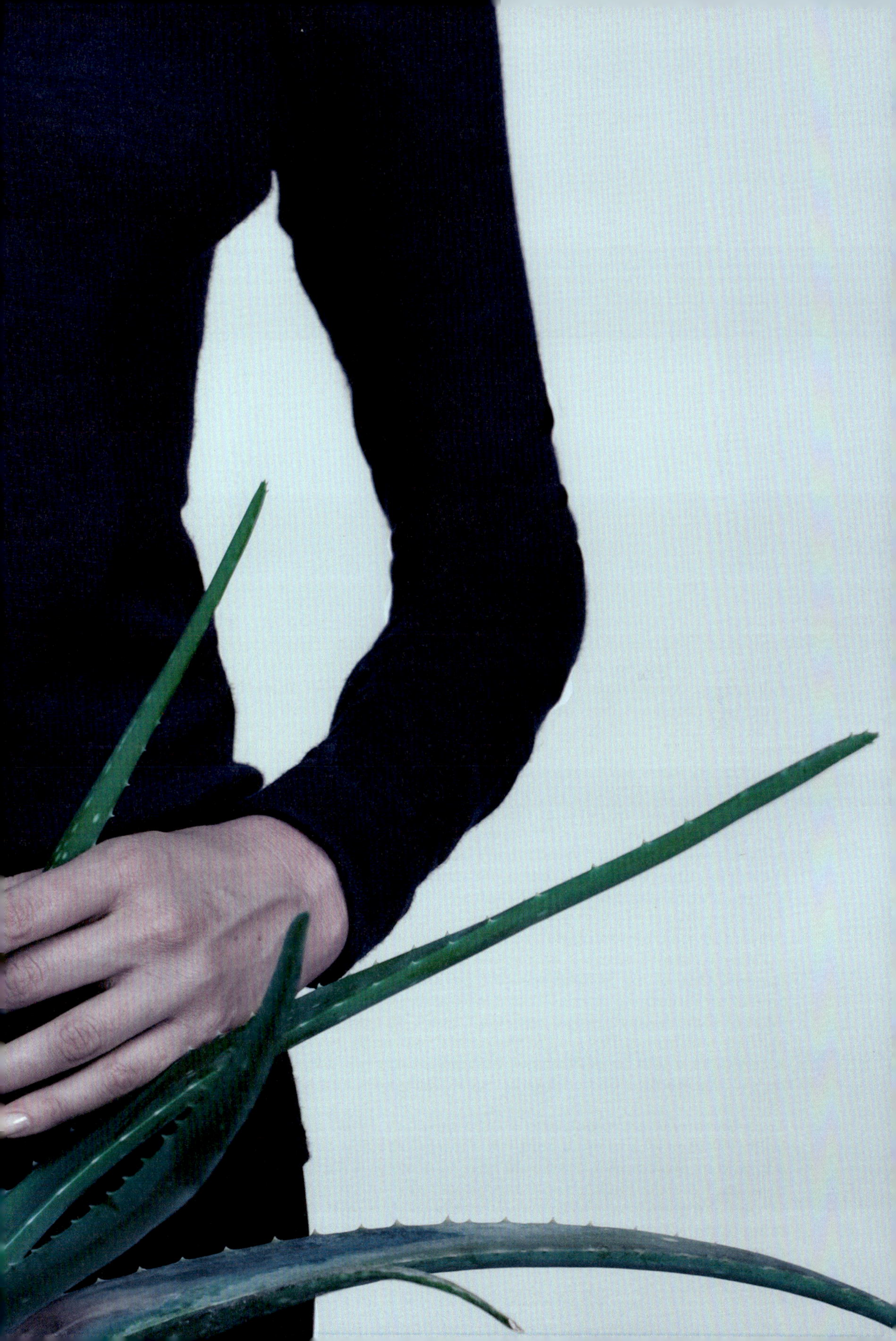

Pretty well all my work doesn't satisfy me, looked at years later. There are even some works that I've started to think about and they've never seen the light of day, but they're not the ones that torment me. If I could, I would destroy a fair bit of my work. I'd revise it more and more strictly every day, and not much of what I did would be left.

Many of my ideas have actually been rejected, and others I just gave up myself. But it wasn't out of confidence that I managed, for example, to persuade someone to dress up like a giant rabbit penis or drill a hole in a museum. It was more an admission of weakness. It was like saying: "I need you, I need you to be part of this, to risk as much or as little as I'm risking." What I really like is seeing what people are willing to do when they're together, when they're sharing something. Challenges per se don't really interest me. It's not about breaking the rules or setting new standards.

I've often dreamed I was walking naked in the street, but a very practical problem prevented me from doing it in reality: where would I put my wallet? More seriously, if I didn't dare to embark on certain projects, it was because they weren't strong enough. One of my failures was the barking birds project. I thought of making an animal do something else, so that it looked like another animal. I like it when you're in front of something you know very well, but it isn't the way it should be: a bird barking instead of chirping. The idea of the animal learning another language is simply about survival, as a test to understand how adaptable we are. Perhaps this is unrealistic today. The margins of freedom are getting smaller and smaller and we simply have to adapt.

Then there was a project with a little goldfish. I had a two-dimensional aquarium built. The idea was to put a goldfish in it from the day it was born, so it would have to adapt to its environment: it would have to grow as a flatfish, a two-dimensional creature, as if there'd been a spontaneous genetic mutation. It's about finding out how far you can go to adapt to a system hostile to your own. Another idea that had something to do with hostility was the project for Central Saint Martins, which of course turned it down. I wanted all the teachers at the school to wear their underwear in public for one day. And the students wouldn't be allowed to laugh. There would be a system of punishments for students who laughed at the teachers. It was about the idea of respect and power, a kind of upside-down day, with the roles subverted and exchanged.

Another rejected project was for a group exhibition on violence at the Andrea Rosen Gallery in New York. I didn't want to present an old work, so I said: "Well, I can give you something else, something new." I've always liked exhibitions to be a public rehearsal, like processes of trial and error. So I worked on a new project, but they rejected it. The idea was to have a dog on a leash. The leash had to be as long as a part of the gallery, so that the moment someone entered the space, they would have the impression that the dog was rushing at them. I wanted a very mean, very savage dog. Visitors could walk around the gallery, but they would be afraid of the dog. It was a form of psychological threat.

For the most part, these projects are more interesting as unrealized ideas. I'm sure that many would be a total disaster if did them, like the one I imagined for Stefano Basilico (*Ileana, I Love You*, 1996). At any rate, a project that hasn't been performed is a project that doesn't exist. It's a defeat, and shouldn't even be talked about it.

[45] ***Super Us***, 1992
50 acetate sheets
29.8 × 21 cm each

This piece is about how the people around you perceive you in ways that differ from how you really are. I was thinking about visualizing the idea of the self. So I asked a friend who worked in the police if they knew anyone who could make portraits based on other people's descriptions of me. Fifty people, apart from my parents and including relatives and friends, described me to the police so they could do these drawings. They really looked like me, but at the same time they're like cartoons. Each provided only one of many likenesses of me. They're terrible. I don't know if it was a fluke.

[45]   *Super Us*, 1992



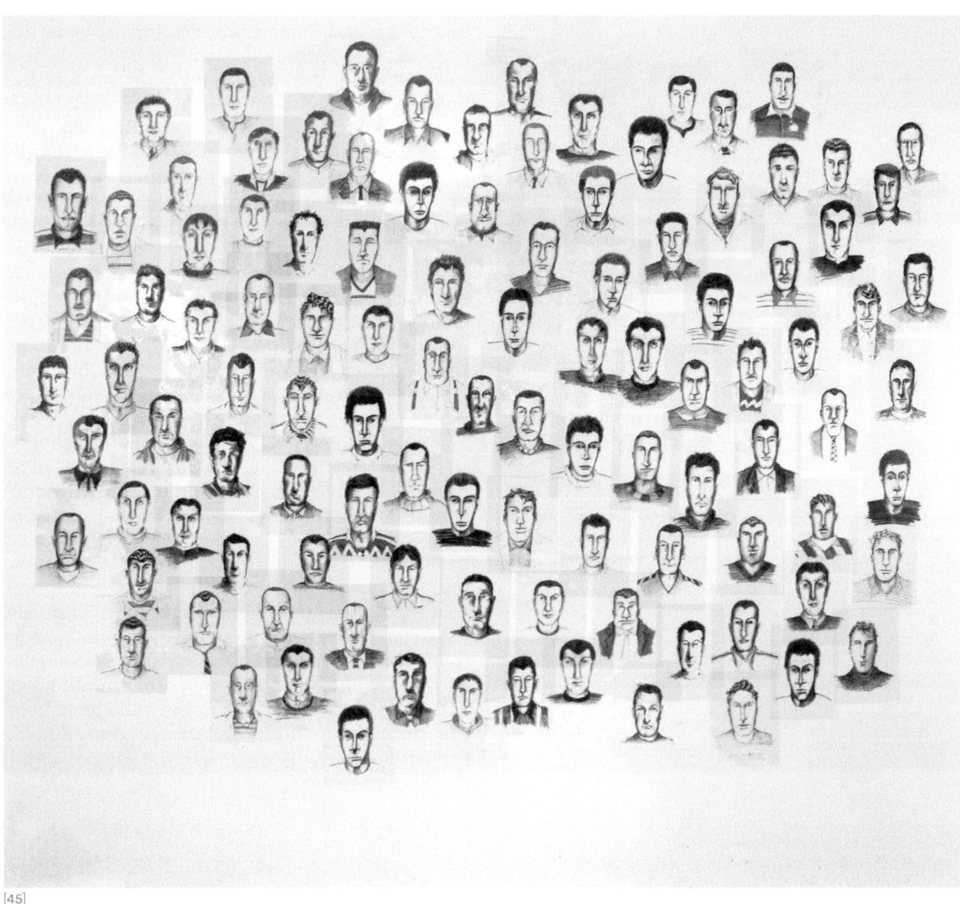

[45]

## [46] Sonsbeek, 1993
Project for "Sonsbeek 93," 1993. Unrealized

For "Sonsbeek 93" I proposed using the whole city for a chemical experiment about fear. I had gone to Amsterdam on my way to Arnhem for Sonsbeek and while there I had casually eaten some cake, without knowing it had been laced with some drug. For one day I was completely out of my mind. The experience was so surreal and intense that I thought afterwards: "Yes, this is what I want to do for the Sonsbeek exhibition." I wanted to alter people's perception of the city in this total, all-encompassing way. But at first I didn't know how I could accomplish this without using a drug, without lacing a cake for everybody to eat. Then I realized I could cover the entire city with a poster campaign and decided to use one that advertised an underground meeting of neo-Nazi skinheads during the week of the opening. I thought this was perfect because the neo-Nazi reference would create a fiction of a fiction, as long as nobody knew that it wasn't for real. I had this kind of experience in Amsterdam and thought it would be interesting to emulate it in some way for a large number of people. The opening of the show was scheduled to include a visit from the Queen, so there was already a massive police presence, which might have made the whole thing more believable, more hallucinatory. So everything was perfect. But the curator didn't like the idea of neo-Nazis. She thought it was too strong a comment about the Second World War and about the atrocities that they had experienced here directly. She said that I had no right to use those symbols. It was too presumptuous. In a way, she was right. But in another way, it was an overreaction. All the same, they kicked me out. But again, the intention wasn't to irritate. I wanted the city of Arnhem (not only a place or a building defined by precise borders) to be under the same pressure and fear that I'd experienced. I could have spread the fake news and stopped there, without the skinhead gathering actually taking place, or I could have actually found a way to get them all together in Arnhem (traveling to major European cities and inviting them with leaflets and other systems), and then see what happened in the town. During the days before the opening I would have liked to evaluate how the town tried to defend itself from this meeting, what tools and means were used. As for my other projects, it could have been a way to get closer to a reality that's obviously remote from my own world.

Some explanations: I see myself in the art world acting more as a researcher than as an artist. I don't support any ideology, least of all the fascist ideology. An aesthetic happening is the result of a process that emphasizes the content, not the form.

I have two friends who were beaten up by skinheads. They're really dangerous but they're the product of this society. The junkie introjects all his existential negativity; the skinhead feeds his emptiness with the nightmares of our recent history.

Search to understand, understand to grow up, grow up to be more civilized. Art can only serve to understand the mystery of life intuitively, but nobody has an answer.

I never really believed that organizing the gathering would be possible. The reactions of the citizens of Arnhem to the fake news might have been heated, but my project would only have been of any interest if a lot of different people were involved in such a primitive feeling as fear. Fear is the only emotion I want to arouse. I'm aware of the problems that realizing the project would have entailed and the moral positions, but the sincerity of my intentions has to be believed. Later I thought of another project for Sonsbeek, which still provides a very important setting for me to develop fundamental ideas for my work. The new project, likewise not done, was simple: to ask citizens for a quick description of some people in Arnhem and, with the help of the police scientific team, to transform their descriptions into a series of real identikits. People would have seen those portraits posted around the town, some completely different from the person, others identical, others dramatic. Basically, they could have been shown to everyone. I would think about how to print the material and display it (in the streets, on buses or in other public spaces). The examples to start from would have been the identikits made by police designers for my project *Super Us* (1992). I liked the idea of a multitude of portraits.



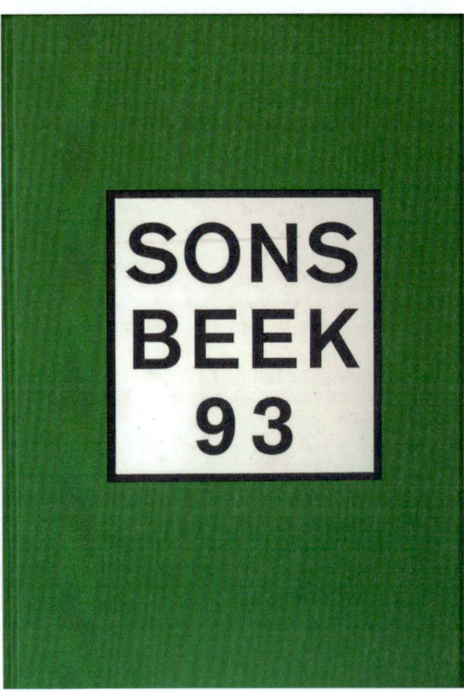


[46]

[46] Cover of the catalogue published on the occasion of "Sonsbeek 93," curated by Valerie Smith, June 5– September 26, 1993 (group show)

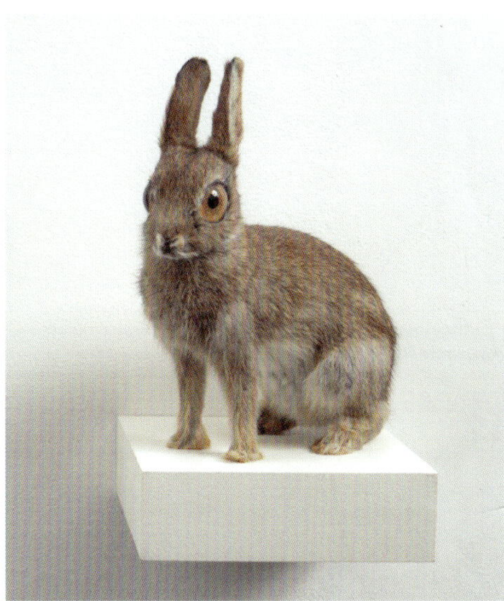

[47]

[47] **Untitled**, 1995
[Initially titled: *Richard*]
Taxidermied rabbit,
lion glass eyes
23 × 9 × 22 cm

[48] **Untitled**, 1996
[Initially titled: *Free Carrot*]
Taxidermied rabbit,
rabbit parts
250 × 10 × 20 cm

[49] **Untitled**, 1996
2 taxidermied hares,
glass eyes
Overall dimensions:
20.3 × 29.8 × 20.3 cm

[50] **Untitled**, 1996
[Initially titled: *Richard*]
Taxidermied rabbit,
lion glass eyes
18 × 9 × 8 cm

I've worked a lot with animals. Following the production of those works, I often visited the taxidermist's workshop. During one of the visits, I must have seen hares and rabbits and thought: "Let's pretend someone pulled their ears." Poor rabbit, it had become a swing. The ears are very long, more than two meters, and are hung wherever they can be hung, so the animal rocks to and fro.
I also made variations with rabbits, putting strange eyes on them or the huge eyes of stuffed lions. The title of a few of them was *Richard*, meaning Richard the Lionheart, in his own way also a hybrid, a sort of cross between species, a weak soul and a strong one together.

105

[47]  *Untitled*, 1995

[48]  *Untitled*, 1996

[49]  *Untitled*, 1996

[50]  *Untitled*, 1996

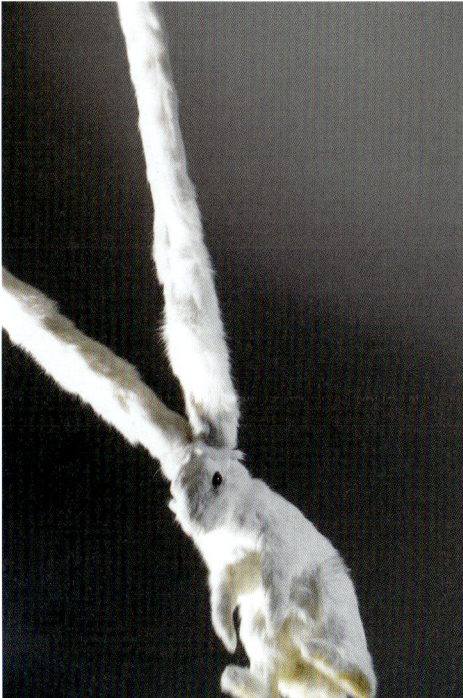

[48]

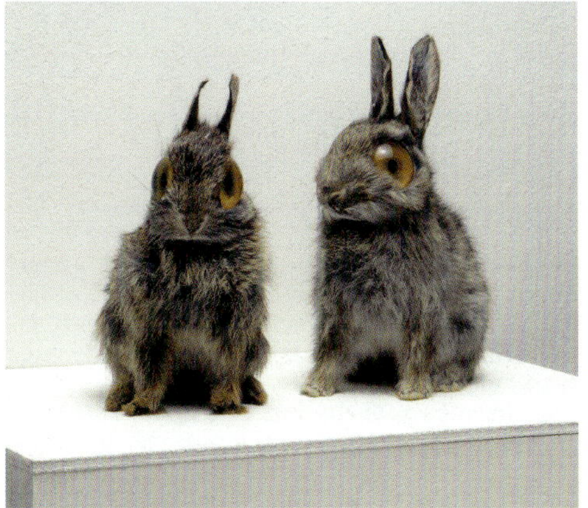

[49]

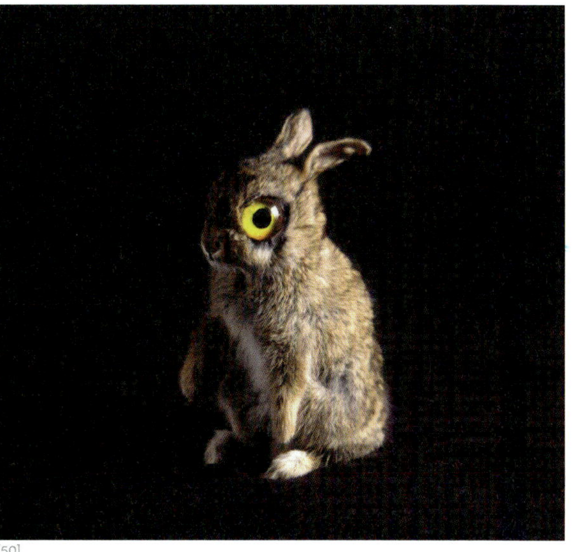

[50]

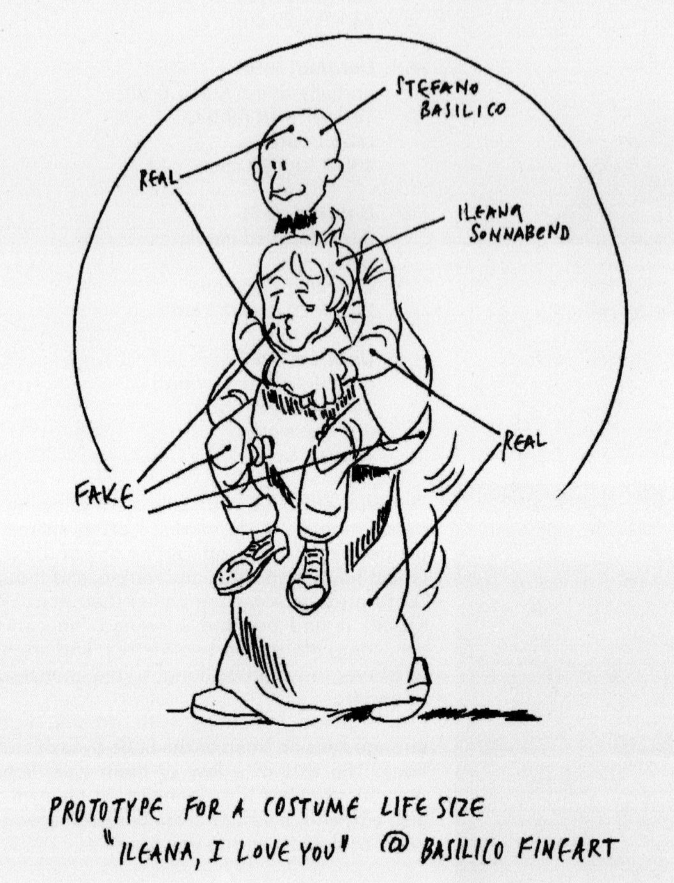





[51]



[51]    ***Ileana, I Love You*, 1996**
Ink on paper
29 × 21 cm
Project for lifesize costume for Basilico Fine
Art, New York; pre-production drawing
done with Umberto Manfrin; published
in *Unbuilt Roads: 107 Unrealized Projects*,
eds. Hans Ulrich Obrist and Guy Tortosa
(Ostfildern-Ruit: Hatje, 1997), n.p.

A lot of people who know Stefano Basilico because of the gallery he had in New York also
know he worked for about ten years for the
Sonnabend Gallery. This close tie with his past
intrigued me, so I suggested doing a project
about it. The meeting with Stefano turned out to
be positive, showing he was wryly self-deprecat-
ing. The project, entitled *Ileana, I Love You*, took
shape immediately and we also decided on the
exhibition date.
I thought about using a costume that would
show Stefano on Ileana Sonnabend's shoulders.
A costume of this type, very popular in the past,
enables you to play two characters at the same
time. And his office would have to be moved to
the space where the works were usually shown.

In this way Stefano would continue to work away
while wearing the costume. A few months after I
started designing the costume itself, Stefano expressed serious doubts about the project, which
by its nature would have increased the excessive
interest that already focused on his person rather than on the artists in the gallery. I disagreed
with the suggestion that I should think of a new
project for the gallery, so plans for the exhibition
fell through.

[52]    ***Untitled*, 1997**
[Initially titled: *Out of the Blue*]
Latex, clothing
Height 170 cm

For Skulptur Projekte I wanted to create a story
about the lake in Münster. I liked the idea of giving it a ghostly aura, which it didn't have before. I
put a mannequin in the lake, a female body fixed
with heavy ropes. It was just below the surface
and the idea was that no one could see it except when passing nearby in a boat. Just after
the installation, a photo was taken, but in a short
while the work sank, without anyone having ac-

tually been able to see it. A few months later, the citizens of Münster demanded that the work be removed, because even imagining a body in the lake was disturbing. They even called out the fire brigade. For my part, I changed the title of the work. *Out of the Blue* became *Untitled*.

Women are often featured in my work, apart from in the lake in Münster. For example, as Georgia O'Keeffe, who welcomes visitors to an exhibition (*Georgia on My Mind*, 1997), or the nice old woman shut in a refrigerator among the carrots and mayonnaise (*Betsy*, 2002). Maybe not all of my works with female figures are exactly a triumph, but they're unexpected and disruptive apparitions. Salvation sometimes comes from where you least expect it. After all, art only works if someone wants to be surprised.

[53] ***Untitled*, 2000**
Project for gravestone. Unrealized

This work was meant to be the grave of a well-known collector. We went to the town where he lives and where he'll be buried, but then he backed out. The render remains. The idea for the inscription on the tombstone, "Pourquoi moi," probably came to me when I saw something in that cemetery.

[54] ***Untitled*, 2016**
Action during Manifesta 11, curated by Christian Jankowski, Zurich, June 11–September 18, 2016 (group show)

The idea for this work was to see in the distance the Paralympic athlete Edith Wolf-Hunkeler in a wheelchair floating on the surface of Lake Aasee in Zurich, where Manifesta 11 was being held. But it didn't work the way I had in mind. It was supposed to be an apparition, without seeing the preparatory phase of the performance, as instead happened. Unfortunately, I couldn't be there when the presentation was finalized, so I didn't have any control over it. Nothing went as it should have done. Moral: never contract out the work. Even when you don't make them yourself, things need to be done to your standards.

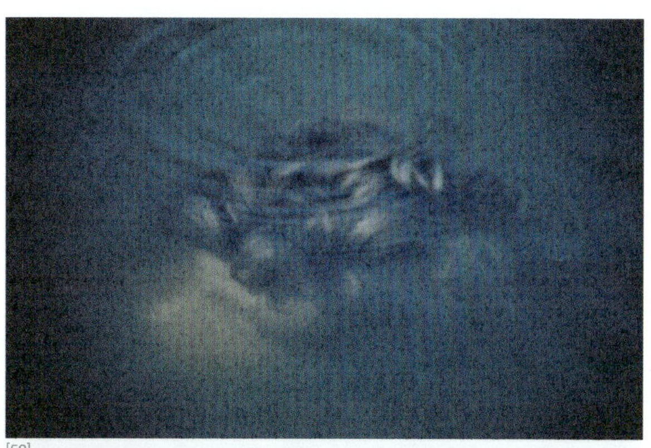

[52]

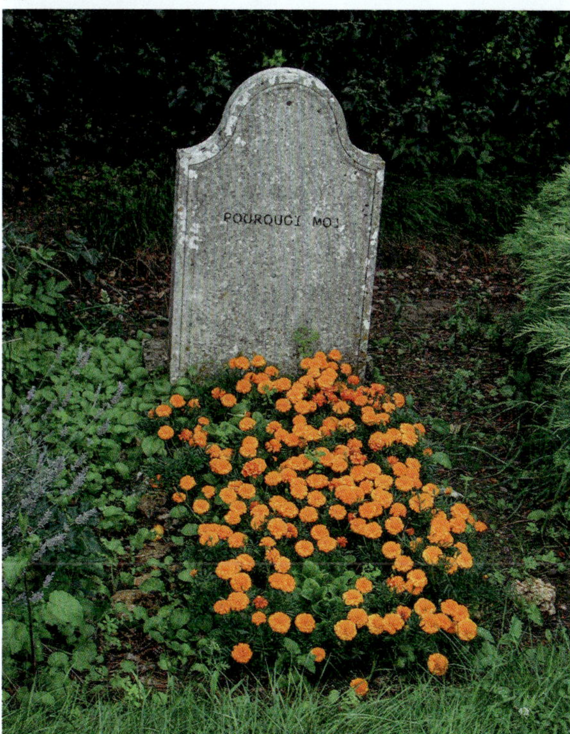


[53]

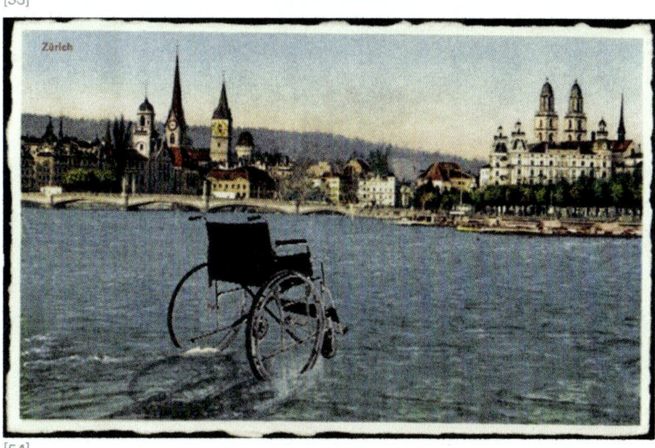


[54]

[52]  *Untitled*, 1997
"Skulptur. Projekte in Münster 1997," curated by Kasper König, Münster, June 22–September 28, 1997 (group show), installation in Lake Aasee

[53]  *Untitled*, 2000

[54]  Postcard realized for the action *Untitled* (2016) at Manifesta 11, Zurich, 1997

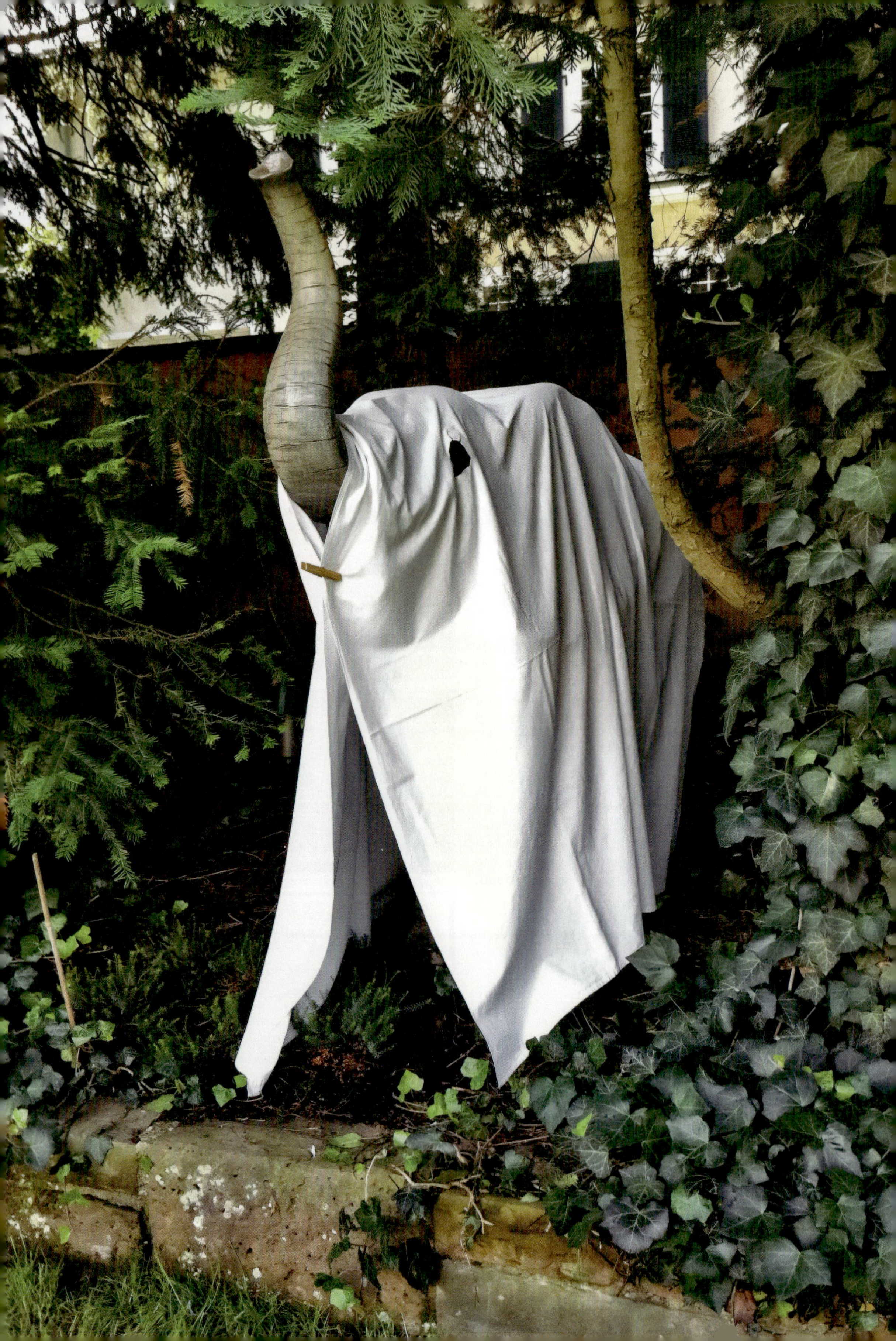

Fear is an elegant weapon, because people can use it against others without ever staining their hands. It's terribly effective. It touches something visceral, it comes from our being animals. I make a daily effort to free myself from my fears. At the same time, it's important to feel fear. Together with desire, it's the great driving force in our lives. It serves as a reminder that we're here on loan and we will have to return what has been given us.

The fear of falling back into poverty is a great theme for me. In fact it's not a theme: it is pure fear, terror. It's the nightmare that makes me wake up with a start. I'm also afraid of having to go back to a regular job, to a world where no part of you is allowed to be alive and you're trapped in a process where you put all your energy into producing something that means nothing to you. I've been afraid since day one and I will always be. But I'm not afraid of losing my talent so much as of failing or being exposed. You can't lose something you don't have.

In the face of fear, I think we have defense mechanisms that we can't even see, or admit to ourselves. Every day we experience fears collectively: fear of foreigners, fear of growing old. The billboards are full of them. Our society is built on this. The system sells you those fears and feeds you with those fears. The fear of failure starts in elementary school. What would our society be like if making a mistake became a way of learning, instead of one where you lose your privileges?

Violence has also always scared me a lot. I understand how it develops, but it disturbs me deeply. You could say the same about power, its fellow traveler. I've always kept away from power and authority, except for the times when I've tried to question them or deconstruct them. On the contrary, many people stop and kneel before the authority of someone who states the absolutes of who is who and what is what.

Power and resistance to power are a dialectical pairing that has characterized human history from the start. I guess that's why I find them such interesting subjects. Power, spirituality and control still exist, despite the changes and revolutions of history. They're a part of humanity, in the changing forms and ways they're exercised. In fact, every age has its own special manifestation of power, but in the end it's always about creating a mystery. As long as the sign remains empty enough, it can be filled with all kinds of concepts and so gains power. The more elusive and ambiguous a symbol is, the greater the meaning and power it can gain.

**My mother always said it's impossible to clean a window if you can't see where it's dirty. To defeat power, you first have to get close to it. You have to flush it out, take it over, replicate it endlessly, as in a laboratory. Practice on dummies, too, if you need to. Every system has its own laws, which you have to learn by heart to understand its weaknesses and avoid becoming numbed. Contemporary art has a natural relationship of conflict with power. Art is the form of expression that probes the wound. It can't be anything else.**

[55]  ***Untitled***, 1996
Gelatin silver print
101.6 × 152.4 cm

I used the image of a star as an invitation to an exhibition in Zurich, at the Ars Futura Galerie. It was perhaps the best thing about the exhibition. If I have to remember the ugliest exhibition I've ever done, it's this one. I had reconstructed the room in which a collective suicide had taken place in Switzerland two years earlier, one of those linked to a sect, the Order of the Solar Temple. In reconstructing the room I'd believed that the place retained the charge of that tragic image, but it wasn't so.
Although I did this work in 1996, the idea dates back to the same period as *Lessico familiare* (1989), the self-portrait in which I'm making the heart sign with my hands, and to the works with the five-pointed star that recalls the symbol of the Red Brigades (*Untitled*, 1994; *Christmas '95*, 1995). It was my response to the power structures and violence common in extremist groups, whether Swiss or Italian.

[56]  ***La Nona Ora***, 1999
Polyester resin, wax, pigment, natural hair, fabric, clothing, accessories, stone, carpet
Variable dimensions

If I was bothered about making something epoch-making in my work, I'd probably be terrified to the point of not doing anything anymore. *La Nona Ora* interested me only as an image. With this work I've never consciously tried to create scandals and controversies. It wasn't meant to be a provocation, let alone anti-Catholic. Not on my part, brought up among pictures of saints on prayer cards and altar boys singing in the church choir. And who in their right mind would represent the pope struck by a meteorite to convey a political message about the Church? *La Nona Ora* is more of a way of remembering that power, all power, has a best-by date, like milk. Religion has nothing to do with it. I'm interested in people in their roles, not so much in historical figures. Being an icon doesn't necessarily mean being untouchable. I think there's nothing wrong with showing the vulnerable side of people. I don't think it weakens their status. Rather, it reinforces

110

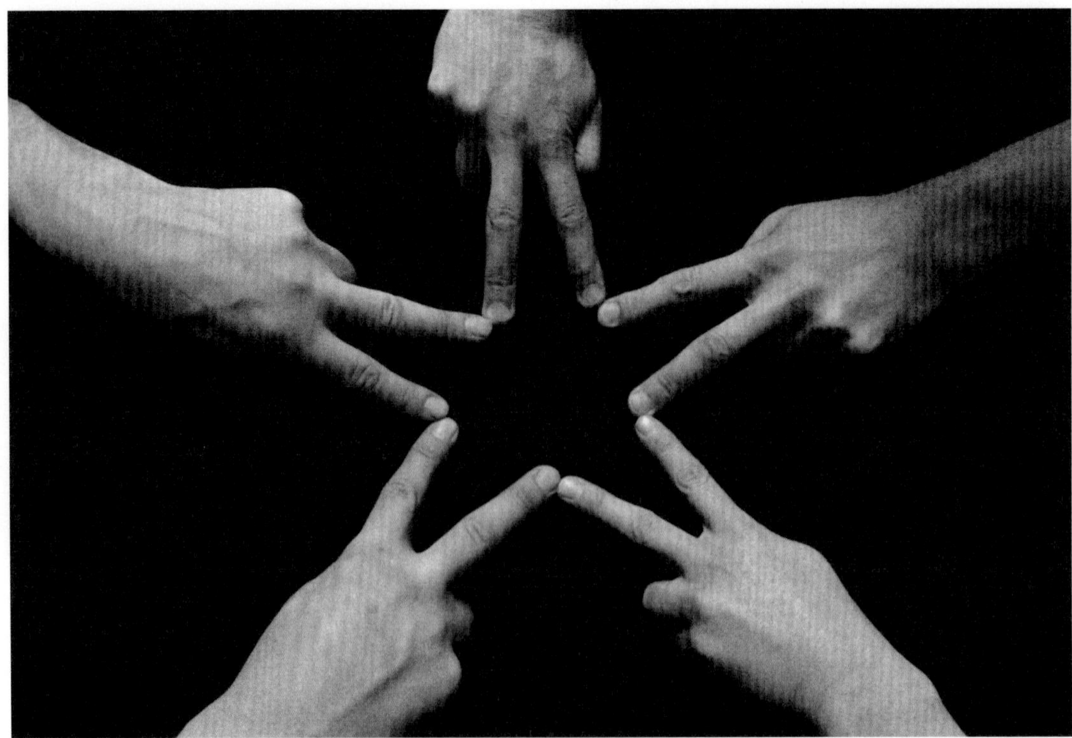

[55]

[55]  ***Untitled***, 1996

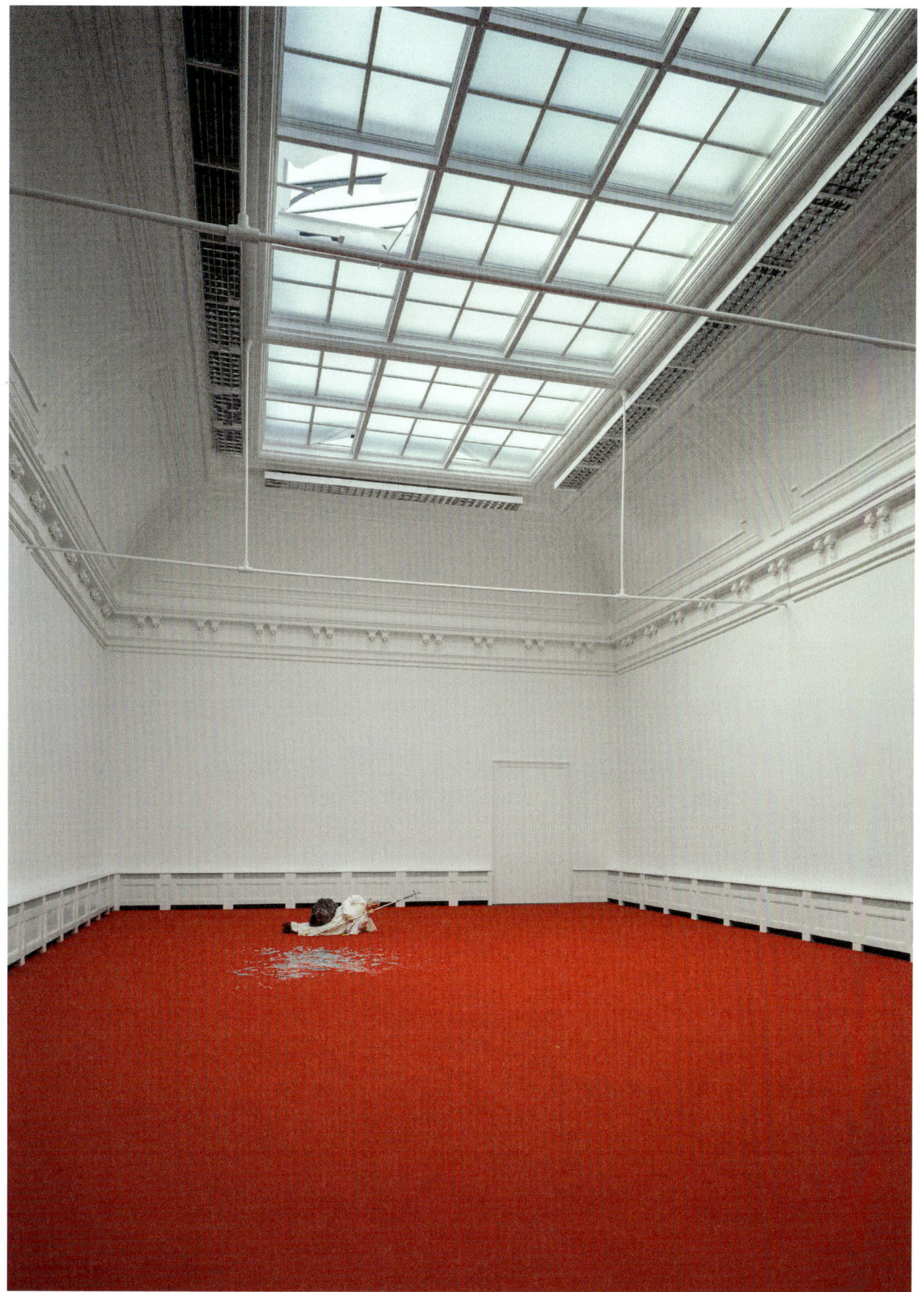

[56.1]

[56.1]  *La Nona Ora*, 1999
        Polyester resin, wax, pigment, natural hair, fabric,
        clothing, accessories, stone, carpet, glass
        Variable dimensions
"Maurizio Cattelan," curated by Madeleine Schuppli,
Kunsthalle Basel, October 16–November 21, 1999
(solo show)

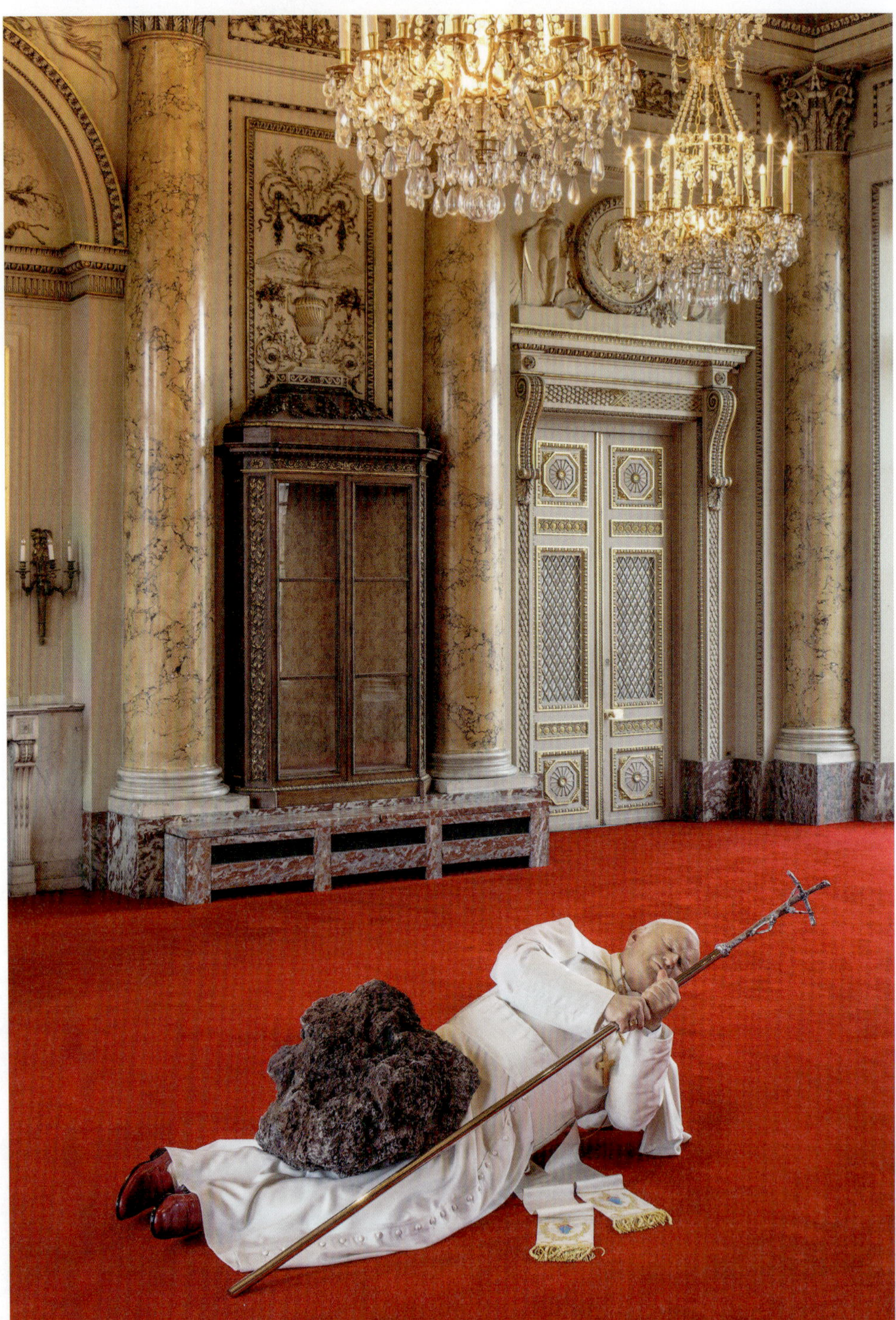

[56.2]

[56.2]  *La Nona Ora*, 1999
"Not Afraid of Love," curated by Chiara Parisi, Monnaie
de Paris, Octotber 21, 2016–January 8, 2017 (solo show)

their position, as well as the belief that they're sacred cows. I think Pope Wojtyła knew this quite well, so he didn't need a meteorite.

On a more personal note, perhaps *La Nona Ora* was also an attempt to solve the problem with my father. Some people choose to spend years in analysis, and then others, like me, decide to exorcise their demons independently, in self-analysis. It's sometimes painful, sometimes satisfying, but it's always a work on oneself that lasts a lifetime. Seen from this viewpoint, *La Nona Ora* perhaps meant killing the father, the most classic of psychoanalytical figures. The pope is the authority. When I first installed the piece, at the Kunsthalle Basel in 1999, it took me two days to decide to lay hands on his body. It was no joke for me. It was very difficult for me to physically touch him. In my original conception, it was going to consist of an empty room with the statue of the pope welcoming visitors. But then, a month before the show, I was like: "Oh my God, this is so bad, I can't show it." So I modified it, using a chainsaw. I asked everybody to leave the room, because I couldn't cut through it with people standing around. Even if I was damaging it, I was dealing with someone who had to be treated with respect.

To tell truth, what was needed was something very simple, as always. It lacked drama, and perhaps also the ability to convey the feeling of witnessing an extraordinary and powerful event. There was no sense of failure and defeat. This gave me the idea of destruction by something powerful, the idea of the sky breaking through the ceiling. I often want to give the impression that an event has just happened, in a flash. Then, even when I had to put the meteorite on the figure, it took me a whole day. It wasn't easy.

The Royal Academy in London, where I showed the work in September 2000, received a letter from the Vatican expressing surprise at how the religious themes were treated so inadequately in the show. My work was perhaps truly inadequate, because it wasn't about the historical person or the public figure so much as the precariousness of power, of defeat and failure, which are always lying in wait. And all men are equal when facing fear.

A few months later, in December 2000, I presented *La Nona Ora* in an exhibition curated by Harald Szeemann for the centennial of the Zachęta National Art Gallery in Warsaw. Szeemann wanted to return the pope to the Poles and I liked the idea that sculpture could travel at the same speed as the pope himself. Wojtyła was the first mobile pope, the first televisual pope. His image was multiplied worldwide. Precisely for this reason I never expected *La Nona Ora* to outrage anyone. I felt it was impossible to mistake an image for reality, but evidently religion, like advertising, still has the power to turn smoke into roast beef. During an official visit, two Catholic deputies grappled with the sculpture, trying to free the pope from the meteorite. It was a premeditated action, accompanied by an open letter that was immediately published by all the Polish newspapers. The case was then dragged into parliament, where *La Nona Ora* became an excuse for demanding the resignation of the museum director, Anda Rottenberg. She was attacked for her Jewish origins and accused of wanting to

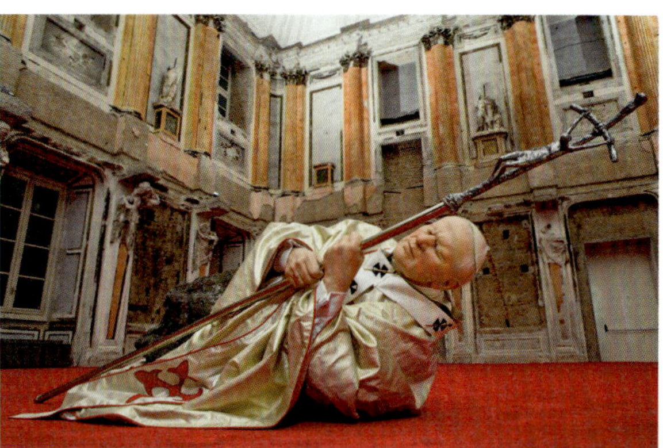

[56.3]

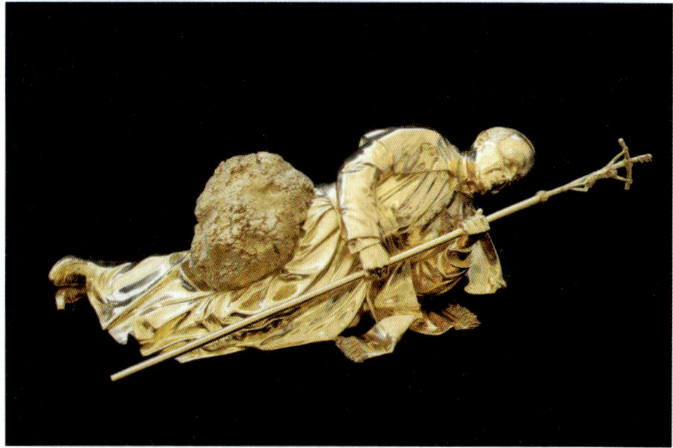

[56.4]

besmirch the symbols of the Catholic religion. The idea of salvation coming for the pope from earth rather than heaven struck me deeply.

I have never sought polemics or pursued strategies of rebellion. When the work was exhibited in Milan, at Palazzo Reale, in 2010, I was delighted that the episcopal vicar for culture of the diocese of Milan, consulted by the city council so as not to offend the curia, saw what the statue of the pope actually is: a spiritual work that speaks of suffering. The title *La Nona Ora* alludes to the hour at which Christ on the cross asks the Father why he has abandoned him, but the pope in succumbing clings to the crucifix. It takes time for some things to sink in.

*La Nona Ora* is a figure of complexity, a sculpture that tries to make religion and blasphemy, passion and spectacle coincide. I like to think of this work as a sculpture that doesn't exist. A three-dimensional image that dissolves into pure communication, into the media noise. A sculpture that becomes background buzz. And this work was also a turning point, the one where I finally felt like part of the system.

[56.3] *La Nona Ora*, 1999
"Maurizio Cattelan. Contro le ideologie," curated by Francesco Bonami, Sala delle Cariatidi, Palazzo Reale, Milan, September 25–October 24, 2010 (solo show)

[56.4] *La Nona Ora*, 2005
    Gold 18 karat
    17 × 63 × 22 cm

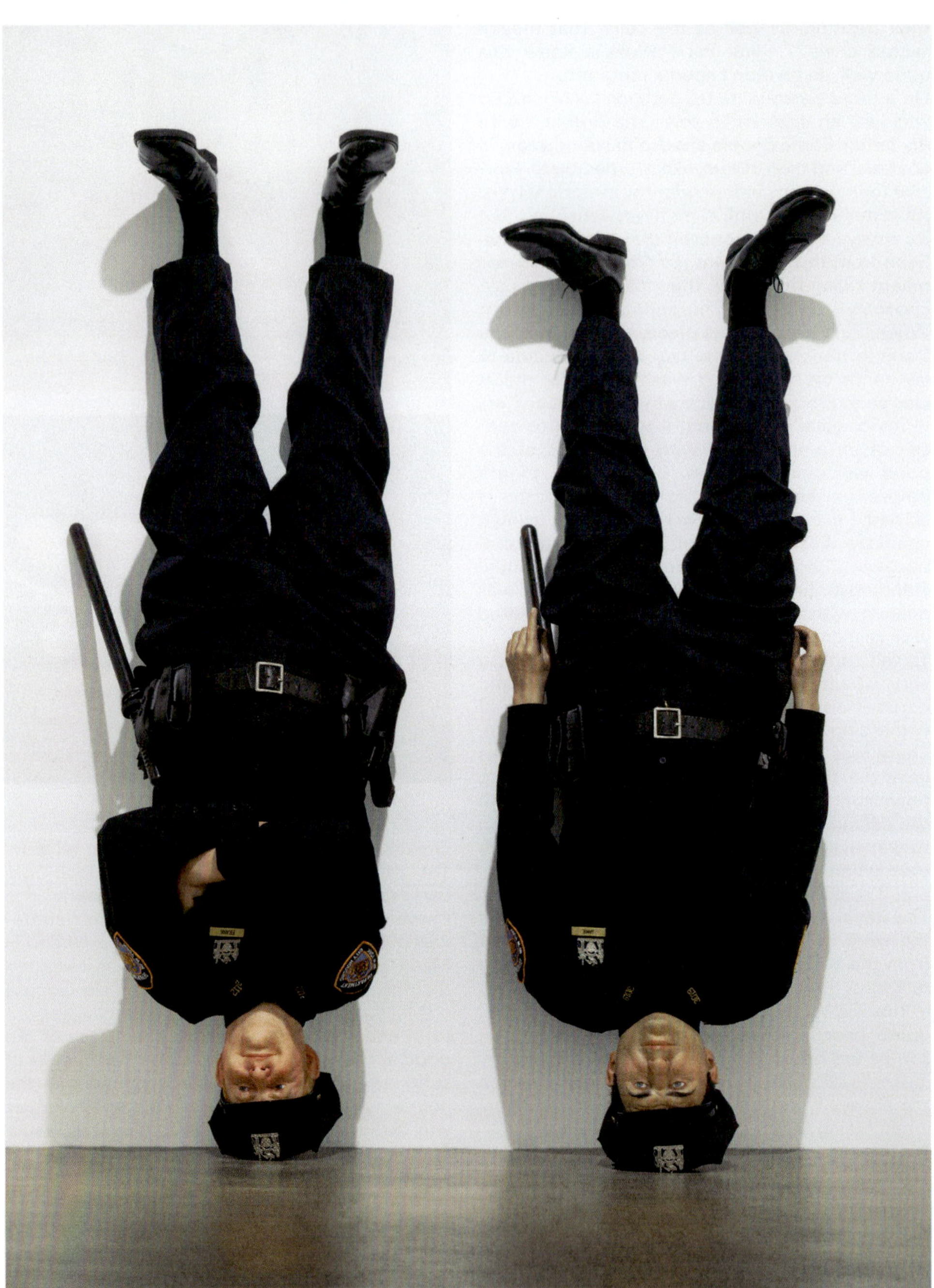

[57]



**[57]** ***Frank and Jamie*, 2002**
Polyester resin, wax, pigment, natural
hair, clothing, shoes, accessories
Frank: 191.8 × 63.5 × 50.8 cm;
Jamie: 182.3 × 62.9 × 45.7 cm

*Frank and Jamie*, presented at my first solo show at the Marian Goodman Gallery in New York in April 2002, are iconic cops, like the ones in the movies, but they're a monument in reverse, a monument erected to celebrate a defeat and warn against any victory. They were necessary as a statement. They concern a general theme. The police have always been here—they count for as much as religion. I felt completely surrounded by them, everywhere, a kind of reaction from the right, and nobody was saying anything. This work was a reaction to oppression. I felt that something strong was coming and it was a good moment to say so, because it was the wrong moment. It was also the perfect moment to do something. I didn't want to make a comment about the New York City police or September 11 or Amadou Diallo, a boy killed in 1999 by four NYPD policemen. In my mind it's the third part of a trilogy about power.

[58]  *Ave Maria*, 2007
Polyurethane, paint, clothing, metal
Overall width: 65 cm;
74 × Ø 13 cm each of the 3 elements

Images are always a bit of one thing and a bit of another, and I've always worked with their ambiguity, avoiding the temptation to tell some absolute truth. To me the outstretched arm is an extraordinary symbol of power, an erection to the nth degree, and at the same time the absolute suspension of judgment. No one has ever been able to really understand the origin of the Roman salute, but doubt has not succeeded in undermining its strength over time. And in the end, if I have to choose between two evils, I always choose the worse.

[57]  *Frank and Jamie*, 2002
"Maurizio Cattelan," Marian Goodman Gallery, New York, April 30–June 15, 2002 (solo show)

[58]  *Ave Maria*, 2007
"Maurizio Cattelan," curated by Andreas Bee and Udo Kittelmann, MMK – Museum für Moderne Kunst, Frankfurt, March 1–September 23, 2007 (solo show)



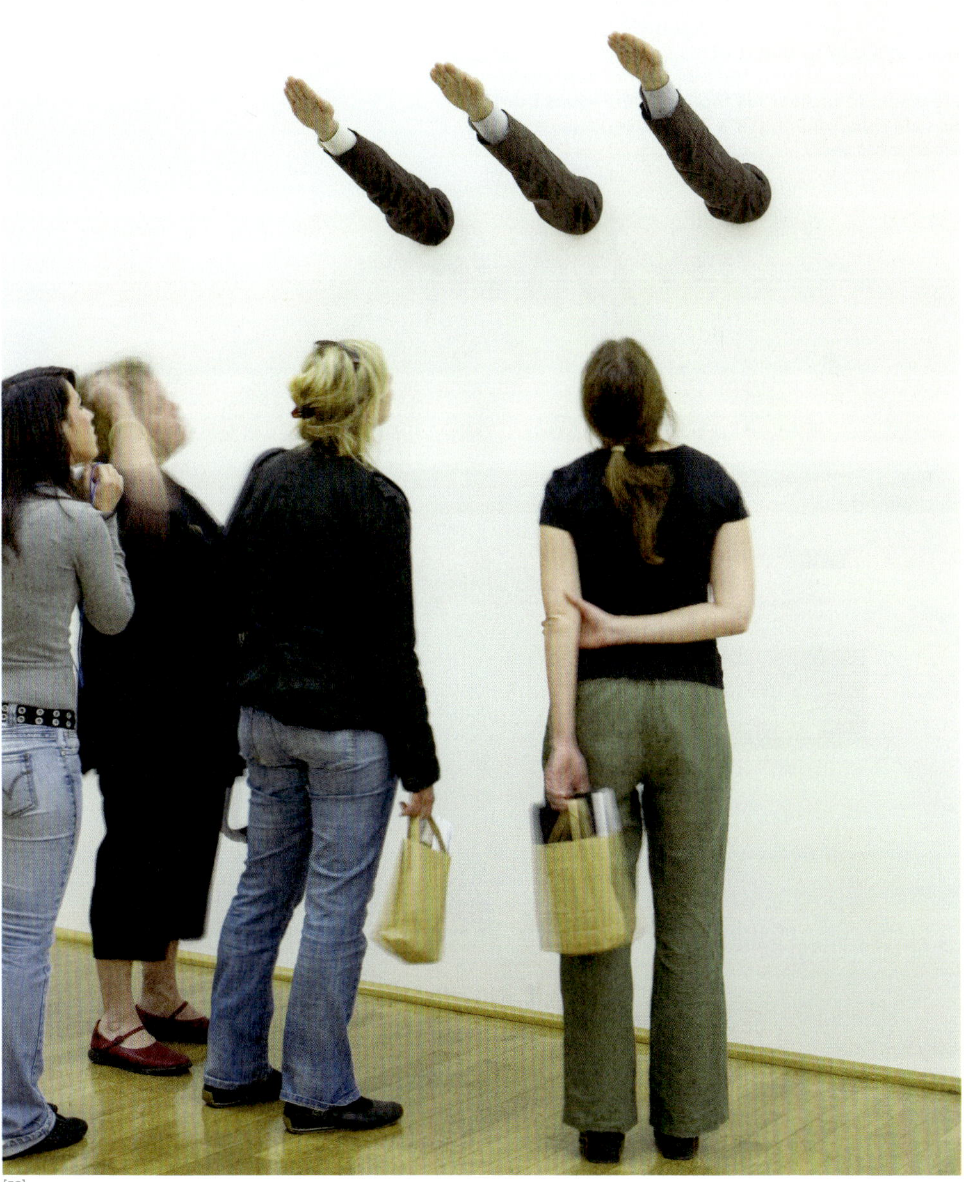

[58]

**[59]** *No,* **2021**
Platinum silicone, resin, hair, clothing,
boots, paper bag
101 × 41 × 53 cm

I've always been fascinated by the hypocritical compromise around the laws in much of the United States that prohibit drinking alcohol in public, and then the police allow them to be broken provided the bottle is hidden. Most of the time you just have to look at the drinker's face to figure out that it isn't a bottle of soda water in the brown paper bag. So I thought I could hide the face of Hitler in *Him* (2001) simply by putting a paper bag over his head. In my work, the bag is a kind of device of the lowest technology that allows the head inside to be projected into a completely different dimension. I like the simplicity of a paper bag and what it can make you imagine. As if it was a tool to experience some extremely sophisticated augmented reality. Plus the bag came in handy for presenting the work in a complicated context like Beijing, where I exhibited it like this. Or maybe my figure has his head in a bag so that it helps him not to see the violence around him, the violence of the world. He wants to protect his thoughts and ideas from possible disruption. It's a kind of protective device for his soul.

[59.1]    *No,* 2021
"Maurizio Cattelan. The Last Judgment," curated by Francesco Bonami, UCCA Center for Contemporary Art, Beijing, November 20, 2021–February 20, 2022 (solo show)

[59.2]    *No,* 2021, and *Novecento,* 1997 [201]
"Maurizio Cattelan. The Last Judgment," curated by Francesco Bonami, UCCA Center for Contemporary Art, Beijing, November 20, 2021–February 20, 2022 (solo show)



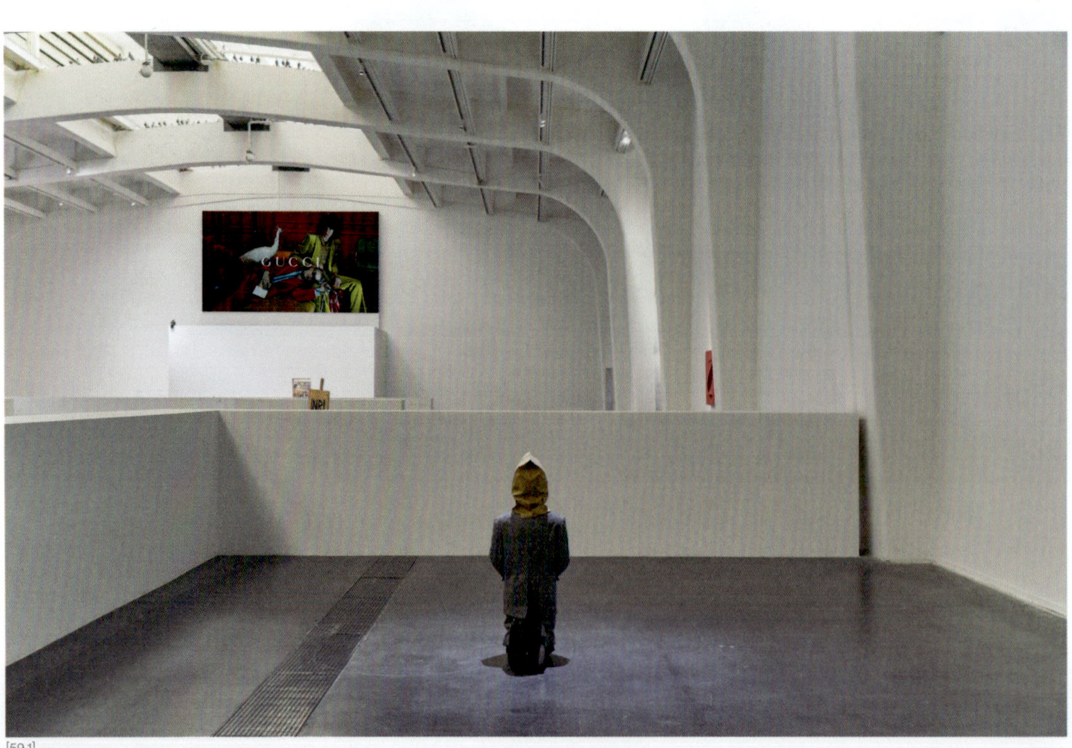

[59.1]

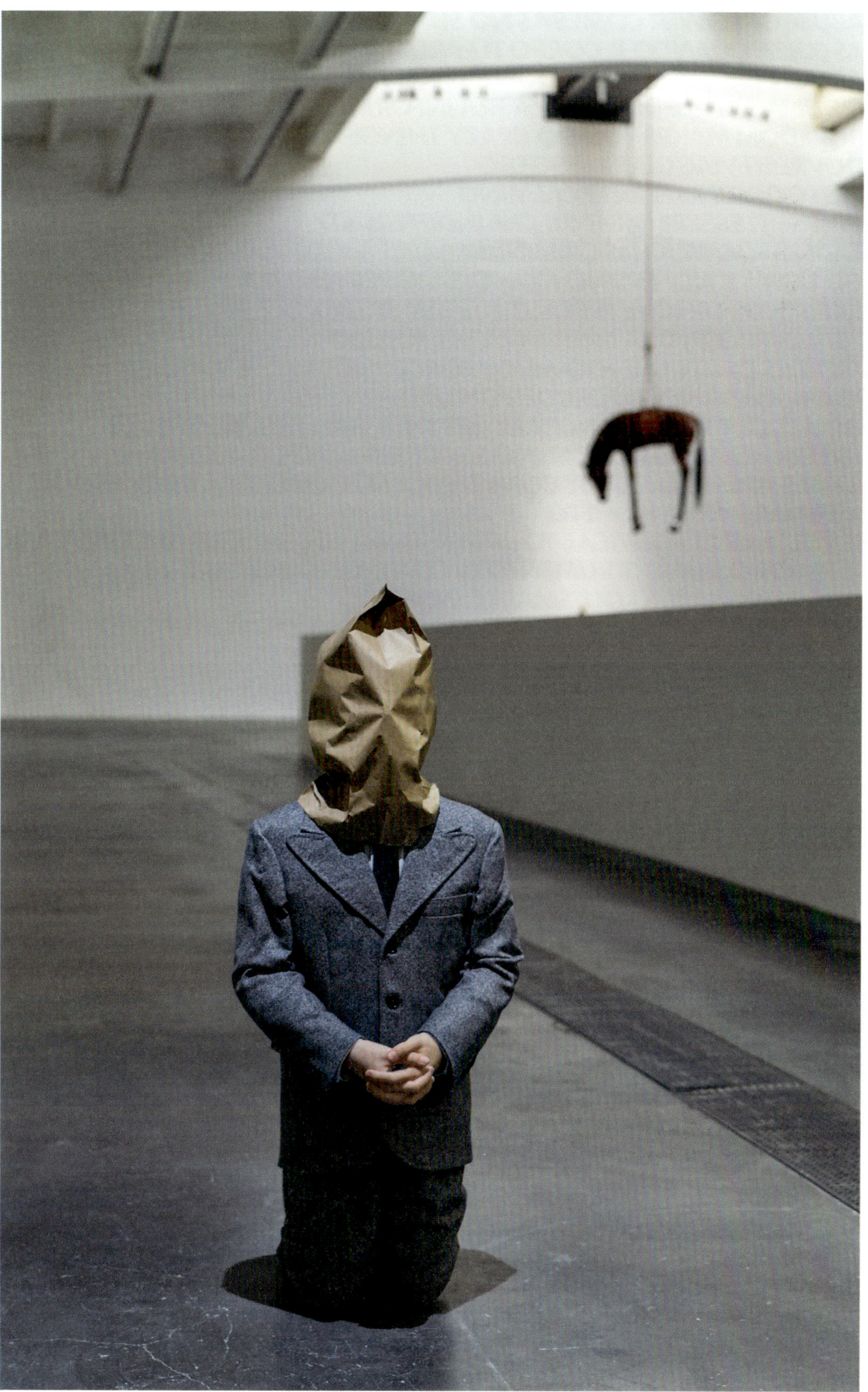

[59.2]

ABUSE OF POWER COMES AS NO SURPRISE
ASCOLTA QUANDO IL CORPO TI PARLA
ACTION CAUSES MORE TROUBLE THAN THOUGHT
C'È UNA SOTTILE DIFFERENZA TRA INFORMAZIONE E PROPAGANDA
BOREDOM MAKES YOU DO CRAZY THINGS
DOVRESTI VIAGGIARE LEGGERO
CATEGORIZING FEAR IS CALMING
È MEGLIO ESSERE INGENUI CHE INDIFFERENTI
EATING TOO MUCH IS CRIMINAL
GLI UOMINI NON SONO MONOGAMI PER NATURA
EXPIRING FOR LOVE IS BEAUTIFUL BUT STUPID
I BAMBINI SONO LA SPERANZA DEL FUTURO
FATHERS OFTEN USE TOO MUCH FORCE
I BAMBINI SONO PIÙ CRUDELI DI TUTTI
GO ALL OUT IN ROMANCE AND LET THE CHIPS FALL WHEREVER
I DESIDERI ARTIFICIALI STANNO SACCHEGGIANDO LA TERRA
IDEALS ARE REPLACED BY CONVENTIONAL GOALS AT A CERTAIN AGE
IL DENARO CREA IL GUSTO
IF YOU AREN'T POLITICAL YOUR PERSONAL LIFE SHOULD BE EXEMPLARY
IL PECCATO È UNO STRUMENTO DI CONTROLLO SOCIALE
IT IS MAN'S FATE TO OUTSMART HIMSELF
L'AMORE INCONDIZIONATO DIMOSTRA GENEROSITÀ DI SPIRITO
IT'S A GIFT TO THE WORLD NOT TO HAVE BABIES
L'INACCESSIBILE IMMANCABILMENTE ATTRAE
LACK OF CHARISMA CAN BE FATAL
LA DISORGANIZZAZIONE È UNA SPECIE DI ANESTESIA
MOTHERS SHOULDN'T MAKE TOO MANY SACRIFICES
LA MODERAZIONE UCCIDE LO SPIRITO
PEOPLE WHO DON'T WORK WITH THEIR HANDS ARE PARASITES
LA RELIGIONE CREA TANTI PROBLEMI QUANTI NE RISOLVE
PRIVATE PROPERTY CREATED CRIME
LE PAURE ATAVICHE SONO LE PEGGIORI
RAISE BOYS AND GIRLS THE SAME WAY
OGNI SURPLUS È IMMORALE
SLOPPY THINKING GETS WORSE OVER TIME
RICORDATI CHE HAI SEMPRE LA LIBERTÀ DI SCELTA
THERE'S A FINE LINE BETWEEN INFORMATION AND PROPAGANDA
UCCIDERE È INEVITABILE MA NON BISOGNA ESSERNE FIERI
YOU ARE GUILELESS IN YOUR DREAMS
UN UNICO EVENTO PUÒ AVERE INFINITE INTERPRETAZIONI

NON SCRIVERE MAI CAZZATE

←    Poster received as a gift from Alighiero Boetti in 1990, reprinted by Maurizio Cattelan and donated to visitors on "Alighiero e Boetti Day," organized by Artissima and Fondazione Nicola Trussardi at the Auditorium Rai in Turin on May 28, 2011, and at the exhibition "Take Me (I'm Yours)," at Pirelli HangarBicocca, Milan, 2017–18.
On the back are these words by Maurizio Cattelan: "I met Alighiero Boetti in 1990, at the Venice Biennale, in the American Pavilion, next to a stack of posters by Jenny Holzer. We talked for a while and before I could say goodbye, he had picked up one of the posters, and added a new truism to Holzer's list—"Do Not Bullshit"—signed it and gave it to me.
I've always thought there was a certain restless generosity in that gesture. I finally had the chance to return him his present."

Making a work is the least fun part. The most enjoyable is the part when you conceive it. I think that's true of every artist. You can do it in a minute in the shower or for days one end when you're obsessed with an idea that's still not enough for you. In the end, creating art is definitely a solitary pleasure, one that you wouldn't share with other artists for all the gold in the world. When you're conceiving a work, everything is new and exciting. The more I get into the practical phase, the more impatient I become to start another job. I don't like things I already know.

What disturbs me outside my artistic practice sooner or later becomes a part of it, so that it's hard to tell what's outside and what's inside. When I conceive a work, I simply spend time collecting my ideas, and once I have enough of them, I start editing all these thoughts, testing their resistance in a kind of virtual battle. Ultimately, the standard that has to be met is mine alone. I do the work first of all for myself, and I'm often unable to clarify the chain of reasoning that led me to that result. There is a line, but there are also passages that are inexplicable, and there are mistakes that you would be happy to repeat, because the error gives rise to the process that often makes the idea stronger.

Something is always wrong before it's right, and then it's wrong again. So, I'd rather keep in mind that from the sublime to the ridiculous it's but a step. I don't know anything except what I see and perceive every day, together with what I've experienced in my life so far. All I can do is share my own anxieties and worries, they're the only things I can count on. Everything else would just be the pretense of knowledge without any depth. The work of every creator is about his biography, even if he doesn't know it or wish it, even if his work is "abstract."

Where I'm concerned, being an artist can be therapeutic, though it doesn't always have this effect. But, if you're lucky, you can be find yourself faced with moments of revelation. Things come to the surface that have happened, that you repressed, tragic moments obviously. I'm always grateful when it happens, but making art can be very painful. It's like having a fast track to your traumas. At other times it's an exploration that leads you to discover sides of yourself that you weren't aware of. Often it's just the anxiety of a long voyage without any certainty you'll make landfall. Looking at all my works as a whole, there's a common thread running through them. I used to not see it

119

but now it's very clear: power, death and identity. And there's definitely a lot of repression, too. When they say that the sins of the fathers shall be visited on their children, it's true in a way. Very true, in fact. In this case, art is a therapy that, when it works, helps you understand what made you become who you are. If you're good, you use it not to change yourself but to understand yourself. So being an artist can help me understand myself, and this is already a major victory. All the other things, such as financial rewards or public acclaim, may be important but in any case they're ephemeral. In the end, if you stay lucid and try to understand why you're doing this job, you don't do it for those reasons. The more material things you have, the more time and concentration you have to put into them. They won't take you away from your obsessions, because the obsessions remain.

"Kill your darlings" is the best advice I've ever been given. Everyone should always try to be skeptical of their own creative output. On the other hand, it isn't easy to avoid being obsessed with every single vision. The best artists I know are objective in judging their work, plus they have the honesty and courage not to kid themselves about it. I try to discuss my work with everyone. Every piece is a test, and needs to be looked at, criticized, destroyed and rebuilt. I tend to avoid my own opinions and trust other people's. I see creation as a maieutic process that doesn't always have a happy ending. But I have to admit that I'm sadder about the failed works than happy at the successful ones. Failure leaves a bitter taste, the feeling of not having been able to extract the juice despite having the right ingredients. But in the end, failure—and I've had my share—is just part of your experience.

Creation comes to me very slowly. When I receive a commission for a work, I don't know where to start. I concentrate, but it's useless. If you think insistently about one thing, you find the solution to another. When the delivery date approaches, I panic, I start calling friends, I go around looking for a clue, then I spend four days staring at a window and, snap! I get the idea. The one for *La Nona Ora* (1999) came to me shortly before the inauguration. The figure was ready, but it no longer convinced me, I wanted to destroy it. And so I thought of shooting it down with a meteorite. The most difficult thing is precisely to find the balance between all the elements to ensure that one doesn't prevail over the others. It works like grandma's recipes: no written recipe works, the result is all in the tasting before its placed on the table. And in having enough courage to make the last-minute adjustments.

The production of an artwork has always been a collective process—just think of the Renaissance masters and their *botteghe*. I don't have a studio. I work directly with the artisans who make the work. All artists, to a greater or lesser extent, need outside help when it comes to turning their ideas into objects. But unlike in the Renaissance, the digital age means you don't need a studio. In turn I contact goldsmiths, marble workers, taxidermists… I never wanted to learn how to do anything, to ensure I didn't become a slave to a particular medium. There's always the risk of crushing good ideas under the weight of technical feasibility. My studio consists of sharing the screen in calls with the people I work with from time to time. For example, when I work on the *Toiletpaper* photoshoots with Pierpaolo Ferrari, we spend our days at the computer. We don't need meetings with anyone, except with the producer who has to organize the casting.

Since I don't have a studio, a piece is ready just for the show it's made for. And what I see is what the public is about to see. At that moment a work is a part of me that I don't want to have anything more to do with. Once a job is over, there's no reason to keep it in front of your eyes. It would only remind you that you could have done it better. Anyway, I've always preferred an empty room and a full mind.

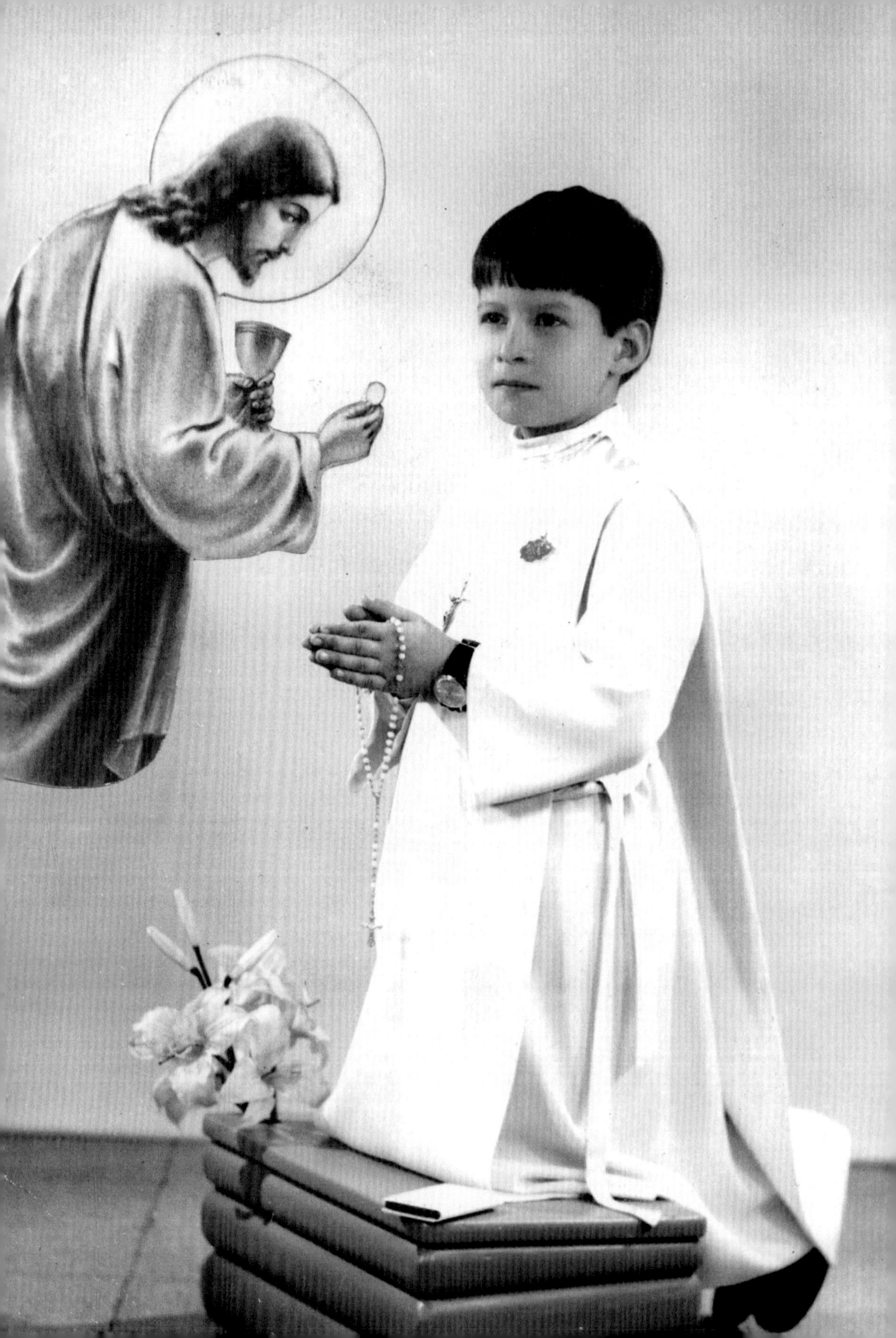

I grew up in a very religious environment. I was an altar boy and I spent a lot of time at the parish center and in church, because it was a way to be free. Am I religious? It's hard to say that nihilism means anything to me. If I weren't in some way a believer, some of my works wouldn't exist. I haven't had to grapple with sickness and suffering yet, so I haven't thought about these matters very clearly, but there's a part of me that feels something.

It's that I'm afraid to face that dimension, just as I'm not a great lover of abstract painting. When I think about spirituality, I always think of my family, which was terribly religious. I grew up immersed in a Catholic education to the core. No matter how much time has passed, it's like original sin, it's a burden you carry with you, and you can't get rid of it. When I was twelve I flunked school and it was a real trauma. My parents thought there was something sick in my spirit, but before they made up their minds about how to treat me, I chose to volunteer as a stretcher-bearer at Lourdes. Well, perhaps one thing I would like to do again today is volunteer work. Even if only to remember that there are other people who have nothing to do with us. Taking a few hours of the day and devoting them to someone else, rather than giving money, which is a passive way of helping. Time is worth a lot more than money.

One of the biggest differences between people lies only in their having more or less access to knowledge, and in making the effort to get it when your original conditions make it hard. All the choices I made were aimed at getting that access. I believe in free will much more than in destiny. I'm convinced that destiny is nothing more than the sum of our choices.

I believe in a world where credit cards and debit cards are useless, a life where ambition doesn't mean serving the ego or false ideals. I believe in silence, which sometimes says more than words. I believe in religion. Humans are religious animals, and this characteristic trait of human behavior can't be ignored or dismissed. I also believe in the power of religion. For centuries it was the only means of enduring suffering. Today we've replaced it with many other methods, none of which strikes me as so effective.

In other respects I feel closer to other monotheistic religions. No image can really come close to God. It's like wanting to depict alien beings. Maybe even God is green and has glowing fingertips.

The Church has managed perfectly to achieve a goal that all artists have. To be iconic and memorable. I wish someone could say the same about my work. In the past, many patrons of the arts belonged to the Church, but today artists find patronage in the fashion industry or among the great collectors. If the Church were to return to its role of commissioning artworks, I'm sure there would be a way to create a fruitful dialogue. After all, Catholicism is one of the greatest reserves of symbolism in our cultural landscape, and it possesses incredible spaces in which artists would be delighted to work. As for me, if the friar in Padua who kicked me out for drawing mustaches on the statuettes of St. Anthony that I was selling as a boy saw what I am today, I'm afraid he wouldn't even let me go home and get my toothbrush. He'd send me straight to hell.

[60] *Catttelan*, 1994
Neon
40 × 130 × 3 cm

I made this neon for a corner in the Laure Genillard Gallery in London, and exhibited it together with *Lullaby* (1994). The three *T*s are the crosses of Golgotha, but apart from being religious, the allusion is obviously also personal. I wanted to measure myself with artists who had come before me who had used neon, in Arte Povera as well as in American Minimalism. This was my version. I put myself on the cross. Damnation and redemption.

[60.1]  *Catttelan*, 1994, and *Lullaby*, 1994 [218]
"Maurizio Cattelan," Laure Genillard Gallery, London, January 28–March 5, 1994 (solo show)

[60.2]  *Catttelan*, 1994

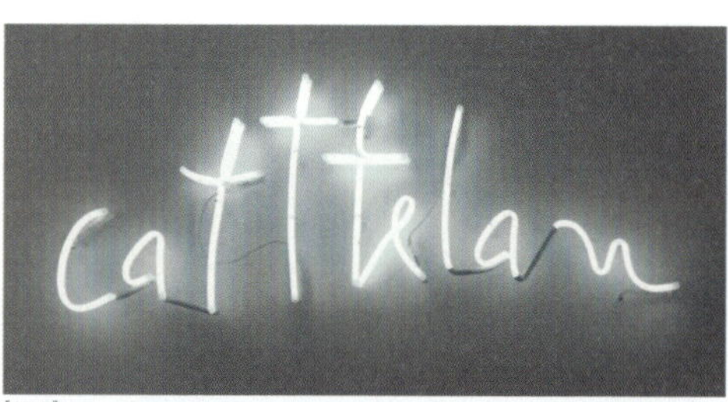

[60.2]

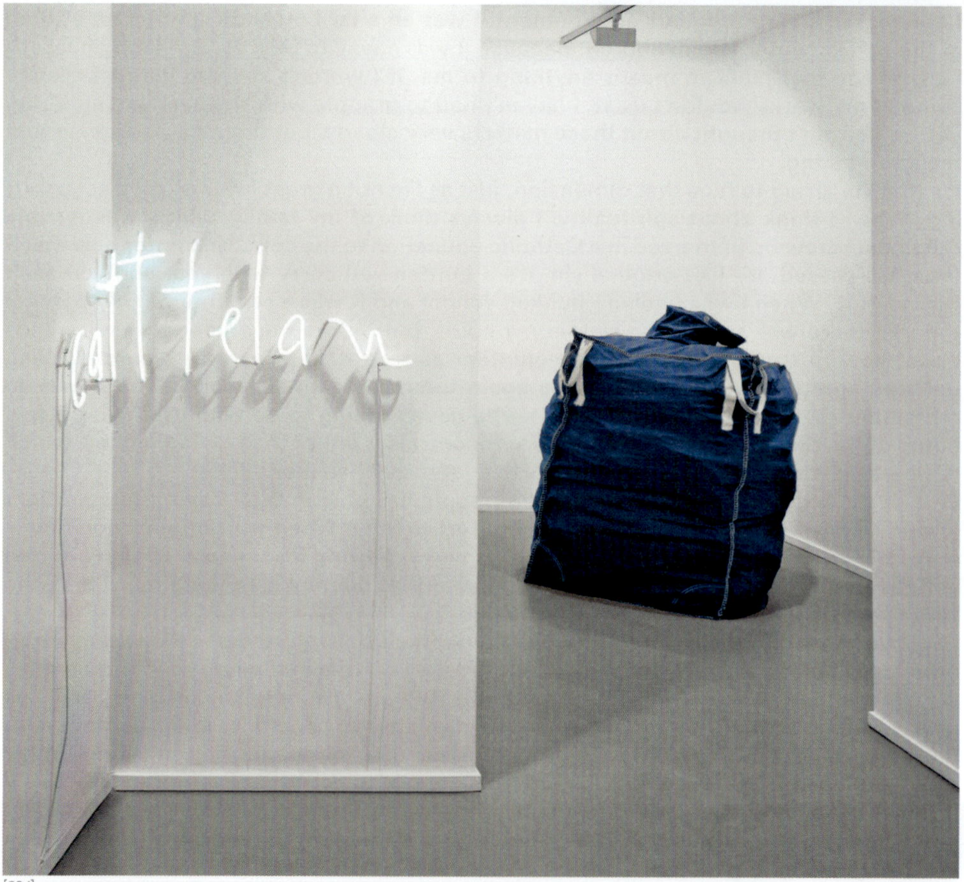

124

[60.1]

[61] **Christmas '94, 1994**
[Initially titled: *Il giardino delle delizie*]
Painted plaster, incandescent lightbulbs
20 × 30 × 15 cm

[62] **Christmas '95, 1995**
Neon
38 × 82 × 4 cm

[63] **Christmas '96, 1996**
Rubber, model trees, artificial snow
35 × 16.5 × 17.5 cm

[64] **Christmas '97, 1997**
Print on mouse pad
19.8 × 23.5 × 1 cm

*Il giardino delle delizie* is a rather strange nativity scene. It also became, with the title *Christmas '94*, the first image in a series of Christmas works that I did four years running. The decision to create a work periodically was interesting, because it made me work to a deadline. That had never happened before.

They're all my versions of a Christmas greeting. After the surreal trio of *Christmas '94*, I did a neon: the comet of the Magi with the star of the Red Brigades. In 1996 I did one of my first hands, which is not skewered and has all its fingers: in fact fir trees are growing from the fingertips. They're just trees, though, without the decorations. Certainly the work recalls the mountains and the Christmas period, but it seems to be more about someone turning into trees. You're just earth.

My last Christmas work, from 1997, is a worn-out mousepad I'd found, and I had printed on it an impossible request, "Give us God," which I'd read on a wall. Perhaps it's actually not an impossible request, but a desperate one, or a prayer, a necessity, an imperative. It's strange that some-

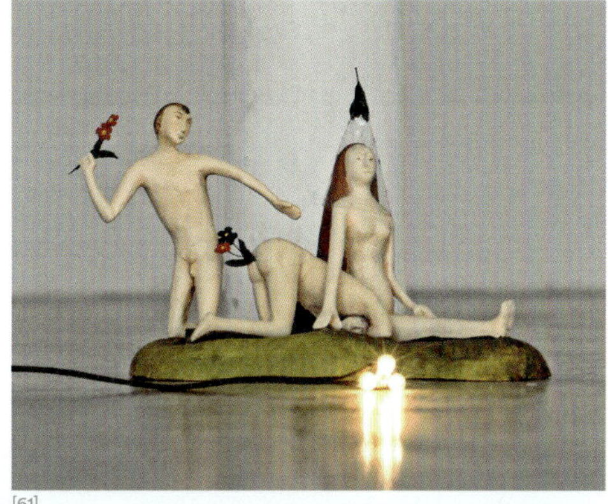

[61]

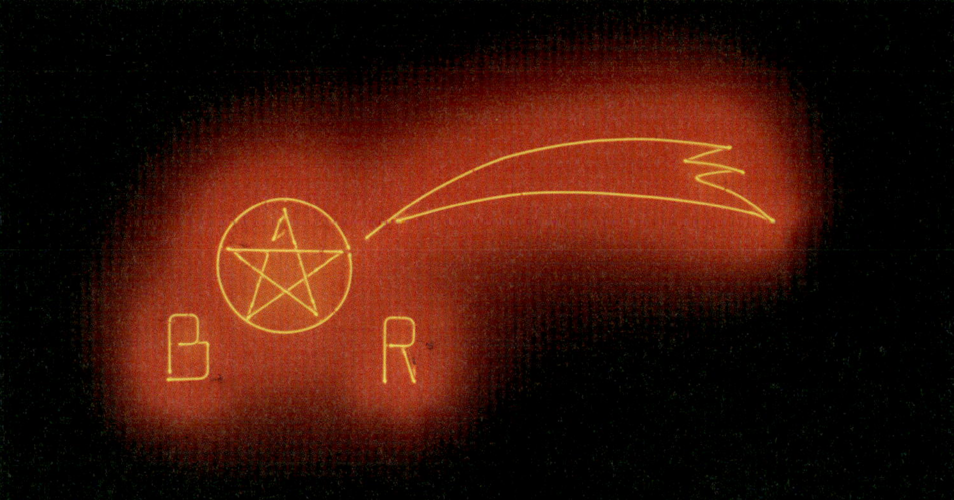

[62]

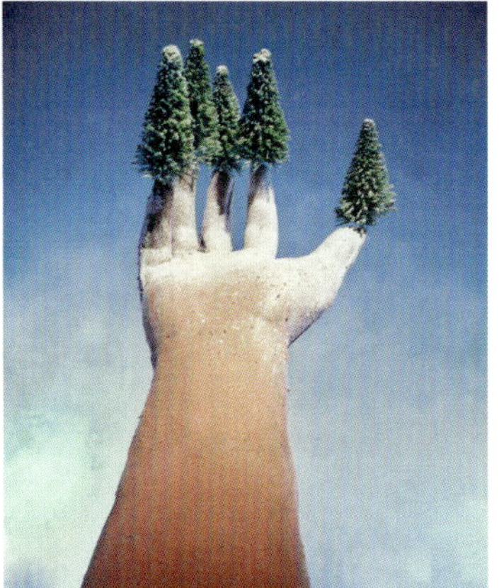

[63]

[64]



125

one went around graffitiing a phrase of that type instead of one of the usual protests. However, there was also a period of romanticism in the streets. Probably the words were written by someone who had experienced a religious, mystical moment. It was an inner appeal, for faith. Each year the work was linked to Christmas, but they're all images or references that I had in mind and was interested in. It doesn't surprise me that I thought of Christmas instead of some other time of the year. That's where I come from, from religion, from family. All my crap, which has stuck to me, is there.

[65.1] **Mother**, 1999
Cibachrome print face mounted on plexiglas
156.2 × 122 cm
Performance with fakir during "dAPERTutto," 48th Venice Biennale, curated by Harald Szeemann, June 13–November 17, 1999 (group show)

[65.2] **Mother**, 1999
Black and white photographic print
88.9 × 71.1 cm
Performance with fakir during "dAPERTutto," 48th Venice Biennale, curated by Harald Szeemann, June 13–November 17, 1999 (group show)

[66] **Shadow**, 2023
Platinum silicone, glass fiber, steel, hair, clothing, refrigerator, food
180 × 75 × 50 cm



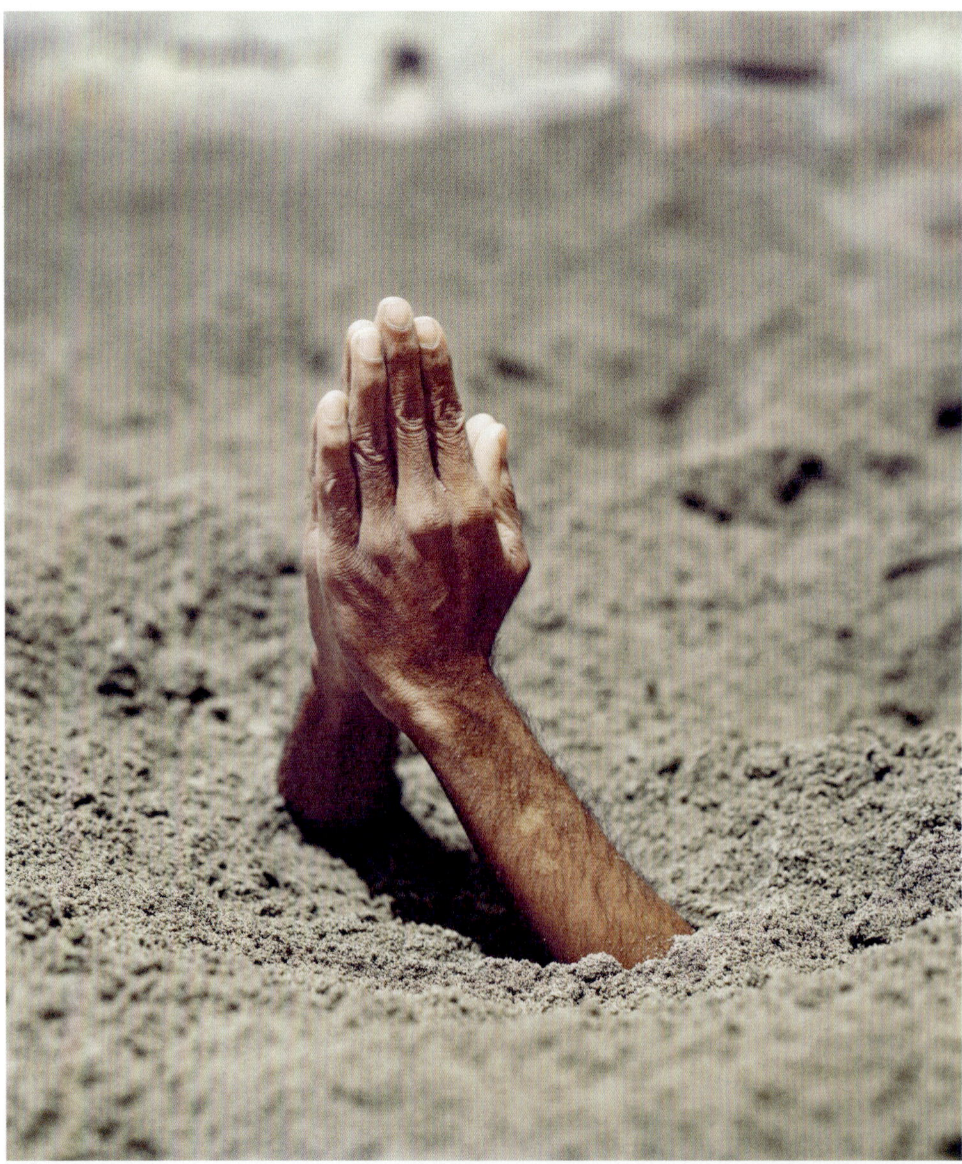

[65.1]

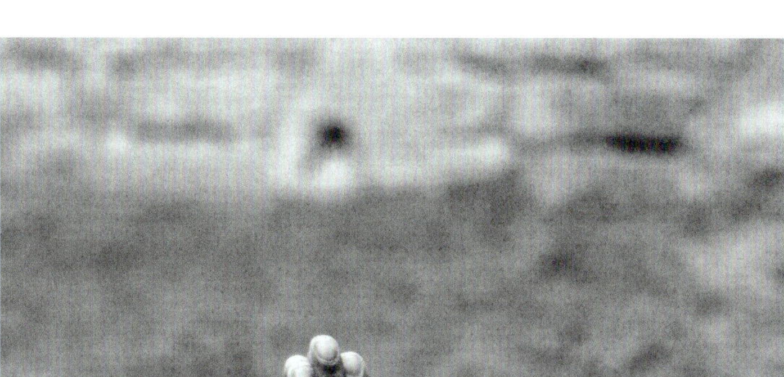

[65.1]   *Mother*, 1999

[65.2]   *Mother*, 1999

[66]   *Shadow*, 2023
"WE," curated by Sungwon Kim, Leeum Museum of Art, Seoul, January 31–July 16, 2023 (solo show)

127

[65.2]

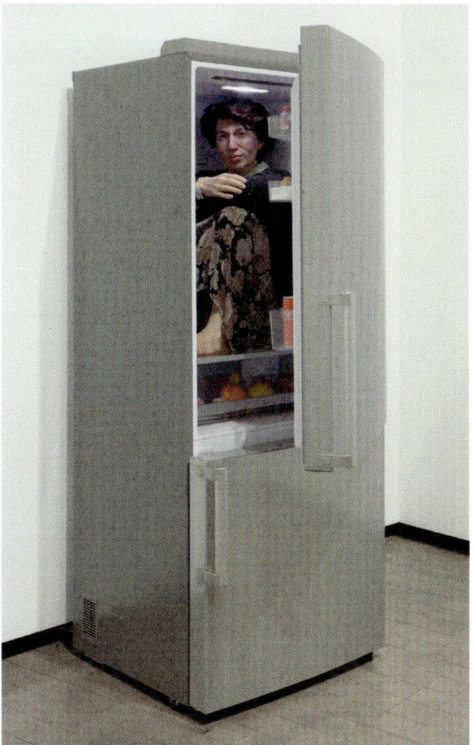

[66]

For my participation in the 1999 Venice Biennale, directed by Harald Szeemann, I initially wanted a person buried upside down, with their legs in the air, as if doing a handstand. At the end of a round of contacts, when I was passing through London, they told me: "Regrettably, we don't have the professional you're looking for here, because he's already in Venice." I think he had teleported. He was too good, and maybe I needed someone less good… In the end, this fakir capable of unbelievable acts of endurance was buried in the ground with only his hands showing in a gesture of prayer or meditation. By just leaving a trace of a body, I forced the viewers to make up their own story.

I decided to call the work *Mother*, because while I was burying the fakir I had a cathartic moment: I was holding my mother's funeral, which I hadn't attended. Years after, I also made her a monument. In "WE," my solo show at the Leeum Museum in Seoul, I wanted to exhibit *Betsy* (2002), but I couldn't. So I decided to redo the work, but it made no sense to replicate Betsy. So I did my mother.

 ***Untitled*, 2007 (first version)**
Resin, paint, natural hair, clothes
Site-specific installation at the
Kunsthaus Bregenz

 ***Untitled*, 2007**
Resin, paint, natural hair, clothes,
wrapping paper, wood, screws
235.6 × 137.2 × 47 cm

I presented this work for the first time at the
Kunsthaus Bregenz in 2008. In that exhibition,
the figure was installed hanging frontally, exactly as Francesca Woodman appears in her photo
where she's hanging by her hands from a door
frame. I had thought of setting up that solo exhibition with one work per floor, but then I asked
them to close the third floor and placed the work
on the door giving access to it, at the top of the
stairs. Then, after setting up the exhibition, I saw
a photo of the sculpture packed in a transport
crate and I changed my mind. I thought it should
be displayed exactly like this, without being
taken out of the crate. Straight after Bregenz I
presented it in a small town in Germany, for the
Kunstprojekt Synagoge Stommeln, like that, inside the crate, hung on the outside of a church.

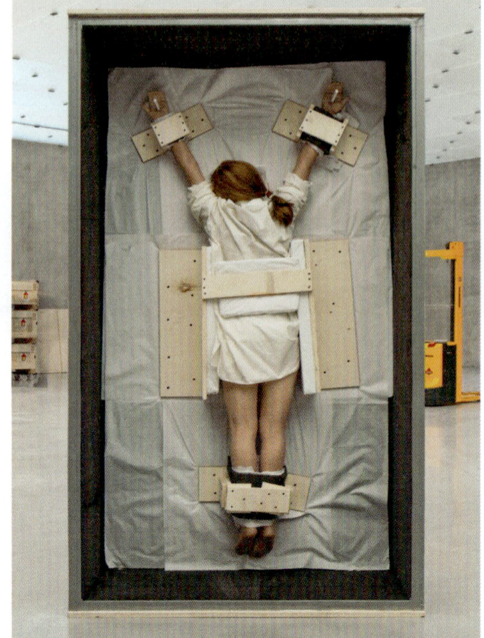

[67.2]

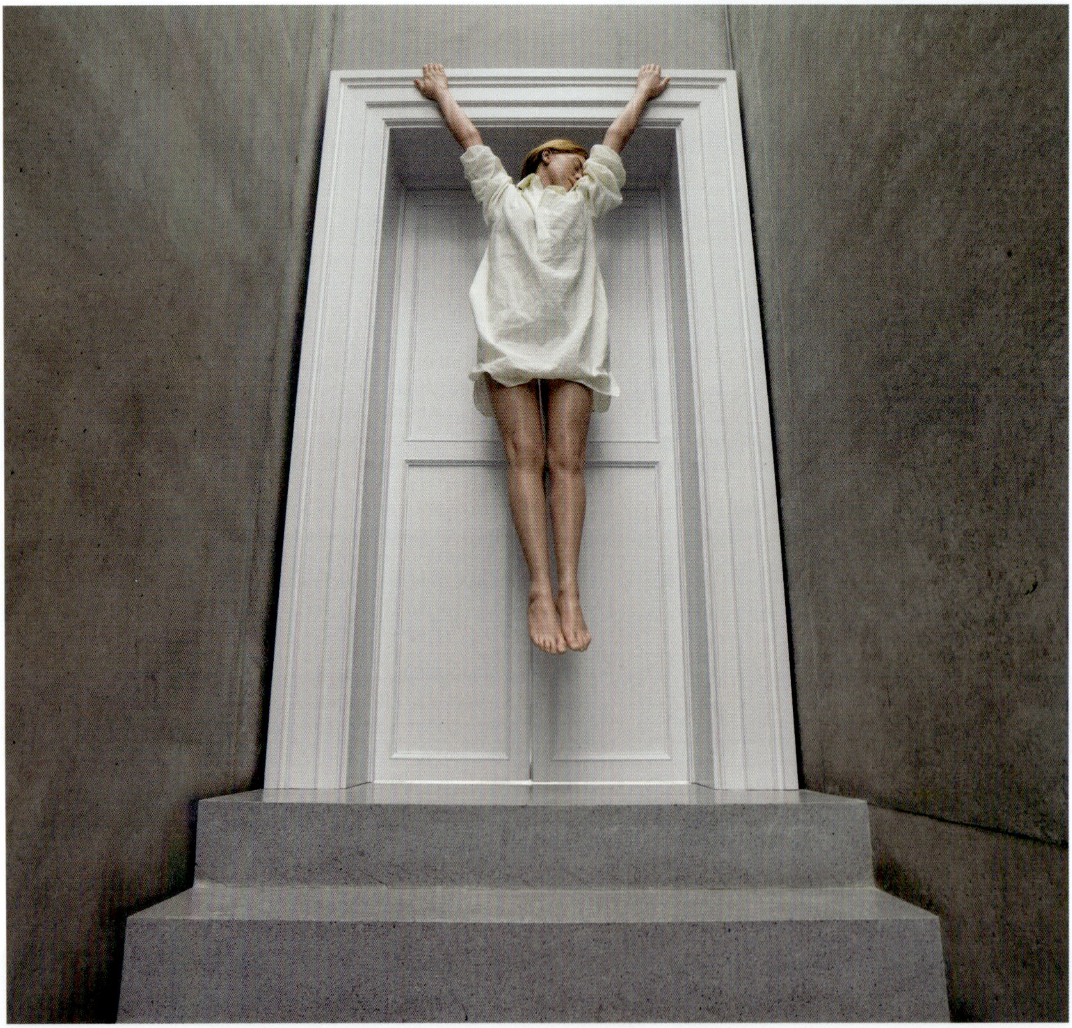

[67.1]

[68] *Frau C.*, 2007
Polyester resin, paint, natural hair,
clothing, shoes
190 × 140 × 38 cm

I don't know how far *Frau C.* is trying to save
humanity or rather whether she's trying to tell
us what a mess we're in. To me she looks like a
revelation, a religious apparition. To be honest, I
still haven't figured out whether she's rising into
the sky or slowly descending to the ground, as if
we've knocked her down. It's certainly a unique
event, like those moments when, as if by a miracle, you suddenly realize the absurdity of what
you've always eaten or the uselessness of what
you've been saying for years.

[67.1]  *Untitled*, 2007
"Maurizio Cattelan," curated by Eckhard Schneider,
Kunsthaus Bregenz, February 2–March 24, 2008
(solo show)

[67.2]  *Untitled*, 2007
"Maurizio Cattelan," curated by Eckhard Schneider,
Kunsthaus Bregenz, February 2–March 24, 2008
(solo show), during the set-up

[67.3]  *Untitled*, 2007
"Maurizio Cattelan," Kunstprojekt Synagoge Stommeln,
June 1–August 10, 2008 (solo show)

[68]  *Frau C.*, 2007
"Maurizio Cattelan. A Miracle in Frankfurt," curated by
Andreas Bee and Udo Kittelmann, Portikus, Frankfurt,
June 13–September 23, 2007 (solo show)

129

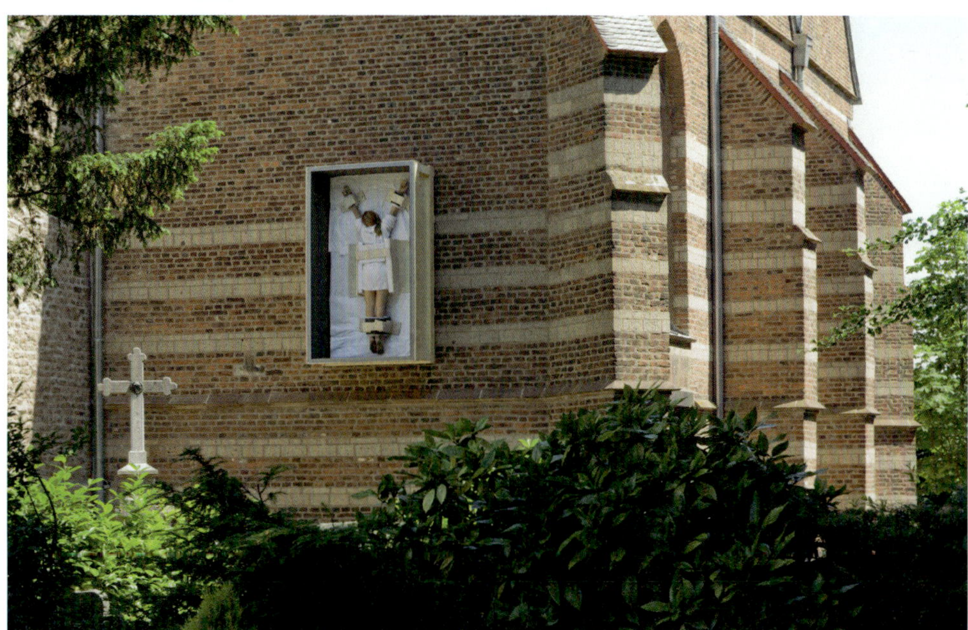

[67.3]

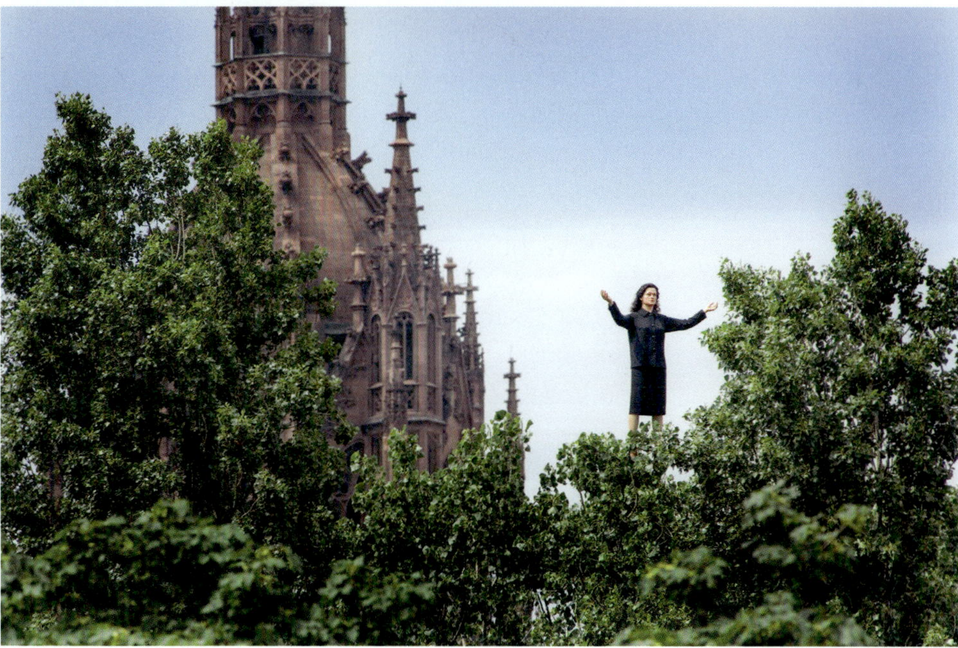

[68]

[69] **"Maurizio Cattelan," 2008**
Solo show, Kunstprojekt Synagoge
Stommeln, June 1–August 10, 2008

[70] *Untitled*, 2008
Boots, plants, soil
Variable dimensions

I exhibited pepper plants growing from old shoes in a former synagogue in Germany, for the Kunstprojekt Synagoge Stommeln, placing the work in front of the place where the Torah was kept. It's life and death together. For the same exhibition I also installed the female figure that I had already exhibited shortly before at the Kunsthaus Bregenz (*Untitled*, 2007), this time leaving it inside its transport crate and hanging it on an external wall of St. Martin's Church, near the synagogue. At one time, the Jewish community of Stommeln and the Christian community had a celebration in common. On the days of the Christian Passover, a procession would leave the synagogue to light the Easter candle in St. Martin's. They walked together through the village and across the railway line. That railway brings with it many memories, some unfortunately horrible. So as not to forget its meaning, I wanted to place it at the center of my project and it became the poster of the exhibition.



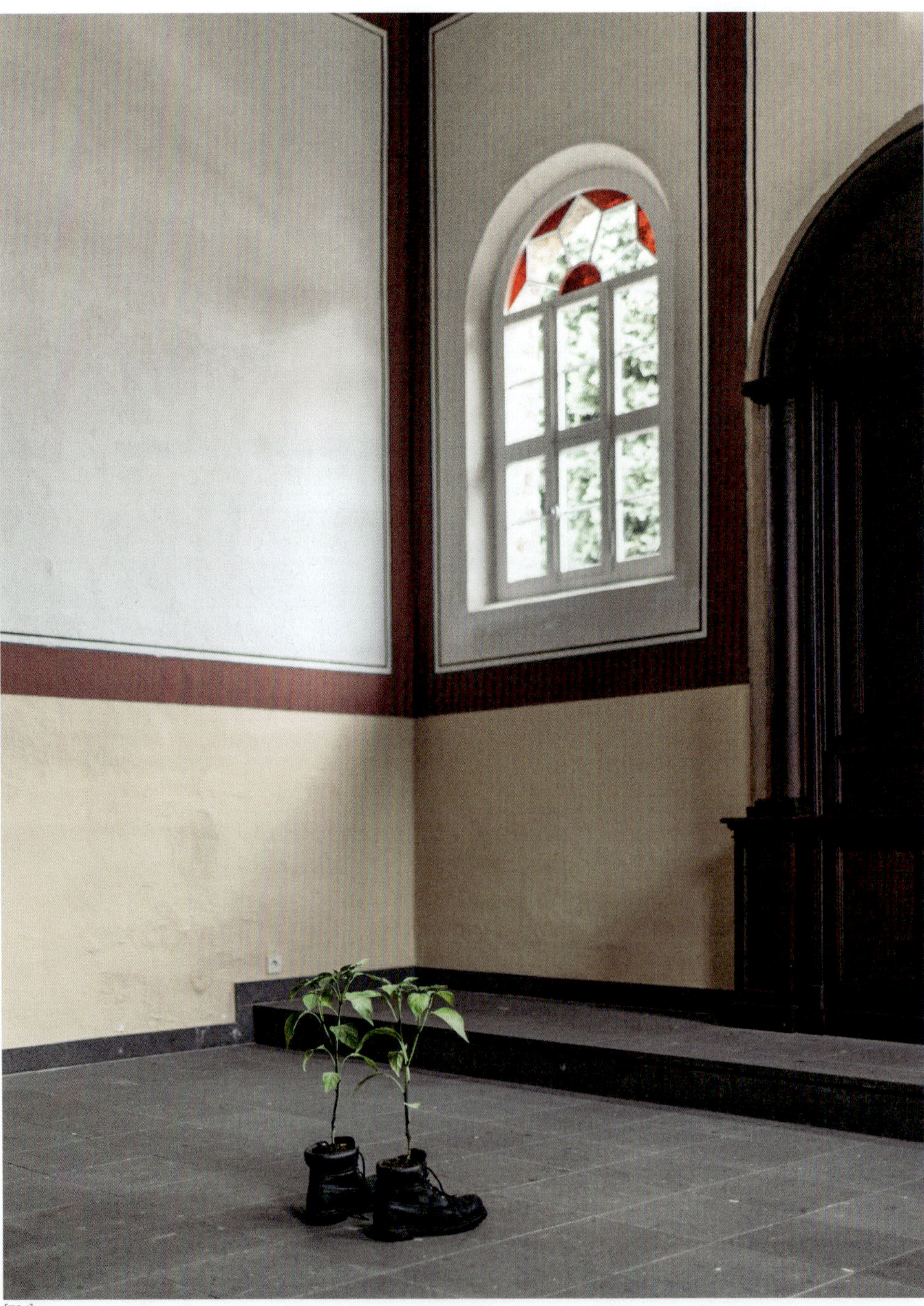

[70.1]

[70.1-2]  *Untitled*, 2008
Boots, pepper plants, soil
Variable dimensions
"Maurizio Cattelan," Kunstprojekt Synagoge Stommeln, 2008

[69]  "Maurizio Cattelan," 2008
Invitation for the exhibition

[70.3]  *Untitled*, 2008
Boots, plants, soil
Variable dimensions
"Maurizio Cattelan. Wish You Were Here," curated by Francesco Bonami, Sea World Culture and Arts Center (SWCAC), Shenzhen, July 9–October 16, 2022 (solo show)

[70.4]  *Untitled*, 2008
Boots, cactus, soil
Variable dimensions
"The Last Judgment," curated by Francesco Bonami, UCCA Center for Contemporary Art, Beijing, November 20, 2021–February 20, 2022 (solo show)

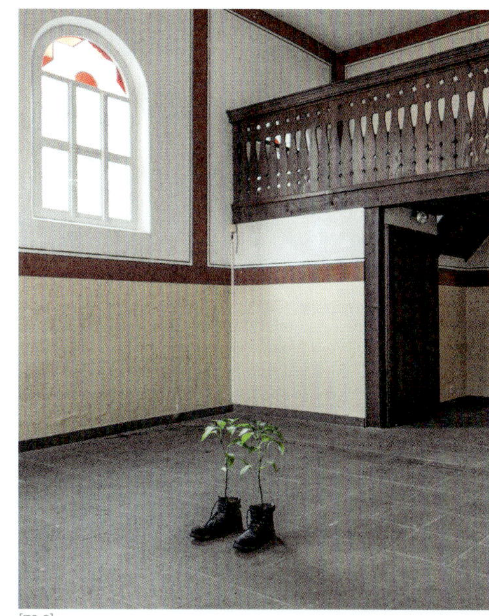

[70.2]

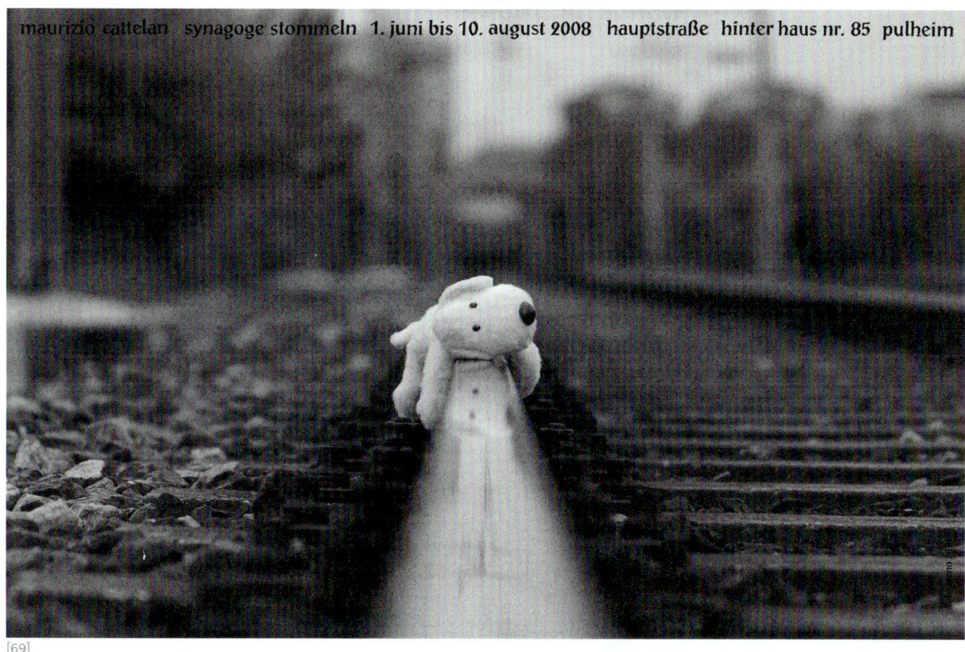


[69]

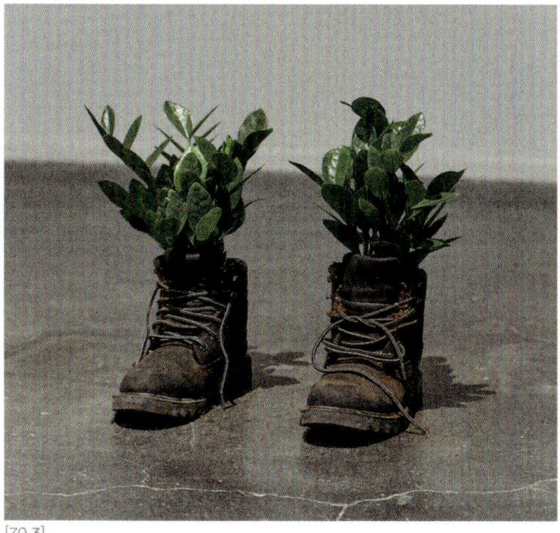

[70.3]

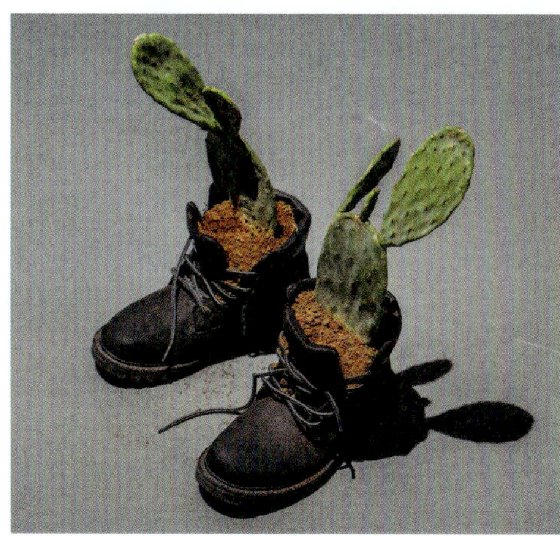

[70.4]

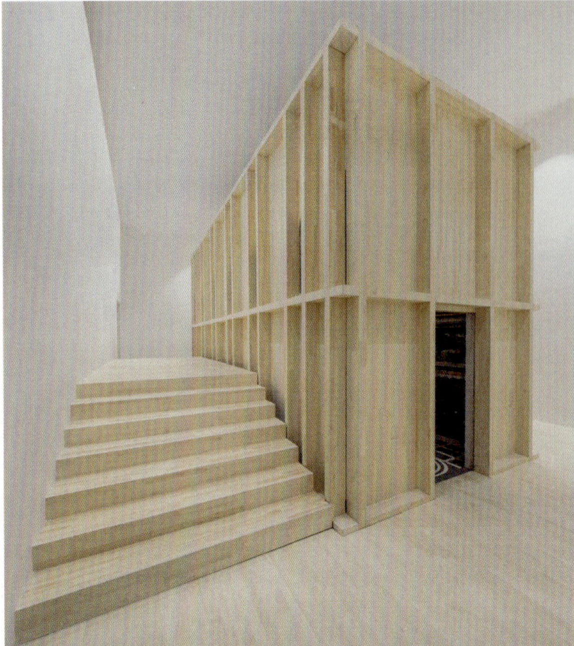

[71.1]

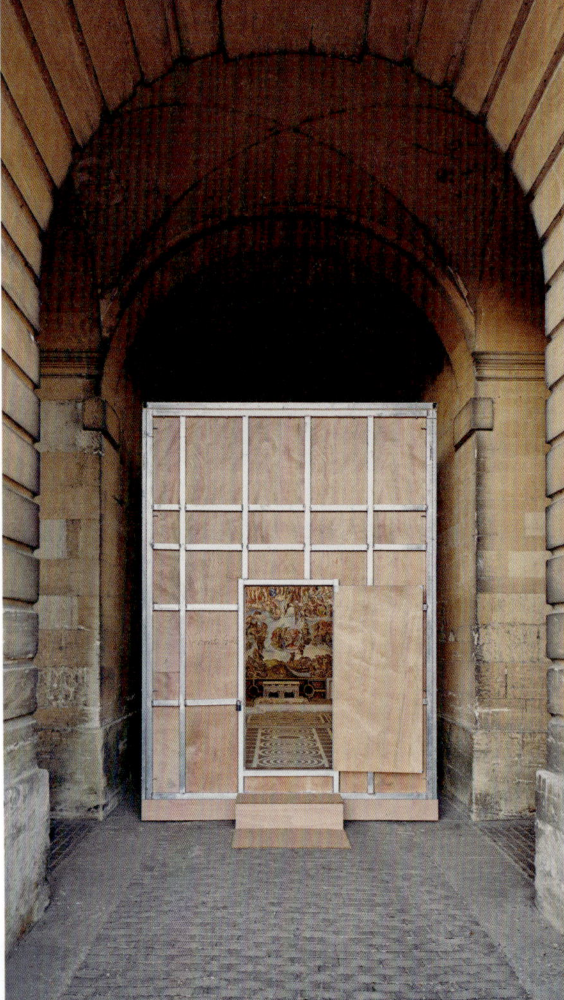

[71.2]

 *Untitled*, **2018**
Fresco painting, pine wood, steel
Interior: 365 × 730 × 243 cm;
exterior: 376 × 830 × 333 cm

The Sistine Chapel contains everything, from genesis to the end of the world, but it's also a place of power and grief. It's where the cardinals meet after the death of a pope: out with one, in with the next. History is cyclical, and so is its representation.

The painted replica of the Sistine Chapel is the only true artwork I signed as an artist in the show "The Artist Is Present," which I co-curated at the Yuz Museum in Shanghai. I'd dreamed for a long time of remaking Michelangelo's masterpiece and the works of the fifteenth century artists before him, making it accessible as an immersive experience: identical to the original but on a smaller, more human scale. Otherwise you can only see it in art history books or by going to Rome and queuing for hours to catch a glimpse of it for a couple of seconds. According to one account, during Michelangelo's absence from Rome, Pope Julius II was annoyed with him because he wouldn't let him see any of the work he was doing. Apparently the pope then bribed Michelangelo's assistants to let him in and see the unfinished masterpiece. Since then, the Sistine Chapel has been visited by millions of people and has been reproduced endlessly: a masterpiece made "portable." Is it still a masterpiece if it travels to us, instead of getting us to go on a pilgrimage to it? In this work I wanted to question whether the copy will save us from a museum-like world where artworks become objects with which the observer no longer has a vital bond, objects about to die.

When it comes to proportions, my Sistine Chapel is much smaller than the one Michelangelo painted, and this is the leitmotif of my feelings towards art history. I've always felt inadequate. It's even truer of the Sistine Chapel.

[71.1,3] *Untitled*, 2018
Fresco painting, pine wood, steel
Interior: 343 × 693 × 242 cm;
exterior: 376 × 719 × 272 cm
"The Artist Is Present," curated by Maurizio Cattelan and Alessandro Michele, Yuz Museum, Shanghai, October 11–December 16, 2018 (group show)

[71.2] *Untitled*, 2018
Fresco painting, pine wood, steel
Interior: 343 × 693 × 242 cm;
exterior: 376 × 719 × 272 cm
"Victory Is Not An Option," curated by Michael Frahm, Blenheim Palace, Woodstock, United Kingdom, September 12–October 27, 2019 (solo show)

[71.4] *Untitled*, 2018, and *La Nona Ora*, 1999 [56]
"WE," curated by Sungwon Kim, Leeum Museum of Art, Seoul, January 31–July 16, 2023 (solo show)

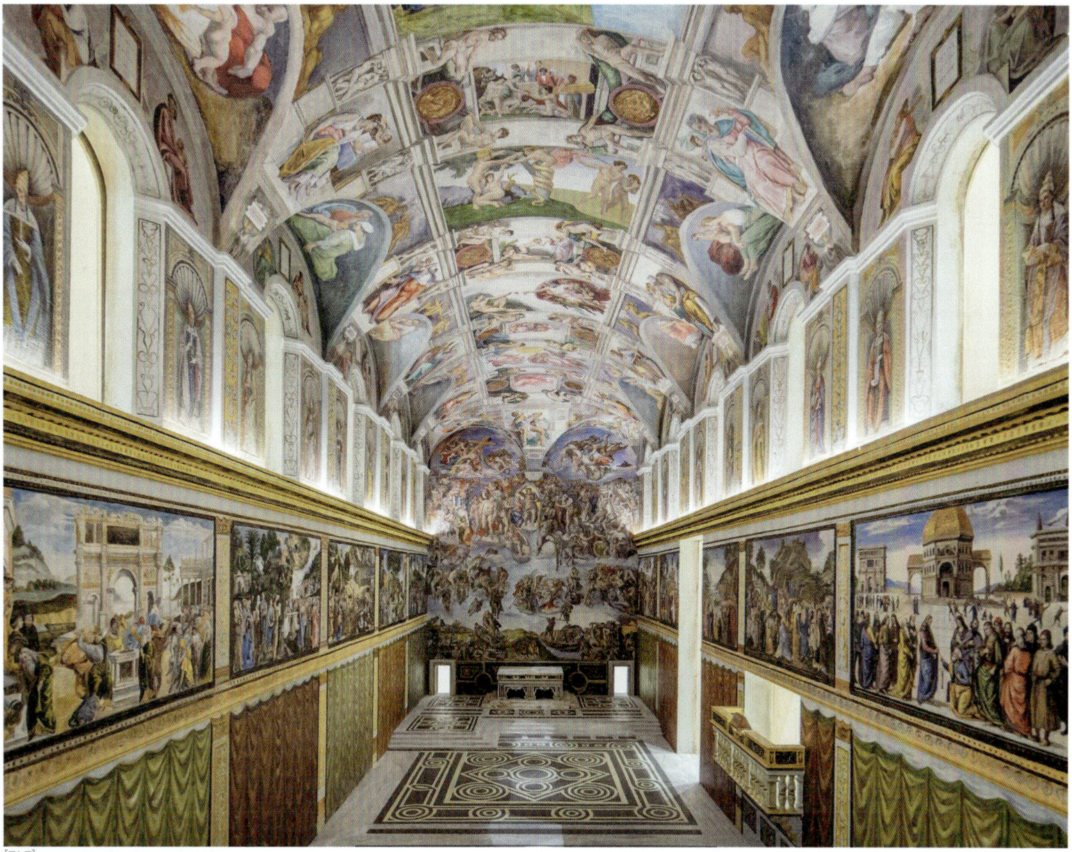

[71.3]

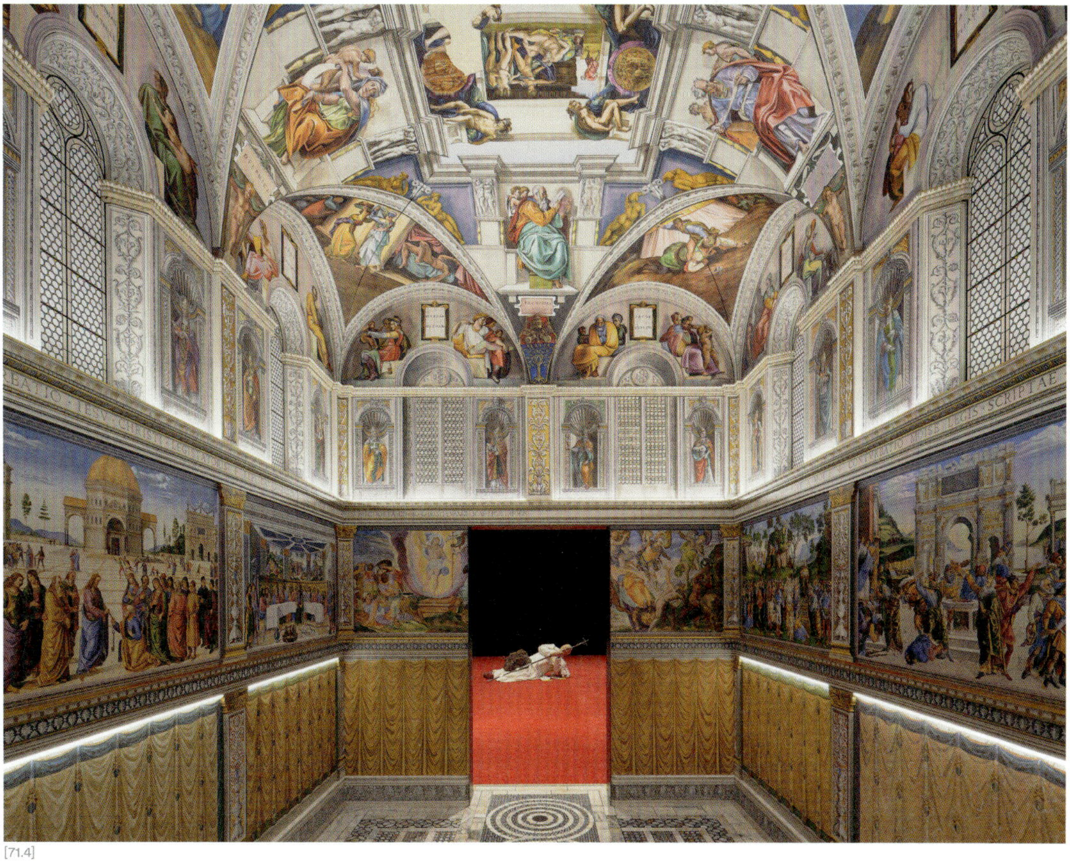

[71.4]

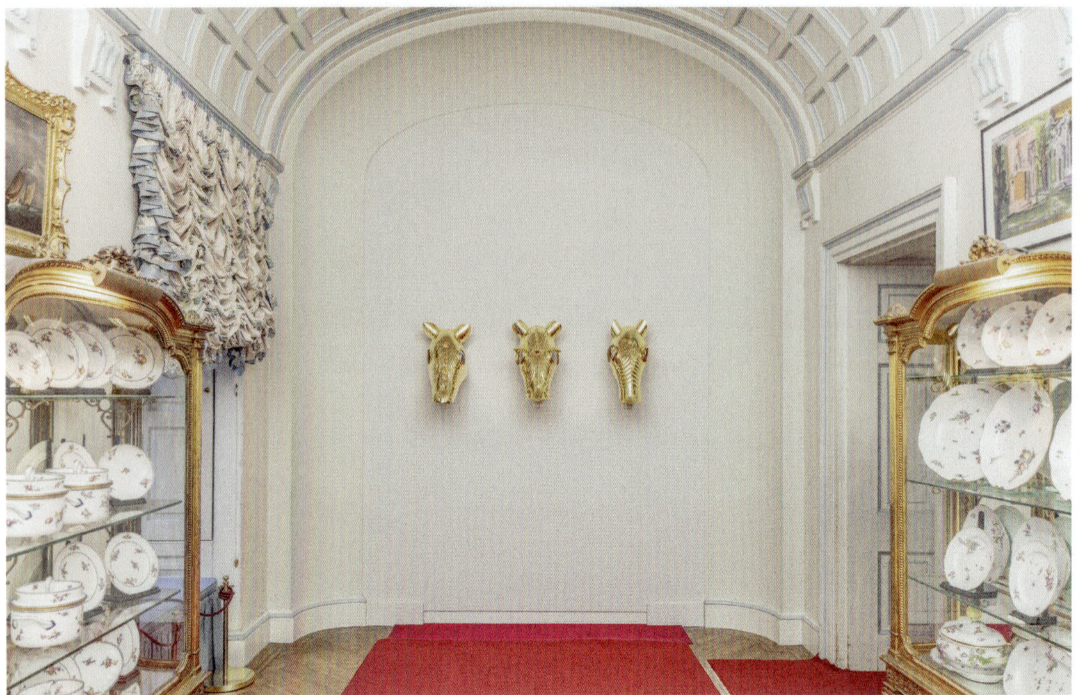

[72]

[72] **_Glory Glory Hallelujah_, 2019**
Bone, 24 karat gold-plates steel
66 × 25 × 35 cm each element

134

Gold is the most highly symbolic material that humanity has used. We've designated it the material of God, but at the same time it is the symbol and basis of capitalism. It's controversial, and for this reason I find it interesting.
For one of the works in the Blenheim Palace exhibition, I thought of horse armor, normally exhibited without horses. In this case the horses are there, or at least their skulls. But this is meant to be a work to be buried, like the one at the Whitney (_Untitled_, 2004). At least I managed to give the work at the Whitney a second life, or take it away. _Glory Glory Hallelujah_ still awaits burial.

[73] **_Ego_, 2019**
Taxidermied crocodile, rope
Variable dimensions

Crocodiles have been at the center of rituals, religions, magical beliefs, and urban legends. They're creatures that both frighten and fascinate, seen as deeply symbolic since the origins of humanity.
Being hung up makes you harmless. It deprives your body of its ability to react. A body suspended has had the ground pulled out from under its feet and is powerless, unable to influence its own destiny. Hanging up a body is a very violent gesture, and turning it against my own work was also therapeutic.
What fascinates me in particular about the crocodile is that everyone is scared of it, but nobody has actually seen it. Captain Hook, Peter Pan's antagonist, if you think about it, just has to hear the ticking of the alarm clock that the crocodile swallowed and he starts to panic, without even seeing its eyes above the surface of the water. And the very fact that the crocodile is Captain Hook's terror shows it has always stood for our deepest fears, those that reduce us to the state of a prey.

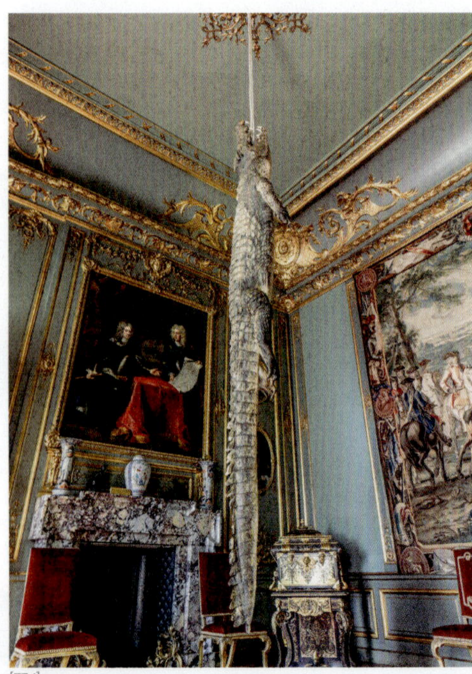

[73.1]

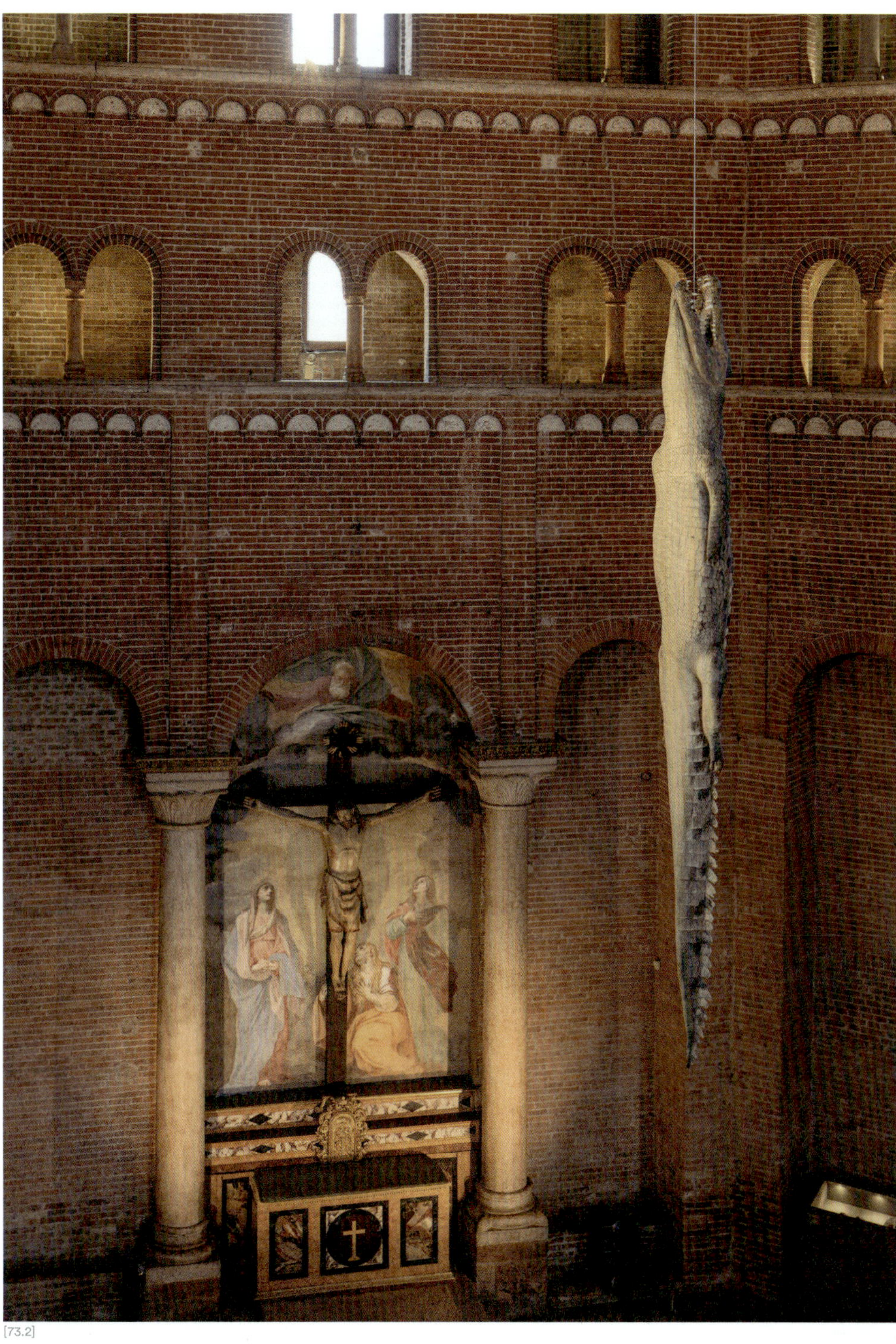

[73.2]



[72]  *Glory Glory Hallelujah*, 2019
"Victory Is Not An Option," curated by Michael Frahm,
Blenheim Palace, Woodstock, United Kingdom,
September 12–October 27, 2019 (solo show)

[73.1]  *Ego*, 2019
Taxidermied crocodile, rope
346 × 60 × 36 cm
"Victory Is Not An Option," curated by Michael Frahm,
Blenheim Palace, Woodstock, United Kingdom,
September 12–October 27, 2019 (solo show)

[73.2]  *Ego*, 2019
Taxidermied crocodile, rope
433 × 70 × 40 cm
Project for Cremona Contemporanea – Art Week,
May 27–June 4, 2023, curated by Rossella Farinotti
(group show), installation at the Battistero di San Giovanni,
Cremona, May 27, 2023–January 14, 2024

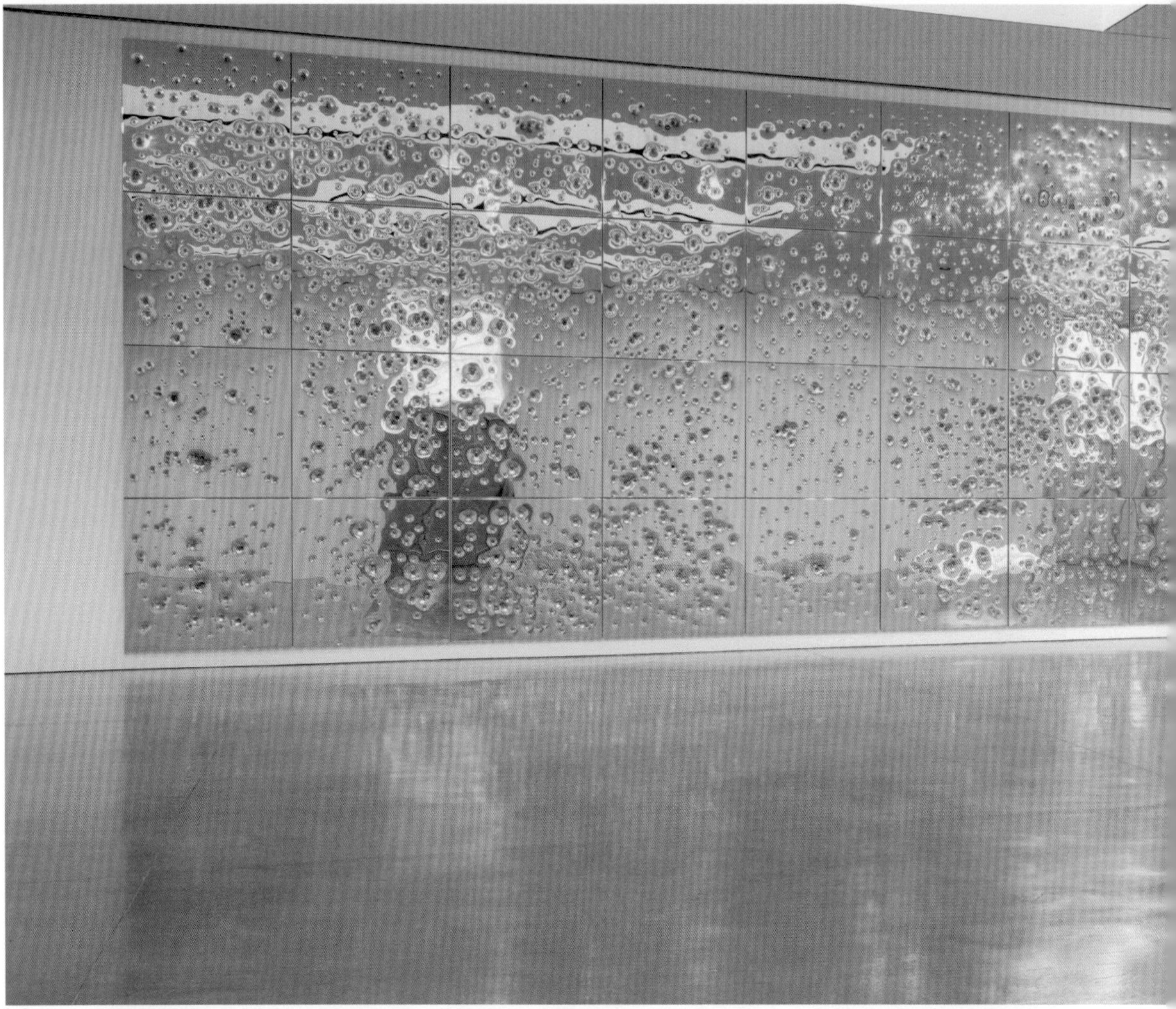

[74]

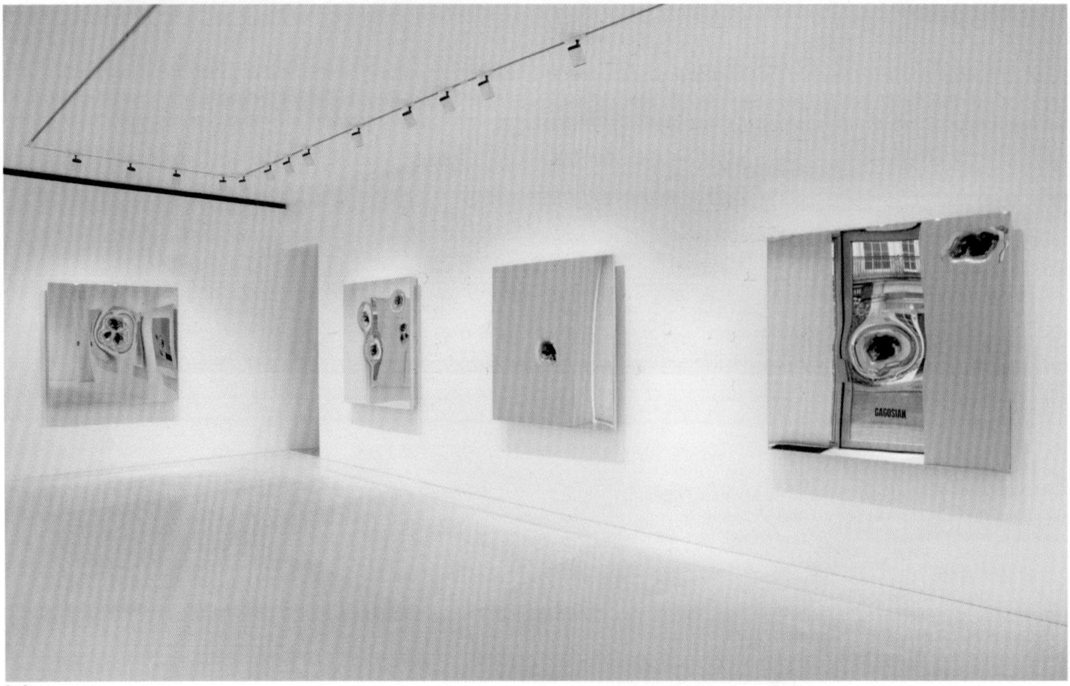

[75]

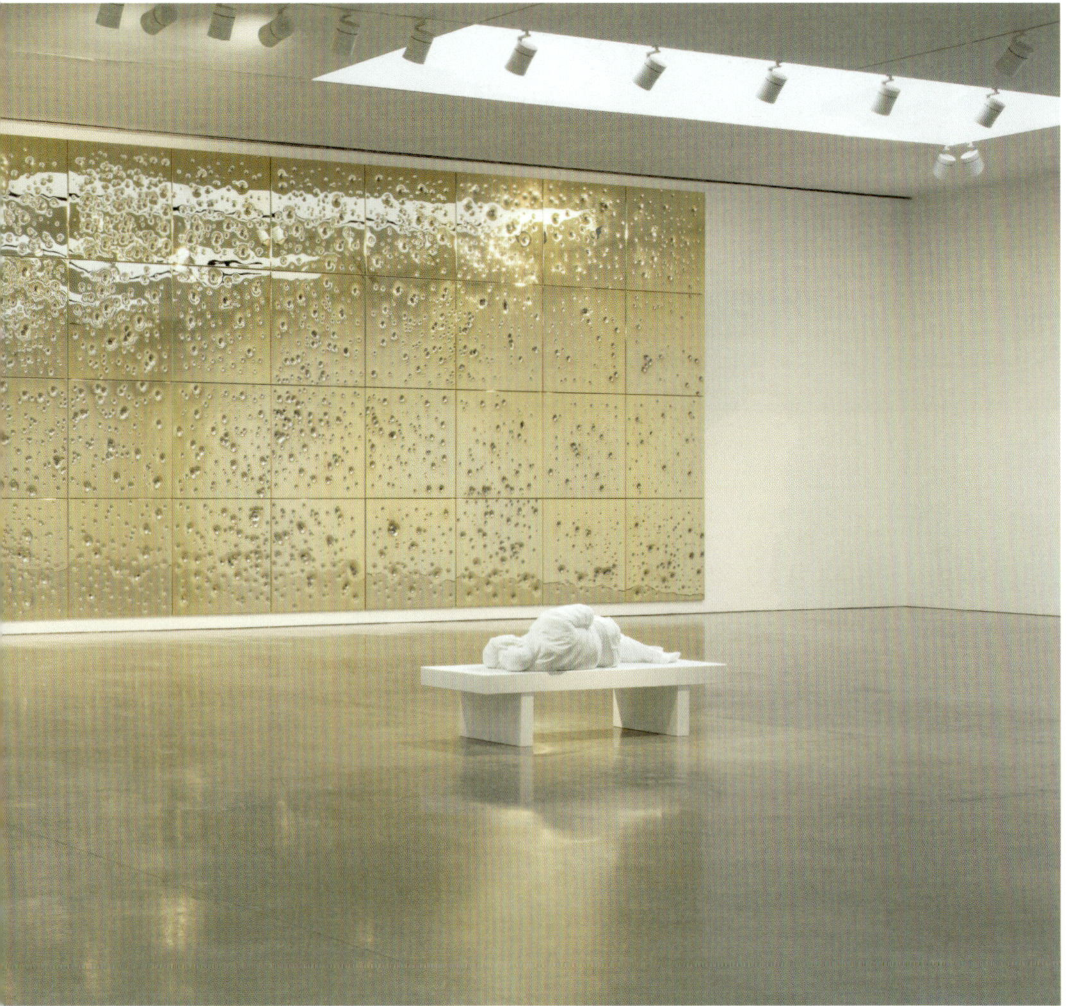



[74]  ***Sunday*, 2024**
64 panels of stainless steel, plated in
24 karat gold
136 × 136 × 4 cm each; overall dimensions:
544 × 2176 × 4 cm

[75]  ***Mouth*, 2025**
24 karat gold-plated steel panel shot with
12-gauge weapon
136 × 136 × 4 cm each

*Sunday*, a Sunday like any other. *Sunday* is part of the journey on flags, which began in 2021 with those of the United Kingdom (*Tears*, 2020) and the United States (*Night*, 2021). I was talking to Lucio Zotti and telling him that we would have to do a test with a completely clean panel, without any filigree design. There were the usual endless times and we did dozens of tests—in mirrored steel, in plated steel, and so on. In the end, we understood that the most appropriate material would be gold, because, as a symbol of inequality, it would create a continuity with *America* (2016). But this work would also be given its own independent code: beauty, luxury, and violence. *Sunday*, the title, works well. I admit that Francesco Bonami invented it, but I like it. Sunday is

the day when people go out, go to the park with the dog, set up the easel and paint. But sometimes, instead of doing a painting, someone will start shooting, and on Sunday it seems scarier. But what is even more frightening is how accustomed we are to stories of everyday violence. Like my other works, *Sunday* also takes us back to the Catholicism of my origins. Sunday is the holy day when everything in Christian countries comes to a stop, although no longer necessarily because people go to church. Associating Sunday with gold and gunshots makes it all strange. In a certain sense it is as if the work celebrates a God, a God who glitters but who brings with him a sin, a virus, something incomprehensible. I've realized that God and sin are not separable. With *Mouth* I worked on the same thought, and this idea of the hunger for power as something insatiable.

[74]    *Sunday*, 2024
"Sunday," curated by Francesco Bonami, Gagosian, West 21st Street, New York, April 30–June 29, 2024 (solo show)

[75]    *Mouth*, 2025
"Maurizio Cattelan. Bones," Gagosian, Davies Street, London, April 8–May 24, 2025 (solo show)

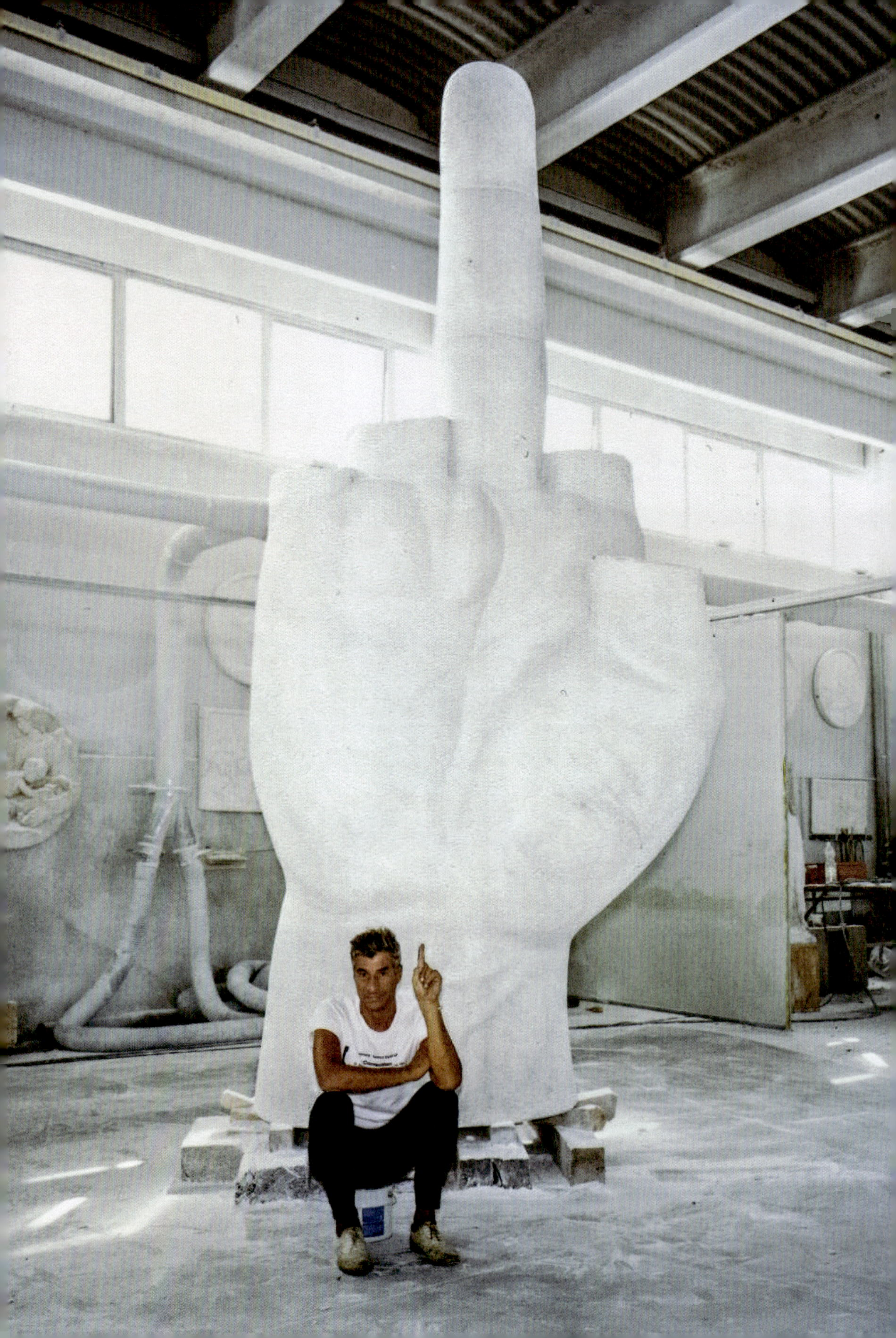

No one has ever invented anything, and this has been true since the beginning of time. Energies and ideas from around the world alter, mingle, hybridize, merge. I guess it's the same with art and ideas, without believing in anything like originality. I'm not afraid of stealing or being stolen from. If an idea of mine is seen as so strong that someone reworks it, that doesn't worry me.

Originality has never existed. We always start from what we know, then combine, change, mix different things and create "new" ideas. Humans started off by copying nature. In the Lascaux Caves wonderful minds decided to copy the animals they hunted. Then people's minds gradually became more complex, and they copied from other humans who had copied someone or something else before. The concept's as old as humanity itself. Copying has to do with the transmission and diffusion of knowledge, both among contemporaries and for people who haven't been born yet. The ancient Romans endlessly copied classical Greek statues because they wanted everyone to be able to admire them, from the senator to the blacksmith.

I don't believe originality is even a notion that human beings can understand. To me, growing up in a Catholic environment, the very first original act was the creation of Adam out of mud. Whatever has come since has been influenced by what went before. We probably continue to aspire to the new and original, because it's something that has more to do with divinity. The quest for originality is our way of getting closer to God. In this respect I can say I'm a complete atheist. The religions that have come down to the present took many of their customs and beliefs from earlier religions, and earlier religions drew heavily from even earlier ones. This doesn't make them any less strong or original. It's another way of looking at what's always happened. Artists have stolen from everywhere since the beginning of time. Now we're just owning up to it. So, in a way, we could say that the act of creation never began.

When they discovered in 1988 that the Shroud exhibited in Turin is an artifact from the thirteenth or fourteenth century and not the imprint of Christ's body on his shroud, no one thought of stopping venerating it as if it were real. I always wondered how this was possible, until I realized that the difference between copy and original is just a matter of faith. If I said that the Eiffel Tower is not original but a copy, would it make any difference to the object? Or to the impression you get when you look at it? I think it's all about faith and it's easier to believe in whatever we see. So the moment something exists in front of us, we'll end up believing in it rather than in an unseen original. The nature of originality derives only from what you see first. It's like the sense of alienation you feel when you look at the big fashion brands' displays in their store windows, which reflect street vendors selling the same bags seen in the store. When I see something that works, it seems so simple to me. There are no rules or copyright or conventions that could convince me it's a fake. If it gives me something and prompts me to question myself, then it's a real work, an original.

The culture of copying or perpetual recreation is part of a context where revolutionary discontinuities are replaced by a continuum in which today is just yesterday reprocessed, changed and transformed. People always look for originality because they believe that history is a process of continuous evolution, but now we realize that it isn't like that. Originality belongs to nature, while copying is a common way for humans to show their understanding of an object. Copying means paying attention to the value of the object being copied. In this way copying makes sense, and even adds value to the original idea. I intentionally speak of copying, rather than imitation. A parrot imitates what it hears but without understanding its meaning, while copying is an act of deep awareness of the subject. My newsvendor says: "Start copying what you love. Copy copy copy copy. In the end you'll find yourself."

Being copied makes you a mentor; copying is a part of learning. A kid learning to play soccer reproduces the moves of champions, and perhaps he'll become a phenomenon thanks to the way he interprets those moves. No one would slap copyright on a bicycle kick. In art, if can't copy your hero's header, it would be better for you take up crochet.

I don't want to be naive. In the art business there's a lot of money at stake and plagiarism can cause losses, but I still think that ideas aren't private property if you can take them to another level of meaning. Copying takes creativity, just as walking on a tightrope calls for balance, so the copy becomes the original the moment it exists.

I believe that at the heart of this obsession with originality lies a persistent reduction of resources in the world of work, while the craving for self-affirmation and self-representation is felt to be increasingly urgent. If I produce something, it has to be mine, so I can make the most of it. It's a principle from the last century. There was a time when copying was a declaration of pure love. We've abandoned this view in favor of the idea that property and copyright are fundamental to capitalist society, while reproduction is only a technique of preservation. The existence of originality is closely bound up with the power of individualism, but we can all perceive that this power is steadily growing weaker. Things are changing. Copying is the gesture we perform most often in the course of the day. We copy every time we share content online. It's true that the idea of intellectual property and the author was already dead in Benjamin's time, but we bury it even deeper every day. The battles for copyright have been lost for the sake of a sharing lifestyle, a concept that has arisen in recent decades and is stronger than copying. In the act of sharing, copying is freed from blame.

Copying is one of humans' outstanding characteristics, and this is especially evident today, when ideas of gender, politics, mass culture, art, fashion and identity are increasingly fluid. Deep down, everyone thinks they're different from everyone else, but even deeper down they know they're just the same as everyone else.

A few years ago, a study was published showing that our genes are modified by experience, a discovery that goes beyond any Darwinian theory of evolution that we've based our whole contemporary culture on. We have to accept that our consciousness and identity change all the time, along with our interpretation of reality. Remaining stuck with originality sounds a bit like not accepting that our traditions are interwoven with other people's. Those who don't accept the changes of our time end up behind the walls and borders built by the Trumps and Salvinis of the world. You can never know what comes from copying, mixing, emigrating and immigrating. Everyone has their own way of copying and this is originality.

Being in touch with Far Eastern culture has confirmed my idea that originality is the fruit of the imagination and the quest for it is hopeless. The cultural difference is particularly striking if you think of the musealization of past glories in the West. I find the model of the Far East much more fascinating, where nature provides the example. Every living organism renews itself by continuously replacing its cells. Basically, we're all replicas of ourselves and our identity, which is always changing. Eastern culture has been based on the concept of reincarnation for centuries. Is there a better way than this to start looking at the idea of copying in a new way? Because they see time as circular, they're indifferent to the idea of progress, typical of cultures that think of time as a straight line. The classic example is Buddhist temples, which are continually being demolished and rebuilt. Where we see a new building, Eastern culture sees the reincarnation of the previous one. My feeling is that ancient cultures, traditionally and geographically very distant from each other for centuries, have never been as close as they are today.

In China, East and West manage to seem close. The famous concept of "Made in China" developed between 1980 and 2000, when the country was starting to open its market to the world. At that time, China was famous for its low-cost, high-volume, low-quality manufacturing industry that flooded the markets with fakes and imitations. Today the Chinese economy is moving away from this stereotype. But, above all, an age when everything is being reproduced suggests the urgency of overcoming the old concept of counterfeiting in favor of a new way of understanding copying as an indispensable tool for dealing with contemporary society.

Once I'm gone, I'd like someone to look through all my activities, even those not normally considered artistic, and show that all the projects undertaken in my life, every task I performed, reflected my effort to question the concepts of originality and reproduction. Honestly, if I decided to be an artist, it's because I wasn't good enough as a forger.

[76]  *-43.500.000*, 1992
2 broken safes
73 × 85 × 32 cm each

[77]  *-76.000.000*, 1992
Broken safe

[78]  *-157.000.000*, 1992
Broken safe
142 × 74 × 79 cm

[79]  *-74.400.000*, 1996
Broken safe
140 × 85 × 64 cm

There is a story behind how the I picked up the first safe as a work, and it's anything but a movie. The first year I arrived in Milan I was staying in a furniture store called Dilmos. The shop shared one wall with a jewelry store. One of those weekends I was there and the jewelry store was robbed. The following Monday there were cops all over the place. I walked in and asked: "My God, what happened?" They just said: "A robbery, do you know anything about it?" I hadn't heard a single thing. Everything had been stolen. I knew the jeweler, and I went to see him inside and saw the actual safe that had been cracked. I asked him what would happen to the safe. "It needs to be replaced." So I asked if he minded if I took the broken one, which of course he didn't, saying that I would spare him the trouble of having someone take it away.

I've made a number of works with safes. Finding the safes involved going through the process from the end to the beginning. Whenever I read about a burglary in the papers, I went to the scene of the crime and tried to get the safe that had been broken open. Then I discovered a place where they stored them, providing assistance to the banks. The amount of money that was stolen became the title of the piece. I had no sociological or be-

havioral interest in doing this; to me it was spiritual support to a process that had already taken place. Like fraud, burglary has always fascinated me. After all, the check faked by Duchamp follows the same line of thought. The piece with the safes was really about my love for certain cops and robbers movies. Inside of everyone there is a little thief. So it was a romantic, sentimental piece. The safe is really a magic object, a projection of our inner selves. It certainly wasn't a comment on the art world.

Then safes, with their gigantic dimensions and their weight, are quite close formally to the tradition of monumental art, and I really like the idea of going back to something so full-bodied and sturdy. However, it's heavy to lift, move, install, and transport. Sometimes you should think before making a work.

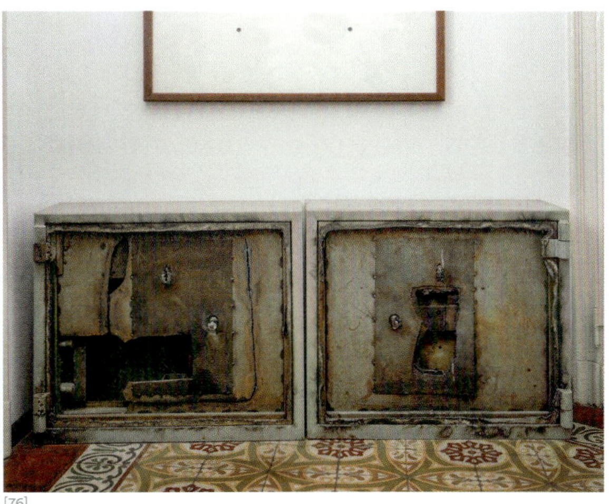

[76]

[76]  *-43.500.000*, 1992
Private house, Milan

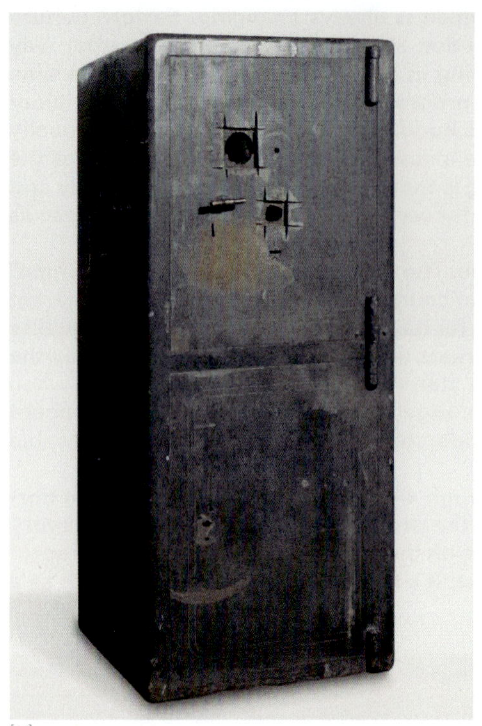

[77]

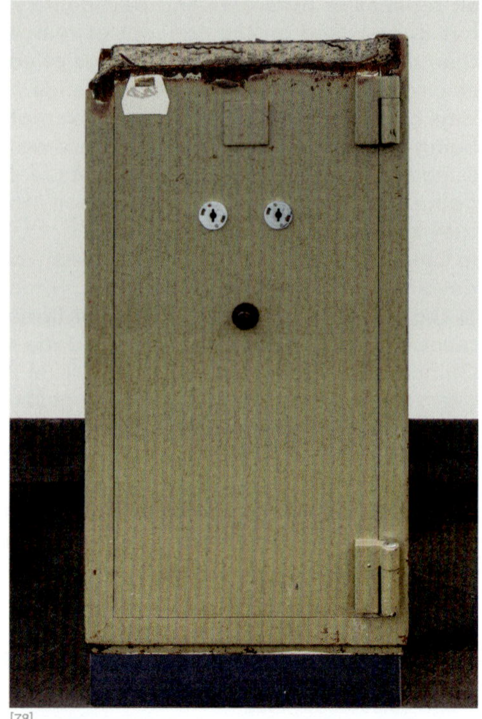

[78]

142

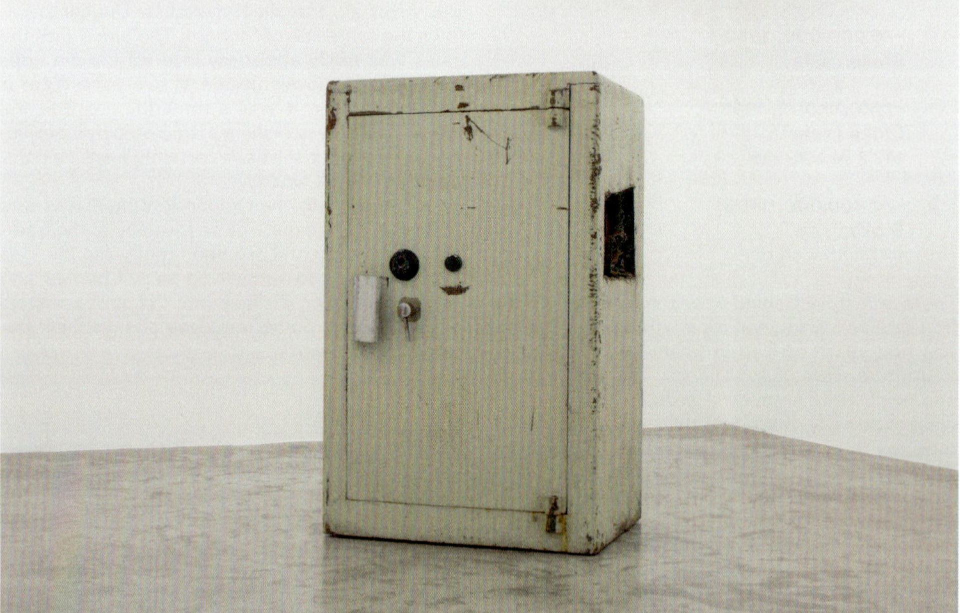

[79]

[77]  *-76.000.000*, 1992

[78]  *-157.000.000*, 1992
"Ottovolante. Per una collezione d'arte contemporanea,"
curated by Attilio Pizzigoni and Francesco Rossi,
GAMeC – Galleria d'Arte Moderna e Contemporanea
di Bergamo, June 6–July 26, 1992 (group show)

[79]  *-74.400.000*, 1996

[80] ***Esaurita*, 1992**
Black and white photographic print
35.6 × 27.9 cm

One day I found myself with a ballpoint pen that had run out of ink. I think I'd never finished a pen or pencil before. I was so surprised that it happened to me! I had it in my pocket. I met my gallerist Massimo De Carlo and asked him: "So, has it ever happened to you?" Blah blah blah blah blah. I thought it would be nice to do something with it, and that it would also be interesting to sell it, but Massimo didn't think it was possible. So as a bet I said that I would prove I could sell it. I took the pen, took the photo, which also became the cover of the Italian art magazine *Juliet*, then I found the collector and we sold it. The image evokes a state of mind of mine. Sometimes you feel drained and don't know what to do, and you're also aware that you're easily replaceable.

[81] ***Hotline*, 1994**
Printed cards
C. 6 × 10 cm each

One of many experiments. I've always been fascinated by the theme of death. It's stronger than me. I found a card with a hotline phone number in case you get a bit burned out and need support. I printed off copies, made a stack of them and put them in the gallery. Anyone who wanted could take one.

[82] ***Untitled*, 1996**
2 chairs, Nutella
Lifesize

I created these chairs slathered with Nutella for a group show in New York. That's how I discovered that if you spread it with a brush, Nutella becomes a kind of fur, but it always remains a bit damp. So if someone sat on it... Anyway, that's your problem, if you sit on the art!
I liked the idea of appropriating an object by applying another material to it, and I did two or three works using a food product. Another is *I Found My Love in Portofino* (1994), where I put some mice in with a Bel Paese cheese.
I also wanted to make soccer balls out of concrete and leave them around on a beach. Like these chairs, it would have been rather a malicious work.

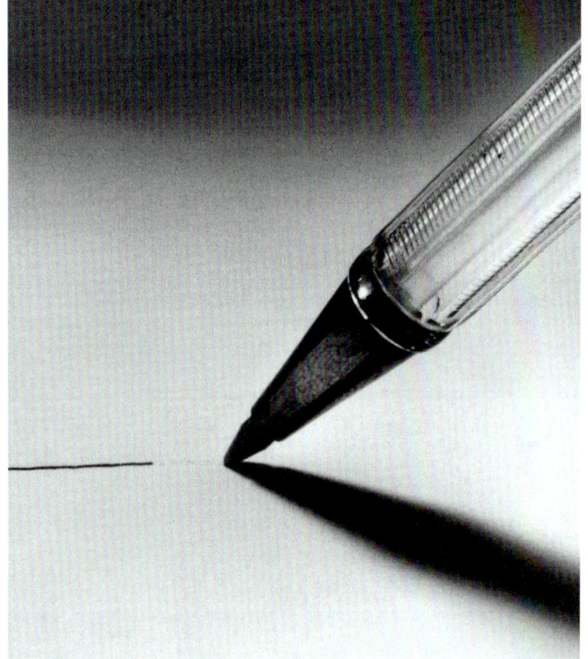

[80]

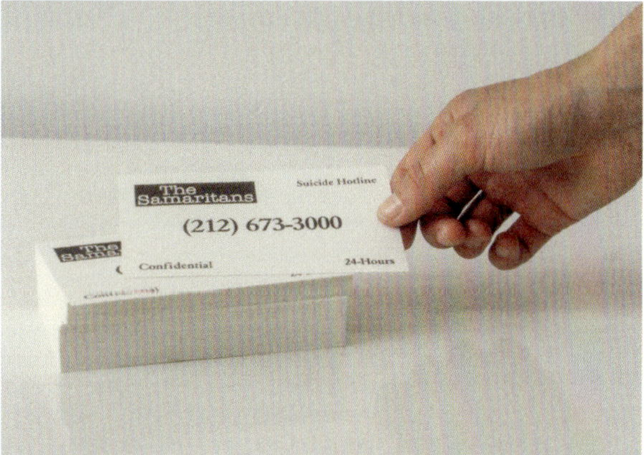



[81]

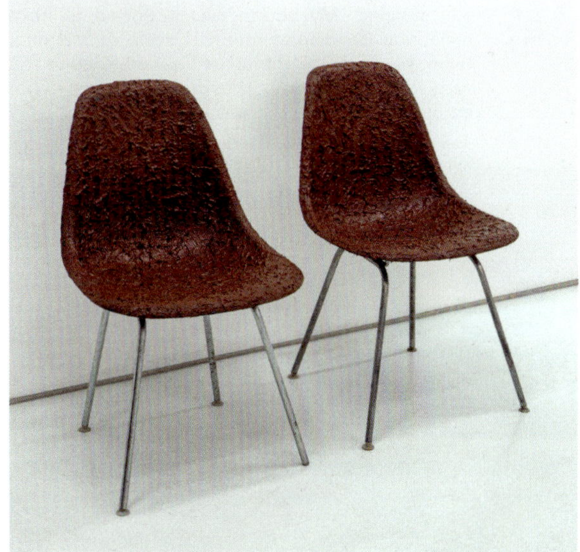

[82]

[80]    *Esaurita*, 1992

[81]    *Hotline*, 1994

[82]    *Untitled*, 1996
"Departure Lounge," Clocktower Gallery (run by P.S.1 Contemporary Art Center), New York, May 3–June 30, 1996 (group show)

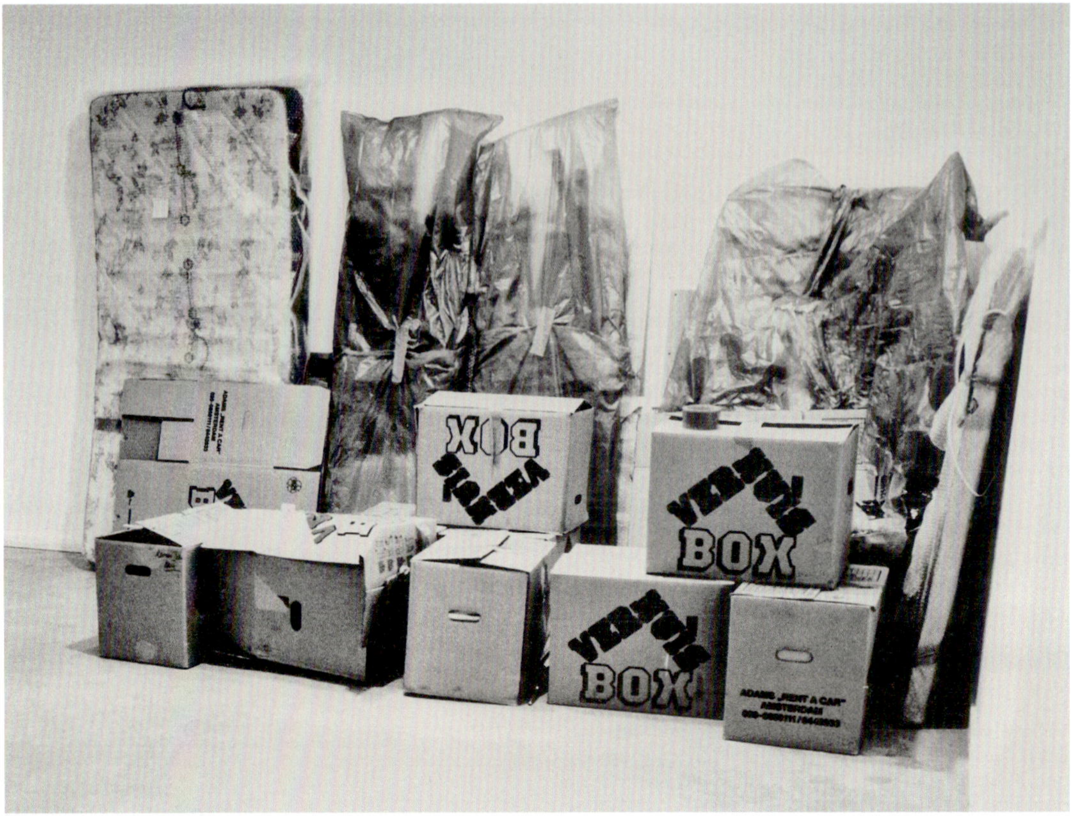

[83]

144

[83] **Another Fucking Readymade**, 1996
Crated and wrapped gallery
contents
Environmental dimension

The theft I did in Amsterdam was more of a sur-vival tactic. De Appel had asked me to prepare a project in two weeks. It usually takes me six months to come up with something. I just took the path of the least resistance, by doing the quickest and easiest thing. I stole from a near-by gallery, the Galerie Bloom. But it wasn't re-ally stealing. My action was intended to be a reflection on displacement. I stole everything, from the works by the artist Paul de Reus to the furnishings, including the garbage cans. I got caught, and before the vernissage all the objects were returned to where they came from. Only a photo remains as a record of the operation, showing the objects packed up and some boxes stacked at de Appel.

[84] **Untitled**, 1996
Exact replicas of adjacent works by John Armleder, fabricated on instructions of the artist for the exhibition "Cabin de bain" in Fribourg, 1996

John Armleder was curating an exhibition in a swimming pool in Fribourg, Switzerland, and asked me to take part. I told him I would do his same piece over again, which occupied two changing cabins. In one there was a picture hanging, in the other there were stacked coat racks with mirrors. I created a duplicate and then turned the principle into a method, since the following year I applied the idea to "Moi-Même-Soi-Même," Carsten Höller's exhibition in Paris. In that case I created even more confusion, be-cause you entered a gallery and saw an exhibi-tion, then you left to go to the gallery next door and there you found the same exhibition.

[83]    *Another Fucking Readymade*, 1996
"Crap Shoot," curated by Annie Fletcher, Nina Folkersma, Clive Kellner, Kay C. Pallister, and Adam Szymczyk, de Appel, Amsterdam, April 12–May 19, 1996 (group show). Work removed before opening

[84]    *Untitled*, 1996
"Cabin de bain," curated by John Armleder, Piscine de la Motta, Fribourg, 1996 (group show)

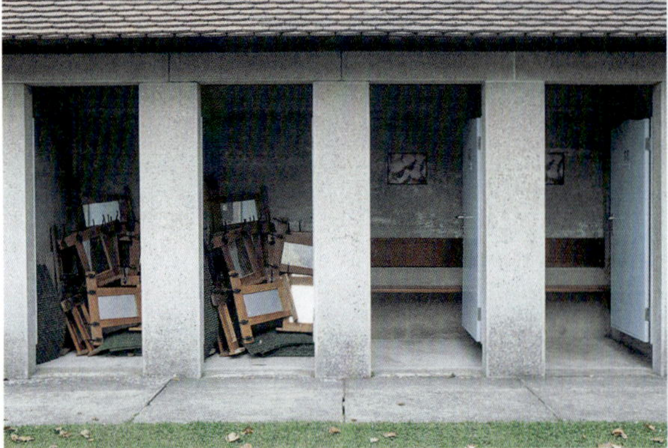

[84]

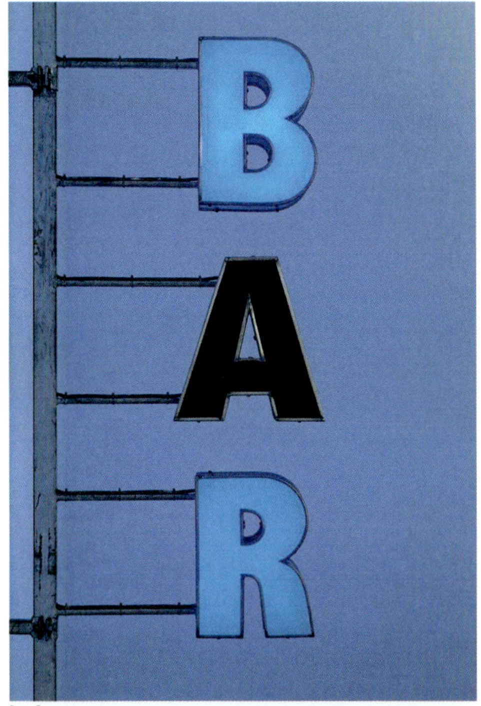

[85.1]

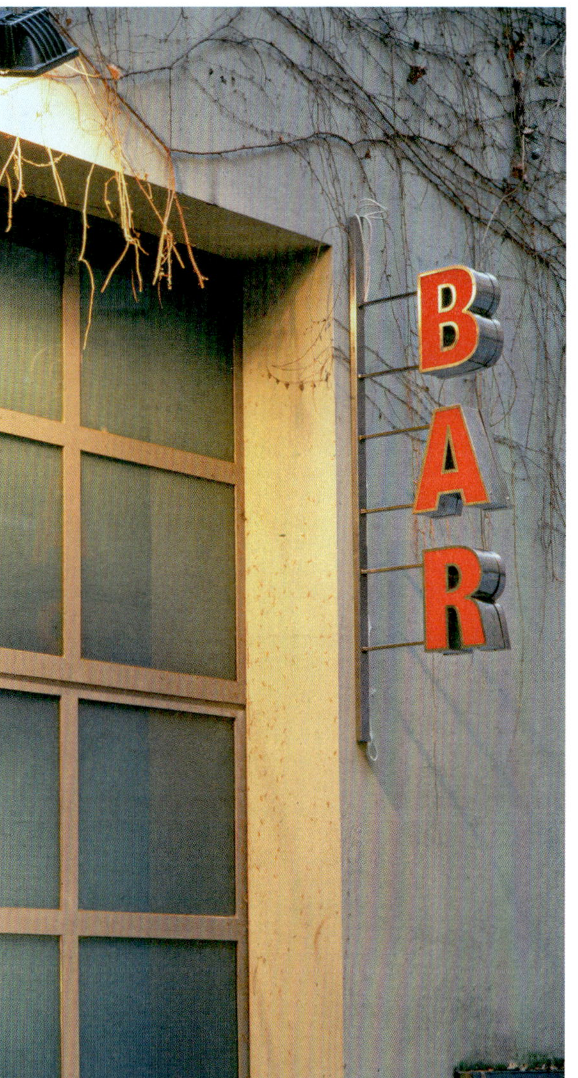

[85.2]

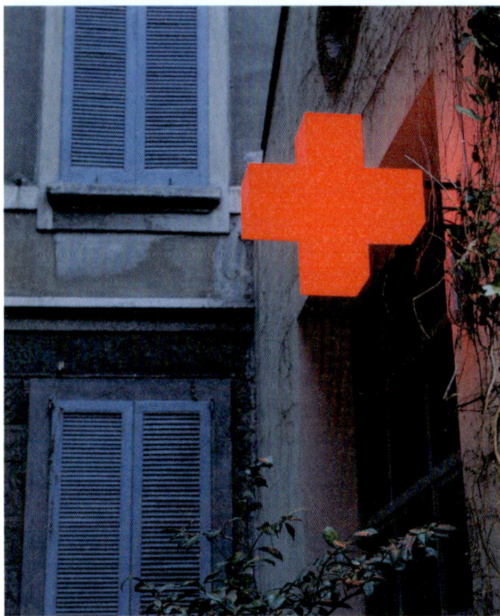

[86]

[85.1]  *Untitled*, 1997
"Odisseo (Ulysses)," curated by Giacinto Di Pietrantonio,
Stadio della Vittoria, Bari, May 1–June 23, 1997 (group
show)

[85.2]  *Untitled*, 1997
"Light Show," Galleria Massimo De Carlo, Milan, 1997
(group show)

[86]  *Untitled*, 1997
"Light Show," Galleria Massimo De Carlo, Milan, 1997
(group show)

[85.1]  **Untitled**, **1997**
Plexiglas, neon, stainless steel
160.8 × 54 × 16 cm

[85.2]  **Untitled**, **1997**
[Titolo iniziale: *Bar Bocconi*]
Plexiglas, neon, stainless steel
160.8 × 54 × 16 cm

[86]  **Untitled**, **1997**
Plexiglas, neon
60 × 60 × 18 cm

For a group show in Bari, at the local stadium, I
placed the sign "Bar" outside the space. The idea
was to confuse visitors, and it worked: people
came in and ordered a coffee.
I made a version in Milan at Massimo De Carlo's
gallery, which was in Via Bocconi at the time, initially calling it *Bar Bocconi*. I also created another variant that looked like a pharmacy sign. They
were all misleading signs.

[87] **_Moi-Même-Soi-Même_, 1997**
Exact replica of exhibition installation by
Carsten Höller "Moi-Même-Soi-Même,"
Air de Paris, Paris, May 24–July 19, 1997,
at the Galerie Emmanuel Perrotin, Paris,
same dates

In 1997, I created an exact replica of Carsten Höller's exhibition "Moi-Même-Soi-Même" in Paris at the gallery Air de Paris. Carsten and I had met the year before, I think, at the exhibition "Traffic" in Bordeaux. Like many of the other artists who participated in that exhibition, we discovered that we had much in common, and we found it quite natural to collaborate on some occasions. For me, at that time, collaboration had to do with simply admitting my inadequacy: I wanted to work with people who were better than me. And it was also a political statement, even though I hate describing it explicitly that way, but I grew up believing there was a strange power in numbers and that artists had to work together. For Carsten, I think, collaboration had more to do with a scientific model of research: his interest in working with other artists derived from his training as an entomologist. (By the way, I have always believed that stated professional background to be just one of Carsten's carefully engineered myths.) When Carsten worked with other artists—such as Philippe Parreno, Rirkrit Tiravanija, Rosemarie Trockel—it always felt like he was putting together a team of visionary thinkers, a pooling of knowledge that seemed to operate like the think tanks of researchers and scientists in universities and labs.

Then again, technically, Carsten and I didn't really collaborate. I simply copied him, perfectly reconstructing his exhibition. Obviously, in order to do so, I had to ask for his permission, and Carsten was very generous—he even put me in touch with his fabricators so that the two shows could be literally identical.

The two exhibitions opened on the same night—his at Air de Paris, mine at Galerie Perrotin; the two galleries were located next to each other on Rue Louise Weiss in Paris. The spaces were identical, symmetrical modules: simple, rather plain white cubes, with that industrial feel that only French utilitarian architecture has. If you visited my show first, then Carsten's would appear to be a replica of mine. And if you first visited Carsten's, I would look like some lazy student who had to copy his friend's paper to be able to pass an exam.

For all the talk about the death of the author, I have always found the art world to be rather conservative on the myth of originality. Yet this wasn't even the issue that concerned me; I was more interested in finding the artistic equivalent of a knockoff. And so much of Carsten's work is about seeing double, so it seemed only natural to copy him.

Some people found the whole idea of reproducing the show quite mean and cynical, but then again, do ethics apply to photocopy machines? Personally, I saw it more as a form of xerox Buddhism or a small experiment in democracy: I wanted Carsten and me to be perfectly equal. Carsten's work has always been about the future, and I'd like to think of the future as a place where anybody can become anybody else. A future in which identity theft will turn into existential timesharing. Which, in other words, is like saying that a rose is a rose is a rose. And, most important, that a rose has no teeth.

["Double," text published in _Carsten Höller: Experience_, ed. Massimiliano Gioni, exhibition catalog (New York, New Museum, October 26, 2011–January 15, 2012) (New York: Skira Rizzoli, 2011), 79–80]

146

[87]     _Moi-Même-Soi-Même_, 1997
"Moi-Même-Soi-Même," Galerie Emmanuel Perrotin, Paris, May 24–July 19, 1997 (solo show)

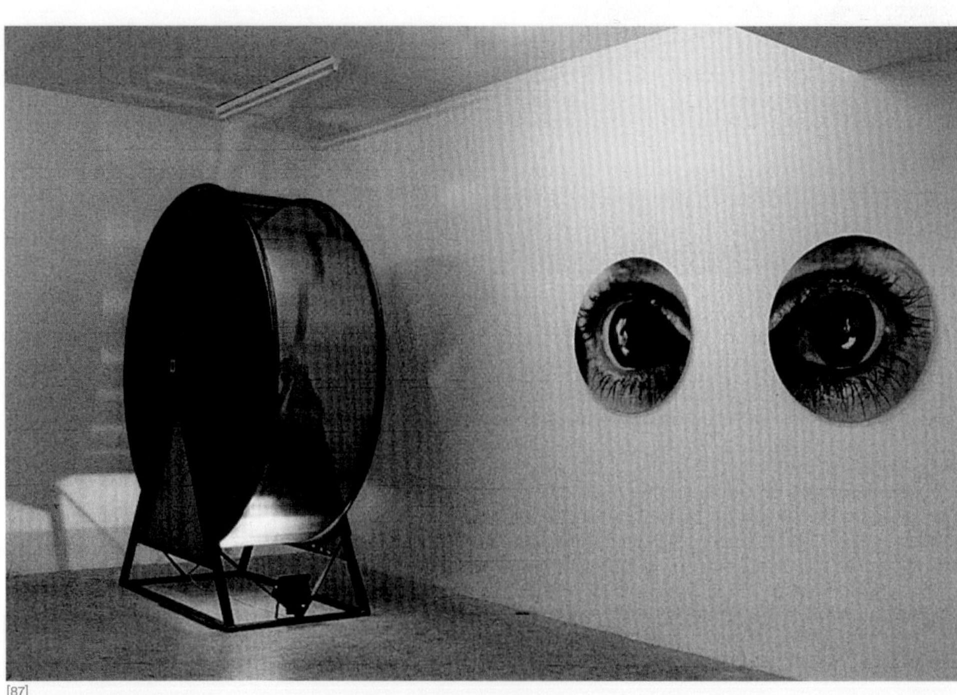

[87]

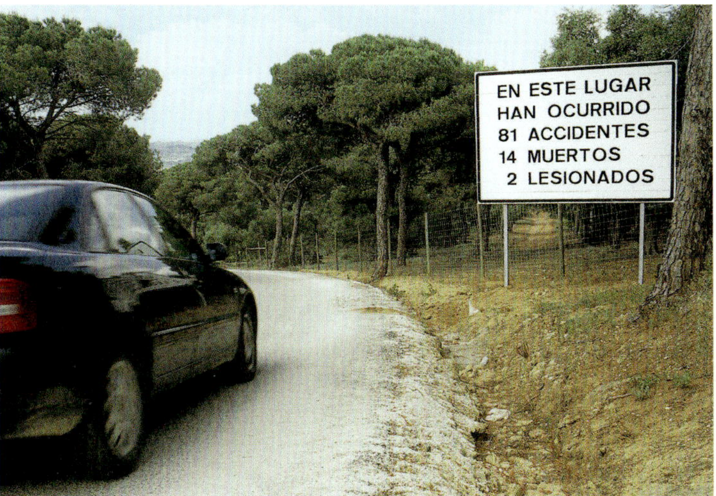



[88]

[88]  *Untitled*, 2001
Installation near the
Fundación NMAC –
Montenmedio
Contemporánea, Vejer
de la Frontera, 2001

[89]  *Untitled*, 2001

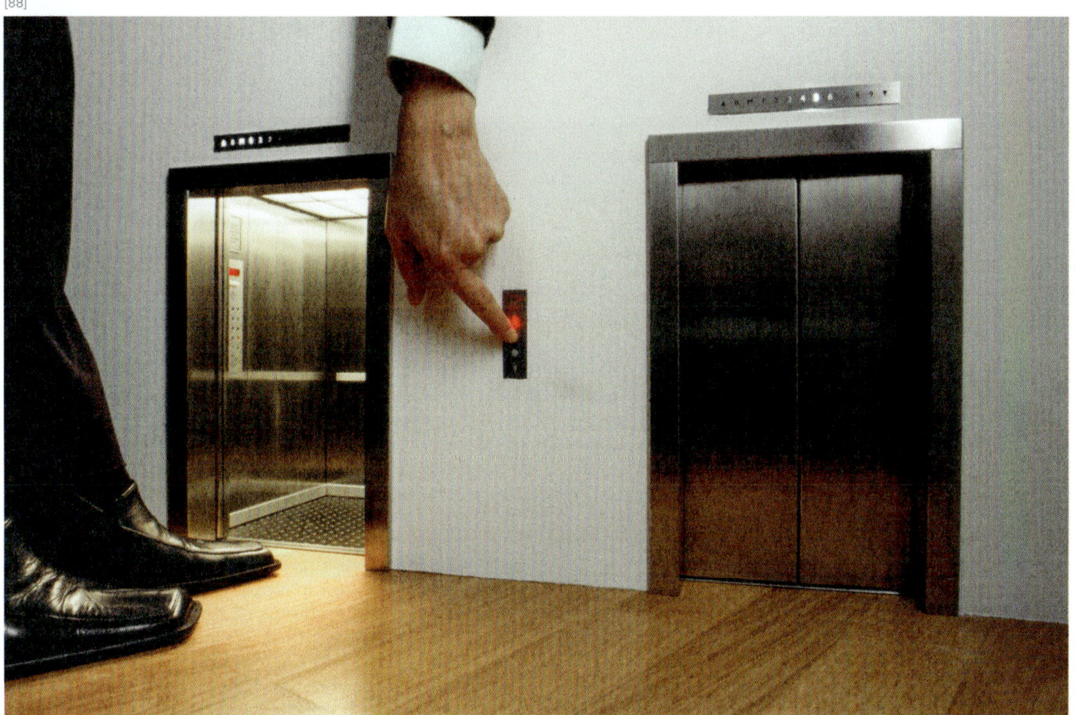

[89]

[88]  **Untitled, 2001**
Aluminum panel
200 × 300 cm

For a Spanish foundation that makes site-spe-cific projects, I used a sign I had seen in Cuba. On a road with little traffic I had one installed that read, "En este lugar han ocurrido 81 acci-dentes 14 muertos 2 lesionados," meaning, "In this place there have been 81 accidents with 14 deaths and 2 injured." A warning not to speed. It appealed to me.

[89]  **Untitled, 2001**
Stainless steel, wood, electric motor, light, bell, computer
59.7 × 85.4 × 47.3 cm

Like stairs, which I haven't yet been able to em-body in a work, I always thought about the eleva-tor. I liked the idea of making the elevator a way of appropriating a whole building without seeing it. An elevator, even on the ground floor or the first floor, makes you imagine many floors.
The elevators in my work are identical to real ones, but in miniature. It's all timed: the numbers in the panels above the doors light up as if the elevators were going up and down, stopping at one floor and then traveling on again.
People have asked me a lot of questions about the elevators and I never really knew what to say. They've been interpreted in many ways. They might stand for working without actually doing anything.

MAURIZIO CATTELAN
1-2/210 3192
175
DATE JUNE 5 2004
PAY TO THE ORDER OF BETH SWOFFORD
$ 1
ONE DOLLAR
DOLLARS
CHASE
The Chase Manhattan Bank
Worldwide Consumer Banking Group
300 Jericho Quadrangle
Jericho, NY 11753
MEMO 25TH ANN. A. AUCTION
SAFETY PAPER

[90]

[90] **_Untitled_, 2004**
Check with additions in ink
7 × 15.2 cm

In 2004, a Californian collector, Beth Swofford, was organizing a charity auction for the MOCA in Los Angeles and asked me to join in. As usual, I had no ideas and again I thought of copying from someone better than me. Duchamp came to mind. Among the many things he turned into art are checks, though he didn't use a real check but created a fake that looks realistic at a glance. Instead, I signed a real dollar check, which of course was never cashed, otherwise the work would have disappeared. It was sold for 15,000 dollars. Over the years I did others, always for a dollar and always to contribute to charity auctions for American museums.

The principle is the same as the banana in _Comedian_ (2019). You have an object and it's you who add value to it. Without the signature, the check is just a piece of paper, but in finance as in art, an autograph makes all the difference.

[91] **"The Artist Is Present," 2018**
Group show organized by Gucci and curated by Maurizio Cattelan and Alessandro Michele, Yuz Museum, Shanghai, October 11–December 16, 2018

Alessandro Michele, at that time Artistic Director of Gucci, came to me one day with this "crazy" idea that he wanted to host an exhibition in Shanghai to discuss the value of copying. And I think he asked me because fashion in past years has been fighting against counterfeit products, while art had more often embraced and accepted appropriation as a pure creative act. We spoke different languages, but we were both fascinated witnesses to the overcoming of originality in our contemporary society. We shared ideas about iconography and icons. I'd say that he works with the former, I with the latter. We met halfway, where iconography meets icons and where celebrated originals become timeless icons through a simple act of repetition and propagation.

Although the concept of the exhibition was undoubtedly evolved under Western philosophy, the issue of copying is universal. We started by questioning the most sacred principles of art in modernity: originality, truth, and identity. How can this trinity be reached through the act of repetition, and how can the originals themselves be preserved through copies? With "The Artist Is Present," Alessandro and I tried to trace a path where nothing was exactly what it seemed, where appropriation was needed to see things more clearly, and where we have to doubt our convictions as being possibly false.

Holding the exhibition in Shanghai was important, because the city allowed for an encounter between civilizations that conceive the copy in profoundly different ways. Various cultures, not only Chinese but Far Eastern in general, played an important part in the conception of "The Artist Is Present." If time is circular, there is the loss of the notion of progress, of old versus new. Reincarnation is the first premise in order to understand the equation "copy=original" that lies behind the entire show.

We also wanted to play with an old stereotype about Shanghai and China, and go beyond the traditional idea of counterfeiting, by proposing that the appreciation of a work is based on an engagement with the ideas behind the work itself, rather than on simple aesthetic gratification. With these concepts in mind, from the beginning we tried to build the architecture of the exhibition on a vision of circularity. While the space of the Yuz Museum is incredible, we decided for a great operation of imagining a new space within the space. We worked with architects and builders to create a path for the viewers to get lost inside our heads for a while. Obviously this would not have been possible without a beautiful space to start from.

The works really came from all over the world, from Mexico to Hong Kong by way of Iceland. Each room in the exhibition was a variation on the theme. Some of the works openly came to terms with the copy-original relationship, in the widest possible range of its manifestations in art, while others were quite distant from the idea, so much so that it was hard to justify their inclusion seen in isolation from the whole visual complex. This was true starting from the exhibition title itself. Marina Abramović's "The Artist Is Present," held at the MoMA in 2010, was the mother of every contemporary art show in the following years. It's the one that everyone knew. Thanks to the images that presented the show in the media, Marina had become a contemporary Virgin Mary, a powerful and venerated icon. Copying the title and drawing inspiration from the MoMA advertising campaign seemed the most natural thing to do for an exhibition that claimed to be the realm of copying in all its possible forms. Marina and her practice had nothing to do with the exhibition, but we were interested in testing the power of an image and a title presented in a completely different context, as in the "Shit and Die" exhibition in Turin, which I curated with Myriam Ben Salah and Marta Papini in 2014. In this way, the exhibition project overcame the physical boundaries of the exhibition itself and became part of the media discussion. Our intention was to give a second life to things that had already happened by copying them. The presence of the copy instead of the original, so that the copy becomes the original. Which artist wouldn't want to become Marina for a while? Every act of appropriation should not start with a question, but with a statement. In the parish where I spent all my childhood, the priest used to say: "Ask for pardon, not permission." I'm pretty sure Marina shares this vision and understands that to copy is to love.

Sturtevant is without a doubt a significant example of the exercise we wanted to focus on. She didn't like labeling her work "imitation," because her intention was not to create replicas of existing works, but to address the notions of authenticity, artistic celebrity and originality. It was precisely the difference between the two works, the initial one and her own, that interested her. These differences encourage the viewer to go beyond the superficial similarities. When they asked Warhol how he created his works, he always replied: "Ask Elaine Sturtevant." For me, this is where the originality of imitation lies.

Original works of art never existed. What can be seen as postmodern is the end of the concept of originality, and this is especially evident in a time when there is a craving for individual affirmation in the creative crafts. But even in the Renaissance, one of the most creative ages, originality had no value. In the end, the best artist is always the one who imitates best.

Years before "The Artist Is Present," I visited Dafen, a village in China known since 1989 as a place to get perfect replicas of art masterpieces, and ever since I've been tormented by a vision that this show enabled me to realize: a replica of the Sistine Chapel on a 1:6 scale. I still had the business cards of Dafen's finest painters, and I took them out of the drawer and called some of them to create a real work "made in China" (*Untitled*, 2018). Through this work, a masterpiece is made accessible on a human scale and allows everyone to see the Sistine Chapel in a closer and unrestricted view. If the greatest wish of humanity is to become God, the ultimate aspiration of imitation is to become original. The truth is that, within these scaled-down walls, we can all be more useful to God.

[Artists exhibited: John Ahearn (with Rigoberto Torres), John Armleder, Nina Beier, Brian Belott, Anne Collier, Jose Dávila, Wim Delvoye, Eric Doeringer, Sayre Gomez, Andy Hung Chi-Kin, Matt Johnson, Jamian Juliano-Villani, Kapwani Kiwanga, Ragnar Kjartansson, Josh Kline, Louise Lawler, Margaret Lee, Hannah Levy, Ma Jun, Nevine Mahmoud, Aleksandra Mir, Pentti Monkkonen, Philippe Parreno, Yan Pei-Ming, Lu Pingyuan, Jon Rafman, Mika Rottenberg, Reena Spaulings, Sturtevant, Superflex, Oscar Tuazon, Kaari Upson, Gillian Wearing, Lawrence Weiner, Christopher Williams, XU ZHEN®, Damon Zucconi]



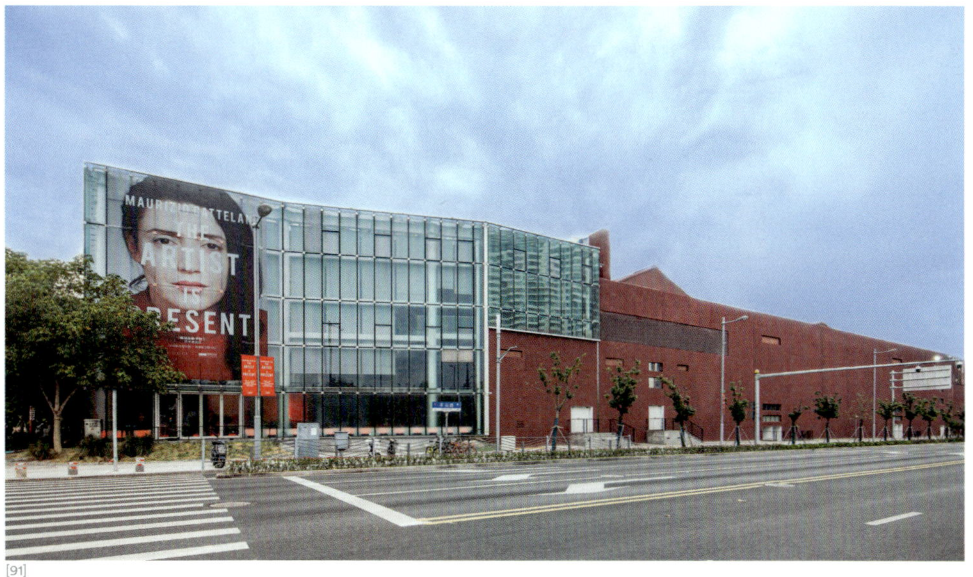

[91]

[90]   *Untitled*, 2004

[91]   Banner of "The Artist Is Present" exhibition on the exterior of the Yuz Museum, Shanghai, 2018

[92] *Comedian*, 2019
Banana, duct tape
Variable dimensions

[93] *Clown*, 2024
Watercolor on Fabriano paper, collage
of UV-printed Japanese paper, rubber
stamped
41.9 × 47 cm
Edition
Series of 20 variants

The banana of *Comedian* is exactly like an apple
for Cézanne: the lowest common denominator
that everybody recognizes. But you need to alter
its condition. Cézanne does it with brushstrokes,
I do it with gaffer tape. Why do some people
pay millions for Cézanne's apples? You don't buy
either apples or bananas, you buy their altered
state as seen through the mind of an artist. If I
am ridiculous, Cézanne is too, which is absolutely okay with me.
One of my biggest frustrations is not being able
to paint. I tried many times in different ways but
I'm the negation of a painter. I can't, that's it. I
have to live with it. I was in New York and I was
going through galleries and looking at auction
results. Painting, painting, painting. Most of
them sold for absurd prices. But I also thought
about the idea of painting and what a painting

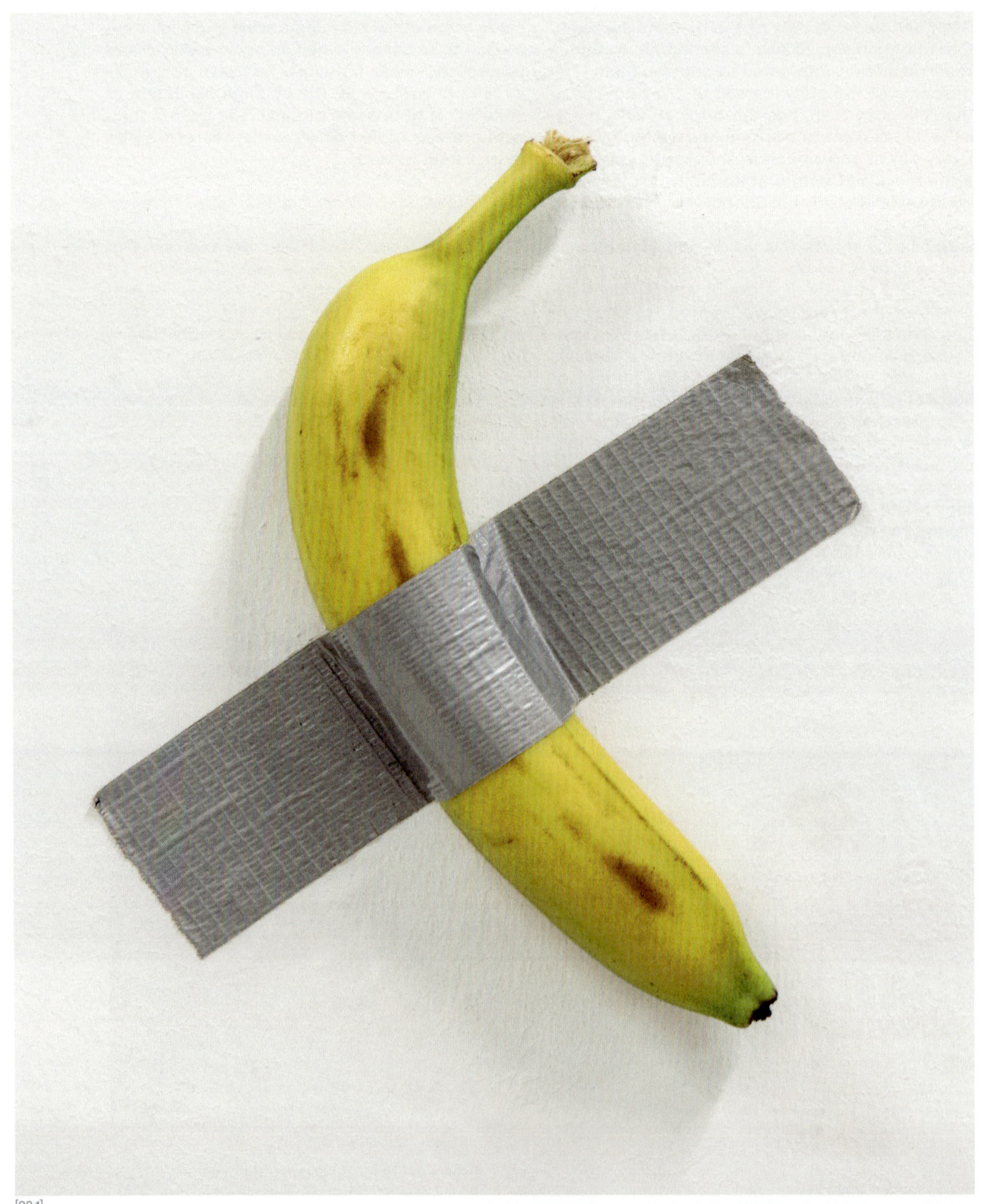

is. A painting is the most recognizable symbolic space in the history of art. Anybody, really anybody, can take a rectangular or square piece of wood, canvas or paper, put something over it—color, shit, straw—and hang it on the wall, and whoever sees it will call it a painting. Never mind good or bad. So I thought about something that, without being a painting, could compete with a painting. Something that anybody could see and know what it was. I think everybody knows what a banana is.

My first attempt was with an eggplant. It didn't work out. This piece took me a year. It became an obsession. I produced many replicas, our of different materials. I played with a banana for a few months, first of plastic, then of metal, but no version convinced me enough to show it. I still have some of those tests at home. At one point, the simpler idea won. Why not present a banana as it was, without reinterpretations? It worked to such an extent that others found it beneficial to appropriate it. After all, art is a matter of recycling, a sort of funny relay between incompetents.

A comedian is not an actor, but not a normal person either. A comedian lives in limbo between fiction and reality, and is someone who can fail very easily. A comedian is doomed to make people laugh—an actor has the option of making people cry. *Comedian* is not a painting.

It's between conceptual art and a joke. Conceptual art doesn't have any emotion. A joke normally doesn't usually carry any big thought. Placed in between, *Comedian* is a sincere commentary and reflection on what we value. At art fairs, speed and business reign, so I saw it like this: if I had to be at a fair, I could sell a banana like others sell their paintings. I could play within the system, but with my own rules. I couldn't say how people would react but I hoped a work like this would break up the normal viewing habits and open a discussion on what really matters. We're surrounded by conversations based on immaterial structures, social values, and hierarchies that we created, but usually we prefer to forget this. It's like being anesthetized.

All ideologies have symbols: an elephant, a donkey, a hammer and sickle... Perhaps it's now time for the banana to find its own republic.

*Comedian* was turned into an edition, *Clown*: the image of a banana peel posted on the wall with a piece of tape with the logo of a museum on it. There are a number of versions, each bearing the name of a different museum. An idea like the Museum League scarves.

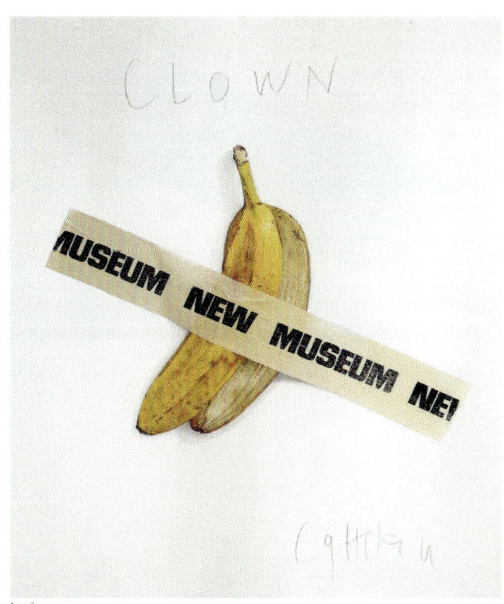


[93]

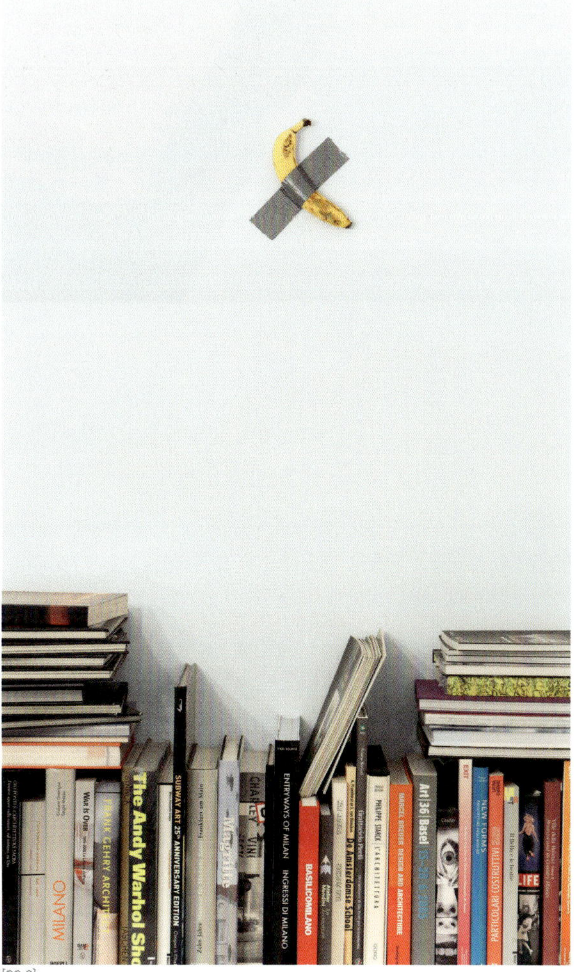

[92.1]  *Comedian*, 2019

[93]  *Clown*, 2024

[92.2]  *Comedian*, 2019
Private house, Milan

[92.2]

**[94]** ***BREAD*, 2021**
Artist's book of one hundred US one-dollar
bills bound in a fabric hardcover volume
inserted in a slipcase set in a box; published by Three Star Books, Paris
Pages: 6.6 × 15.5 cm each;
closed book: 7.6 × 15.9 × 1.9 cm; slipcase:
8.3 × 16.1 × 2.5 cm; box: 16.7 × 22,7 × 3.8 cm

**[95]** ***Crumbs*, 2025**
Acrylic on paper, wood frame with
gold finish
70 × 50 cm

*BREAD* is *Comedian* (2019) in the paper version
and edition. I collected a 100-dollar bills in perfect condition and bound them in red cloth: you
flip through them like a book, but it costs 500
dollars. It's less pop than *Comedian*, but the concept is the same.
*Crumbs* are miniature one-dollar bills drawn by
hand. A magnifying glass is needed to see them.

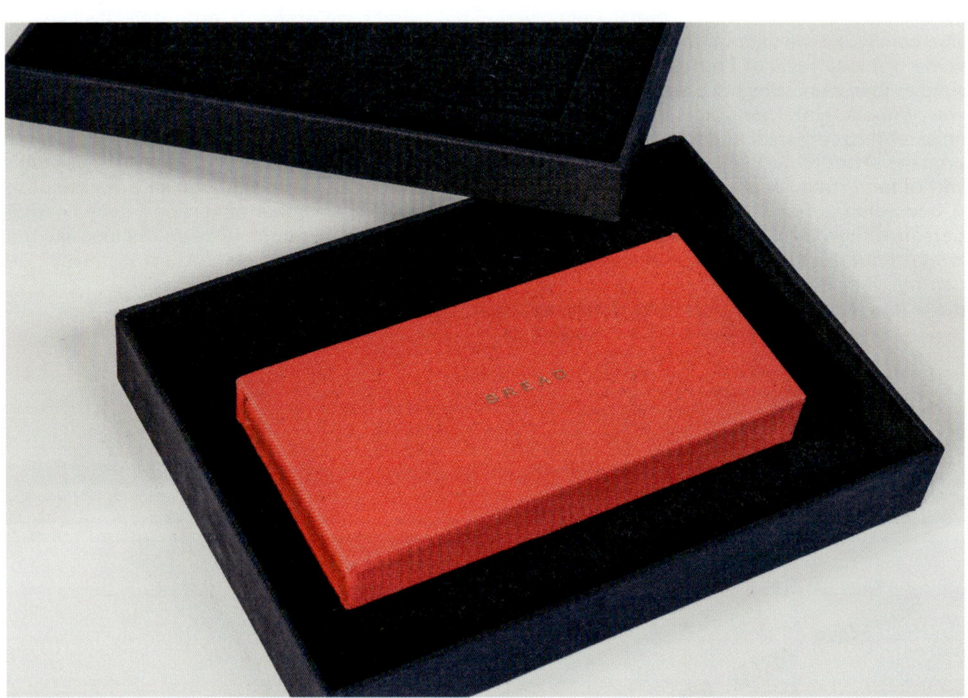

[94.1]

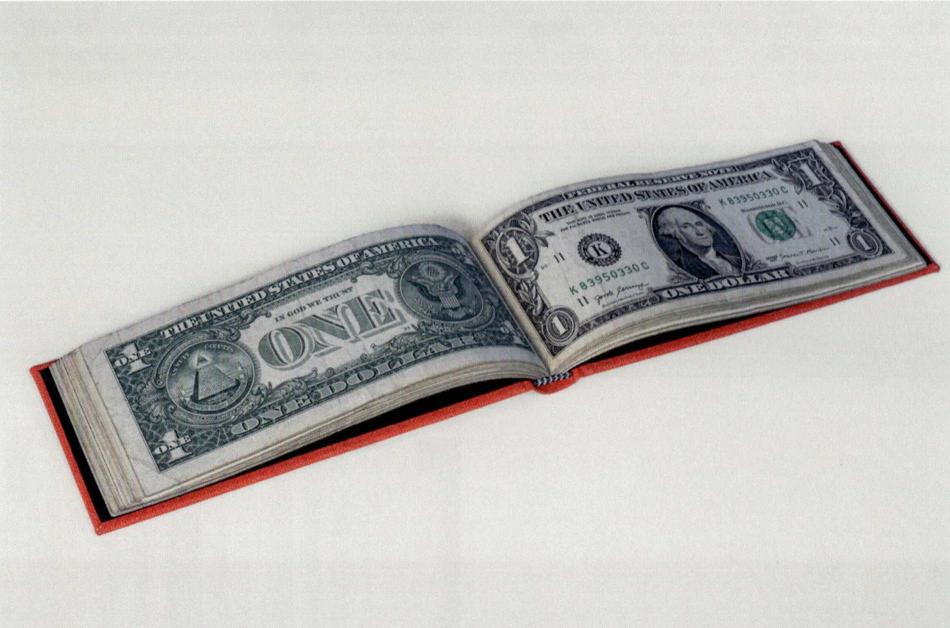

[94.2]

152

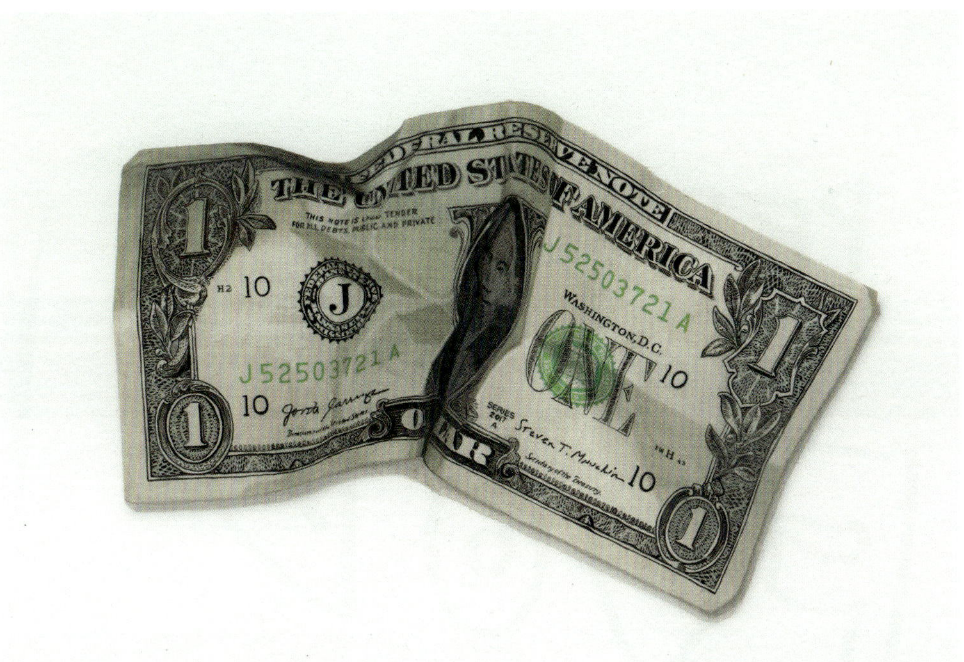

[95.1]

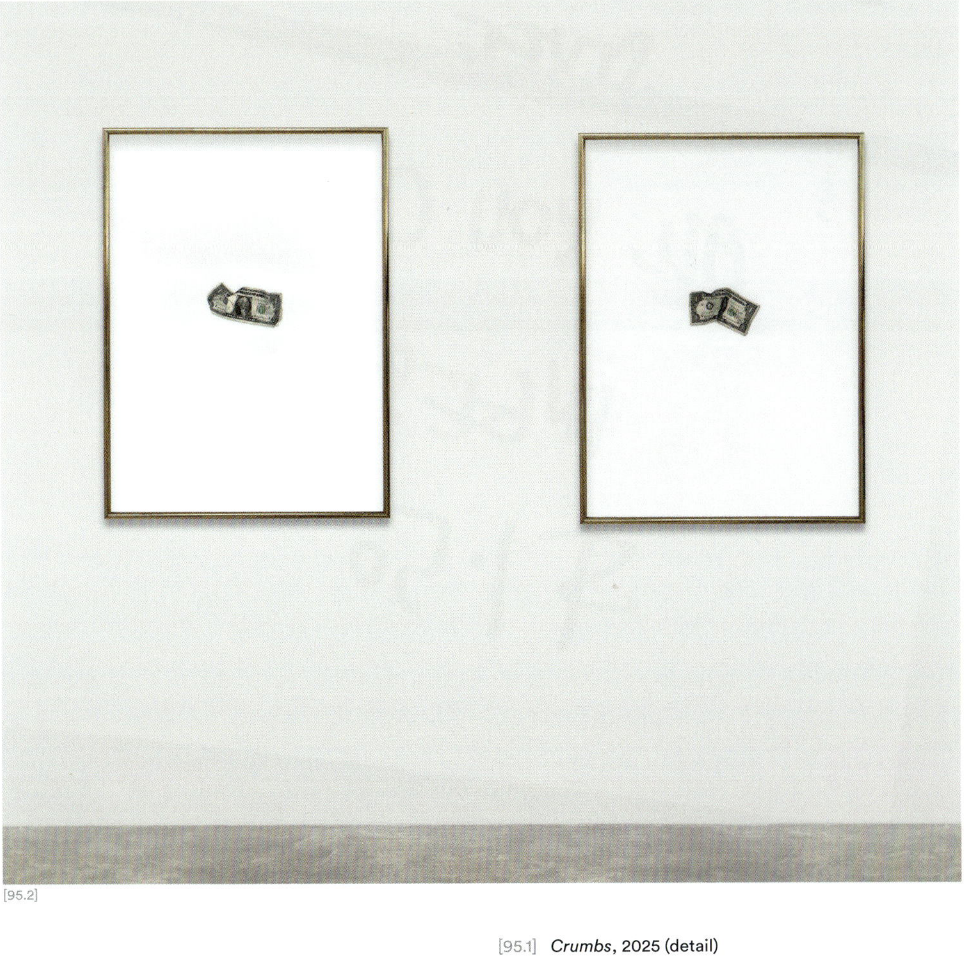

[95.2]



[95.1]  *Crumbs*, 2025 (detail)

[94.1-2]  *BREAD*, 2021

[95.2]  *Crumbs*, 2025

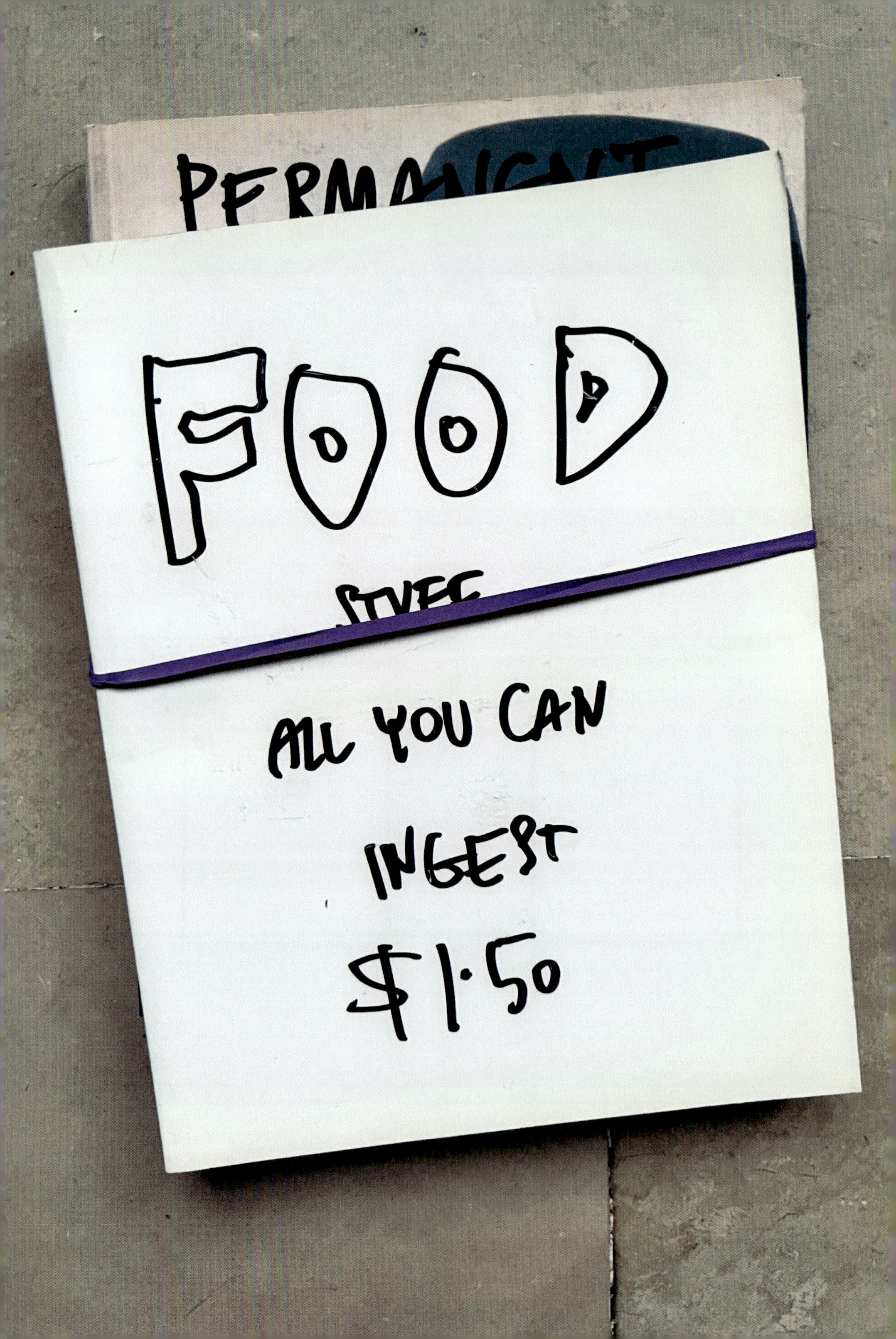

PERMANENT
FOOD
STUFF
ALL YOU CAN
INGEST
$1·50

When I was a kid, my neighbors were nearly all Jewish. There were no sacred images in their homes, while my parents had plastered our walls with saints and Madonnas. Maybe my obsession with images comes from this, from those bare houses and my family's superstition. I learned to fear icons, and at the same time I realized you can't trust images. On the other hand, while I'm well aware that most of our childhood is preserved not in photos but in certain types of cookies, a quality of light, scents or the textures of carpets, as Proust teaches us, and although this is true of my memories, it's not the way I think.

The power of images lies in their seduction. What fascinates me most is that we use them as if they were real, but they aren't. Even though we know this, we continue to be taken in. I believe it's intrinsic to human nature: the need to believe what we see. In a world that feeds on consumerism and images, and consumes images that disappear or are digested and return to the dust they came from, reality and image come together in a whole that is difficult to break down. Think of a chef who lives all day depending on the dishes that will disappear into your stomach that night. His creations will be photographed and eaten. The images will be as real as the flavor of those dishes, if you can remake them at home. The image is the reality, even the image that we keep in mind after seeing something beautiful. Then our memory will soon start to distort it, until in the end it's nothing like the real thing.

The question is, where does an image take place? In your head or in front of your eyes? And can an idea be an image for more people instead of just myself? I limit myself to looking for images that arouse an instinctive gut reaction, amid the flood of useless information that overwhelms us every day. From the very beginning, my sculptures are conceived as images, and in this form they go on living in the media. If they're powerful at first glance, they'll work. Actually, calling them sculptures sounds strange to me. It's not a question of the medium but of images. I never use my hands to create my works. It is not the sculptures but the images that interest me. I've never handled a chisel, never had a studio.

Ever since there's been art, there's been iconoclasm. Images are always the butts of attacks, sometimes symbolic, at others physical. By contrast, I'm affected by an acute form of iconophilia. If I don't see at least a hundred images a day, my face comes out in boils. The images never sleep, and I feed off them constantly. It's my way of interpreting reality, of discovering what I don't know and also my way of getting bored with reality. And as I look at all those images, I realize that an image without content deteriorates very quickly and is bound to vanish. But the best images are the ones that last, that speak of the stranger inside us.

Images are a statistical variant of reality. I'm interested in the sort of things we encounter every day: a thought, something seen on television or read in a newspaper, or something that sticks in your mind while you're browsing the internet. Images have the power to encapsulate the present and perhaps turn it into an anticipation of the future. Maybe my works are just a magnifying glass that makes you see the most hidden details of reality.

I've been called a conceptual artist, but I don't know what that means. I don't think about what I do. I go by images. Over time I've become positive that the best images appear only when I don't think. If I were asked what my works are about, I couldn't say. I work so that the image comes first. Thinking always follows, and anyway I find thinking very boring.

I'm interested in images, no matter whether they're mine or somebody else's. In the end, we're all part of the same digestive system. Everyone consumes images and ideas how they like and spits them out completely transformed and enriched. Many things I have done have been chewed up and digested by others. The important thing is to get your daily dose of calories.

156

[96]    *Untitled*, **1998**
Olive tree, soil, water, wood and metal structure
800 × 500 × 500 cm

[97]    *Untitled*, **1999**
Wood, soil
Height c. 500 cm

I like it when the work becomes an image. I make a distinction between works that function as an idea or a project—like the soccer memorial wall I did in London (*Untitled*, 1999)—and those that get transformed into a memorable image. These are more readably repeatable, like the tree I made for Manifesta 2 in Luxembourg. It started as something I just wanted to see; a huge clump of earth with a tree growing out of it, as if you could glimpse it from below the ground. When

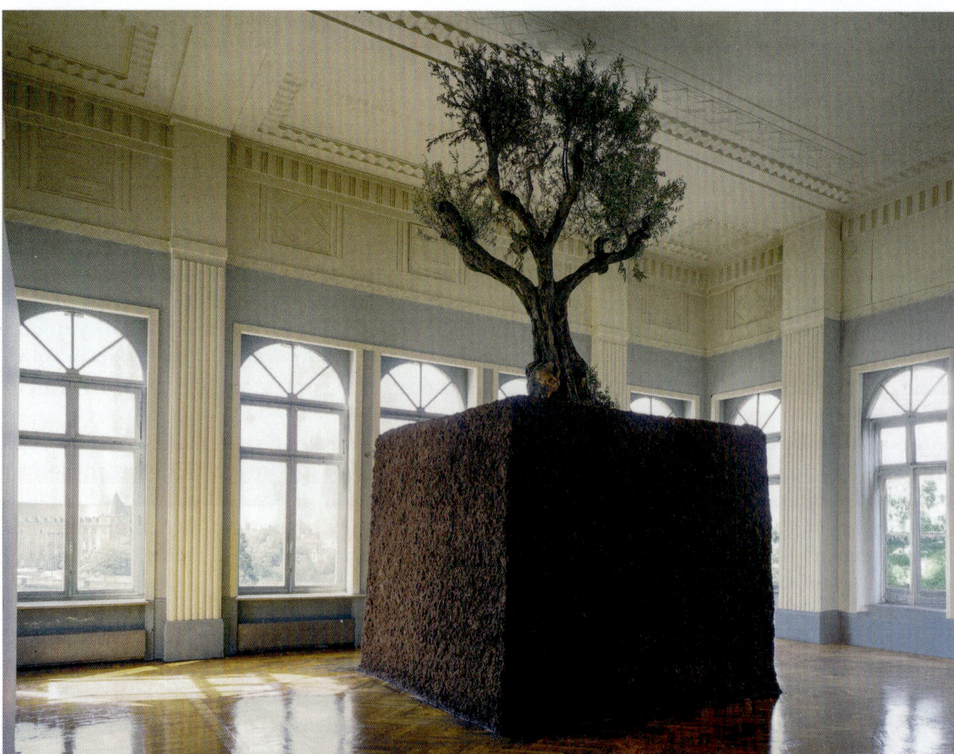

[96.1]

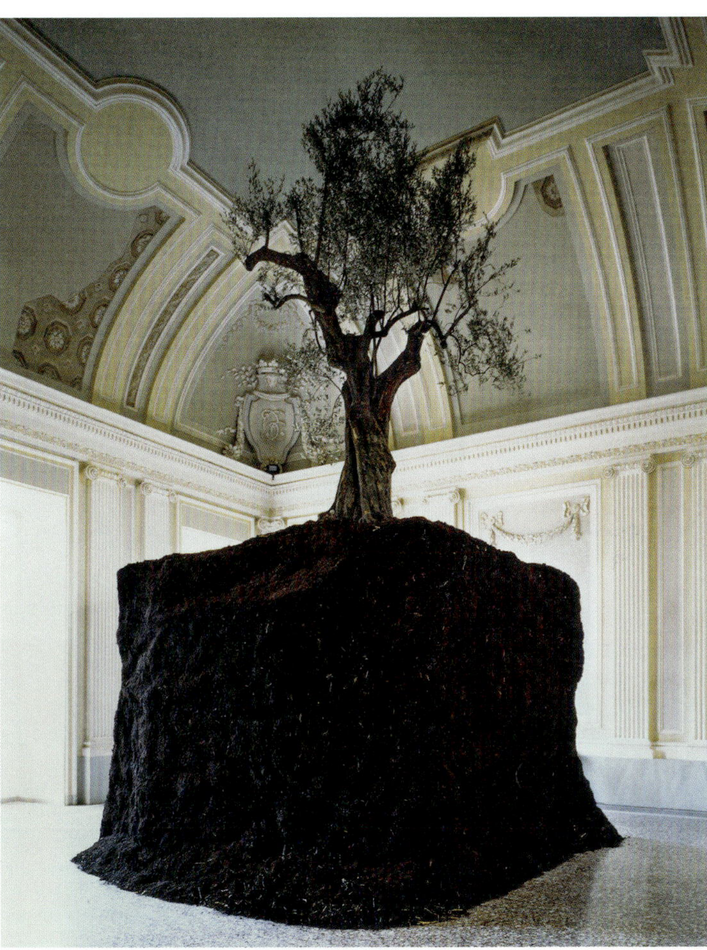

[96.2]



[96.1] *Untitled*, 1998
Manifesta 2, curated by
Robert Fleck, Maria Lind,
and Barbara Vanderlinden,
Luxembourg, June 28–
November 11, 1998 (group
show), installation at the
Casino Luxembourg

[96.2] *Untitled*, 1998
Castello di Rivoli Museo
d'Arte Contemporanea,
Rivoli-Turin, 1998

[97] *Untitled*, 1999
"Zeitwended-Ausblick,"
Rheinisches Landesmuseum
and Kunstmuseum Bonn,
December 4, 1999–June 4,
2000 (group show)

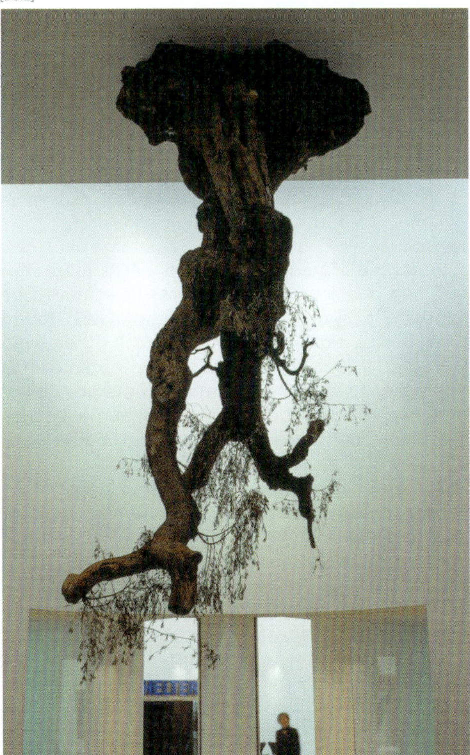

[97]

I first thought of the piece, I imagined a more natural shape than the one they constructed in Luxembourg. They made a cube out of the earth and I found the shape too related to art—but after all, I created this piece over the phone. But when I showed it again at the Castello di Rivoli, in Turin, with a rounder, less rigid base, it worked much better for me.

Since I don't have a studio, I have to work these things out in the public eye. Every time I produce a piece, I show it at the same time. I see the piece for the first time in the exhibition. That's when I assess the failure, if it's a failure. When I arrived in Luxembourg, it was crazy. There were 2,000 kilos of earth on the second floor. There were structural problems, technical problems, organizational problems. Then, when it was done I thought: "Okay, now we'll see what the result is. If I get another chance, I'll want to make it better." It's as if my exhibitions are my studio. I think that many pieces of mine are public failures. Some things could have been better, presented in a different way.

I also tried inverting it. At an exhibition in Bonn I installed the tree upside-down. It's certainly not something that plants like, but over time they show a surprising resilience and capacity for adaptation.

**[98]** *Untitled*, **2004**
Resin, fiberglass, synthetic hair, clothing, rope
Variable dimensions; 130 × 50 × 55 cm each of the 3 figures

I never say anything about my works before they're exhibited. Partly out of superstition, partly because I don't think it's my job to describe or interpret them. In 2004 I was invited to think of a work for Milan by the Fondazione Nicola Trussardi. I chose to work in Piazza XXIV Maggio, on the large oak tree at its center, a tree resembling the ones in fairy tales, as impressive as a skyscraper in the midst of the noisy and relentless flow of traffic. Everything had been negotiated with the authorities and we worked at night. I had a hunch: how long will it last? In my head, the work was like a small urban legend with a tragic ending, perhaps a way of reflecting the present, with its tensions and nightmares. Looking fear in the face perhaps serves to push it away. Anyway, a few hours later the work no longer existed in the piazza, but only in the pages of the newspapers and on television.

I never know where images come from. I only know that in Piazza XXIV Maggio I wanted to send a signal about childhood and violence. Childhood, that strange age when you suffer from traumas and have incredible dreams, is a time I always return to. When you create a work like that you also do it against yourself. And you think: have I exaggerated? I hope not. The knots around the children's necks were not tight and the expressions on their faces almost of resignation. The bodies seemed to levitate, float above the ground rather than hang down. It was an almost angelic image. They looked like living children looking down on us, like three judges or three prophets. The installation showed a condition to which we have forced childhood: from that position childhood looked at us and told us what we're still doing to ourselves and our future. The work represented the way we're treating our dreams. It was an evocation, an inner manifestation, extremely sacred, strangely spiritual. One of the three figures was placed a little higher than the other two. It was a crucifixion, perhaps a ritual sacrifice. The installation was not supposed to draw further attention to me, but only to the world out there.

I did nothing illegal and nothing more inappropriate than a lot of the things that are around us and are there for all to see. It was very important for the work to be exhibited in a public place. That was the reason that made people find it so insufferable. Tucked away safely inside a museum it would have been a huge success; being outside one inevitably made the vision darker. When we hear the news we're certainly shocked, but our emotions are muted and we get accustomed to the atrocity of the images. Art is a matter of distance: you can look away from it, but the thing that disturbs you is still there.

I don't believe in generalizations. In Milan there were people who hated the work and others who would have liked to continue to see it in the square. I was aware of the possibility that someone would be disturbed by it. The public is made up of many stories, everyone brings one. I passed through Piazza XXIV Maggio several times and



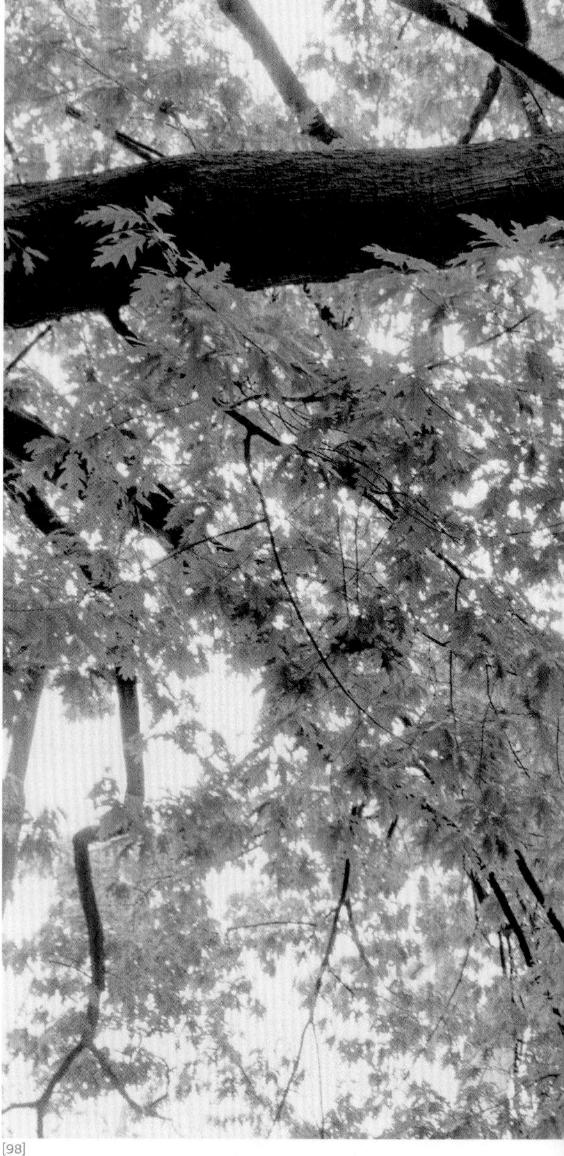

[98]

saw people arguing civilly. Those 40 square meters had come back to life. A result achieved by mistake? Still a good result. People who found time, desire, energy to talk with each other, even the elderly. Everyone expressed their opinion. It's important to shift the attention to the possibility of exchanging opinions, of looking at reality with the wide open eyes of my children. Some people said: "It's an anti-war work." Some else said: "It's in defense of trees." Others said indignantly: "We're for life, not death." If I could have collected those comments all together, I would have considered them the true work of art.

I expected discussion and debate. That the installation also became the subject of a political clash perhaps not, but I think that as a whole the affair was really interesting. Art also has this task, it has to be a catalyst for different opinions, a litmus test of our paranoia. Above all, I was struck by the fact that the work triggered debate about freedom of expression. We live in an age

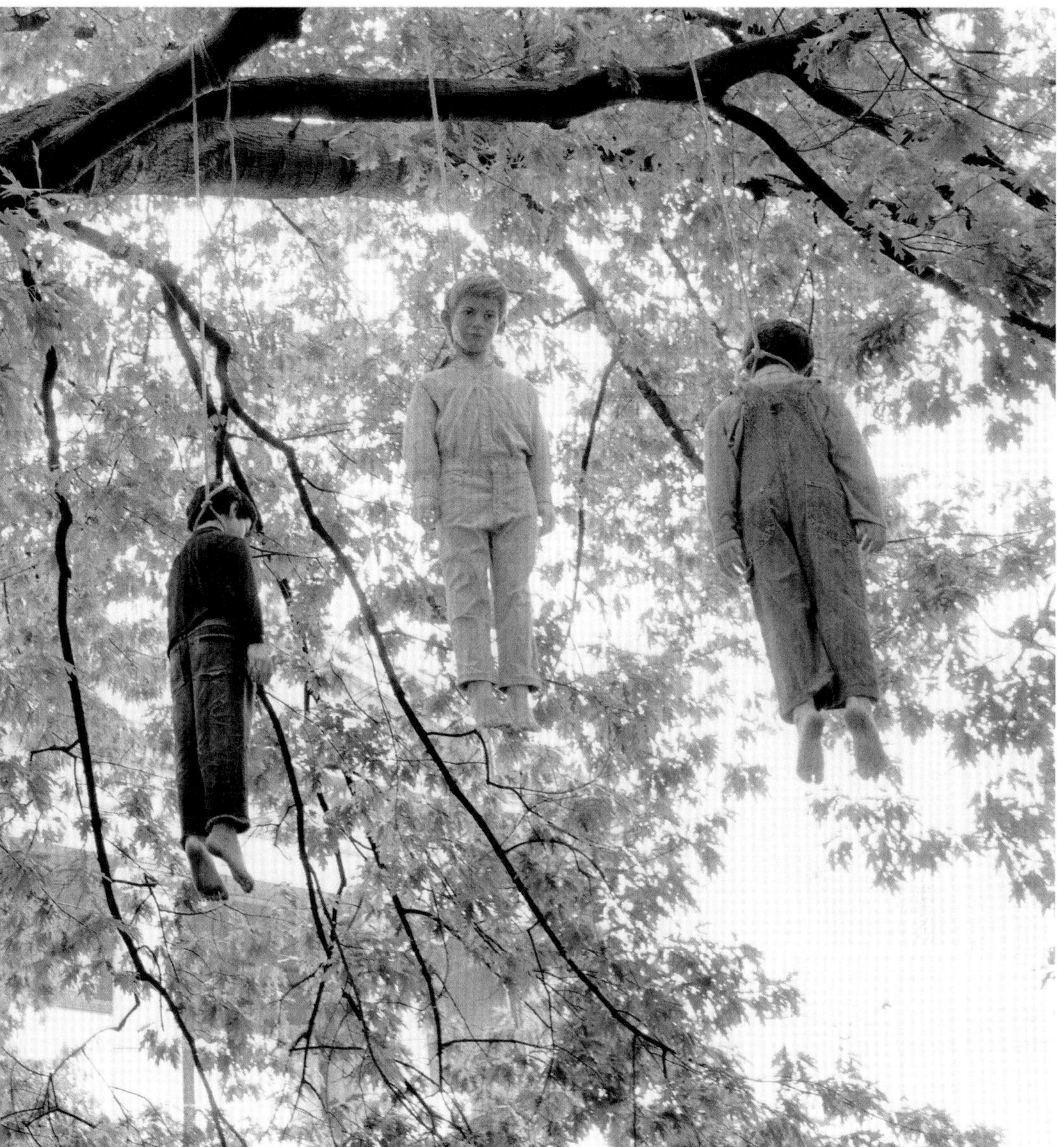

159

when rights are taken for granted, and often for-gotten. You need to stop from time to time and try to talk about them.

I was also interested to read the criticisms of me in the newspapers. I was surprised that people were suddenly scandalized by my work instead of questioning what it represented. The real prob-lem is that this type of violence exists, it's com-mon currency. Perhaps the debate should center not on the violence of artworks but on the vio-lence that artworks evoke. I don't want to make comparisons, but when Goya etched the *Disasters of War* he produced some very harsh images. But the problem was precisely those disasters, not that someone had the courage to depict them.

All the same, I think that every reaction is legit-imate. The real regret I felt only at that person who climbed the tree and cut the ropes that the children were hanging from. His reaction was violent: he wanted to destroy the work. Pre-cisely that work about everyday violence that it

[98]  *Untitled*, 2004
"Maurizio Cattelan," curated by Massimiliano Gioni,
Fondazione Nicola Trussardi, Piazza XXIV Maggio, Milan,
May 5–June 6, 2004 (solo show). Work destroyed one day
after the opening

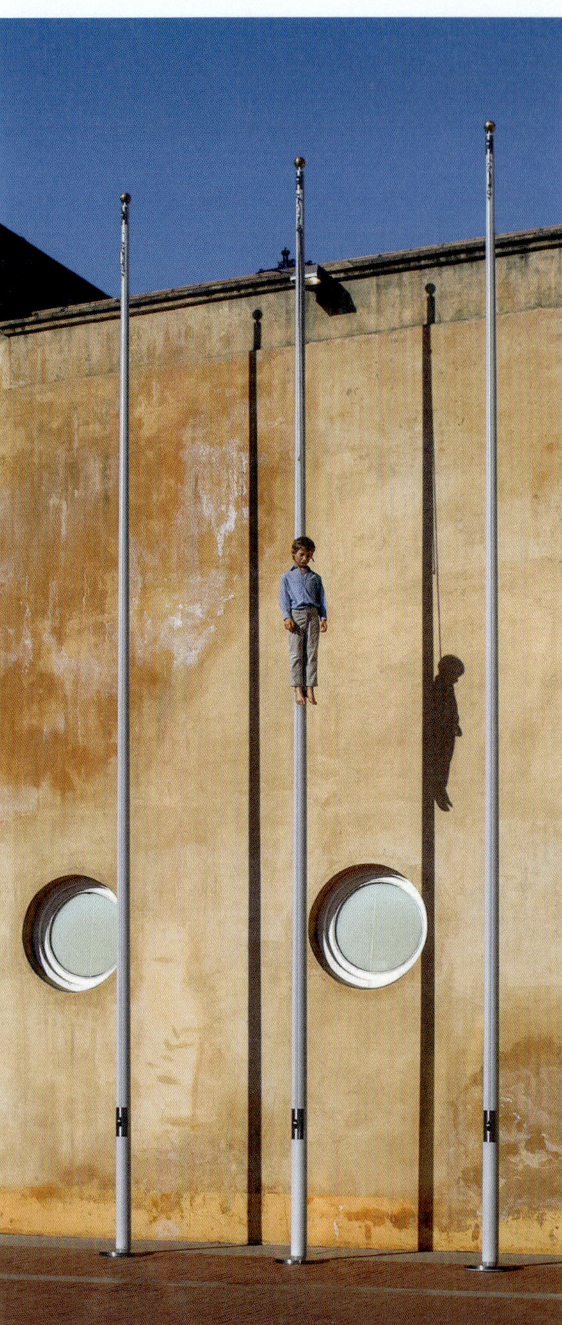

[99.1]

was meant to make us think about. Not to mention that, for some reason, after their removal, nobody thought it was indecent that it was reproduced in all the newspapers and broadcasted on all the TV channels. It was incredible: an image that according to some was intolerable in a square became acceptable in the pages of a newspaper or a television program.

The work was gone, after only two days, but the story continued. On the other hand, I was somehow happy, because that's the type of work that loses its power if it stays too long. The fact that it was taken down gave it even more history and background, and the memory was even stronger. All the same, giving explanations or writing footnotes is not my job. It's a task for viewers and critics. And then I actually wanted the work not to seem mine alone. I didn't hang the children on the tree. We were all doing much worse, and still are, directly or through others.

Maybe it was time to make less noise, and it still is. The children in the tree were so quiet, in spite of the traffic all around. Maybe you have to start from there. You certainly can't cut off an ear every day, always be a hero or an exhibitionist. Silence is golden.

[99]  *Untitled*, 2004
3 flag poles, polyurethane, polyester resin, paint, synthetic hair, clothing, rope
Figure: 130 × 50 × 55 cm; flag poles: 900 × 20 × 20 cm each

The first suspended child was to have been made for a Whitney Biennial with Chrissie Iles. I had suggested installing it on Madison Avenue. She kindly told me they didn't want to distract attention from the other artists, and it would be better if I brought a different work. An excuse to say no. Then, with Massimiliano Gioni, I decided the work absolutely had to be done—sometimes you make a commitment not to a person but a work. With some difficulty we succeeded in Milan, in Piazza XXIV Maggio, in 2004. Another version of the work was presented at the end of the same year in Seville, in an exhibition curated by Harald Szeemann. Szeemann realized there always had to be something that makes a noise. Already in 2000 he had wanted *La Nona Ora* (1999) in Warsaw, in an exhibition of Polish artists. I asked him: "What's it got to do with me?" And he replied: "Well, the pope's Polish."

I presented other versions of the suspended child years later, one in Warsaw and another, in 2016, at "Not Afraid of Love," my solo show at the Monnaie de Paris, where it remained on display for one day only. The child was hanged from a flagpole. It could only vaguely be seen but, knowing of its existence and looking for it, it could be made out from the Seine. But somebody complained, and a day later it was removed.

[99.1]  *Untitled*, 2004
"La alegría de mis sueños," curated by Harald Szeemann, Centro Andaluz de Arte Contemporáneo, Monasterio de la Cartuja, Seville, October 3–December 5, 2004 (group show)

[99.2]  *Untitled*, 2004
"Amen," curated by Justyna Wesołowska, Centre for Contemporary Art, Ujazdowski Castle, Warsaw, November 15, 2012–February 24, 2013 (solo show)

[99.3]  *Untitled*, 2004
"Not Afraid of Love," curated by Chiara Parisi, Monnaie de Paris, Octotber 21, 2016–January 8, 2017 (solo show)

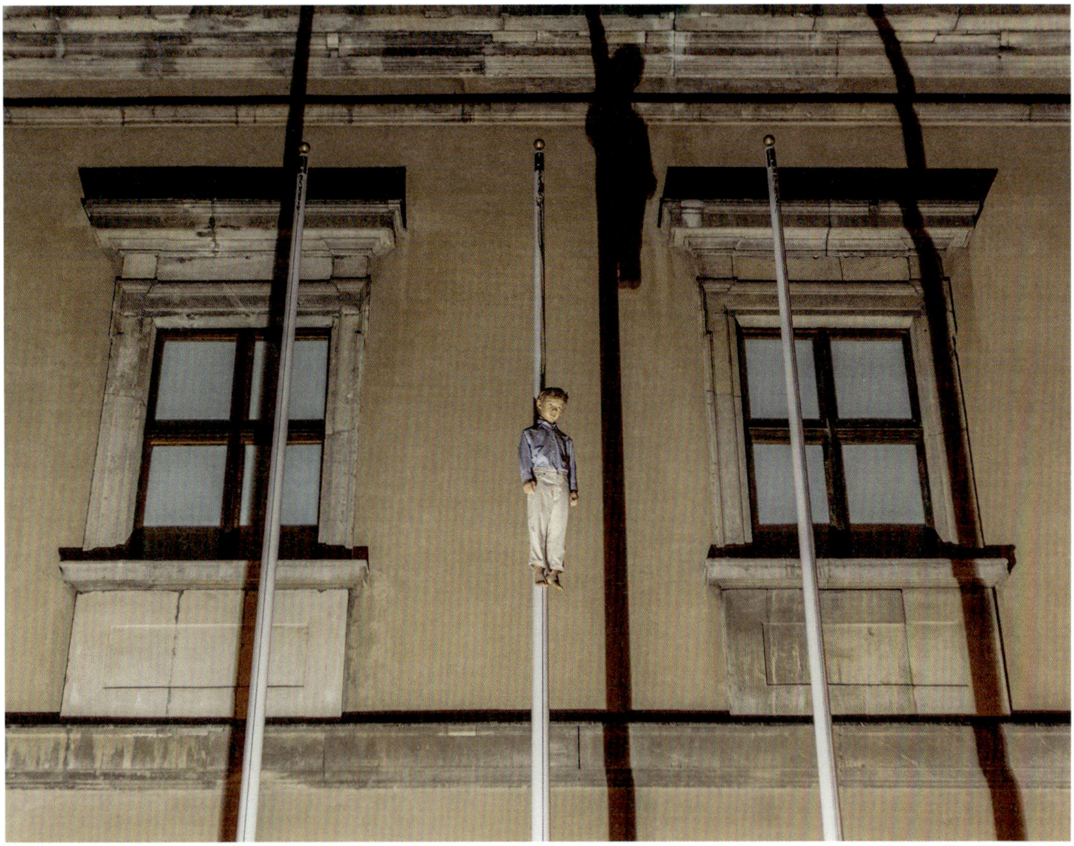

[99.2]

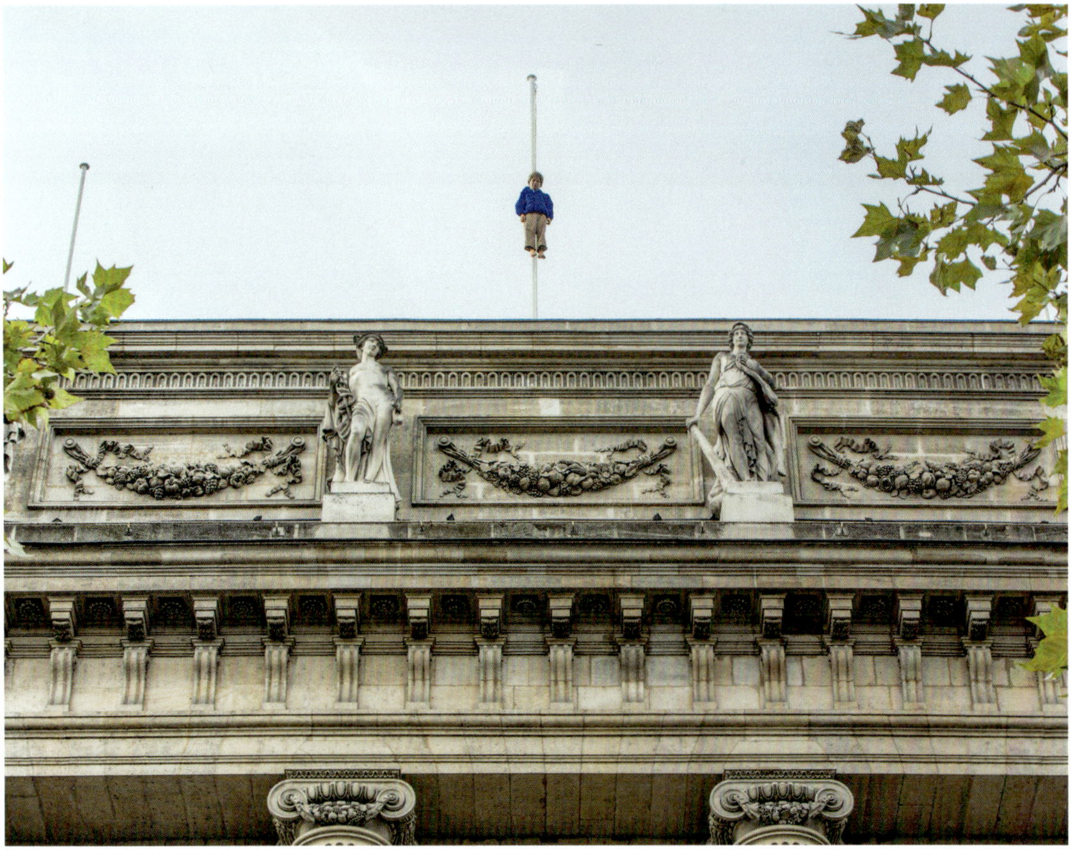

[99.3]

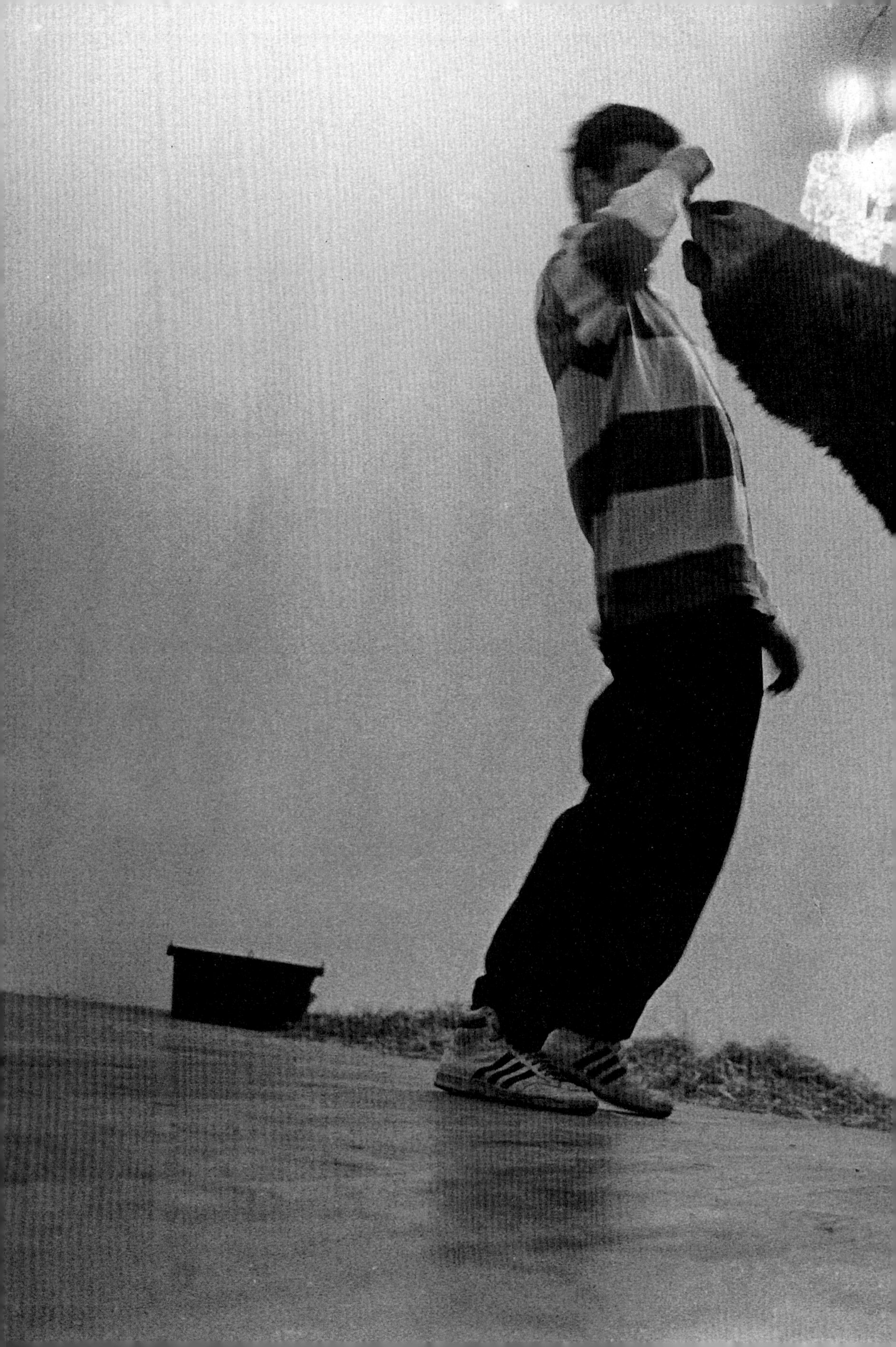

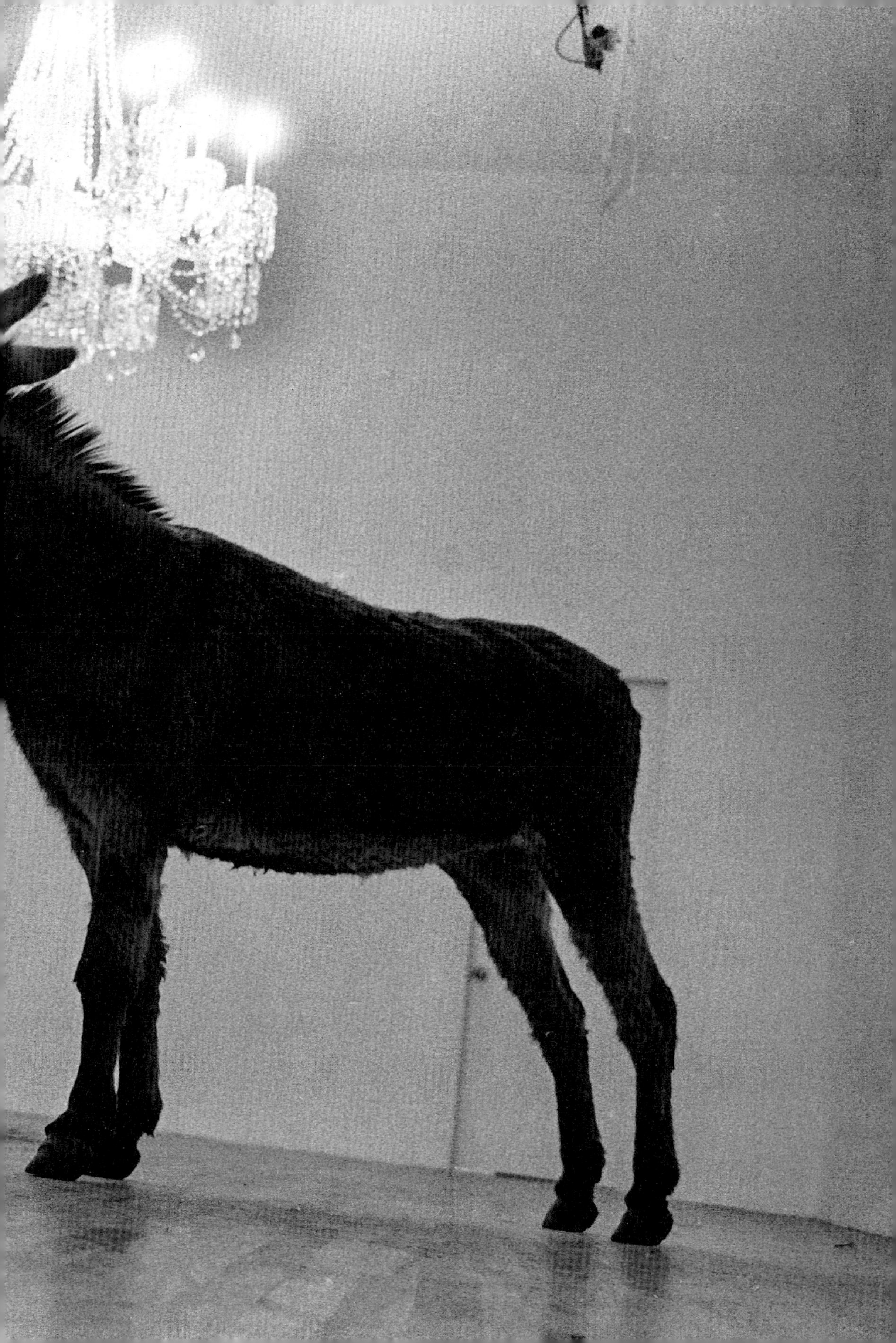

**[Lectio Magistralis Given at the Faculty of Sociology, University of Trento, March 30, 2004]**

Maurizio Cattelan portrayed by Lina Bertucci at his exhibition "Warning! Enter at your own risk. Do not touch, do not feed, no smoking, no photographs, no dogs, thank you," Daniel Newburg Gallery, New York, May 28–29, 1994

I'm ashamed. What else can I say? You are presenting me with this award, according me this recognition, and I feel like a thief, robbing you of your trust. Yet, I cannot help but accept your flattery, before you change your mind.

As always, with every victory comes a defeat. And I never know which side to join: the winners or the losers. Shame is a healthy feeling, and unjustly despised. Somewhere I once read that when man blushes, his noblest being begins. Of all animals, we are the only ones that feel embarrassment, or at least the only ones that show it. Shame, perhaps, is a discreet way of emerging from anonymity. The face that previously seemed identical to others becomes all at once conspicuous. It can be seen, its cheeks tinged with embarrassment.

I have many reasons to be embarrassed today, here before you. At school—it is useless to conceal it from you—I was a terrible student. In third grade, at the year's end, together with the report card, they handed me a Form I-9. I had spent so much time in the corridor that they meant to hire me as a janitor.

And now I find myself lecturing you. It's a role that just doesn't suit me. In fact, if it weren't for you, I wouldn't even be here. I find this slightly reassuring, because once again I can share a success, or yet another failure, with various accomplices, more or less voluntary.

This, after all, is a degree that you bestow firstly on yourselves, on your magnanimity, and secondly on everyone who has shared part of my work and my insecurities. In reality, this lecture ought to be a mere list, like the closing credits of a movie.

Without others, I'm nobody. I'm truly empty. I even wrote this speech with a friend, stealing a few phrases from here and there. I've been going on like this since my school days. My teacher always got angry at me because I wasn't even smart enough to copy from the cleverest kids.

As you can see, I'm a bad role model. At times I even believe that my work embodies certain values that we should be embarrassed about. But art is a mirror: it presents us with the image of what we are or will become. And mirrors are attractive, even when they're unflattering.

Seeing it like this, reflected in the mirror of art, the world does not seem a very welcoming place. In art and reality, sometimes the world appears as if it were temporarily in the hands of the wrong god, while the real one is standing on the sidelines.

Perhaps I'm a pessimist, but at the same time I believe that the world offers many other consolations we can take advantage of: love, food, music, the immense variety of languages and faces, and then the continuous buzz of images.

Well, maybe I should talk to you about images, because after all, it's through images that I speak. If I've ended up being an artist–whatever that means–it must have been precisely as an escape from words, a way to invent a language that would be more my own. Not that I've invented anything special. On the contrary, sometimes I've been content to move an image from one place to another, quite simply. This creates a small short circuit, producing a thousand sparks, sometimes quite dangerous ones.

Perhaps I'm fascinated by this ambiguity of images, by the possibility of never fully controlling them. I don't quite know why, but I always feel that images never belong to anyone, and instead there they are, available to everyone.

So unlike words, I feel that images always ask to be interpreted. In words you can say yes or no, but in images things get more complicated. In fact, if I had the courage to teach anything, I would say: "Always be wary of unambiguous images." One-way images are garbage for the eyes and brain: pure visual pollution.

The images that interest me most are the ones I don't understand. Or rather ones that seem to contain an endless multiplicity of meanings. I don't know anything about sociology, but maybe the images I really like–no matter whether they're my own or someone else created them–resemble what I insist on imagining as an ideal society: they're a chorus of voices, a din of interpretations and discordant sounds that mysteriously attain a balance. And this balance, moreover, doesn't rest on any hierarchy: no voice dominates the others, no interpretation can claim a right to superiority, no sound is a noise. The best images are like so many small towers of Babel that mysteriously remain standing. They may tremble, but they don't collapse. In fact they draw new strength from the continuous quaking that shakes their foundations.

From images I've also learned something about the world: I've learned to accept everything. And above all, I've learned not to underestimate anyone. I certainly cannot enlighten you about our society: you know far more about it. Yet I can testify that there is no one who is unable to change your life. Taken in small doses, man is a rather extraordinary animal, capable of foolish gestures of generosity, sometimes verging on self-harm. The degree you are giving me is a further demonstration of this. After all, it's like joining an exclusive club. If it accepts my nomination, then it can't have been so very exclusive. Here's what I like about this degree, and what I'd really like to thank you for. For a moment, all these professors, and all the professors in the world, and professors of professors, they all seem closer to me, and if they're closer to me, then it really means they can be closer to everyone. For me, this degree is not a promotion. It's not me rising, but perhaps it's the professors who have decided to sink, to lower themselves to my level. And this strikes me as a good sign: a way to get closer together, to shuffle the cards.

My mother used to say that without a piece of paper you will never get anywhere. While I thank you, I cannot keep it from you that I am scared to death. I hope that this ceremony does not mark a point of arrival. I like to think of it as only one stage in the journey, not the end of the line. I don't know who usually receives honorary degrees, or degrees in general, but I hope they're intended for those who still want to learn, and not for those who think they already know everything.

["Lectio magistralis all'Università di Trento," text published in *Work: Art in Progress*, no. 9 (Summer 2004): 94]

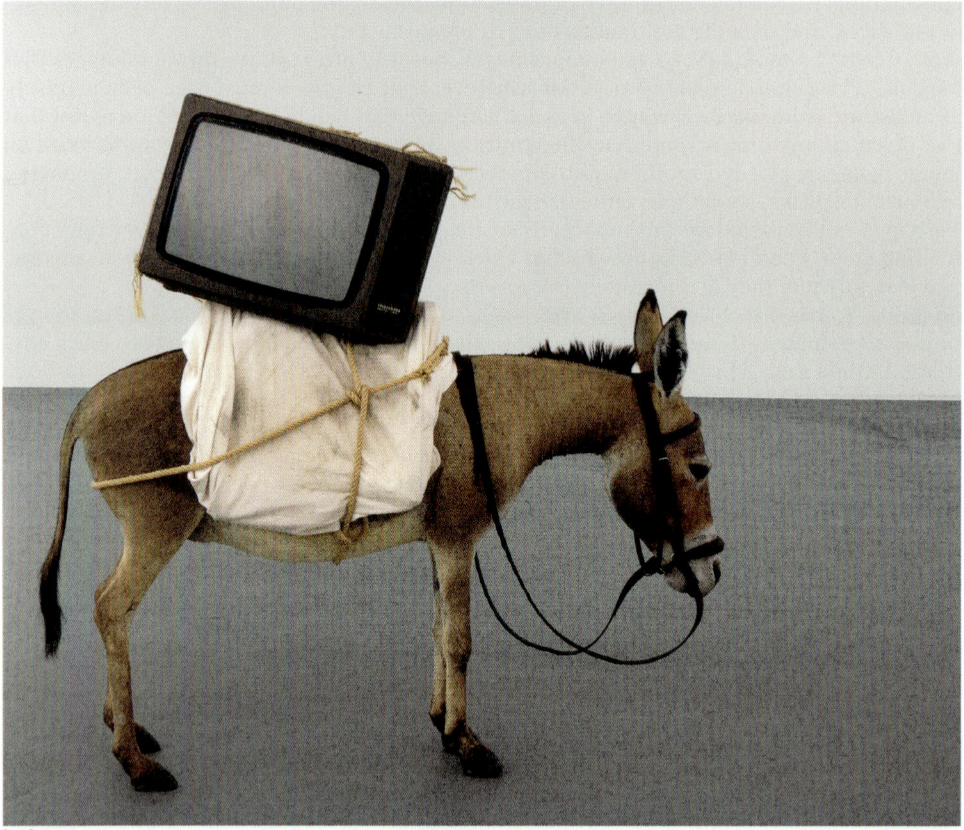

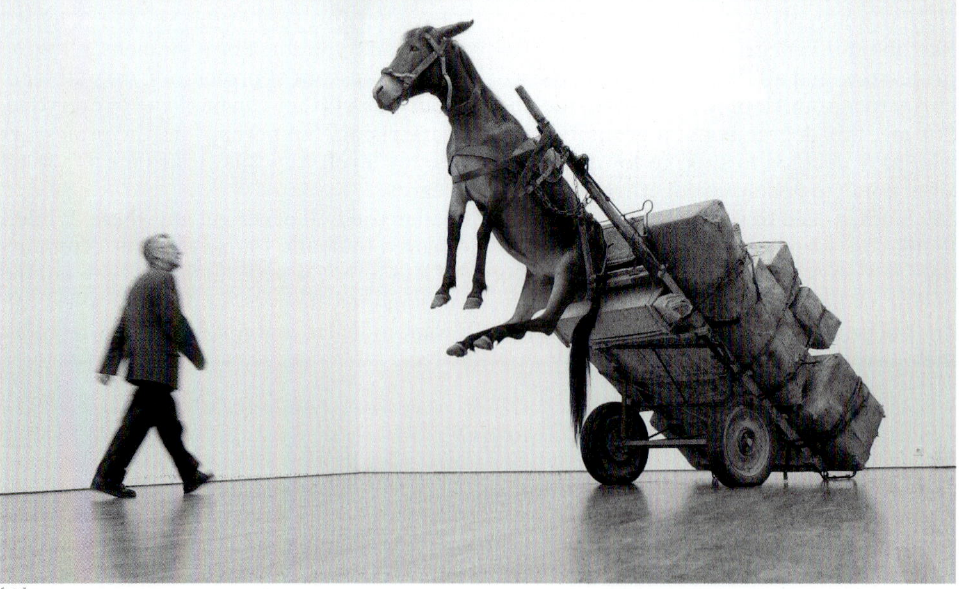



[100]

[101]

[100]   *If a Tree Falls in the Forest and There Is No One
        Around It, Does It Make a Sound?*, 1998
"Ironisch/Ironic," curated by Rein Wolfs, Migros Museum
für Gegenwartskunst, Zurich, June 26–August 9, 1998
(group show)

[101]   *Untitled*, 2002
"Public Affairs. Von Beuys bis Zittel: das Öffentliche in der
Kunst," curated by Bice Curiger, Kunsthaus Zürich, Zurich,
September 15–December 1, 2002 (group show)

[102]   *Untitled*, 2004
University of Trento, Faculty of Sociology,
March 31–September 26, 2004

[100]  **If a Tree Falls in the Forest and There Is No One Around It, Does It Make a Sound?**, 1998
Taxidermied donkey, television, rope, saddle, blanket
150 × 154 × 46 cm

[101]  **Untitled**, 2002
Taxidermized donkey, wood, metal, fabric, paper, rope, rubber
250 × 400 × 165 cm

[102]  **Untitled**, 2004
Taxidermied donkey
160 × 80 × 175 cm

After the failure of the exhibition with the live donkey in New York ("Warning! Enter at your own risk. Do not touch, do not feed, no smoking, no photographs, no dogs, thank you," 1994), I decided to try again. This time the donkey was embalmed, in a strange mix with technology. Past and future together.

Another stuffed donkey is the one overcome by the weight of its burden. Overwork creates a surreal image. Thinking about it, it's like an overworked laborer who eventually explodes.

When they presented me with an honorary degree at the University of Trento—me of all people, who'd always been a dunce at school—I did another one. They called it "A donkey among the doctors," but I didn't give it a title. It could very well be an image by Goya, humanizing donkeys in a beautiful way. A work is fantastic when you succeed in evoking a strong feeling with very little energy. This, with a lot of energy, doesn't evoke any feeling. On the other hand, I took home my degree. It was the trade-off to get it.

167

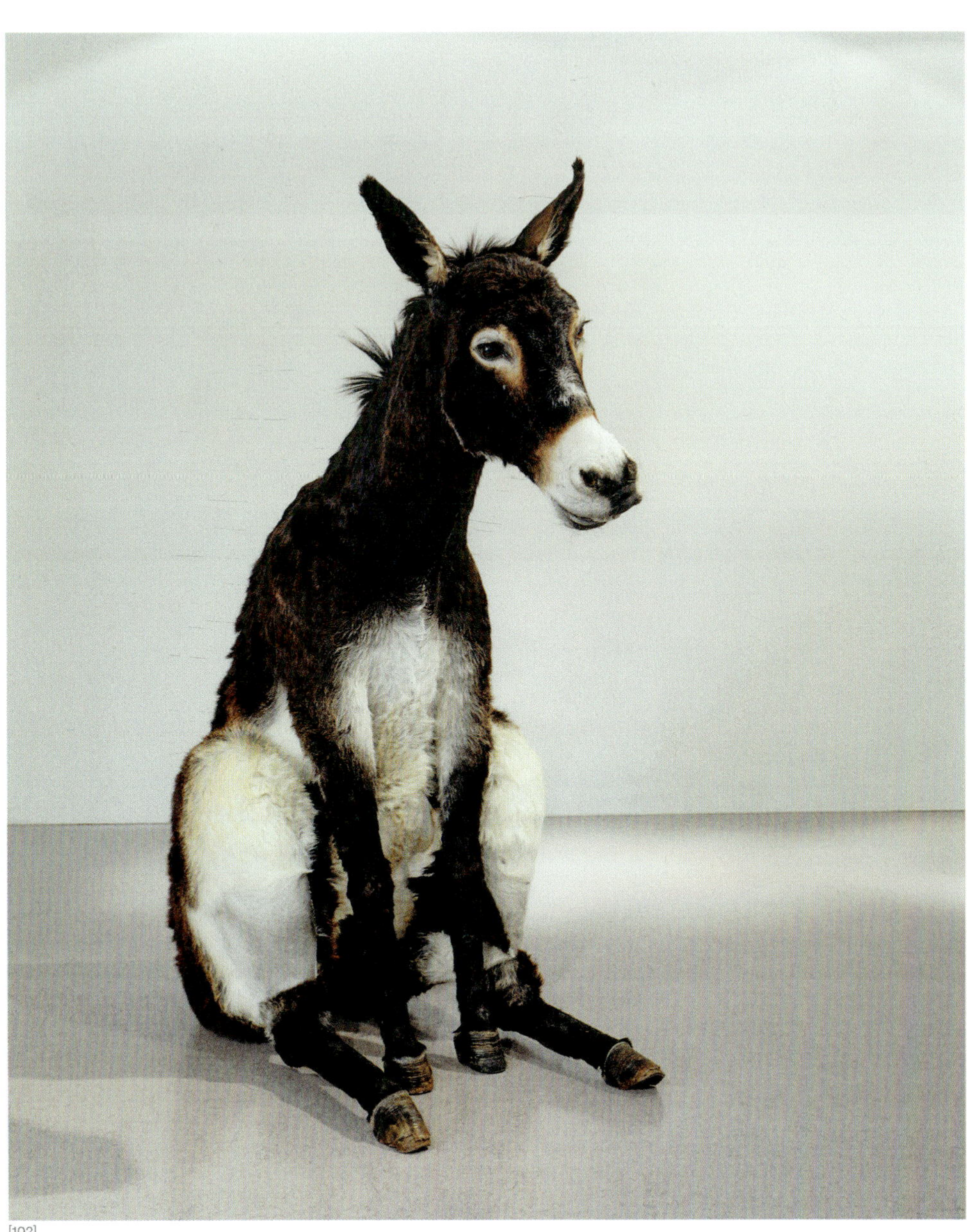

[102]

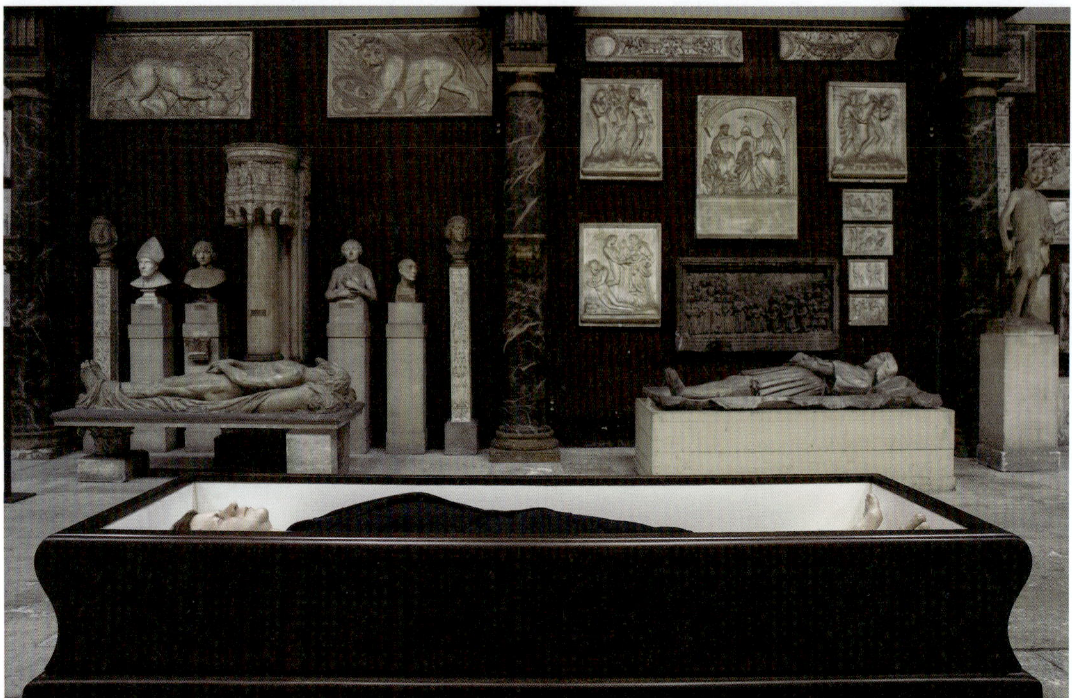

[103.1]

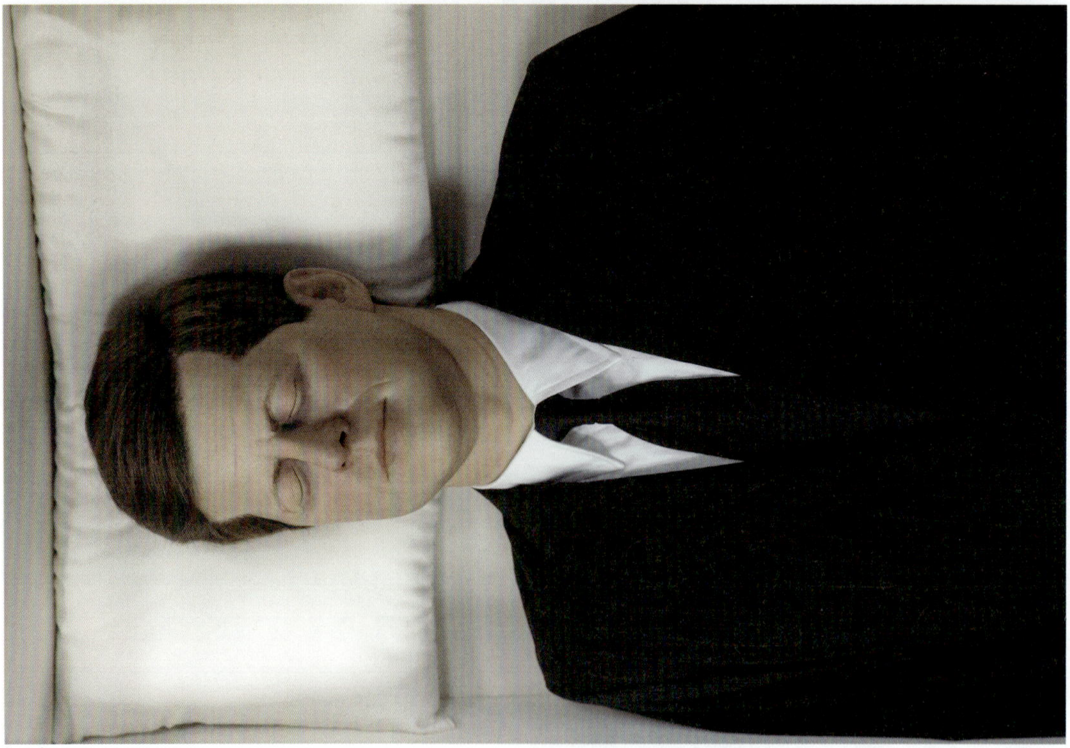

[103.2]

[103.1-2] *Now*, 2004
"Now," curated by Laurence Bossé, Hans Ulrich Obrist and Angeline Scherf, Chapelle des Petits Augustins, École nationale supérieure des Beaux-Arts, Paris, October 1–31, 2004 (solo show)

[104] *Untitled*, 2009
"Pop Life. Art in a Material World," curated by Jack Bankowsky, Alison M. Gingeras, and Catherine Wood, Tate Modern, London, October 1, 2009–January 17, 2010 (group show)

**[103]** ***Now*, 2004**
Polyester resin, wax, pigment, natural
hair, clothing, wood
85 × 225 × 78 cm

I'm not very much interested in history or politicians. I mainly deal with mass fears and personal hysterias. Kennedy is no longer a person or a character anymore; he has become a sign, an image. It reminds you that power and fame are always paths to something else, and failure is always around the corner.

For me, the work is on the one hand an allusion to Mantegna's *Dead Christ*, on the other a corpse not fully dressed and not yet buried. Because Kennedy's dream is dead anyway, because his assassination was the end of an era, and because, when I made the work, you could feel the threat to democracy in the air, just like today.

I spoke at length about the work with Calvin Tomkins, who had come to Paris specially to see it, and he wrote an essay about it in an issue of *The New Yorker* in October of the same year that was much better than my words. In brief, it went more or less like this: "On the day of our visit to the École des Beaux-Arts, only a few people were aware that his new piece, called *Now*, would be a life-size sculpture of John Fitzgerald Kennedy lying in a coffin. [...] Cattelan wanted it kept secret from the rumor-hungry art world, to preserve the impact of its first appearance. [...] Cattelan often worries that his art works will fail. Many of them have been failures, in his view. His sculptures depend on the power of images to embody social issues. [When I first saw it] Kennedy was lying on a low pallet in the middle of the room, face up, dressed in a black pin-striped suit and black shoes. The skin tones hadn't been painted yet—Cattelan had expected they would be—but the handsome Irish features were instantly recognizable, under a bushy head of hair. [...] I wanted to know about the thought process that had led to a sculpture of J.F.K. in a coffin. 'But I am not a conceptual artist!' Cattelan protested. [...] After some further evasive tactics, he allowed that the idea of using Kennedy had been in his head for about three years: 'Why? Because he's a kind of icon, even if he's not. He has all the elements. He had a fantastic life, a mixture of society, politics, so many elements. But Kennedy is so difficult to touch. I mean, every time you have a loss of hope, Kennedy comes to my mind. Now it is more contemporary than ever, don't you think?' [...] Cattelan [then] called from Europe: 'Lucio [Zotti] kept saying the shoes were not right, so I finally said O.K., no shoes, and no socks. It reminds me more of someone who's a saint. Also, we decided to do closed eyes. The guy is definitely dead, but there's no finality. It has to be ungraspable.'"

**[104]** ***Untitled*, 2009**
Taxidermied horse, steel, felt-tip pen
on wood
Horse: 55.3 × 201.1 × 188.9 cm

A terrible image in the series of my works with horses, but I didn't invent it. I took it from a photo in a news story.

We're so used to seeing the cross that we often forget how closely it is bound up with an act of violence. Associating the inscription affixed to the cross of Christ with the body of an animal brings the tragedy back to the surface. The horse is an animal that even sleeps standing up, but here it's lying on the ground. You can't misunderstand it.

169

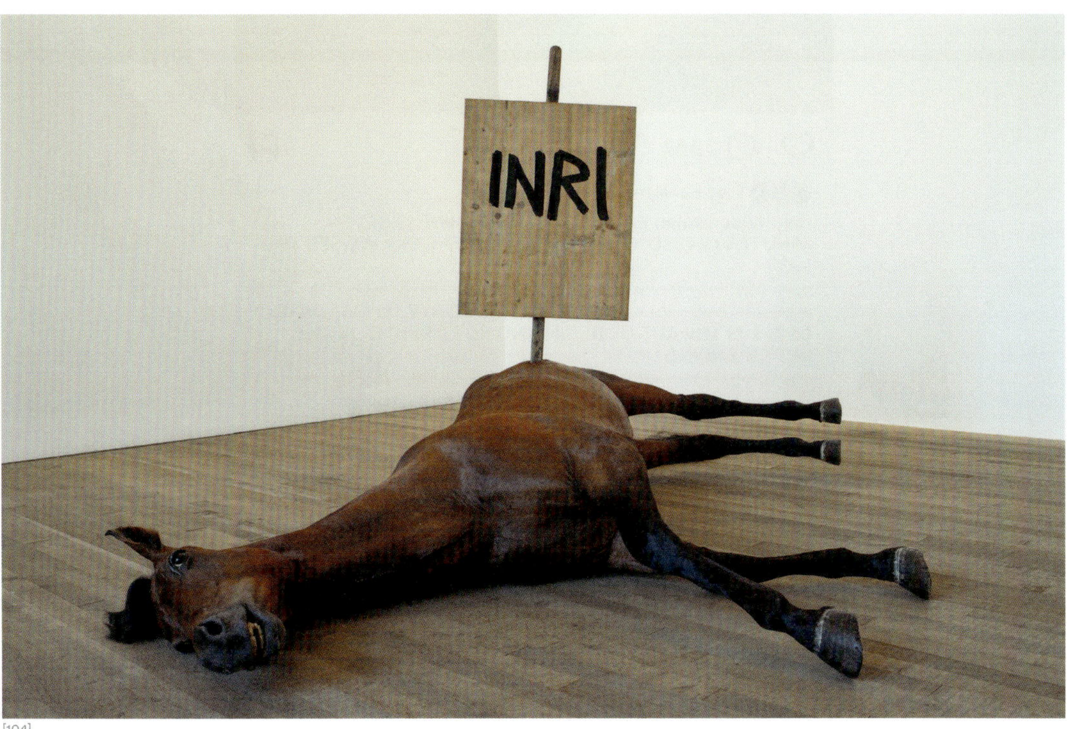


[104]

13:11

MAURIZIOCATTELAN
Post

mauriziocattelan


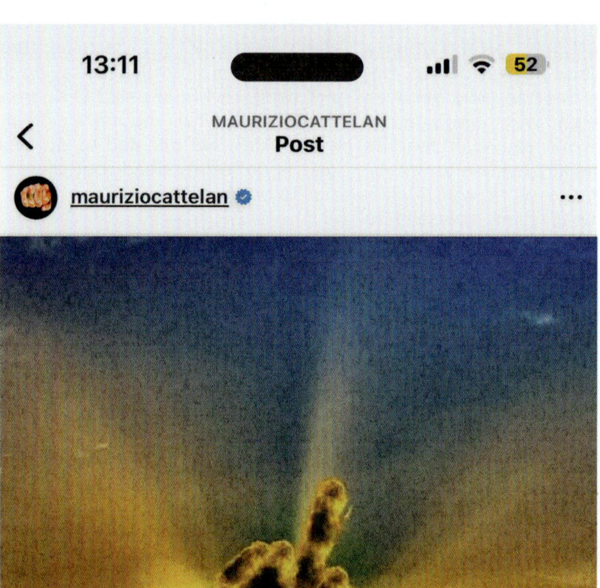

3.652

Piace a ileniadurazzi e altri
mauriziocattelan EACH RAY OF SUNSHINE IS SEVEN
MINUTES OLD SO WHEN WE LOOK A THE SKY WE SEE THE
PAST
——————————————————————————————————
——————————————————————————GOODBYE TO EVERYONE,
GREAT IS THE ART OF BEGINNING BUT GREATER IS THE
ART OF ENDING
——————————————————————————————————
——————————————————————@andrewbmyers

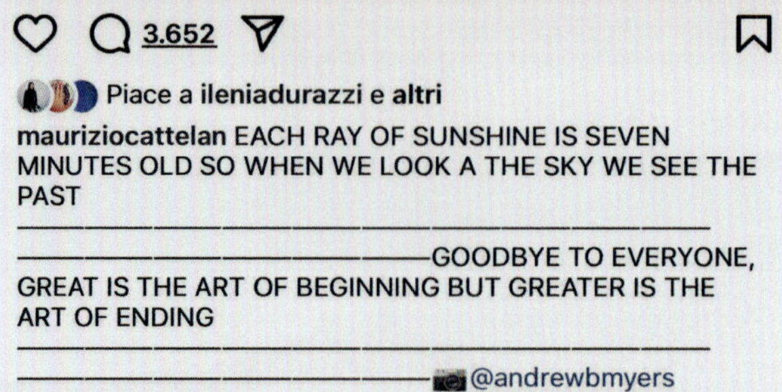

Images and texts, no matter whether they were made just now or hundreds of years ago, have at least two lives: one printed, the other virtual. What strikes me most is that almost anybody can create printed material or a blog, but, if everyone's a content producer, who's left to be the audience? I consider re-blogging to be blasphemy. Until a few years ago I had a Motorola without a built-in camera. Whenever I'm on the point of buying a smartphone, I'm reminded of what my newsvendor always says: "One of the few good things about our times is that, if you die horribly on the web, you won't have died in vain—you'll have entertained people around the world." Sincerely speaking, I feel I'm not good at playing this game. The only way it works for me is to think that nothing is permanent and everything forgettable. So for a while I was interested in having an Instagram profile that broke with the dynamics of obsessive self-archiving. Emptiness became content when fullness wasn't content any more. So I started *The Single Post Instagram* page to feature a new story every day, keeping just one post in my feed at all times. I used that page as a display to underscore the things I saw out there that had struck me. I didn't like the idea of saving posts. It distracted me and made me feel vulnerable. Instagram is like a peep show—sometimes I think you could call it Pervertgram—but you couldn't spy on all of mine. I had nothing to do with the X-ray image of myself on display. The idea of looking back at previous posts and reviewing what I'd posted also seemed anachronistic, egoistic and useless. So I followed my own rules, dismantling the most obvious ones and trying to find my way in this case too. Posting a single photo that deletes the previous one each time was no different from making an exhibition leaving the gallery empty with the sign "Back soon." At the same time, it was a challenge to myself. A page with just one post and not following anyone makes it much more difficult to increase the number of followers. It was obviously controversial. If all profiles followed my rules, Instagram wouldn't exist.

I was active for a year and a half. It wasn't easy but it was fun. I enjoyed working on my photos and captions. In short, it was fun until I stopped learning. That's why I gave up. I prefer to soothe my existential angst with other things, like seeing friends, reading, working, and visiting galleries. At this point I'd rather sit and watch the work on a building site. To me it's more exciting than scrolling on Instagram.

I stopped using Instagram, but clearly I haven't stopped using images. Digital images have changed the way the players in the field look at artworks, whether as collectors, curators, artists, or gallery owners. In some cases this has even changed the works themselves and the way they're presented. Every technology has had the power to shape the art of the age in which it spread, starting from printing with movable type. I no longer use images on paper. I suffer from an addiction to images on the net. The difficulty is to resist confusion. Being online is like going to New York, London or Paris when you're young. If you don't know what you're looking for, if you don't have a purpose, after three months you're completely lost, because those metropolises can offer everything.

The digitization of reality that we're experiencing also produces new ways of thinking. For example, it can hardly be denied that the concept of the copy, as well as of true versus false, is being profoundly redefined on social media. Thousands of new images are available online every day, and each of us looks at them or shares them obsessively, often without going into the merits of the contents. The absolution of the act of copying lies in the act of sharing itself.

The digital dimension is a beautiful lie. You can finally be what you aren't in real life. And so make up for your failure. I'm not fascinated or repelled by likes, but they certainly don't leave you indifferent. They're now dictators in our lives, on or off any social platform. They could lead to a form of social control with some disquieting effects, to standardization, with anyone who deviates from the rule being sacrificed to keep the majority more compact. It's as if we're in the Wild West, the version depicted in the movies, where the law wasn't the same everywhere and enforcing it was tough. What we're experiencing is the digital version of that period. Sooner or later, hopefully not too late, laws and rights will arrive and be respected on the internet as well.

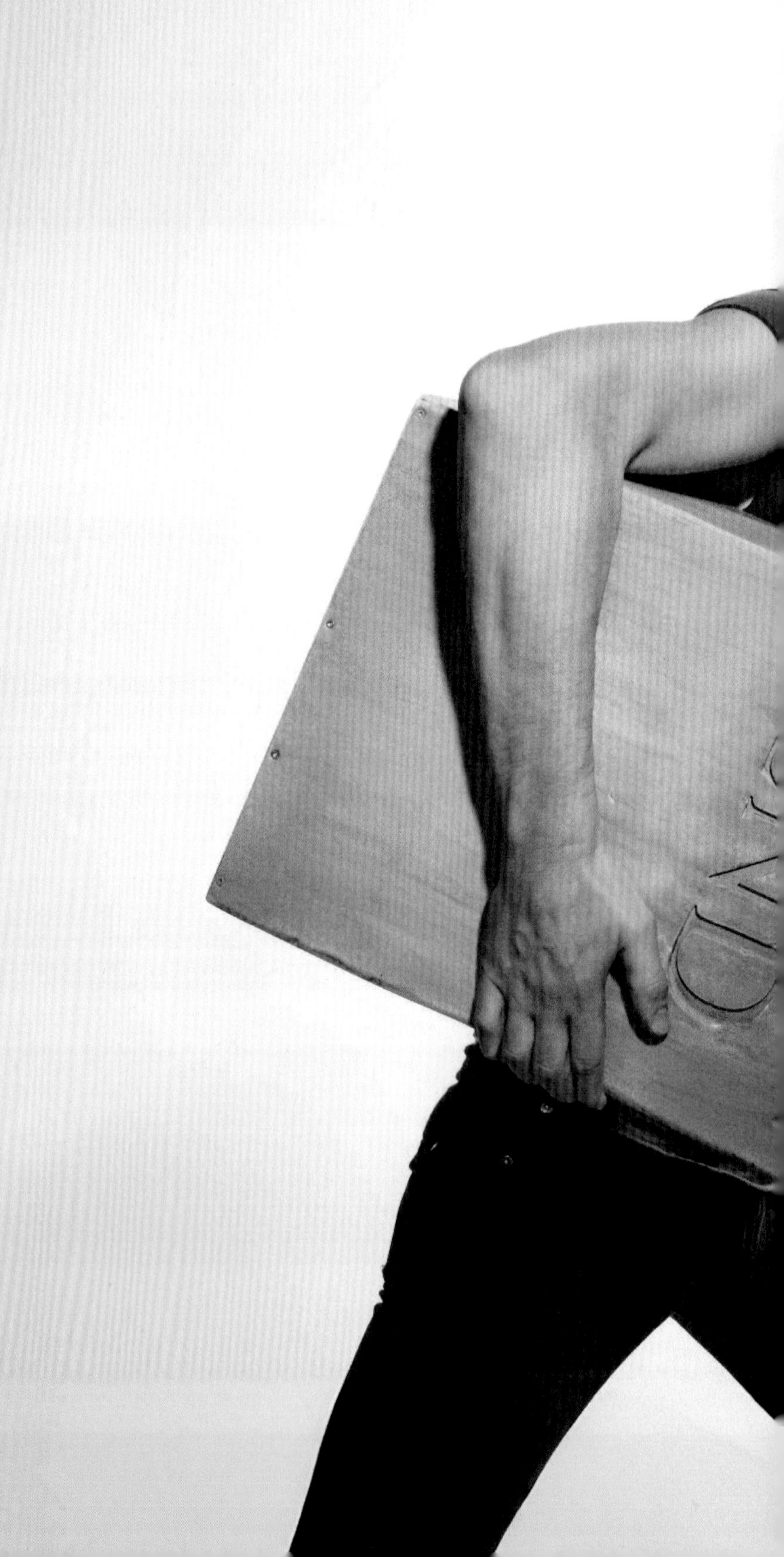

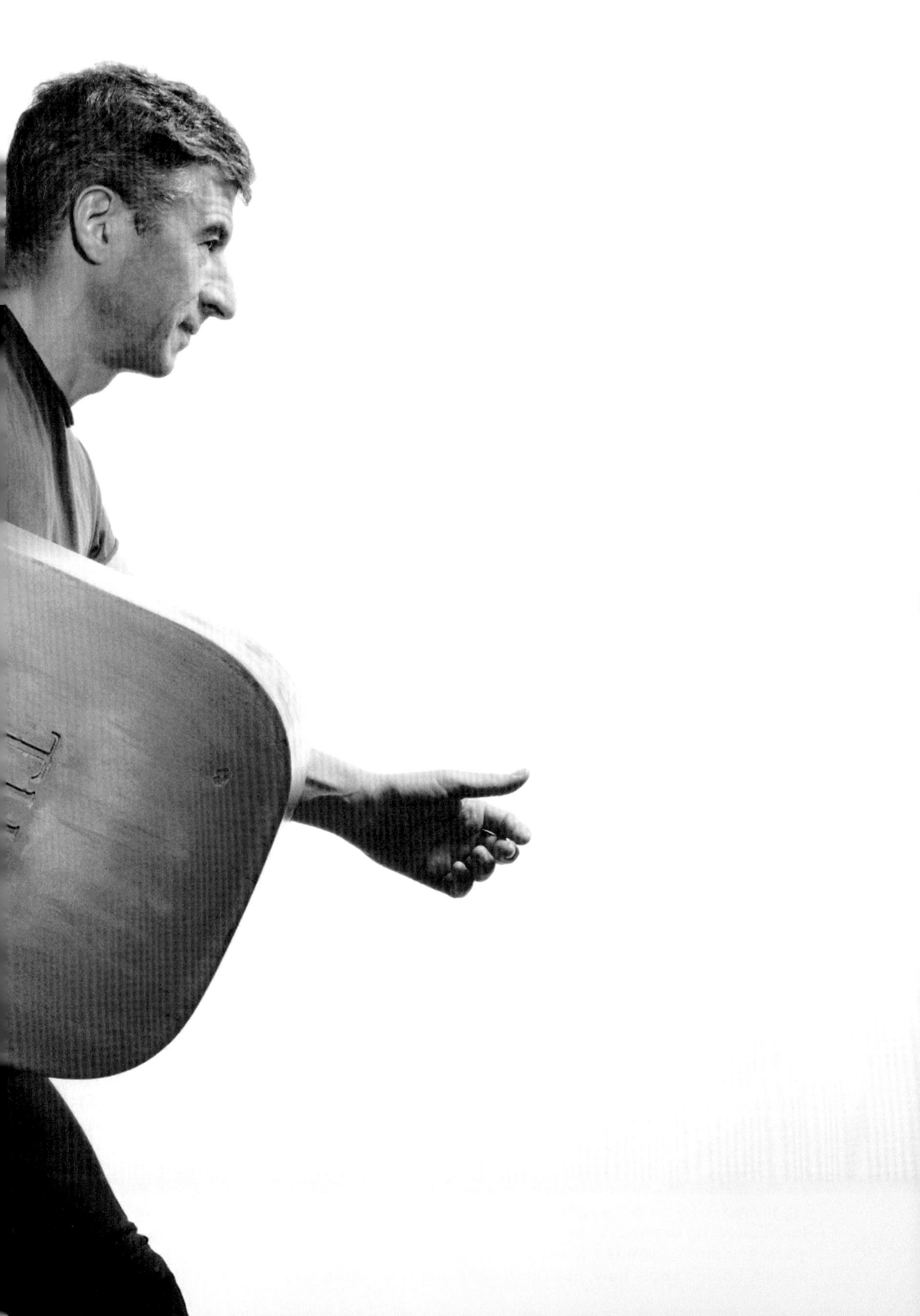

One of the most wonderful things about being an artist is you can be free, really free. So I can stop and start again whenever I feel like it. More than that, we have a duty to stop when we feel the time is right, because producing tasteless and uninteresting works is the worst crime an artist can commit.

As a kid, I wanted with all my might to free myself from the authority of my parents. I ran away from home and went to work so I could live on my own. At that point the urge became to get rid of my employers, and I started to become an artist. When I retired, it was because I was feeling the same urge about gallery owners. Being an artist had become a job like any other. It was no longer the anarchic and forbidden pleasure that had made it appealing and desirable, that unpredictable quality that had fueled me when I started being an artist. I felt forced into a vise, compelled to give answers and make decisions about matters that didn't strike me as important. And wasting time doing things that bring you no fulfilment is a luxury no one should indulge. I've spent my life trying to strike a balance between the desire to do more and better and the temptation to stop and wriggle out of all the mechanisms of expectation. I believe that the announcement of my early retirement was the response to the second of these pressures. Then, to me, art is not about gaining something; it's more about getting rid of the darkness I've accumulated. In the years leading to my retirement, I'd collected a lot of junk and I felt it was time to get rid of some of it. I needed to put higher hurdles in my way and figure out if I'd be able to jump over them. Believe me if I say that retirement was really one of the biggest challenges I've had to face in my life.

In any case, given that I once called myself an "imagination worker," retirement seemed the most appropriate goal. In 2011 I felt I was repeating a pattern I'd already seen, I had a feeling of déjà-vu. If I'd gone on working, I'd probably have ended up having a style, which can be a form of early death. I wasn't feeling too happy, and oddly I also felt too comfortable with what I was doing. That's not a good combination. I drifted, floating on the surface of a daily schedule, insensitive to everything around me. I was also asking myself: why do we assume that a personal path has to become a career and has to function along the lines of predictable productivity? In short, I wasn't enjoying the art game any more. I wanted to start playing something different. It was time to reinvent myself. I didn't know how, but there were lots of possible ways. All endings are simultaneously new beginnings. Retirement would be an extra project, another phase of my development. Certainly I would keep working on my publishing projects. While earlier I'd only thought about *Permanent Food* or *Toiletpaper* during my vacations, from then on I could devote myself to my side projects every day, with the care a pensioner puts into gardening. It's amazing how the word *retire* can suddenly change your life. There's something magical about it. It frees you from anxiety, from the urgency to prove something. And it gives you the illusion of an egoless, timeless future, where everything is possible again and nothing is necessary.

With retirement I drew a line between me and my work, and that same line became a challenge to the curators and the archive itself. All my works were available for them to build their exhibitions, test the strength of the works and exploit their potential, without asking my permission. And without my interfering with the experiments. So my interest was to sit on a bench and see how my works would go on living independently of me, without being around as the artist. And it was a chance to get rid of the prankster label, which cast a shadow also over my work. Once all the rumors about me subsided, I was sure the public would take moments of silence to delve into all the aspects of my work that hadn't been analyzed until then.

It was the "death of the author" applied to the letter. Those years were like a Shakespeare tragedy or a tale by Poe. I pretended to be dead, but I could still see and hear what was happening around me. I guess it was like being the father of grown-up kids. You start losing authority over them, and it's clear that you'll never be in complete control again, but you still want to keep in touch.

Sometimes the decision not to do something is more important than the decision to do something, until the moment when the decision to do something becomes more important than the decision not to do something. I realized this later, after being retired for a while. It didn't matter what I decided to do or not do, since I was stressed out. In the end it wasn't about the art world, the problem was me, so I might as well start doing something more spiritually fulfilling. Like those porno stars who suddenly convert and decide to marry God. I played dead for a while. But then, like Dante after his tour of hell, I chose to come back to life. I realized that I preferred to work. Work always brings challenges and excitement. To be honest, not having a job is more boring than having one. I think I simply discovered that I can't sit idly by. It's stronger than me. Distancing myself from what I'd achieved in the past was incredibly helpful for a deeper understanding of my career, but then I could say that only stupid people never change their minds. I needed to be free to make mistakes, to strip myself of all the clutter acquired by habit or inertia. Announcing my retirement had been a striking gesture but it proved useful as a way to free myself from the dynamics that were stifling me. I cleaned myself up and I could start thinking freely again. The truth is that you don't stop being who you are just because you decide to be, and after a while my obsessions came looking for me again. So, in a world where incredible things were happening, after resting I thought at some point about returning.

My affair with art is a troubled one, but it's by far the longest relationship I've ever had. It happens that even the best and strongest couples make mistakes and try to break up, but true love always wins out in the end.

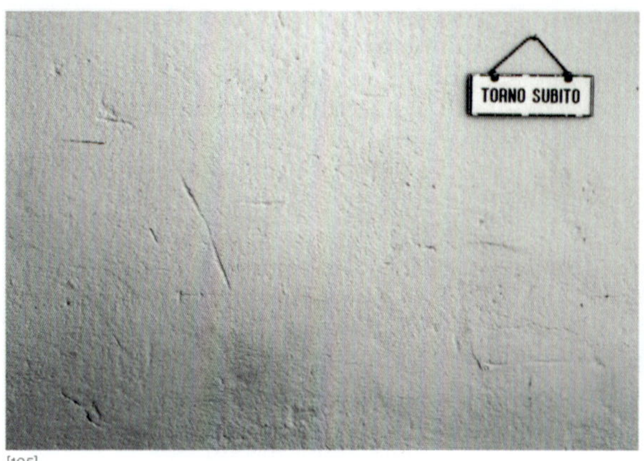


[105]

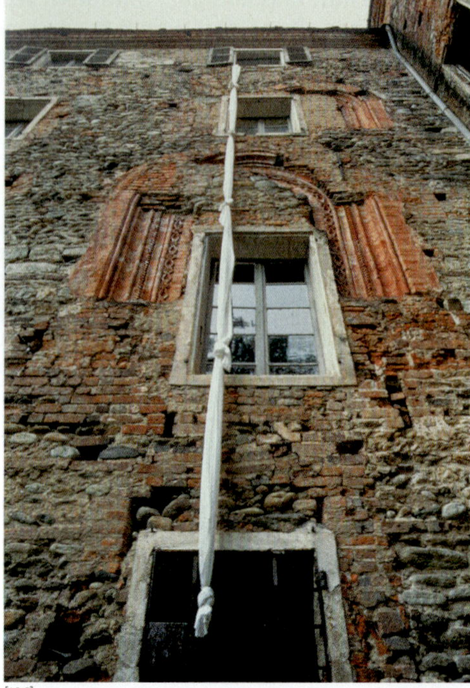

[106]

**[105]** ***Torno subito*, 1989**
Engraved plexiglas
4 × 12 cm

My first serious exhibition was in Bologna. At that time, I was interested in furniture, in working with my hands, and I went through a process that developed from furniture-making into art. I had prepared ten pieces, but the day before the show I looked at them and thought: "Oh my God, I don't like them." I felt that my clumsiness was unacceptable. Instead of exhibiting the work I put a sign in the gallery window: "Back soon." I'm also considering this phrase as an epitaph, although I think the truly insuperable one is: "I don't rule out my return."

178

**[106]** ***Una Domenica a Rivara*, 1992**
Knotted sheets
Length 12 m

The Rivara exhibition was curated by Gregorio Magnani. I can't say how he knew my work. He'd invited some interesting artists, and I still can't say what I was doing there. But I knew—someone had told me—that if I went to Rivara I would eat for free for a week. An unmissable opportunity! It was the first time I'd taken part in a themed exhibition and it was really interesting. I liked to see what the other artists were doing, how they reacted to the situation. Some were deeply involved and tried to make a work in keeping with the theme; others regarded it as a routine exhibition and showed old works.
Anyway, I stayed in a room in the castle for most of the time, leaving it only when dinner was ready. I was there with a friend, and when it was time to present the work I left. Instead of leaving a note explaining why I'd split, I knotted a few sheets together and hung them out the window. It wasn't just metaphorical, because to get away, the night before the opening I let myself down on the sheets instead of going down the stairs normally. It wasn't a radical gesture, but one of the games I was always playing at the time. I don't know if it's a good defense against the charge of provocation, but it's the truth.

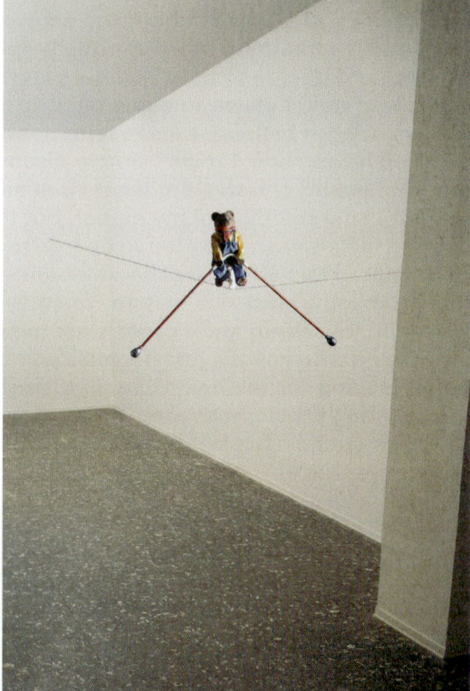

[107]

[105] *Torno subito*, 1989
"Biologia delle passioni," Galleria Neon, Bologna, May 6–June 12, 1989 (solo show)

[106] *Una Domenica a Rivara*, 1992
"Una Domenica a Rivara," curated by Gregorio Magnani, Castello di Rivara Museo d'Arte Contemporanea, July 4–31, 1992 (group show)

[107] *Untitled*, 1993
"Maurizio Cattelan," Galleria Massimo De Carlo, Milan, January–February 14, 1993 (solo show)

[107]  ***Untitled**, 1993*
Plastic, fabric, wood, lead, strings
Environmental dimensions

This is the work I created for my first exhibition in the Massimo De Carlo gallery in Milan. I saw a mechanical bear in a bakery on Madison Avenue in New York, where I went occasionally. He kept going up and down and his movement stayed in my head. When we decided to do the exhibition, I told Massimo I would like to do something that was visible from outside, without entering the gallery, which at the time was in Via Castaldi. So I had the entrance walled up. When a visitor rang the doorbell, the door would open automatically and the lights in the hall would switch on. But beyond the door there was a wall. You then looked through the two windows to see inside, where the bear was going back and forth. I also wanted to see Massimo De Carlo outside the gallery for a month. It was the first time I'd used the figure of an animal. In some way it represented me. It was funny and sad at the same time in the way it was isolated and unapproachable.

It was thanks to this work that I arrived in London, at the gallery run by Laure Genillard, who had seen the show in Milan.

[108]  ***Lavorare è un brutto mestiere**, 1993*
Inkjet print on plastic
280 × 580 cm

I took part in the Venice Biennale for the first time when I was invited to the "Aperto '93" section by one of the curators, Francesco Bonami. I just didn't know what to do. Like that Beck lyric: "I'm a loser baby, so why don't you kill me?" It was such a big space and I was so young and inexperienced. Francesco was brave, in a way, to let me do it. Precisely because I was nobody, I had nothing to lose. I hope this principle will always accompany me. I think it's essential to be able to do my job well. I didn't start making art to find myself afraid to say or do something, that's a cage I'd never want to put myself in. I chose art

to remain free from this kind of restraint and fear, and I still feel the responsibility of that decision. I rented out the space assigned to me by Bonami to the Armando Testa advertising agency, which offered me three options: a brand of toilet paper, the launch of a political party still without a name but with a leader already known as an entrepreneur (it would later become Forza Italia), and a perfume. The first risked shifting the meaning of the work and becoming insulting, while I didn't want to insult anyone. I sensed the second would have excessive implications, beyond my control. Perfume seemed the most neutral choice. After all, the content was not so important. Finding a billboard in the Biennale could be enough.

At the time, people interpreted it as a comment on the value of information and advertising. To me, it was more about admitting my failures in public. Products can change, their advertisements can change, but the concept is the same: someone else is paying for my lack of ideas.

Anyway, *Lavorare è un brutto mestiere* was my way to realize that in being invited to the Biennale, I was given a real opportunity to transform working, which is generally a very hard, ugly, unavoidable activity, into something beautiful. So when you call me an impostor, I feel you deny me the credit of having worked to transform my life into something better, not to make other people's lives worse. Which is what a real impostor does.

179

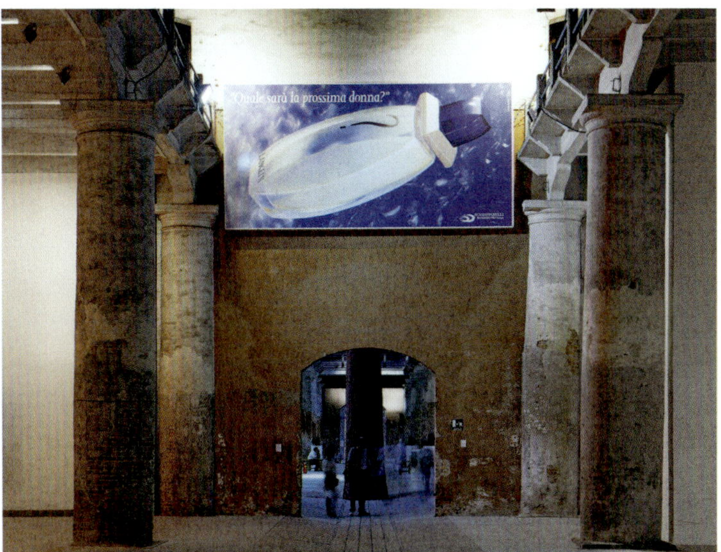

[108]  *Lavorare è un brutto mestiere*, 1993
"Cardinal Points of Art,"
45th Venice Biennale d'Arte, curated by Achille Bonito Oliva, June 14–October 10, 1993, section "Aperto '93. Emergency," curated by Francesco Bonami, coordination by Helena Kontova (group show)

[108]

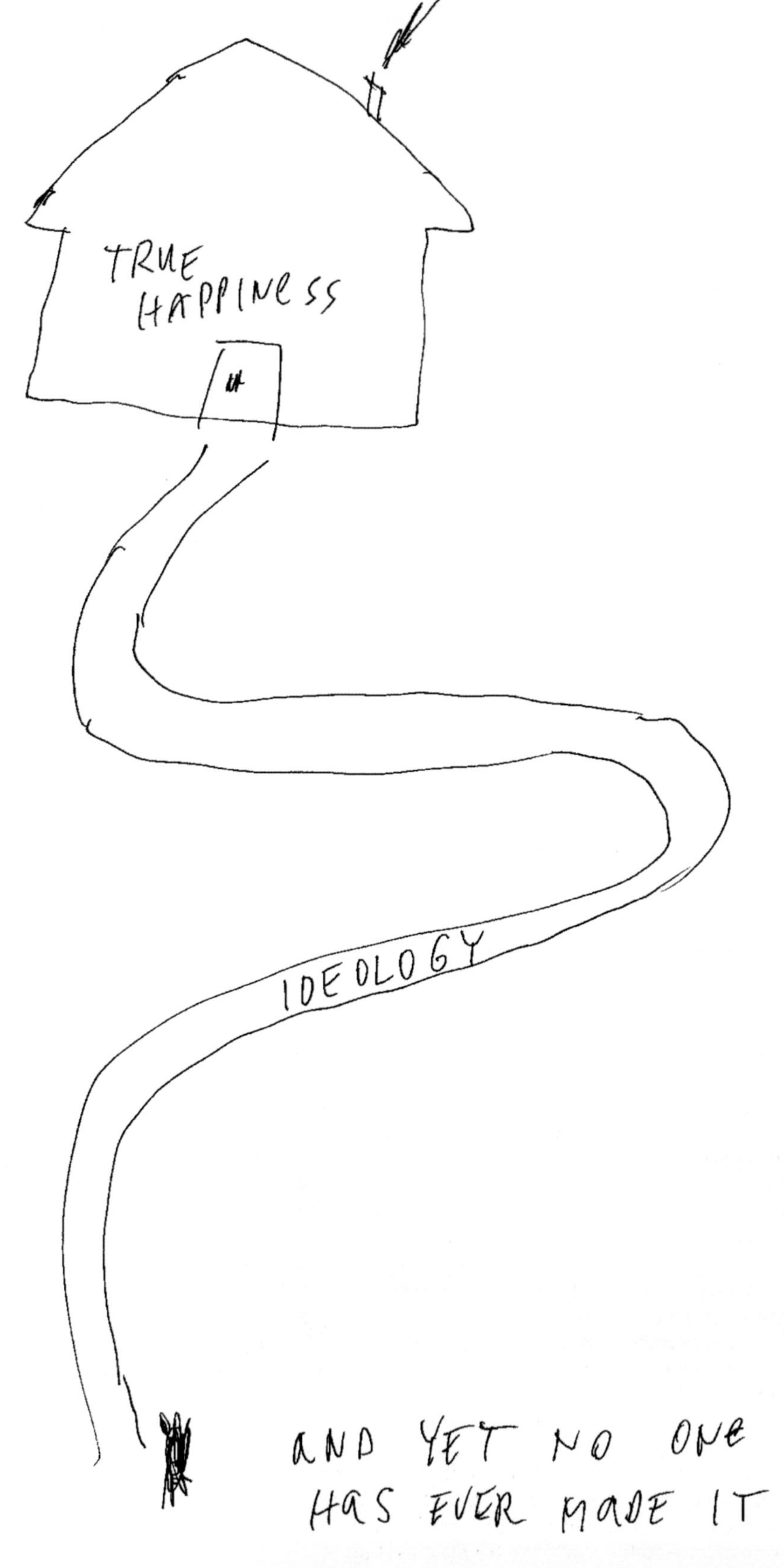

TRUE HAPPINESS
IDEOLOGY
AND YET NO ONE HAS EVER MADE IT

My parents wanted a girl, they were all set for a girl, but then I came along. I guess I must have been a disappointment. In fact, they didn't even have a backup name, and for days I went without one. After a while, since I hadn't been registered, the police even showed up. They opened the calendar of saints' names at random and out popped Maurizio. In this way, I'm the fruit of chance. So why are we born? They say we ought to be grateful to be born, but that's no answer. Could I have been born into a different family? No, otherwise I wouldn't be me, Maurizio Cattelan, born in Padua on September 21, 1960. That's the mystery of the universe, in a nutshell.

My parents were unfortunate. When I was born, my mother had cancer. Then another illness and then another. What would my analyst say? From the age of six months, I was sent from one public caregiver to another because my mother was in hospital. So, as a child I must have suffered from a lack of affection. No one read me fairy tales and I don't remember having any toys. I guess that then many of my works serve as customized toys for grown-ups.

Once, coming back by bus from one of the usual periods at summer camp, a seaside holiday for kids who couldn't afford any other holiday. The other families were there, on the lookout, waiting for their kids. All except mine. The driver saw me looking sad, asked me if I remembered my home address and took me back to the fold. It was a very sad day and that loneliness remained inside me for a long time. Near my home there was an orphanage. Passing in front of it every day, I used to meet two kids my own age. One day on impulse I gave them my collection of trading cards, a whole stack of cards. But then the teacher turned up and confiscated them, got all the kids together and shared the cards out equally among them. It was a great lesson.

When my mother wasn't in hospital she went to work to supplement my father's earnings. In this situation, becoming the babysitter of my two sisters became routine. But as a kid I also kept getting it in the neck from everyone: from my family, from school, practically from every established authority. The thing I learned best in childhood was to escape punishment, to avoid being a moving target. It wasn't a successful tactic, but it saved me from worse trouble than being an artist.

Between home, church and school, everybody did their best to leave their mark on me. I have a collection of educational episodes that are not very edifying for how we conceive the relationship with childhood today. Hanging on the wall of my classroom in first and second grade was a carpet beater. I never saw it at work, but I don't think it was there for dusting carpets. Things were different in those days. It was quite common for physical punishment to be inflicted on the unruliest kids. As for me, perhaps I was a trouble-maker, much more than now. My mother, in despair, came and asked what was wrong with me. I remember a half hour of silence. In my head there were thousands of beginnings of possible dialogues that never took verbal form. It wasn't just the inability to express my needs, it was an emotional block. I didn't have a drum, but I used silence.

At home I never saw a book or a magazine, except *Famiglia Cristiana*. We grew up with very little. There was TV, because I haven't forgotten *Carosello* and Neil Armstrong setting foot on the moon, but we only had a shower at home when I was ten years old. Before, after doing the laundry, my mother would fill a tub with the leftover water and everyone would get in. There was no running water and there wasn't gas either. We used to make great trips to the cellar to fetch the coal.

Even as a teenager my urgent need was to make myself financially independent. Between the second and third year of high school they flunked me in three subjects, so I said to myself: "In September I won't go back to school. I'll go to night school, find a job and leave home." Eight hours of work and five hours of evening school, where I learned a sense of discipline.

On the one hand I was too independent, and on the other I wanted to reassure my parents. My mother kept telling me: "You're a slob and a red terrorist." Both terms were off the mark, but the period was rife with paranoia, shadows and suspicions. She'd got this idea into her head and my father went along with it. When I was sixteen the Carabinieri even called at our door. I used to practice shooting at the gun range, and this had aroused their suspicions, so they came to ask me to explain this strange hobby.

When I was seventeen I was working as a trainee bookkeeper and they gave me a week's vacation. I left home, telling my mother I was off to Spain, but I don't think she realized I meant the country. I drove from Padua to Barcelona with bags of gasoline instead of suitcases, because my trusty Califfo moped had a one-liter tank. It went well downhill and along the flat, but you had to pedal uphill. It juddered so much that I used to wake up shaking in the mornings.

In the battle for independence, I left home at eighteen, but I'd already decided to do leave when I was fourteen. It was 1978. I wasn't very far from certain political circles, but I had my own plans. Changing the world seemed endless, while I had to try and change my own situation first. And I couldn't take any chances. If I blew it, I'd have to go back home. That would have been a huge defeat for me. My struggle for independence meant being self-sufficient, freeing myself from family arguments over every decision. And then I needed silence around me. Our place was small and there were too many of us. I remember my eighteenth birthday clearly. I had two plastic bags. My mother asked me: "Where are you going?" I said: "Away from home." "Away from home where?" "It's nothing to do with you. I'm just leaving. Ciao." "Come on, don't be silly, no one leaves home with plastic bags." But I only had my underwear and socks to take with me... At first my mother took it very badly, as a rejection. She'd been an orphan and she re-experienced the sense of abandonment. My father, on the other hand, took it in his stride. One less mouth to feed.

If I think of what I was and where my friends from that distant time are, I tell myself that I've managed to do what I wanted to. At times I think back to the day I quit the hospital, one of my many old jobs. At the personnel office they all froze, with amazement and dismay written on their faces. They said: "Are you crazy? It's a secure job. Think about your parents. What are you going to do tomorrow?" "I don't know. We'll see." At home it was a shock. In 2000 my father was still urging me to change my mind. "If you come back to Padua, maybe they'll take you on again at the hospital."

Padua is the place I come from, but it's also the one I don't want to go back to. My childhood is archived there. I prefer to leave it tightly closed in boxes that I sometimes open at a distance. Padua is also the city where I discovered art for the first time. There was the statue of *Gattamelata* in the piazza; then there was a gigantic wooden horse kept in Palazzo della Ragione; and finally there was the forerunner of a concept store bound up with the cult of the Saint and relics. These are all images that have left an indelible mark on me. One day as a child I went to the square with paper and pencils to draw

*Gattamelata*, but I failed in the attempt and asked someone to draw it for me. This is a vice I haven't lost even as an adult.

In the end, I learned a lot from my family. They never confused what they were and what I was. They never had the Maradona syndrome. They're a healthy and inexhaustible reservoir of insecurity. I don't have any kids, but I've given birth to many offspring by splitting and duplication. Perhaps this is why I like dummies and self-portraits. They're a small army of kids, though with the heads of grown-ups. But mine is a family made up of orphans with many adoptive fathers, who have taken care of my works better than I ever did.

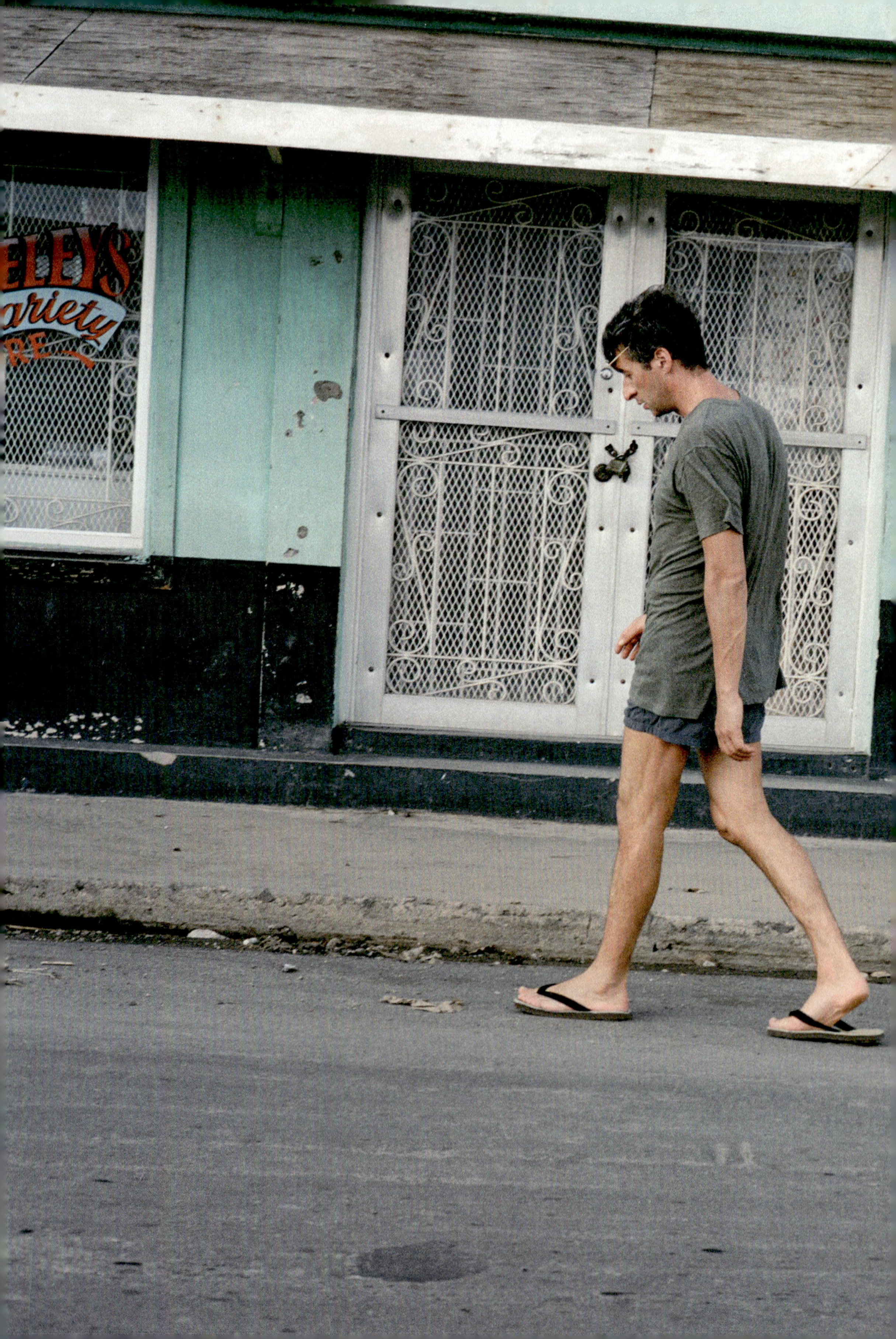
ELEYS'
riety
RE

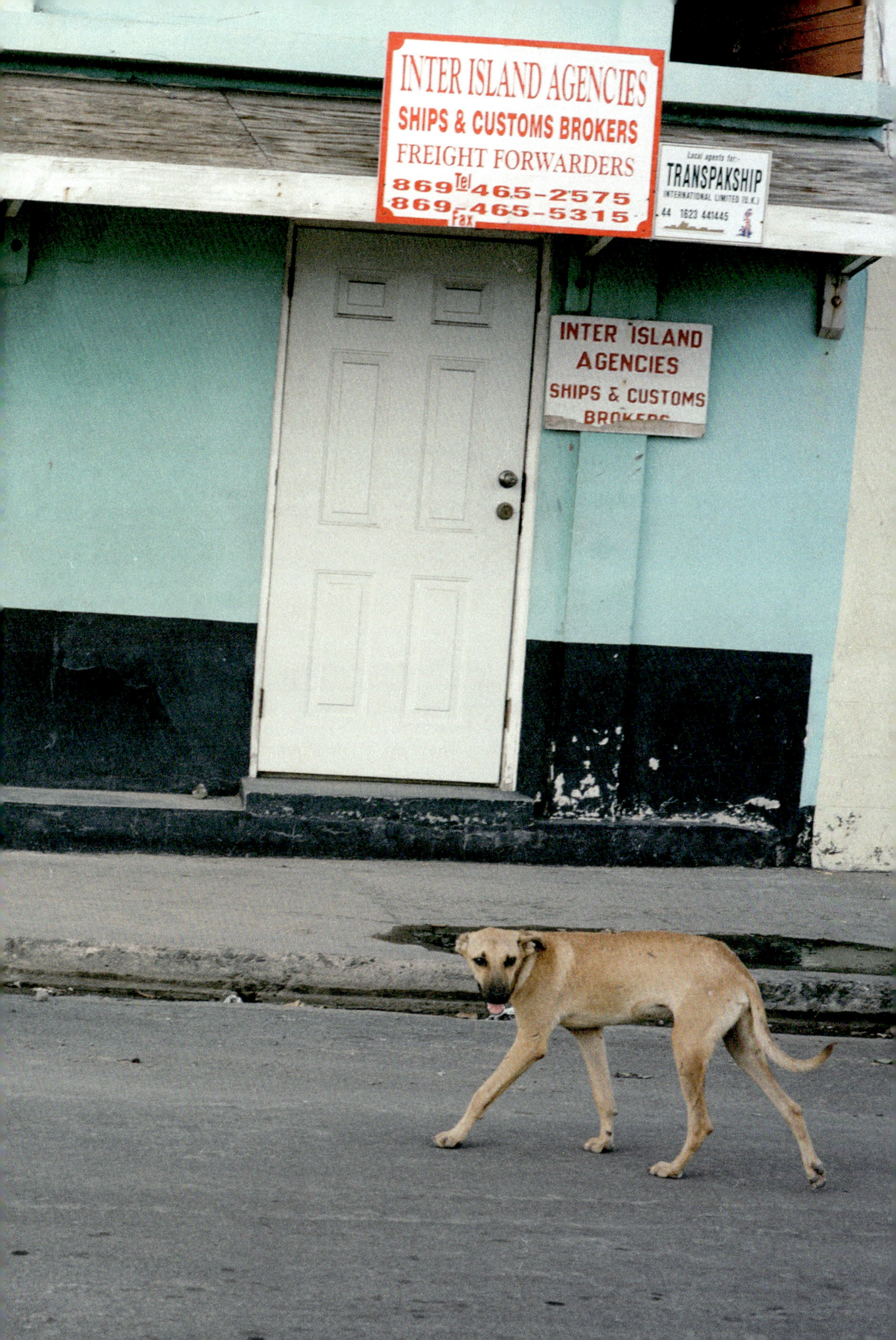
INTER ISLAND AGENCIES
SHIPS & CUSTOMS BROKERS
FREIGHT FORWARDERS
Tel 869 465-2575
Fax 869 465-5315
Local agents for:-
TRANSPAKSHIP
INTERNATIONAL LIMITED (U.K.)
44 1623 441445
INTER ISLAND
AGENCIES
SHIPS & CUSTOMS
BROKERS

I did a lot of different jobs before I ended up as an artist. Independence has always been what I most desired, and while working I was looking for a way to find some freedom, to escape from authority in those days. But I came to realize that working eight hours a day was a waste of time. My aim was to reach zero hours a week, meaning not working but to have an income anyway. I kept dreaming of empty spaces where I could live without feeling hemmed in. But first I had to detox, not so much from work as my upbringing. I came from a traditional working-class Catholic family, where they said: "If you don't work, you don't eat." There was a punitive atmosphere at home. To detox I had to get rid of everything that wasn't a part of me: inherited habits, false beliefs, imaginary fetters and everything I'd always considered normal just because everyone accepted them. An extenuating cleanout that was the price for gaining emancipation and independence. But I did have one lucky break: I was able to distinguish necessity from desire.

From the time I was twelve, I would spend every summer working. When I was thirteen I lost my summer job. Now it may seem funny but at the time it wasn't, because that job provided all my spending money. I was working at the Basilica of Saint Anthony in Padua, in the souvenir shop where they sold statuettes of the saint, postcards and so forth. Everyone needs an outlet when they work eight to ten hours a day with a bunch of other kids. We were having a break and laughing. I had drawn mustaches on the little statues. As soon as the friars saw them, they came straight over to me, without asking the other twenty kids anything. They knew right away it must have been Maurizio. Another time they fired me was in 1978. I was working as a cleaner in a laundry, and they found me doing my own laundry at work. They said: "What are you doing here?" And I said: "Washing! Washing my laundry! It's my uniform! Where else can I do it?" They fired me.

When I was a kid I was asked what I wanted to be when I grew up. I said: "A waiter." That was one of the few jobs I never did, because for the rest, from being a gardener to a cook to a cleaner, passing through a postman, a trainee bookkeeper who went around paying the bills, and even a sperm donor in Verona, I went in for practically everything. The jobs mostly lasted three months. My first regular, secure, potentially permanent job was in a hospital. First the nursing course, then working in the departments. I was the gofer in the various wards. I worked forty-two hours a week plus four hours of the nursing course. To do that kind of work you need to have a vocation, like being a priest. Your contribution is more than just what you do, it's also the human contribution you can make. It challenges you continuously, because you have to forget your own problems, and at the same time not let your day be affected by other people's. After a while I was moved to the intensive care unit. There, of course, no one says anything, there are no emotional exchanges. It's full of instruments beeping in an endless variety of electronic tones. It's like living in the realm of the machine. At the hospital I actually did a bit of everything, I even swept the wards. Wearing a white coat, invariably dirty, I emptied the garbage cans, I got rained on when the weather was bad, every now and then I cursed, and I was busy keeping a citadel of 3,000 people neat and clean. After a while they asked me whether I was willing to work in the morgue. I didn't say no and I did another six months, almost like a mortician. From intensive care, the world of the living who were dying, I was moved downstairs to the world of the dead. Both places taught me that if you work with the living you can't be moody. This is probably why I find life much more serious than death. The relationship with a patient is much stronger and more demanding than with a corpse, which only leaves you with a sense of peace. As a nurse I realized that my agitation wouldn't help the patients. The energy of the people around you when you're so fragile is vital. So the solitary deaths caused by Covid affected me deeply. In the past, people gave birth and died at home, perhaps even in the same bed. It's only in recent days that life and death have happened in remote places, cut off from everyday life. I can't say whether it was better or worse, but personally I feel I'm very lucky to have had these experiences. Dealing with the sick and then the dead taught me to see the true value of every event in my life, to keep things in perspective.

After a while I'd had enough. I'd reached this point psychologically. I found a sympathetic doctor, who understood my state of mind. He decided I was having a bit of a breakdown and gave me a couple of months' sick leave. I still received my salary, but for the first time I also had a chance to finally look around. My peers were getting up in the morning, if they got up, they did what they had to do, if they wanted to do it, and then had to fill the day with nothing. "Well, that's great," I said to myself. "I want to do that too." I had all the time I wanted, a privilege that can't be bought. It's not written anywhere that you have to work. It's not written that someone has to pay you because you can't or don't want to work. But that's life. I've always managed to get by.

I quit in 1984, spent another year in Padua, and then moved to Forlì. When I got there, I started a course in Bologna, a European Community pilot course, and spent six months at a computer for eight hours a day. My head was really getting bigger and my body was getting smaller. It reached the point, whenever I got home, that I was beginning to think: "When am I going to kill myself?" At the start of the course I had the feeling of having a good power over something that seems not just unattainable but incomprehensible—to dominate the machine. Then, when you realize that there's only one set of instructions, which might be used to program a washing machine, you lose interest, unless you can combine what you're doing with your research. So I started doing experiments with automatic writing until it palled. Instead, after the hospital and the morgue, I discovered that I enjoyed working with my hands, so I began to make the furniture and lamps that eventually took me to Milan. The impulse that drove me was a reflection. I was coming out of a moment of extreme fatigue, hence the question: "Why am I tired?" Because I hadn't understood that the terms of work weren't quantity but quality. Suddenly everything became new. There were no more rules and I was finally the only person in charge of my life. Existence was waiting to be discovered.

In practice, I came to doing art by running away from other jobs. And then I had far more work than before. Seeking freedom, I found the real prison. But at least it's the prison that I chose for myself.

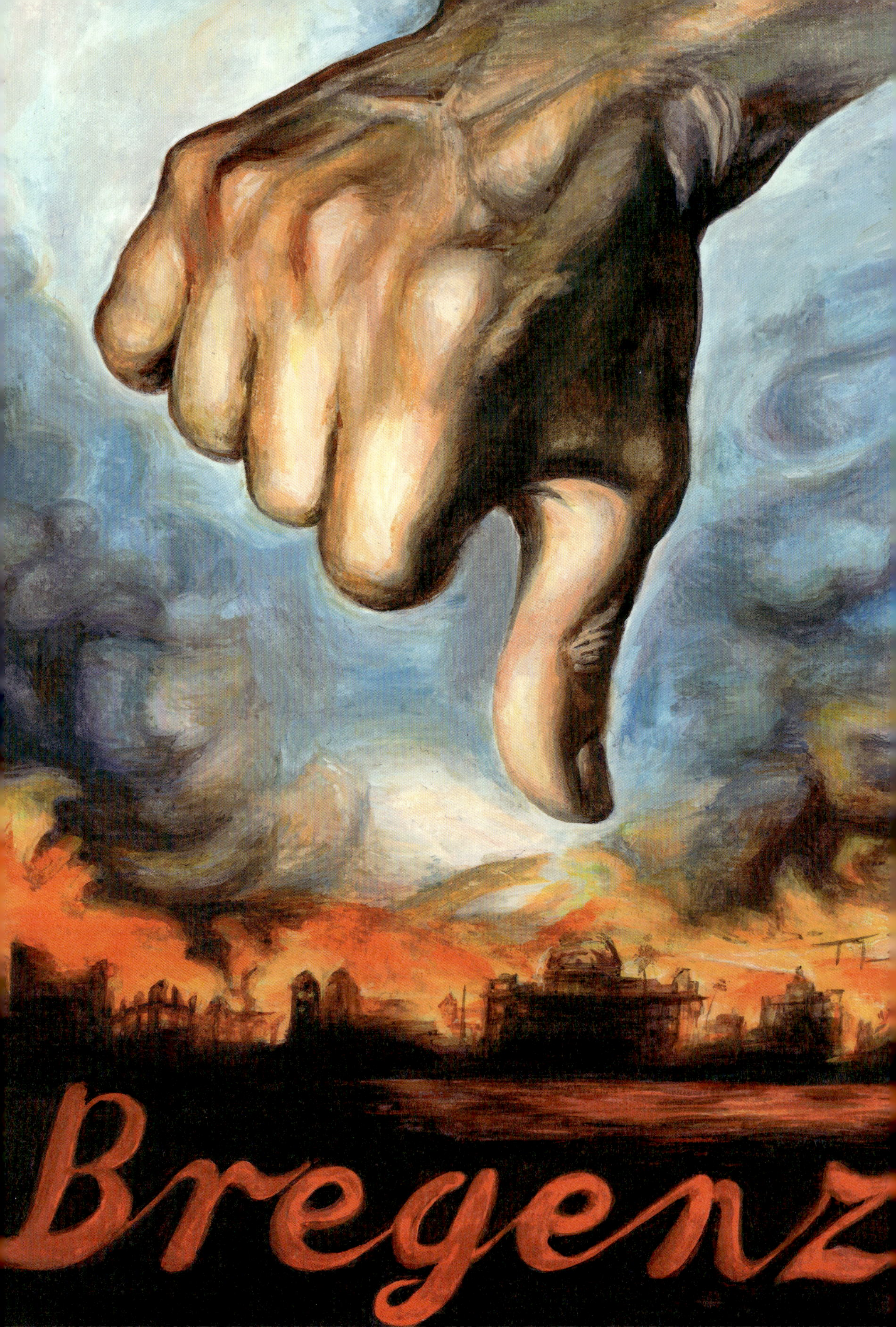
Bregenz

**Death is a theme. My art is very basic, it deals with simple, essential topics: death, money, power. Not sex, because I don't think it's so interesting, at the end of the day. It's like eating: you need it to survive, not to create. It's not a subject; it's an activity. You can't avoid death, you always need at least some money, and power is the driving force of life.**

**Life itself is very often the subject of art, and death is part of it. There really isn't much more certainty in our lives than that sooner or later we won't be here anymore. And around this certainty everyone rotates at their own speed. I have to admit that I'm the first to be surprised when I consider all my works taken together. From the very beginning, many were associated with death, and it wasn't a conscious choice.**

**Before becoming an artist I worked in a hospital for three or four years. There the relationship with life and death is intense. Perhaps to overcome that very harrowing experience, after a while I became cynical, unfeeling faced with the circle of life, and then I was unconsciously compelled to work with that very material. Probably also to play it down. It's the other side of me.**

**The pyramids, luxurious, colossal tombs, are among the world's most widely visited monuments. The mystery of death is perhaps the only one that humanity, and with it art, has never ceased to question. However technologically evolved we may be, life is always governed by two basic laws: we're born and we die. The symbolic, universal themes are always the same. Signs change and take on the value of symbols, the signs that the artist identifies and exhibits to the public. In this way art can have the arduous task of displaying what everyone is afraid to express.**

**Every artwork is a way of defeating death. There are three ways to ensure continuity: to reproduce, become an organ donor, and create artworks that, if you're a good artist, will endure. Each of my works, or maybe any artwork in general, is consequently a desperate attempt to distract death from you for a while. Like the chess game in Ingmar Bergman's movie *The Seventh Seal*, where the knight is trying to distract Death. He knows he can't get the better of Death, but he can put off his defeat. At a lower level than Bergman, this is what I've been trying to do ever since I was a kid, by creating distractions.**

**Anyhow, as I see it, the highest form of human art is tragedy, because we're perhaps**

the only creatures intimately aware they will have to die, even when death isn't imminent. Death always unnerves us. Other creatures are afraid only when it's present, when a huge gaping maw is about to eat them. We humans, on the other hand, all sit around quietly and suddenly come out with: "Aw shit! I have to die." We find tragedy in every century: in opera, in theatre, sometimes in music. But in the twentieth century, at the height of the appreciation of tragedy, of loss, there's the blues. "I'm going to get up this morning, and I'm going to put my shoes on." The idea of putting your shoes on in the morning is the hardest thing in the world.

Death is an exclamation mark. It makes sense of everything, but destroys the suspense. Worrying about death is like worrying about the growth of a flower. We all know that every process is bound to end sooner or later. The terrible thing in people's lives is when there's nothing left to die. You can play them the great music of the centuries and they can't hear it.

They say you've never really lived until you've risked dying. When you rest in peace, and your image fades, and your image of the world fades, and your idea of others fades, what's left? A glow, a radiant emptiness that is simply who you are.

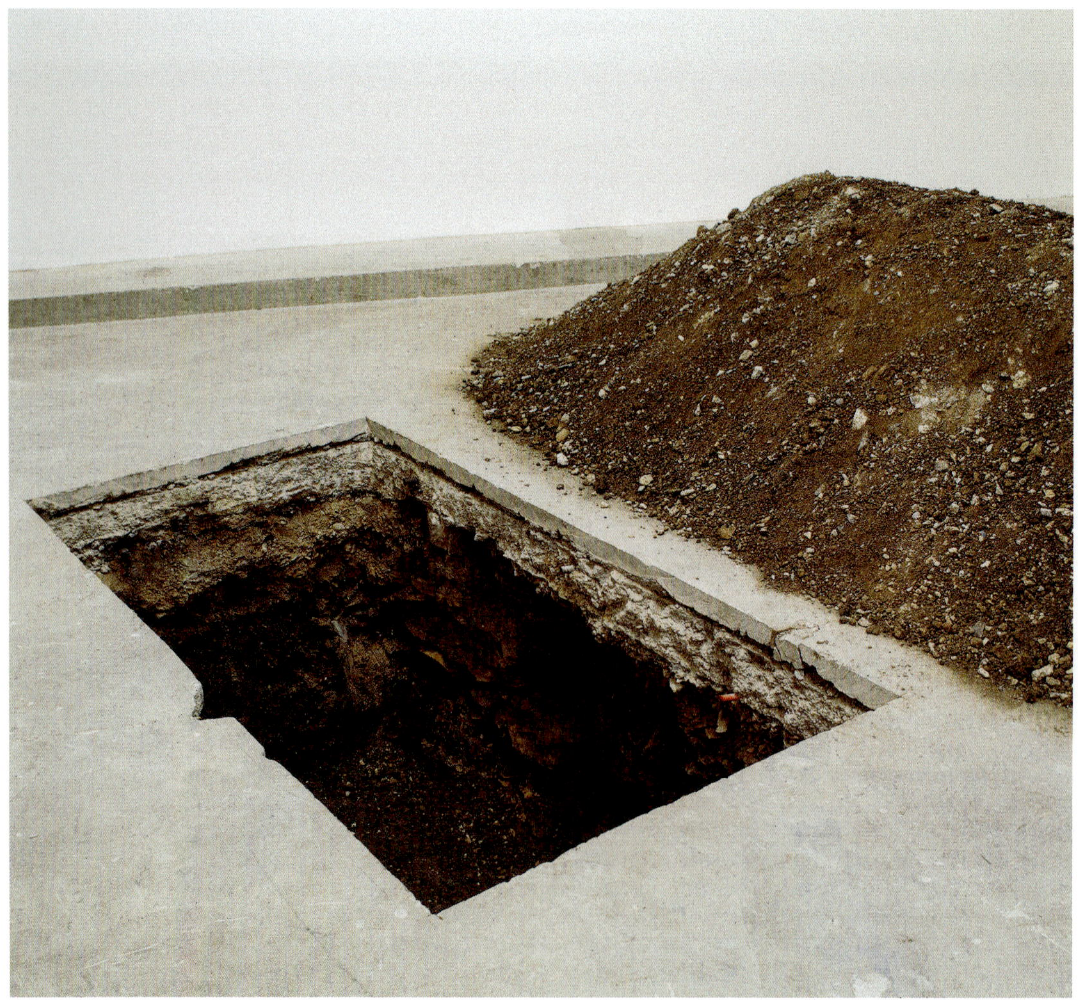

[109]

[109]  *Untitled*, 1997
"Maurizio Cattelan," Le Consortium – Centre d'art
contemporain, Dijon, January 24–March 22, 1997
(solo show)

[109]   ***Untitled**, 1997*
Rectangular hole, pile of removed soil
200 × 100 × 150 cm

[110]   ***Untitled**, 1997*
Wardrobe door (wood, paint, metal)
installed in a museum doorway
C. 200 × 100 × 40 cm

I was invited to Dijon for a solo show at Le Consortium. The first time I saw the space, the lighting reminded me of a morgue. So it was a kind of natural decision to dig a hole. I guess it reminded people of a grave, but it was just a hole with some dirt beside it. In fact, I hadn't added anything to the place, I had just taken something away, and I'd created an escape route for myself. I also moved a metal cabinet that I found there and placed it in front of the office door. Also in this case I worked by subtraction: I had cut off the back of the cabinet and the museum staff had to go through that absurd portal to get to work.

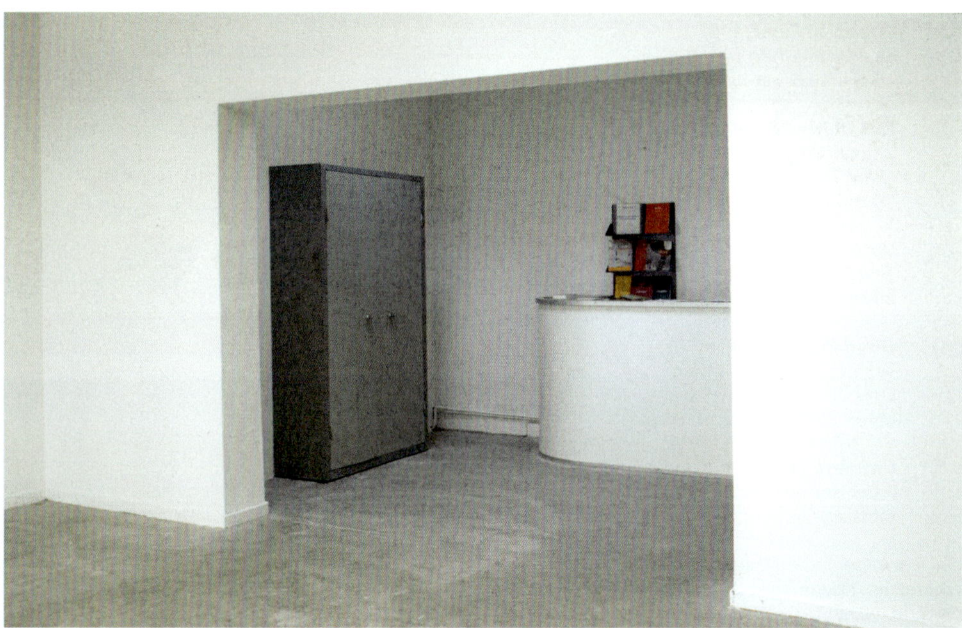

[110.1]

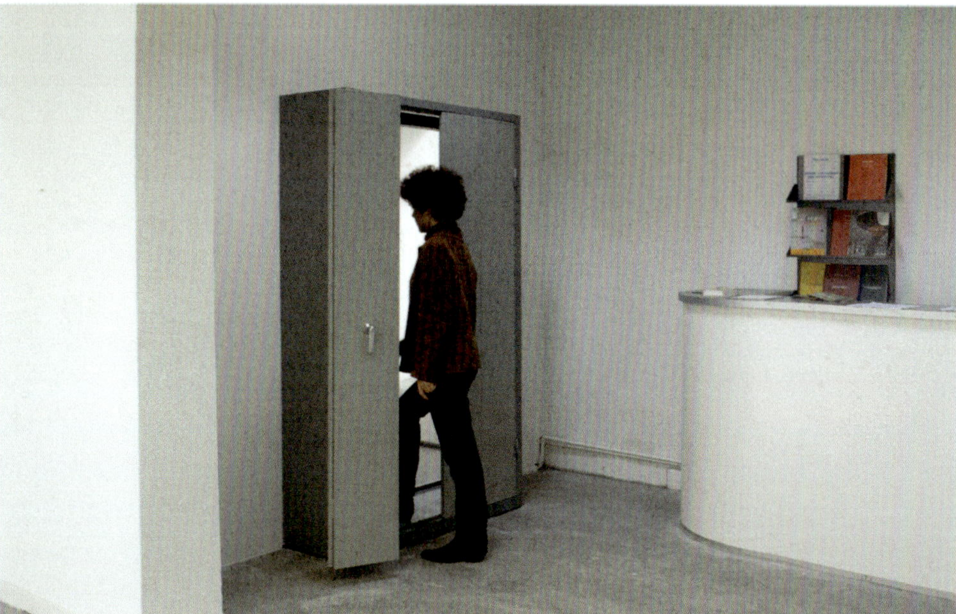

[110.2]

[110.1-2]   ***Untitled**, 1997*
Installation created for "Maurizio Cattelan," Le Consortium – Centre d'art contemporain, Dijon, January 24–March 22, 1997 (solo show)

[111] ***Untitled***, **1995**
Black and white photographic print
mounted on aluminum
125 × 190 cm

[112] ***Untitled***, **1995**
Black and white photographic print
mounted on aluminum
125 × 190 cm

[113] ***Stone Dead***, **1997**
Taxidermied dog
30 × 38 × 15 cm

[114] ***Cheap to Feed***, **1997**
Taxidermied dog
40.5 × 35.5 × 16.5 cm

[115] ***13.3.81 My Last Kiss***, **1997**
2 taxidermied dogs
Overall dimensions:
30.5 × 135.9 × 94 cm

[116] ***Untitled***, **1997**
Taxidermied dog
Lifesize

[117] ***Good Boy***, **1998**
Taxidermied dog, chair
Dog: 12.7 × 40.6 × 27.9 cm;
chair: 81.3 × 45.7 × 50.8 cm

[118] ***Untitled***, **2007**
2 taxidermied dogs, taxidermied chick
Lifesize

192

On a trip to India, I saw dogs sleeping every-where, an image that stuck in my head. Once back in New York, I came across a couple of dogs that kept following me, and they too stayed in my mind. The first work that I used a dog in was *Stone Dead*. Curled up under a large man-telpiece in the Castello di Rivoli, he looked in his perfect place and made the museum room look homely. A series of works followed. For my ex-hibition at the Kunsthaus Bregenz in 2008 I re-used this subject, but in a family scene, almost a nativity: two Labradors and a little chick in the middle, though it isn't clear whether it's really safe between them (*Untitled*, 2007). I also re-turned to this theme using marble, when the dog finally found his best friend (*Breath*, 2021). And on the other hand, I impersonated the first dog myself, having myself photographed lying on the ground, curled up and with my tongue out like in a cartoon (*Untitled*, 1995; *Untitled*, 1995).

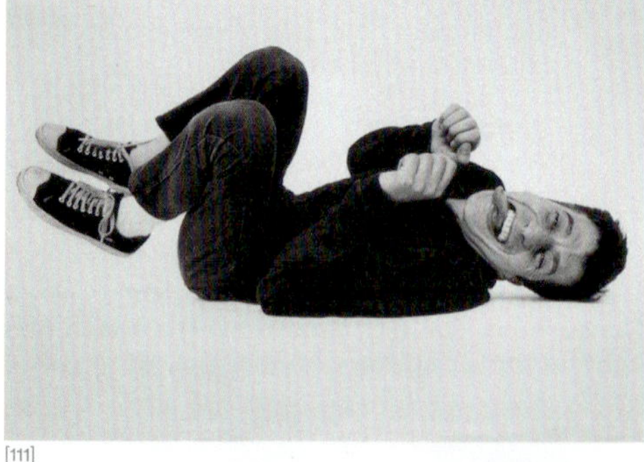

[111]

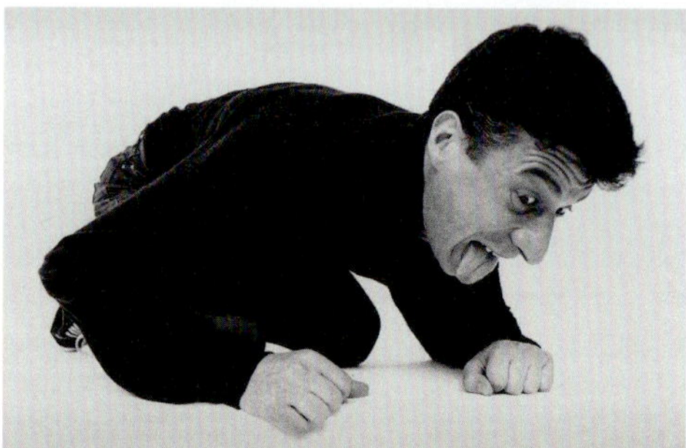

[112]

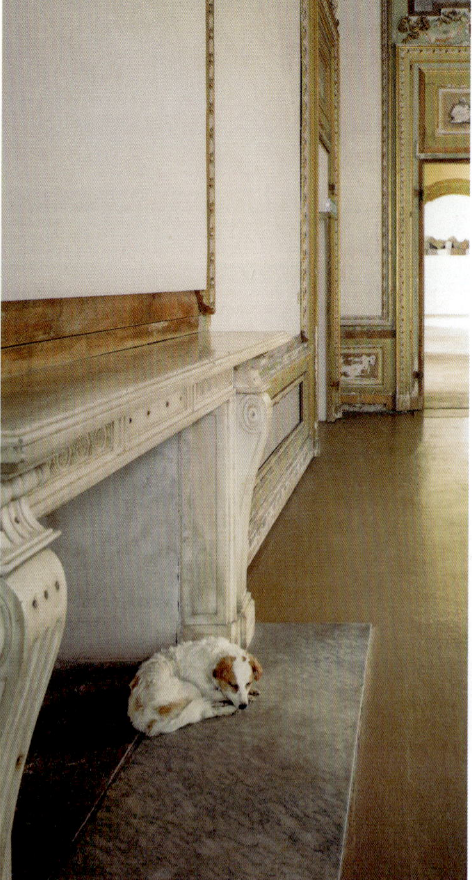

[113]

[111]   *Untitled*, 1995

[112]   *Untitled*, 1995

[113]   *Stone Dead*, 1997
"Maurizio Cattelan. Tre installazioni per il Castello,"
curated by Giorgio Verzotti, Castello di Rivoli Museo d'Arte
Contemporanea, Rivoli-Turin, September 25, 1997–January
18, 1988 (solo show)

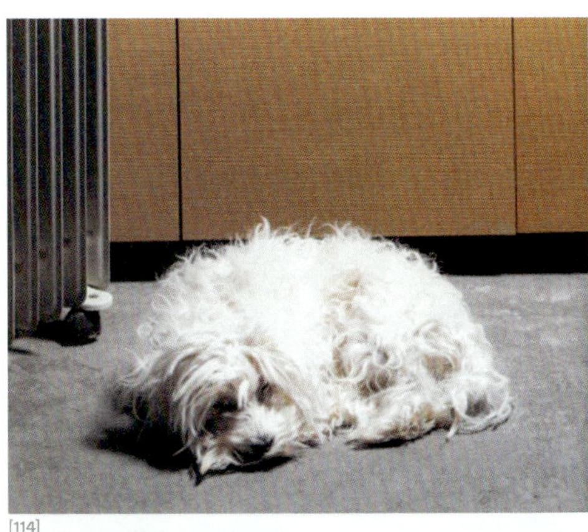

[114]

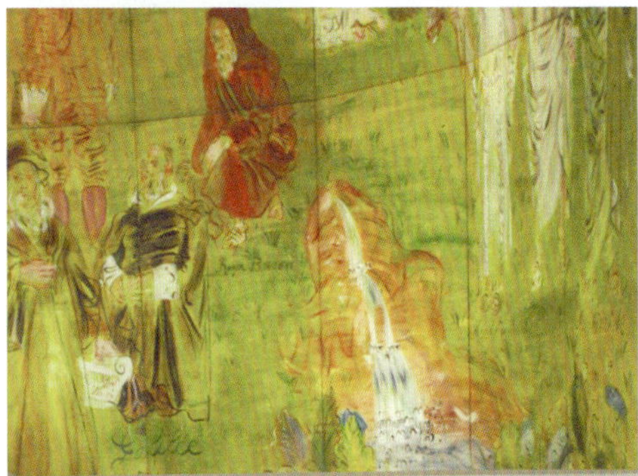

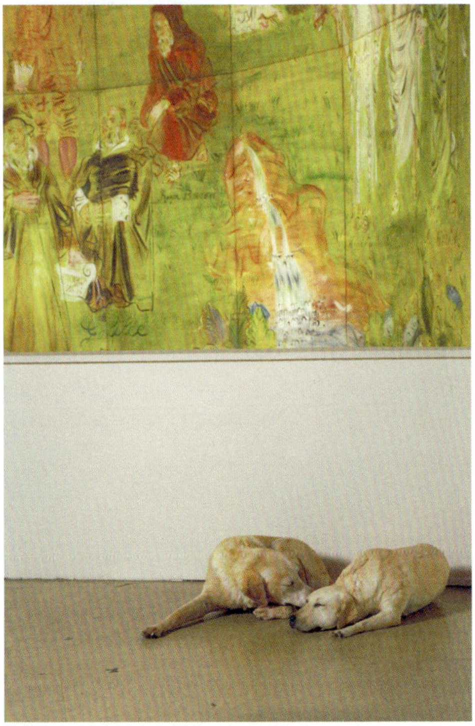

[115]

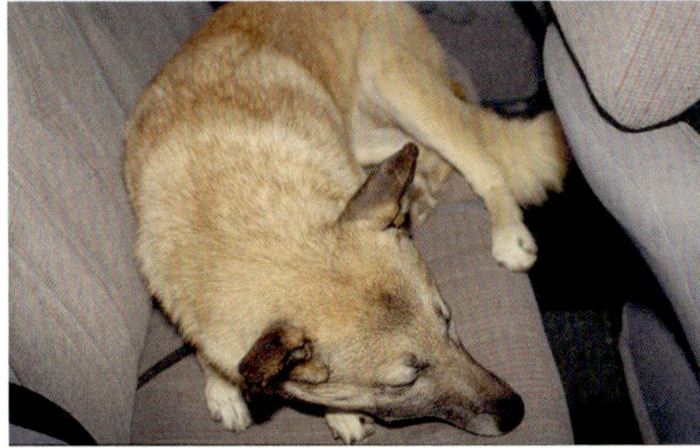

[116]

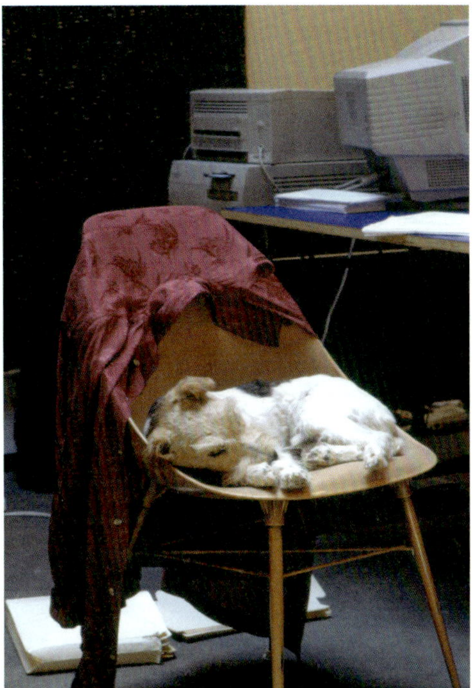

[117]

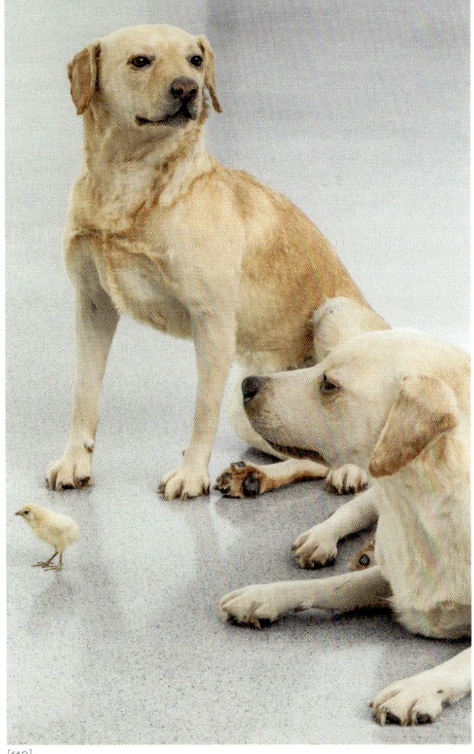

[118]



[114]   *Cheap to Feed*, 1997

[115]   *13.3.81 My Last Kiss*, 1997
"Delta," curated by Francesco Bonami, Musée d'Art
Moderne de la Ville de Paris, December 4, 1997–
January 18, 1998 (group show)

[116]   *Untitled*, 1997

[117]   *Good Boy*, 1998
Gavin Brown's Enterprise, New York, 1998

[118]   *Untitled*, 2007 (detail)
"Maurizio Cattelan," curated by Eckhard Schneider,
Kunsthaus Bregenz, February 2–March 24, 2008
(solo show)

[119] **_Untitled_, 1997**
[Initially titled: *Pluto*]
Dog skeleton, newspaper
50 × 80 × 40 cm

I did this work just before Skulptur Projekte in Münster, where I showed *Love Lasts Forever* (1997), made with the skeletons of a rooster, a cat, a dog, and a donkey placed one on top of the other. But this dog, which I'd nicknamed Pluto, is alone. He's waiting for someone to take the newspaper to. It's the idea of fidelity that is timeless.

[120] **_Piumino_, 1999**
Marble
56 × 35 × 14 cm

[121] **_Sparky_, 1999**
Marble
14 × 34.9 × 55.9 cm

[122] **_Sparky_, 1999**
Marble

[123] **_Lupetto_, 1999**
Marble
35 × 56 × 14 cm

Piumino was the name of a friend's dog. He died and I asked his owner if I could bury him at Villa Medici, in Rome. His tomb was the work with which to close the animal period. Then, while I was at the villa, I discovered that a dog was already buried in the gardens, belonging to a lieutenant who had lived there. This dog was called Sparky, and so the second version of the work was born. *Lupetto* is yet another.

194

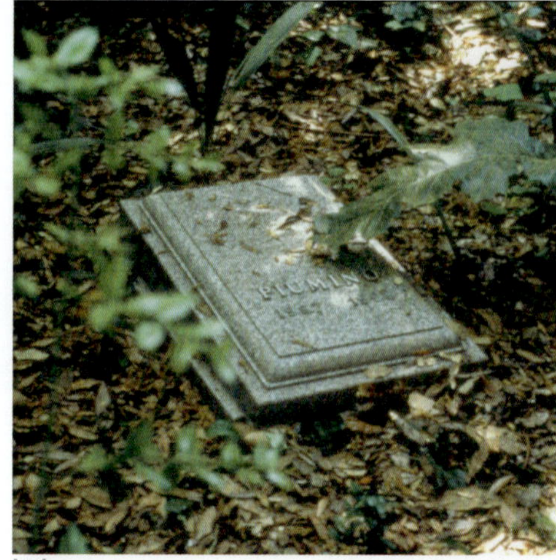

[120]

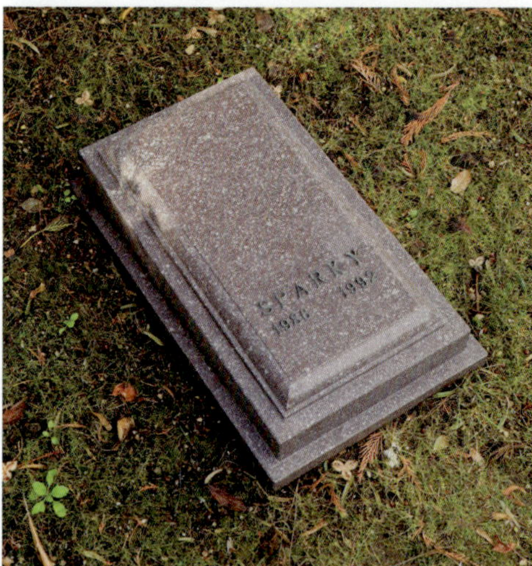

[121]

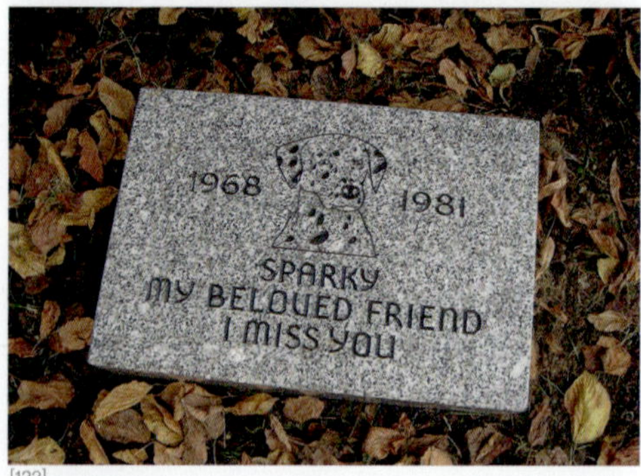



[122]

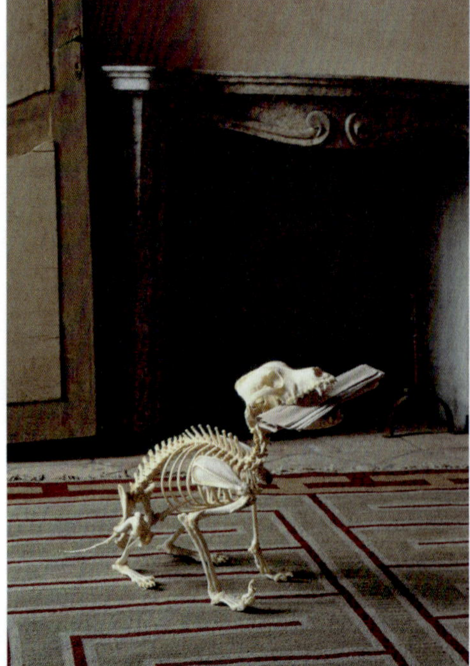

[119]

[119]  *Untitled*, 1997
"Ironisch/Ironic," curated by Rein Wolfs, Migros Museum für Gegenwartskunst, Zurich, June 26–August 9, 1998 (group show)

[120]  *Piumino*, 1999
Académie de France, Villa Medici, Rome, permanent installation created on the occasion of "La Ville, le jardin, la mémoire," curated by Laurence Bossé, Carolyn Christov-Bakargiev, and Hans Ulrich Obrist, May 28–August 29, 1998 (group show)

[121]  *Sparky*, 1999

[122]  *Sparky*, 1999

[124] ***Untitled*, 2000**
Polyesther resin, paint, synthetic flowers
30.5 × 43.2 × 43.2 cm

[125] ***Untitled*, 2000**
Polyesther resin, paint, synthetic flowers

[126] ***Deaf*, 2025**
Glass, bronze, wood, cork, silver,
fabric
27.5 × Ø 12 cm

Somewhere I'd seen a skull with holes in it, perhaps even with painted flowers, anyway a skull-shaped vase. They say it brings good luck and so I decided to make one too. My skull is waiting for luck with folded arms, but he has the freedom to change his hair. At any rate, it's death that gives rise to life.

I had a period when I worked on the signs or symbols of existence. I happened to see one and decided to do it again. The pope of *La Nona Ora* (1999) had the same origin. In creating the work I realized that reproducing the symbol wasn't enough. I managed to modify the pope, and not this one, but it would be interesting to redo it in marble. I only managed to add his legs and place him waiting seated (*Untitled*).

Recently I tried again. I put the skeleton in a bottle. He's playing the guitar and lulling himself in a rocking chair with his face covered by a balaclava. It's called *Deaf*, and it's not clear if he's isolated himself or is imprisoned, if he doesn't want to be seen or heard, or if it's other people who won't listen to him.

[124] *Untitled*, 2000

[125] *Untitled*, 2000
Cimetière du Père-Lachaise, Paris

[126] *Deaf*, 2025

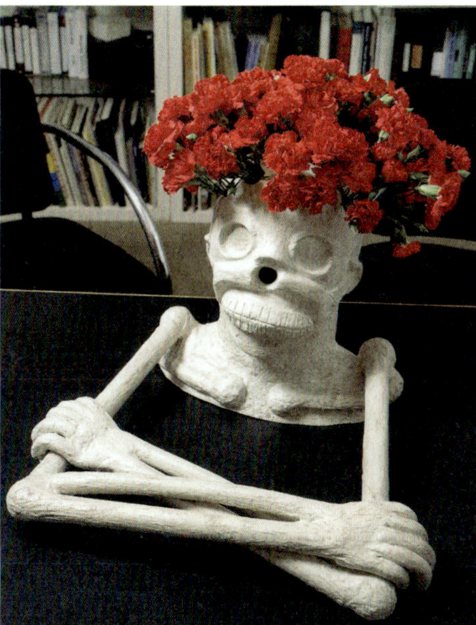
[124]

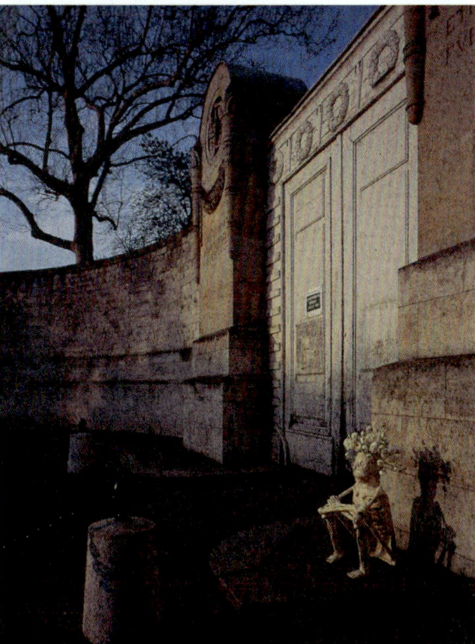
[125]

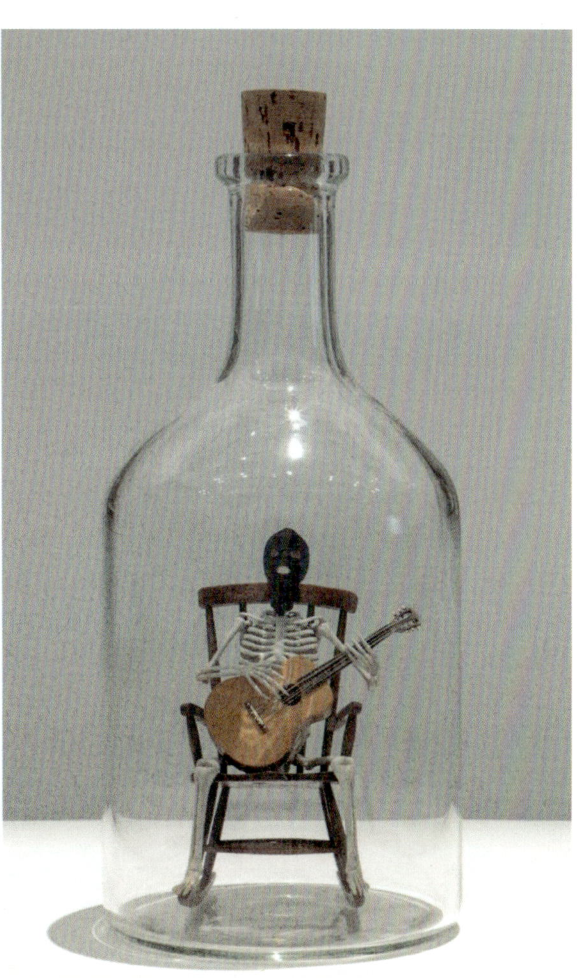
[126]

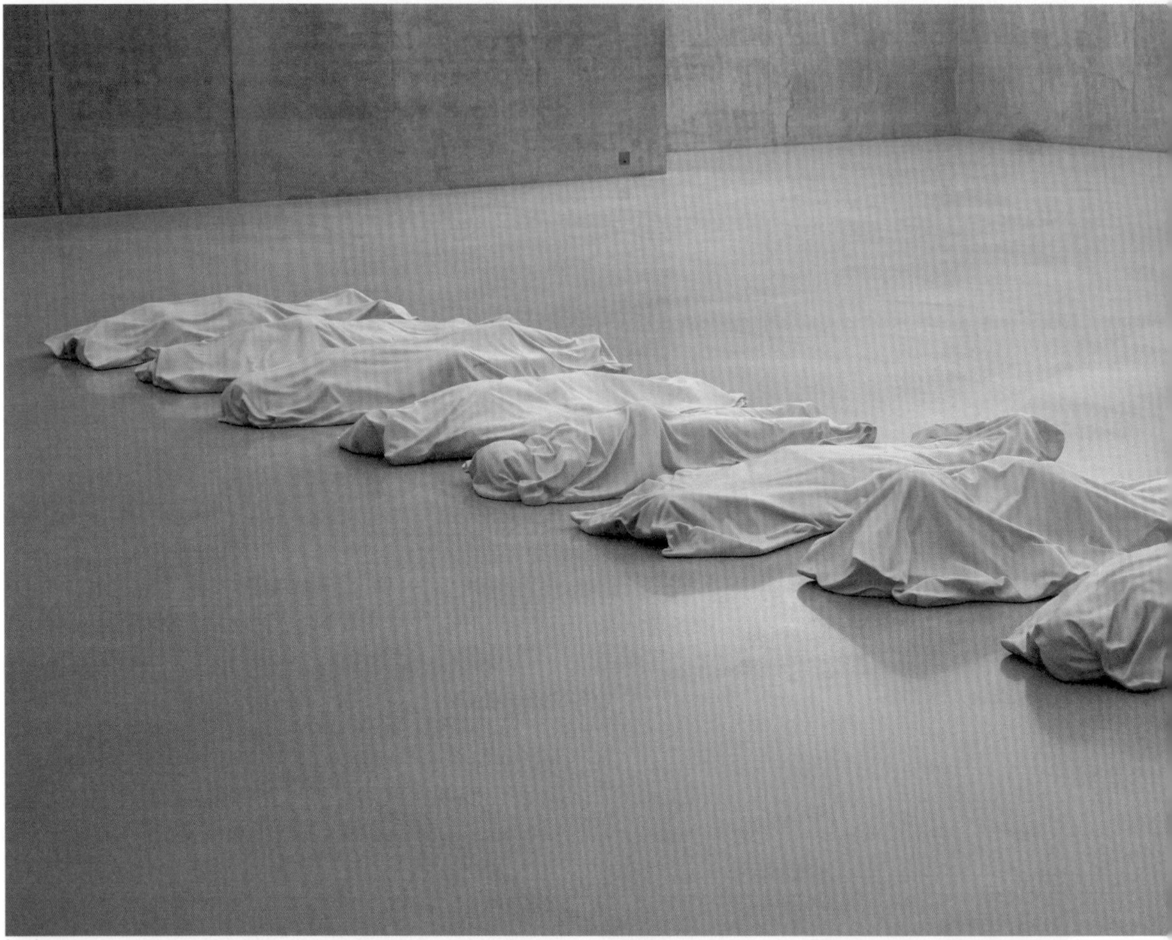

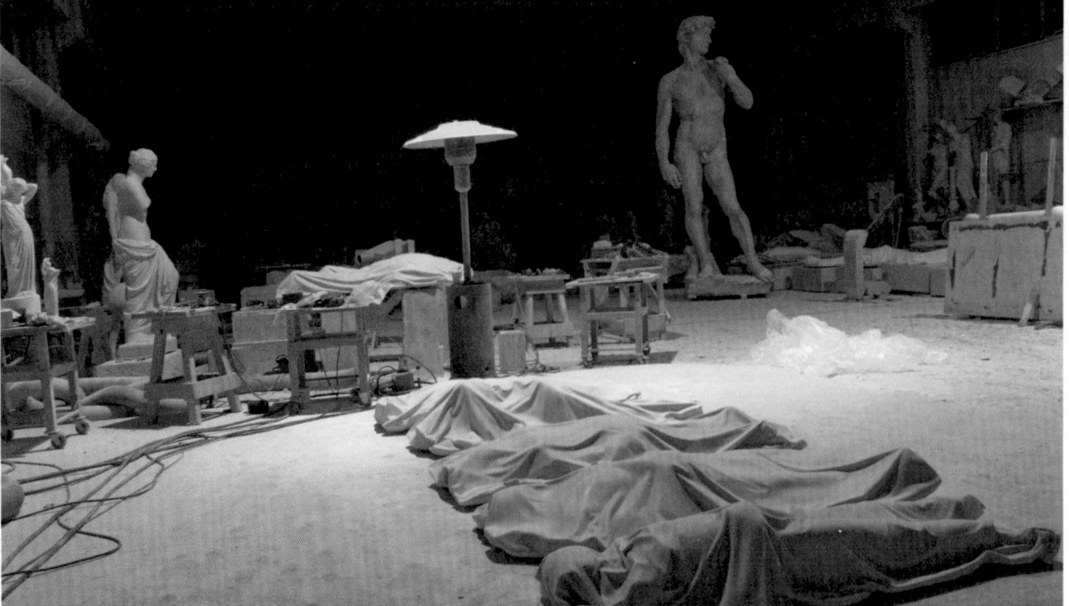

[127.1]

[127.2]

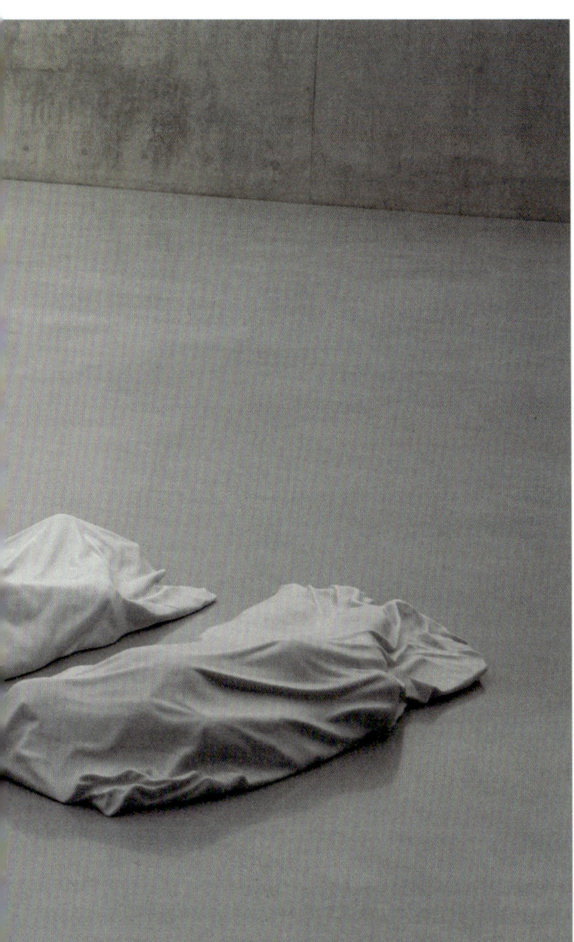

**[128]** ***Eternity*, 2018**
Gravestones, mixed media
Variable dimensions

My favorite dream has always been the one where I get to go to my own funeral. I've always liked cemeteries, so quiet and inspiring. Maybe we should create a place where we go and laugh at the people who have to die. In Italy they say that whenever you dream of someone dying, you're making their life longer. So I hoped that my work *Eternity* would prolong the lives of many people. The idea came to me when I was given an honorary Professorship of Sculpture at the Academy of Fine Arts in Carrara, in 2018. And I thought why not build a cemetery for the living? Maybe it would make our lives easier, because we would learn to coexist with the end. In Carrara I involved the students in making the work, and associated it with the awarding of scholarships. They created the tombstones of the artists of their choice.

It was ironic to take the pop-up cemetery project to Buenos Aires a few months later, as part of "Hopscotch (Rayuela)," the program curated by Cecilia Alemani for Art Basel Cities. There *Eternity* brought together more than 200 local artists who each did their interpretation of the tombstone. At a particularly precarious moment in Argentina's recent history, it could just as easily have been a cemetery to bury the nation's debt in.

197

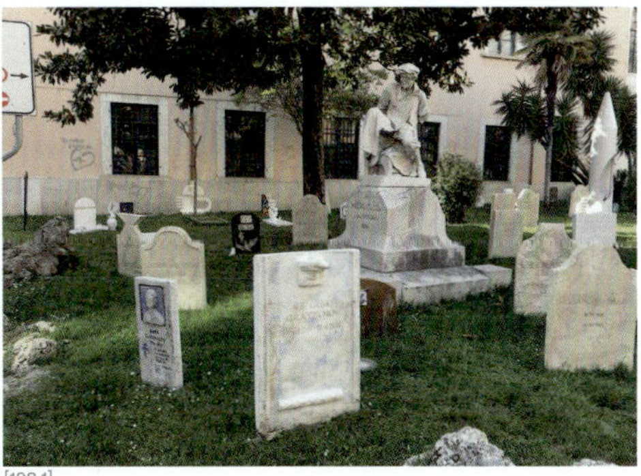

[128.1]

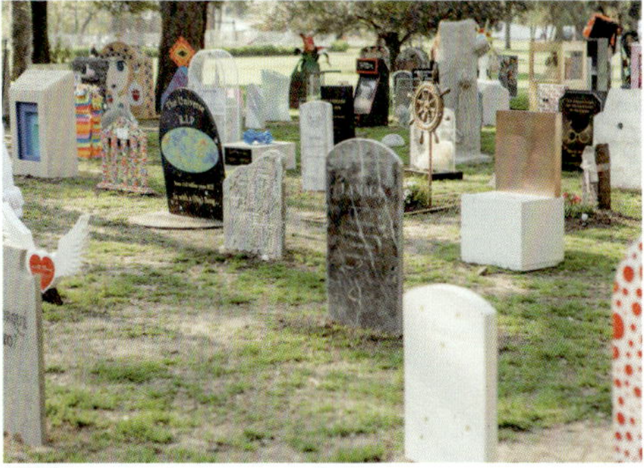

[128.2]

**[127]** ***All*, 2007**
Carrara marble
C. 30 × 100 × 200 cm each
of the 9 elements

When I first saw them finished, the tragedy and the silence of the nine bodies under the sheets in *All* set the veins trembling under my skin. I had handled real corpses while working in the Padua hospital morgue, and they seemed so deaf and distant. Perhaps because of that job, whenever I think of a sculpture I imagine it every time just as distant, somehow already dead. And I'm always surprised that people laugh when they see some of my works. Perhaps it's natural to react to death with laughter.

When I arrange the nine bodies under the shrouds and lay them on the ground, I'm not creating an allusion to a specific war or disaster. This work is about death, the death of everybody. To some extent it remains a political work, but it stands above all on the side of religion, of the spiritual.

[127.1]   *All*, 2007
"Maurizio Cattelan," curated by Eckhard Schneider, Kunsthaus Bregenz, February 2–March 24, 2008 (solo show)

[127.2]   *All*, 2007
The work being made at the Studi d'Arte – Cave Michelangelo, Carrara, 2007

[128.1]   *Eternity*, 2018
Gardens of the Academy of Fine Arts, Carrara, April 23–September 28, 2018

[128.2]   *Eternity*, 2018
"Hopscotch (Rayuela)," curated by Cecilia Alemani for Art Basel Cities, Buenos Aires, September 6–12, 2018 (group show, commissioned by the city of Buenos Aires and Art Basel)

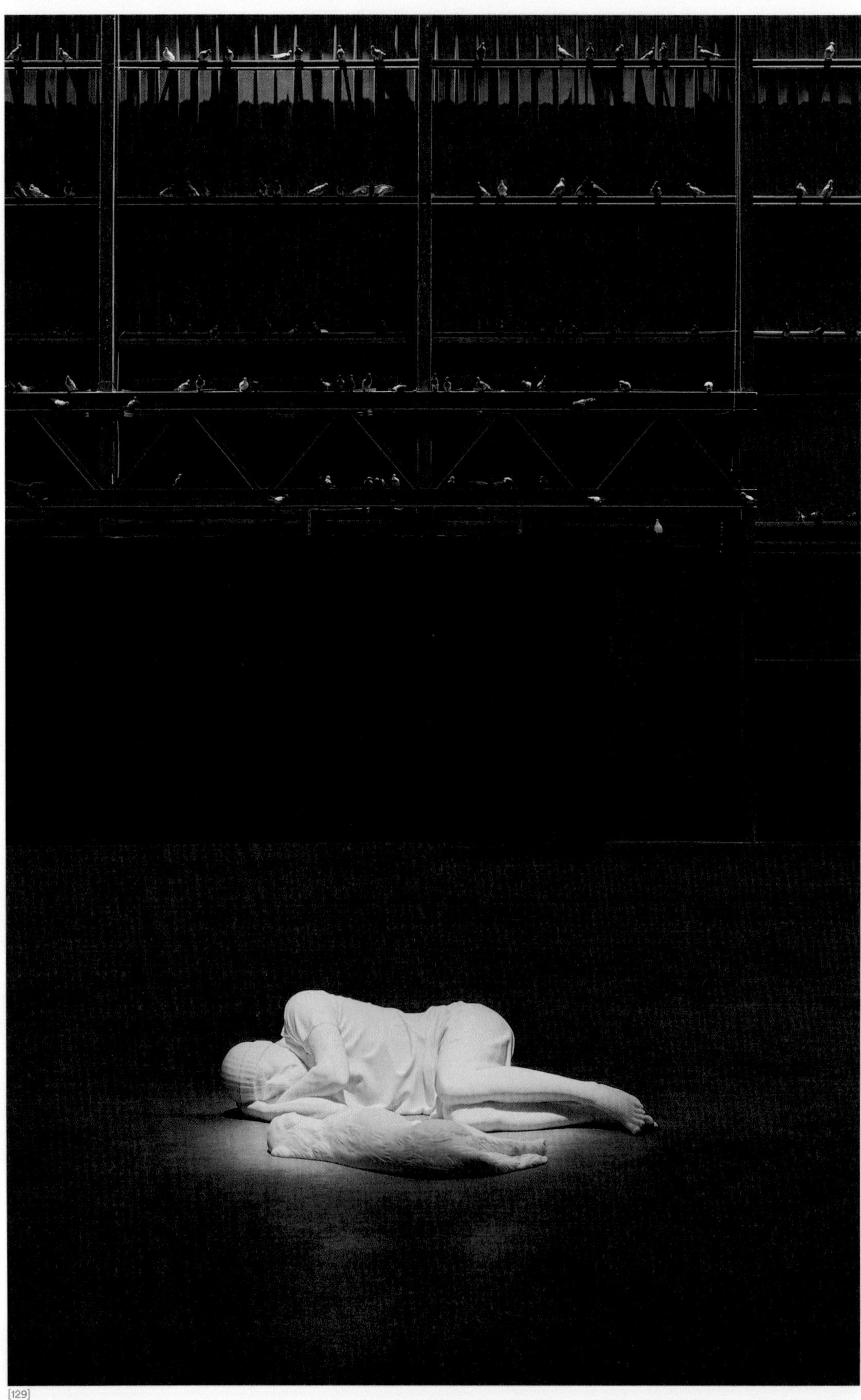

[In Carrara the project was coordinated by Luciano Massari, a teacher at the Academy of Fine Arts. The scholarships were awarded to the following students: Selene Bertagnini, Marco Arcolini and Matias E. Reyes, Jonathan Campisi and Michela Tabaton Osbourne, Francesco Carapelli, Ennio Castellano, Matteo Cracchi, Gennifer Deri, Filippo Gallorini, Naeim Ghomorlou, Greta Maggi, Despoina Shekine Naindi, Quan Luo, Fabio Quattrocolo, Marianna Quintiliani, Gruppo Cooperativa Monterosso, Gruppo Scuola di Grafica, Gruppo Tecniche Speciali (Alfredi Calasso, Marina Corazza, Hyun Wook Park, Davide Vanzo), Gruppo Cessi (Paolo Bacci, Denise Ceragioli, Niccolò Fagnini, Niccolò Forcieri, Maria Ilaria Melis and Michela Tabaton Osbourne, Renata Vinchesi, Seung Wan Park), Gruppo Strano (Martin Brusinelli, Francesca Claudia De Leonardis, Nicola Moracchioli, Federico Zurani, Lorenzo Gardinali). Honorable mentions went to Camilla Dalmazio and Claudia Zanaga]

[129]  ***Breath*, 2021**
Carrara marble
Figure: 40 × 78 × 131 cm;
dog: 30 × 65 × 40 cm

*Breath* is about fear, hope, and patience. I remember when I was a little kid, I would go into my parents' room when they were sleeping, and I would check that they were breathing. If we wait long enough, maybe dead people will wake up. It may recall a nativity scene. But you could also say the image was inspired by the funeral monument of Ilaria del Carretto in Lucca Cathedral by Jacopo della Quercia. There is a small dog crouching at her feet. It looks like it's waiting for her to wake up.
Animals are the mirrors of human beings. We understand ourselves in them. How many and what meanings and powers have we invested in animals in human history? Many more than you could attribute to a single human being. I've always wondered what it meant to say that the dog is man's best friend, and I tried to understand it with *Breath*.
The use of marble is interesting because there is already a meaning and value in the material that seem to be upended by the subject. What is really negligible? What is remarkable? If you've made a work that expires, like milk, it means it wasn't good enough and has to be thrown out. What difference will it make a hundred years from now whether it's mine or not? It will matter more if the breath I'm talking about is still there.

[129]  *Breath*, 2021
"Maurizio Cattelan. Breath Ghosts Blind," curated by Roberta Tenconi and Vicente Todolí, Pirelli HangarBicocca, Milan, July 15, 2021–February 20, 2022 (solo show)

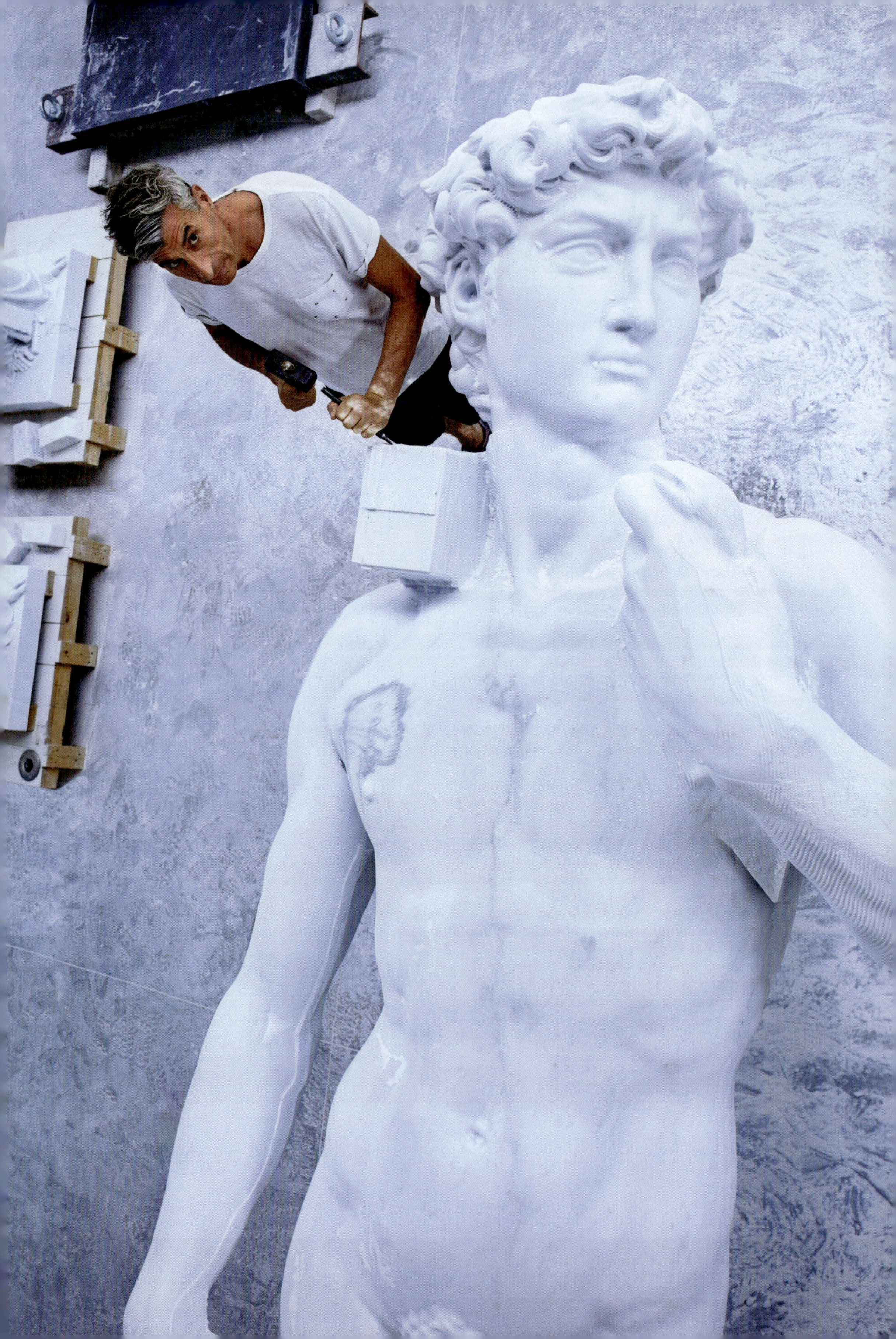

Art doesn't come from inspiration so much as the obsessions and fears haunting us every day. I've never been able to escape from the world around me, shut myself away in a room, sit down at a desk and say: "I'm an artist. I have to create." Having a studio might be relaxing. Sometimes I could choose not to go, I could call in sick. Art is above all a way of looking at reality. There are no Sundays or days off. Art is a continuous obsession: you can't take a vacation from yourself.

I believe that everything connected with reality can be interesting, if it's told in the right way. I read the newspaper every morning from cover to cover. You can even find inspiration in the obituaries or the list of bankruptcy auctions, if you're in the right frame of mind. I don't do anything, I just continue to feed on things, meaning on images and information. And then there's a process of selection and separation that's not really conscious. I work more with my stomach than my brain; it's a digestive process, I don't know what of. Anyhow, I believe that having ideas is all about allowing your mind to stray far enough from the obvious. It's a risky business, because you can discover things about yourself that you'd rather not know.

I've never properly examined the reasons that prompt me to do something. Each time it simply seems like the right thing to do at that moment. This is true of my whole output. I leave it to others to say whether my work or whatever I do changes or challenges anything. I just keep going, without bothering about the comments. The next chapter is suggested between the lines of what is already written. At any rate, a state of mind doesn't influence a work of art. In my case, the most interesting works have always been the result of great anxiety. But anxiety can be the vehicle, not the gasoline to produce something. If masterpieces stemmed from anxiety, they'd be everywhere and we wouldn't know where to put them. Creating an artwork is a kind of solitary, painful, revelatory journey, but the torment doesn't necessarily make you creative.

Every work I see is important. Very good pieces are inspiring. They give you the will to improve your own work. Bad pieces are useful: you learn what mistakes you should try to avoid. Mediocre ones show where your works will end up, supposing you don't manage either of the above.

I try to learn from everyone. Being overconfident is the biggest risk for anyone. I've always loved smart people, but I don't mind dullards either. Artists have been copying since ancient times, and I try to learn as much as I can from them, and from everything else I'm capable of achieving, even from know-it-alls. Being self-taught could be an advantage. I have no debts to anyone. But while I reckon I didn't have any teachers, I do have a lot of schoolmates, and I can try to work out the math problems with them.

I would have liked to visit Louise Bourgeois at one of her *Sundays, bloody Sundays* at her home at 347 West 20th Street in Chelsea, New York. Every Sunday afternoon, starting in the 1970s until her death at the age of ninety-eight, in 2010, she welcomed young artists who came to show her their work. She would ask them questions and criticize them. Anyone could go, you just had to bring your work and not have a cold.

I would have liked to get to know Antonio Ligabue, visit him at Gualtieri and spend an afternoon with him. I'd like to share the experience of an *artiste maudit*, struggling with his demons every day and still managing, despite everything or because of it, to make art that is also significant for others.

I would have liked to spend an afternoon at the Bar Jamaica in Milan, to chat with Piero Manzoni over a spritz, to see Aldo Mondino arrive riding on a camel... I would have liked to know the non-artistic side of many of them, to look at their works in a less historical and more vital light.

Conceptually, Dadaism is the father of a lot of contemporary art, and it's impossible not to pay tribute to it for its irrational approach and freedom of association. I admire the Futurists for their vitality and combativeness. Some even died in wartime for the sake of their ideals. They might have been mad, but they can't be blamed for lacking integrity. They were basically fanatics, but they anticipated a lot of what's going on today. Their blind faith in progress has many similarities with the positions of people who are now advocating change through an extremist ideology. Bruce Nauman's silence, Joseph Beuys's severity, Raphael's affectation, Bernini's eccentricity, Gino de Dominicis's alchemy, Caravaggio's doomed soul... The whole history of art can teach something, no matter whether it's positive or negative. But most of all I believe there's something to be learned from those who risked everything for their ideas, like Jesus or Giordano Bruno.

I've come to the realization that there are three different types of revolutionaries. There are the ones who want to change things; the ones who are into the struggle, but couldn't care less whether things change or not; and the ones who work instinctively, reacting to a situation in their own way, which can end up having a collective effect and influencing the world to a much greater extent. The last kind perhaps interests me most. Take Gerhard Richter or Andy Warhol. Warhol is proof that you can be a revolutionary without being a militant.

Anyway, more than the people, I care about the works. Perhaps my inconstancy is to blame, or simply because I get bored easily, but I'd like to think of the whole history of art as the work of a single artist, so perhaps placing Jeff Koons's *Puppy* or Géricault's *The Raft of the Medusa* next to the paintings in the prehistoric caves and then Warhol's portraits. After all, the signature never really matters. What remains are the images, especially the ones that have managed to climb over the fence of art and become a part of common feeling. That's why I also like things that aren't art but seem to be.

I can't remember when I first saw the Surrealists' mannequins, but I'm pretty sure it was in the early 1980s. It happened in Padua, in a barber's shop. At the time it was still quite common to find those men-only magazines that cost very little. They were soft-porn mags, often put together with recycled photos from various sources. They were produced without a budget, without photographers, without anything, so they used images stolen from art books, newspapers and the fashion pages, accompanied by a story written by some underpaid writer. In the same issue you could find a photo of Henri Cartier-Bresson transformed into the setting of an erotic encounter, or a portrait of Buster Keaton represented as a sex fiend. The story featuring the Surrealist mannequins was about a murderer who had filled his cellar with bizarre statues with birdcages on their heads. A few years later, I was sitting in a library browsing some art books, trying to find something—an idea or at least an image that would stick with me for a while—and I came across a reproduction of those same mannequins. This time the photo had a caption identifying them as the products of the imagination of Breton, Dalí, Duchamp and Co. The book went on to explain the Surrealist attraction to fetishes and *cadavres exquis*. But to me those mannequins were simpler and so much more bewildering. They seemed to make more sense when they were published in the barber's shop magazines. In that context, their utter weirdness turned into a perfect reflection of our cheap perversions. They functioned as mirrors of our mediocrity. I can't say I was influenced by that image, but it was probably one of the first times that I realized that art can actually hide behind reality, and that reality can easily function as art.

**Influences**



Once a friend of mine asked me what had influenced me and my work as an artist.
I was influenced by:
My father, who used to say I would go blind if I didn't stop that thing
Moby Dick
Listening to my uncle Franco
Sniffing gun powder in Salerno and Anzio
My former wife
Reading *Popeye, Toots and Casper* and *Chris Crustie*
Some rumors about albino alligators in New York
Some story about a pill that you can put in the tank of a car with just a drop of water and drive around with no fuel
The story that George Gershwin actually never wrote a single song–it was his twin who could play and George would keep him tied to a rock down in the cellar
That other story about James Dean–he never actually died and he's now living with Elvis; and Hitler is waiting for them in Argentina and they are gonna write a movie all together.
You know, it's just a stupid question:
I was influenced by every single second I spent riding my bicycle.
I never understood if birth helps life anyway.

[Text published in *Maurizio Cattelan*, eds. Francesco Bonami, Nancy Spector, and Barbara Vanderlinden (London: Phaidon, 2000), 125]

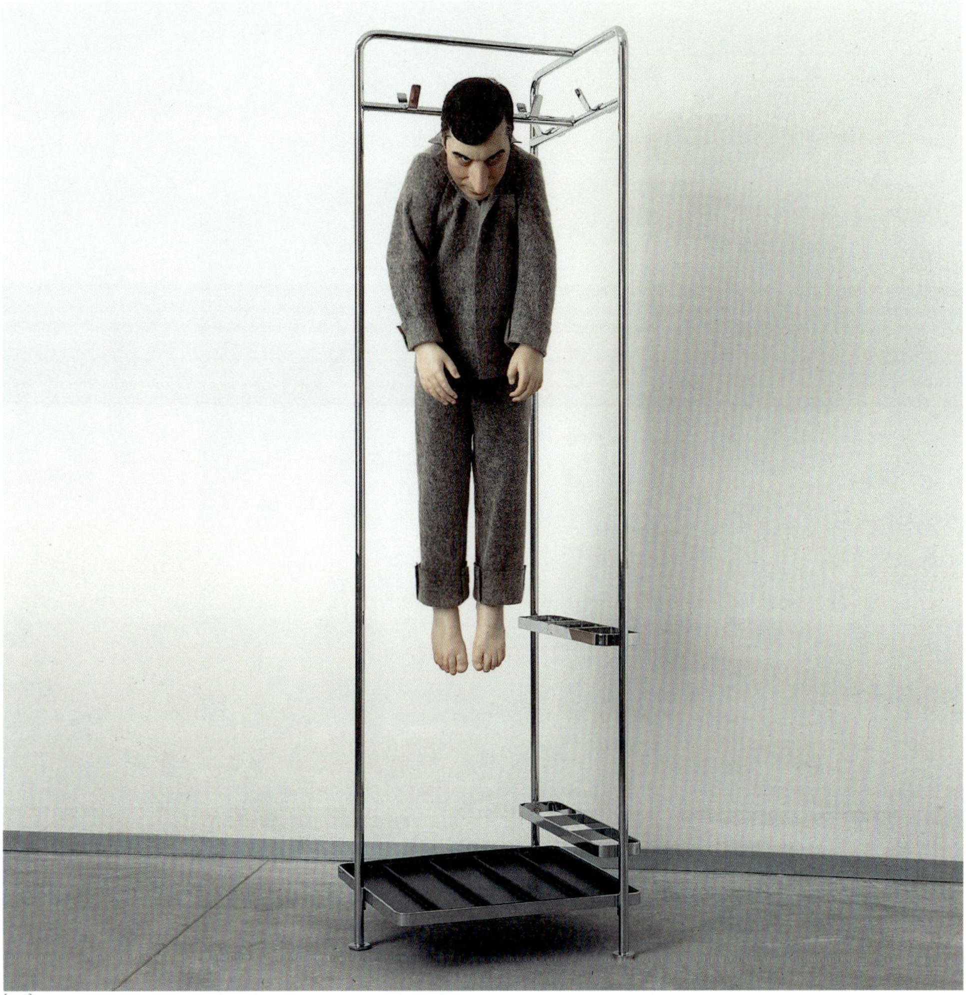

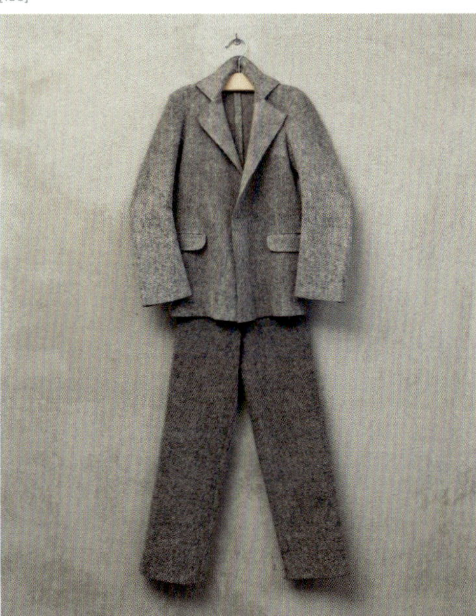

[130]

[131]

[130]  *La Rivoluzione siamo noi*, 2000

[131]  *Untitled*, 2000

[130]  ***La Rivoluzione siamo noi*, 2000**
Polyester resin, wax, pigment, hair,
felt suit, metal coat rack
Figure: 123.8 × 35.6 × 43.2 cm;
overall dimensions: 190 × 47 × 52 cm

[131]  ***Untitled*, 2000**
Felt suit, wooden hanger
110.8 × 48.3 × 5.7 cm

[132]  ***Untitled*, 2000**
Polyester resin, wax, pigment, hair,
clothes
Figure: 123.8 × 35.6 × 43.2 cm

I think for every given space there is only one
solution. When I was invited to show at the Migros Museum in Zurich, the place had ten different rooms. I said: "I can't do a show here." I
asked them to take down all the walls, and they
did. A good way to concentrate the energy. But
I left this space empty and had steps added to
get to a room on the floor below. This was a
completely new setting, which could only have
one work. I did the Beuys self-portrait. It was
obvious. There couldn't be anything, as it was
Switzerland, which is almost Germany. It was

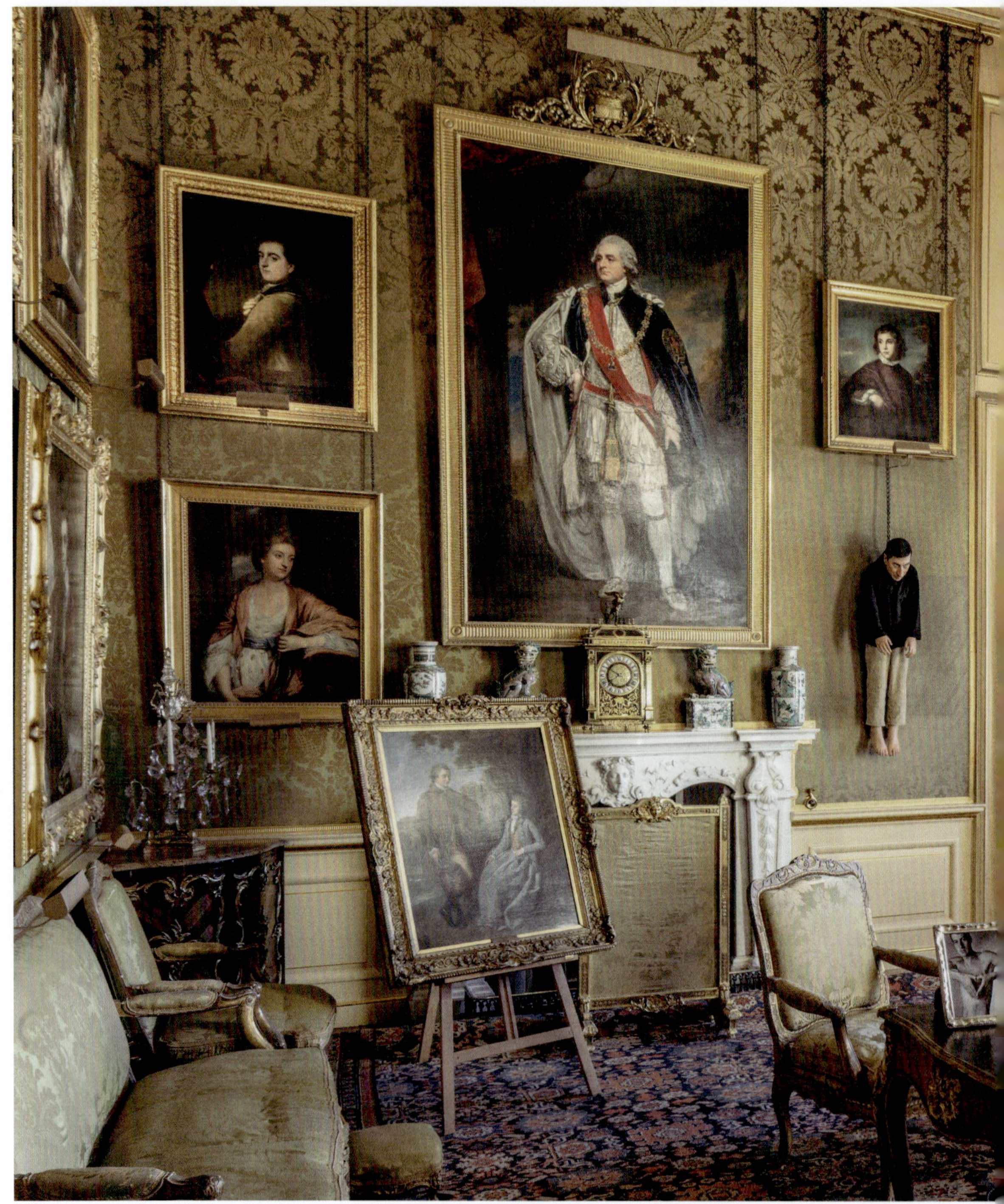



perfect. I literally put myself in Beuys's shoes and also borrowed the title of his manifesto. But I'm no good at keeping my feet on the ground, and even with the best teachers my head is always in the clouds. And anyway I also felt a lot smaller. In fact, I didn't think I was putting myself in a humiliating position. I've always been in a humiliating position, so it was like doing my regular job.

[132]  *Untitled*, 2000, and *Lessico familiare*, 1989 [16]
"Victory Is Not An Option," curated by Michael Frahm, Blenheim Palace, United Kingdom, September 12–October 27, 2019 (solo show)

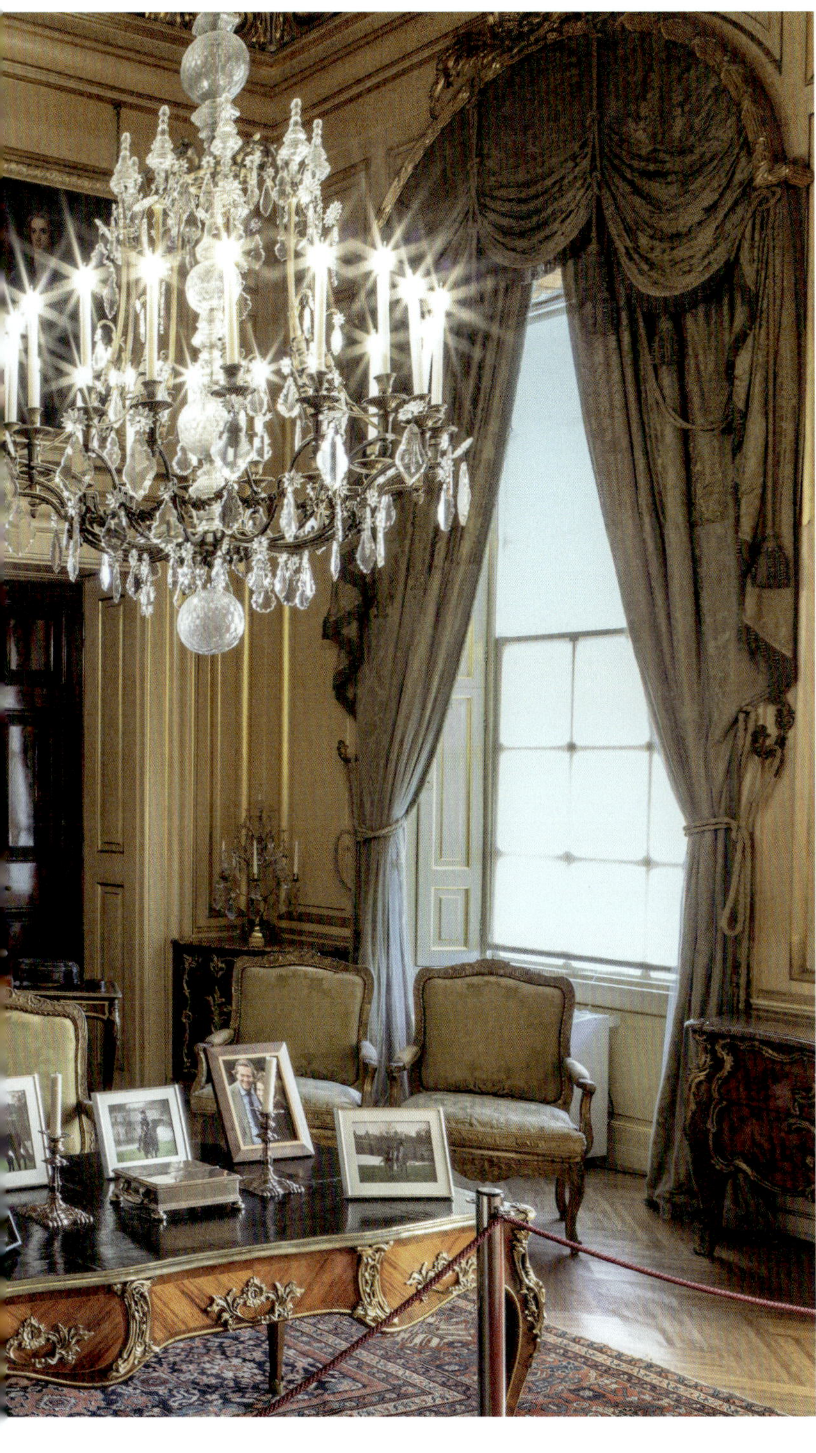

**The Fat Is on the Table: Maurizio Cattelan on Joseph Beuys**



beuys is dead
beuys is also uniting love and knowledge
beuys is more present in a desert freak
beuys is sponsored by museum für moderne kunst
beuys is appointed professor of sculpture at the düsseldorf academy of art
beuys extends ulysses by two chapters at the request of james joyce
beuys is surely not a sartre follower, but of course there are many parallels
beuys is mentioned next to steiner
beuys is back in town
beuys is back in belgium, in berlin, US, active in germany
beuys is the contemporary artist responsible for the popular notion that politics is an aesthetic activity that anyone can engage in
beuys is inspired by steiner
beuys is not so reactionary as to deny the existence of the entire art history repertoire
beuys is widely acknowledged as one of the most influential postwar german artists
beuys is the identification with everything from mythological figures and historical personages to writers and artists
beuys is a mythical figure in the art world, however
beuys is particularly significant in the light of his introspective research on the possible reunification of human and natural life
beuys is in the creation of the social sculpture
beuys is either loved or hated
beuys is considered one of the most
beuys is widely regarded as one of the most important german artists since world war II
beuys is demanding sun instead of rain/reagan
beuys is more like an evangelist
beuys is famous for an extraordinary body of drawings
beuys is such an obvious candidate; he started making art following a breakdown that was a result of his experiences in world war II
beuys is represented in depth in dia's permanent collection

beuys is
beuys is among the most famous of today's artists
beuys is one of the most famous performance artists
beuys is valid because wolfgang laib shares his belief in the transcendent power of art
beuys is another sculptor that
beuys is one of the major figures in postwar german art
beuys is known for his shamanistic artist's persona
beuys is among the world's most comprehensive
beuys is in these digital photographs represented not by him directly
beuys is a real people's artist understood by a professor
beuys is *megjelent a kövek mellett és hamarosan heves vita bontakozott ki közte és a közönség között*
beuys is a 1972 lithograph in which the essential feature is that of beuys as everyman
beuys is *elvesztette*
beuys is *átvett és ami interszubjektiv jellege miatt nem volt*
beuys is called to account by his presumptive offspring
beuys is *veel materiaal verdwenen*
beuys is questioned by the activities of maclennan
beuys is instructive
beuys is very important in mail art
beuys is understandable
beuys is known to
beuys is not completed by his death
beuys is i was never secure and happy in the world of galleries from the very beginning
beuys is and how it is pronounced
beuys is cleverly recontextualized in
beuys is of course enormously interesting
beuys is *l'éminence grise* of community building as an art form
beuys is interested in the proportions between crystal and amorphous states
beuys is able to evoke the experience of the past
beuys is a magnificent
beuys is based on three stages
beuys is a special case because of the buildup of a curious sense of obligation to respond positively
beuys is the generation of my father
beuys is talking about the much wider concept of creative potential
beuys is regarded as one of the most significant personalities of the past
beuys is steeped in the struggle of world war II
beuys is a big influence right now
beuys is unavoidable
beuys is purely a decorative artist
beuys is hype
beuys is cited as the great collaborator of the twentieth century because
beuys believed everybody was a potential artist
beuys is on e-bay
beuys is a mythical figure in
beuys is one artist i wanted to ask you about
beuys is one of the biggest art world phonies of recent years
beuys is probably unique in the history of art
beuys is supposed
beuys is a very controversial sculptor
beuys is grounded in a tradition of narrative sources that is often absent in american art of the same period
beuys is hardly a household name in the history of twentieth-century art
beuys is the great shaman of twentieth-century art
beuys is represented with his monumental work created shortly before his death, *lightning with stag in its glare*
beuys is best known for declaring "everyone an artist"; koons seems to declare that everyone is a consumer

[Text published in *Tate Etc.*, no. 3 (Spring 2005): 80–81]

209

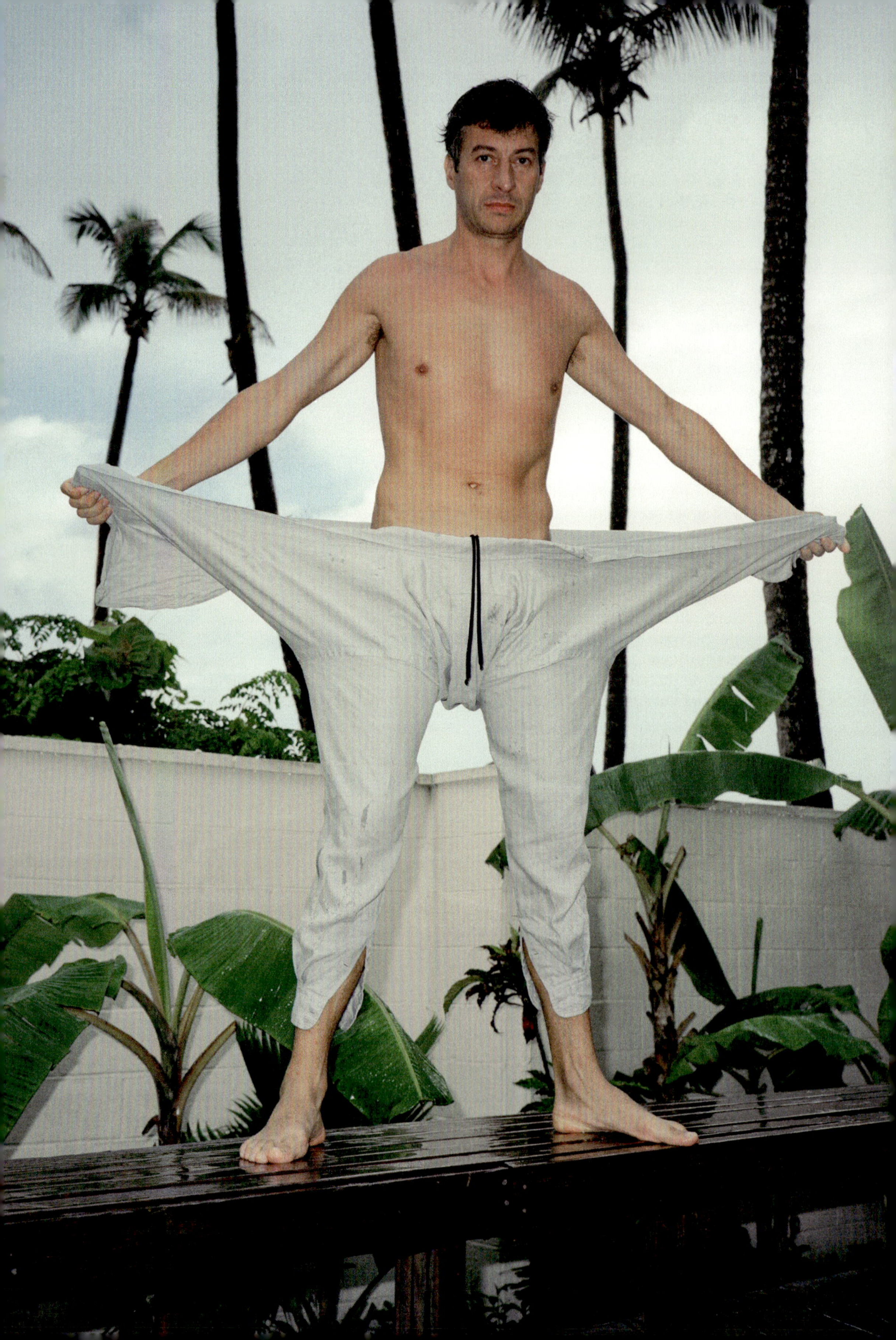

I can't led a day pass without working. Work has always been therapy for me. It's like a doctor's prescription: you can't skip a dose. And I can't start my workday without swimming for at least an hour. Repeating the gestures has a meditative effect on me and saves me. I guess it could be seen as a religious workout, but in my case it's only a matter of order. I always try to be as methodical as possible, though in the end each of us is a slave to deadlines and everything tends to get out of control.

I'm a monk with many sins. I don't like having too many people around—I don't have a secretary or a family—and I'm quite maniacal and repetitive. I also get rid of everything that bothers me. I try not to own anything. I struggle every day to be free, and freedom from the slavery of things is a substantial part of this quest. Every two or three months I throw everything out. For me it's a matter of organic cleanliness. I prefer memories to objects. I admit that I'm sensitive to the seduction of things, but I know that, much as I desire an object, as soon as I've got it I lose interest. Objects are memories that have taken shape in reality. They're there to remind you at all times that time is inexorably passing and there's a past in which those objects meant something. Living without this burden of things and thoughts enables me to look ahead lightly and lucidly. And then I like the idea of always being ready to move to the other side of the world, without looking back. So, in my house I sleep easy. There are only two chairs, a table and a closet full of white T-shirts and black jeans. Wherever it may be, my home will always be empty. It's funny: between the home I have now, the ones I had before and the one I lived in with my parents, nothing has changed. Only the address. I have a spacious home in New York, but I still work in a corner near the bed, in front of a window. The privilege is perhaps that instead of being on the ground floor I'm up on the tenth. But the highlight of my Saturday is still vacuuming the place, which also reminds me where I'm from.

I pay much more attention to what it's important to have around my apartment than to what's inside it. In an ideal world, my house would be as wide as the space between two mountains, with only the echo around me. True luxury means not needing things. If we talk about spiritual wealth, I have room for improvement. On a material level, I believe there's a maximum point, which corresponds to the real needs of each person. This is the limit beyond which it no longer makes sense to accumulate. The people who exceed it need help, because when wealth serves only to produce more wealth, it's stripped of all interest.

Money has given me stability, but I have a strange attitude to money. I'm almost afraid of it, and I've tried to go on living as if nothing had changed. Money is a means of developing ideas. The paradox is that when you're young your mind's full of ideas, but you don't have the money to carry them out. When you're old, the opposite happens more often. You have the means, but the fertility of when you were twenty is gone. I believe that the worst misfortune that can happen to a person is to forget that money is not an end. It becomes just numbers and no longer has any value. I spend money rather than accumulating it. To me, money is a transmission mechanism, an extraordinary means of communication, perhaps even more effective than religion. But then it doesn't matter how much money you have: it only matters how and where the money goes.

An Italian writer once said that you should enjoy life, but always bear in mind that at any moment everything could vanish in a cloud of smoke. I try to follow his advice every day, and also to pass it on to others.

As for my impact on the world, if I were a curator, or a collector, I would try to make the works travel by land, instead of by plane. As an artist and a human being, I don't think I can do much more than I already do. I use very little heating and light, I eat almost nothing but vegetables and rice... All the same, I'm always ready to change my mind and improve.

I live in a condition of continuous desire for what I don't have. I miss everything and nothing at the same time. It's a restlessness that I've learned to transform into curiosity, and that's why I can't say I have any regrets. I feel rather like an outside observer of everything, both in Italy and the United States. And sometimes I'm not comfortable with myself. The problems may seem very obscure to me and the solutions very far away. At those times I feel I have to take a break from my life, a break from being myself. So I go to the movies, where I can stop thinking. A movie gives me eighty-eight minutes of escape from myself, whether I'm crying or laughing. Whenever I see a masterpiece I find myself thinking about the head of the filmmaker. Being able to perfectly hold together all those ingredients (the writing, the light, the shots, the camera movements, the management of the actors) is the closest thing to having superpowers that I can imagine. In addition to the cinema, I'm an avid consumer of stories in books. The ones I like best can combine details of real life and journalism with fiction and take the reader midway between those two worlds. I love the magical moment when you accept a pact with the author and, as if by a leap of faith, you start to think that what you're reading is true, while they're just images of a parallel reality.

By my nature, on the other hand, in most cases I act instinctively, which in practical life leads me to the right thing at the right time more than any reasoning. However, I certainly have a rational part as well, a sort of safety net to stem anxieties and insecurities. But there's a saying that sums up my attitude to life. It's Russian. If you wake up and you're not in pain, you know you're dead.

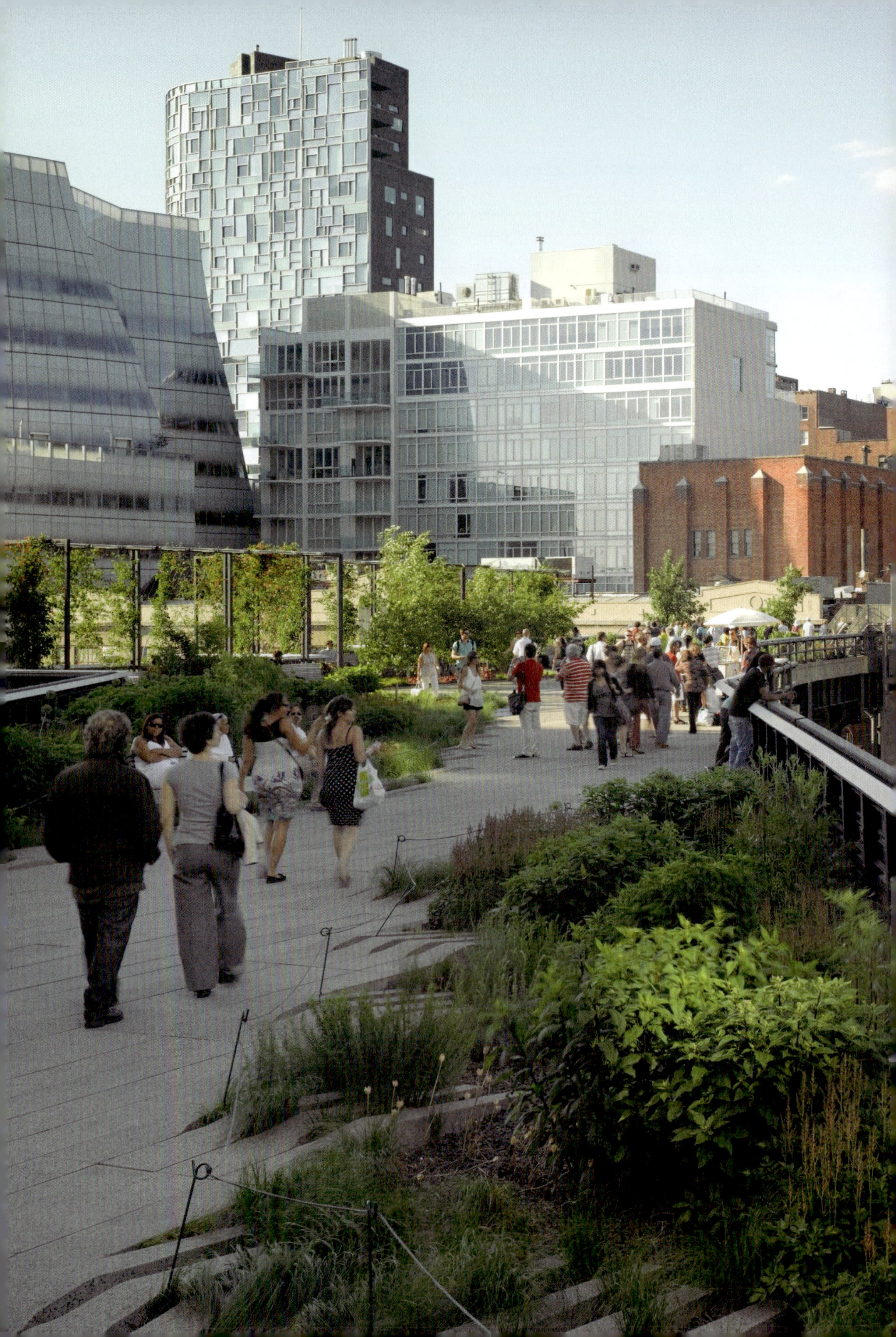

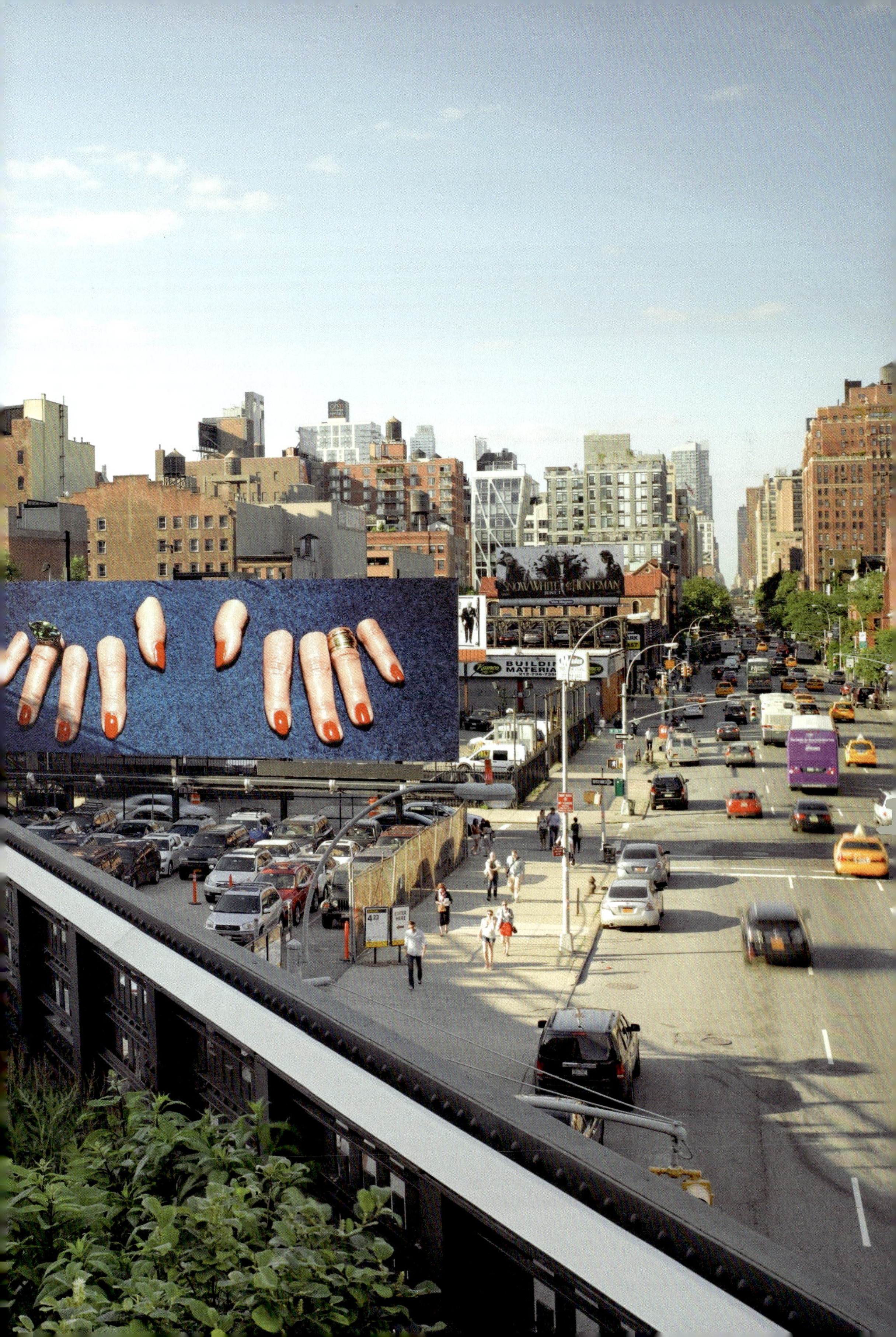

SNOW WHITE & THE HUNTSMAN
JUNE 1
Kamco
BUILDING
MATERIAL
212-734-75
ENTER
HERE
4 23

Maurizio Cattelan and Pierpaolo Ferrari for *Toiletpaper*, *Untitled*, 2012, billboard for The High Line, installation at Edison ParkFast, West 18th Street 10th Avenue, New York, May 31–July 1, 2012. Photo by Austin Kennedy



I spent many years in other places before arriving in New York. After twenty-five years in Padua, I moved to Forlì, which at the time struck me as the mirage of an active universe. Today Forlì still strikes me as unique, but mostly because they serve an excellent piadina with prosciutto there. I'm not passing any kind of judgment, I'm the last person who should do that. But I'm aware that living in New York is really special, because the city is like a giant office that never stops working around the clock.

In Italy I had explored all my possibilities. New York was the place par excellence for art. I gave myself three years to make it. I arrived in 1993 without knowing a word of English and spent three months sleeping. In Milan I'd met a guy from New York who sublet me two rooms on 12th Street in the East Village for 700 dollars. I earned zero, I lived on five dollars a day, but it's not true that I used to steal bicycles. To get to the gallery that represents me, the Marian Goodman Gallery on 57th Street, I did cycle for at least an hour. That helped me think and if I had bad vibes, I worked them off.

I see myself as lucky. Ever since I moved here, New York has remained the most stimulating city on the art scene. I think what makes it special is that every new theory or movement here is embraced without too much fuss about what's wrong and what's not. You're always able to find a new "faith" and there's always time to change your mind the next day.

I don't really care much about the art system or the most powerful galleries. To me, New York remains a compressed space, full of images, of contrasts all packed in and locked up on an island covering a few square kilometers. It's a kind of city-state. And you always have the illusion that everything is within reach. This is what really interests me and what I think other artists and gallery owners like too: the impression of having an immediate impact on everything around you. The most interesting thing today is that for some things whether you're in Milan, New York or Mumbai no longer matters, but for others it's fundamental. In New York, even if you're holed up at home, you can feel the energy of the city. Just two blocks away you'll find 150 art galleries: 150 young thinking heads, and a stroll will take you to them.

Art has always been an indicator of the temperature of the world and current affairs. If you move about while you have a thermometer, your temperature shoots up immediately, so my grandma used to say. In this, America is perhaps the greatest power in the world. It's difficult anywhere else to find such a large range of opposition and dissent, as well as of handshakes and pats on the back. The real problem with being creative is never how to come up with new ideas, but rather how to chase away the thoughts that have been buzzing in your head for a lifetime and which you've got so accustomed to that you sink into them comfortably. Well, there are cities like New York that certainly help you forget everything in your head and force you to completely reinvent yourself every day. I don't know if you can make a comparison, but when I arrived in New York in 1993 I think I suffered a culture shock identical to what you'll feel today when you go to Buenos Aires or Cape Town or Shanghai. Everything is so different from what you know and from your expectations that it stuns you and changes you forever.

When I landed in New York, I felt like a citizen of some non-Western country. The experience of being an emigrant is fundamental. I would recommend it to everyone, because it's a way to cut yourself down to size and learn to talk even with people who don't understand you or don't want to listen to you. Even in Milan I prefer to live as if it weren't my home. After all, I like geographical boundaries: if they weren't there it would be impossible to cross them. I always believe in obstacles, because it's only when you find yourself trapped that you have to start looking for the escape routes.

[133] *Oblomov Foundation*, 1992
Engraved glass plate (100 × 100 cm) installed on the exterior of the Brera Academy of Fine Arts, Milan, 1992–93

Oblomov was someone who had understood everything. He is the title character of a novel written and set in mid-nineteenth-century Russia. Oblomov fails to measure up to life. For the first fifty pages he moves only from his bed to a chair. He is the hero of anti-heroes: instead of embarking on great feats, he just chooses not to. He isn't an invention of the author, Goncharov. There is a long tradition of searching for time freed from work, starting with Greek and Roman culture. At the time, you needed leisure to ennoble yourself, to be able to call yourself free. More recently, before industrialization, this same concept was rendered in Italian as *il dolce far niente*. The industrial age, capitalism and its latest degenerations have upended this idea. Today everybody works all the time, everywhere, and they're proud to do so. So in a short time we've became the burnout society. Work today can be a disease. It's scary. The pandemic has shown us what we gave up. It would be much better if the Italian Constitution opened with the words: "Italy is a democratic Republic, founded on leisure and work."
I created the *Oblomov Foundation*, which offered 10,000 dollars to an artist who agreed not to produce any art and not exhibit for a whole year. It was a kind of scholarship. It was my way of expressing the fact that a group of artists had become that of the usual suspects who exhibited at all the international exhibitions. There must have been a photocopied list of the artists invited to the exhibitions of the last three years. Why bother with advertising? There was no need. Everybody already knew the list.
It was an early project of mine, perhaps too early. I really liked the idea of involving a hundred or so people, contacting them individually to raise funds for the grant. I began to make a list of people who might contribute to the project. It wasn't easy. Every day I spent four or five hours on the phone saying: "Hi, do you know me?" No one knew me at the time, so it was really hard to introduce myself quickly. I had to get their atten-

[133.1]

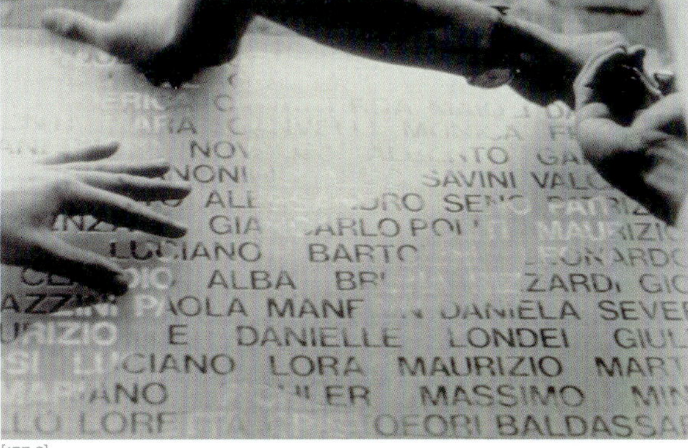

[133.2]

[133.1]  *Oblomov Foundation*, 1992

[133.2]  *Oblomov Foundation* (detail), 1992

tion and then say: "Can you give me a hundred dollars for this project?" I had to sell my position. Another tough job. I convinced a hundred people to donate a hundred dollars each, so I raised 10,000 dollars. But the young artists I contacted declined the offer. They said: "Are you crazy?" For an artist, stopping exhibiting for a year meant falling completely out of the loop, disappearing from the art world. Sure enough, the *Oblomov Foundation* was an institution to teach failure.

I made a plaque with all the donors' names on it, the kind you see in museums, and I placed it outside the Brera Academy of Fine Arts in Milan. I went there early one morning with fake documents and fixed the plaque to the wall under some scaffolding. The people in charge of the place came and said: "What are you doing?" I just claimed a company had ordered me to post it. The plaque was there for a whole year. Whenever I walked past it, I thought: "Hey, that's me!" It was very nice that to have this piece on the wall. But the story needed an ending, so that money paid for my move to New York.

[134]    *Warning! Enter at your own risk. Do not touch, do not feed, no smoking, no photographs, no dogs, thank you, 1994*
"Warning! Enter at your own risk. Do not touch, do not feed, no smoking, no photograph, no dogs, thank you," Daniel Newburg Gallery, New York, May 28–29, 1994 (solo show)

[134]    ***Warning! Enter at your own risk. Do not touch, do not feed, no smoking, no photographs, no dogs, thank you, 1994***
Donkey, crystal chandelier
Environmental dimensions

I can explain the process that led to this work. If I was asked: "What does the donkey mean?" I couldn't say. But I'm sure the process could be interesting.

I didn't know what to do for my debut show in New York, at the Daniel Newburg Gallery. Everything I wanted to do was too expensive for the gallery. I had the idea only five days before the opening. I really liked the live donkey.

In that show I was visualizing myself for the first time. At school they used to put a dunce's cap on your head with two big ears and say: "Donkey!" And I thought: "Oh God, I'm a donkey..." The exhibition was the perfect opportunity. There was an elaborate crystal chandelier and the donkey. I imagined that when the Communists took over in Russia you would have seen something like this in the Winter Palace in St. Petersburg. So the work was like a little story. The donkey made a fantastic noise. The din was so great that the exhibition closed after only one day.

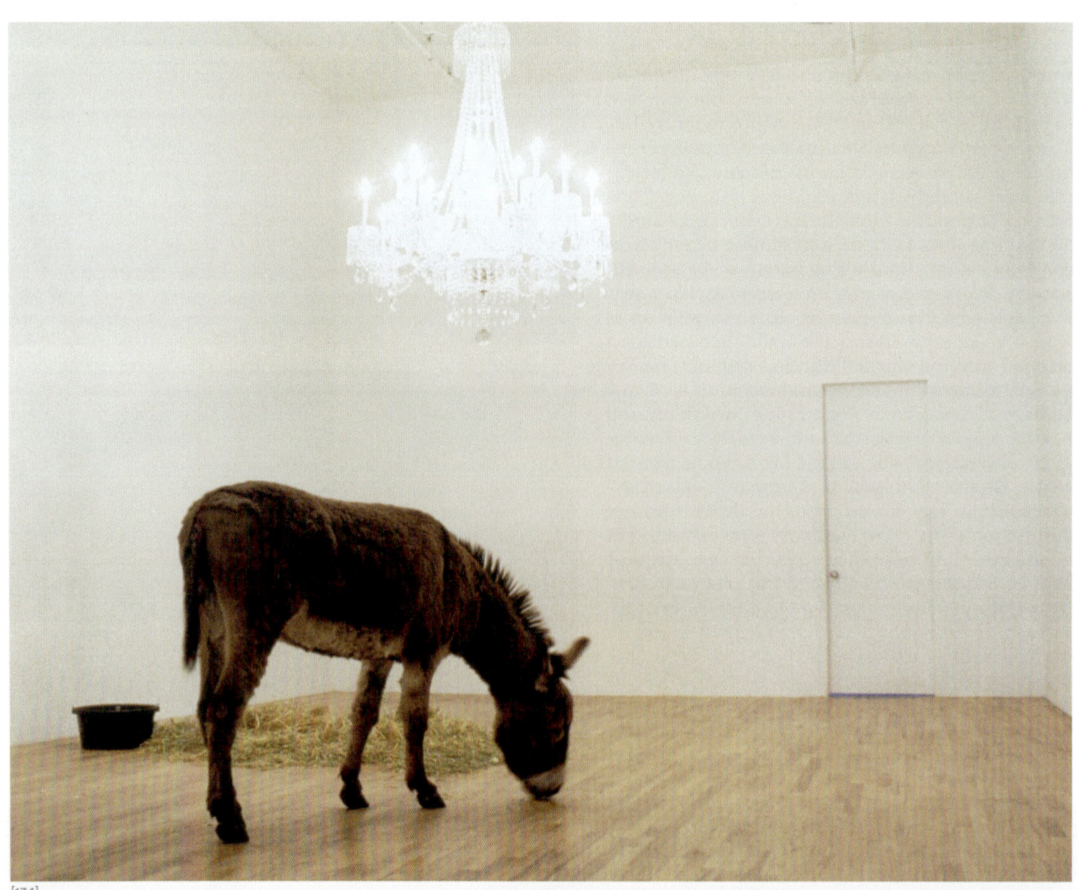

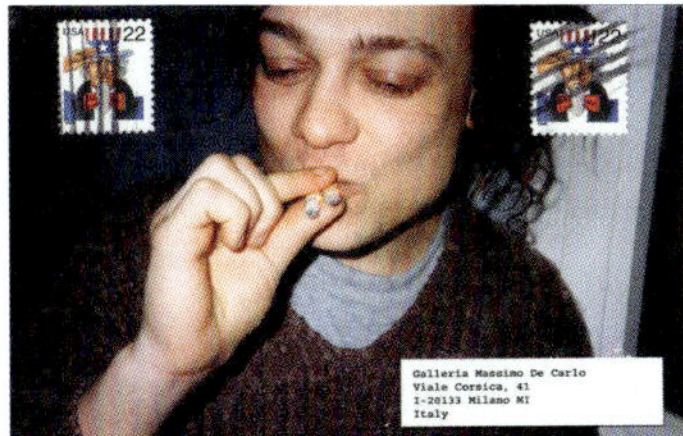

[135.1]

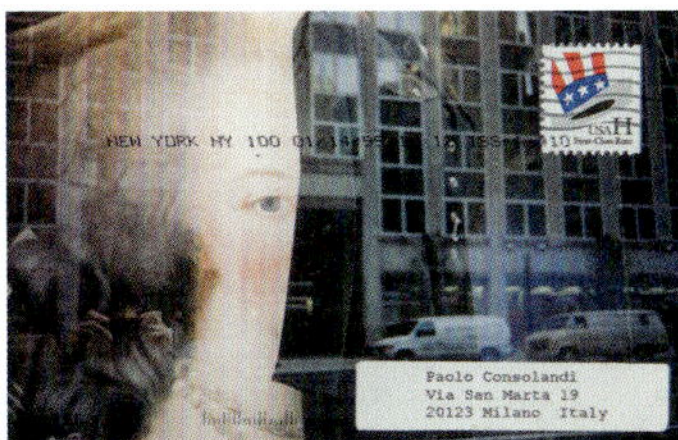

[135.2]

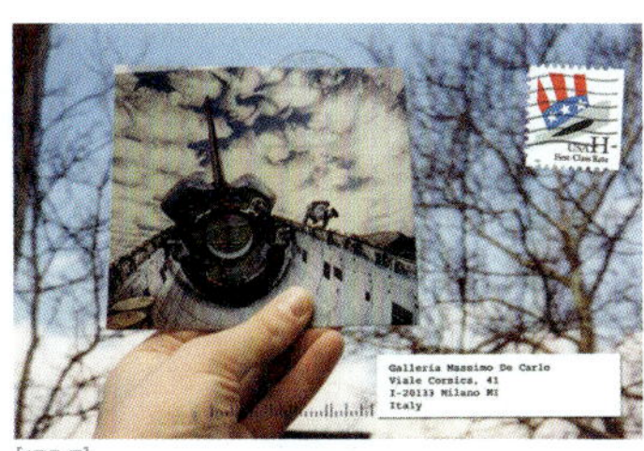

[135.3]

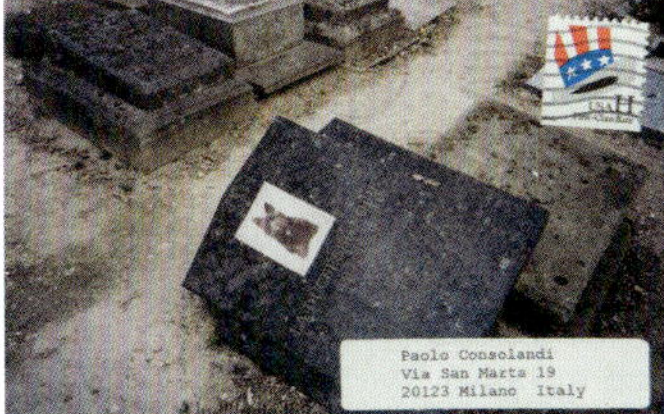

[135.4]

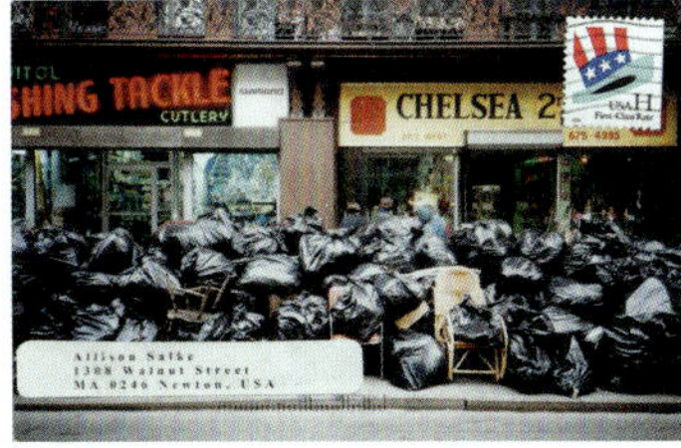

[135.5]

[135.6]

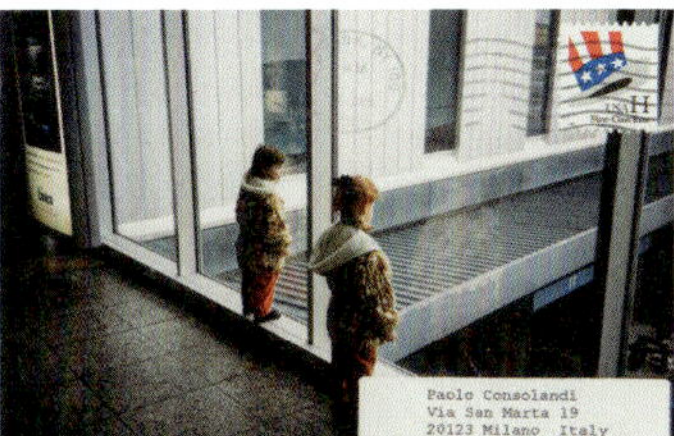

[135.7]

[135.8]

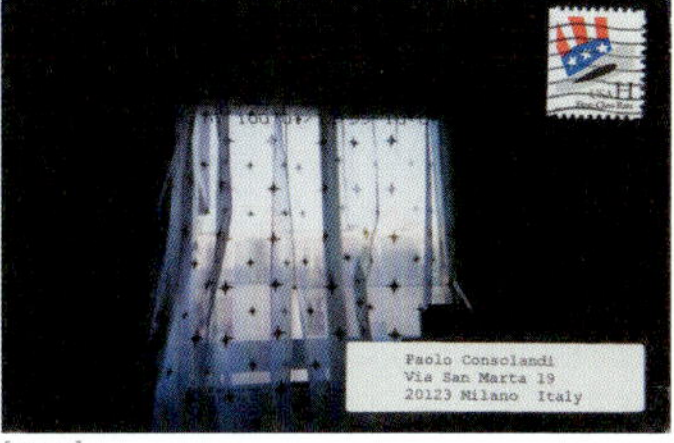

[135.9]

[135]   **_Ten Part Story_, 1999**
10 chromogenic prints, postal stamps,
labels
10.2 × 15.2 cm each

[136]   **_Monday Nothing_, 1995**
Collage for the exhibition "Fuori Uso '95.
Caravanserraglio Arte Contemporanea,"
curated by Giacinto Di Pietrantonio,
Pescara, 1995

In the late 1990s I used to take a lot of photos,
for no special reason, in streets and shops and
parks. After a while I started sending them, as
if they were postcards, from New York to Bologna, putting a stamp and a label with the address
directly on the photo. Others were marketed
through Emmanuel Perrotin, who was fantastic
at making the work saleable. He made the offer
to some collector, and I then sent the photos to
him, always by mail. In other cases I sent them
to myself at my New York address. I always sent
them in batches of ten. They had nothing to do
with each other, but in seeing them together
they became a story. The truth is I never really
understood how to use them, though I'd already
made a (failed) attempt for the 1995 edition of
"Fuori Uso" in Pescara, where I made a collage of
photographs.

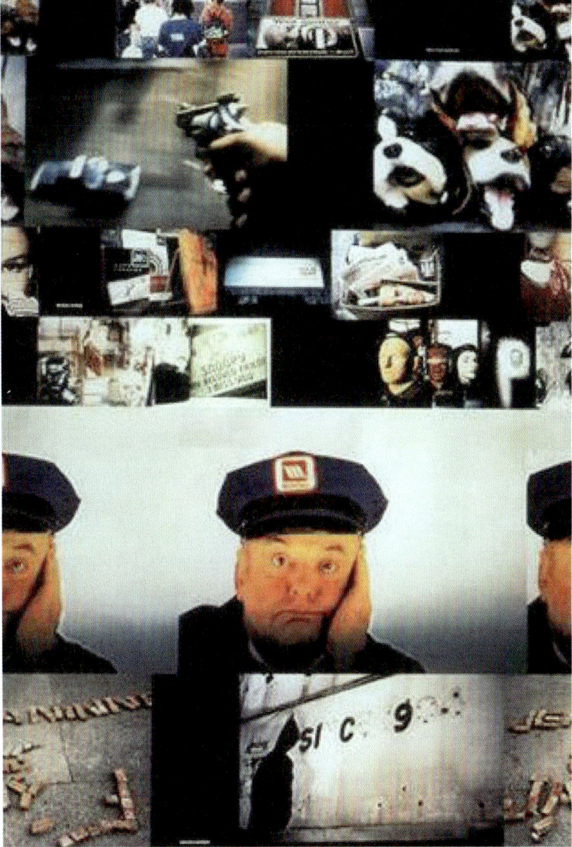

[135.1-9]   _Ten Part Story_, 1999 (detail)

[136]   _Monday, Nothing_, 1995

[136]

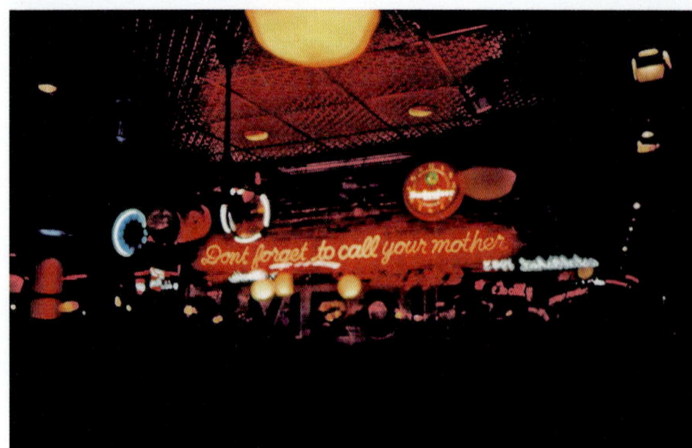

[137]

[137] ***Don't forget to call your mother**, 2000*
Silver dye bleach print face-mounted
to acrylic
66 × 101.6 cm

This is another experiment with photography. I
took the photo in a bar near my home, in East
Village, New York. Being a university neighbor-
hood, the phrase was probably meant to be a
way of saying: "Don't get wasted." I don't think
it worked, in fact it sounded more like invitation
to disobedience.

[138] ***Untitled**, 2000*
Resin, clothes, table, chair
Environmental dimensions

220

[139] ***Untitled**, 2004*
Concrete, fiberglass
39.4 × 48.3 × 37.5 cm

AI did this work in 2000 for the Center for Contemporary Art in Kitakyūshū, Japan, but I wasn't
convinced by it. I had set it up in a room that
couldn't be entered. The door was ajar and you
could see the work, a man bent over a table, only
from a distance.
I didn't sell it. Then for the 2004 Whitney Biennial, I suggested to Chrissie Iles that we could

bury it. There are a lot of works that I'd like to
have buried because they don't deserve to exist,
but I'd never done it. At the time, the Whitney
was still in the Breuer Building on Madison Avenue. We ran a steamroller over the sculpture, like
in cartoons. Whatever was left became a crate
that we inserted in the cavity between the first
and second floors. Crushing it made me want
to make some more mistakes, to kill a piece by
some different means. Instead of steamrolling
it, throwing it out of an airplane or sinking it, or
using a laser.
A few years later, when work on the Whitney's
new premises in the Meatpacking District was
nearly complete, they asked me to bury the work
for real. So, before they finished the floor of the
lobby, we dug a hole and put it underground.
We added a sort of epitaph, which is still there
somewhere, accompanied by a quote from Man-
dela. Today I'd avoid the epitaph. There's always
someone who for their own needs tells you how
you ought to finish something, but I should have
put just the date of burial. All the same, it's nice
that people are walking over it. We're constantly
walking on our dead. It's like archeology. A body,
pasta and tomato sauce. Maybe I should have
buried a bottle of wine with it.

[140] **"Maurizio Cattelan. All,"** 2011–12
Solo show curated by Nancy Spector,
Solomon R. Guggenheim Museum, New
York, November 4, 2011–January 22, 2012

The Guggenheim is perhaps the most strongly
characterized museum ever built. It's practically
impossible to do a conventional exhibition there,
with so many imponderables to take into account. It's by far the most difficult space in which
to show sculpture. Frank Lloyd Wright liked the
idea of the rotunda and just followed that, completely disregarding the basics that up till then
had been considered the foundations of any good
museum. It's no secret that he loathed New York
and his attitude towards modern art was luke-
warm. When someone objected that low ceilings
weren't suitable for displaying large paintings, he
suggested they be cut in half. You can only be
impressed by the nerve shown by the Guggenheim family. Calling on someone like Wright to
design a museum for their collection in New York
was the equivalent of calling on Richard Nixon to
talk about the importance of a free press! It was
either the greatest act of confidence ever made,
or else a display of total madness.

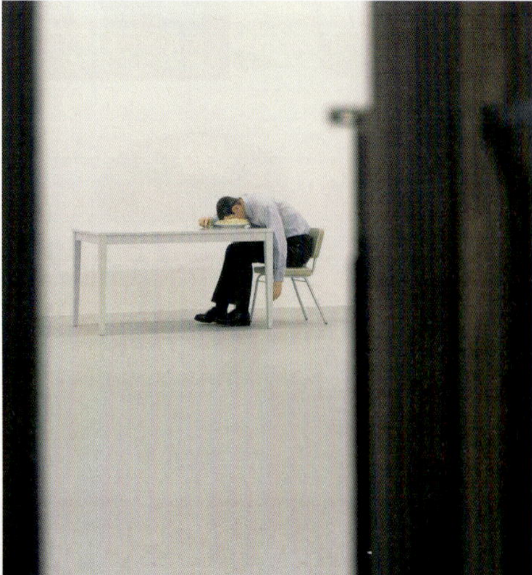

[138]

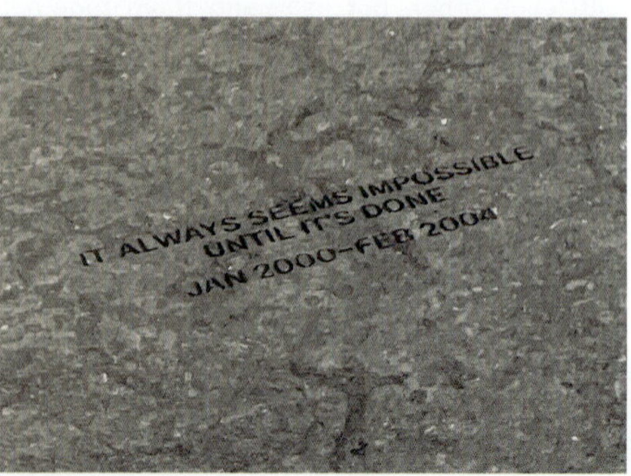


[139]

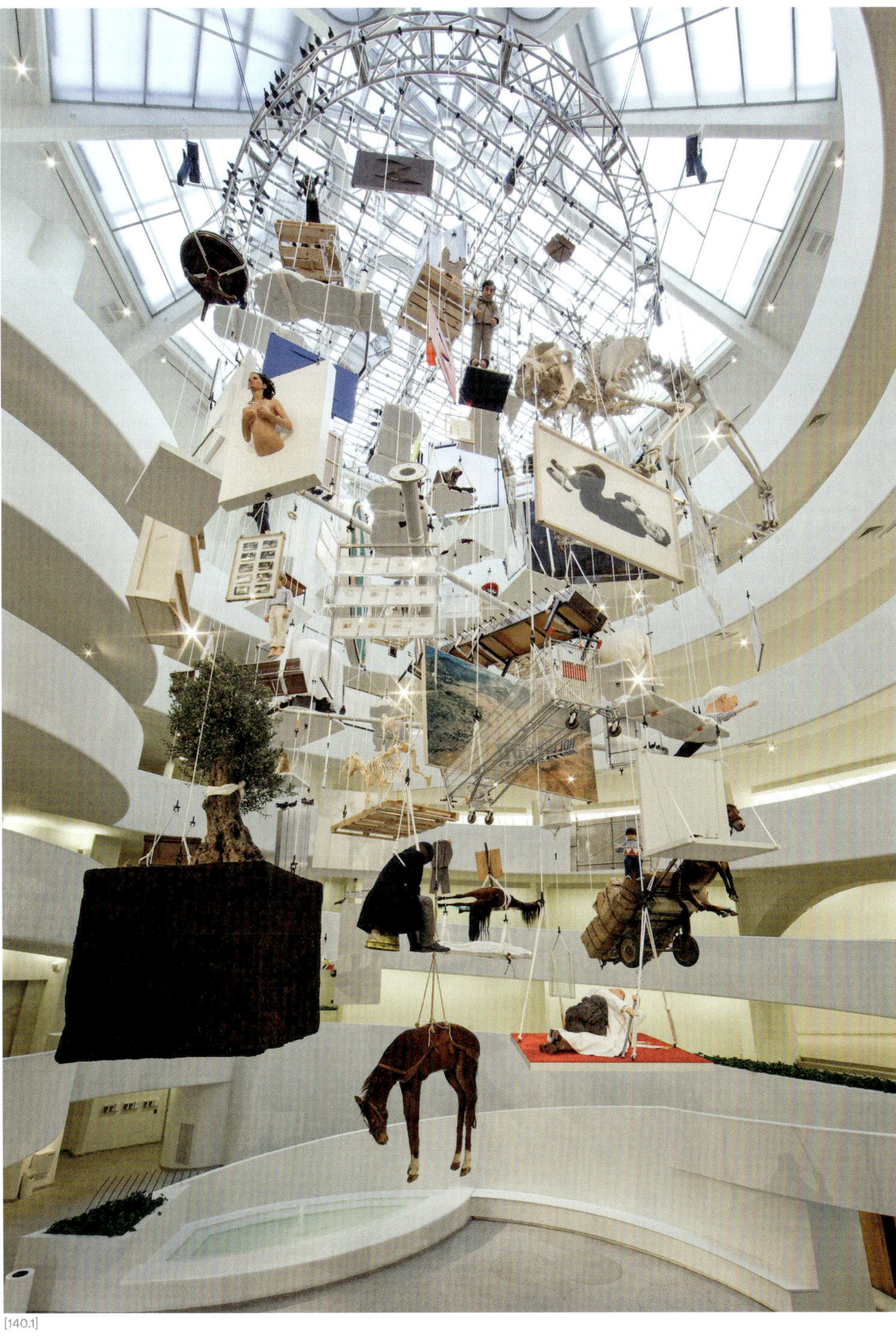

[140.1]

221

Then I was fairly familiar with the museum and how it operates. The curator Nancy Spector was a longtime supporter of my work. Mutual trust is a key factor in this kind of venture. Nancy knew how I worked, and I knew how she worked. My previous involvement with the Guggenheim had been limited to group exhibitions, but even then a part of my brain couldn't help looking out of my corner and focusing on the rest. I guess it's a bit like when you prune a tree. You inevitably end up thinking about how the rest of the garden would look if you were to prune everything else.

In a way, it was as it always is with me, a question of turning constraints into advantages. The purpose of the rotunda is to instill a democratic vision of art. No area is more important than another. Everything is placed on the same level, with a structure that encourages viewers to spend the same amount of time before each work. I'd already concluded that it was infeasible to show my works in a way that would have preserved their primary intention.

There were occasions when combinations of my works had worked. An example was the exhibition "Contro le ideologie" in Milan in 2010, where the pope of *La Nona Ora* (1999), the crucified woman (*Untitled*, 2007), and the kid banging the drum (*Untitled*, 2003) composed a sort of dysfunctional family. But showing more than a hundred pieces was another story. Duane Hanson once said that what prevented him from making very large groups was ultimately that bringing too many of his figures together into the same room would end up undermining their credibility. Look at what I had—headless horses, cat skeletons, mini-dictators, popes, policemen, old ladies, trees, deceased presidents, hanged kids... The whole thing would have looked like the craziest of nativity scenes or a scene in a Fellini film. So what I decided was to follow the logic of the architecture. I considered the center of the rotunda the most important part of the museum. I thought it was the only part to be taken into consideration. Everything was there, hanging. It didn't matter where you were: all the sculptures looked the same, as they should, the well-known and the lesser-known. There was no longer any hierarchy. Every episode was important to me. I don't have any favorite children. The exhibition was not an act of institutional criticism, but the way it was set up could be seen as a critique of the idea of a retrospective. In any case, bad works remained bad works and good ones remained good ones. The installation didn't hide anything. From a technical point of view, it was the most challenging project I'd ever done.

The Guggenheim has a cinematic quality. If you work in that space it unwinds. I'd say that my installation is static but the way the visitors see it could be a personal cinematic viewing. It was like the sculptures themselves were movies compressed into a single still suggesting a scene or a

222

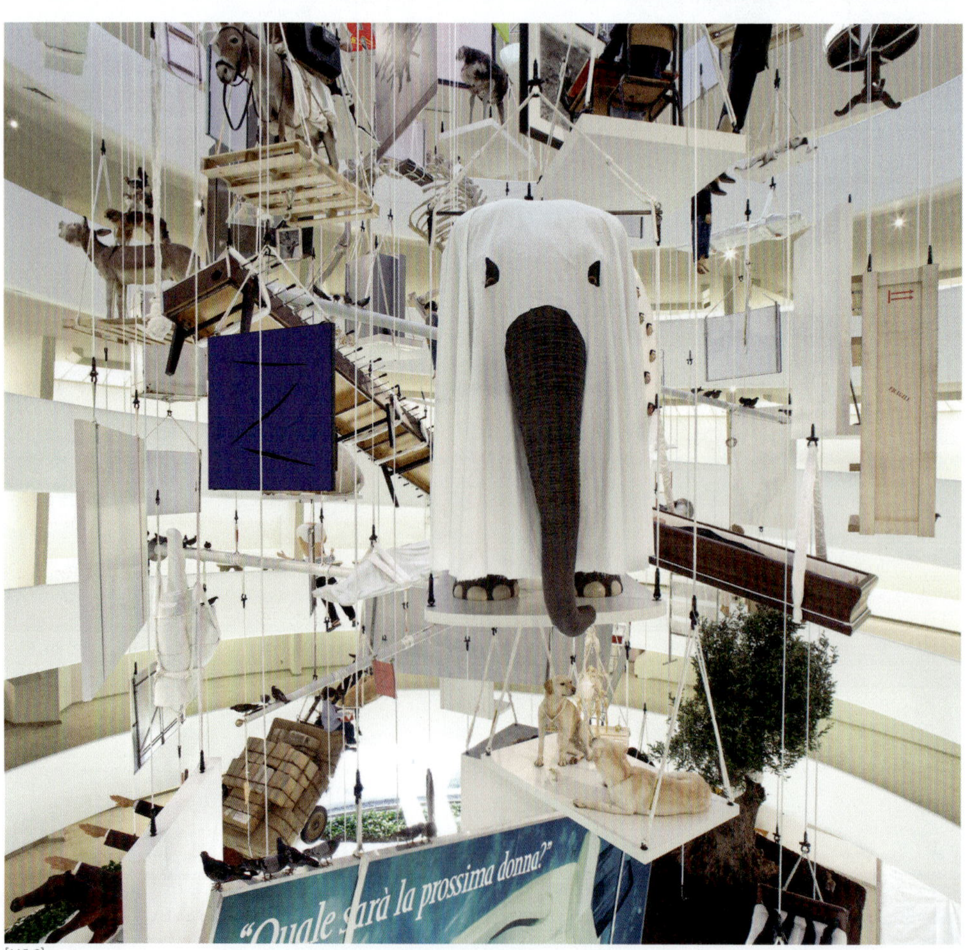


[140.2]

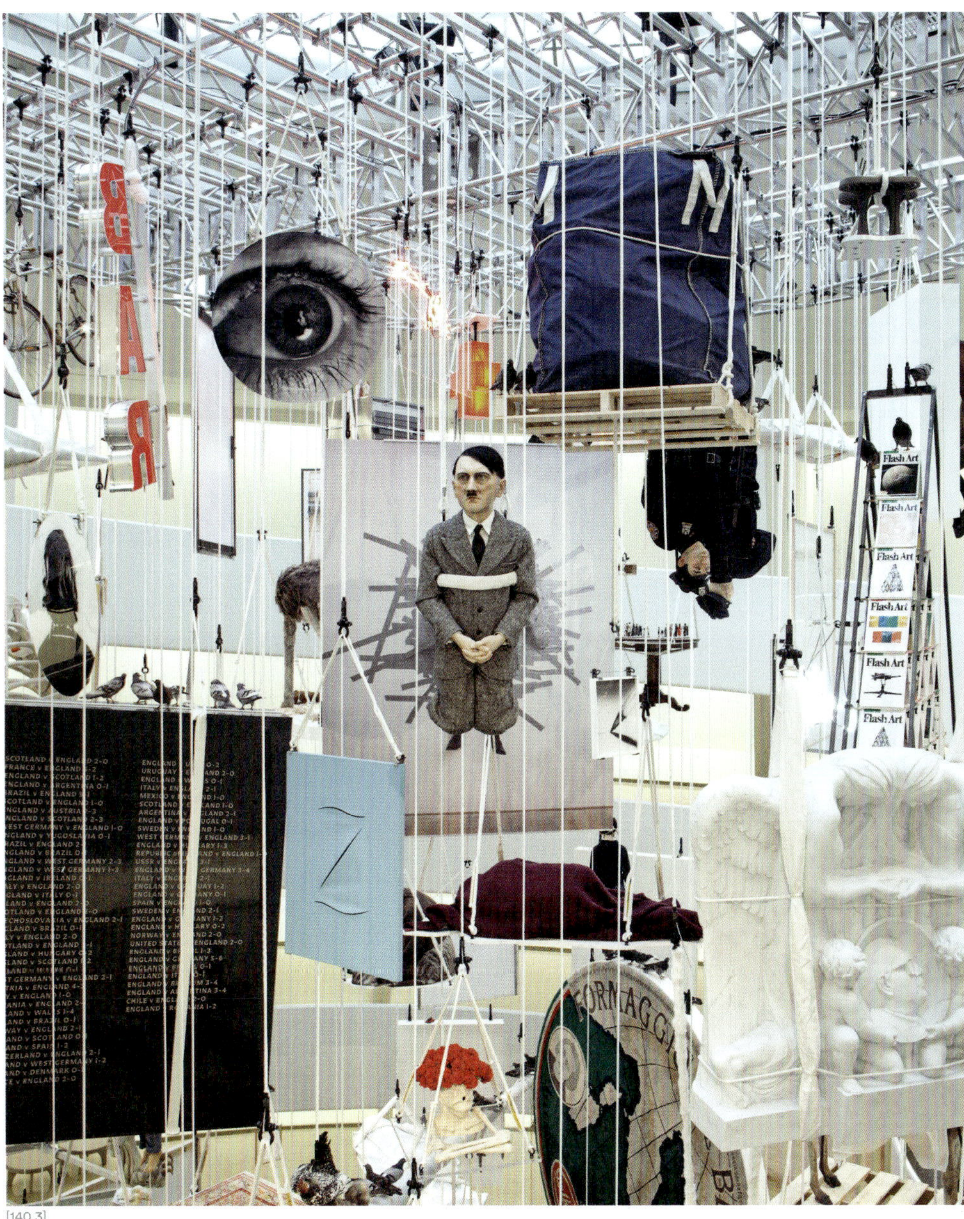

[140.3]

223

story. Maybe the whole show could be seen as a movie—unconnected scenes, each with its own theme. If an exhibition could be a movie, it would only be at the Guggenheim.

With "All," maybe I was just trying to rectify some of the inaccuracies written about me, or to shake off the image of the guy who just comes up with a random idea, creates some havoc and runs. I always had the impression of being misrepresented in the past. There are some really serious aspects in my work that have been overlooked or ignored. Maybe the Guggenheim exhibition helped in the sense that for the first time in my life I found myself giving a hard look at my past. I had to select old works and track them down, and that process quite naturally brought up a lot of memories attached to them about who I was and what I was trying to say.

At the Guggenheim there were all the works I'd produced down to 2011. The exhibition was ultimately a piece in itself: an imposing work that could be considered the last of that period of my life. The idea of retirement came together with that exhibition, not after. It stemmed from the need to draw a line between myself and what I'd done till then. That overall view helped me digest many mistakes, close a circle. Having to deal with all those works was the experience that I imagine closest to seeing images of your life pass before your eyes on the verge of death. Perhaps retirement was this: a small death from a change of state.

[140.2-3]  "Maurizio Cattelan. All," Solomon R. Guggenheim Museum, New York, 2011–12

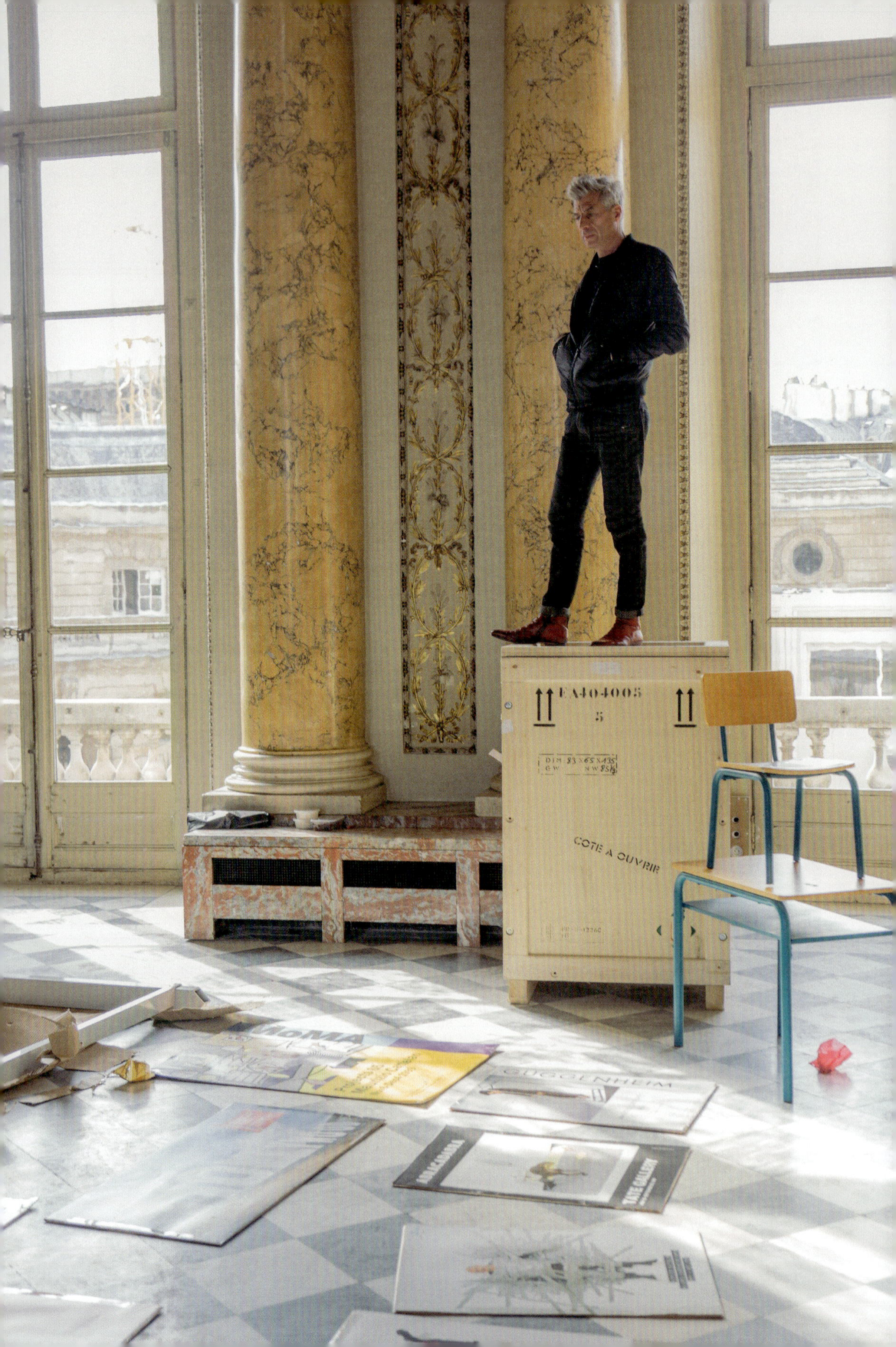

The word *exhibition* has always bothered me: it's so exhibitionist and brash. Maybe that's why my works, even the most frontal ones, are usually displayed in corners or hanging from a ceiling, always off-center. I like to lose my balance, fall, and maybe even vanish.

Anyway, when I think of an exhibition, I imagine the course that visitors will follow, what will be the first thing they see, what they'll have to examine close-up and when they'll have to take a step back to get a full view of something else. It's like a movie or a concert. You can't choose the players in an orchestra if you don't know the concert hall they're going to be performing in, and you can't edit anything without the music. I believe that building an exhibition is in a way like building a new house. Every detail is important, even deciding where to put the toilet. It's like working on a book or a magazine, because you have to imagine the sequence of images and the way they'll work together. The most difficult task is having to eliminate the superfluous. It's a painful operation, and at the same time it calls for great care. I strongly believe that the editing process is one of the most important actions in everyday life. Every decision often leads to exciting developments that you didn't always foresee.

In my show at the Kunsthaus Bregenz in 2008 I presented all brand-new works. But for the first time I had multiple pieces in different parts of the space dialoguing with each other, rather than a single strong centerpiece, like the little Hitler at the Färgfabriken in Stockholm in 2001, or the pope struck by a meteorite at the Kunsthalle Basel in 1999. I realized the potential of this opportunity, how the sum of three or four independent pieces can form a larger picture while retaining their intrinsic meaning. Since then, it's been a gradual process. The next step was the exhibition at the Menil Collection in Texas in 2010. This is a relatively small but very interesting museum, with an excellent collection and very distinctive architecture. It was encouraging to discover that I could put together a project on that scale and interact with the existing fabric without compromising my vision. In the meantime, the Guggenheim had offered me a mid-career review. I've turned down many solo shows, even prestigious ones, but I knew that sooner or later I'd have to accept such an invitation, and I thought the Guggenheim was the right place for it.

Some of my previous refusals were certainly driven by the idea of resisting time. Even the simple word "retrospective" is something I associate with the Old Masters, and being able to look back over the different stages of a career from its end point. Influences are stated, developments analyzed and works contextualized. It's all very flattering, especially if you're a living artist, but the subtext of this kind of treatment is that your best days are over, your role is clear, and any projects you might wish to do in future could never make the same impact as whatever you've done to date.

I'm only interested in what I'm doing now. Another thing that bothers me about retrospectives is the resurrection aspect, which is that people who missed the artist's work the first time around think that the artist himself or the retrospective can recreate the original experience for them. Intellectually, in terms of what the work means or how it really looks, this might be true, but the historical conditions have changed.

Anyhow, retrospectives have never particularly impressed me. There are of course some exceptions, but curators mostly tend to adopt a very traditional line. And in their eagerness to discuss an artist's work in scholarly terms they often forget that, unlike technological progress, art doesn't follow a straight line. There are many elements you have to factor in—unexpected breakthroughs, moments of reflection, historical shifts and site-specific projects—that just can't be recreated anywhere else without losing the initial impulse that gave rise to them. I believe the best retrospectives are ones that leave the door open to questions instead of just providing answers, where the original spirit of the artist is reflected and respected, to the point of prevailing over the place and the comfort zone created by the lapse of time.

I felt that the idea of putting together a bunch of pieces that had been installed separately would be ridiculous. If I had to hold a retrospective, I would have liked the works to be set up not in a museum but in different places to suit the nature of each piece. People would choose when to see them and in what order.

These are the reasons why I thought for a long time that it would be impossible for me to accept a retrospective, that I would find it repulsive. In my work, it's the ideas that make the difference. If I present something in an aesthetic key, I'm finished. That's why I sometimes say I'm not an artist but a creator of projects, a creator of situations.

Then the retrospectives gave me opportunities to reflect. I was able to do several exhibitions with the same works but in different atmospheres, depending on how I managed them. Some shows, like the ones at the Menil Collection, the Guggenheim and the one at the Monnaie de Paris in 2016–17, enabled me to take stock of what I'd achieved. I would never have imagined that an exhibition could help you analyze your output and see its main lines. Not that you can understand why you did certain things and not others, but you can spot some obsessions. And you can see what led you to produce your weakest works. My mistakes are undoubtedly due to my not having a studio, so the moment of truth is the show itself. That's where you see whether a piece works or not. In this way, awareness of whether you've bungled it or hit the spot is never a private matter.

It's a serious moment when you start seeing certain repetitions and obsessions and you wonder why you should ever reiterate them. This book brings together everything I've done. I'm closing a cycle of my work and going beyond it. Goodness knows whether I will retire again. At some point, everything that's shown will necessarily come from the archive of the works created. I've seen many artists repeat themselves and their work fall apart. I don't want to be just another one.

It's a bit like in in love affairs. As long as you don't lose the habit of seeing each other, you never come to the end of a relationship. In my case I haven't ended the relationship with any of my gallerists, but I always try to put an end to the bad habit of being tempted by gallery shows. It's like smoking. I can't say I won't start smoking again, but it's unlikely. I've trapped myself in a kind of public sphere and now I can't escape. I think it was the same for Christo and Jeanne-Claude. Once you've wrapped the Reichstag, you can't go back to wrapping a chair for a gallery show.

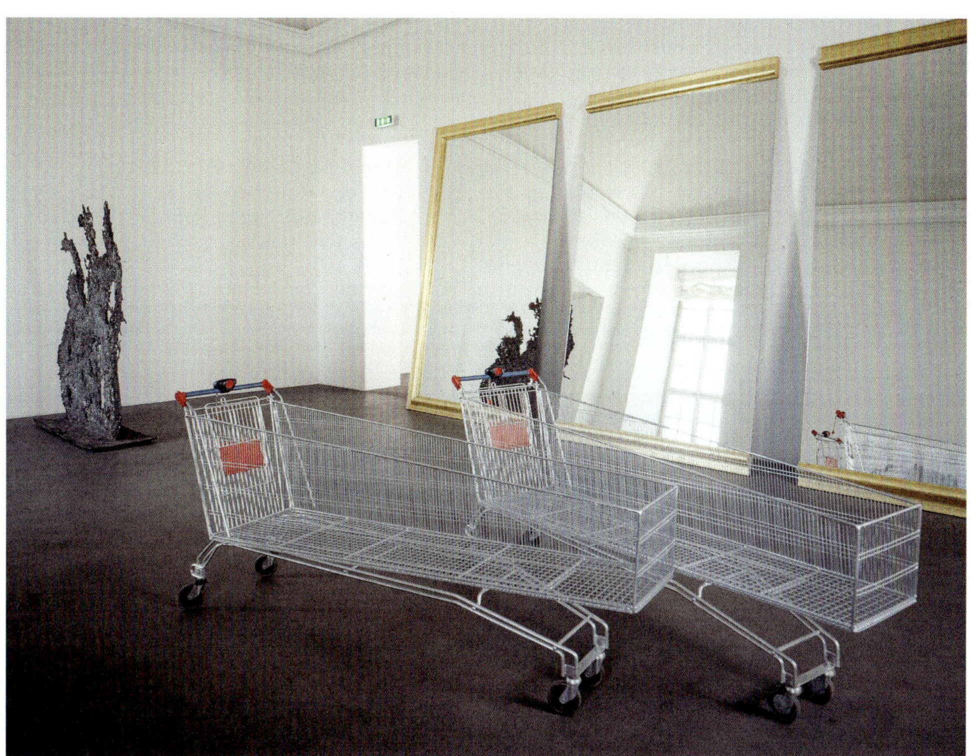

[142]



[141] **"Maurizio Cattelan. Tre installazioni
per il Castello," 1997–98**
Solo show curated by Giorgio Verzotti,
Castello di Rivoli Museo d'Arte
Contemporanea, Rivoli-Turin, September
25, 1997–January 8, 1988

    [142] *Less than ten items*, 1997
    Steel, rubber, plastic
    120 × 220 × 60 cm

[143] **"Is There Life Before Death?," 2010**
Solo show curated by Franklin Sirmans,
The Menil Collection, Houston, February
12–August 15, 2010

    [144] *Untitled*, 2009
    Canvas, broom
    210 × 85 × 60 cm

    [145] *Untitled*, 2010
    Silicone, paint, natural hair,
    metal grid
    18 × 13 cm

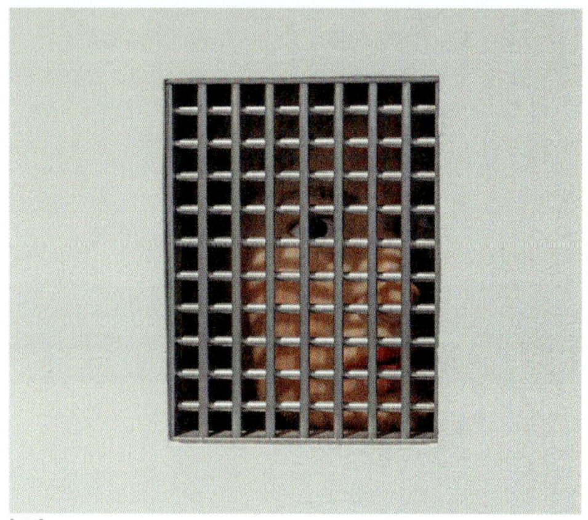

[145]

The exhibition at the Castello di Rivoli was my
first show in a museum. I was invited by the director Ida Gianelli, who had very clear ideas about
what the museum needed and what worked. She
guided me and we came up with the idea of presenting three works in the different rooms of the
collection. I set up one of my first dogs, *Stone
Dead* (1997), camouflaged with one of the fire-
places in the castle, the child seen from behind to
him who has run away from school but not from
his desk, *Charlie Don't Surf* (1997), and a work designed specifically for the room with Pistoletto's
mirrors, *Less than ten items*. They were two shopping carts put there as if they were meant to be
filled with works from the collection. They were
enormous, like the voracity of the market. I'm surprised that today trolleys are not all like that.
I did a similar operation years later, in 2010, for
the exhibition at the Menil Collection in Houston,
inserting ten of my works in the rooms of the museum in relation to the works in the collection. I
trod warily, with the attitude of one hiding himself from the great masters. Perhaps that's also
why I came up with the idea of the face peering
from behind a grate, a small note of humility.

[142] *Less than ten items*, 1997
"Maurizio Cattelan. Tre installazioni per il Castello,"
Castello di Rivoli Museo d'Arte Contemporanea,
Rivoli-Turin, 1997–98

[145] *Untitled*, 2010
"Is There Life Before Death?," The Menil Collection,
Houston, 2010

[146] **"Amen," 2012–13**
Solo show curated by Justyna Wesołowska, Centre for Contemporary Art, Ujazdowski Castle, Warsaw, November 15, 2012–February 24, 2013

Fabio Cavallucci, who was directing it at the time director, invited me to create this exhibition at the Centre for Contemporary Art at Ujazdowski Castle in Warsaw. I presented seven works. I was especially interested in showing artworks in an urban setting. For this reason I installed one of my children hanging from a flagpole (*Untitled*, 2004) in the museum courtyard, and the figure of

Hitler kneeling (*Him*, 2001) in the entrance hall of a building in the former ghetto. From the street you could only see a figure from behind praying alone in his corner.

[147] **"Maurizio Cattelan," 2008**
Solo show curated by Eckhard Schneider, Kunsthaus Bregenz, February 2–March 24, 2008

The Kunsthaus Bregenz building, designed by Peter Zumthor, is extremely minimalist, all exposed concrete. I decided to match the austerity



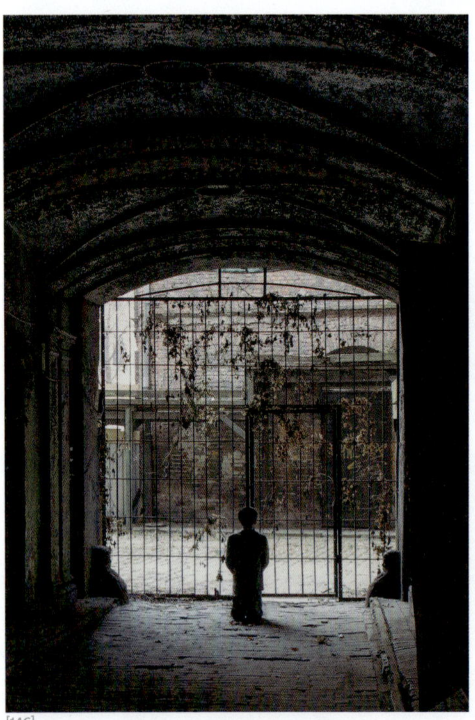

[146]

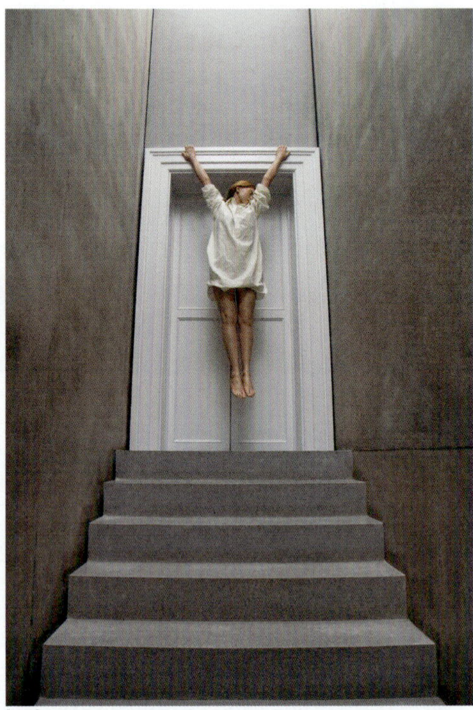

[147.1]

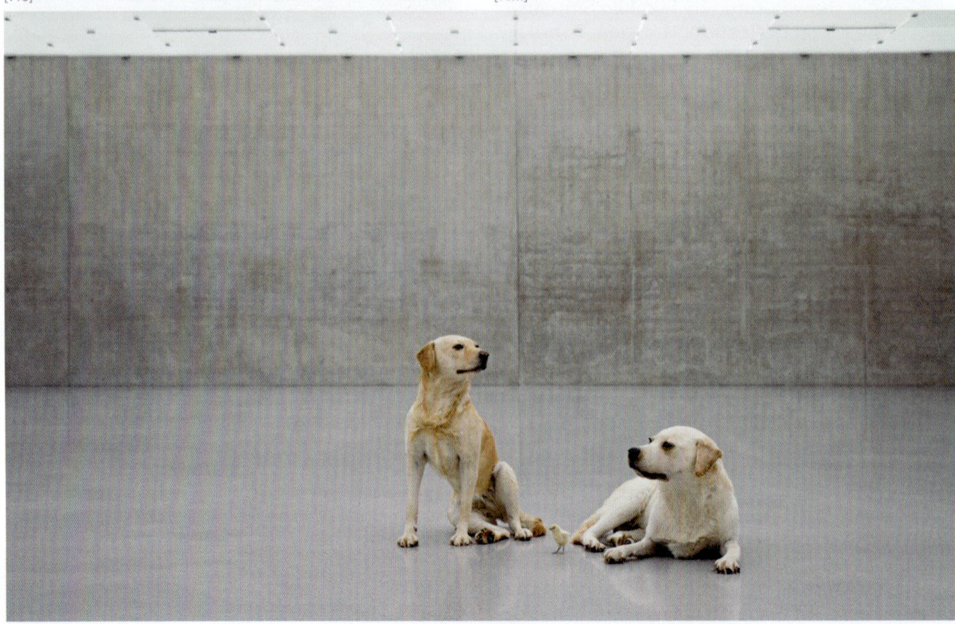

[147.2]

of the architecture, leaving the three floors of the museum practically empty. I even asked to turn off the heating system, and the exhibition was being held in Austria in winter. I presented three new works, one on each floor, developing a sort of trilogy on the theme of death, hence necessarily of life. Then, on the ground floor, at the entrance to the museum, hung the exhibition poster, as a small prelude, a divine judgment over a city in flames. On the first floor, at the start of the layout, I placed the sculptures of two Labradors and, between them, of a chick, a tiny presence that could only be discovered by looking at it closely (*Untitled*, 2007). On the second floor I set up the veiled marble bodies of *All* (2007), while the third was in fact inaccessible, because I'd installed a work right at the top of the staircase, hanging in front of the entrance door to the floor. It was the sculpture that recalls a self-portrait of Francesca Woodman, a sort of crucifixion, or even resurrection (*Untitled*, 2007). I only presented the work like that in Bregenz, because since then I've always shown it by leaving it in its transport crate.

[148]  *Kaputt*, 2013
       5 taxidermied horses
       C. 300 × 170 × 80 cm each

After it had been in my mind for many years, in 2007 I returned to the horse, installing its body directly on the wall, as if the head were buried in the wall, or simply hidden. A hunting trophy

in reverse. The horse is a fixed appointment with death. Death is an extraordinary subject, the only one that has the same weight as life. If you want to talk about life, you have to think about death first.

In 2013 I resumed this work on an exhibition at the Fondation Beyeler. It was the time of my retirement from the art world, but the project didn't change my status, as it grew out of an existing work shown in a new context. No novelty, no new production. My archive and the curators of the Fondation Beyeler were able to devise an exhibition with a single work, without new ones being made, simply by exhibiting that horse in all its three editions, plus the two artist's proofs. It was not a new work but in a way it became one. I think that exhibition is an example of how a good work can be presented as something new without being one. In a situation of international crisis, such as that of the time, the choice could also be interpreted as a question of economy: why continue to produce new works when there were already so many in circulation?

In the museum my work was surrounded by rooms filled with masterpieces of contemporary art history. On one side the collection, on the other a Max Ernst exhibition. In the middle of it there was a foreign body crushed between giants. It was the allegory of a heroic effort, a desperate attempt in search of salvation, thwarted by the reality of History.

229

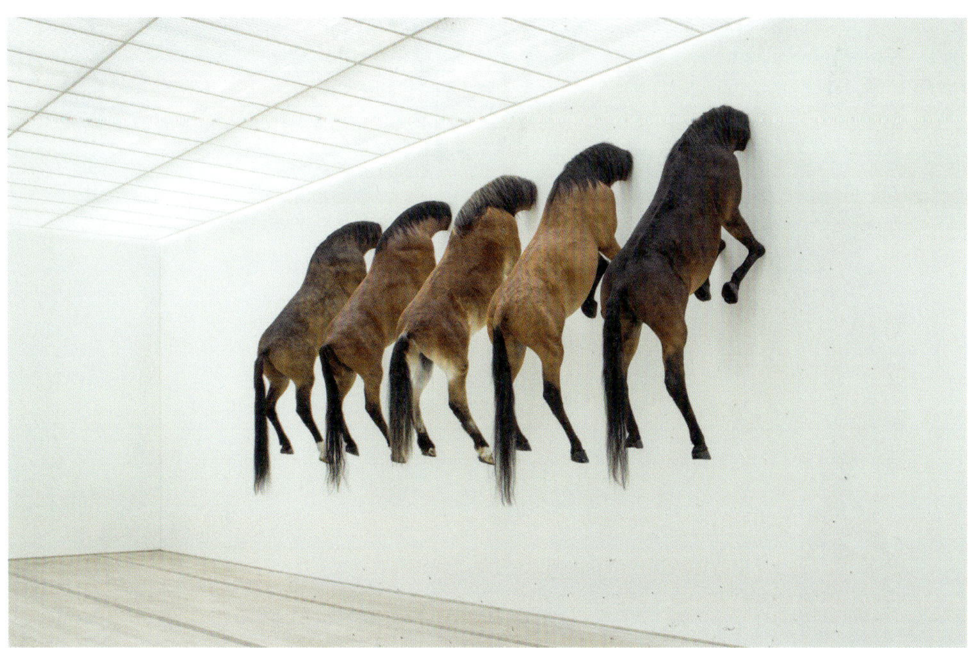

[148]

[146]  *Him*, 2001 [203]
"Amen," Centre for Contemporary Art, Ujazdowski Castle, Warsaw, 2012–13

[147.1]  *Untitled*, 2007 [67.1]
"Maurizio Cattelan," Kunsthaus Bregenz, 2008

[147.2]  *Untitled*, 2007 [118]
"Maurizio Cattelan," Kunsthaus Bregenz, 2008

[148]  *Kaputt*, 2013
"Maurizio Cattelan. Kaputt," curated by Michiko Kono and Sam Keller, Fondation Beyeler, Basel, June 8–October 6, 2013 (solo show)

[149]  **"Not Afraid of Love," 2016**
Solo show curated by Chiara Parisi,
Monnaie de Paris, Octotber 21, 2016–
January 8, 2017

"All" at the Guggenheim was definitely my most challenging exhibition project, "Not Afraid of Love" at the Monnaie the most revealing. It was a post-mortem exhibition. A great opportunity to exhibit some of my works in silence, without being overshadowed by the image of a jester foisted onto me.

Of the 129 works presented at the Guggenheim in 2011–12, I consider many of them no longer useful to anyone. I'd be happy for them to pass into oblivion. I see them as transitional, necessary to get to those ten or at most fifteen works that I'd save on most days. It was clear to me after the exhibition at the Monnaie. We had made a very narrow selection of truly significant works. Those works in particular, when placed side by side, open up to a variety of new and different meanings. They were designed for different settings. Forcing them to stay together might weaken or strengthen them.

230

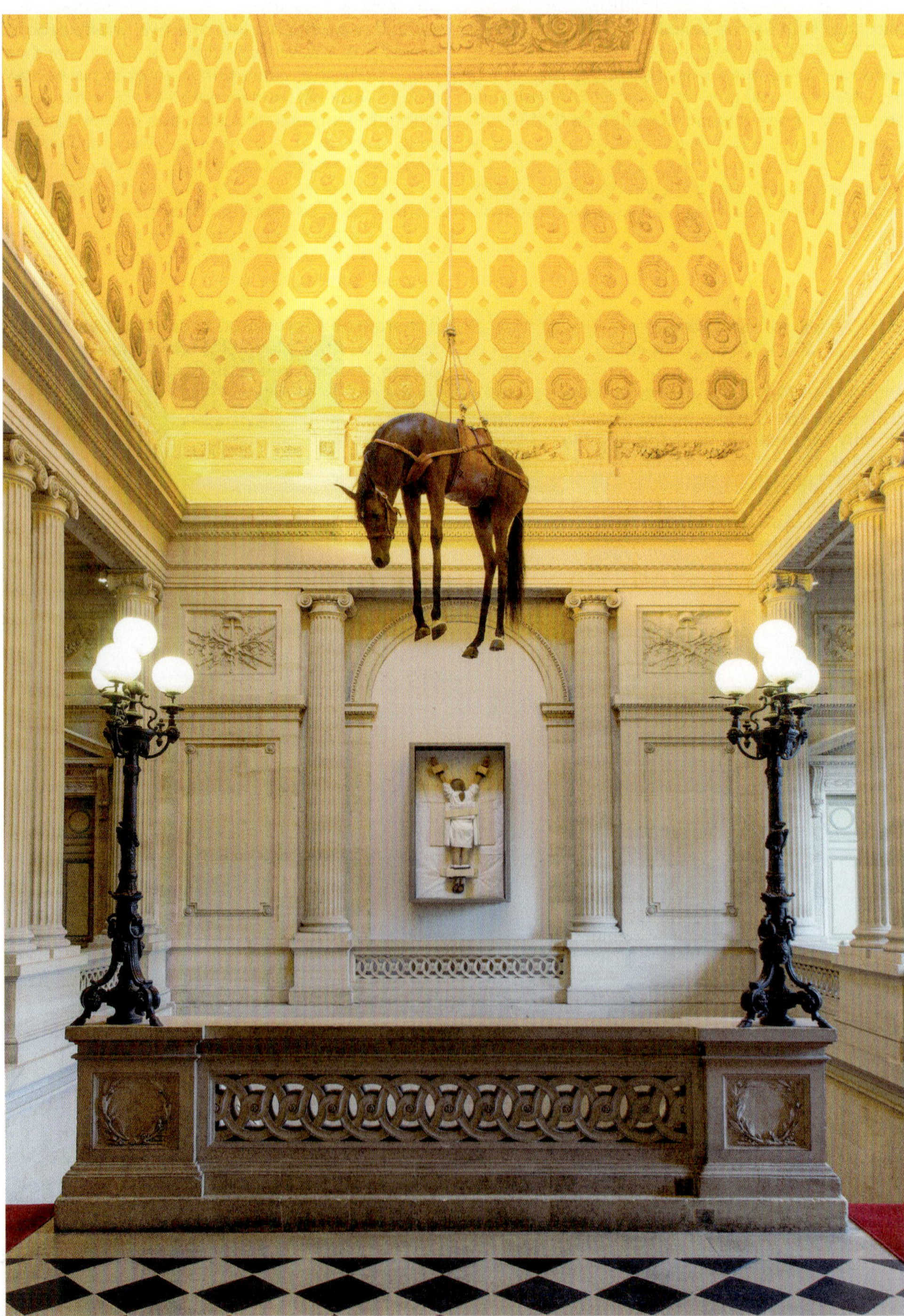

A work of art has to go through a phase when it's famous, a waning period and then a comeback. At that point, if the work has survived through to the third phase, we can say whether it's a major work, or even a masterpiece. Today we can tell which are the masterpieces of the 1990s, but it would be misleading to go further. Only from a long perspective can we say whether a work has the right combination of importance in the media and relevance in the history of art, and isn't just a matter of media hype.

Like many events in a career, the show in Paris started out as a completely different project. But if life is not always linear, neither are exhibitions. At first the idea was not to exhibit old works. Chiara Parisi, the then director of cultural programs at the Monnaie, asked me to do something new, but I couldn't find the right idea. I then realized that I could stay behind the scenes and direct a new edit of some of my works. So we designed the exhibition working they way you do with a book or a magazine. The editing process is one of the most important in everyday life, beyond exhibitions. A single decision often leads to interesting and unexpected developments that you hadn't in least envisioned at first. The most difficult task is eliminating the superfluous. It's both painful and necessary.

It was an interesting experiment, like listening to a group of individual voices that slowly tune in and eventually become a real choir. I was the first to be surprised by the result.

The architecture of the setting also shapes an exhibition. This is true of every show I ever did. In the case of the Monnaie, the rooms were at the same time passageways, and you could view the whole sequence from three key points. It was like seeing the title of the next chapter before you've finished the one you're reading. Then the captions created shifts in meaning. They'd been written by different people and were opinionated, with arguments for and against the works, so that the visitors could join in the conversation and form their own opinions.

From my point of view, love was the missing answer to all the works on show. It was more about the lack of love and a desperate lifetime quest for it. It might have a happy ending or not. It was completely up to the public. Or maybe the exhibition was more about the fear of love. At any rate, a common misunderstanding of novelists also needs to be dispelled in my case. Not everything they write is based on real life and it's not strictly autobiographical.

After the Paris exhibition, bringing together existing works continued to be an exercise in thinking about different combinations, which I repeated for exhibitions at the UCCA Beijing in 2021–22 ("The Last Judgment"), the Leeum Museum in Seoul in 2023 ("WE"), and at the Fundação de Serralves in Porto in 2025 ("Sussurro").

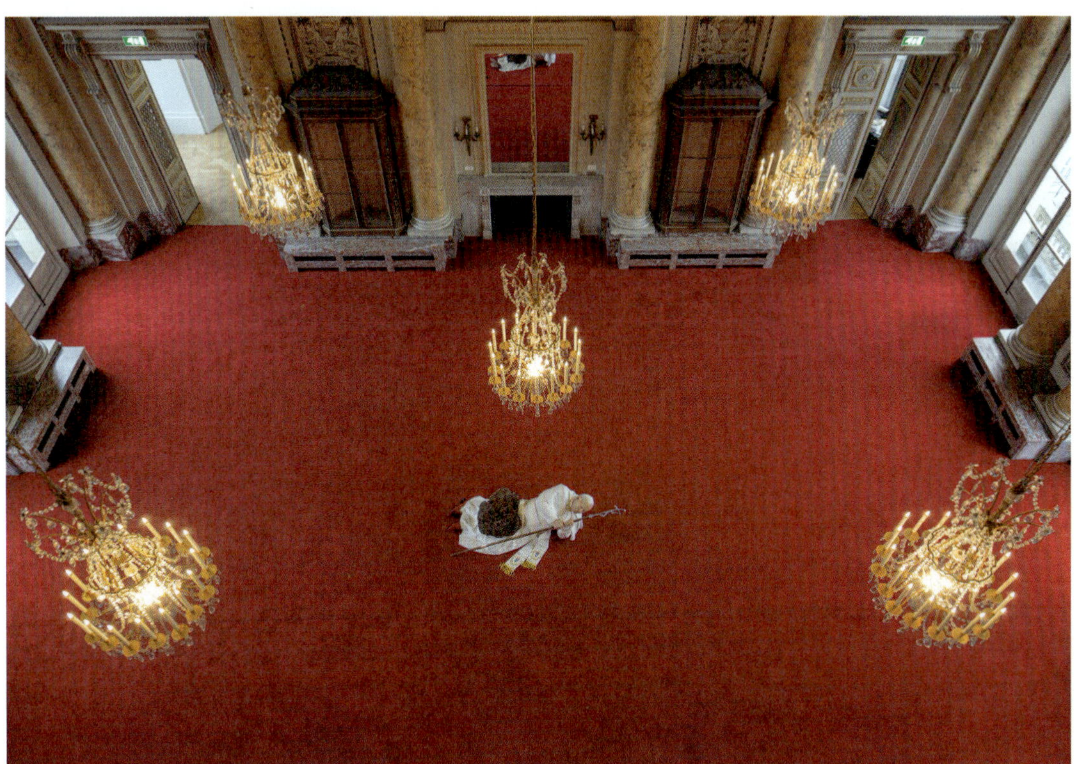

[149.2]

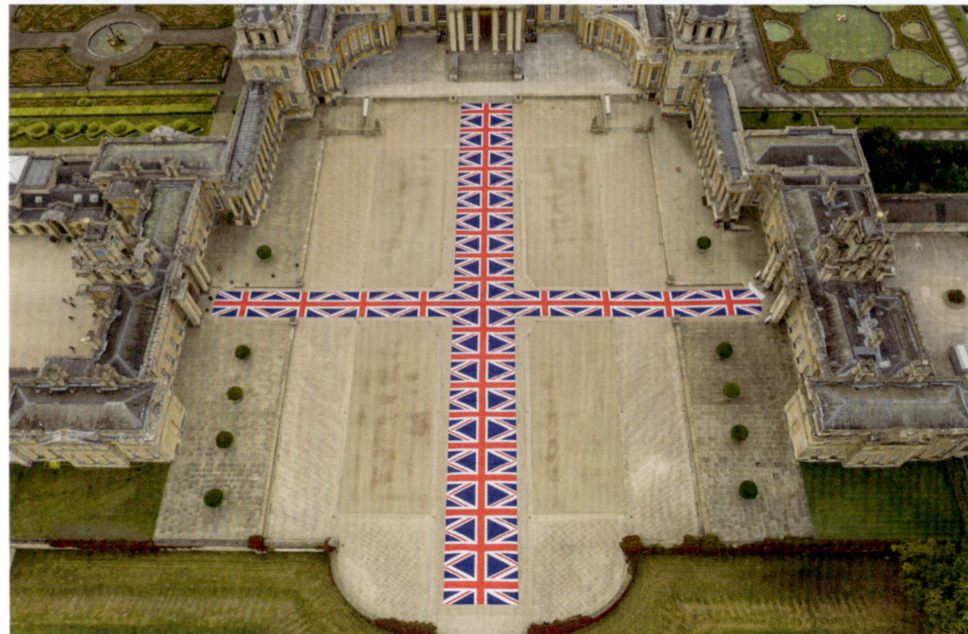

[151.1]

**[150]** **"Victory Is Not An Option," 2019**
Solo show curated by Michael Frahm, Blenheim Palace, Woodstock, United Kingdom, September 12–October 27, 2019

232

[151] *Victory Is Not An Option*, 2019
Decotex 220 g/m², rubber matting, felt
2048 m²

I'm slow to make decisions. It took me years to recover from the 2011–12 Guggenheim exhibition. For a long time I thought I wouldn't be able to make anything new out of my earlier work any more. But with the show at the Monnaie in Paris in 2016–17, I think I slowly realized that by carefully editing my work I could still deal with it without feeling sick. In 2019 I decided to accept the proposal from Blenheim Palace. If I'd been a Jane Austen character, I would have died unmarried.
Going to Blenheim is like taking a trip back in time or being on the set of *Downton Abbey*. I'm fascinated by the way power expresses itself in splendid architectural masterpieces. "We shape our buildings, and afterwards our buildings shape us," a wise inhabitant of Blenheim once said.
There isn't any specific criterion for selecting works for exhibitions like the one at Blenheim Palace. You start from a focal point and work your way up from that. You include a work that links to the previous one you thought of, as if you were sewing, and then add the next one advancing in the same way. When you get to the end of the thread you're back at the beginning, and you can close the circle without even being aware of it. The most important thing is not to sew alone. You have to keep talking with the curatorial team and your friends, and that makes the circle perfect.
Artists are like sponges. They absorb all kinds of things from their environment, then they re-

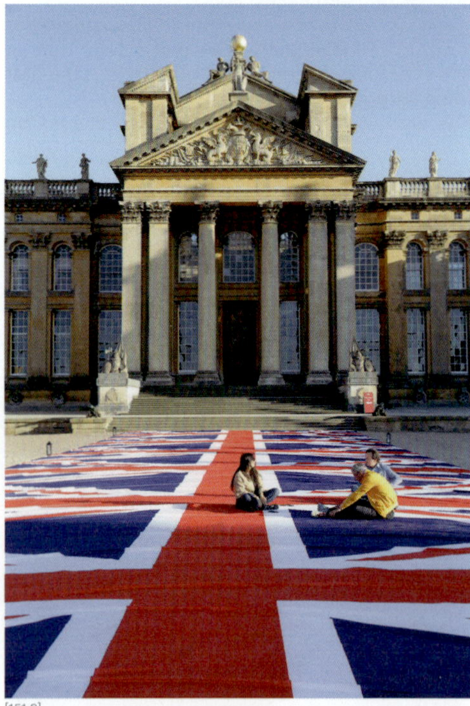

[151.2]

[151.1-2] *Victory Is Not An Option*, 2019
"Victory Is Not An Option," Blenheim Palace, Woodstock, United Kingdom, 2019

[150.1] *Him*, 2001 [203]
"Victory Is Not An Option," Blenheim Palace, Woodstock, United Kingdom, 2019

gurgitate it in their work without really knowing where it all came from. I was surprised myself by all those flags popping up in the show, but then I took a look at the front pages of the newspapers and found an explanation. We're living in dark times, when nationalisms and borders seem to be vanquishing the dream of a larger and more open society. I believe it's a climate that we can dispel, but we can't ignore its existence, how it has come about and what it means to be living through it. And works of art have a good memory.

The two rows of Union Jacks that were trampled on to enter the palace could be considered the overture to the show. They worked as a visual title. The actual title of the work, and the whole exhibition, *Victory Is Not an Option*, is as controversial as the flags are. Both prompt us to reflect on how the meaning of victory and failure can change depending which side of the battle we consider. At any rate, the first work is always the most important, because it sets the temperature of the exhibition. It's the standpoint from which you'll view all subsequent works. In this respect, I feel that *Victory Is Not an Option* also said something like "Enter at your own risk."

Old houses are always full of furniture and ghosts,

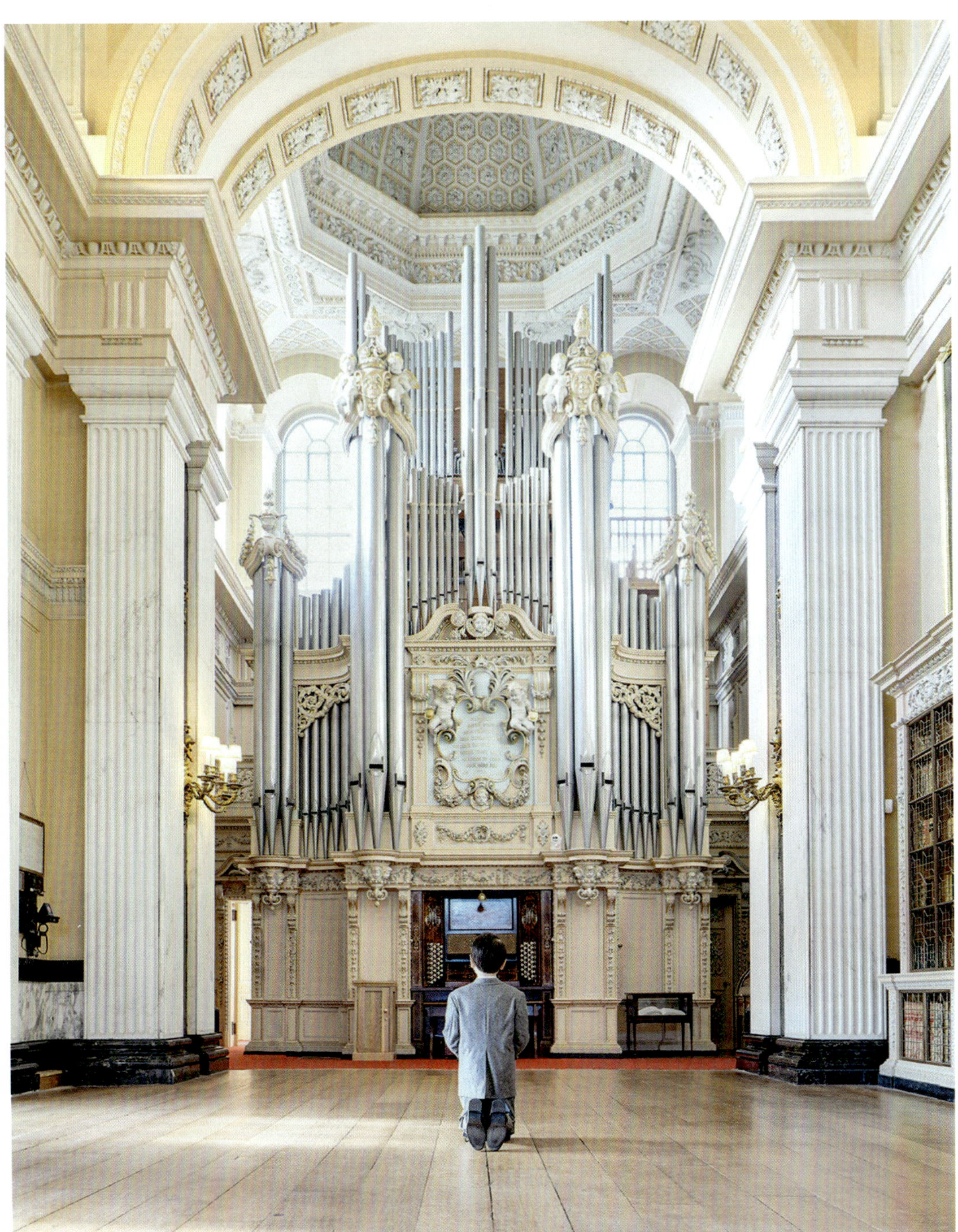

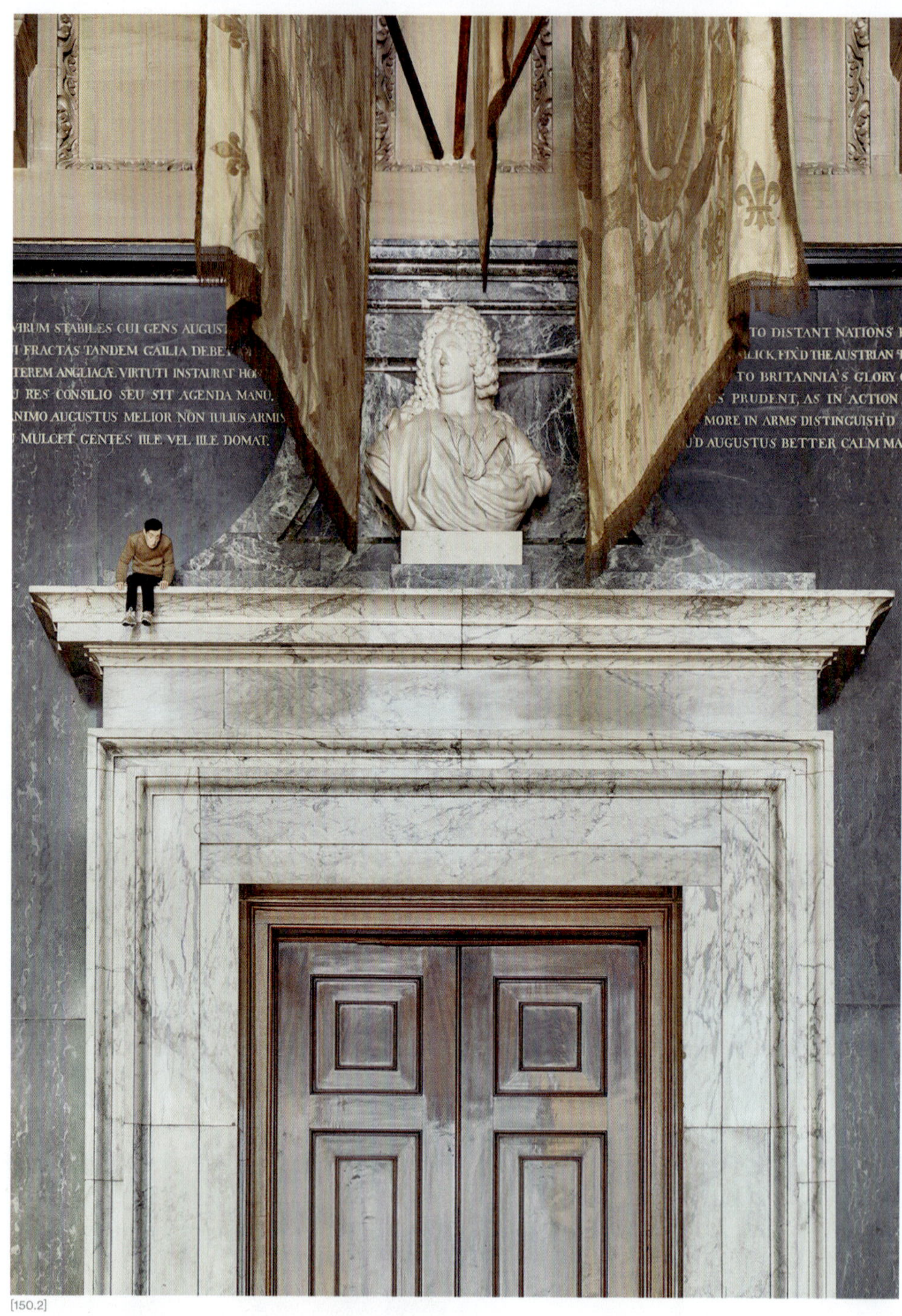

[150.2]

and the only way to deal with them is to approach them, to establish a relationship. You can't avoid or ignore them, because you're the intruder, not vice versa. From room to room, you're either a threat to their place or you gently enter into symbiosis, like a chameleon. The crocodile from *Ego* (2019) had long been swimming in the depths of my mind, as the real one would have done, until I saw the rooms at Blenheim and it peeped out. I found the (perhaps perverse) idea that those walls had seen so much history and were then forced to witness my exhibition very thought-provoking.

[150.2]   *Mini-me*, 1999 [3]
"Victory Is Not An Option," Blenheim Palace, Woodstock, United Kingdom, 2019

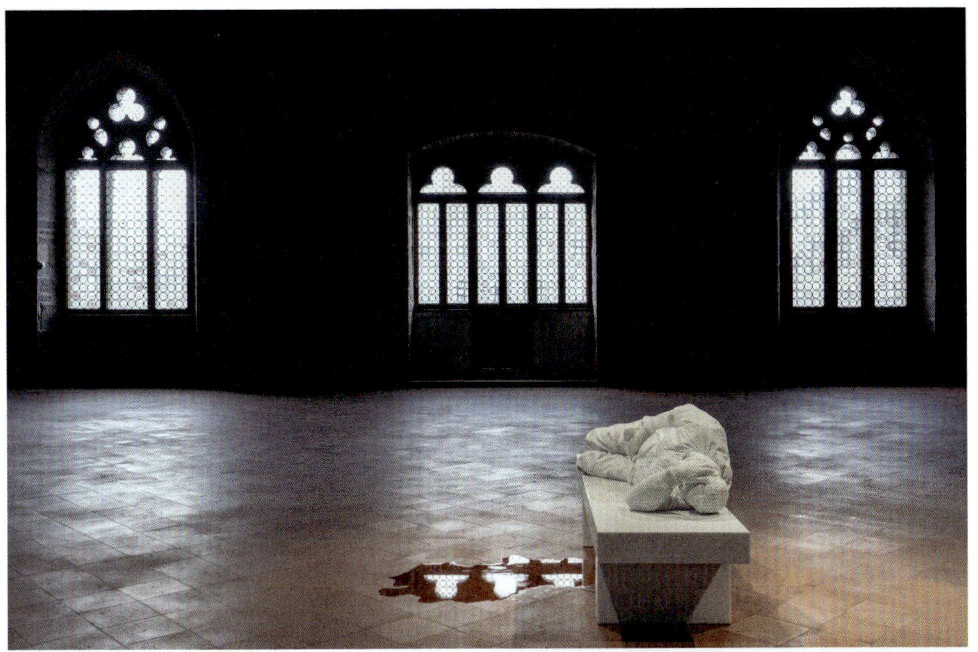

[152]



[152] **"Maurizio Cattelan. Seasons," 2025**
Solo show curated by Lorenzo Giusti,
GAMeC – Galleria d'Arte Moderna e
Contemporanea di Bergamo and other
venues, June 7–October 26, 2025

    [153] *Empire*, 2025
    Glass, cork, brick
    41 × Ø 12 cm

    [154] *Bones*, 2025
    Michelangelo statuary marble
    35 × 270 × 174 cm

    [155] *One*, 2025
    Silicone, resin, steel, synthetic
    hair, clothing, wood
    153 × 87 × 100 cm

I didn't need an analyst to tell me I have a bent
for stories of loneliness and defeat, which return
cyclically in my work, a bit like a seasonal de-
pression. This is the thread that unites the five
works I presented for a project with the GAMeC
in Bergamo, aptly titled "Seasons."
In the Palazzo della Ragione I installed *November*
(2024), which as in New York is seen first from
behind. From there the figure seems to be looking at the frescoes, while when you look more
closely you find that it's also a fountain. It des-
ecrates the sacredness of a historic place, but it
also confers a monumental quality on the marginality of the man, who is in fact peeing. It has
something irreverent about it. It's a scene that
might make you uncomfortable, but it makes
me think more than anything else about social
inequalities. And in this story of loneliness I think
we can also glimpse a possibility of renewal.
With a not very distant idea of play and light-
ness towards history, I tried to renew a symbol,
a monument to Garibaldi. Until you touch them,
the monuments in town squares are always in-

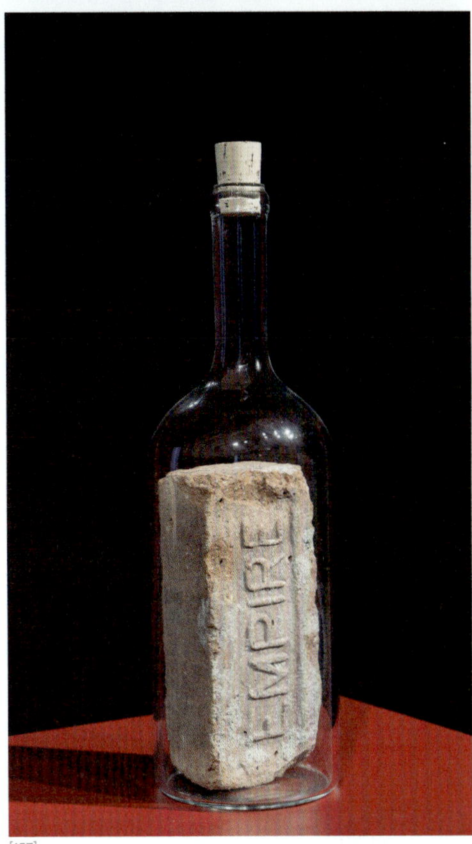



[153]

[152] *November*, 2024 [245]
"Maurizio Cattelan. Seasons," GAMeC – Galleria d'Arte
Moderna e Contemporanea di Bergamo and other venues,
2025, installation at the Palazzo della Ragione, Bergamo

[153] *Empire*, 2025
"Maurizio Cattelan. Seasons," GAMeC – Galleria d'Arte
Moderna e Contemporanea di Bergamo and other venues,
2025, installation in the museum

visible, but as soon as you lay hands on them, everyone has something to say. And in the new generations I perceive an innocence towards history. Everyone sees Garibaldi as a hero of the unification of Italy, but he was also a controversial character, with a life full of shadows. That's why with *One* I turned him into a horse, or maybe into a father with a child straddling, an irreverent mini-me.

There are stories forgotten and stories omitted, but they do not cease to exist. Doing research for the project, I discovered that in Dalmine, an industrial city founded near Bergamo after World War I, the workers in the steel factories invented the so-called "creative strike," one that didn't involve stopping production, but during which they discussed their rights while continuing to work. In 1919 Mussolini gave a speech to the workers of the Dalmine steel mill, and in memory of that event in 1939 a sculpture of an eagle was made. The eagle is often a symbol of royalty and power, even imperial rule—in Bergamo it's in the coat of arms of the province and it's the symbol of the Bergamasque Alps. After the fall of fascism the eagle was removed but, since history can't be erased, I made another one. Mine, however, has nothing victorious or royal about it. On the contrary, it's an emblem of defeat (*Bones*). But it should not be surprising that a certain idea of power, which seemed to have finnaly faded, can persist and finds its way back in the most unexpected forms: In one room of the museum, I exhibited *Empire*, a brick enclosed in a glass bottle, together with *No* (2021).

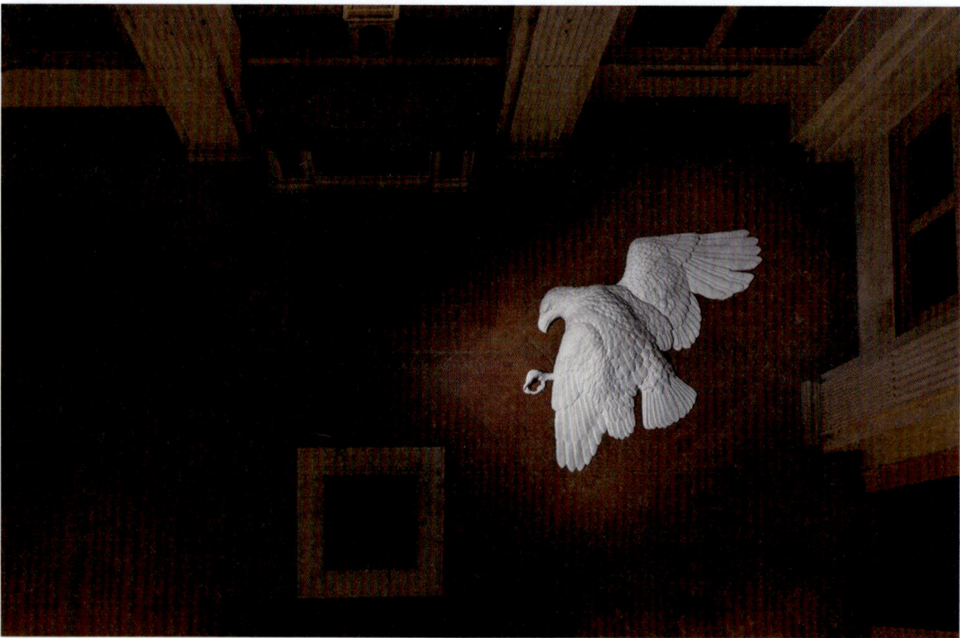

[154]

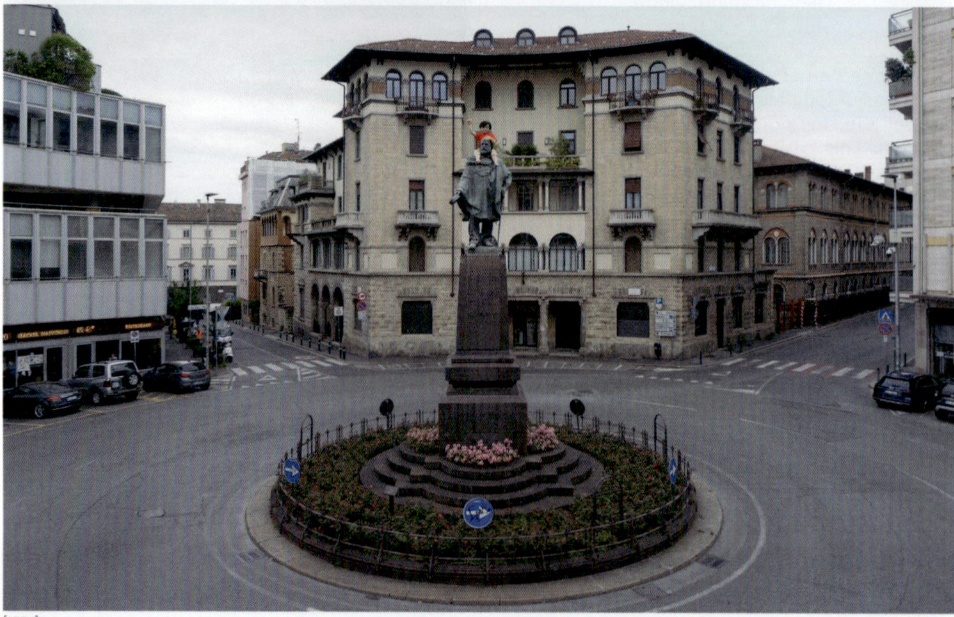

[155.1]

237

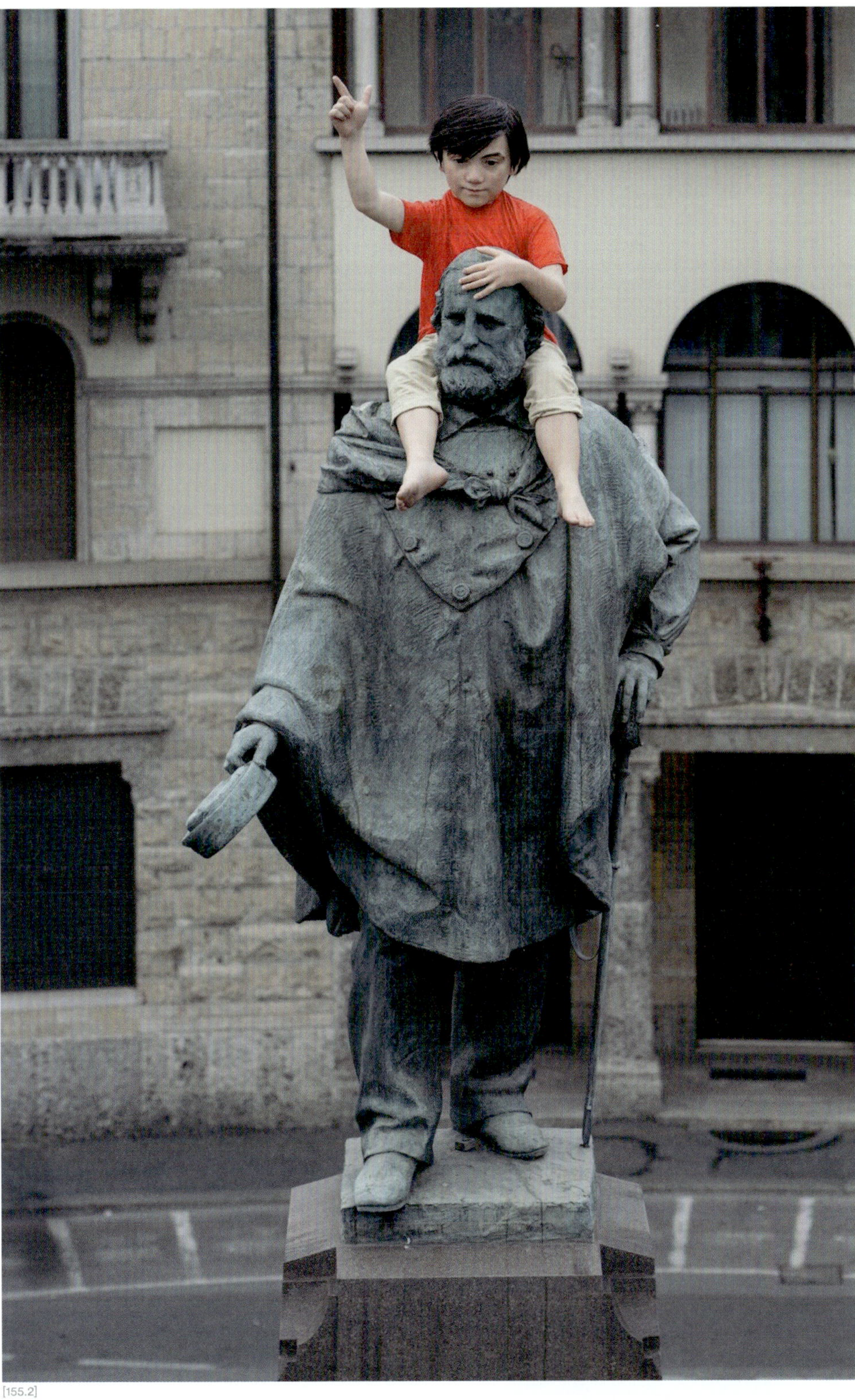

[155.2]

[154]    *Bones*, 2025
"Maurizio Cattelan. Seasons," GAMeC – Galleria d'Arte
Moderna e Contemporanea di Bergamo and other venues,
2025, installation in the former Oratorio di San Lupo,
Bergamo

[155.1-2]    *One*, 2025
"Maurizio Cattelan. Seasons," GAMeC – Galleria d'Arte
Moderna e Contemporanea di Bergamo and other venues,
2025, installation at the Rotonda dei Mille, Bergamo

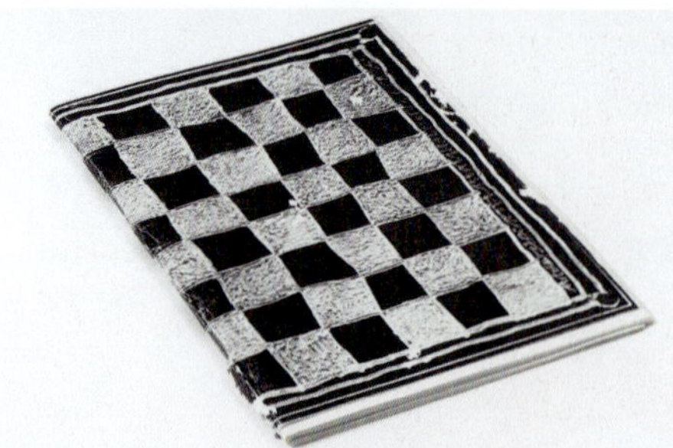

[156.1]

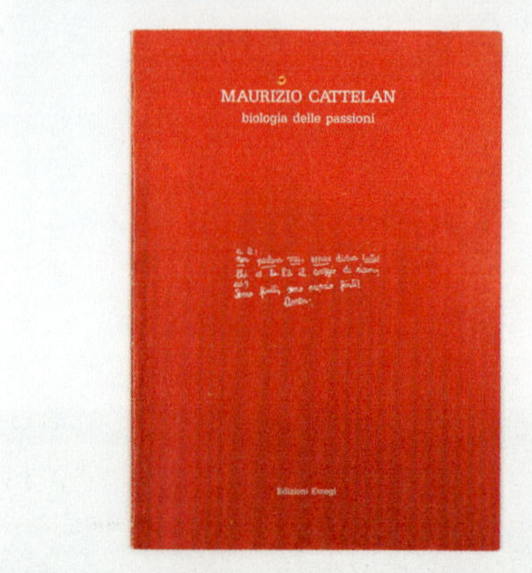

[156.2]

238

## [156] Monographs

Like retrospectives, monographs have always scared me. In the late 1980s, I published two books—*Natura Codarda* and *Biologia delle passioni*—but it was more to publicize my experiments at the time than as a record of them. The first real book, published by Phaidon in 2000, embarrassed me so much that when, three years later, I was asked to reprint it, I decided to do it in the smallest possible format: the volume is almost identical to the first, but reading it is a challenge. In 2008, for the show in Bregenz, the request for a book was insistently repeated and after a while I could no longer put it off, but I did it my way. I contacted a Chinese calligrapher and commissioned a book in which the text and images were handmade. This led to the project with Three Star Books in Paris, which continues to this day, without a precise calendar. In sixteen years four publications have been issued, all on loose sheets contained in a folder, with illustrations of my works and each with a single long text written by a person who has been close to me: in order Bice Curiger, Francesco Bonami, Massimiliano Gioni, Nancy Spector. The monograph *All*, released for the exhibition at the Guggenheim, is another story. The cover looks like a Bible, and inside it has a short text devoted to each of the works on display. *Un salto nel vuoto* is a special case in its turn, though it comes from the same period. I wanted to retire and abandon the world of images and it came naturally to me to talk with Catherine Grenier for hours on end.

[156.1]   *Maurizio Cattelan: Natura Codarda*, 1988
Texts by Stefano Verdicchio and Angelo Ventrone; published by the Galleria Neon, Bologna
15 × 10.5 cm, n.p.

[156.2]   *Maurizio Cattelan: Biologia delle passioni*, 1989
Texts by Bruno Bandini, Franco Bolelli, Stefano Casciani, Clara Mantica, and Alessandro Mendini; published by Palazzo del Diavolo Edizioni and Essegi, Ravenna, on the occasion of his solo exhibitions at the Galleria Fuxia in Verona, the Galleria Neon in Bologna, and the Loggetta Lombardesca in Ravenna, May 1989
23 × 16.3 cm, 48 pages

[156.3]   *Maurizio Cattelan*, 2000
Edited by Francesco Bonami, Nancy Spector, and Barbara Vanderlinden; published by Phaidon, London
29.2 × 25.4 cm, 160 pages

[156.4]   *Maurizio Cattelan*, 2003
Edited by Francesco Bonami, Nancy Spector, and Barbara Vanderlinden; second edition revised and enlarged; published by Phaidon, London
15.8 × 13.6 cm, 212 pages

[156.5]   *Die / Die More / Die Better / Die Again*, 2008
Text by Bice Curiger; published by Three Star Books, Paris, in 1000 copies
32.5 × 43.2 cm, portfolio of 43 sheets printed only on the recto

[156.6]   *The Three Qattelan*, 2010
Text by Francesco Bonami; published by Three Star Books, Paris, in 1000 copies
32.5 × 43.2 cm, portfolio of 49 sheets printed only on the recto

[156.7]   *The Taste of Others*, 2011
Text by Massimiliano Gioni; published by Three Star Books, Paris, in 1000 copies
32.5 × 43.2 cm, portfolio of 56 sheets printed only on the recto

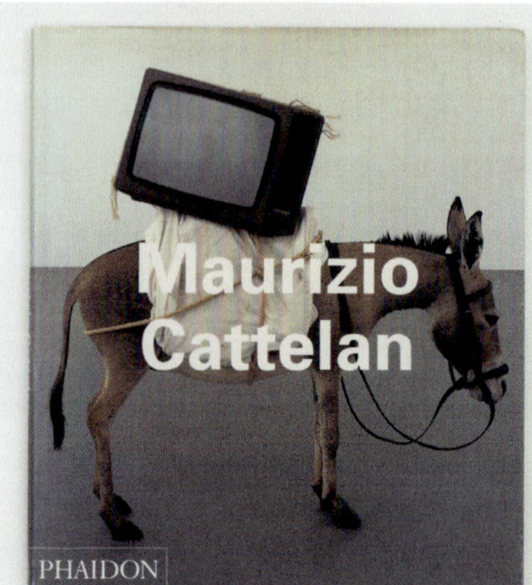



[156.3]

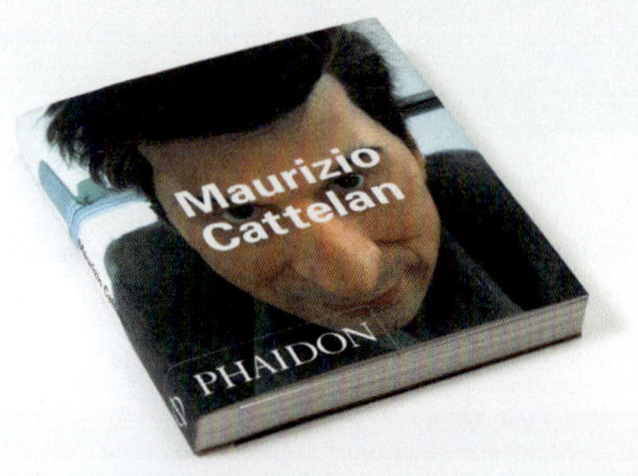



[156.4]

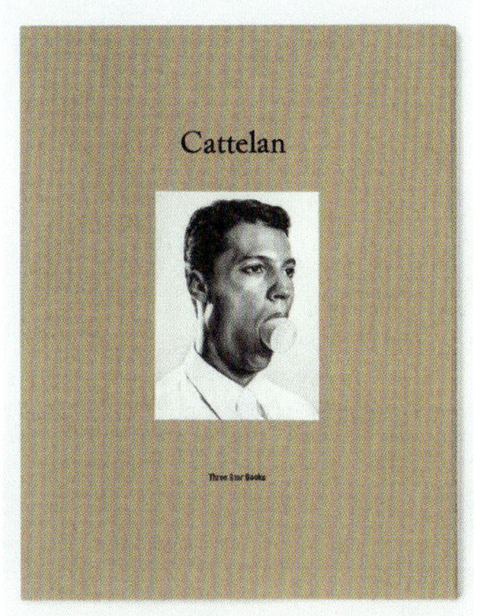

[156.5]

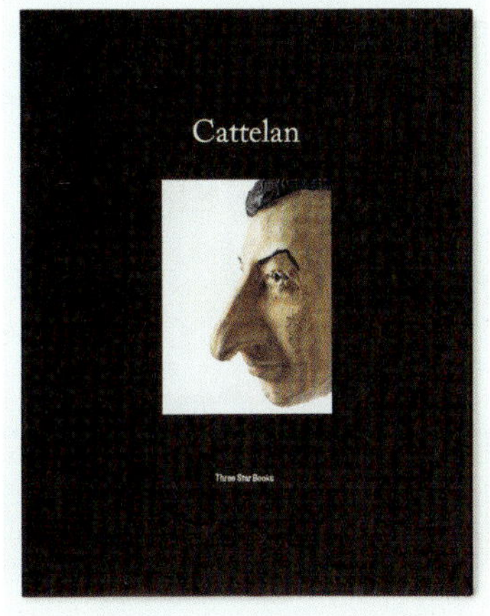

[156.6]

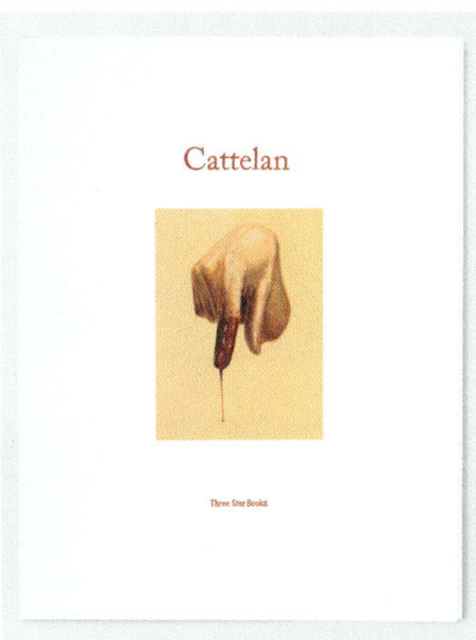

[156.7]

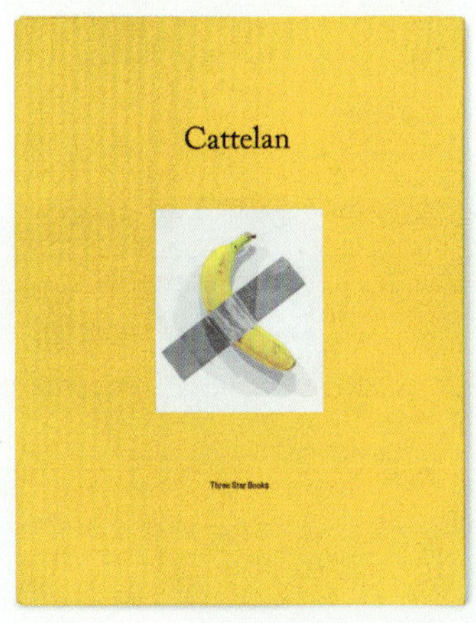

[156.8]

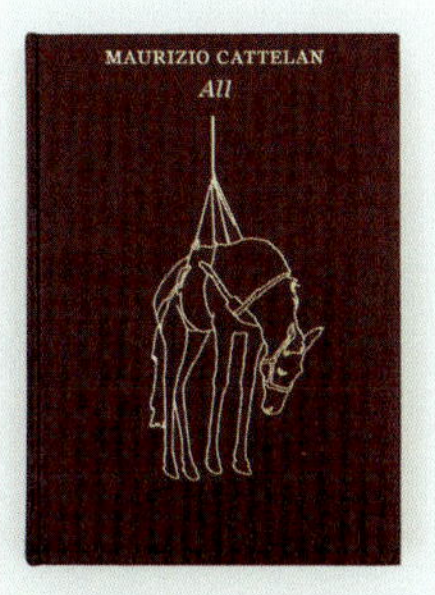

[156.9]

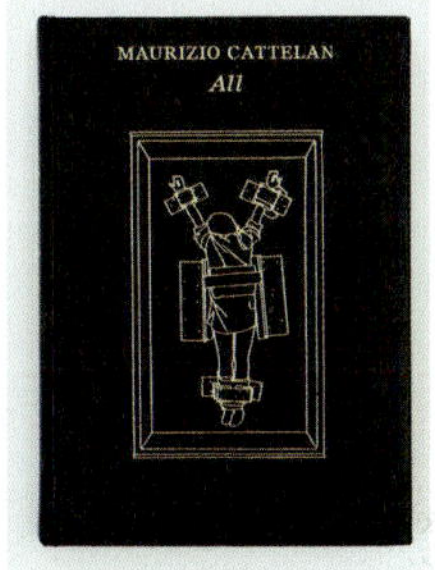

[156.10]

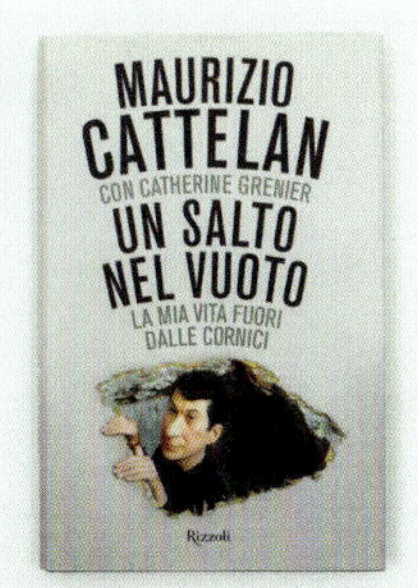

[156.11]

[156.8]   *The 11th Commandment*, 2024
Text by Nancy Spector; published by Three Star Books,
Paris, in 500 copies
32.5 × 43.2 cm, portfolio of 33 sheets printed only
on the recto

[156.9]   *Maurizio Cattelan: All*, 2011
Edited by Nancy Spector; Italian edition of the volume
published in the same year by the Solomon R. Guggenheim
Foundation, New York, and Skira, Milan, on the occasion
of his solo show at the Solomon R. Guggenheim Museum
25 × 17.5 cm, 256 pages

[156.10]   *Maurizio Cattelan: All*, 2016
Edited by Nancy Spector; second revised edition of the
volume published in 2011 by the Solomon R. Guggenheim
Foundation, New York, on the occasion of his solo show
at the Solomon R. Guggenheim Museum
25 × 17.5 cm, 259 pages

[156.11]   Maurizio Cattelan with Catherine Grenier,
*Un salto nel vuoto: La mia vita fuori dalle cornici*; published
by Rizzoli, Milan
22.5 × 14.5 cm, 145 pages

[156.12]   *Maurizio Cattelan*, 1998
Published on the occasion of the exhibitions at Centre
d'art – Espace Jules Verne, Brétigny-sur-Orge, December
13, 1997–February 21, 1998, at Le Consortium – Centre d'art
contemporain, Dijon, January 24–March 22, 1997, and at
the Galerie Emmanuel Perrotin, Paris, January 26–March 11,
1995 and May 24–July 19, 1998
26 × 24 cm, 150 pages

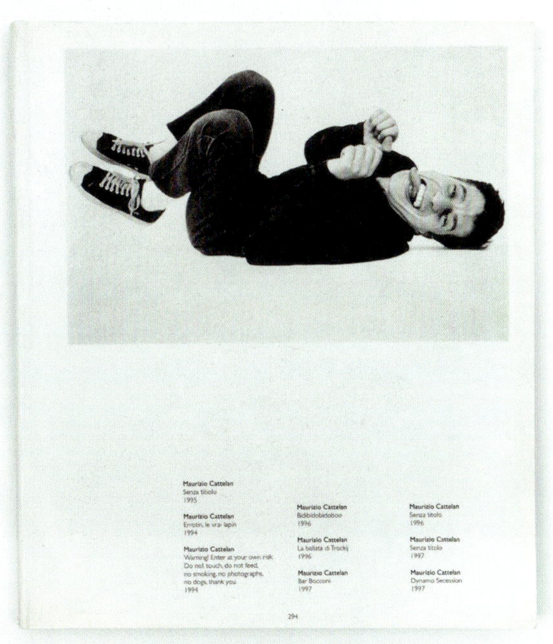

[156.12]

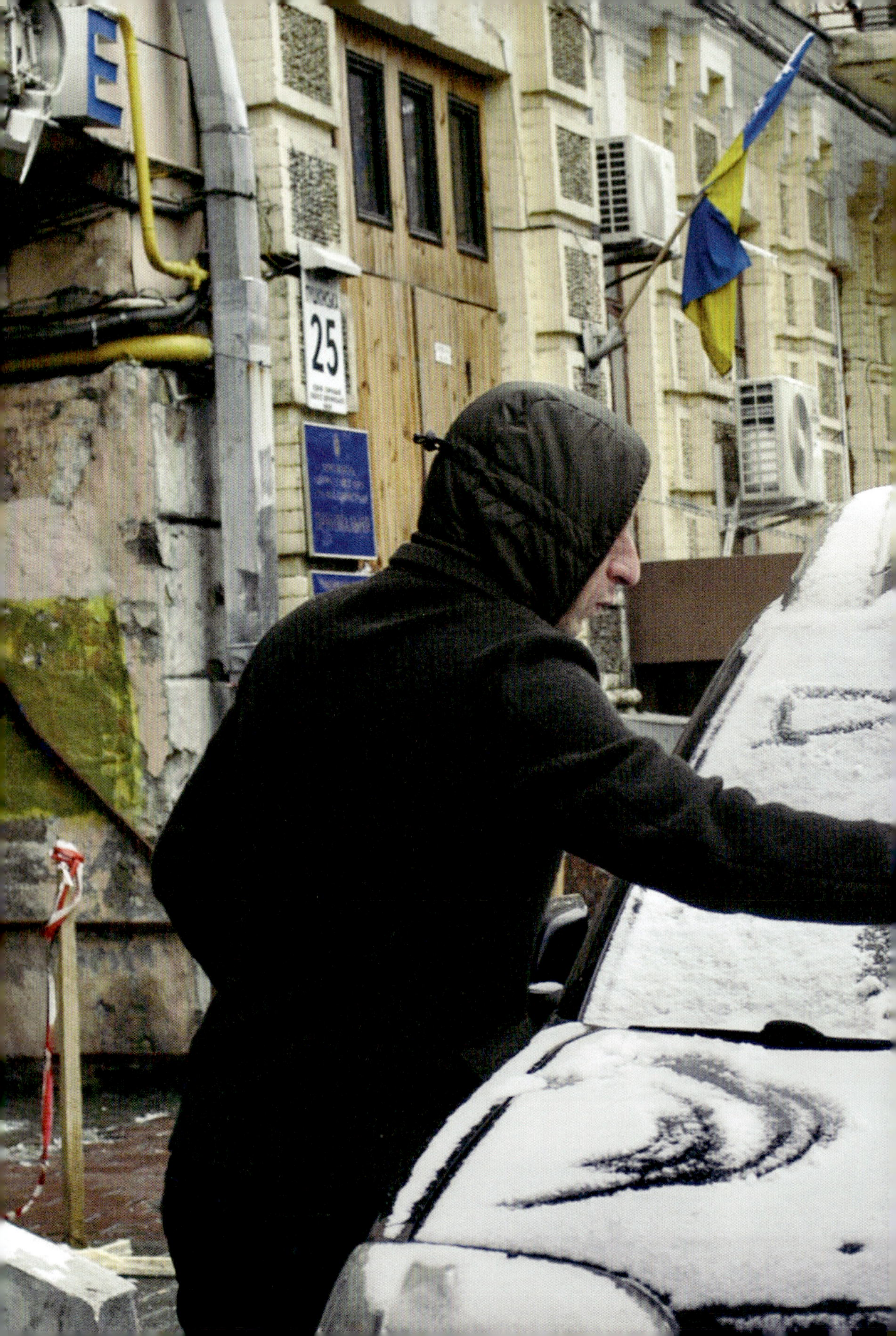
E
25

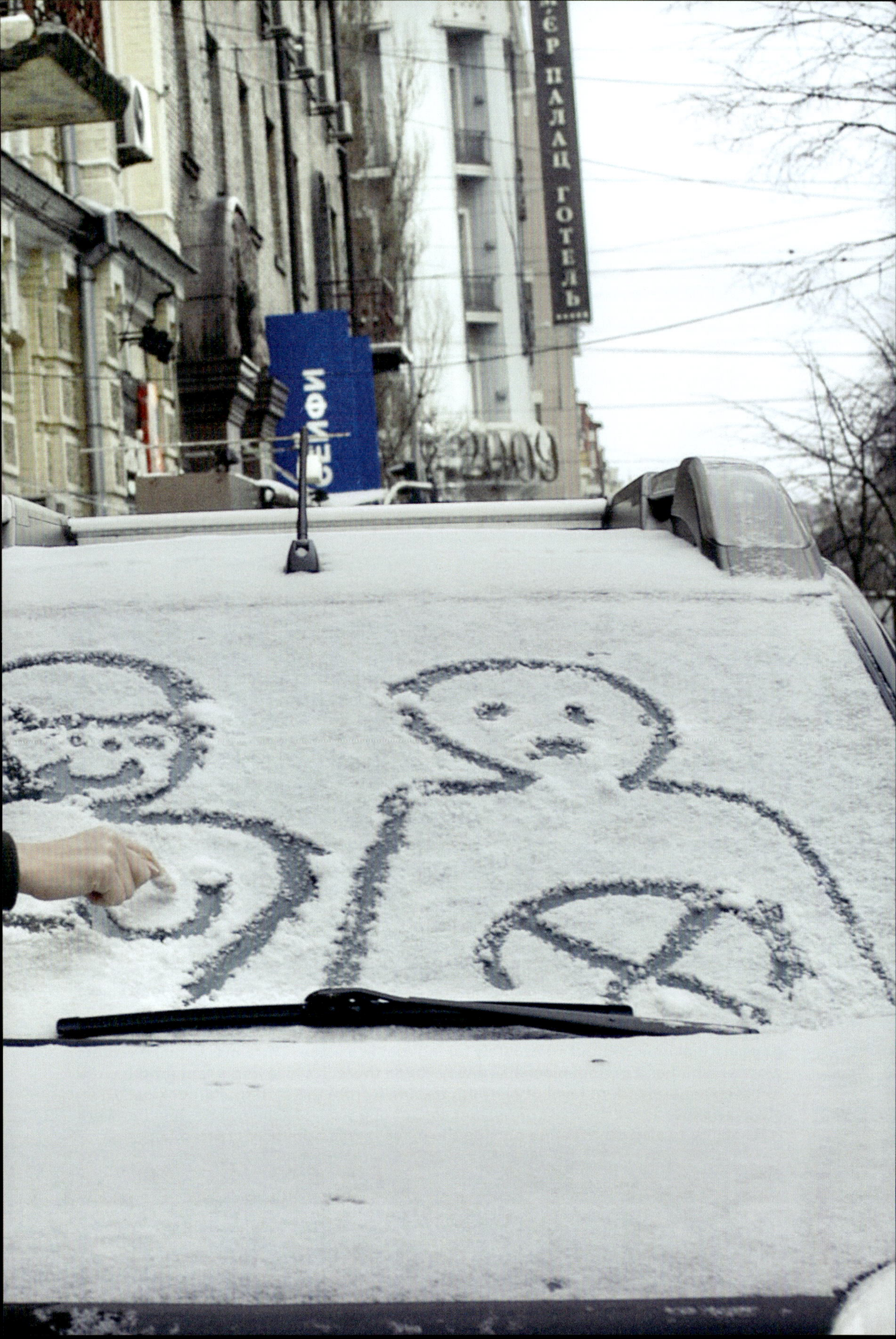
ЕР ПАЛАЦ ГОТЕЛЬ
СЕНФОН

If the viewpoint of the observer is part of the artwork's significance, since art is the realm of subjective interpretation, the context also is a part of this. Understanding the context means creating the perfect setting to complete the works.

We know what happened to the children suspended from a tree in 2004 in Milan. They were vandalized, and at that moment the work turned into something else. But even if it hadn't happened, the presence of the work at the Seville Biennial only a few months later would still not have been the same as in Milan. It wasn't possible. And this is not necessarily a bad thing, if the new installation is done intelligently, because the work can acquire new, unexpected meanings. *La Nona Ora* (1999) has been exhibited in Basel, Warsaw, Milan, New York, Paris, Stockholm and Venice, and each time there has been a different but equally interesting response.

When I start a new work, I start from a space, from the very place for which the work is intended. I can't work in a void. I would end up losing my bearings. A work is always conceived for an occasion, for a context. You can have an idea that's been swirling around in your head for a while, and then it finds its perfect place the moment you receive an invitation to an exhibition. You need a situation where the work and the setting create a short-circuit. It's intriguing that for each space there's only one viable solution, a single answer that works.

But while the context influences my choices, I always try to avoid the obvious, to engage in a dialogue without completely taking root in a place. The aim is to make visitors wonder whether a certain piece has always been there. It's also important for the work to have an independent level of reading, freeing it from the setting. Paradoxically, I've always believed that the most important aspect of a well-conceived site-specific work is its ability to also be effective outside the place it was originally created for.

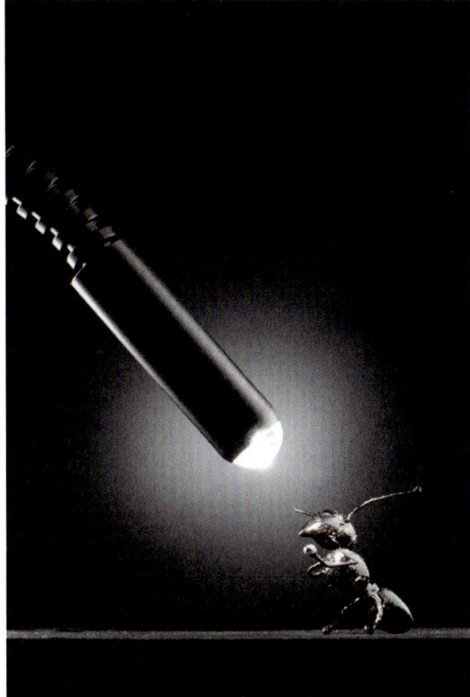

[157]

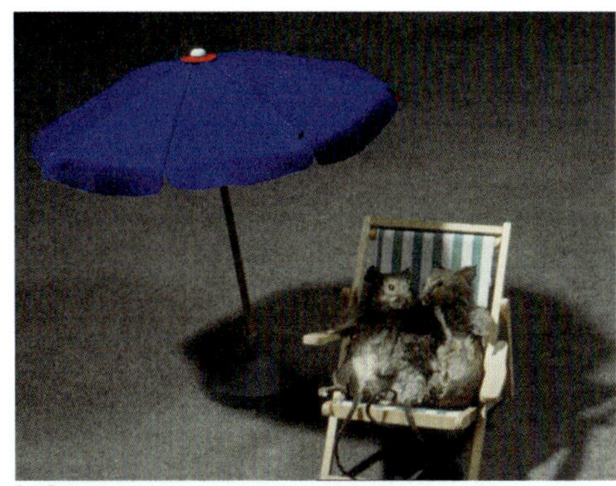

[158]

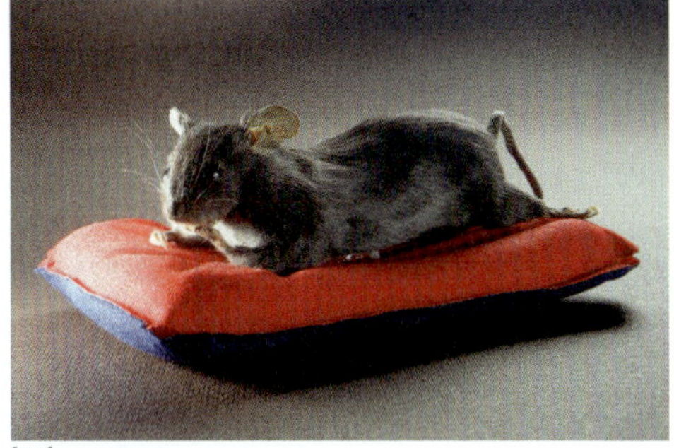

[159]

[157]   ***Untitled*, 1995**
Metal, paint, plastic, lightbulb
Ant: 2.1 × 1.4 × 1 cm

I made this work for the 1st Gwangju Biennial. I had a gigantic room at my disposal, so I decided to do a work as small as possible: an ant doing the forearm jerk in complete darkness, except for a small lamp that illuminates it. Obviously you could only discover it by going close up and the gesture, though it might strike a lot of people as offensive, to me was a way to rid myself of a burden and my sense of inadequacy, the inability to act.

[158]   ***Untitled*, 1997**
Taxidermied mice, wood, fabric

[159]   ***Untitled*, 1997**
Taxidermied mouse, fabric
4 × 13 × 6 cm

[160]   ***Untitled*, 2000**
Polyester resin, brass fixture, digital audio soundtrack, electric lights
Door: 13 × 4 cm; garbage can: 6 × Ø 2.5 cm

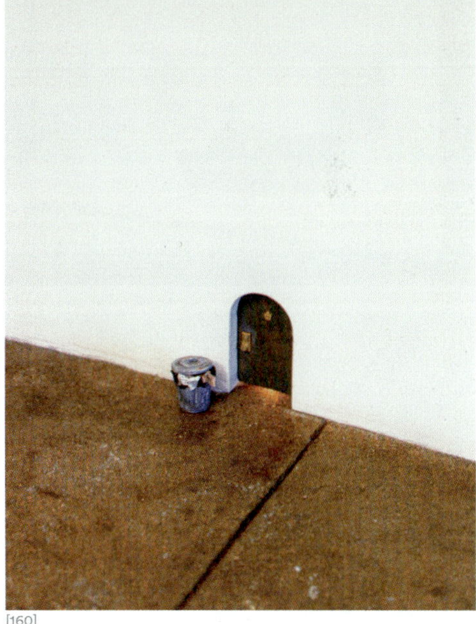

[160]

243

I imagined various scenes with mice. The first time I took part in a group show at the Marian Goodman Gallery in New York, which was held in the summer I did mice on vacation. After all, New York is the city with the highest number of mice per person in the world. For a group show in San Antonio, Texas, I created a domestic scene, but one that you only overhear from outside a tiny door. There's a light on inside the mouse's nest, a garbage can outside, and there's an audio tape playing two mice arguing, without them being seen. I'd asked the director of the gallery if I could record a tiff between her and her husband.

[157]   *Untitled*, 1995
"Beyond the Borders," 1st Gwangju Biennale, curated by Lim Young-bang *et al.*, September 20–November 20, 1995 (group show)

[158]   *Untitled*, 1997
"A Summer Show," Marian Goodman Gallery, New York, July-August 1997 (group show)

[159]   *Untitled*, 1997

[160]   *Untitled*, 2000
"Maurizio Cattelan," Artpace, San Antonio, June 8–July 16, 2000 (solo show)

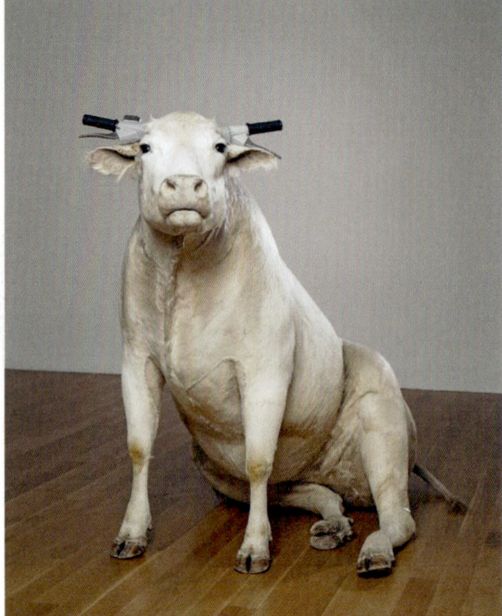

[161]

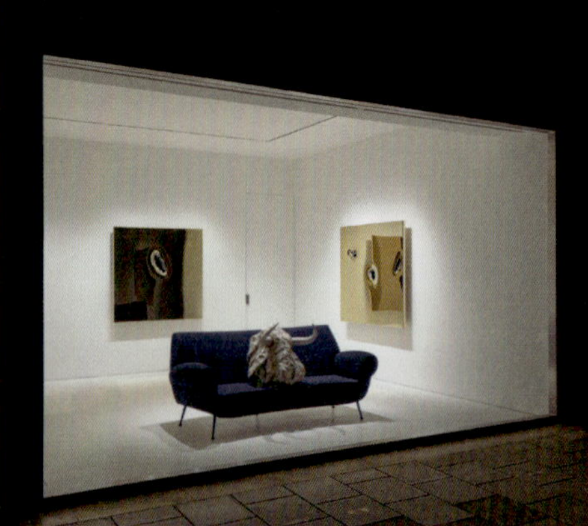

[162]

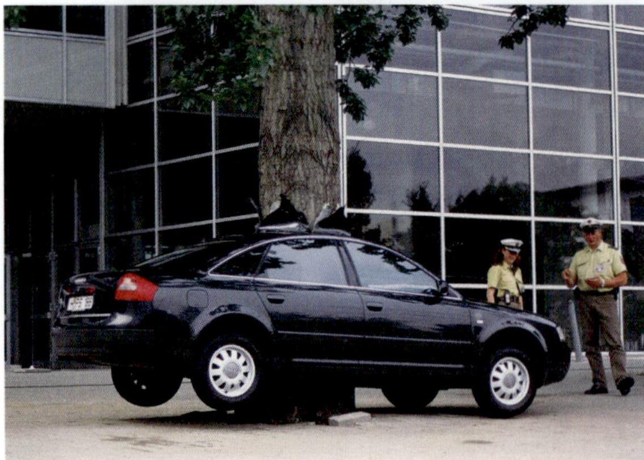

[163]

244

[161]    *Untitled*, 1997

[162]    *Notre Dame*, 2025
"Maurizio Cattelan. Bones," Gagosian, Davies Street,
London, April 8–May 24, 2025 (solo show)

[163]    *Untitled*, 2000
"In Between," curated by Wilfried Dickhoff and Kasper
König, Expo 2000, Hanover, June 1–October 31, 2000
(group show)

[161]    ***Untitled***, 1997
Taxidermied cow, scooter handles
231.6 × 140.3 × 160 cm

[162]    ***Notre Dame***, 2025
Carrara marble, fabric sofa
100 × 197.4 × 81 cm

For the 1997 Triennale India in New Delhi I
thought of doing of an embalmed cow a little
smaller than average size, lying down, in the
position of cows resting in pasture, and with
the handlebars of a Vespa instead of horns. It
seemed interesting to me to put together in
that context an animal sacred to Hindus and a
reminder of the chaos of the daily traffic of Indian cities. Unfortunately, the work was not done
as I'd planned, because the cow was sitting up
and was much larger. The whole thing ended up
being a bit strange. In any case, the work never made it to the Triennale, because it got stuck
at the Indian customs. (I would only be able to
present it at the Guggenheim show in 2011–12.)
Anyway, what could I expect?
And to be honest, I don't even know what I expected when I returned to the subject of the cow
many years later, for an exhibition in London.
This time I did away with the body, replacing it
with a sofa, one of those often found in galleries.
The head, made of solid marble, rests on it, and
it seems to be there waiting to engage in conversation.

[163]    ***Untitled***, 2000
Audi car, tree
Environmental dimensions

I'm deeply involved with a bicycle, and that's another world. But I do have a car. Originally, for
Expo 2000 in Hanover, I wanted to create an
invisible car, but then I realized it was not such
an original idea. Benedict Radcliffe had already
done it. Plus, I'd already had an "invisible" artwork stolen from my car before, and doing another project on invisibility would have been
overkill. And let's not forget that Robert Raus-
chenberg wanted to design a transparent car
for Renault, in the late 1960s... In short, I found
myself in a *cul-de-sac*. But then I had an epiphany, because it was the end of the century. The
previous one marked the end of the horse, while
then it was the end of the mechanical century.

[164]    ***Felix***, 2001
Oil on polyvinyl resin, fiberglass
610 × 183 × 792 cm

My works are like reminders of the relationships
with the people I made them for. *Felix* is a reminder of my experience in Chicago at the Museum of Contemporary Art whom I produced it
for. It embedded in time and space.
I wanted to turn domesticity into horror and for
this reason I created the skeleton of an out-of-
scale cat, looking like a dinosaur skeleton. In a
way it resembled the *Tyrannosaurus rex* called
Sue, the star of the city's Field Museum of Natural History. Then I called my skeleton Felix, a
great classic that also evoked my childhood.

[164]   *Felix*, 2001
"Maurizio Cattelan. Felix," curated by Francesco Bonami,
MCA – Museum of Contemporary Art Chicago,
November 28, 2002–April 4, 2003 (solo show)

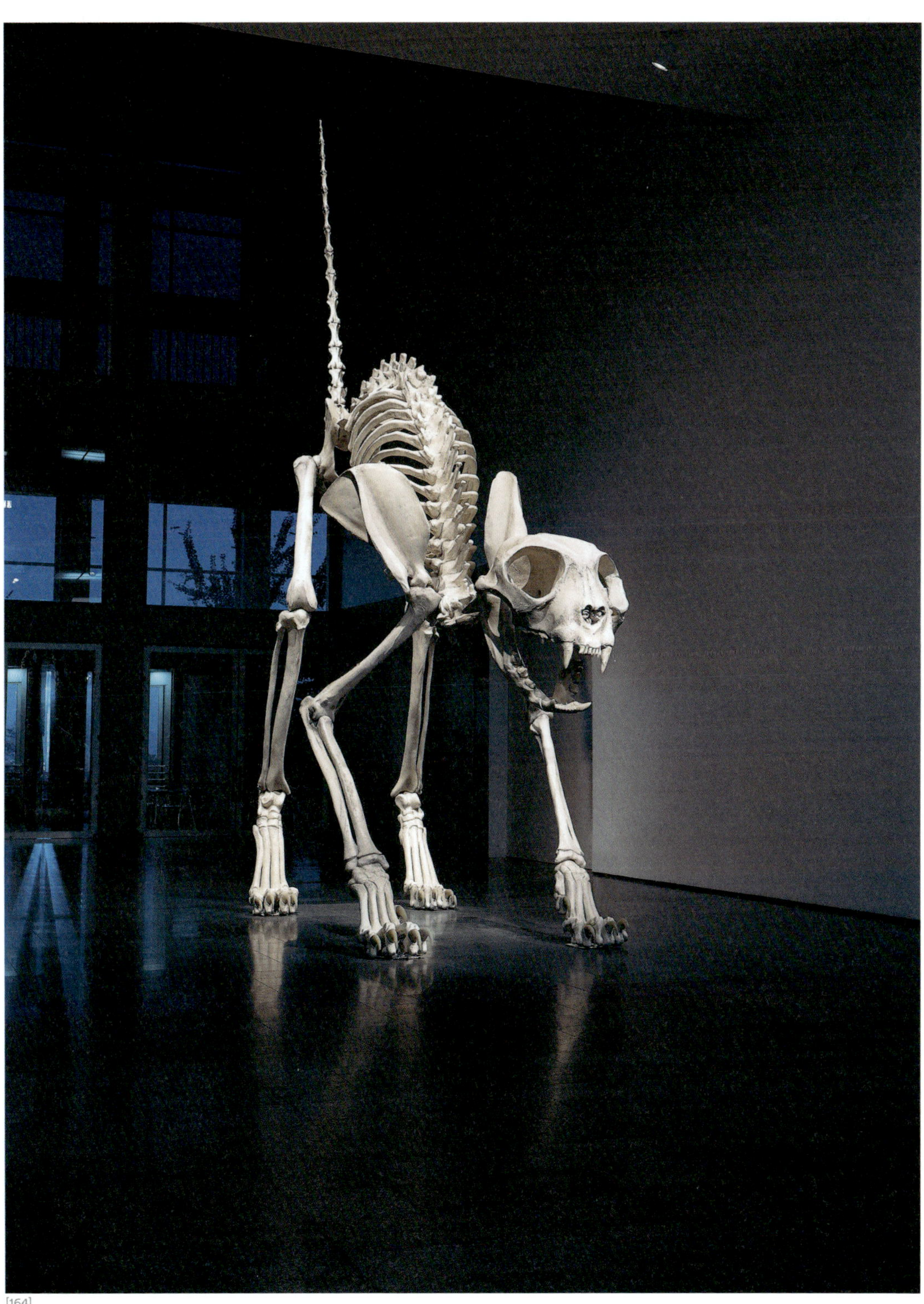

[164]   *Felix*, 2001
"Maurizio Cattelan. Felix," curated by Francesco Bonami,
MCA – Museum of Contemporary Art Chicago,
November 28, 2002–April 4, 2003 (solo show)

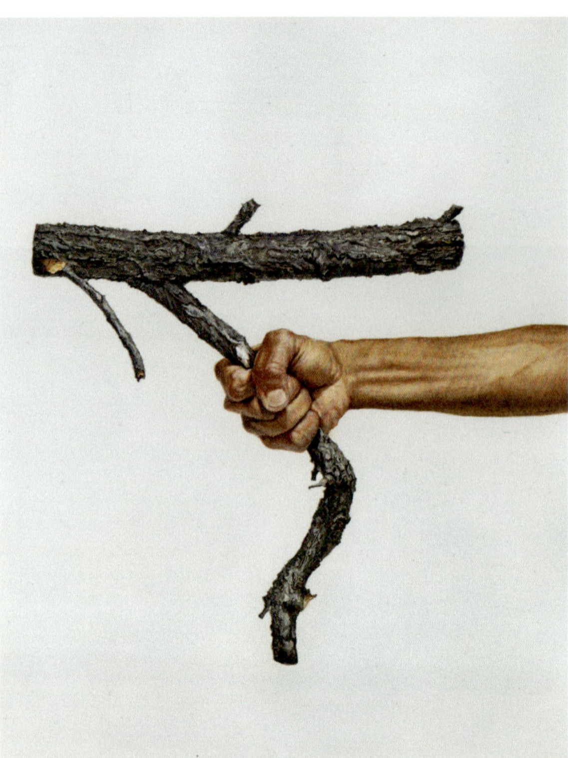

[166]

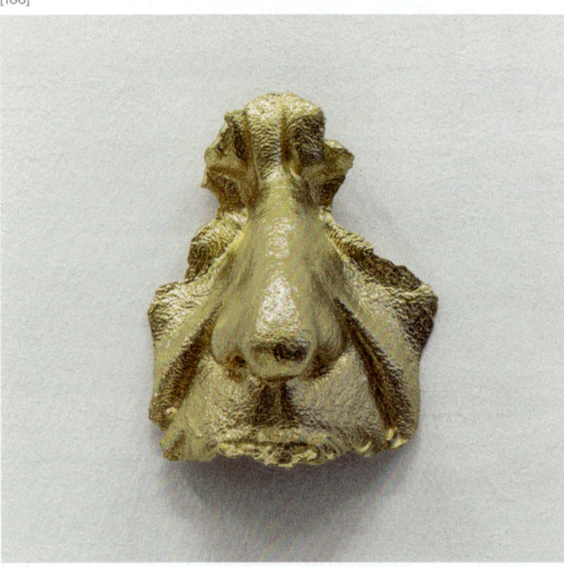

[167]



**[165]** **"Smoke," 2021**
Exhibition in the stands of Massimo
De Carlo, Marian Goodman Gallery
and Perrotin, Art Basel, September
21–26, 2021

[166] *Untitled*, 2019
Watercolor
43 × 32.5 cm
Image used as invitation
for the exhibition "Smoke"

[167] *Brother*, 2021
18 karat gold
12.5 × 10 × 6 cm

[168] *Ghosts*, 2021 + found work
Taxidermied pigeons, found work
Found work: 180 × 163 × 11 cm;
overall dimensions:
200 × 163 × 11 cm



*Brother* is a self-portrait of myself in gold, but as
if the face was embedded in the wall and hidden,
leaving only the nose sticking out. A way of being present while also disappearing. I set it up at
Perrotin's stand.
In my New York gallery, Marian Goodman, I presented two canvases that I'd bought years earlier
at a market in the city. They were probably devised by someone immediately after September
11 to commemorate the event. Around the "I love
NY" logo, hundreds of people wrote something
by hand, such as their feeling after the attacks
or their reaction. I'd always kept the two canvases with me, even hanging in the house for a
while. Then I told myself that either I would do
something with them or they should go to the
Smithsonian, because they're a piece of history.
"Smoke" was an opportunity to share them.
Also for the project in Massimo De Carlo's stand
I thought of referring to history and so exhibited
*Night* (2021). It's a flag, something that should
unite but very often divides. This has lost its colors. It's unrecognizable and has been injured.
Scattered around the three stands like ghostly
presences uniting these works, I installed hun-
dreds of the pigeons from *Ghosts* (2021).



[166] *Untitled*, 2019

[167] *Brother*, 2021

[168] *Ghosts*, 2021 + found work

[165] *Night*, 2021 [210]

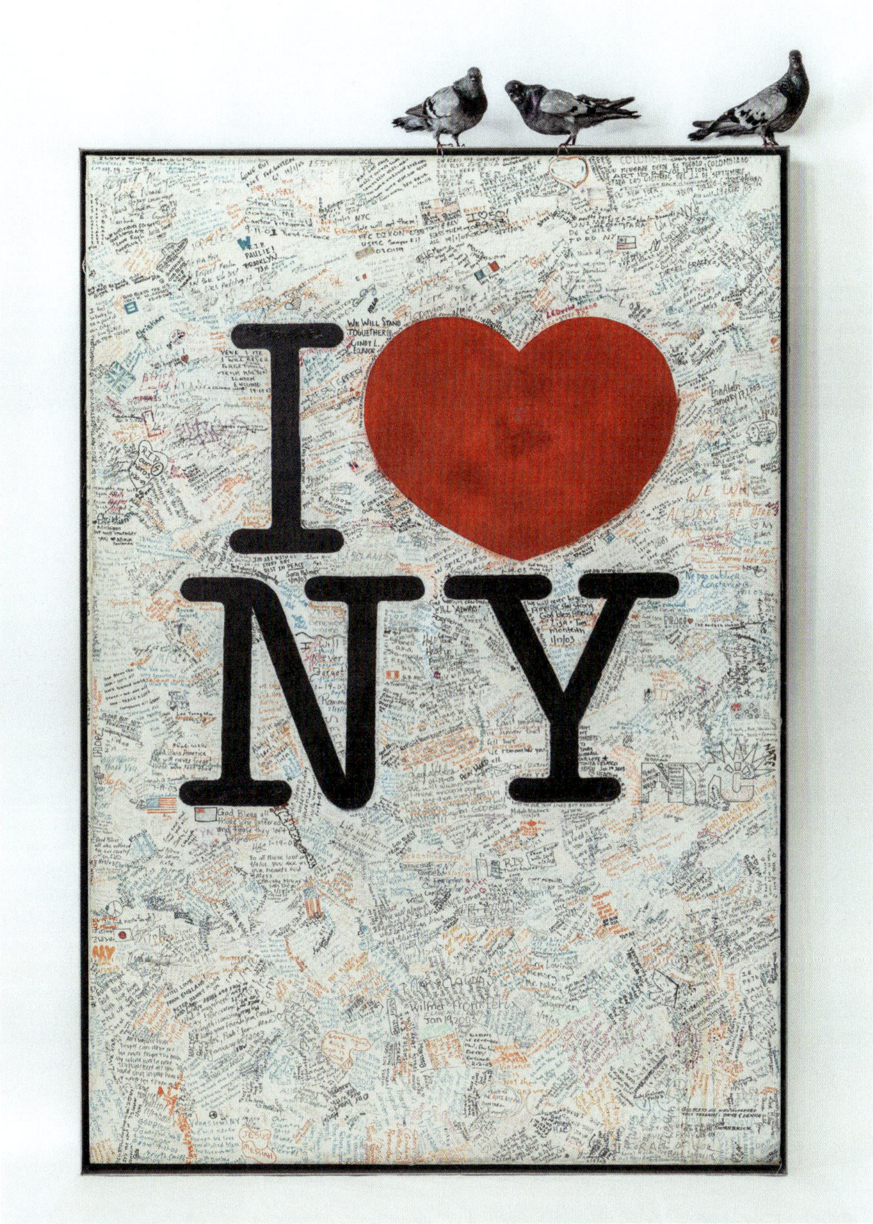

247

[168]

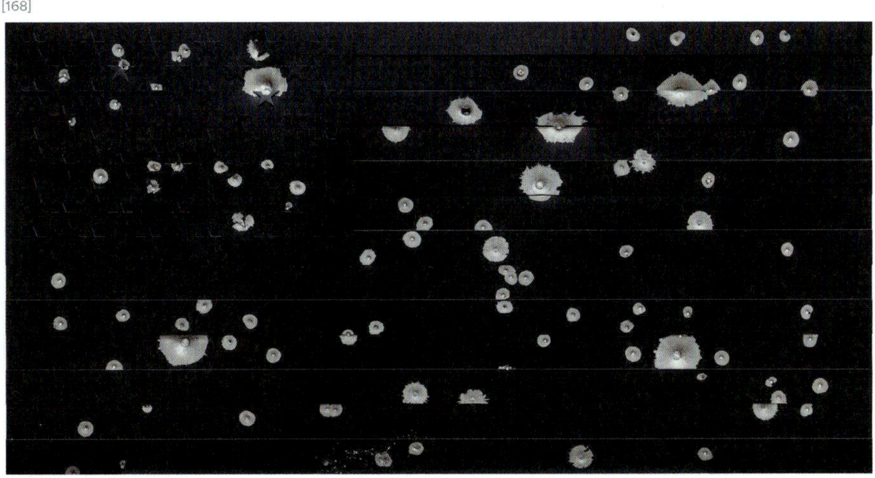

[165]

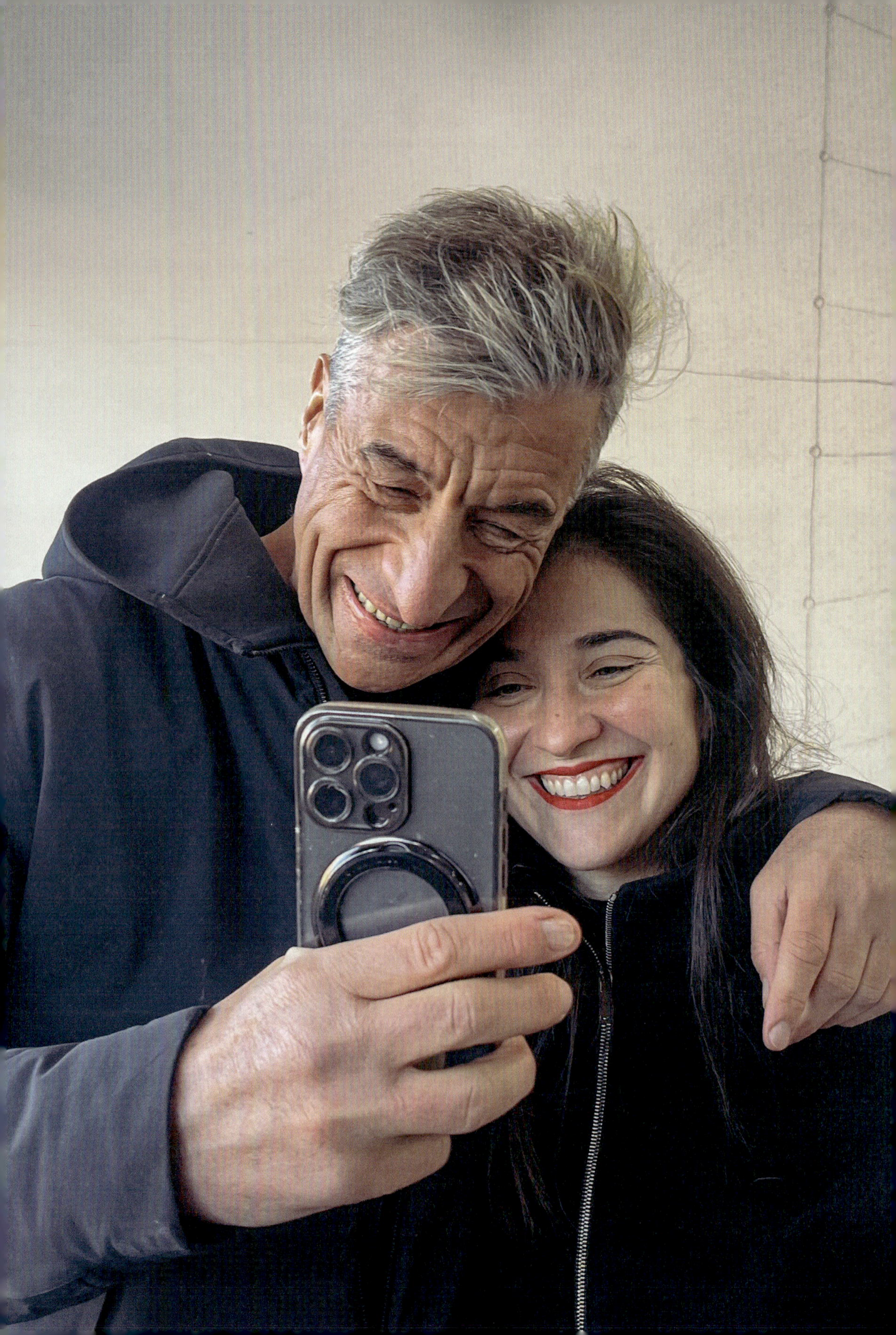

Some studies have shown that being trained in a specific field can help solve problems that have completely different bearings. I read somewhere about an acrobat who became a ski champion. It's all very likely, if you think about it. In my case, producing a magazine increases my sensitivity to iconic images and editing skills. Designing furniture opens up a world of possibilities for your work to be seen also in terms of its utility. This possibility often goes begging, but not always, as happened, for example, with *America* (2016). Running a non-profit space keeps you modest, while curating exhibitions makes you feel like God and at the same time very fragile, because as an artist you're always on the other side as well. So, to keep shuffling the cards, I curate exhibitions in museums and galleries as well as non-profit venues. I like to think that in this way I'm giving a voice to artists who don't receive enough attention, as in the case of Birgit Jürgenssen and Cinzia Ruggeri.

I see being a curator as bringing me into close contact with a hidden secret. I'm sure that, as with all words, the meaning of *curate* has changed over time. In Italian *curare* still means "to assist," while in English the meaning is slightly different, but it still means bringing something to the point where we can be sure that it's presented at its best. As a curator, I always try to be very respectful of other people's works, but without being submissive. Being aware of what other artists are doing is a vital part of being an artist, and you can occasionally find it exciting to focus on creating an exhibition instead of a work. I think this has to do with scale and self-awareness. Working with others is like multiplying yourself until you lose yourself, and then you find yourself again. Like Alice, who is tiny at one moment and towers over everything the next.

I've always wanted to wear a lot of different hats, because I've never liked professional labels and I believe in role-playing. All the same, I find being a curator an interesting experience but a temporary one. I believe that a good curator is someone who manages to make chaos legible. Orderly and obsessive as I am, being a curator every day is not for me. I couldn't sacrifice the moments of pure and healthy loss of control.

Apart from me, artist-curated shows are quite interesting because they challenge people's common understanding of concepts such as the autonomy of art or authorship, until they dismantle the meanings of exhibitions themselves. Obviously, this might lead some artists to be skeptical of the result, but, as they say, nothing ventured nothing gained. We lack a bit of courage in the art world. I think we need to start taking some risks, as both artists and curators. Of course, not all exhibitions can be works of art, just as not all artists can be curators, but it does happen.

I really like to have an exchange of views with the curators, because they have generally clear ideas. This gives me a lot of confidence, but it troubles me, because of the lack of misgivings, and if there are no misgivings there are no questions, so the why and the wherefore are missing. And in that case we know how things will end up. I see the work of a curator as not so much about finding answers as asking questions, which is what artists try to do. Undoubtedly over the years artists have let curators take some of the weight from their shoulders, but it's a gamble that doesn't seem to have paid off. Because of their position, as catalysts between the institutions and the visionary dimension, curators fail to perform this task. There are exceptions, of course, but the great majority of curators are focused on defining their role and what this entails more than anything else. 90% of the discussions at panels and round tables are about formats. What does it mean to curate in the new millennium? What is the collector's role? How should art fairs and biennials be held? And so forth. They only talk about structure, hardly any of them about theory. And, since no one else does it, I think artists ought to. Who knows? Maybe it's time to write a new manifesto.

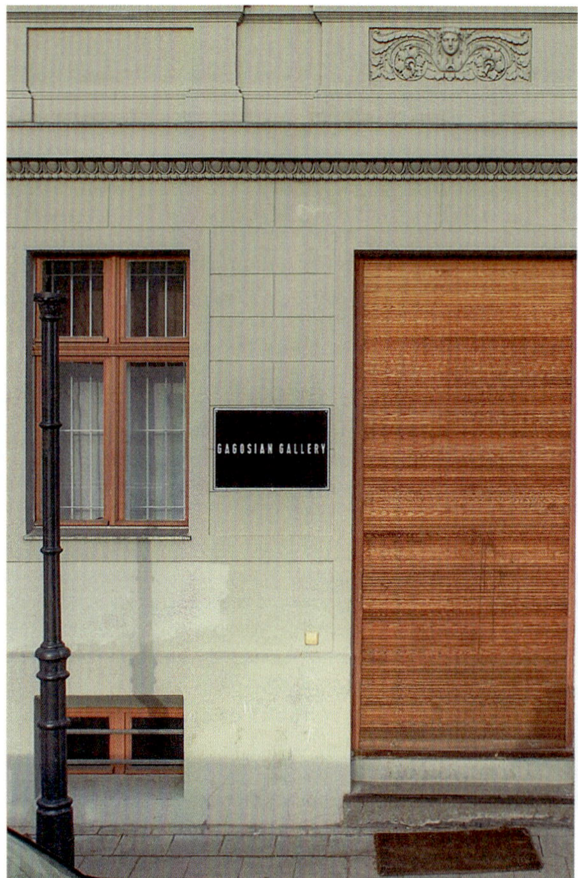


[169]

[169]   Gagosian Gallery, Auguststraße 50A Berlin, 2005–06

[170]   Maurizio Cattelan, Massimiliano Gioni, and Ali Subotnick portrayed by Jason Nocito, image used for the communication of the exhibition "Of Mice and Men," Berlin, 2006

[169]   **Gagosian Gallery, 2005–06**
Project by Maurizio Cattelan, Massimiliano Gioni, and Ali Subotnick for the 4th Berlin Biennale for Contemporary Art, Auguststraße 50A, Berlin, September 2005–June 2006

Gagosian Gallery was a project for the 4th Berlin Biennale that preceded its opening with the presentation of a different exhibition every month. The gallery referred to the art market in ways that went far beyond those of The Wrong Gallery, which Ali Subotnick, Massimiliano Gioni and I had opened a few years before in New York, first and foremost by having a real, physical space. The Wrong Gallery was more a deception, a given space with limited opportunities for the artists to express themselves. What we were interested in was that such a specific framework would give us a chance to see some outstanding ideas appear. Gagosian was more like we were playing, not on the other side of the fence but within it. The fact that we chose such a name was like an evolution without strong compromises. So, you play, you're joyful, but you still make a critical statement, though I'm not interested in criticism. Actually, the project had a kind of double layer. We knew that we had only four or five months as a lifespan for this project, and we wanted something from it. We wanted to be recognized from the inside and the outside as being part of the artworld. Part of the network, and the name Gagosian immediately made that possible. It could be both a marketing tool and a double take.

We never talked with Gagosian himself about opening our gallery in Berlin. I think it was tolerated as long as we don't didn't deal. We practiced a sort of guerrilla franchising, an irreverent joke to place art on the level of Chinese industry by inventing the mass falsification of a mass brand like Gagosian. It was also an opportunity to rethink exhibitions and high-speed events. It is not right for biennials, art fairs, and large galleries to be the only catalysts for art. We wanted to remind artists, institutions and ourselves that equally striking effects can be achieved by working even at a microscopic level.

[Exhibitions held:
— "Berlin Beauties," curated by Maurizio Cattelan, Massimiliano Gioni, and Ali Subotnick, September 27–October 22, 2005 (artists: Dorothy Iannone, Dieter Roth, Emmett Williams);
— "The Addiction," curated by Anna-Catharina Gebbers, November 1–22, 2005 (artists: Markus Amm, John Bock, Roberto Cuoghi, Christian Flamm, Ellen Gronemeyer, Alexander Heim, Richard Hughes, Dorothy Iannone, Gareth Jones, Karsten Konrad, Olaf Metzel, Bernhard Prinz, Anselm Reyle, Thomas Scheibitz, Andreas Slominski, Katja Strunz, Patrick Tuttofuoco, Paloma Varga Weisz, Nicole Wermers, Johannes Wohnseifer);
— "The Gone Wait," curated by Tobias Buche and Martin Germann, November 29–December 31, 2005 (artists: J. Depp/Gibson Haynes/John Frusciante, Rainald Goetz, Jacob Holdt, Jandek, Josef Kramhöller, Kitty Kraus, Jonas Lipps, Josef Strau, Herbert Volkmann, Maximilian Zentz Zlomovitz);
— "Friends and Enemies," curated by Autocenter (Joep van Liefland and Maik Schierloh), Starship (Martin Ebner, Ariane Müller and Hans-Christian Dany), and Tilman Wendland, January 9–February 1, 2006;
— "YBA – YOUNG BAVARIAN ART," curated by Olaf Metzel, February 7–March 11, 2006 (artists: Benjamin Bergmann, Nick Bötticher, Christian Engelmann, Beate Engl, Andrea Faciu, Alexander Laner, Florian Morlat, Stephanie Pelz, Michael Sailstorfer, Michael Schrattenthaler, Marco Schuler, Stefan Wischnewski, Martin Wöhrl);
— "Happiness," curated by Martin Germann, March 24–April 18, 2006 (artists: Gerry Bibby, Henning Bohl, Peter Coffin, Simone Gilges, Kim Hiorthøy, Judith Hopf, Chris Johanson, Sean Landers, Tere Recarens, Mungo Thomson, Kerry Tribe, Geerten Verheus, Katharina Wulff);
— "Homework," curated by Zdravka Bajovic, Anna Hermann, Anne Kayser, Sylvia Lysko, Katia Reich, Stephanie von Spreter, Roberta Tenconi, and Renate Wagner, April 24–May 28, 2006 (artists: Safaa Erruas, goldiechiari, Sofia Hultén, Katja Mater, Peter Rösel, Michael Schultze, Nedko Solakov, Kathrin Sonntag, Lorenz Straßl)]

[170] **"Of Mice and Men," 2006**
4th Berlin Biennale for Contemporary Art, group show curated by Maurizio Cattelan, Massimiliano Gioni, and Ali Subotnick, various venues, Berlin, March 25–June 5, 2006

Curating the Berlin Biennale with Ali Subotnick and Massimiliano Gioni was an eye-opener. It was a more institutional experience than anything I'd ever done before, with a level of organization and bureaucracy that I never expected to find. You could do very big things but there were also incredible limits. On the other hand, the assignment allowed us to explore areas where we'd never been before in other projects. But stepping out of the limitations dictated by being an artist or a curator wasn't a novelty for us. From The Wrong Gallery to *Charley*, we were always trying to do something different.
Unlike a lot of curators, in preparing the Berlin Biennale, we avoided running around the world in search of new names and unknown faces. In-

251

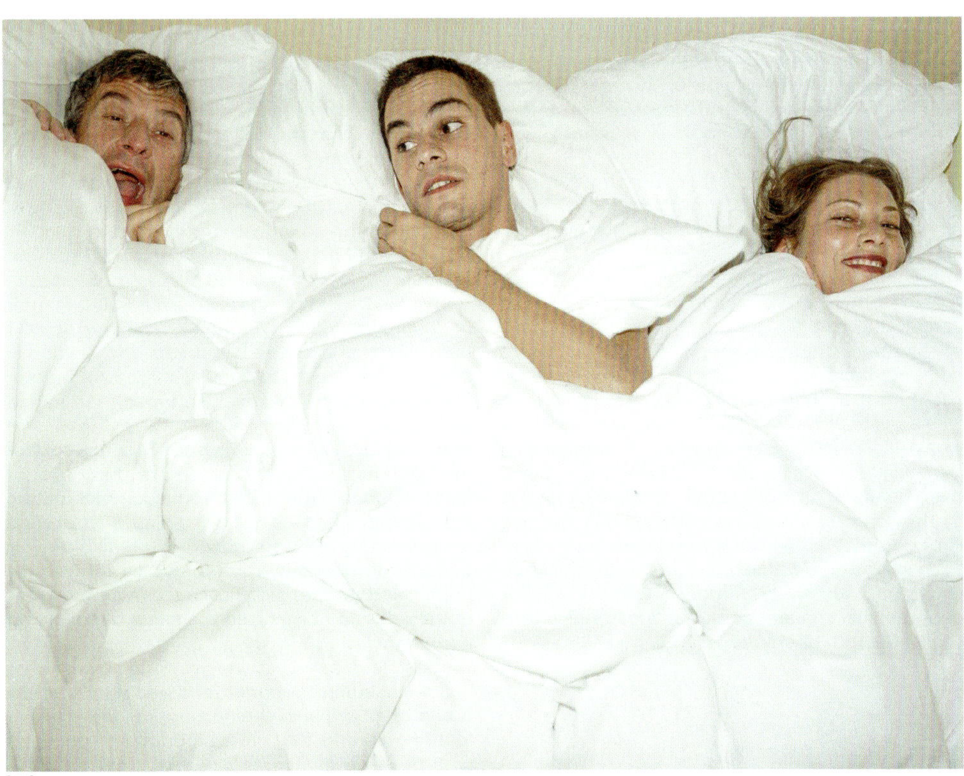

[170]

stead, we focused on the idea of implanting solid roots and establishing connections with the city and its surroundings. For example, we opened a gallery, the Gagosian Gallery, a few months before the Biennale and did our research mostly in Germany. We even did most of our traveling by train. This was to say that anything can become interesting if you look at it long enough. Often even the smallest and most insignificant details conceal the whole universe.

Over the years, Germany had been able to develop such a widespread network of museums and institutions that almost on every street corner there was a gallery, a space for artists or someone trying to show their works. I don't think I'd seen such urgency anywhere else in the world. There was almost an overexposure of art, a magnifying glass constantly pointed at the world, always ready to reveal its contradictions and ambiguities.

As for the exhibition to be created, at first we played with a lot of different ideas. Of a biennial without art (like the 6th Caribbean Biennial of 1999), or an exhibition without objects, or one with many objects but without any art, and so on. In the end we chose to set up an exhibition that we ourselves would have liked to see and that reflected the attitude of many contemporary artists who had replaced spectacle and provocation as ends in themselves with a more silent, obscure, and introspective research. We wanted to create a story that followed different plot-lines and open-ended narratives, not be a themed show or an exhibition with a thesis. "Of Mice and Men," its title taken from Steinbeck's novel, was an exhibition about birth and loss, death and surrender, grief and nostalgia. In Berlin the cries of the past still echo in every building and even on the street corners. By contract we had to live in the city for a year. We set up the entire Biennale along a street, the Auguststraße, where we had already opened the Gagosian Gallery. The exhibition itinerary began at a deconsecrated church, passed through a former Jewish girls' school, apartments, cellars, offices, and ended in a cemetery. By their works, the artists made the everyday life of a street extraordinary. As in a Perec novel, people looked at their own city and rediscovered it completely.

The choice of a street was a way of using what was in front of us. We would never have noticed it and transformed it into an exhibition space if—like many more fashionable curators, more interested in spectacle and the art system—we had gone proselytizing in China or Thailand. So it was a political choice, because in that other way we would have risked making an all-encompassing exhibition, where the difference would have been defended in words but in fact canceled out by the compression of any distance. Instead, we kept our distance, made up of details and traces of many stories, official and intimate. "Of Mice and Men" was an exhibition not of stylistic or geographical similarities but of proximity, intensity, and depth of emotions.



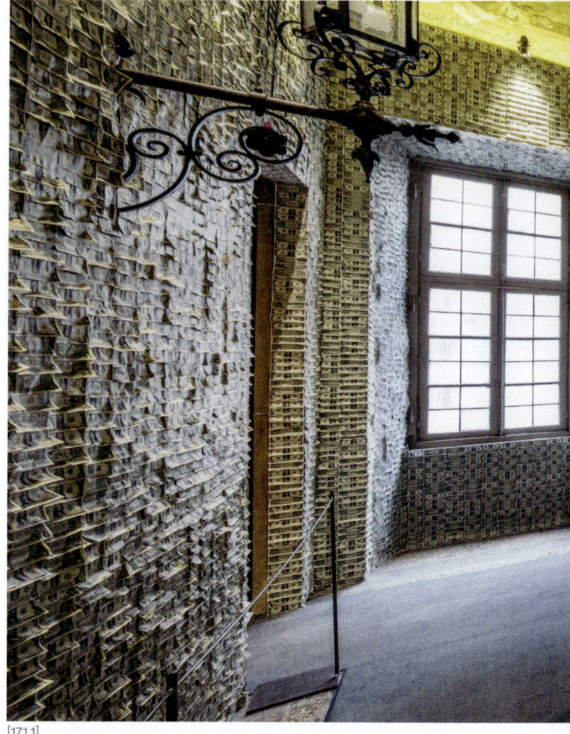

[171.1]

[171] **"Shit and Die," 2014–15**
Group show curated by Maurizio Cattelan, Myriam Ben Salah, and Marta Papini, Palazzo Cavour, Turin, November 6, 2014–January 11, 2015

I was invited by Artissima to curate an exhibition, and "Shit and Die" was the result of teamwork with Myriam Ben Salah and Marta Papini. We devised it and built it together, with six hands and three heads.

We thought of the exhibition as a story in images: objects from the collections of Turin's museums made to engage in a dialogue with existing contemporary works or new ones commissioned from young artists in Italy or abroad. In this way, Turin's past as an industrial city then in decline, the fascination with collecting and the fetishism for objects were put on display in a non-didactic way. In the end it worked a bit like a Tumblr or Instagram page. We just chose the objects and works and related them to each other in space, giving rise to new visual associations. We worked very intuitively, although we ended up building a strongly structured and cohesive significance. There was probably some sort of hijacking in the show: hijacking of traditions, of some exhibition gimmicks, some communication clichés that we were happy to play with to shed an interesting light on the works on display. Not being professional curators gave all three of us more freedom. We didn't care about any conventional rules and organized the show by following our instincts.

We started from whatever we found in the city, in the museum collections, and patiently embroidered on it all, broadening out the circle as we identified works that we felt could best dialogue with those finds. It was also like creating a tai-

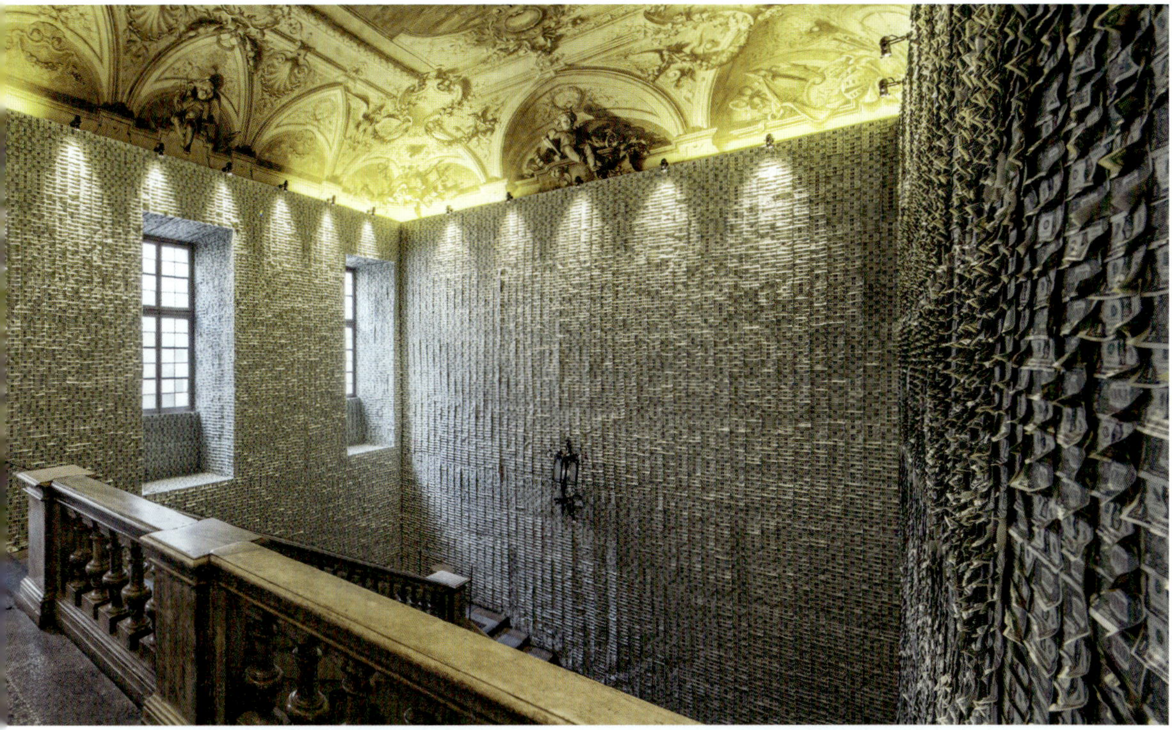

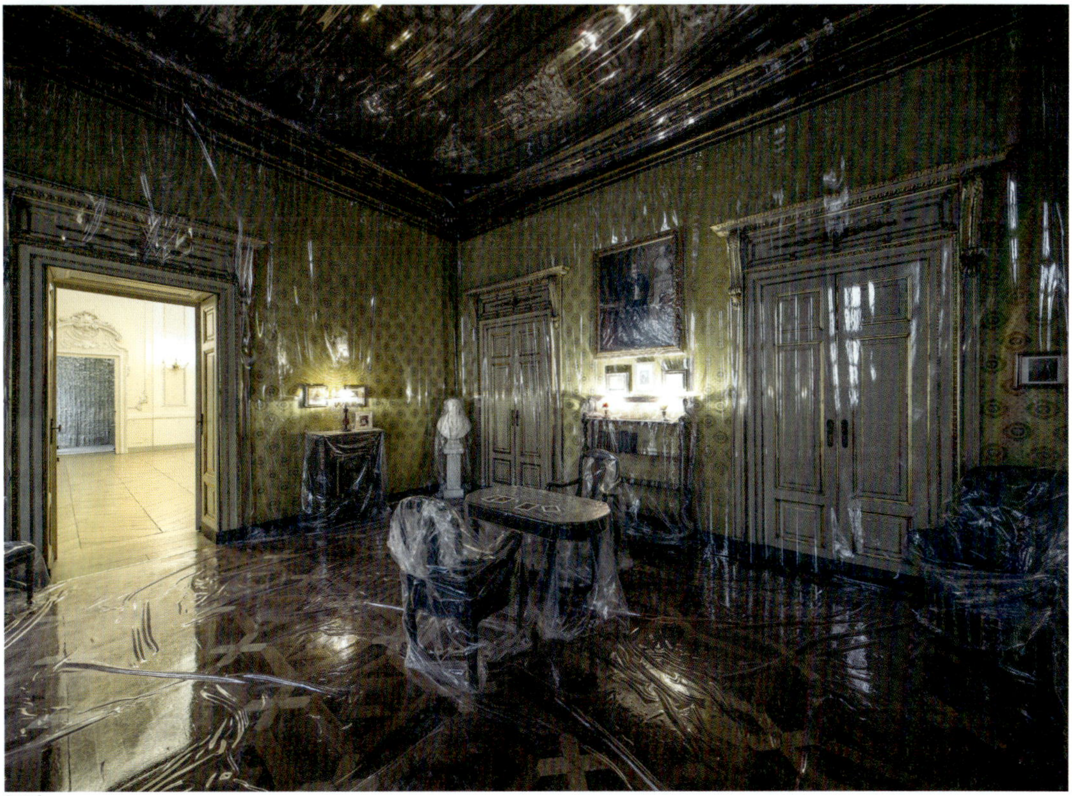

[171.2]

[171.1]   "Shit and Die," Palazzo Cavour, Turin, 2014–15
Intervention by Eric Doeringer on the grand staircase

[171.2]   "Shit and Die," Palazzo Cavour, Turin, 2014–15
Cavour's study, reconstructed and wrapped in celophane
from floor to ceiling

lor-made suit for the exhibition venue in Palazzo Cavour. The exhibition could not have been moved anywhere else, not even to an identical building in another city, because somehow, even though it wasn't obvious, it was the image and likeness of Turin.

We were less interested in historical events than gossip and urban legends. In the end, these tell you most about a place and its inhabitants. We often described the show as an archaeology of the chimera, as we presented unreliable sources as much as reliable ones, perhaps more so. From our first visits to Turin, when we said that we were organizing an exhibition at Palazzo Cavour, various people referred right away to Cavour's alleged coprophilia. A story like this was more inspiring than his work for the unification of Italy, perhaps because we wanted to delve into human weirdness in general.

Our exploration of the city went ahead like a kind of *cadavre exquis*. We didn't have any plan of where to go or what to exhibit. Some characters were key points in the process. For instance, Fulvio and Napoleone Ferrari, the founders of the Museo Casa Mollino, were incredible sources of inspiration, as they knew the most unexpected treasures of the city. The Cesare Lombroso Museum of Criminal Anthropology was another major place. Not only because of the objects we borrowed from it (a gallows and the pitchers of prisoners with their graffiti on them), but also all the stories that the staff told us and the materials they showed us.

We wanted the show to extend beyond the exhibition venue, and so we started a series of parallel projects, including *Séance*, a film made by Yuri Ancarani about the eclectic Carlo Mollino. The catalogue was anything but a regular exhibition catalogue. It was a sort of missing room with exclusive contributions by artists and commissioned texts that explored and extended some of the topics dealt with in the installation. The Olivetti advertisement on the cover had a timeless quality, very rare today, and at the same time it was a reminder of Italy's brilliant industrial past, tragic in comparison with the subsequent decline. There was even a fanzine conceived by the photographer Ari Marcopoulos, which offered a completely alternative view of the exhibition. Then part of the process was the blog on Tumblr. We inserted images that we swapped while reflecting on the exhibition, and they nurtured our ravenous imaginations, even though they didn't go directly into "Shit and Die."

Then there was the title "Shit and Die," which first of all was very intriguing, just what you'd expect from a title in the first place. We took it from Bruce Nauman, who's a genius at hijacking marketing techniques, and clearly we took advantage of that. But there was obviously a deeper connection with the exhibition. Nauman's installation *One Hundred Live and Die*, from 1984, features neon phrases indicating a hundred possible banal and tragic ways of living and dying. "Shit and Die" was one of them, and we thought the combination of communicative immediacy and uncompromising toughness delved deeply into the universal human experience without imposing an unalterable meaning. Echoing the title, and the path of life itself, the exhibition

was a purposeless journey, both sad and hopeful, tough and absurd, silly and tragic, slight and profound. It wasn't provocative. In three words it summed up one of the few certainties we have in life. Whatever you do, you'll live and die without distinction of class, origin or gender. I believe that you can't ask for anything better from a title than to be so concise and so meaningful. In fact, I didn't invent it.

254

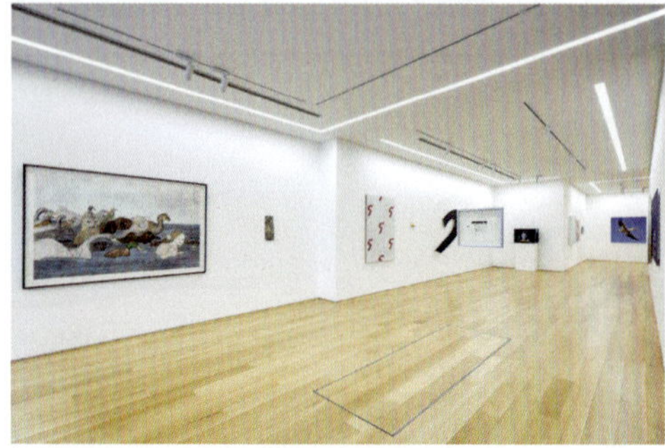

[172.1]

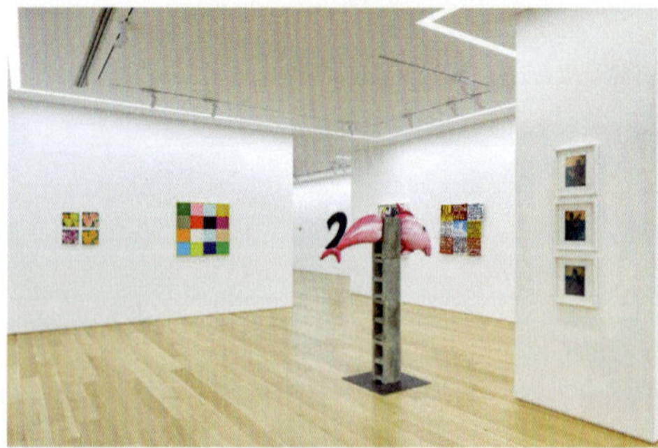

[172.2]

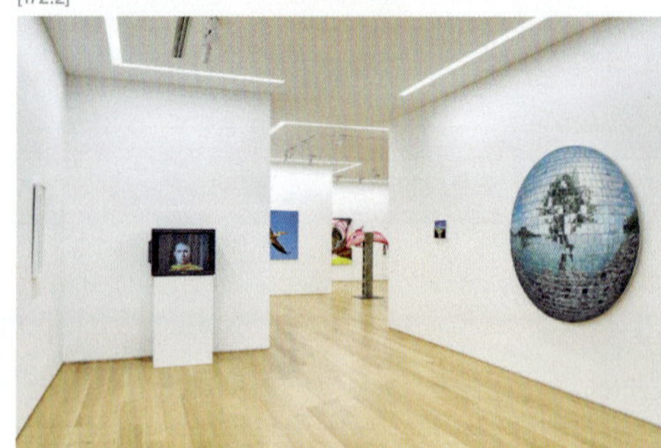

[172.3]

[172.1-3]  "The Smiths," Marlborough Gallery, London, 2019

[173]  *Him*, 2001 [203]
"The Third Hand. Maurizio Cattelan and the Moderna Museet Collection," Moderna Museet, Stockholm, 2024–25

**[172] "The Smiths," 2019**
Group show devised for the Marlborough Gallery, London, July 3–August 2, 2019

Call it short-circuit or serendipity, it is all my in-box's fault: in the very same moment I received three different invites for openings from different venues with artists named Smith showing in it. I took it as a divine sign. Someone needed to grab it and make something good out of it. Obviously, it was not me.
On that same Smiths day, during a tour in Chelsea, I met Pascal Spengemann of the Marlborough Gallery and mentioned the idea. So, I'd say it's the result of the combination of three mini-accidents: the inbox had the idea, the accidental encounter made it possible, and then the gallery made it happen.
I'm not sure about the concept of the show, but its conception was based on a democratic principle. When I saw the show I thought that it worked so well that we should continue the series with the Browns!

[Artists exhibited: Emily Mae Smith, Greg Parma Smith, Lucien Smith, Kambel Smith, Sir Paul Smith, David Smith, Joshua Smith, Patti Smith, Harry Smith, Cary Smith, Zak Smith, Adam Parker Smith, Michael Bell Smith, Sable Elyse Smith, Matt Sheridan Smith, Meryl Smith, Clive Smith, Michael Smith, Barbara T. Smith, Michael E. Smith, Shinique Smith, Molly Smith, Cauleen Smith, Kiki Smith, Tony Smith, Bridget Smith, Bob and Roberta Smith, Anj Smith, Richard Smith, John Smith, Matthew Smith]

**[173] "The Third Hand. Maurizio Cattelan and the Moderna Museet Collection," 2024–25**
Solo show curated by Gitte Ørskou, Moderna Museet, Stockholm, February 24, 2024–January 12, 2025

[174] *L.O.V.E.*, 2024
Cellulose plastic, jesmonite, fiberglass
Overall dimensions:
1000 × 470 × 470 cm

**[175] "Endless Sunday. Maurizio Cattelan and the Centre Pompidou Collection," 2025–27**
Solo show curated by Maurizio Cattelan and Chiara Parisi, with Sophie Bernal, Elia Biezunski, Anne Horvath, Laureen Picaut, Zoe Stillpass, and Marta Papini, Centre Pompidou-Metz, May 8, 2025–February 2, 2027

[176] *Envy*, 2025
Michelangelo statuary marble, nail
36 × 26 × 14 cm

[177] *First*, 2025
Michelangelo statuary marble, nail
12 × 10 × 5 cm

The very concept of a collection scares me. Throughout history, at some point someone decided that it was worth choosing something, picking it up and taking care of it. Being in charge of another selection makes me feel like

255

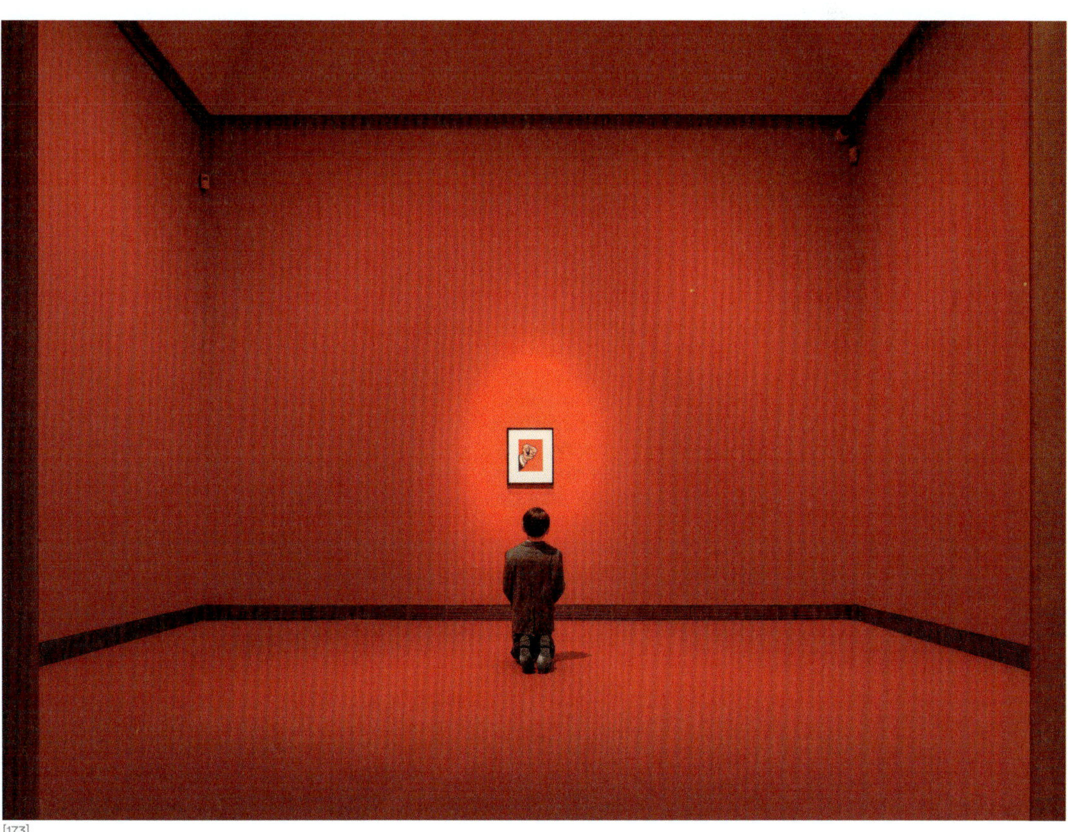

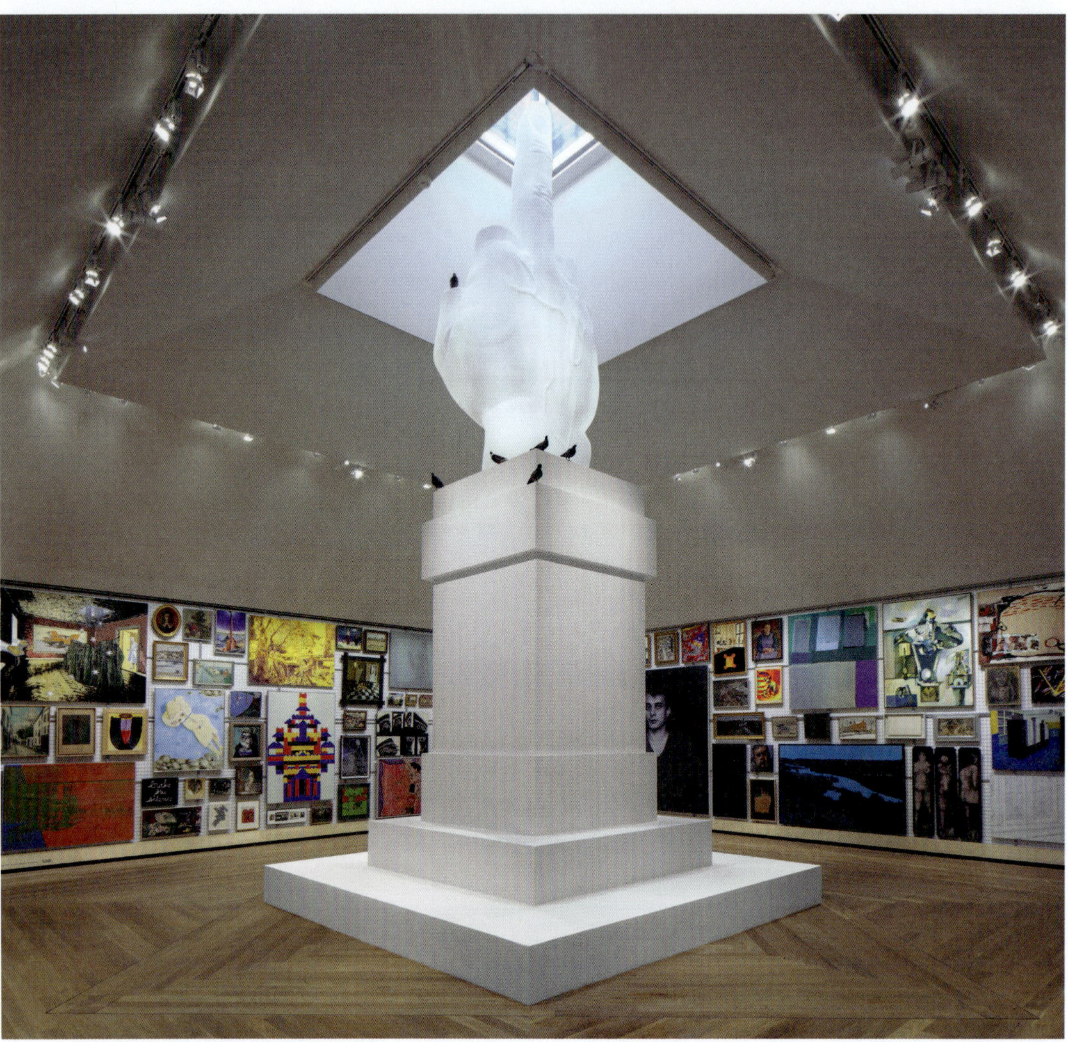



a judge, while for me not choosing is always the best choice. However, I think that doing the things you're afraid of is a good training and for this reason, when the Moderna Museet in Stockholm invited me to work on its collection, I didn't run away. I mixed some works from the museum with my own works, resulting in a reflection on the idea of power and defeat. The exhibition layout opened with *La Nona Ora* (1999) and ended with another figure on the ground, not crushed by a meteorite but who seemed to be sleeping next to a dog (*Breath*, 2021). Why did I do it? I'm the least suitable person to answer. What I do know is that at first I felt I was playing gooseberry between the curators of the museum and the works. Perhaps for this reason I titled the show "The Third Hand." It was also an opportunity to bring *Him* back to Stockholm: the little Hitler kneeling (2001), twenty-three years after the first time. I put it in front of an inquisitorial finger, a print made by Roy Lichtenstein for the Moderna Museet in 1973 (*Finger Pointing*), in a room that was completely red, both the walls and the floor. The project with the Pompidou-Metz, on the other hand, is a hybrid. This was not a museum format, as in the case of Stockholm, but an initiative arising from a long friendship. Already in 2021 I had worked with the museum to curate an exhibition together with the director Chiara Parisi, an exhibition linked to the works of Arcimboldo. Chiara invited me again, but this time there were over 400 works to be put together, almost all from the collection and some of mine. My works are like little intruders; the main narrative is different. And in fact even the new works that I've done draw on the tradition of art. *Envy* is a monochrome, but instead of canvas I used marble, as again in *First*. In both cases something seems to have gone wrong: they're perforated images. I would call both the outcome of the exhibition and the process a Frankenstein. For this reason, to get everyone to agree, we chose the day of inertia, Sunday, as the theme. It was a somewhat unsettling title, but one that has its own sacredness. Besides, a direct title never works..

[171]  *L.O.V.E.*, 2024, and *Ghosts*, 2021 [240]
"The Third Hand. Maurizio Cattelan and the Moderna Museet Collection," Moderna Museet, Stockholm, 2024–25

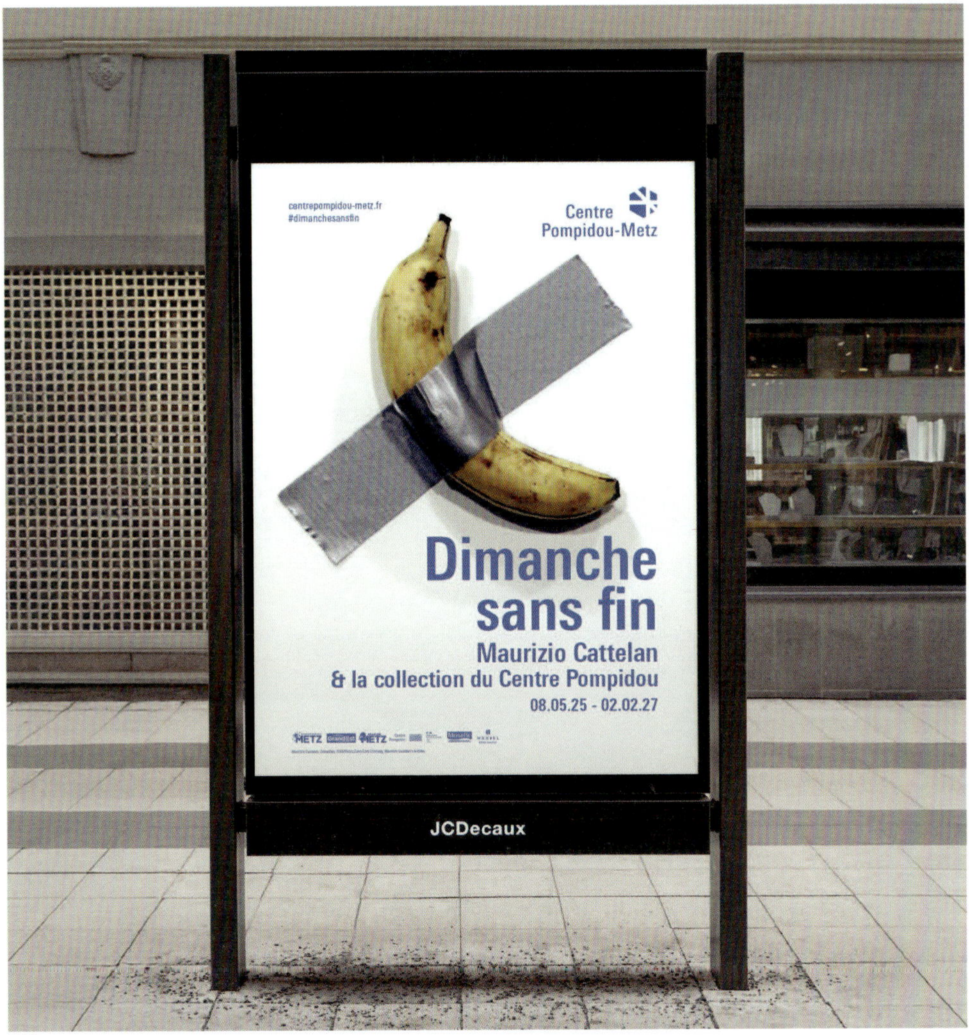

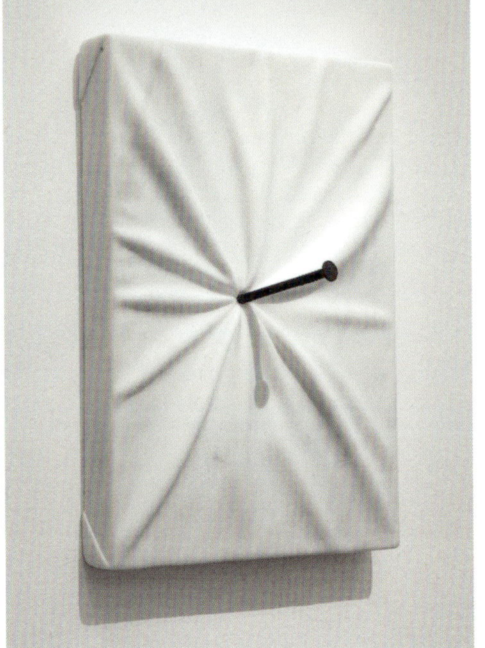



[175]

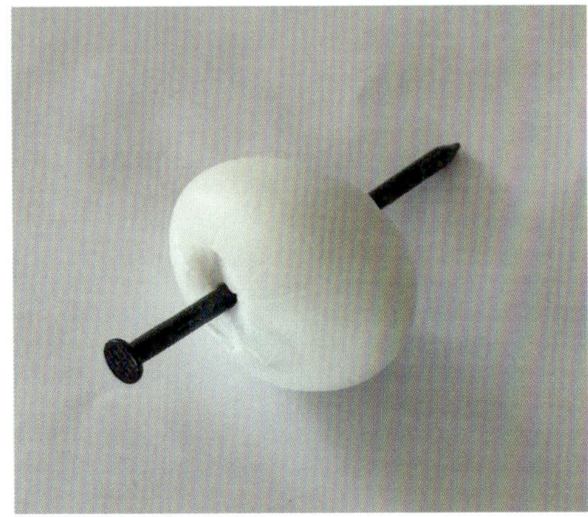

[177]

257

[175]  "Endless Sunday. Maurizio Cattelan and the Centre
       Pompidou Collection," Centre Pompidou-Metz,
       2025–27
       Poster of the exhibition

[176]  *Envy*, 2025

[177]  *First*, 2025

[176]

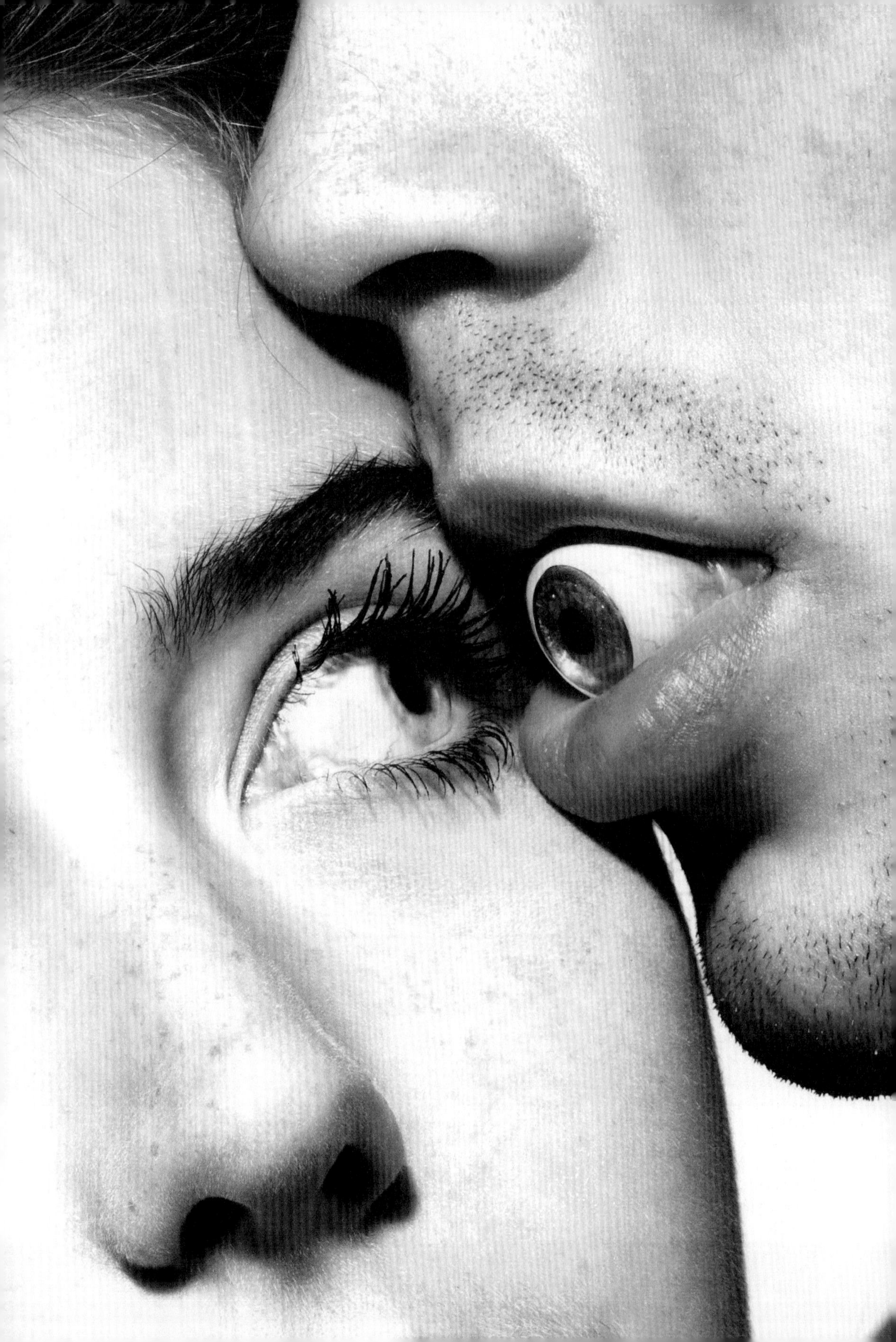

I invariably see my work as reflecting the way I think or understand certain things. What interests me is the personal twist that a person gives everything they do. Sometimes this succeeds better by turning to another field, and besides I perceive my way of being in the art world as fairly broad—I don't want to say it goes the full 360°, but it's a bit wider than just tending my own little corner. I'm really bad at splitting myself into pieces and playing one role at a time. When I think creatively, all the individuals that make up me become one and act accordingly.

What interests me is the way different fields overlap, such as fashion, publishing, advertising, and art. It has been shown that solutions to difficult problems can come from people not directly involved in a given field. I wonder whether, in future, the contemporary art world mightn't be renewed by people from fashion or advertising, and vice versa.

No matter how hard I try, I don't see such clear boundaries between publishing and advertising, design and fashion. Of course, each of these fields has its specifics, but they're all closely linked. And, after all, moving between genres (or skipping over genres) has always been typical of artists. It's probably also due to a pinch of megalomania. Besides, just think of the prehistoric men in the Lascaux caves. They made weapons out of wood and stone to get food by hunting and then decided to draw the scenes of hunting on the cave walls. The weapons were designed to respond to a basic need, hunger, and solve the problem, while the hunting scenes were painted to explore more existential questions: Who are we? Why are we here? Can we leave a trace of our passing?

Today everything is certainly more mixed—art can be socially useful and design totally useless. But I can still see these differences. Like a pendulum, I too swing between these two fields, going back and forth. I store up problems by doing design and shed them by doing art. In my beginning is my end and in my end is my beginning.

Making forays into fields other than those you're used to is an essential way of enriching the creative process. The encounter between different kinds of creativity brings new levels of meaning, and for this reason I've always tried to keep switching hats. I've always needed to devote myself to side projects, taking breaks from my usual work, finding effective ways to express the same things in different modes of expression. At one point, for instance, I got more interested in focusing on team projects such as *Toiletpaper* and Family Business rather than expressing my individual vision in new works. I've always been fascinated by advertising and its viral and pervasive way of reproducing images. *Toiletpaper* proved to be a good way to give it a try in the commercial field. Advertising and art will continue to run side by side, sometimes exchanging a glance of understanding, sometimes grabbing each other's hair. The best advertising gets through. It becomes part of the common language much more easily than art. But the worst publicity is short-lived. You blink and it's gone. Art doesn't reach any of these extremes, but out of ambition or inability it veers towards one and then the other.

Fashion is another field I like to make incursions into. It fascinates me by its dual nature. On the one hand, it's a very advanced industrial and economic system involving lots of people in the production chain. On the other, it seems to depend on a single head, the creative director's, who has to make quick and instinctive choices that all those other people rely on. I work in a completely different way. I prefer not to be tied to anyone who relies on my inspiration to make a living. That's why I've always avoided having a studio.

I don't know if I have a conception of fashion. In any case, I don't even believe in history or art history. I believe in images. I chew them, swallow them and transform them into other images, meaning my works. I see fashion as consisting more of images than a discourse. There can certainly be a fashion discourse, but since my job is to produce images, I think it's the same for fashion designers. When I was young, I wanted to be a fashion designer.

Both fashion designers and artists stand on the shoulders of giants. They don't have to face history directly, but they're grateful for what their predecessors did so that they can look further. We both hold that most of today's innovative work is another exploration of the ready-made, which inevitably touches on the concepts of the circular economy and recycling. It's more than art history. Creating a new object has gradually become an anachronistic idea.

Since Pop Art, the worlds of art and brands have become inseparable. Just think of Andy Warhol's TDK commercials for Japanese television or, more recently, Murakami's work with Vuitton. The difficult thing is to keep the creative process independent of the commercial side. I think a great deal depends on the artist's ego. A lot of artists find it easy to give in to the temptation to multiply themselves through the marketing of their work as a product. Maybe my luck was that I always wanted not to be myself, or for others to be me, so I never really felt this urge to multiply.

[178]  *Permanent Food*, 1995–2007
Magazine founded and edited until 1996 by Maurizio Cattelan and Dominique Gonzalez-Foerster; since 1997 edited by Maurizio Cattelan and Paola Manfrin

CI created *Permanent Food* with Dominique Gonzalez-Foerster. It was based on a very simple idea. If you want a magazine, you need contributors, writers, different people and ideas. We thought that instead of asking, we could simply take what was already out there that we liked. So it's a magazine made up of images and pages we found in other magazines. In one way it's like any other magazine you can buy on the newsstands. In another it's more schizophrenic, as it's a product with no identity per se, because it's made up of all different and weird identities. From the beginning we wanted *Permanent Food* to be a second-generation magazine, something that grew by taking what was already out there. And we also wanted to have a magazine without a personality. So the more personalities were involved, the less it would look like the product of a single author.

The title came from Dominique Gonzalez-Foerster. It was an expression that she just turned up in her head, and we thought it could work for a magazine. Sometimes you just need a name. You can do amazing things thanks to a simple name. It's like creating an authority or a brand. So we first created the name and then came the magazine.

Dominique left *Permanent Food* after the third issue, because she's more like a start-up person in a way. She has fantastic energy and really likes adventure. For her, it was more like setting a trend or launching a company. To me, instead, it was about setting some rules and then following them forever. When you find something really good, you have to continue to the end. If you do a magazine and you only do three issues, it's no longer a magazine. A magazine is something with fifty issues or more. I never thought of using *Permanent Food* as a sort of dream. It's a magazine, and it had to work as a magazine.

*Permanent Food* began as an experiment on visual memory and the power of images: a way to try to collect and disperse fragments of other magazines, books, catalogues. A way to look at what already existed by rereading the information and reorganizing it into something new. Then, like all the funniest games, it became a serious business. The evolution of *Permanent*, the permanent evolution, was dictated more and more by my addiction to images, which I chose together with Paola Manfrin. Between 1995 and 2007, a total of fifteen issues were published, before the project was transformed into another magazine, *Toiletpaper*, launched in 2010.

Someone said that *Permanent Food* was also a kind of admission of weakness, because instead of making a newspaper from scratch, it was made out of waste or by sabotaging other people's newspapers. From another point of view, however, we played to our advantage, turning a weakness into a strength. It's a second-generation, copyright-free magazine. I'm interested in projects with an element of audacity, but also of passivity. *Permanent Food* seems to strike a good

balance, a good imbalance between these two tendencies.

Not many people have been annoyed by the way we worked. Instead, every now and then I discovered people who are doing their own *Permanent Food*, calling it by another name. That was great. Ideas belong to everyone.

[178.1-15]   *Permanent Food*, 1995–2007
Covers of the fifteen issues: no. 1 (1995); no. 2 (1996); no. 3 (1996); no. 4 (1997); no. 5 (1997); no. 6 (1998); no. 7 (1988); no. 8 (2000–01); no. 9 (2003); no. 10 (2003); no. 11 (2003); no. [12], supplement of *Vogue Italia*, no. 634 (2003); no. 13 (2004); no. 14 (2005); no. 15 (2007)

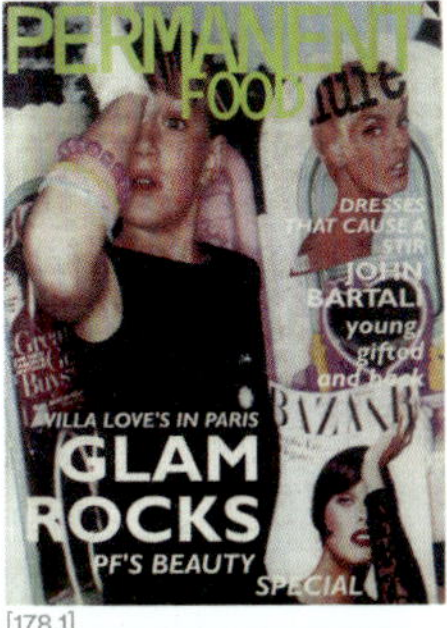
[178.1]

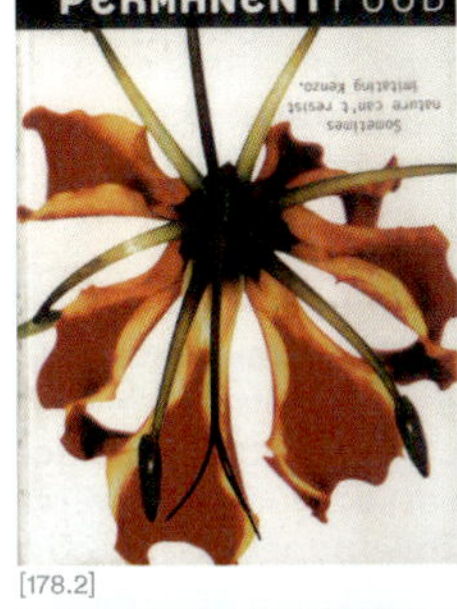
[178.2]

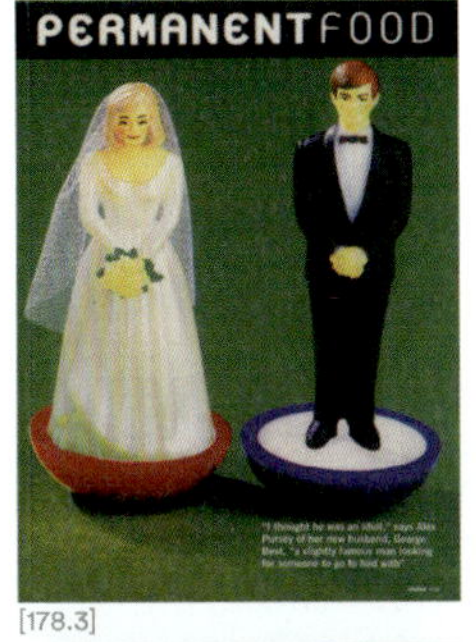
[178.3]

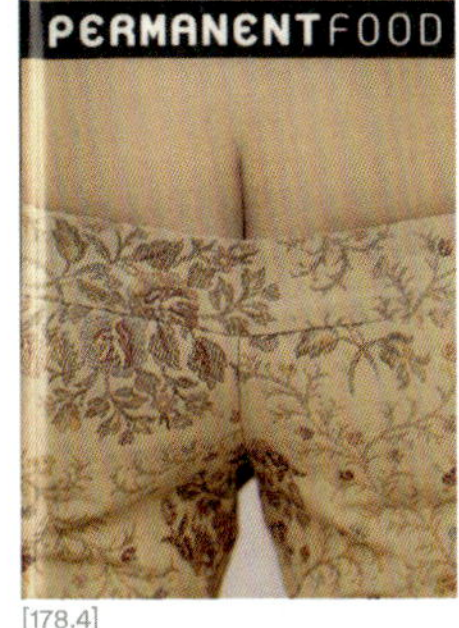
[178.4]

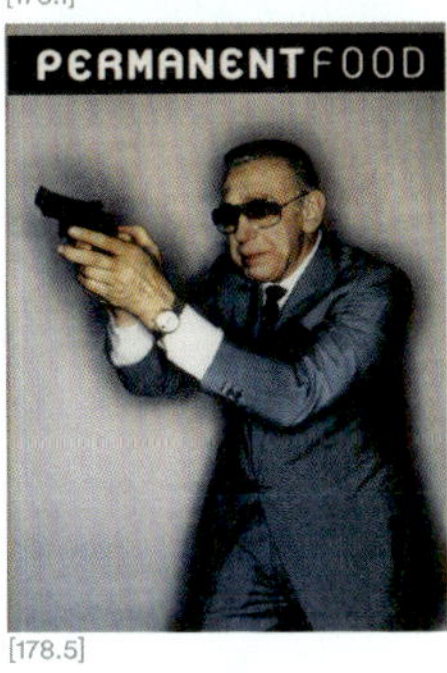
[178.5]

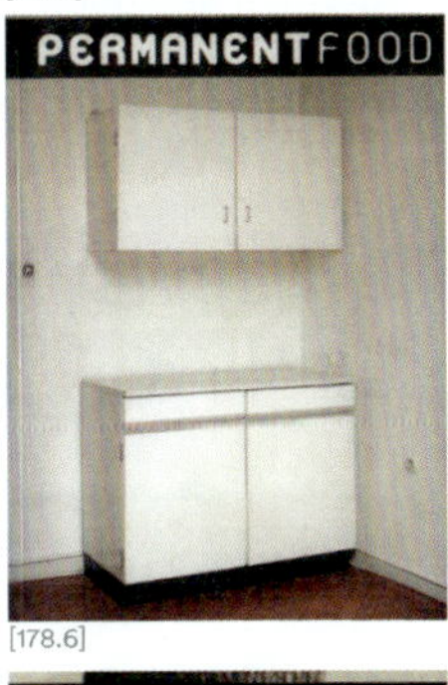
[178.6]

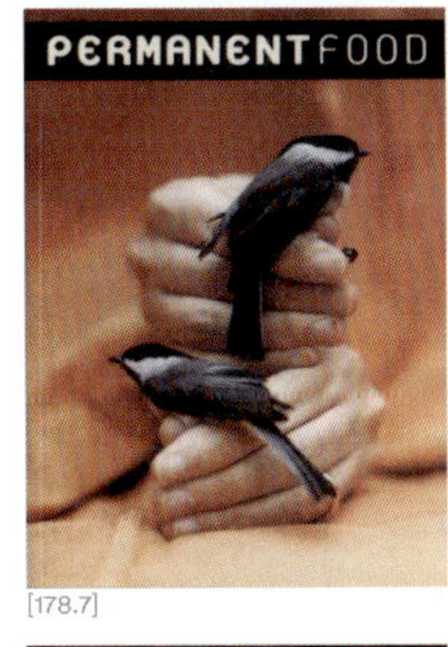
[178.7]

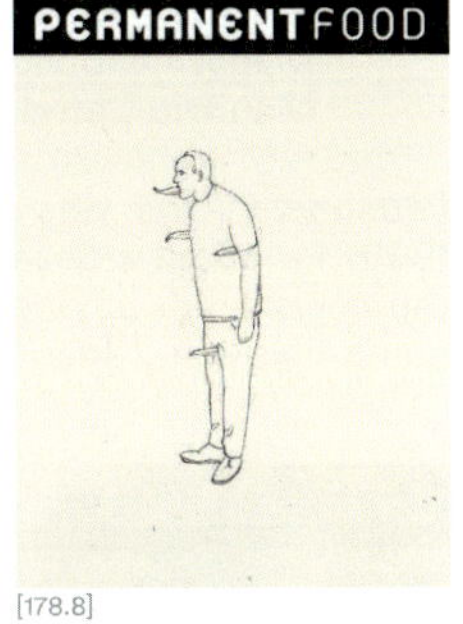
[178.8]

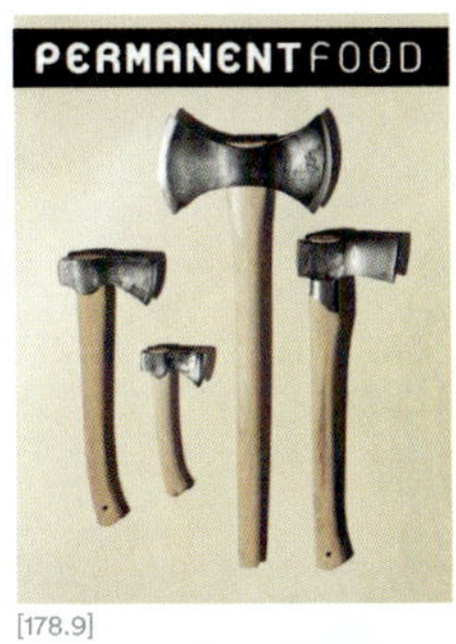
[178.9]

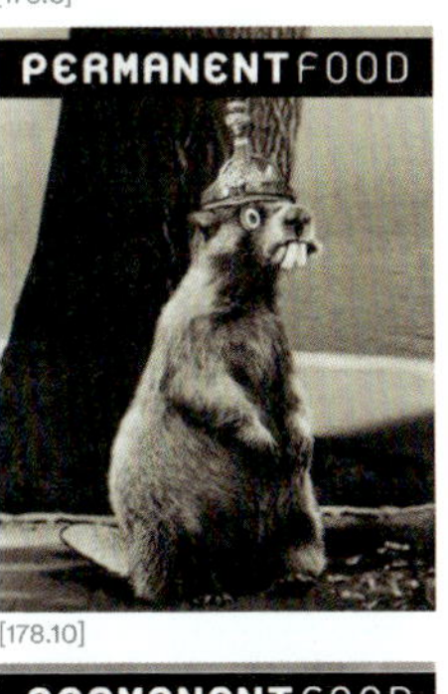
[178.10]

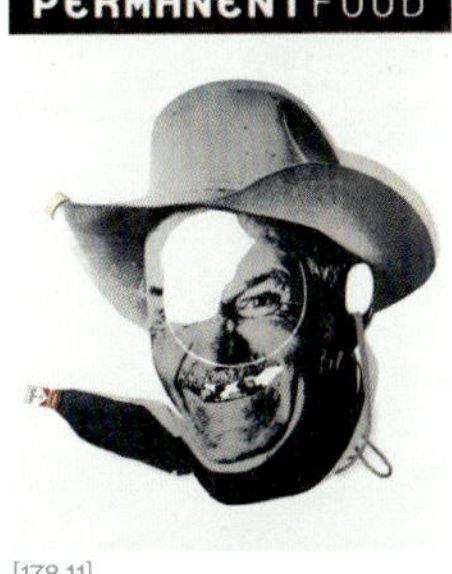
[178.11]

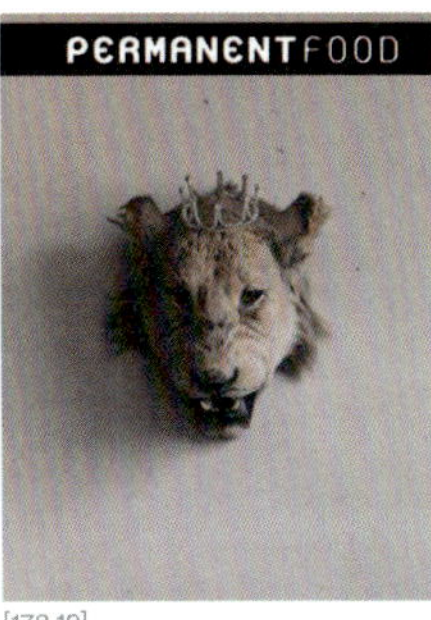
[178.12]

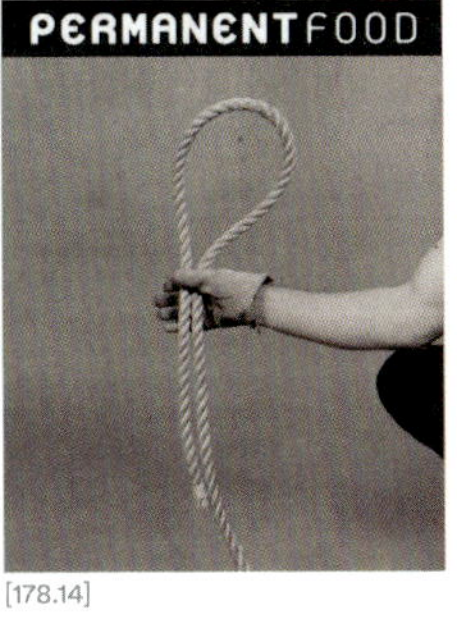
[178.13]

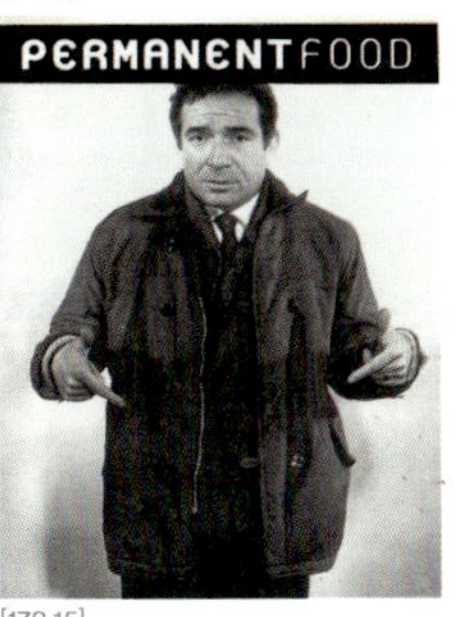
[178.14]

[178.15]

261

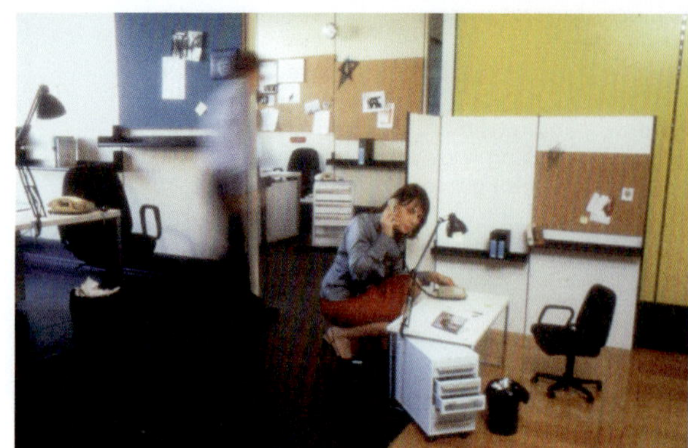

[179]

[179] ***Untitled***, **2000**
Mixed media
Environmental dimensions

*Permanent Food* was done during the closing hours of the agency in Milan where Paola Manfrin worked. With her I developed the magazine we'd started with Dominique Gonzalez-Foerster. After a while I became part of the agency too. The work is a miniature reconstruction of the office where we worked. She then took it home. In the photo you can see Paola herself.

[180] ***Toiletpaper***, **2010–ongoing**
Magazine founded and edited by
Maurizio Cattelan and Pierpaolo Ferrari

*Permanent Food* was published from the mid-1990s for about a decade. It was about going to the newsstand, buying all the magazines there, going home and tearing out the pages that we liked. We reconfigured them and sent them to the printer. It was a second-generation magazine made with images taken from other magazines. The arrival of internet undercut the principles on which *Permanent Food* worked. Already in the mid-2000s, the principle of repurposing existing images outside their initial context were spreading with blogs. Images were reblogged hundreds of times, to the point where you couldn't trace their origin any longer. Presenting the same process on paper lost its meaning. *Toiletpaper* was created with Pierpaolo Ferrari. It was the natural evolution of that practice. It could be said that if *Permanent Food* was based on the functioning of the Dadaist ready-made, *Toiletpaper* is based on the citationist pastiche.

*Toiletpaper* is a purely visual object that investigates the contemporary obsession with images. It's the result of the digestive process that follows an overdose of visual consumption. Aesthetically, its content could be confused with commercial photography, as the magazine's pop imagery catches the eye and manipulates vision the way advertising does. But there is a twist: a *Toiletpaper* image has absolutely no super-ego. It explores in a seemingly harmless way our most intimate, hidden, unspeakable desires and urges. Each picture in the magazine is carefully constructed within a specific mental setting. It is assessed, judged and transformed until it reaches *Toiletpaper* status, conveying a mix of unexpected disquiet and uncanny ambiguity, which could define the magazine's style, if such a definition is possible. What makes it a *Toiletpaper* image is the attempt to say something terrible while keeping quiet.

Clearly, the magazine didn't happen overnight. It was a long process, as with any collaboration. I met Pierpaolo more than twenty years ago, during a photo shoot. We both had fun and I

262

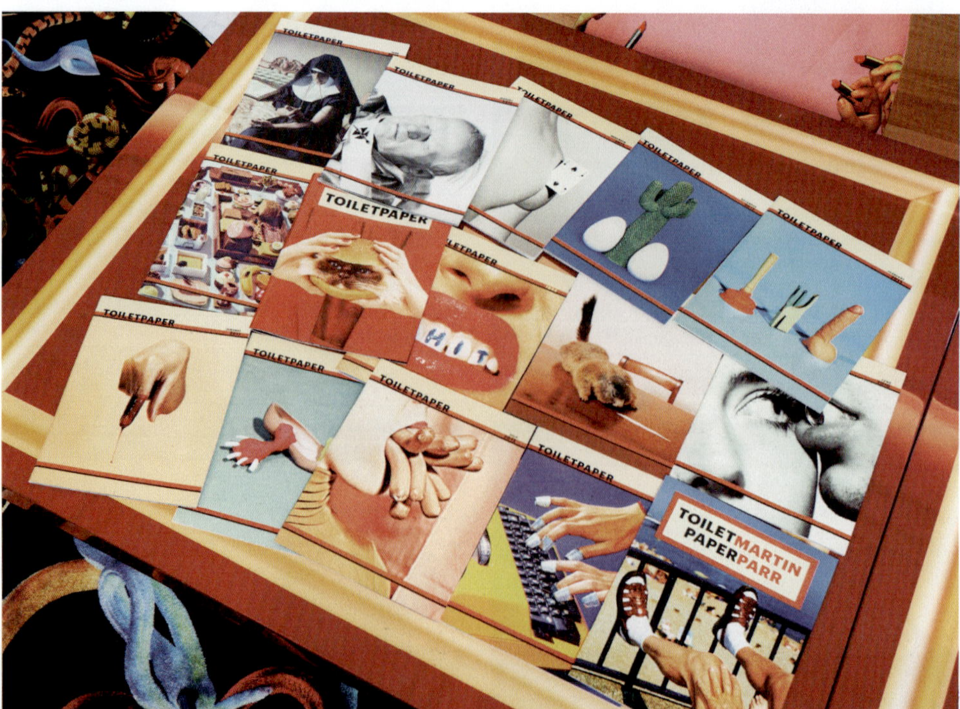


[180.1]

quickly realized that there was a good feeling—especially since we have the same profile! I can't say whether *Toiletpaper* was created at that time or ten years later, when we started doing a photo shoot for the first issue, but in any case it was our way to continue having fun.

If it was a person, we could say that *Toiletpaper* was born and raised in Milan. When I distributed the first issue, friends and collaborators were amazed that it was completely made in Italy. At first we were interested in it not being attributable to a specific context, then later, as a well-known magazine, we're happy that it's characterized as "produced in Milan." Pierpaolo and I are very attached to this city. For both of us it's a familiar place, full of attachments, a real home. *Toiletpaper* is a field of research, a laboratory

[179] *Untitled*, 2000
The work in McCann Erickson's offices, Milan, with Paola Manfrin

[180.1] *Toiletpaper*, 2010—ongoing
Selection of covers of the magazine

[180.2] Selection of objects from the Toilepaper line produced by Seletti

263

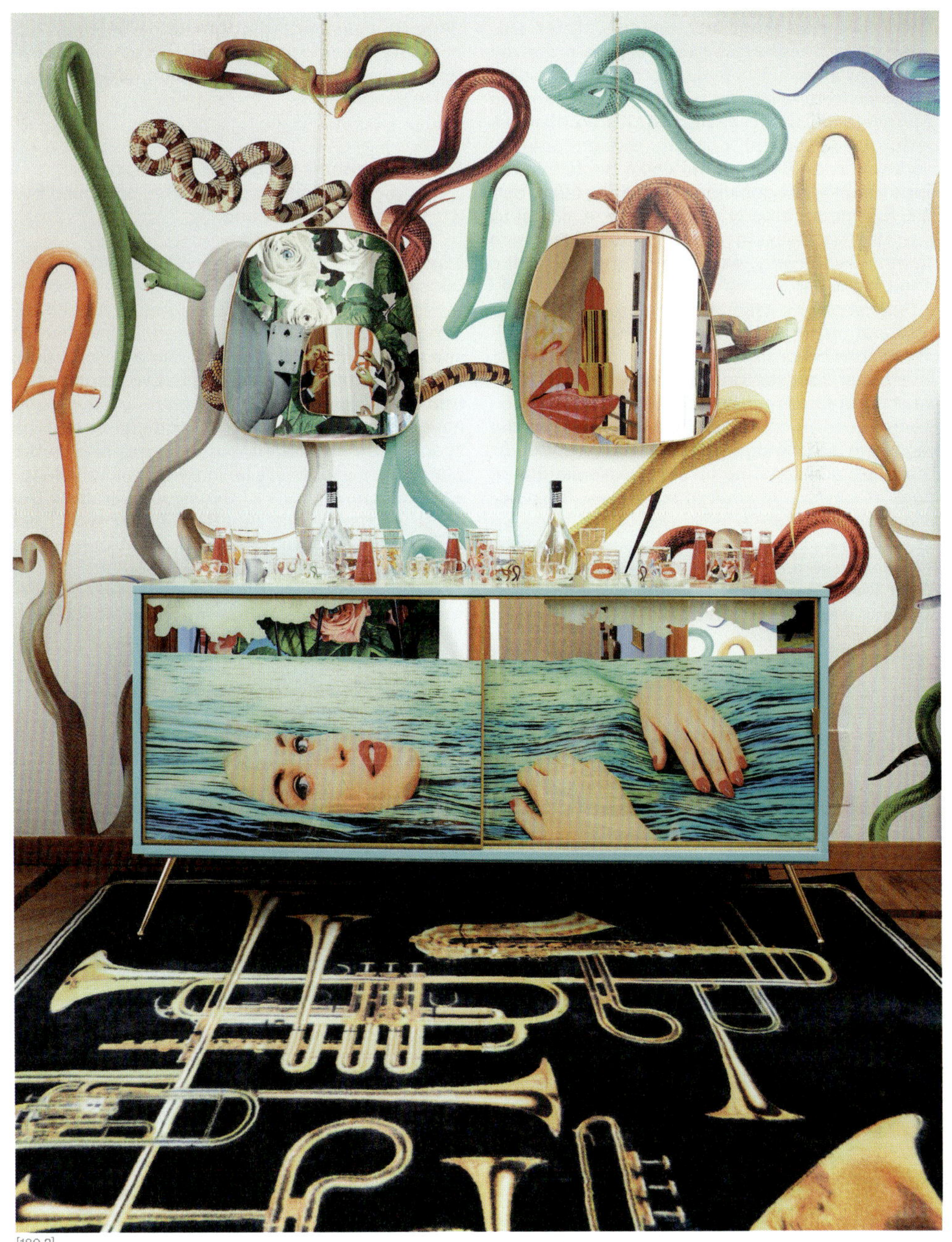

[180.2]

where we give space to our vilest fantasies. The result is a magazine made up of twenty-two photos, without any text. What fascinates me about this format is the speed of creation. In a day of shooting we can turn out as many as twenty or thirty ideas, although many fail to become good photos.

Our studio is screen sharing. When I work on *Toiletpaper* I spend my days in front of the screen together with Pierpaolo on preparing the photo shoot. We don't need meetings with anyone, except with the producer who has to organize the casting. The real *Toiletpaper* circus opens in Milan only three times a year, when we take the images. Post-production, on the other hand, is not as long as you might imagine. Most of our images, crazy as they are, are photos taken for real.

The set of *Toiletpaper* is like an orgy. It's hard to tell who's doing what to whom. Only a DNA test could give you the answer, but that would also mean the end of the fun. We've always preferred to work as a team. We feel that the best ideas often come from engaging with the people around us. *Toiletpaper* is no exception. It's a collective performance out of control, though actually Pierpaolo and I direct it and make the final decisions about what goes in and what to leave out. The *Toiletpaper* credits are in any case almost as important as the images, and it's no coincidence that they're the only text. They show how far the magazine is a group effort. Every person named in that list plays a crucial part in creating the images and making production of the issue possible, each in his or her own way.

*Toiletpaper* focuses on concepts that have always existed: Arcimboldo's works in the sixteenth century, photographic collages at the beginning of photography, the *cadavre exquis*. These are all alienating forms of associations of ideas of a symbolic kind. In some way, the magazine's images create new worlds, or open up parallel ones. On the other hand, violence, sex, the grotesque and the ironic have all been part of art for a long time. They're both ancient and contemporary themes. We'd like the commonest feeling before one of our images to be a sense of both familiarity and disgust. For this reason we take apparently normal situations to an extreme. We'd be satisfied to make someone feel they've been gut-punched.

In the title we were fascinated by the idea of mentioning something that's never talked about but is used every day. It's a real statement, a way of saying to anyone who leafs through the magazine, "Don't take us too seriously, after all it's just toilet paper!" And the same goes for everything that's grown up around the magazine in the meantime. We call it all Toiletpaper, and it's really a many-sided entity. We also became designers, we have a house, we host people, we throw parties, and so much more.

*Toiletpaper* will have an end, that's for sure. I personally hope we'll stop before reaching the boredom stage. Until then, *Toiletpaper* will continue to investigate that gray area between advertising, fashion and art, with no other purpose than exploring. Like scouts at summer camp, but more perverted.

[181]   **Museums League, 2018–ongoing**
Series of scarves in acrylic, produced by Made in Catteland

Museums League, a Made in Catteland project, consists of a series of custom scarves inspired by soccer team scarves. Each one is named for a museum, a foundation, a gallery or another art space or center. Each has its name on one side, together with a phrase that I felt was apt on the other. The colors and lettering are arbitrary, and have nothing to do with the official ones. The scarves can be bought, but each one only in the place it represents. It's an initiative that challenges many conventions of the art market: both the fetish of the unique, unattainable artwork and the creation of limited editions, that only a few people can afford.

The project also has this name because it starts from the observation that museums and similar

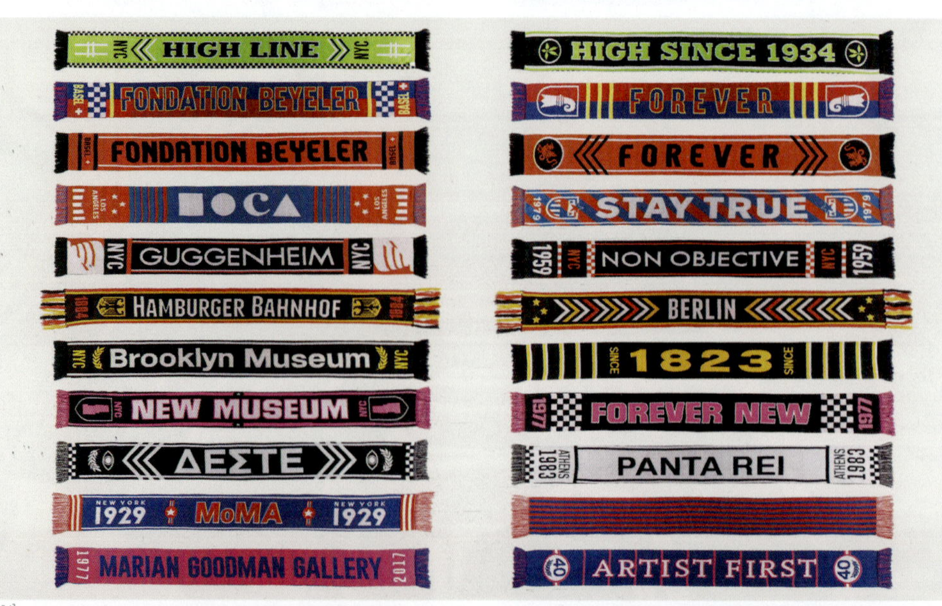

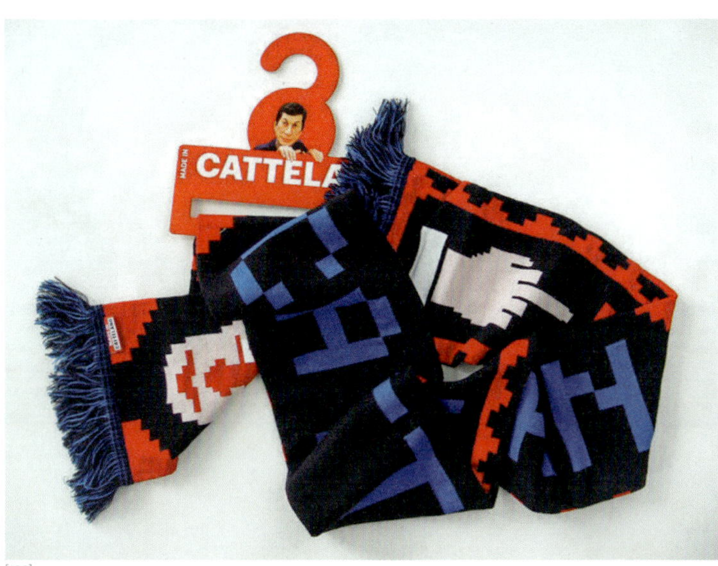



[182]



places are starting to inspire a sense of community, processes of identification, passion and faith. Everyone has their favorite, just as happens with football teams. Museums should be meeting places, where people can get together and share a passionate experience. I hope that attending them will become a ritual event, like the match of someone's home team.

[182]  **Made in Catteland, 2018–ongoing**
       Merchandising products and other
       items made in open editions and sold
       in museum gift shops and online

Made in Catteland is not a real art practice. It's a project devised in 2018 to go beyond the limits of the artwork as we normally understand it and explore the possibility of reaching the public through the creation, or rather the conquest, of new spaces of experience. Made in Catteland attempts to redesign museum gift shops. These places are visited by the art public, but they hardly ever have anything to do with the museum and its contents. Visitors are forced to file through them as if through a shop on the service plaza of some turnpike. Why shouldn't the shop be part of the aesthetic experience?
The motto "Art for all" is one of the guiding principles of the project. To me creativity and impact are inseparable. The more impact you make with your work, the more influence you'll have. The ability to make an artwork go viral seems like a superpower. With Made in Catteland this possibility passes through widespread marketing, avoiding the mistake of deluding oneself that art can be avoid market mechanisms. Warhol was the first to realize this. He produced goods himself, as well as depicting them.

[183]  *Untitled*, **2019**
       Polystyrene, epoxy resin, fiberglass, paint
       150 × 135 × 110 cm

For the project Made in Catteland I replicated all my works in miniature, an initiative that later came to nothing. So I engrafted the miniatures onto a big face, fusing them into a head that can no longer be seen. To be honest, it's a soulless work, like a bank lobby.

265

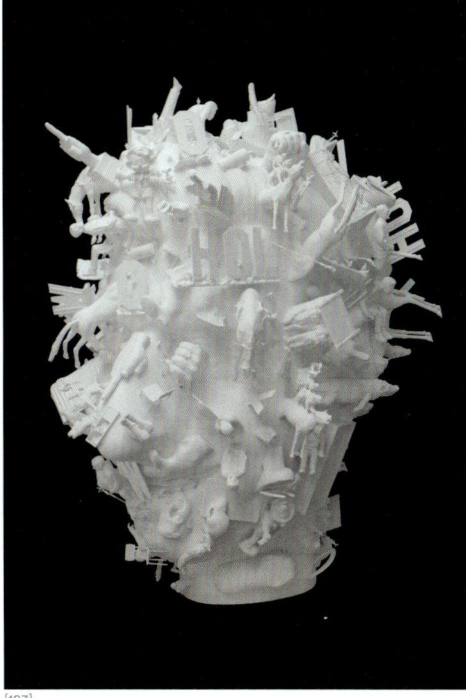

[183]

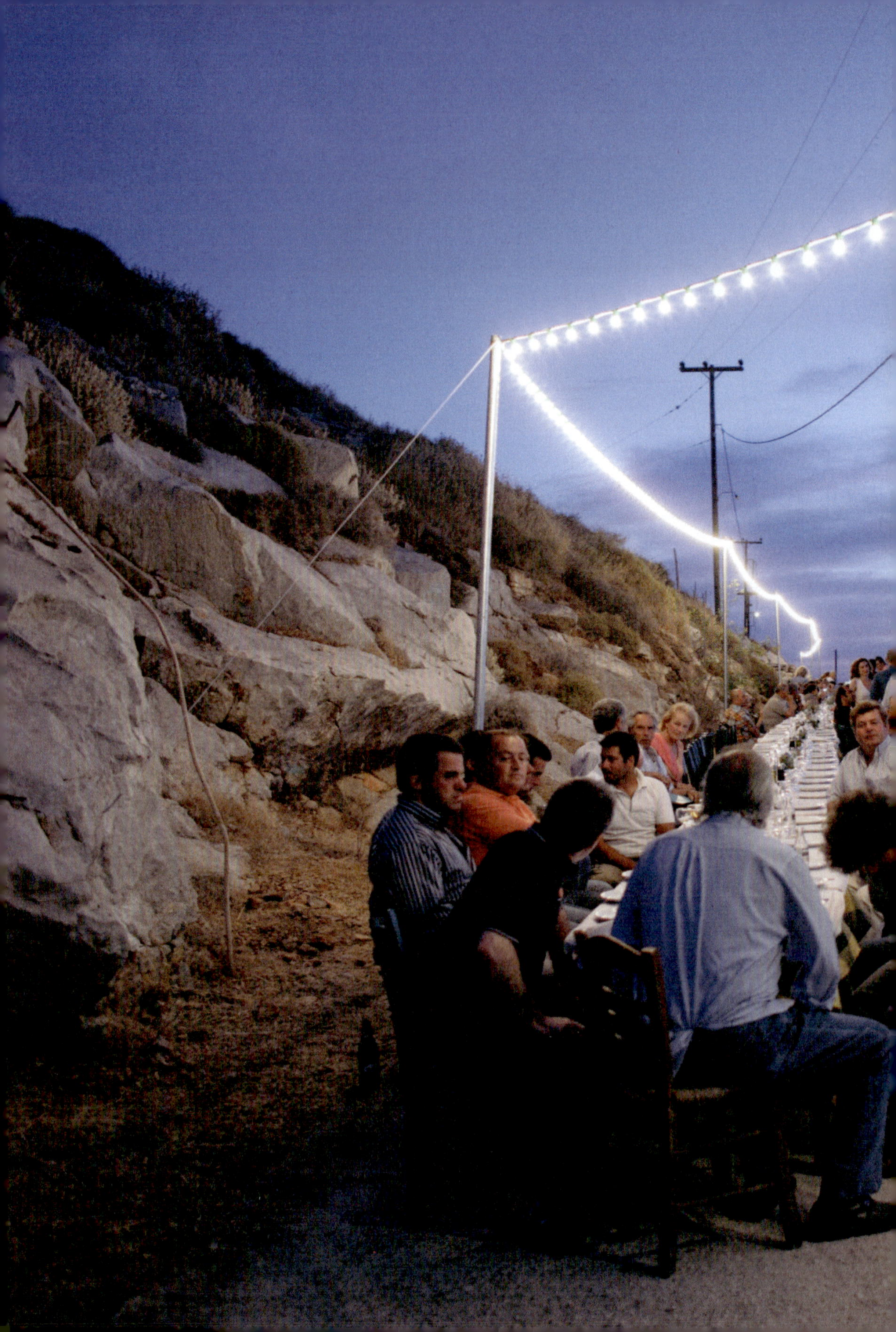

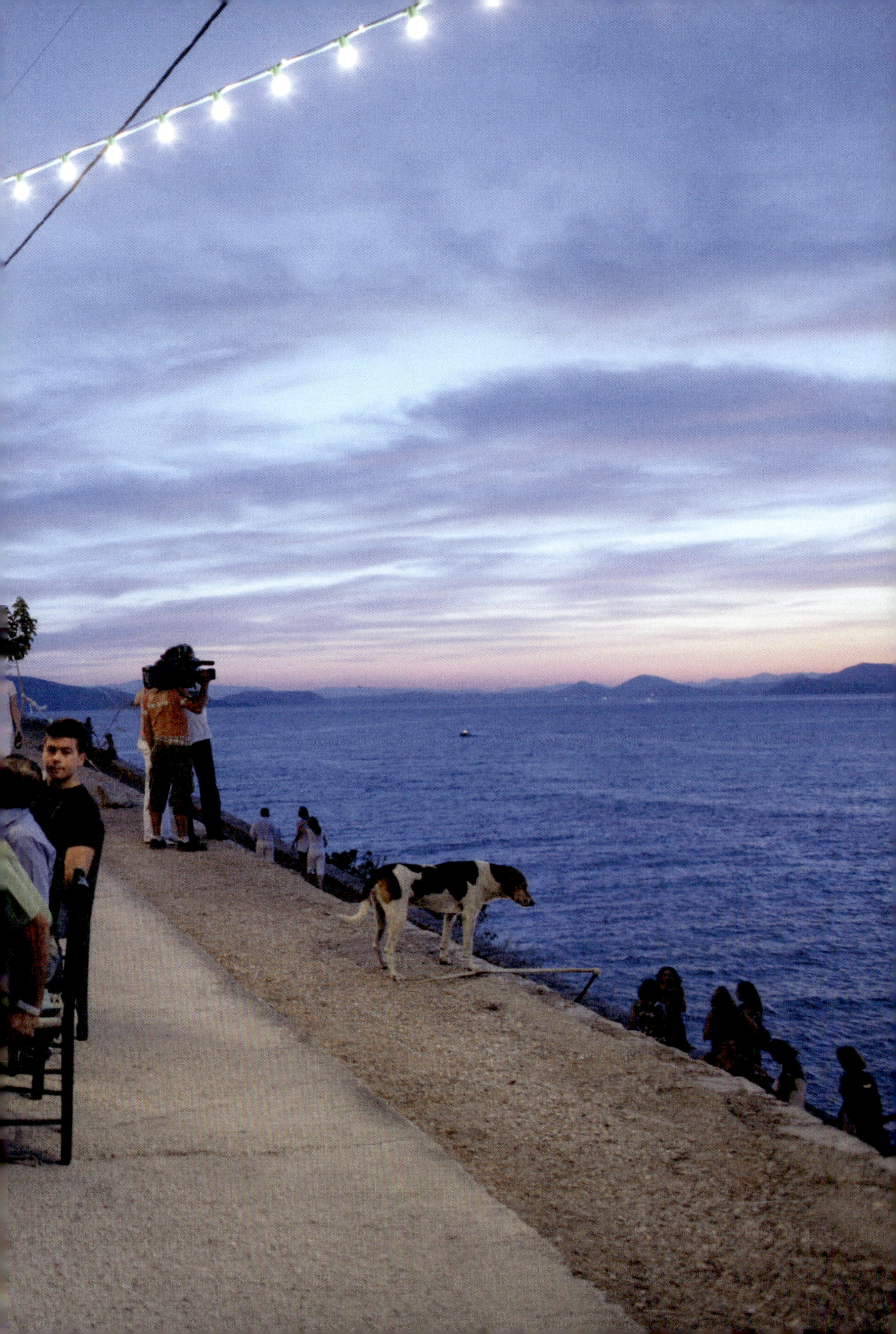

↵    Opening at the DESTE Foundation Project Space, Slaughterhouse, Hydra. Photo by Nicholas Samartis published in *Being Cattelan*, ed. Paola Nicolin, monographic issue of *Abitare*, no. 517 (2011): 63



I've never liked mentors, and even less being in a position of responsibility. That said, I don't think I've ever worked a day but for myself and, at the same time, I've never been alone. Every project has had its team, and if the result is good it's only through teamwork. It's difficult to establish in retrospect who got this or that idea. It only matters that everyone has been indispensable in giving birth to a certain project, because the construction and success of a piece depend partly on the degree of interaction established with the people you come into contact with. I always try to leave the work without ready-marked boundaries, so that it's the relationship with others that completes it.

The creative process fascinates me, but probably only scientific analysis could tell who adds the value to whom. I always like teamwork because I feel that the best ideas come from a mental collision with other people. You talk to them and learn from them. Ultimately, we need to admit that no one's original. Whatever we achieve arises from the collective efforts.

In short, everything good I've done in my life is due above all to collective work. I've always worked like this. I've never deluded myself that I could create something without a continuous dialogue with people I trust and respect. I've always found it easier to pull ideas out of other people's hats, and it's probably mutual. I also practice delegation, which is not a kind of declaration or stance: it's a necessity, a way of solving problems. If there's something to be done, you need to find whoever will do it best, and at any rate there'll always be someone who'll do it better than you. It depends on the type of idea you're working on. You have a project and you go out and look for a consultant, a specialist, an architect, a craftworker... It's the same with interviews. I'm looking for someone who's interesting and funny. There's nothing radical about this, because each of us does it every day. If you think you can control everything, you're screwed.

I'm not really capable of doing anything on my own. The most interesting things happen when there are at least two people in the same room. The moment you start working alone is the moment you start to fail.

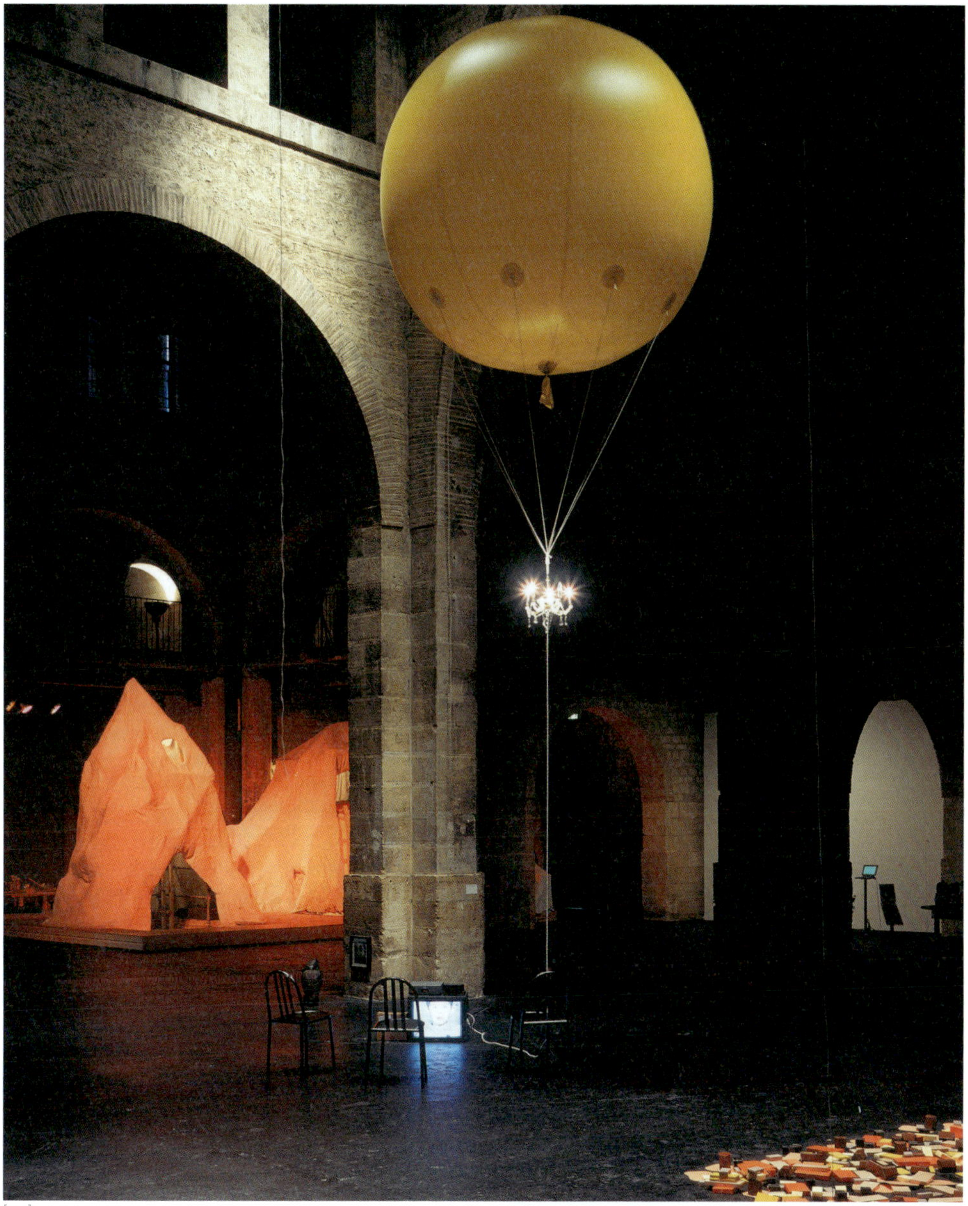

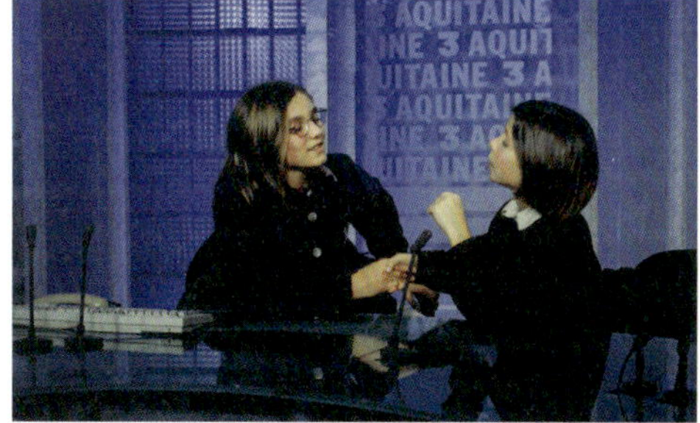



[184]

Maurizio Cattelan and Philippe Parreno
[184] **_La Dolce Utopia_, 1996**
Balloon filled with helium, chandelier
1000 × Ø 400 cm

Maurizio Cattelan and Philippe Parreno
[185] **_CPC Channel_, 1996**
TV station

For the exhibition "Traffic" at the CAPC in Bordeaux, I created two works with Philippe Parreno. Together we wanted to make a TV channel for one person, producing twenty-four hours of scheduled programs for a single viewer, a sort of major contradiction in terms of what television means. The production was meant to take place directly in the exhibition space. We had done all the TV graphics and the set. To make the programs we thought of putting a camera

[185]

[184]  _La Dolce Utopia_, 1996
"Traffic," curated by Nicolas Bourriaud, CAPC Musée d'art contemporain de Bordeaux, January 26–March 24, 1996 (group show). On the floor, a monitor transmitting CPC Channel programs

[185]  _CPC Channel_, 1996
Recording a program

inside a large yellow helium balloon and filming as it went around Bordeaux. Another hour of the program was meant to be made with the footage of a camera hidden inside a teddy bear that kindergarten children played with. But the project never really worked. In the end, the big balloon remained for the installation and we added a monitor underneath.

["Traffic," curated by Nicolas Bourriaud, dealt with projects of sociality and interaction within the conceptual framework of what is termed "relational aesthetics."
The following text is Maurizio Cattelan's contribution to the exchange with Philippe Parreno published in the exhibition catalogue (*Traffic*, curated by Nicolas Bourriaud [Bordeaux: CAPC Musée d'art contemporain de Bordeaux, 1996], n.p.)]

PLAYING OR BROADCASTING?

Imagine producing twenty-four hours of videos. It's impossible to watch in its entirety, unlike being at the movies. People will just live with it, given the possibility of spending a day with the TV switched on. There would be no major problems about receiving a broadcast: simply a VCR, video tapes, and a TV screen would do it. And we've got a cable TV.

- A few ideas. A reading of the late 1960s in France, when thousands of intellectuals left the universities to work in factories and prepare for the revolution. They founded what they called "la gauche prolétarienne," and named themselves "les établis." The revolution never happened, but one of their leaders, Robert Linhart, later wrote a book where he had this line: "Renault or Citroën does not produce only cars but human relationships." It was likely written from the point of view of the witness of a plane crash, full of emotions, with an urgency to speak. In this precise moment he starts to focus on gestures, the way people are looking to each other, a description of how people are linked together. A description of a factory like a movie sequence, where each event, each gesture, each character leads to the next one. An idea of proximity, which slightly changes the idea of context and concept into proximity and feelings.

- "The way you formulate those ideas sounds like a *dolce utopia*."

*The Necessity of Recording*
While walking down a street in London I saw a fire station. One detail was strange, there were movie lights hanging from the ceiling projecting bright daylight. This fire station is used by the BBC as a set for a sitcom, so the production decided to leave the lights on permanently.
Lighting the space, and waiting for the event whether or not a camera would be there to record it. A sitcom without a camera. The script of a sitcom is always this situation where an alien, a foreigner, somebody different arrives in a closed system, waiting for possible stories to appear, just by the presence of someone else.
In the meantime, I think we have to introduce CPC as it is now in our head, not on a magnetic tape, but on paper. A sort of brochure capable of eliciting suggestions that automatically allows one to speak and ask questions; an introduction to the first cable TV without a cable, and without a camera or studios.

*Out of Focus Pictures*
We can design Muppets. A mascot can be a hero.
A camera in plush, like a teddy bear but able to record pictures in a kindergarten, pictures with an out of focus shape.
Now I'm drawing some stupid faces like the ones you saw on the Buchholz's invitation card, and when I go to Milan I want to study different fabrics so as to produce them.

*Mute Section*
I'm thinking that my approach uses fewer words than you, so I'd like to introduce a mute section. A fixed camera where people are allowed to use it consciously or even without knowing they're being filmed. We can build a booth. You will be able to press a button to film five minutes. This booth could be placed in a public square or in a school lobby, so as to obtain different types of interventions. In the end you'd have an incredible amount of material.

*Events*
One idea could be to create situations for CPC. CPC will create events—questioning the creation of events and the recording of events. When you invite people, anything can happen.
Take a firecracker, not a big one but a noisy one, and set it off in the center of a city, so all the car alarms go off.

*Location*
Don't you think that walking inside a white space is as weird as walking on a stage? Anyway the place will come with the city: a bakery, a garage, a bar, or a fire station would be great.
Producing CPC in different countries, the camera will always be an immigrant.

[186]  **6th Caribbean Biennial, 1999**
Project devised by Maurizio Cattelan and Jens Hoffmann, Saint Kitts, November 10–17, 1999

The Caribbean Biennial developed because I was hanging out with Jens Hoffmann. We were talking about a lot of stupid things like opening up a branch of the Guggenheim in Brooklyn. So we went looking for someone else named Guggenheim in Brooklyn for the rights to use the name. But then I thought, instead of doing something about an institution, we should do it about something broader, that would relate to my experience of biennials. A joke can take you to an unexpected place. We started out by studying what a biennial is. Well-known artists, ads in magazines, a catalogue, a press office, a curatorial project, invitation letters, curators, guests. And then we produced it exactly the way a biennale is produced. There was something extremely romantic in our gesture: a certain grandeur and insanity, too, which is what you expect from art. Putting together a show in a few months, gathering all those artists in one place takes as much strength and concentration as painting the biggest canvas. In a way, that biennial was our arena, the place where we tossed our frustrations and tensions and happiness. It wasn't an opportunistic move, but an act of generosity.

The Caribbean Biennial, titled "Blown Away," was not exactly a show, a showcase for artists' projects or objects. It was less and more than that—more or less. What I'm really interested in is the notion of complexity, the idea that there are no fixed roles and definitions. Everybody is forced to change roles every single moment of their lives. One minute you act like a star, and afterwards you have to be all smiley and cheesy and flattery to get the attention of someone who is a better star than you. Or maybe you try to be polite to a waiter and your voice sounds funny and so it comes out in the wrong way, and you have to apologize, otherwise you're not going to get served. Complexity is not an invention of what we call postmodern discourse: it's a matter of every day life. I wanted the Biennial to come out like that, something really everyday-ish. Nobody should be able to tell if it was an artwork or a critical and curatorial statement. Nobody should be able to figure out where the artworks were, if there were any, or what the artists were doing on that Caribbean island.

The problems we were dealing with are much

271

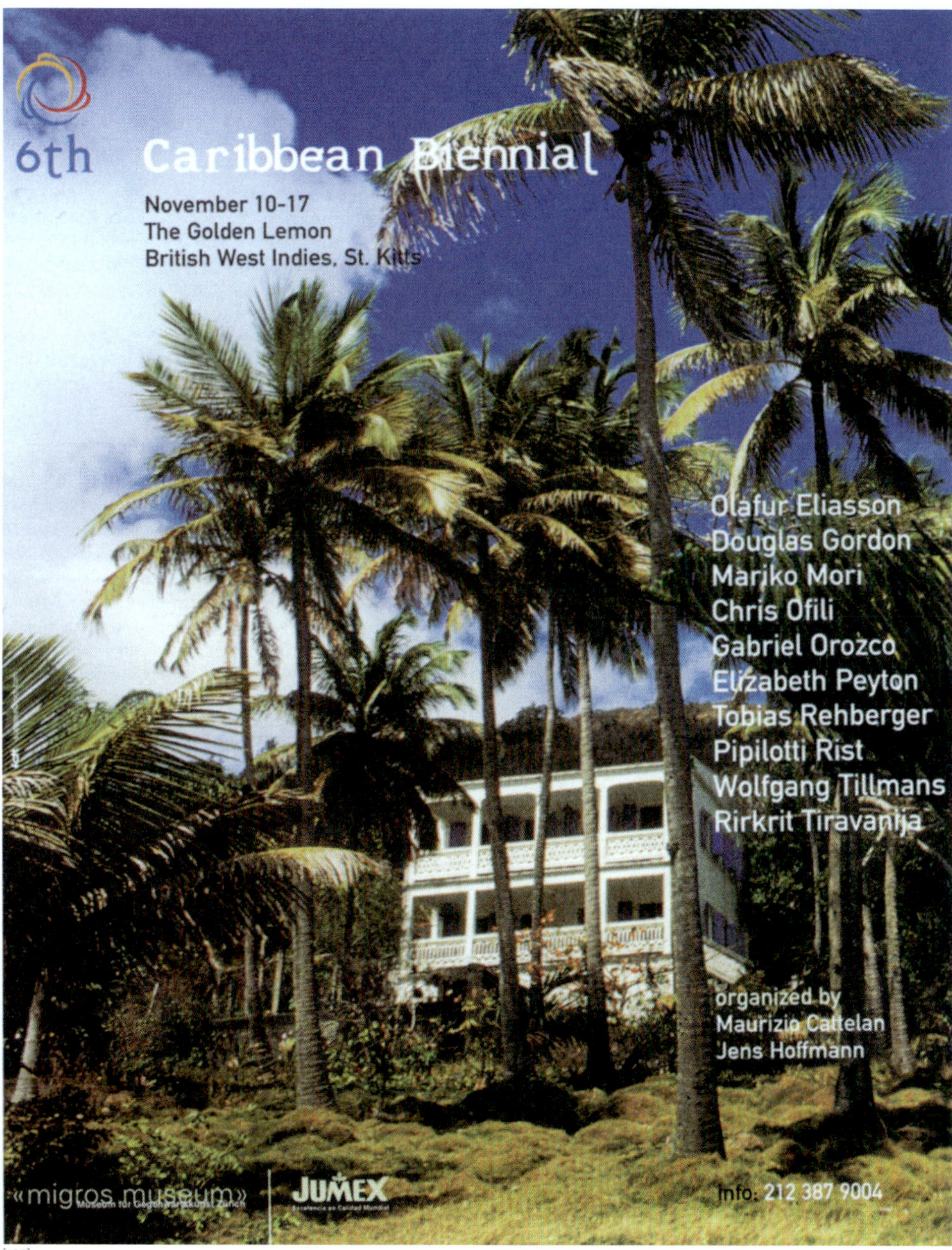



[186]

[186]   6th Caribbean Biennial, 1999
Advertising poster

more down-to-earth. Who's going to pay for the plane tickets? Who's going to send all the press releases? Who's going to make a phone call to place the ads in the magazine? Art is what's left between an email to a gallery, a phone call to a collector, and a reservation at some hip restaurant in Tribeca. This doesn't mean I subscribe to the cynical idea that art is just a matter of visibility, promotion, and public relations. What I'm trying to say is that art is a collision of different systems and levels of reality. And I wanted our Biennial to reflect all this. Besides, complexity is hard to grasp, so our project might have been a total flop. Which was okay because failure is closer to reality than art itself.

Actually the Caribbean Biennial wasn't a holiday at all, because everyone took it so seriously. It even become a way to understand how institutions criticize themselves and write new rules for their practices. It was reconsidered later on, when the proliferation of biennales was so obviously in front of everybody's eyes. It was really weird. It was so difficult to be there and not do anything; to vacation and not feel guilty. It was like each of us was checking on the others suspiciously. Afterwards, it was received and discussed extremely negatively.

So the Biennial experience was dramatic. The image of a world without creativity. This is what we were facing—a meeting of good minds, good artists with, for once, no need to show their egos or their art. It was de-powering people. But then a hurricane came and the Biennial became so alive. What was a problem for so many people on the island was for us the missing element that transformed the whole project. It was showing the real stuff. I remember people crying. It wasn't a joke. The whole island was barricaded, with no connection to the outside world for three days. It was a really memorable time. We played, we talked, we played some more. And then there were a few groups and we got to know each other very well. We were lucky to have that.

There are events that no one sees as mattering, and they disappear precisely because there are no witnesses, such as the famous tree that falls alone in the forest. With the Caribbean Biennial I tried to reverse the parts: there were witnesses, there were all the proofs, while the fact itself, the actual biennial, took a back seat. It wasn't a question of making anything visible, but of continuing to be nothing, while being visible.

[Artists taking part: Vanessa Beecroft, Olafur Eliasson, Douglas Gordon, Mariko Mori, Chris Ofili, Gabriel Orozco, Elizabeth Peyton, Pipilotti Rist, Tobias Rehberger, Rirkrit Tiravanija.
The project was supported by Museo Jumex (Mexico City), Färgfabriken (Stockholm), Migros Museum für Gegenwartskunst (Zurich), Banca Popolare di Ancona, Marian Goodman (New York), Le Consortium – Centre d'art contemporain (Dijon), Janvier (Paris), Golden Lemon (Saint Kitts)]

[187]  **The Wrong Gallery, 2002–10**
Project by Maurizio Cattelan,
Massimiliano Gioni, and Ali Subotnick,
various venues

The Wrong Gallery started as a test, a do-it-yourself affair, capable of reinventing itself for each project. It wasn't a joke, or rather it began as a joke, but it became serious, like a lot of jokes that I like. This makes all the difference: you set up a system and follow it until the end. So it's not about who laughs first, but who laughs last. The Wrong Gallery started in New York as nothing but a door with a few bricks around it. And the door was obviously always locked, one of the things that made it wrong. You couldn't go inside. And it didn't sell or buy anything, so it didn't work as a gallery, so it was completely wrong. We also loved the idea of people saying: "It's a great show, but it's in the wrong gallery." What turned out to be interesting was that artists really connected with the whole idea. They never saw it as a limit but a resource.

The Wrong Gallery was like background noise or a disturbance. When I opened it with Ali Subotnick and Massimiliano Gioni we never thought it was going to last so long. It was a place to show works by others, certainly not mine, where you could discover something new or unexpected. It was a non-profit space, no budget, no everything. You literally worked with nothing, but the challenge was just that: to reinvent its whole organization every time without money or resources and find new accomplices.

The Wrong Gallery was a parasite, in this way a relative of *Charley* or *Permanent Food*. Like the magazines, the gallery also grew by using whatever was already out there. Around that square yard, that door and that window, gravitated the energies of everyone who had something to say or offer, starting with the gallerist Andrew Kreps, who turned the space over to us, a landlord who let you work without asking for rent, a photographer who documented the installations in exchange for nothing, and an installer who one day showed up at our door and set to work. In the end, The Wrong Gallery was perhaps Chelsea's bastard daughter, or more simply the back door of contemporary art.

Chelsea was an epicenter. At that time, SoHo was waning and Brooklyn was an outcast, so the choice of Chelsea was logical. If you want to say something about society, or a part of society, you go to where it's represented most often. Chelsea had more than 200 galleries, and there was a kind of control so visible that you didn't need to explain why you might open something like The Wrong Gallery. So it was quite easy to make our statement. A statement that was understandable. Many gallerists came to the openings. We didn't make the market and so there was no competition. New York can be very welcoming when there's no money involved.

The idea was to have fun with what we liked. The first idea had been to build something in a parking lot, but it wasn't perfect. Then we were in front of Andrew Kreps's gallery and Andrew came out. One thing led to the next. A week later we had the door installed. It all started without thinking too much about it. We started with a project by Martin Creed, because we thought

[187.1-18]   Selection of performances and exhibitions at The Wrong Gallery, New York, 2002–10: [1] Martin Creed, October 12–November 16, 2002; [2] Daniel Squires, Merce Cunningham Dance Company, November 15, 2002; [3] Paul McCarthy and Jason Rhoades, December 12, 2002–January 17, 2003; [4] Sam Durant, March 8–April 3, 2003; [5–7] Paweł Althamer, April 8–29, 2003; [8] Cameron Jamie, November 9–December 10, 2003; [9] Keegan McHargue & Matt Leines, [10] Keegan McHargue, January 31–March 6, 2004; [11] Mark Handforth, March 10–April 3, 2004; [12–13] Michael Wilkinson, April 9–May 21, 2004; [14] Piotr Janas, May 29–June 23, 2004; [15] Tommy White, May 29–June 23, 2004; [16] Carol "Riot" Kane, June 26–July 23, 2004; [17] Justin Lowe, June 26–July 23, 2004; [18] Dara Friedman, September 9–October 6, 2004

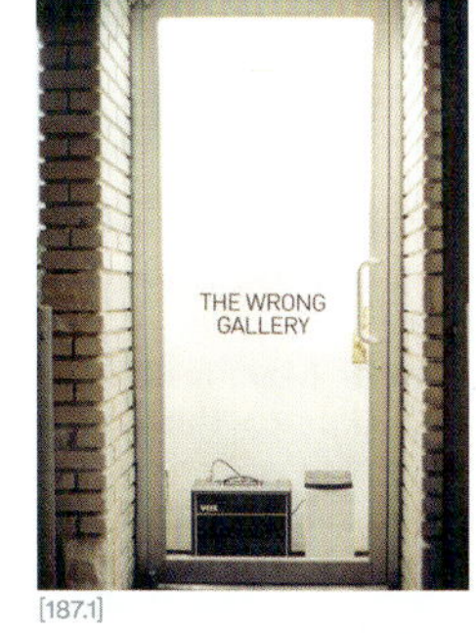
[187.1]

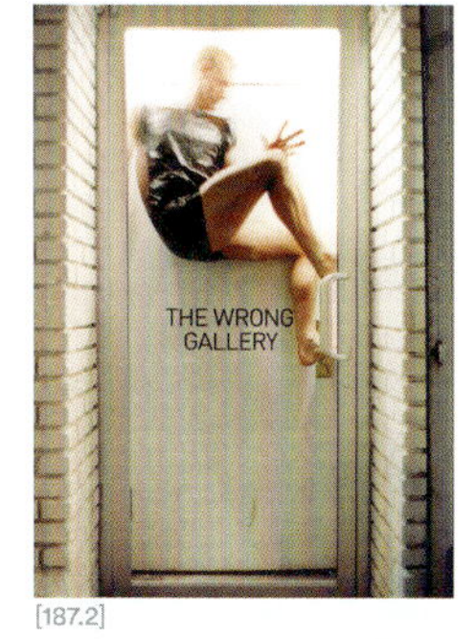
[187.2]

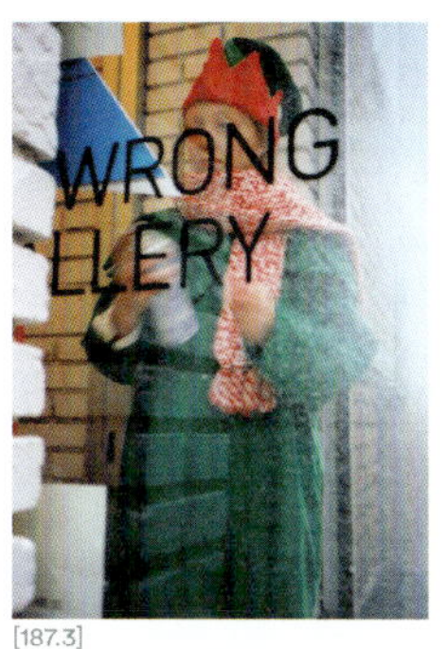

[187.3]

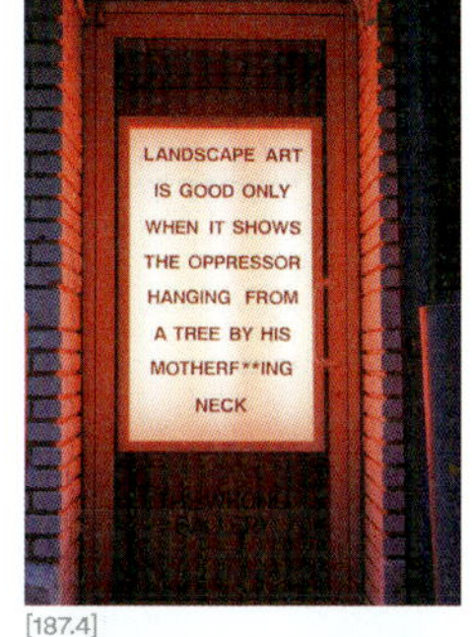

[187.4]

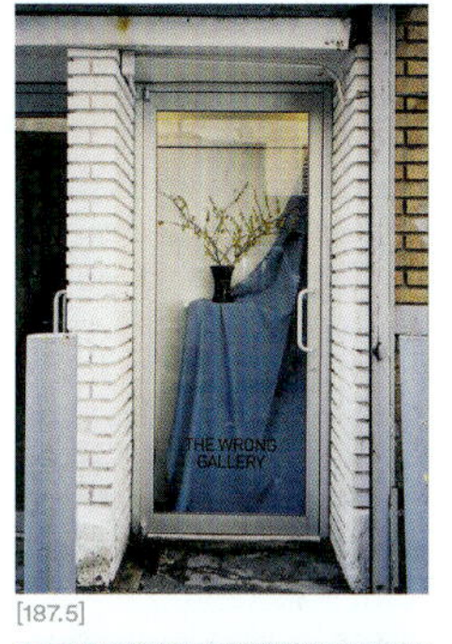
[187.5]

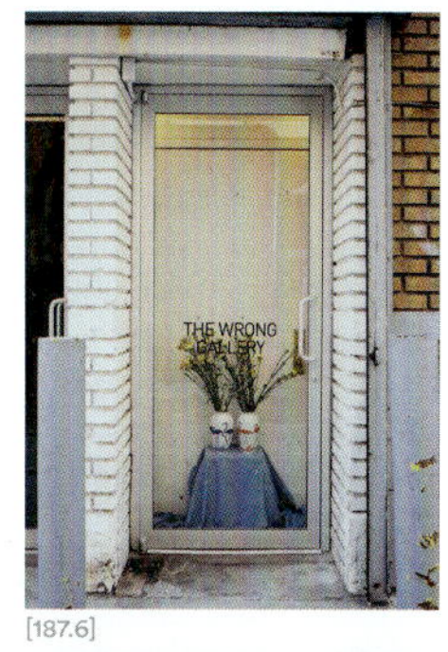
[187.6]

[187.7]

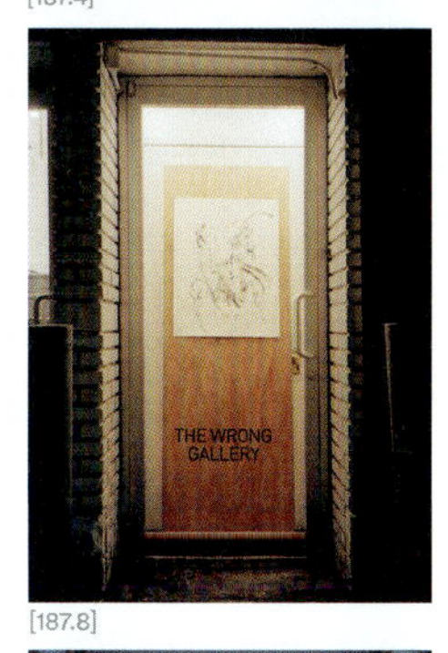
[187.8]

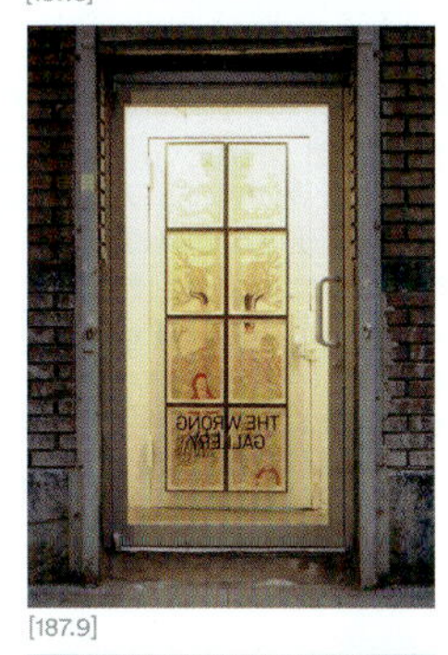
[187.9]

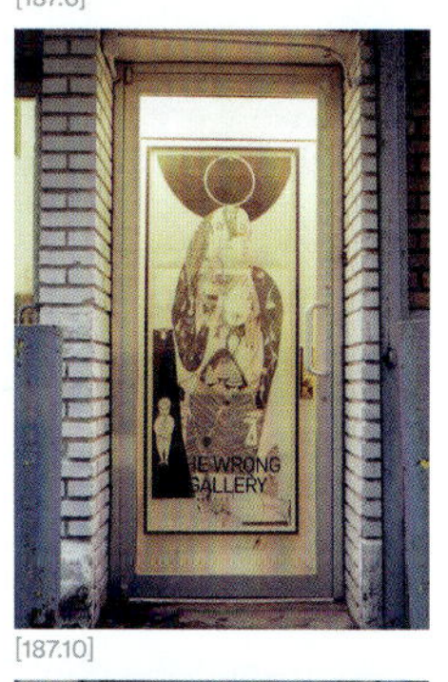
[187.10]

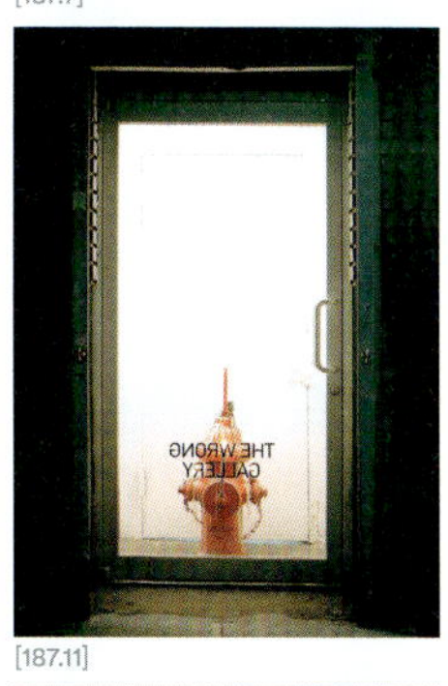
[187.11]

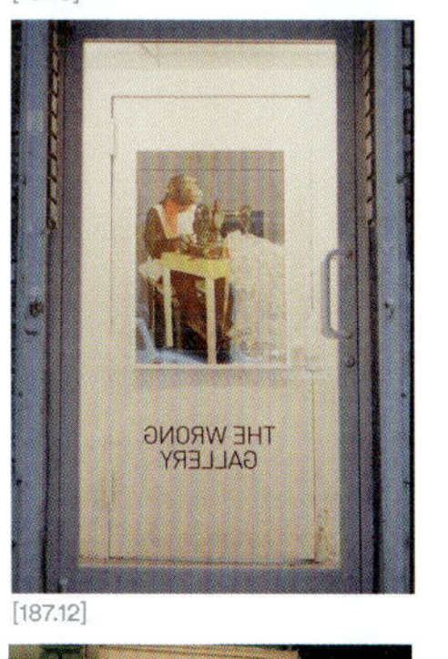
[187.12]

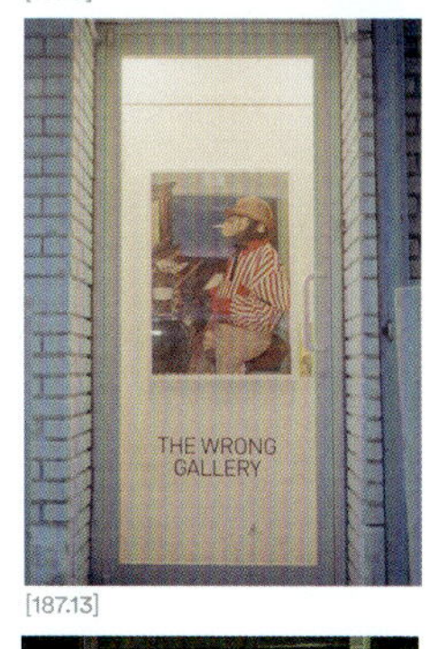

[187.13]

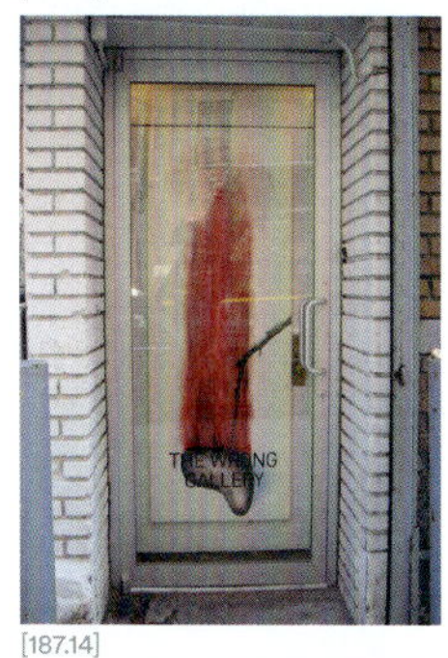
[187.14]

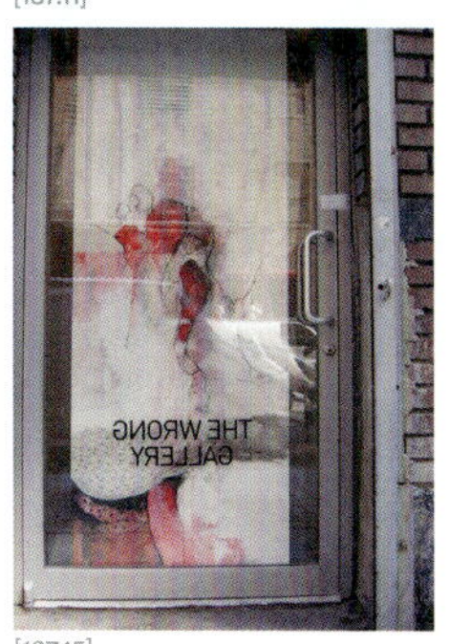
[187.15]

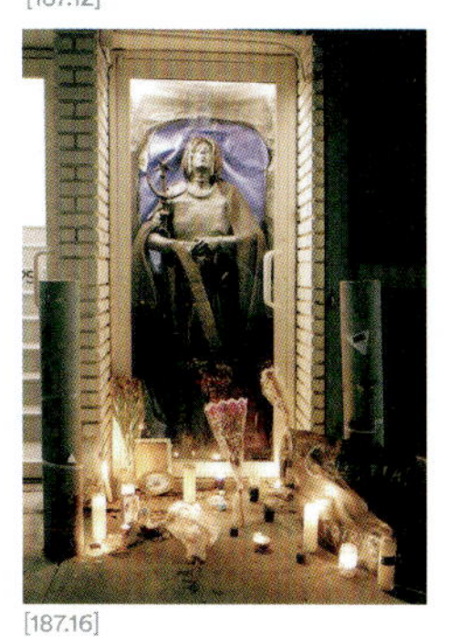
[187.16]

[187.17]

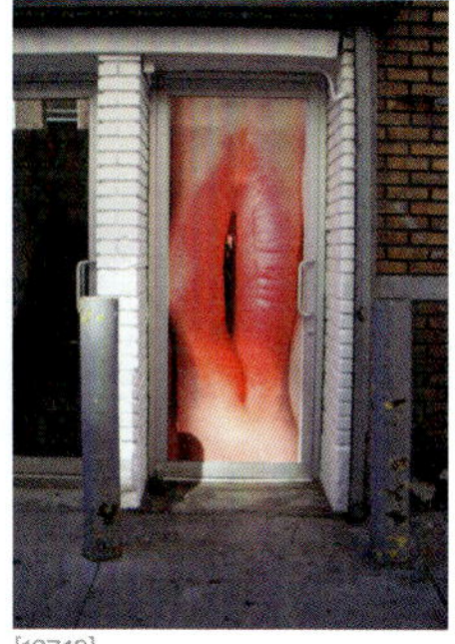
[187.18]

273

it made sense to open the smallest gallery in the world with a Turner Prize winner, as a way to break down certain hierarchies. We worked a lot with the other galleries on the block. On the evening of our inauguration, Anton Kern and Andrew Kreps also opened. The invitation to our exhibition was designed by David Shrigley, who was working on his own show at Kern. Gavin Brown covered the expenses of Martin Creed's work. Then we asked Phil Collins to think of a special project, and he turned the gallery into a light box. Financing the exhibition that time was Michele Maccarone, who at the opening made a little speech to the friends of The Wrong Gallery. Paul McCarthy with Jason Rhoades and many others followed.

One of the weirdest things that happened was that someone called the police for a piece by Elmgreen & Dragset. It was a car parked in front of the gallery with a very realistic sculpture of a baby on the back seat. It had been there for about a week and hadn't even gotten a single ticket. Then someone called the police and said there was a baby inside. The cops came and freaked out. First they wanted to break a window. They, when they saw it was a sculpture, they wanted to confiscate the car. Meanwhile, Andrew Kreps, who had the gallery next door, was taking photos from the window with his staff. It was quite hysterical. But I guess that's what art is about.

When we were evicted in 2005, we received an invitation from the Tate Modern to move there. It was a new experiment. The challenge was to keep The Wrong Gallery weird and awkward enough. It was interesting, because we had to adapt to a different environment, gathering new energy from our neighbors and at the same time working against them, trying to look different. We shaped our identity in response to our surroundings. We had our own independent program and we did what the Tate couldn't do. It was as if the Tate was a limousine and Ali, Massimiliano and I the poor relatives on bicycles.

[The Wrong Gallery opened in October 2002 at 516A1/2 West 20th Street, Chelsea, New York. In January 2003 a second Wrong Gallery was set up nearby, at 520A1/2. After being evicted from both locations in July 2005, due to the sale of the building, the original door was relocated to the Tate Modern in London in January 2006. At the same time, an edition of 2,500 mini-reproductions of the gallery was also produced in collaboration with Cerealart, exhibited worldwide. The gallery gave rise to the newspaper *The Wrong Times*, which ran for three issues (2004, 2005, 2006) and featured interviews with artists hosted at the gallery and many others. Between 2002 and 2010, The Wrong Gallery organized numerous pop-up projects in various institutions and art fairs around the world and published the magazine *Charley*.
Between 2002 and 2005, over fifty events were organized to present individual artistic projects or exhibitions. They included:

— Martin Creed, *Work No. 122: All the sounds on a drum machine*, 1995–2000, October 12–November 16, 2002 (516A1/2);
— Daniel Squires, Merce Cunningham Dance Company, November 15, 2002;

— Phil Collins, *Sinisa and Sanja*, 2002, November 21–December 10, 2002 (516A1/2);
— Paul McCarthy & Jason Rhoades, *Humpback (The Fifth Day of Christmas)*, from the series *13 Days of Christmas Shit Plug*, 2002, December 12, 2002–January 17, 2003 (516A1/2);
— Lawrence Weiner, *Give & Get* and *Have & Take*, from January 12, 2003 to disappearance (spray paint lettering on the sidewalks [516A1/2]);
— Elizabeth Peyton, *593 Napoleon After His Bath*, 1991, February 15–March 5, 2003 (516A1/2);
— Sam Durant, *Landscape Art Sign (Emory Douglas)*, 2003, March 8–April 3, 2003 (516A1/2);
— Paweł Althamer, *The Wrong Gallery*, 2003, April 8–29, 2003 (516A1/2);
— Isa Genzken, *Berlin Headlines*, 2002, April 30–May 12, 2003 (516A1/2);
— Paola Pivi, *Untitled (pearls)*, 2000, May 13–29, 2003 (516A1/2);
— Adam McEwen, *Untitled (Closed)*, 2002–2003, May 30–June 18, 2003 (516A1/2);
— "The Virgins Show," curated by Fernanda Arruda and Michael Clifton, June 23–August 1, 2003 (artists: Philippe Perrot & Chris Caccamise, Yoshua Okón & Torbjörn Vejvi, Shahin Afrassiabi & Alexandre da Cunha [516A1/2]);
— Tomma Abts, *Obbe*, 2003, September 6–October 6, 2003 (516A1/2);
— *Sandwiched (in New York)*, 2003, project by Jacob Fabricius, September 24–October 4, 2003 (artists: Bernadette Corporation, Leon Golub, Sharon Hayes, Ben Kimmont, John Miller, Aleksandra Mir, Adrian Piper, Julia Scher, Michael Snow, Valerie Tevere; Fulton Mall, Brooklyn);
— "The Landlord's Show," October 5–November 8, 2003;
— Tino Sehgal, *This is Right*, 2003, October 16–20, 2003 (Frieze Art Fair, London);
— Cameron Jamie, *"Divine Brown Om,"* Hollywood, 2003, November 9–December 10, 2003 (516A1/2);
— Adam McEwen, *Untitled (Sorry)*, 2002–03, December 12, 2003–January 10, 2004 (516A1/2);
— Aleksandra Mir, *Happy Holidays*, 2003, January 1, 2004;
— Bob Nickas, *Projects & Exhibitions*, 2002–04, January 10–30, 2004;
— Keegan McHargue & Matt Leines, *Untitled*, 2004;
— Keegan McHargue, *Seven Symphonies Play to the Same End*, 2004, January 31–March 6, 2004 (516A1/2);
— Mark Handforth, *Parking Meter (candles)*, 2004, and *Fire Hydrant (candles)*, 2004, March 10–April 3, 2004 (516A1/2 and 520A1/2, respectively);
— Michael Wilkinson, *Sewing Chimp*, 2003, and *The Entertainer*, 2004, April 9–May 21, 2004 (516A1/2 and 520A1/2, respectively);
— Piotr Janas, *Untitled*, 2004, May 29–June 23, 2004 (516A1/2);
— Tommy White, *Untitled*, 2004, May 29–June 23, 2004 (520A1/2);
— Carol "Riot" Kane, *It's All Wrong: Celestial Is Dead*, 2004, June 26–July 23, 2004 (516A1/2);
— Justin Lowe, *Waterfall*, 2004, June 26–July 23, 2004 (520A1/2);
— Dara Friedman, *Vertical Smile*, 2004, September 9–October 6, 2004 (516A1/2);
— "The Landlord's Show," September 9–October 6, 2004 (artist Ali Yaghoubi [520A1/2]);

— "Trailer," September 11–October 10, 2004 (works by Philippe Parreno, Charles Avery, The Wrong Gallery, Jens Hoffmann & Claire Fitzsimmons, Charles De Meaux, Martín Sastre, Liam Gillick & Sean Dack, Makoto Aida, Mathieu Copeland, Norbert Schoerner, Alan Michael, Milena Dragicevic, Gail Pickering, Olivia Plender, Nathaniel Mellors, Roger Hiorns, Keith Wilson, Erik van Lieshout, Doug Fishbone, Carey Young);

— Adam McEwen, *Untitled (Closed)*, 2002–03, October 7–November 5, 2004 (516A1/2);

— Trisha Donnelly, *Untitled (cannon)*, 2004, October 7–November 5, 2004 (520A1/2);

— Noritoshi Hirakawa, *The Home-Coming of Navel String*, 1998, October 14–18, 2004 (Frieze Art Fair, London);

— Shirana Shahbazi, *Untitled*, 2004, and *Untitled*, 2004, November 6–December 5, 2004 (516A1/2 and 520A1/2);

— Andreas Slominski, expedition from the door of 516A1/2 to Hamburg, where he stayed for a week for a dinner, and return to New York, November 23–December 14, 2004;

— On Kawara, *Reading One Million Years (Past and Future)*, from 1993, December 14, 2004–January 15, 2005 (516A1/2 and 520A1/2);

— "We disagree," January 29–February 26, 2005 (works by Peter Peri, Florian Pumhösl, Dieter Roth, Robert Kuśmirowski, Christian Frosi, Jamie Isenstein, Silke Otto-Knapp, Jonathan Monk, Martin Boyce, Hayley Tompkins, Simon Evans, Roman Signer, Michael Sailstorfer, Evan Holloway, Monika Sosnowska, James Yamada; Andrew Kreps Gallery [516A1/2 and 520A1/2]);

— Jamie Isenstein, *Will Return*, 2005, and *Inside Out Winter Hat Dance*, 2005, January 29–February 26, 2005 (516A1/2 and 520A1/2, respectively);

— Roberto Cuoghi, *Untitled*, 2004, March 7–30, 2005 (516A1/2);

— Michael Elmgreen & Ingar Dragset, *Forgotten Baby*, 2005, March 12–22, 2005 (opposite 516A1/2);

— Gedi Sibony, *No Title*, 2005, April 1–30, 2005 (516A1/2);

— Peter Coffin, *Untitled (Absinthe Drinker)*, 2005, April 1–30, 2005 (520A1/2);

— Michael Cline, *Michael's Box*, 2005, May 6–19, 2005 (516A1/2);

— Dave Muller, *Larry's Top Ten (on a door)*, 2005, May 6–19, 2005 (520A1/2);

— Harrell Fletcher, *With Our Little Hands: Reports From The Pacific North West*, 2005, and *Sasquatch*, 2005, May 20–July 8, 2005 (516A1/2 and 520A1/2, respectively);

— "You Only Live Twice," September 23–October 30, 2005 (artists: Annika Eriksson, Jeremy Deller, Sean Landers);

— "The Show That Never Happened" (Delia Gonzalez & Gavin R. Russom, *Goodness Had Nothing to Do With It*);

— For the Whitney Biennial 2006, "Day for Night," The Wrong Gallery organized the exhibition "Down by Law" at the Whitney Museum of American Art in New York, January 21–May 21, 2006 (works by Dennis Adams, Anonymous, Matthew Antezzo, Edgar Arceneaux, Jules de Balincourt, Richard Barnes, Monica Bonvicini, Fernando Bryce, Chris Burden, Paul Cadmus, Paul Chan, Larry Clark, Chivas Clem, Verne Dawson, Jeremy Deller, Sam Durant, Marcel Dzama, Gardar Eide

Einarsson and Oscar Tuazon, Kota Ezawa, Matias Faldbakken, Leon Golub, Félix González-Torres, Boris Gorelick, Gregory Green, Karl Haendel, Barkley Hendricks, Jonathan Horowitz, Matthew Day Jackson and Dan Peyton, Sergej Jensen, Mike Kelley, Christopher Knowles, Glenn Ligon, Mark Lombardi, Nate Lowman, Louis Lozowick, Robert Mapplethorpe, Naeem Mohaiemen, Vik Muniz, Henrik Olesen, Raymond Pettibon, Tim Rollins, Ed Ruscha, Dread Scott, Andres Serrano, David Shrigley, Taryn Simon, Fred Tomaselli, Kerry Tribe, Kara Walker, Andy Warhol, Weegee, Kehinde Wiley, David Wojnarowicz)]

[188]  **Charley, 2001–11**
Editorial project by Maurizio Cattelan, Massimiliano Gioni, and Ali Subotnick; graphic design by Purtill Family Business

*Charley* grew out of a collaboration with Massimiliano Gioni and Ali Subotnick, begun as a necessity. The basic idea was to do something for young artists: in the first issue we published four hundred. Then we realized that we wanted a different idea every time. They were all experiments, of a newspaper in some way second-hand, do-it-yourself.
The second issue was devoted to a season of gallery exhibitions in New York. The third brought together images of one hundred artists famous in New York in the eighties and nineties, but who had then already disappeared or become peripheral. It was like making a catalogue without an exhibition, an operation on the system. All the same, this issue gave rise to two real exhibitions: "Bright Lights Big City" at David Zwirner in New York and "Yesterday Begins Tomorrow" at the DESTE Foundation in Athens.
The fourth issue was supposed to be a compilation of contemporary artworks purchased by the world's most important museums. A bit like sticking your nose into their storage space, to see how art history is constructed (though, it should be remembered, history is like a bottle of milk and you always have to check the best-by date). But in 2004, with Ali and Massimiliano, I started working at the Berlin Biennale, and that issue of *Charley* became something else, in parallel with the research for the exhibition.
*Charley* and also Gagosian Gallery, our project that anticipated the Biennale, were like gambling on different tables, or as if playing different instruments, since in the end you can't go everywhere in a limousine, sometimes you have to walk, sometimes you need a bike. Gagosian was our little bike. Maybe it was rusty, but that's how we wanted it. It could be quicker and more spontaneous than a mass exhibition, and sometimes more fun. This was also the point of every issue of *Charley*, which has always been concerned with appropriating information and mixing it. And then, when you do something you can make mistakes, and only those who do nothing are irreproachable. For us, that issue of *Charley*, entitled *Checkpoint Charley*, was as important as the whole Biennale, perhaps even more so: a visual diary of a year's work, which also contained an endless list of possible biennials.
In 2007 we kept to the same line with the fifth issue, looking at what was considered the "pe-

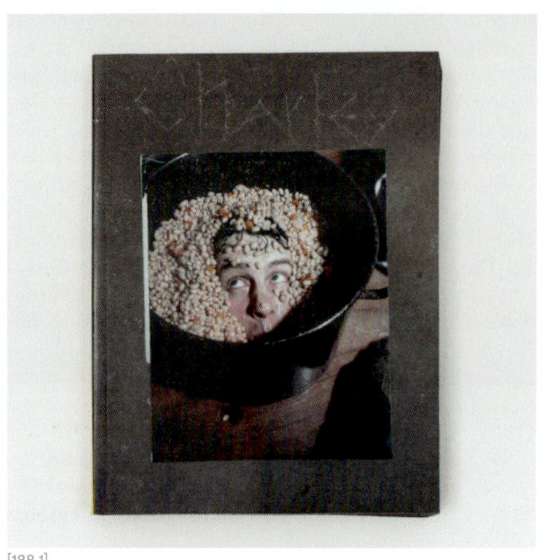

[188.1]

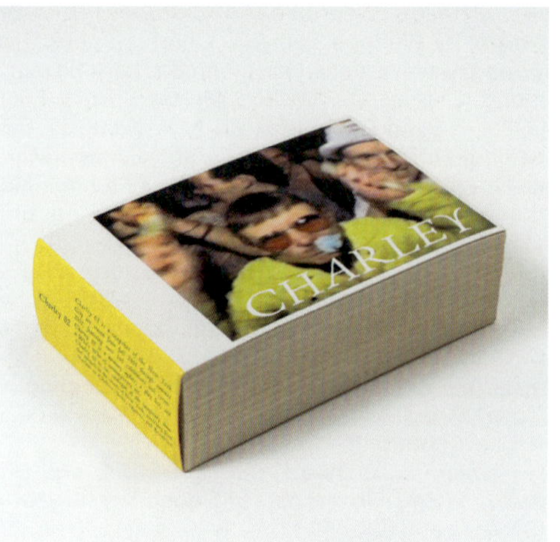

[188.2]



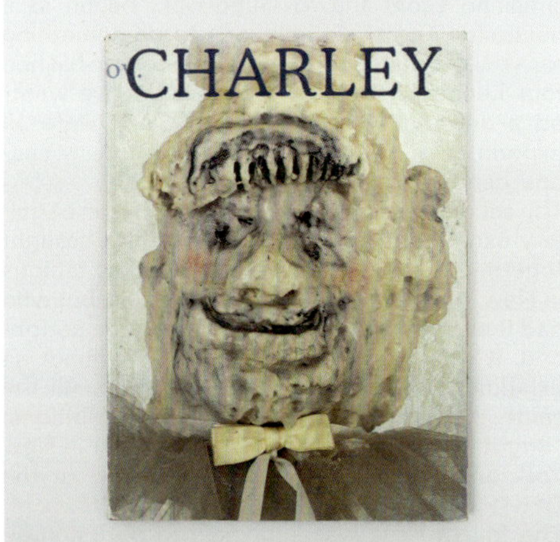

[188.3]

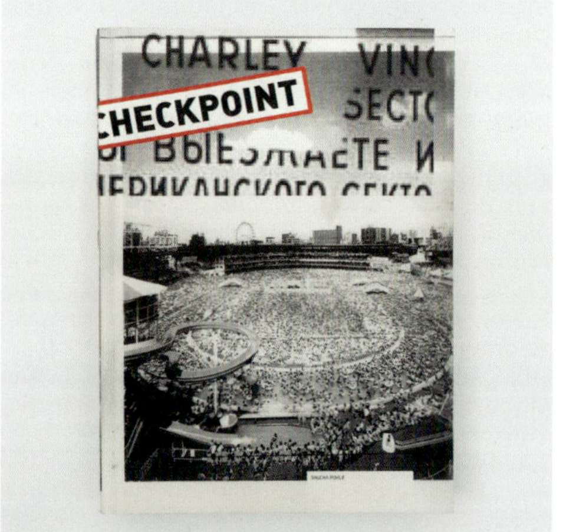

[188.4]

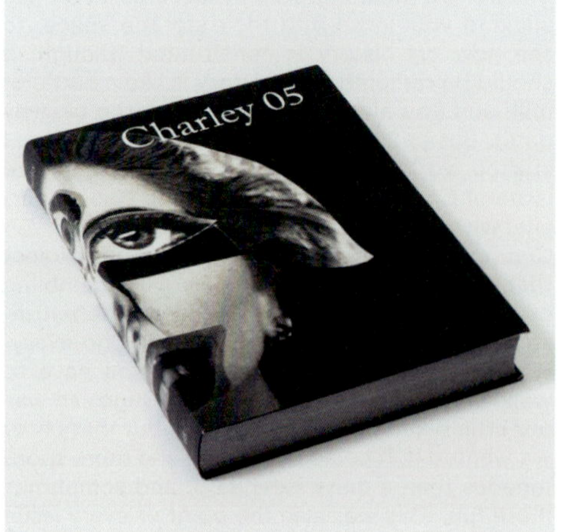

[188.5]

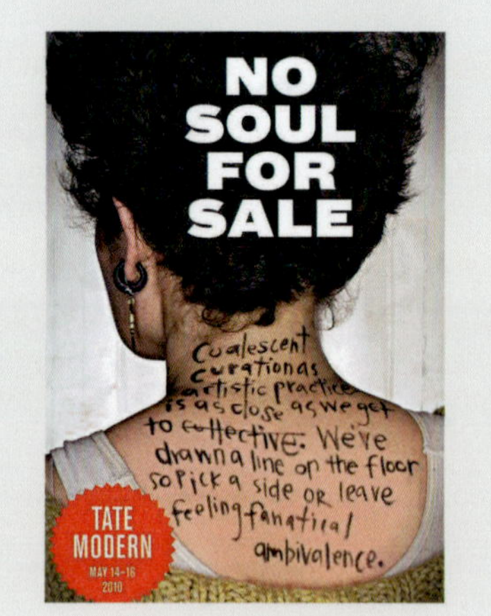


[188.6]

[188.1]   *Charley 01*, 2001
          15 × 20 cm, 192 pages

[188.2]   *Charley 02*, *Postcards*, 2002
          142 colored postcards, 10 × 15 cm each
          Produced by DESTE Foundation for Contemporary
          Art, Athens

[188.3]   *Charley 03*, 2003
          22 × 30 cm, 384 pages

[188.4]   *Charley 04, Checkpoint Charley*, 2005
          21 × 29 cm, 800 pages

[188.5]   *Charley 05*, 2007
          17 × 24.5 cm, 544 pages

[188.6]   *Charley Independents: No Soul For Sale*, 2011
          Edited by Cecilia Alemani, Maurizio Cattelan,
          Massimiliano Gioni, and Ali Subotnick
          24 × 16 cm, 356 pages

riphery" but which for us was only an "alternative center." We collected the work of a hundred artists who remained outside the limelight. It was the only time we added texts, while the format was, as always, different from the previous ones. After that number, we stopped. We made one exception: the festival I organized with Cecilia Alemani, Massimiliano Gioni, and Ali Subotnick at the Tate Modern in London, where for three days we took over the Turbine Hall and invited associations, artist-run spaces, independent publishers, and alternative spaces of all kinds from everywhere. The title was brilliant: "No Soul For Sale."

[189]   **Family Business, 2012–14**
Project by Maurizio Cattelan and
Massimiliano Gioni, various venues

Family Business grew out of the desire, which I shared with Massimiliano Gioni, to repeat the format of The Wrong Gallery, perhaps on a slightly larger scale. We opened Family Business in Chelsea, occupying a part of the Anna Kustera Gallery at 520 West 21st Street. The year was 2012, in the midst of my retirement after "All" at the Guggenheim. I had to do something, and it was a lot of work, unlike The Wrong Gallery, though the space was still tiny.
The name was a kind of celebration of the democracy of misunderstanding. As with The Wrong Gallery, we thought it would be interesting to see what would happen by giving space—albeit relative—and freedom to an artist to exhibit their work. A decision often leads to exciting developments you don't always foresee. The family expanded and we made many new friends. With a fate like The Wrong Gallery, Family Business lived out its last phase elsewhere, at the Palais de Tokyo in Paris.

[Family Business, with 11 square meters of floorspace, was promoted by the Center for Curatorial Studies of Bard College, New York. It also hosted concerts, workshops, presentations and other events.
Exhibitions presented in New York (2012–13):

—   "The Virgins Show," February 16, 2012;
—   "TOASTING TO THE REVOLUTION," April 19, 2012; "Megabodega," June 26–July 6, 2012;
—   "Artists Guarding Artists," August 13, 2012;
—   "Industrial Evolution: Kris Perry & Friends," September 6–29, 2012;
—   "Raspberry Cargo: Duane Linklater," October 5–25, 2012;
—   "Cleopatra's Family Jewels," November 16–December 8, 2012;
—   "DON'T BE A HAM!! (CHRISTMAS PARTY): Ari Marcopoulos," December 12, 2012–January 12, 2013;
—   "LUSTLANDS: Lakis and Aris Ionas," January 24–February 16, 2013;
—   "Cold Castle," February 21–March 9, 2013;
—   "In Praise of Chance and Failure," April 4–20, 2013. Exhibitions presented at the Palais de Tokyo in Paris (2014): "The State of the Sky," February 13–September 7, 2014;
—   "The Order of the Third Bird," March 8–23, 2014;
—   "Salon des Refusés," April 5–20, 2014.
In Saint Petersburg, Family Business organized the exhibition "TAMIZDAT," May 18–June 1, 2013]

277

[189]   Family Business, 2012–14
Image for the communication of the project

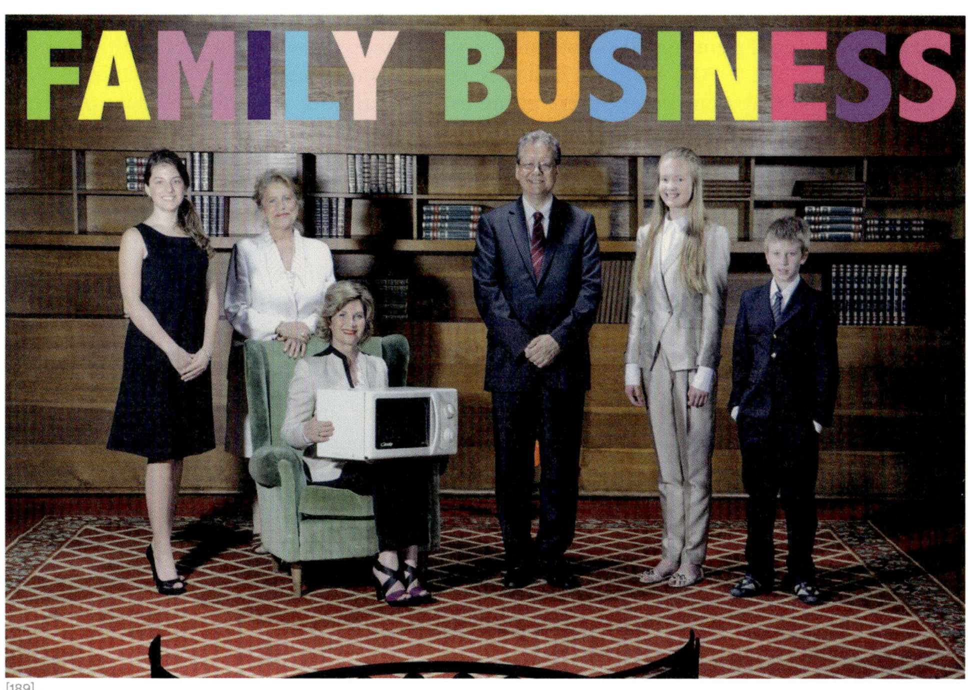


[189]

I'm always a bit perplexed when people talk about the 1990s, 1980s, 1970s… I wonder if it is possible to analyze a period in these terms, and whether the span of time that stretches from the first year of a decade to the tenth is really such a homogeneous and coherent reality. Instead I have the impression that a decade always ends in a radically different way from how it began. The 1930s had opened with an unprecedented economic crisis and a progressive society, only to finish in prosperity and in the grip of dictatorial regimes. The 1960s began under the shadow of the Cold War and social conformity but closed with a revolution. Who would have thought that at the end of the 1950s, in an art dominated by nonrepresentational paintings, Fluxus and Pop Art would arrive to turn everything on its head? Or that in the 1970s, when art had reached its conceptual (and, to a certain extent, austere) heights, that some people were going to start painting again for the pure pleasure of it?

A second problem to consider is that historical periods are often contradictory; diametrically opposed realities lived under the same roof at the same time. One thing that has always struck me, ever since I was at school, is that history books tend to explain things to you vertically, and not horizontally. I suppose that this is more effective from a pedagogical point of view, but I find it strange that no one ever drew my attention to the fact that, at the time when Mazzini and Cavour were trying to create Italy by fighting wars of independence, cowboys and Indians were running around America. It makes me smile when I read things like "the 1970s, the punk era" or "the 1970s, the age of disco," as if an entire generation had chosen to march in one direction rather than another. The truth is that the two things coexisted, that reality was as complex and fragmented as it has always been, and that the predominance of one thing over another is due solely to the viewpoint of whoever is recalling them.

My 1990s, for example, were different from those of many others. My life changed completely in the space of a decade. My first exhibition abroad, my first visit to the Venice Biennale—as an observer as well as a participant, having had rented out the space at my disposal to an advertising agency. In 1990, I was considered and up-and-coming artist, but by 1999 the same people regarded me as one of those artists whom, up until a few years earlier, I had regarded with a mixture of curiosity and fear, as if they were veterans, simply because they had a few more years of activity behind them. My own career, however, fades into the background in comparison with other events during that period. One of the most significant moments of those years for me, for example, was the death of Alighiero Boetti in 1994. It had been Boetti, when he wrote "today is the ninth day of the seventh month of the year one thousand nine hundred and eighty-eight," who had made me realize the fleeting power and ambivalent significance of a date.

But the part of the 1990s I most like to remember is when they came to an end. The year 1999, dawn of the third millennium. I recall the excitement, the fear, the curiosity, the euphoria—all feelings relatively out of proportion to what was actually going on. I thought about what had happened in the year 1000, and about the strange destiny that had allowed me to experience and event so rare on the calendar and yet so totally ordinary at the time.

It is said that the best way to deal with the future is to look at the past. Maybe the opposite was true here. Perhaps the best way to reflect on the 1990s was to wait for the next decade. I remember that in the 1970s, there was a genuine revival of the 1950s: *Happy Days, American Graffiti, Grease*. I watched and didn't understand. The previous two decades were perceived as a period of innocence and positivity, even though in reality those had been the years of McCarthyism, of the threat of the atomic bomb, of the Korean War. Only today, from a safe distance, can I see that those specters were filtered through the perspective of the 1970s.

In the 1980s there was much talk of the 1960s, just as in the 1990s people spoke of a revival of the 1970s. According to this logic, the second decade of the new millennium ought to see a return of the 1990s. Perhaps it will be the best way to understand what has happened, and to get an idea of where we were and where we are going.

[Text published in *Kaleidoscope*, no. 3 (September–October 2009): 64–65]

IS THERE LIFE
BEFORE DEATH?

Being stubborn enough to resist the impositions placed on you from above is certainly crucial to overcoming your first hurdles. When I was young, before I became an artist, I had no idea what life held for me. It's sad when I think about it, but I didn't have any great ambitions. My only big dream was being independent, financially and from my family. I measured the degree of my success by my ability to break the chains that held me back. It's when you prove to yourself that your life is in your hands, when you become the master of your time, that you can find the space to ask yourself questions about the future and be truly ambitious. For the rest of my life I've remained interested in changing my future more than my past, although I can't always do it.

I think that the future, as it's usually understood, doesn't exist. What we think of today as the future isn't the future. People are always afraid of the future and the future has always been a disaster, like the present. Rhetoric about the future bothers me, because we say that almost everything we're doing today is for the future. The future is here and now. Take the Renaissance: it was hardly an accident that it was a period when many artists imagined a new society, a new world and, above all, a new type of life. They were definitely not thinking of the future, and they didn't care about it. We bring about the future by doing it today.

All the same, I'd like to have faith that one of those moments in history will soon come when we can breathe hope and faith in the future every day. As human beings, we constantly raise the bar of our goals and the limits to be overcome, thanks to inspiring images from the arts. How has our age managed to change, starting from the imagination of some visionary? In 1865, Jules Verne's *From the Earth to the Moon* was science fiction. A hundred years later and it's historical fact. The influence of technology on the future of humanity involves a dilemma that has always given rise to a lot of literature and, more recently, a lot of movies. Few people can predict what's going to happen in the long run, rather like what happened when printing with movable type was invented. No one could have imagined that it would become the medium for spreading Luther's heretical ideas. I've always been very interested in recognizing the forerunners among thinkers, writers or directors, those who already knew how our life would change. Marshall McLuhan, Philip K. Dick and Isaac Asimov were some of the most lucid, as I see it. But it fascinates me even more to reflect that somehow, by their thoughts and imagination, they've shaped the way we live now.

What strikes me most today, though, is that we're becoming increasingly technological and increasingly barbaric at the same time. I don't see any civility in using the latest smartphone to take snaps of refugees drowning off our coasts. Creating new technologies to deal with life is a part of human culture and we can't avoid it, but it also has to do with good and evil, as well as with greater or lesser creativity. It's up to us to draw the good from it.

As for art, I believe that no artwork should be closely wrapped up in new technologies, because then tomorrow they'll already be obsolete. We've seen this repeatedly, for example when they tried to use algorithms to create the next hit song of summer. Despite having all the information for a winning song, the machine can't come up with a new hit. There's something about humans that makes a difference, and I'm positive that, in a world increasingly governed by machines and calculations, diversity will be our most precious asset. Exactly the way it was expressed in the final scene of *Blade Runner*. It's the memory of a personal and unique experience that makes us human and, in the best of cases, worthy of remaining in history. The algorithms underpinning artificial intelligence will become more sophisticated and precise, with a computing capacity and productivity that we can't even imagine today, but they'll never be able to invent anything, unless we can teach them to make mistakes. Creativity arises from diversity, accident, a deviation from the norm. Machines will never be able to reproduce imperfections. But in the future, I'd like to be right in the black hole where science and art will finally meet.

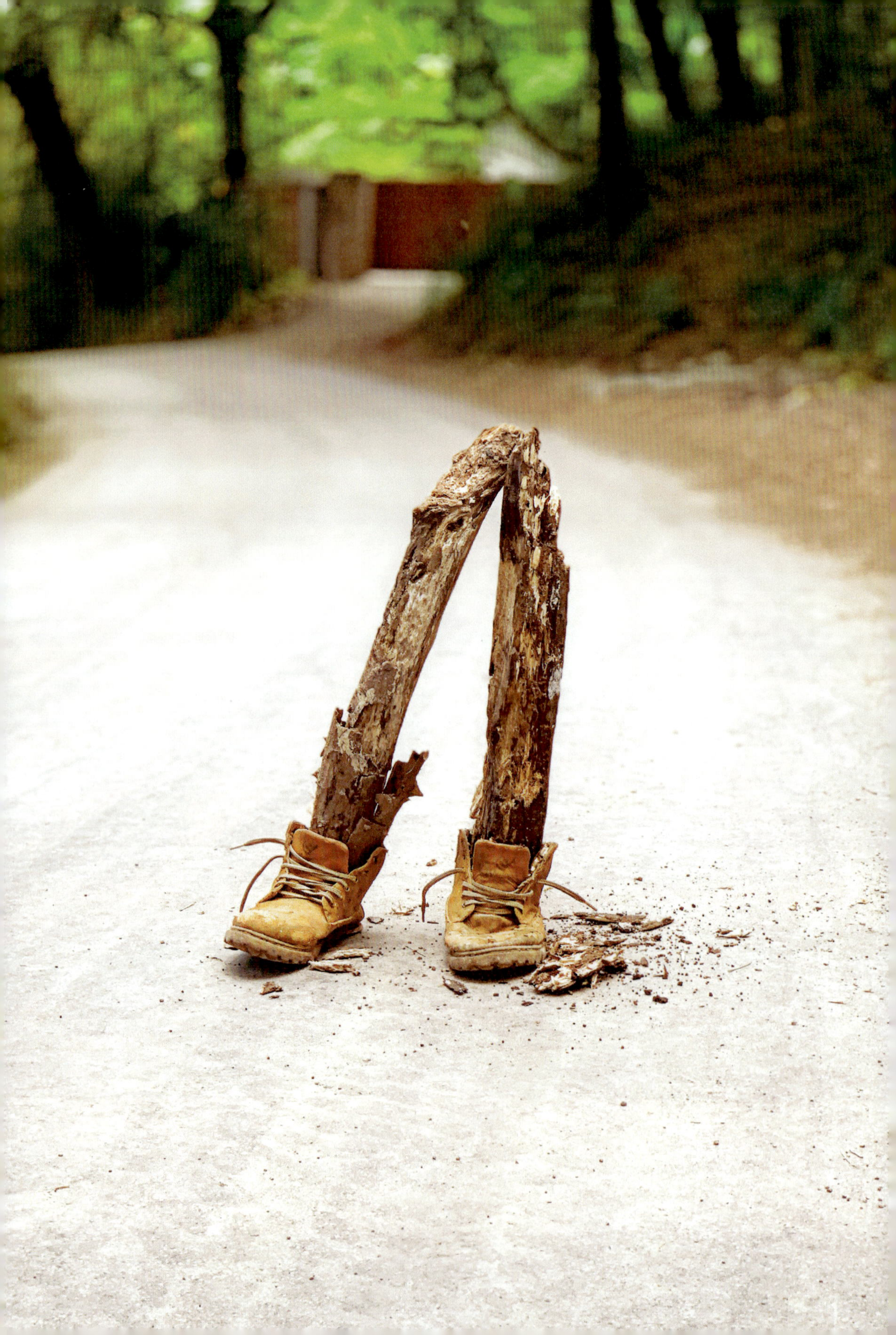

Art has always been between a pandemic and a war. The phase we're going through, seen from the perspective of art history, is just one of many terrible periods in human history. Art isn't someplace else, it's in the world. Sometimes it absorbs and reflects current affairs. Think of Picasso's *Guernica* or Goya's shocking *Black Paintings*. And at times art shuts itself up in its cubbyhole and looks out the window.

Covid has changed the world and all of us. As far as my work goes, it opened up some opportunities and closed others. It boosted dematerialization, after our societies had already been pressing on the accelerator for some time. I found its timing interesting, as if it wasn't due to a series of random events, as it actually was.

The pandemic was an opportunity to keep still. We all had to switch off for a bit, but this led us to reset certain aspects of our lives. It was a collective illness. We weren't stuck in bed, but that's the way it felt, and for a while some basic issues resurfaced—not so much the functioning of the system as a whole, but the ways we enjoy certain rights and benefits, like having a home or a job. The lockdown also taught us we don't need much, and how our attitude to work and relationships is often doped up. The only necessary creation that it taught us was of our inner spaces. Despite experiencing that drama, I hope that some people found the strength to set themselves free. Everybody needs to find their own antidotes.

Because of this possible effect, Covid was perhaps an exception. Normally viruses, attacks and acts of sabotage are only newspaper headlines or commercials; everything else goes on working indefinitely. The center of gravity shifts, we take a new blow, we lick our wounds and try to move on in another direction.

[190]  ***Father*, 2021**
Hand-painted mural
Environmental dimensions

The image of feet is one of the three I thought of during Covid, along with the one where I'm hiding behind a leaf, and the man underwater in a pool. It's a mural painted in different sizes depending on the surface available. The execution is masterly. In Seoul, where the work was made at my solo show "WE," when you went up close to it you couldn't tell that it had been painted by hand.

It's funny how this mental image was formalized in a real work. At my solo show in Beijing in 2021–22 after the third round of censorship, there wasn't much left. The space was large, and there were gaps, so I asked Francesco Bonami, who was curating the exhibition, what we could do. Then I told him: "I've been thinking about this image for a while, I haven't printed it yet and it's not a photo. I can't resolve it. Why don't we so it as a mural?" So we found the solution to the problem of the image that I couldn't turn into a work and also to the problem of the gaps in the exhibition.

The more I think about this work, the more I realize that it's an offshoot of art history, but above all it represents human frailty. This is why I chose it for my work in the Holy See Pavilion at the 60th Venice Biennale in the Giudecca prison for women. In 1999 I took part in the "Aperto" section of the Venice Biennale with a fakir who was buried in the ground for two hours with only his hands visible above the ground in the position of prayer. The work was called *Mother*. Twenty-five years later, I brought its counterpart, *Father*, to the facade of the prison chapel facing the outside.

The black and white image of the soles of a man's feet can recall Renaissance imagery, like Mantegna's *Dead Christ*, or Caravaggio's *Crucifixion of St. Peter*, or some corpse in a movie or the cover of *Abbey Road*. As for me, it brings together the few images that I've brought with me ever since childhood: my parents and the tormented relationship with authority, Catholicism and a bit of art history. Bare feet function as a synecdoche for the human body and its mortal condition. In our society, we show our bare feet when we're children and when we're dead. It's a symbol of vulnerability and a reminder of death, but also a reminder of prison, so to speak. Each of us can find ourselves in a cage, even without wanting to, or even worse without realizing it.

It's a hard thought to embrace when you're free. The decision to place the Vatican Pavilion in the Giudecca prison was very simple and at the same time amazing. It turned the spotlight on the invisible, on the people who live on the margins of society, on all those we consider distant, or keep distant. It was a compassionate gesture, and at the same time revolutionary, because it forced us to set foot in an unexplored region, to look into the eyes of people who had lost their freedom.

286

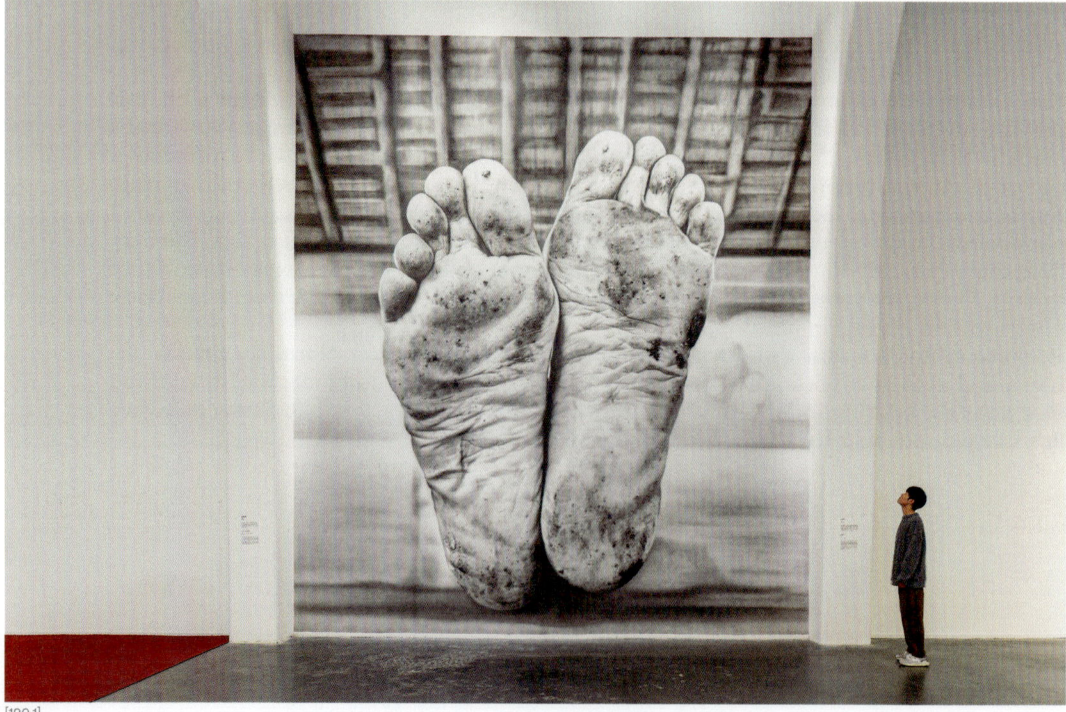

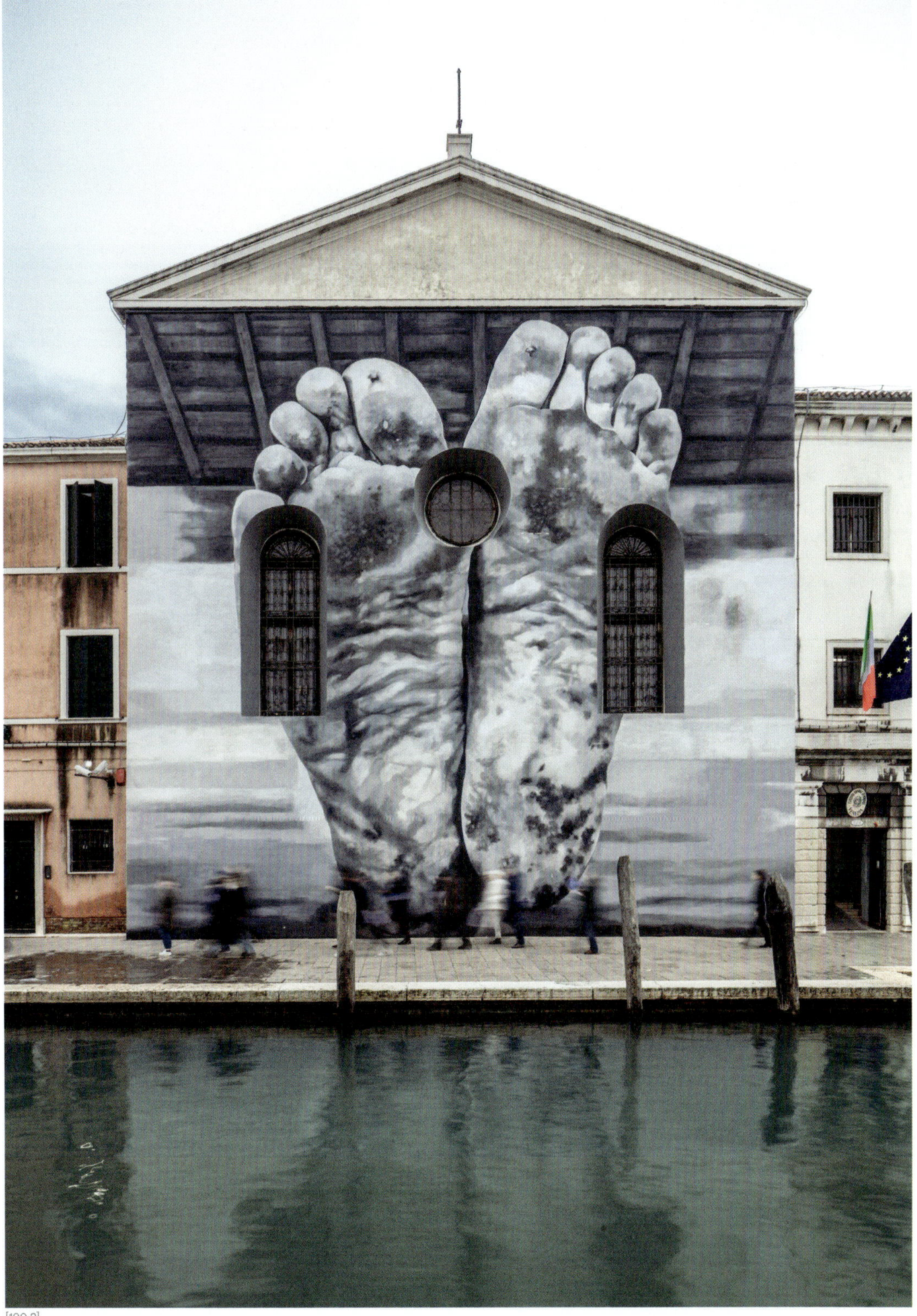

[190.2]

[190.1]   *Father*, 2021
"Maurizio Cattelan. The Last Judgment," curated by
Francesco Bonami, UCCA Center for Contemporary Art,
Beijing, November 20, 2021–February 20, 2022 (solo show)

[190.2]   *Father*, 2021
"Con i miei occhi," curated by Chiara Parisi and Bruno
Racine, 60th Venice Biennale, April 20–November 24,
2024 (group show), Holy See Pavilion, installation at the
Casa di Reclusione Femminile di Venezia-Giudecca

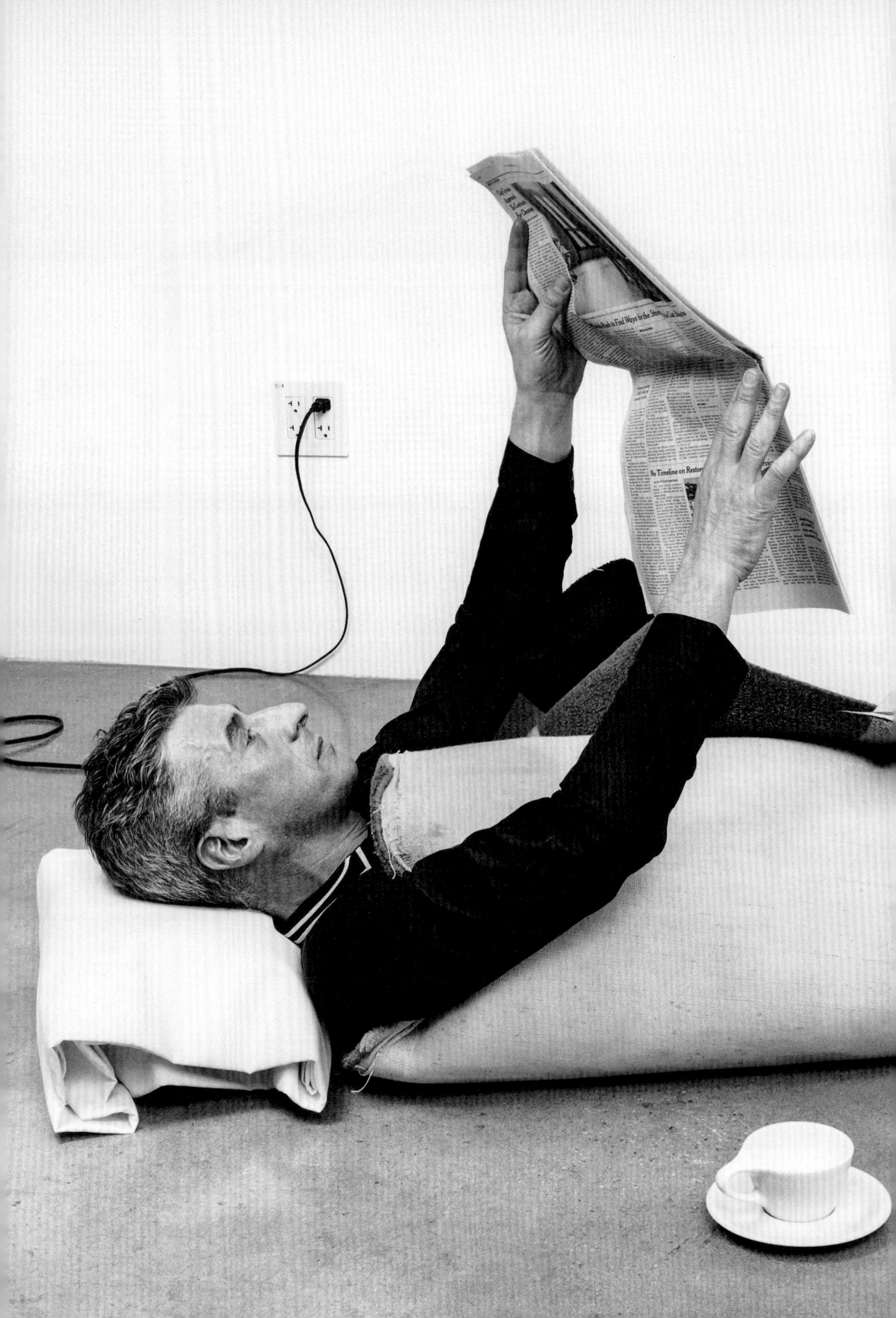

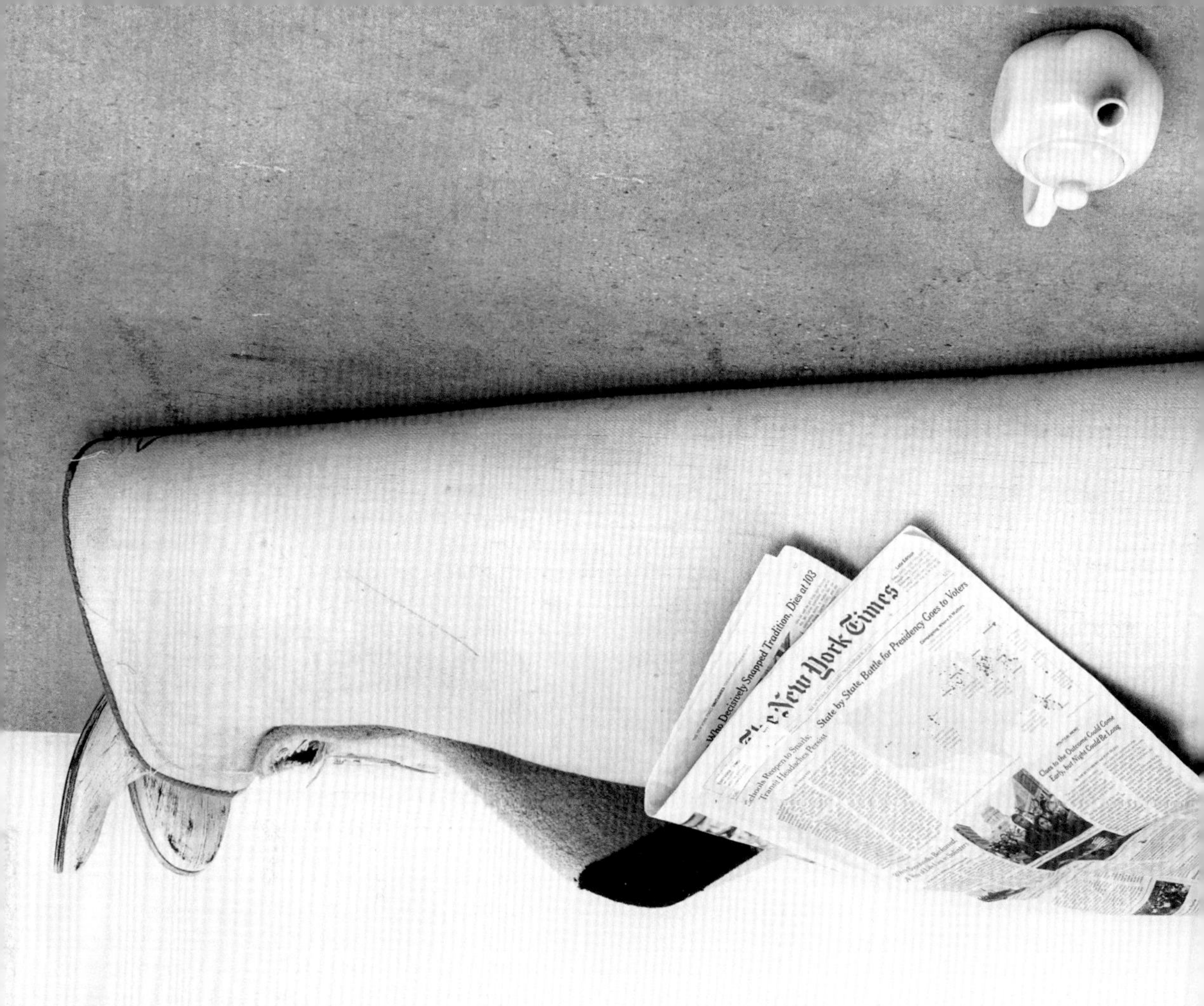
The New York Times
State by State, Battle for Presidency Goes to Voters
Clues to the Outcome Could Come Early, but Night Could Be Long
Schools Reopen to Snarls, Transit Headaches Persist
Who Decisively Snapped Tradition, Dies at 103

Maurizio Cattelan portrayed by Craig McDean, November 2012

290

I believe that everything is a political act and no speech is neutral. Art is no exception: art is political and there's no way it could be otherwise, because life is political. But I admit that the idea scares me, because there's a risk that art could become propaganda for one or another ideology, at that point ceasing to speak to everyone. If artistic expression is reduced to a political message, the only effect is to debase it. Many artworks that are considered political end up being didactic and obvious, like kicking an open door. In any case, I think that the works of all artists are political, because they express a person's viewpoint. Living in a society, the artist offers an indication, an interpretation of that same society.

I think that art still has the power to deal with complex issues and express them simply and immediately, but never simplistically. How to manage this is the challenge that every artist should feel called on to face. The problem is that no one believes in politics anymore. I'm concerned about the effect of the toxic tensions on the integrity of contemporary society. The only way to make people believe in politics is to shock them with an image. I think that, when you look at works like *Him* (2001) or *La Nona Ora* (1999), the accuracy of the garments and the way the work is perfectly detailed down to the clothes is part of the effect it has on the viewer.

So even my art, although deeply personal, is political. After all, as a feminist slogan put it, the personal is political. In fact, as far as I'm concerned, the most naturally political action is to think and work through art. Sometimes I'm afraid I'm being too metaphorical. There's often been a sensationalist media rumpus around my works that has prevented their interpretation in depth, going beyond a joke. I feel that the same thing happens in politics: we read statements in block lettering about the major scandals, but we rarely examine the political platforms. The result is a superficial analysis of the contents. This applies precisely to both art and politics.

On the other hand, politics has become a great trivializing machine that moves around supposedly opposite poles, contrasting black and white, and voters have become ultras filled with hatred. Politics is increasingly a performative activity. I don't think it's a coincidence that in a number of countries showmen have become politicians. Berlusconi was the father of all the Trumpisms in this. On the other hand, comparing Trump's rallies to a performance would mean underestimating him: he combines Berlusconi's jokey performativity with extreme right-wing hatred. I believe that voting is a fundamental step in democracy, the most important expression of everyone's will, but it's also an assumption of responsibility. It means being responsible for a choice. If today most people are a prey to the most vulgar populisms, the candidates are unfortunately nothing more than the expression of the voters' choices. I'm struck by the lack of a spontaneous response, the apparent inability to take to the streets and react. From the era of ideologies we seem to have fallen into the ice age. We've become the spectators of our own ruin. Paraphrasing the title of a 1972 work by Joseph Beuys, today we could say: "We are the crisis." It seems not to concern us directly, yet we're the people that are drowning. In reality, perhaps it's the methods that need to change, not so much the people, but I don't see any changes in this respect. Ideally, I'm fascinated by the potential of direct democracy. We can express our preferences by televoting in reality shows and talent shows, but not on the really important issues. We have out-of-the-box technology, yet we still hide in voting booths every five years. It's as if we needed to communicate something urgently and sent a registered letter instead of using WhatsApp.

[191]    ***Untitled*, 1994**
Photocopy, spray paint
450 × 600 cm

For the solo exhibition at the Galerie Daniel Buchholz in Cologne in December 1994, I took up a wall with an enlargement of two pages of the Catholic newspaper *Avvenire* for March 19, 1978. This was the day when all the newspapers published the first photo of Aldo Moro as a prisoner of the Red Brigades. I exhibited the work together with the mice and the Bel Paese cheese (*I Found My Love in Portofino*, 1994). The pages became a kind of wallpaper. In ink I'd added the tail of a comet to the star symbol of the terrorist group. Both works were a reflection on the stereotypes and conflicts that Italy was experiencing.
I then reused the comet-star in one of the Christmas cards, the neon one (*Christmas '95*, 1995).

[191.1]    *Untitled*, 1994
"Maurizio Cattelan," Galerie Daniel Buchholz, Cologne, December 15, 1994–January 22, 1995 (solo show)

[191.2]    *Untitled*, 1994

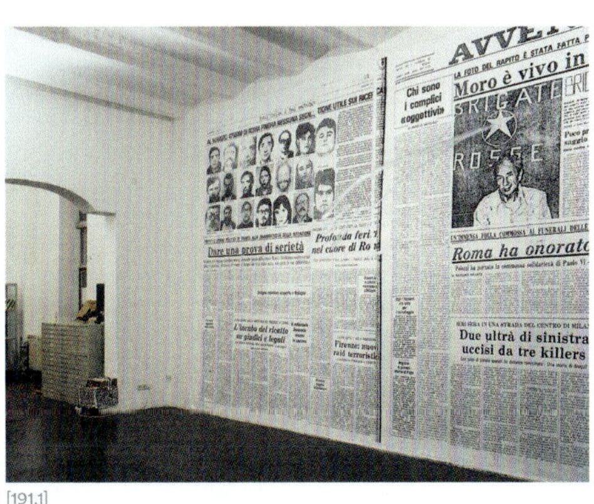

[191.1]

291

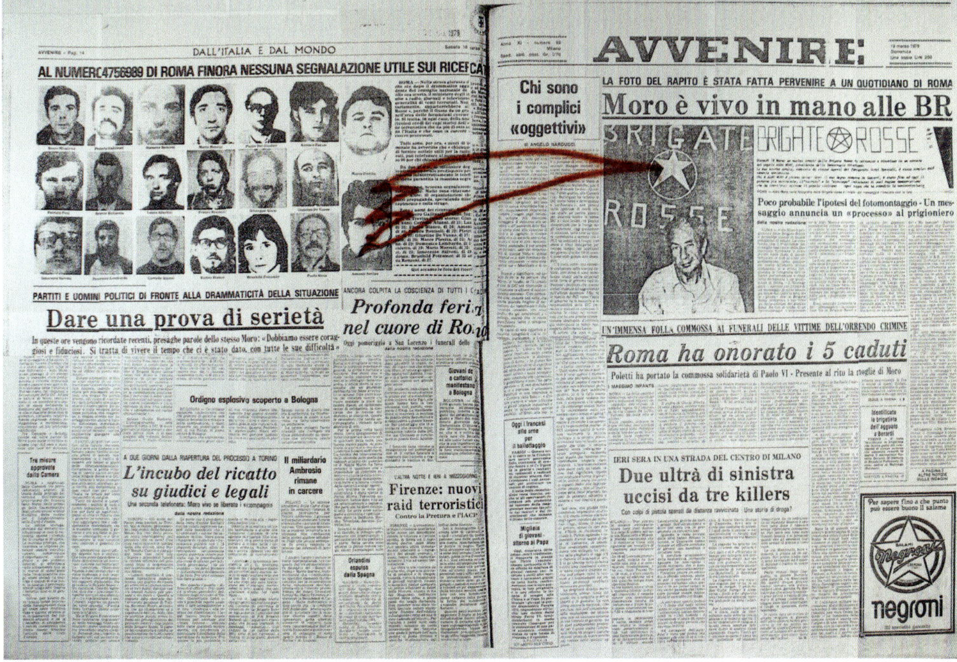

[191.2]

[192] **Andreas e Mattia, 1996**
Stuffed cloth, clothing, shoes

[193] **Kenneth, 1998**
Plastic, clothing, shoes, blanket

[194] **Gérard, 1999**
Plastic, clothing, shoes, blanket
82 × 66 × 87 cm

[195] **Jean-Pierre, 1999**
Stuffed figure, clothing, shoes, blanket
45.7 × 83.8 × 148 cm

[196] **Steve, 2002**
Silicone rubber, blanket, clothes, shoes,
steel

[197] **Tom, 2019**
Clothes, shoes, fabric

[198] **Donghoon, 2023**
Clothes, shoes, fabric

[199] **Junho, 2023**
Wood, polystyrene, stainless steel,
clothing, shoes, accessories
75 × 85 × 115 cm

I like all the little stories behind my works. They make them more alive. I like faces and legends more than I like artworks. In 1998 I did a project on the campus of the University of Wisconsin, Milwaukee, for its Institute of Visual Arts. The project engendered a long story, almost a novel. When I arrived, first I wanted to show a series of films, stealing them from the university cinema. But something went wrong with the equipment, so I had to come up with a new idea in a couple of days. I decided to build a sculpture out of rags and old clothes. It was the effigy of a homeless man: *Kenneth*. I left the poor guy near one of the campus buildings. The next morning it turns out that someone had attached a sign to my sculpture, complaining about the increase in university fees. Homelessness had become a kind of symbol of a struggle I knew nothing about. After that, the neighbors started complaining about my work, and finally someone stole the sculpture, leaving only its shoes. So the police took over the situation, with the officers looking for a missing sculpture. A perfect plot. The police found two different sculptural pop-ups, with a sign that said something like: "We don't need an Italian to teach us what art is."

Actually, when I first made this piece, in 1996 in Italy, when it was called *Andreas e Mattia*, I received some really different reactions. It was another story but with the same characters: the police, some neighbors, a homeless man. Some people got angry and called the police to complain that no one was taking care of this poor old man on the street. So they went to check on his condition, and began to shake him, saying: "Hey, hey, wake up! It's time to go." And when he didn't move, they thought: "Oh God, he's dead!"

Sometimes I like the idea of taking these stories a step further and creating a sequel. I thought of a work that I could do in Buenos Aires that would involve setting up ten or twenty of these fake beggars around the city early in the morning, and then gathering them at the end of the day and collecting the money they'd received.

In doing these pieces, I didn't express any particular fear of being homeless. I was just interested in the dynamics that exist when you walk past someone sleeping in the street. Basically, you ignore them, but at the same time, you can't help noticing them. There is this funny contrast between your instinctive reaction and your eventual decision. In a way it's not very different from walking around an exhibition. There's a strange sense of detachment from what you see, and yet there you are.

[192]  *Andreas e Mattia*, 1996
"Campo 6. Il villaggio a spirale," curated by Francesco Bonami, Galleria Civica d'Arte Moderna e Contemporanea, Turin, September 28–November 3, 1996 (group show), installation outside the museum

[193]  *Kenneth*, 1998
"Maurizio Cattelan, Kelly Wood, Erwin Wurm," Institute of Visual Arts, University of Wisconsin, Milwaukee, March 13–May 3, 1998 (group show)

[194]  *Gérard*, 1999



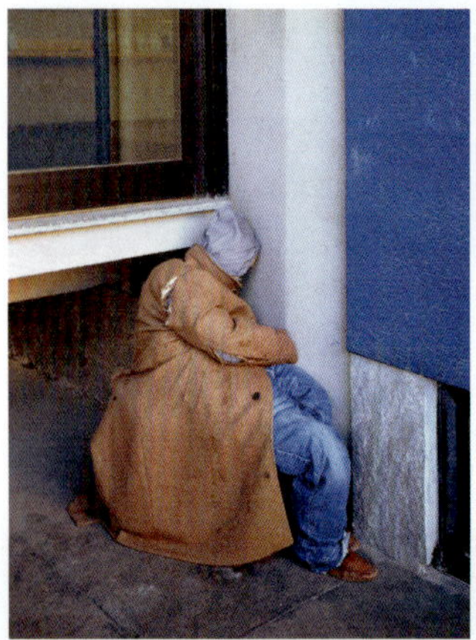

[192]

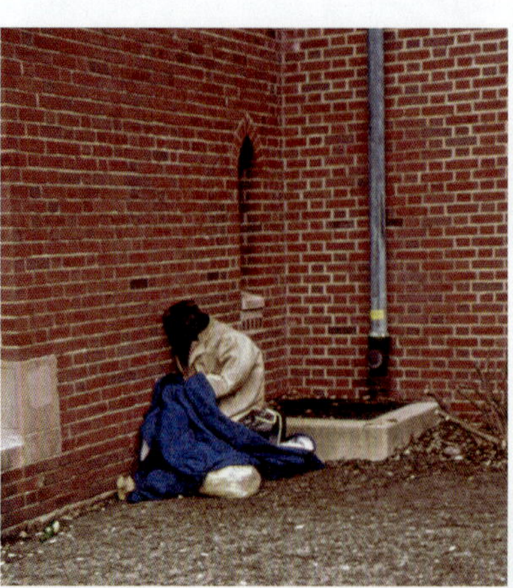

[193]

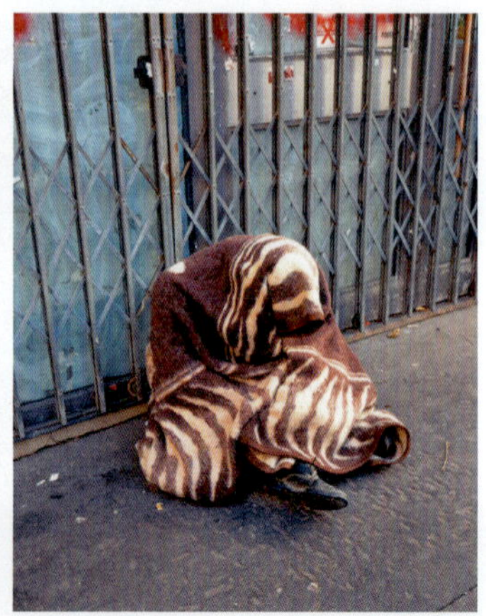

[194]

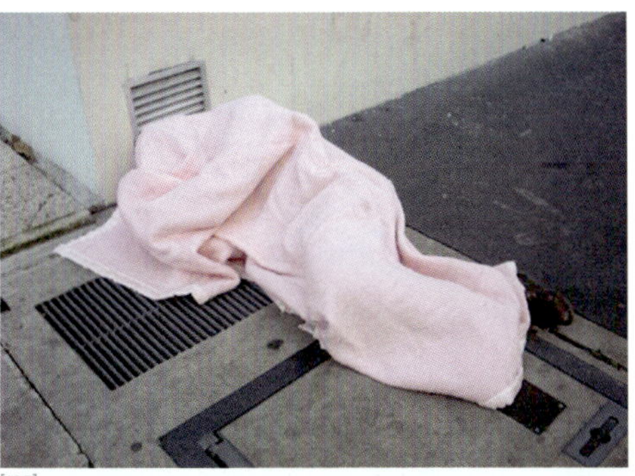

[195]

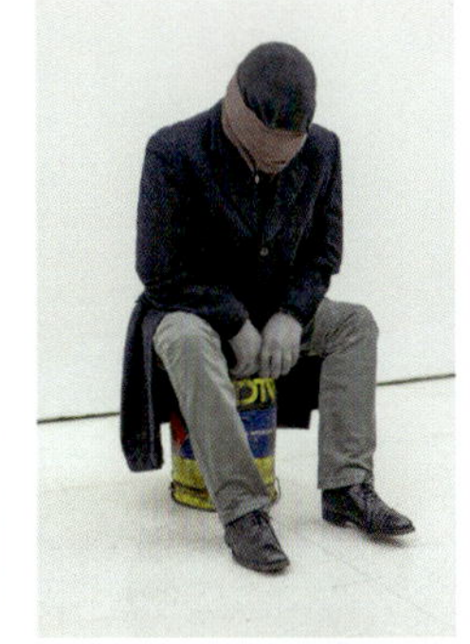

[196]



[195]   *Jean-Pierre*, 1999

[196]   *Steve*, 2002
"Maurizio Cattelan. All,"
curated by Nancy Spector,
Solomon R. Guggenheim
Museum, New York,
November 4, 2011–January
22, 2012 (solo show)

[197]   *Tom*, 2019, and
*Others*, 2011 [239]
"Victory Is Not An Option,"
curated by Michael
Frahm, Blenheim Palace,
Woodstock, United
Kingdom, September 12–
October 27, 2019
(solo show)

[198]   *Donghoon*, 2023
"WE," curated by Sungwon
Kim, Leeum Museum of
Art, Seoul, January 31–July
16, 2023 (solo show)

[199]   *Junho*, 2023
"WE," curated by Sungwon
Kim, Leeum Museum of
Art, Seoul, January 31–July
16, 2023 (solo show)

293

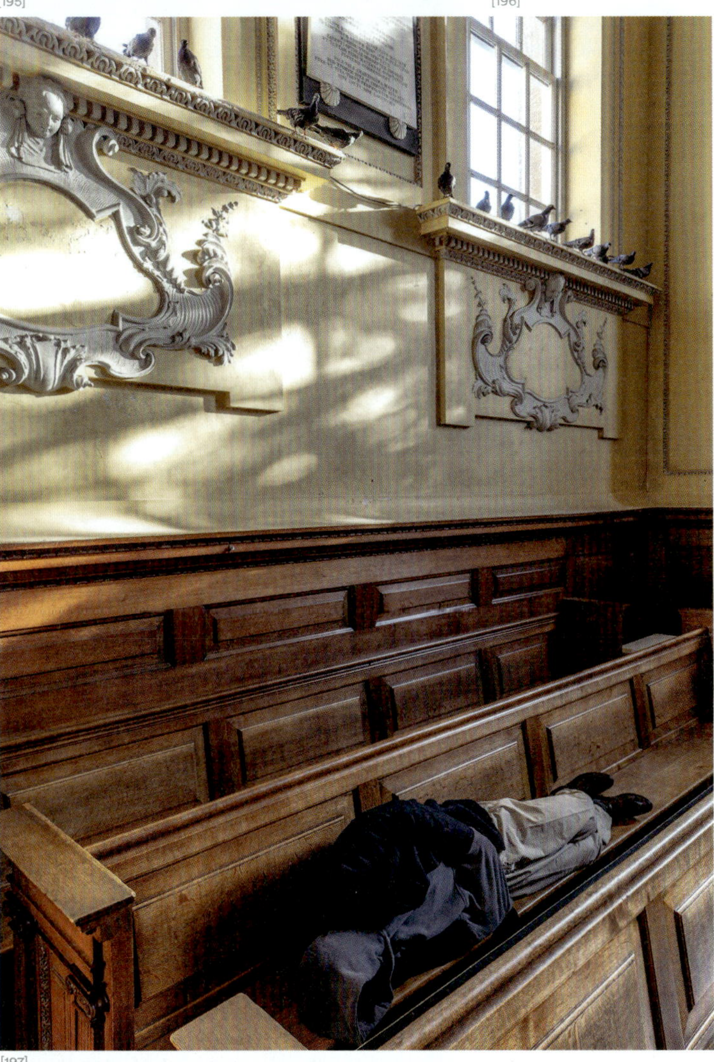

[197]

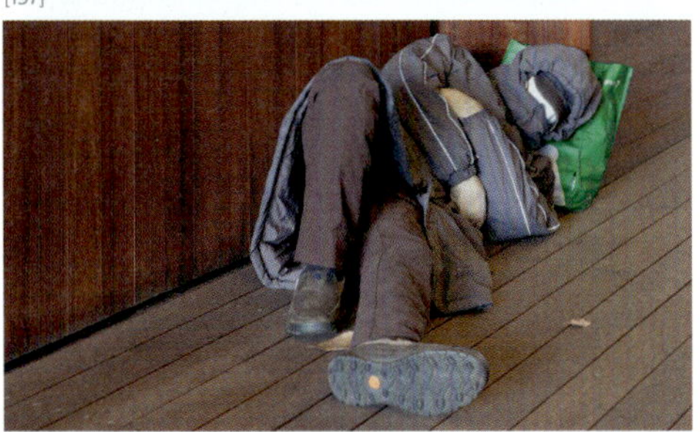

[198]

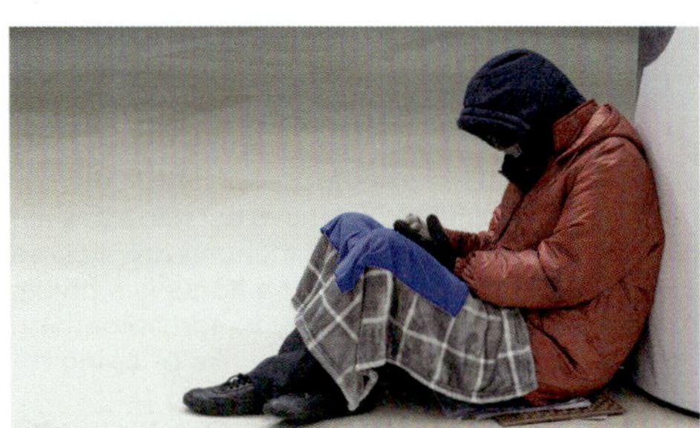

[199]

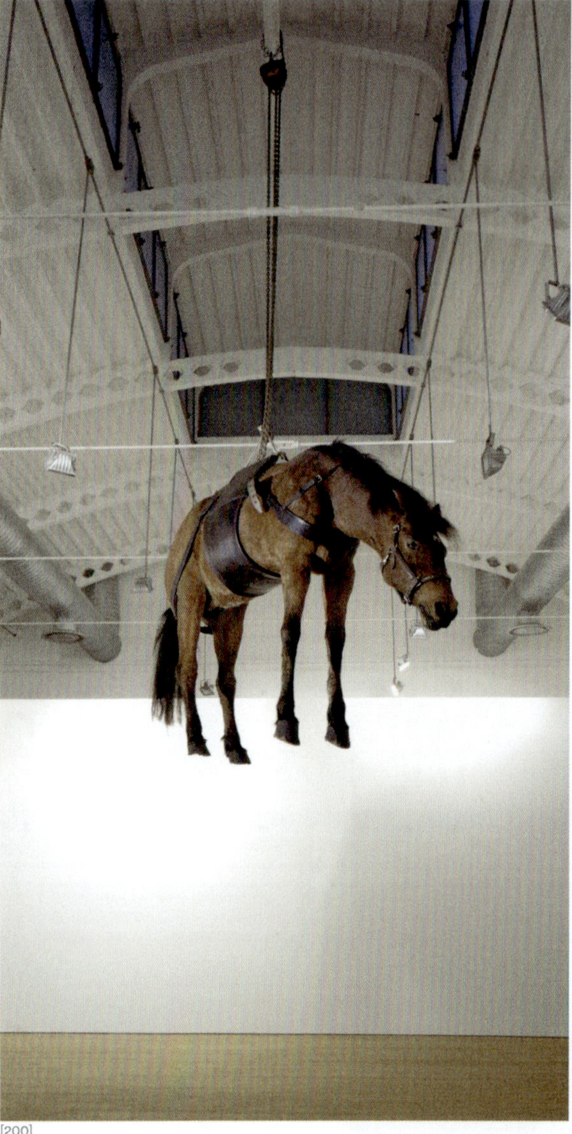

[200] **Untitled, 1996**
[Initially titled: *La Ballata di Trotsky*]
Taxidermied horse, leather saddlery,
rope, pulley
223 × 265 × 85 cm

[201] **Novecento, 1997**
Taxidermied horse, leather saddle, rope
200 × 270 × 70 cm

[202] **Untitled, 2007**
Taxidermized horse
370 × 170 × 80 cm

The horse has been a subject of art since the beginning of humankind. You have horses in prehistoric caves, in paintings, in monuments, and so on. Everybody might say that a horse is a horse, but you can always find a way to add something that will open someone's eyes. I like bringing together different types of emotions.
The horse is a classic subject. I think it's honest

to say that my work has roots, and I really like Kounellis' work. Like him, for *Novecento* I tried to have a live horse, but it was too difficult.
What strikes me whenever I install *Novecento* is the condition of desperation and helplessness it conveys. In art history, the horse is a symbol of dynamic vigor and strength and the embodiment of human empowerment. Immobilizing it suspended from the ceiling turns it into a monument to the frustration that comes from the inability to act, a very human condition. It was actually another self-portrait, since I was in a period where I had a lot of energy but I couldn't do anything with it. It was like having a very good car with the engine revved up, but in neutral. And at that time Italy was in the middle of trying to clean up its politics, to get rid of all the corrupt politicians to make room for new corrupt politicians.
The horse is between earth and sky, and it's trying to reach the floor. The year before *Novecento*, in 1996, I had made two other versions, one of which was entitled *La Ballata di Trotsky* (today

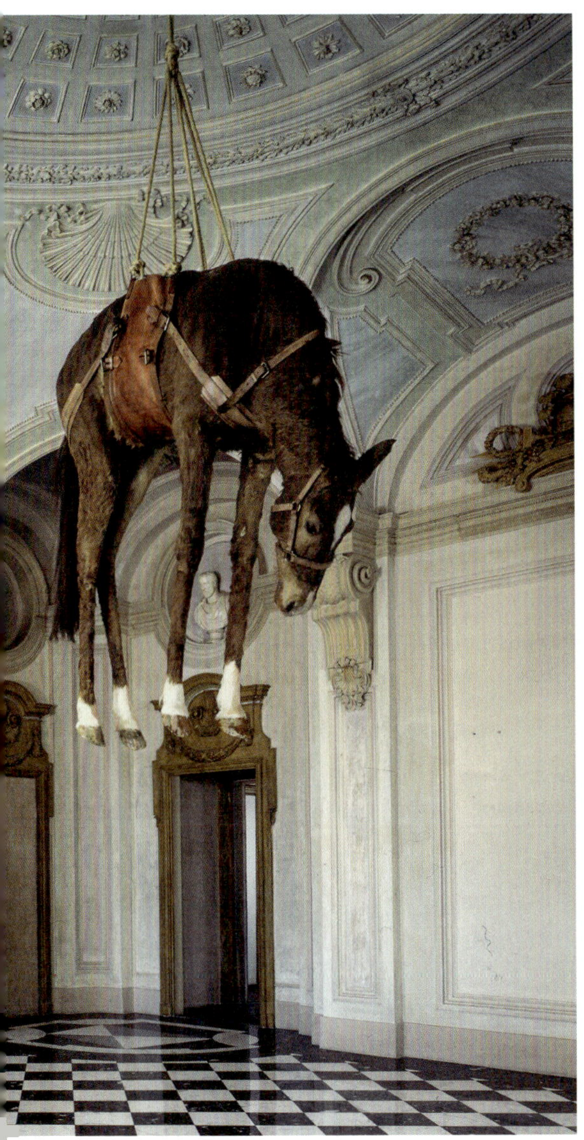

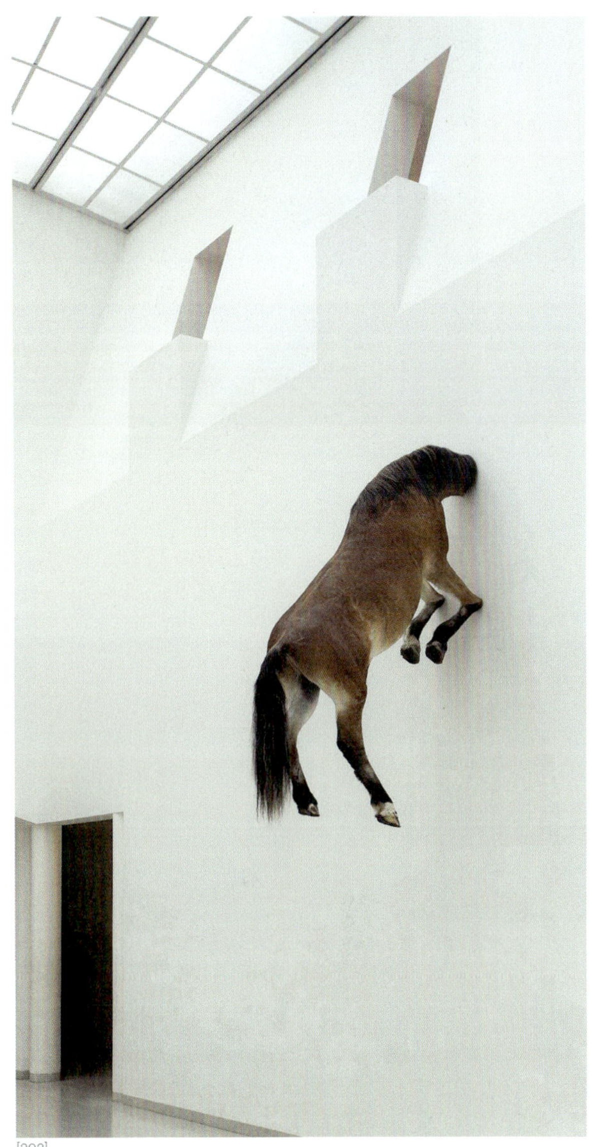

[202]

*Untitled*). I'd had that horse's legs stretched, so it was somehow pulled towards the floor. It was as if there was a magnetic force coming from the ground.
I lost many friends because of *Novecento*. My work was going along one line, and then a different line arrived shifting it to a completely different level. It was like discovering a new tool. You gain something but you lose something else. With *Novecento* I found a new audience and lost the underground one that probably wasn't taking me anywhere. This work is more mature, fuller and less didactic. It touches on a number of things at once and it's actually difficult to say what it's about. It was less obvious than the previous works.

[200]  *Untitled*, 1996
"Maurizio Cattelan," Galleria Massimo De Carlo, Milan, February 16–March 1996 (solo show)

[201]  *Novecento*, 1997
Castello di Rivoli Museo d'Arte Contemporanea, Rivoli-Turin

[202]  *Untitled*, 2007
"Maurizio Cattelan," curated by Andreas Bee and Udo Kittelmann, MMK – Museum Für Moderne Kunst, Frankfurt, March 1–September 23, 2007 (solo show)

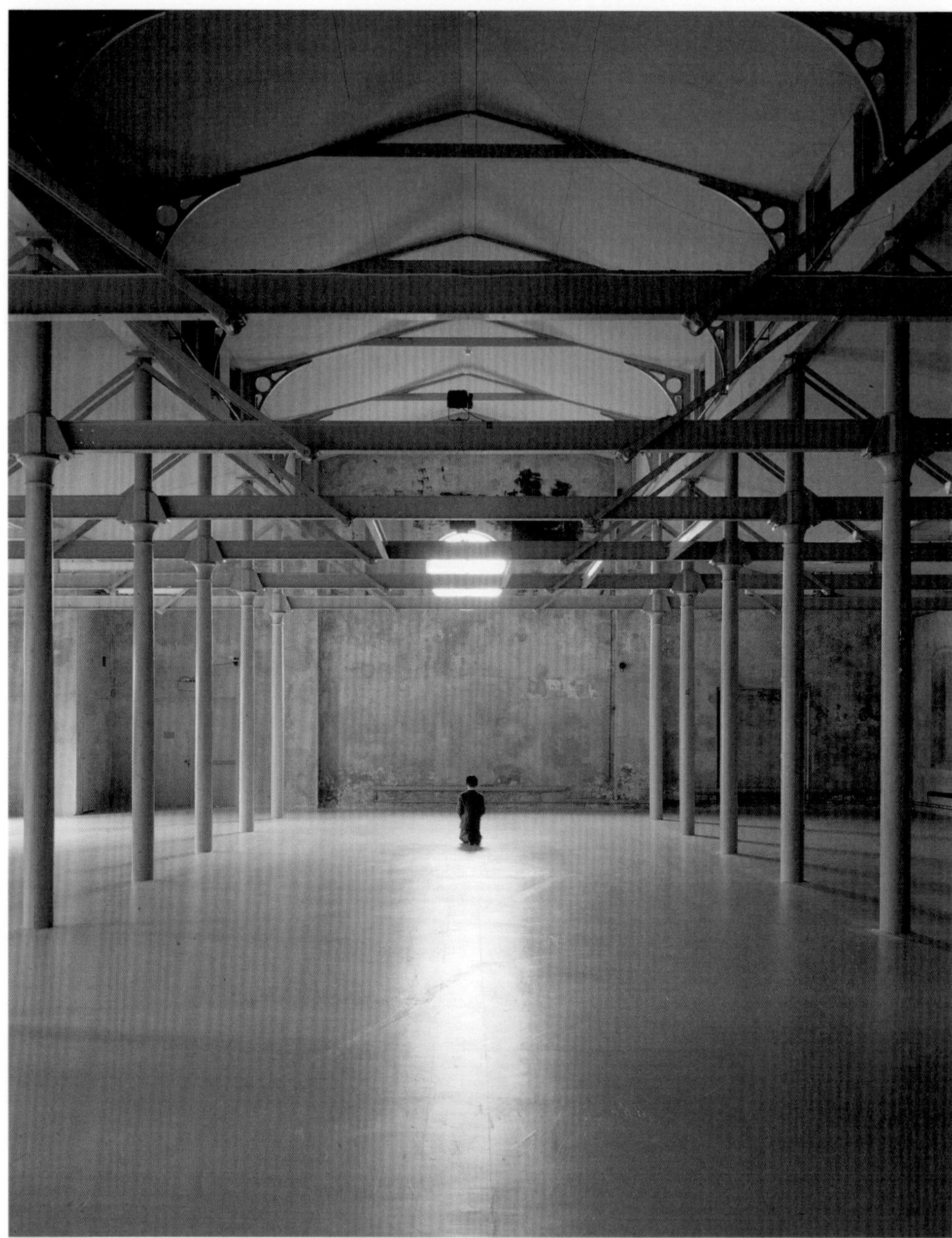

[203.1]



**[203]** *Him*, **2001**
Polyester resin, wax, pigment, natural
hair, suit, boots
100 × 40 × 67 cm

I wanted to represent absolute evil, without knowing how to do it. I'd been invited to an exhibition in Sweden. I thought of the country's ambivalent position during World War II: it was the right place for a difficult work. The figure of Hitler asserted itself. It took me a year to fulfill the task.

We'd made some images to show what the work would look like and how I wanted it to be positioned. But due to delays in the production, which was done in Paris, I didn't see it done until the day before the opening. I was ready to de-stroy it if it didn't strike me as right. Sometimes you're seduced by an idea, but that doesn't mean the result will be equally good. When I opened the packing case I realized that it worked. I saw it went beyond simple provocation and could trigger some reflections on human nature. After all, art is meant to do this. Why is he kneeling? Because it works. Why is he praying? Because it works. Because it's a shock.

At first I thought the figure should be naked, like the emperor in the folktale. I changed my mind a thousand times, every day. Hitler is an image that is frightening. It's still painful to think about him. He's become a part of our memory and yet he's still taboo. Hitler is unmentionable, irreproducible, wrapped in a blanket of silence. I wasn't trying to trigger a conflict or offend anyone. I just wanted that image to become a point where we could meet or a litmus test of our psychoses.

*Him* is mostly about fear. It's a symbol of fear, an icon of fear. You don't know if this Hitler is praying for another six million people to kill or for forgiveness. It's wrong, but it's not wrong. I don't know what the Bible or other sacred texts say, but a Catholic should forgive even the most horrible sins. The work functions silently. In the images he's only Hitler, but when you have him in front of you it's as if you want to give him another chance. *Him* has traveled widely, and its presence has aroused violent reactions each time, almost as if it were Hitler himself traveling around Europe. The evocative power of that image is incredible, and whenever you come face to face with evil you learn something. It's a warning, and God only knows how much we need it in the times we're living in.

[203.1]  *Him*, 2001
"Maurizio Cattelan. Him," Färgfabriken, Stockholm, February 10–April 4, 2001 (solo show)

[203.2]  *Him*, 2001



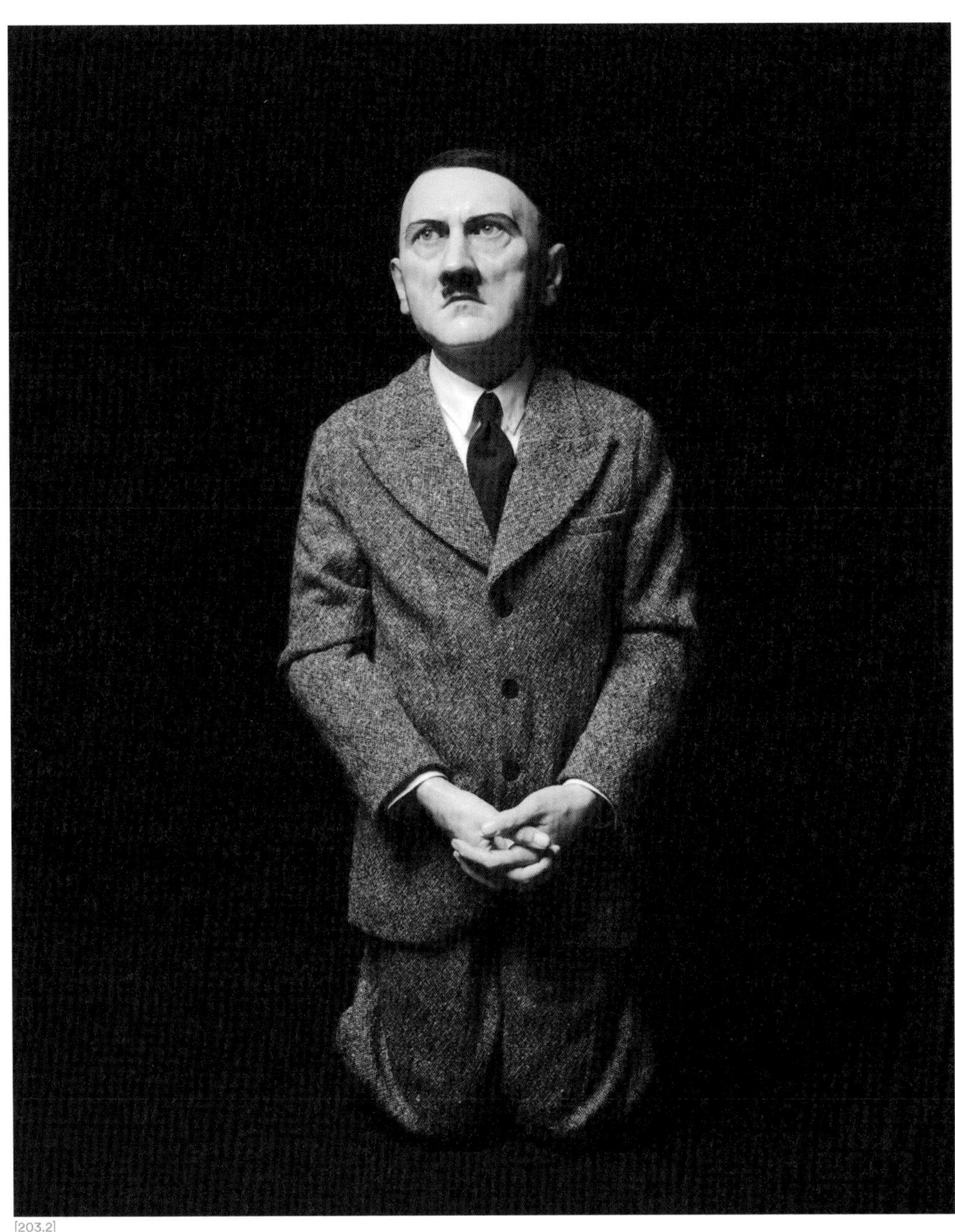

[203.2]

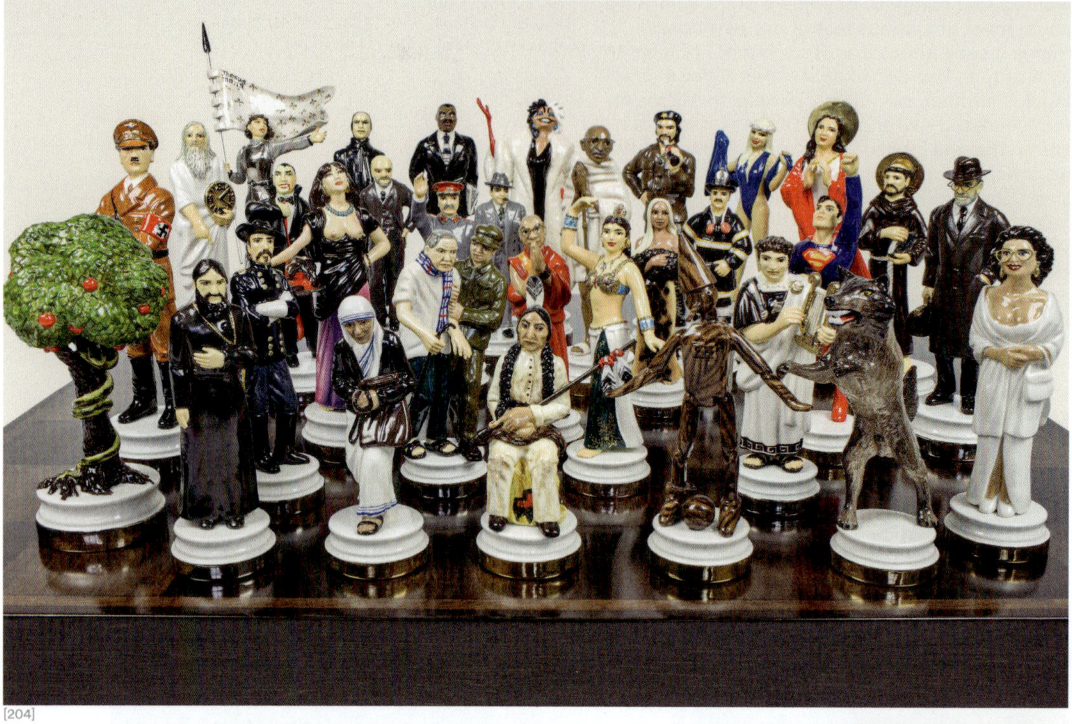

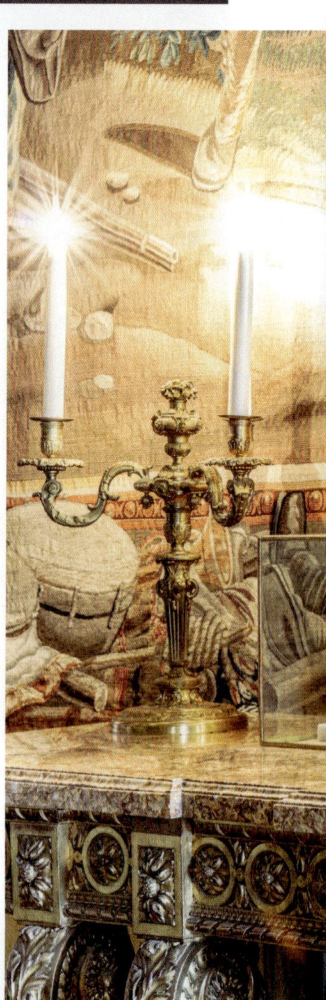

[204]



[204]   ***Good Versus Evil*, 2003**
32 hand-painted porcelain figures, wood,
chessboard, travel case

The pieces in this work are a chess set. A creative
agency in London, RS&A, with various friends in
the art world, invited a series of artists, such as
Yayoi Kusama, Damien Hirst, Rachel Whiteread,
and Barbara Kruger, to do a project together.
They identified chess as the unifying theme and
the result was very fine. We all exhibited together in a show at Luhring Augustine in New York in
2005. I developed the work using ceramics and
depicting figures of the most disparate types,
both imaginary and real, contrasting good and
evil in a final clash. Some figures, though, are un-
classifiable, such as Freud, who is on both sides.
Of course, I didn't make the pieces, which I commissioned from the ceramists Bertozzi & Casoni.

[205]   ***Untitled*, 2009**
Polyurethane rubber, steel
51 × 38 × 18 cm

[206]   ***Untitled*, 2019**
24 karat gold-plated brass
49 × 40.5 × 18 cm

In both versions of this work you can see the
shape of a human head. In the first I generated
it from a black rubber boot, which in Italy might
recall a fascist uniform. I made the gilded variant for the exhibition at Blenheim Palace: history
teaches us that the abuse of power is good at
hiding itself, even by changing its appearance.

[206]

[204]  *Good Versus Evil*, 2003

[205]  *Untitled*, 2009
Private office, Milan

[206]  *Untitled*, 2019
"Victory Is Not An Option,"
curated by Michael
Frahm, Blenheim Palace,
Woodstock, United
Kingdom, September
12–October 27, 2019
(solo show)

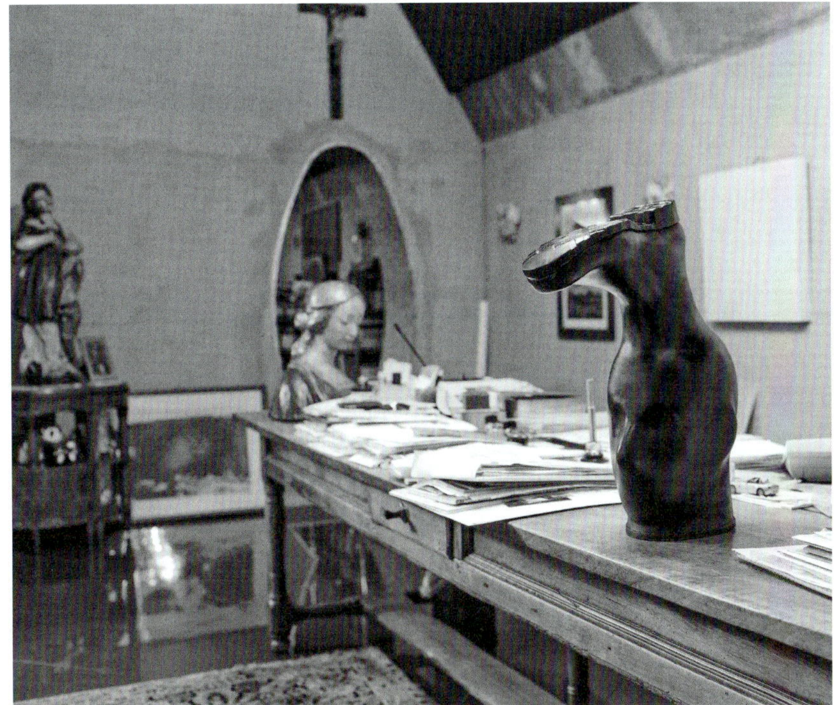
[205]

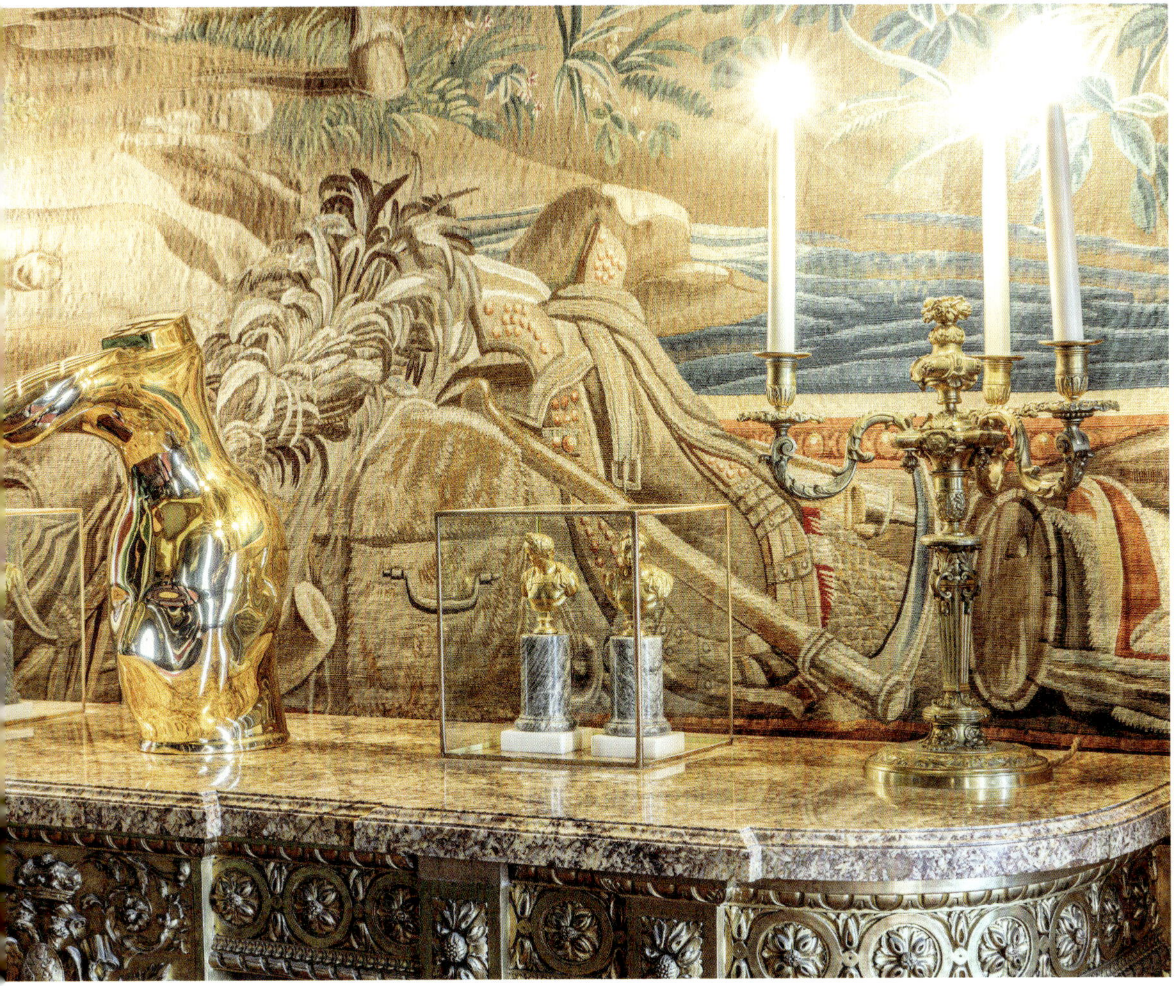

**[207]** *America*, 2016
18 karat gold
48 × 35.6 × 65 cm

*America* was the work that helped me get back on track without selling out.

When I started thinking about this work, in 2015, Donald Trump was just one of many candidates in the 2015 presidential election, and his victory seemed impossible. The social condition that my work grew out of is the same that gave rise to Trump as a politician. They were generated by the same inequality. By making an object that was unattainable for almost everyone universally usable, *America* gave everyone the same opportunity, so somehow exemplifying the American dream.

A toilet is a place that everyone uses in their daily routine. When I started thinking about the work, that point was very inspirational. No matter what you eat, whether it's a 200-dollar lunch or a 2-dollar hot dog, the result is the same, seen from the toilet bowl. Then came the material. Gold is the religious material *par excellence*, as well as the very essence of capitalist culture. I laughed at the idea, talked about it with some friends and we joked about it. I then realized that it could be interesting to combine the rarest material with the commonest place. *America* would be a great leveler. For a brief, intimate moment, the 99% would have the opportunity to enjoy a privilege exclusive to the 1%.

But the work was a two-edged sword. It held out an essential promise of the American dream—access to opportunities and better conditions for all—and at the same time it embodied what is unattainable for most people. From the wall to the pedestal and from the pedestal to the toilet, *America* offered the opportunity of being one to one with the ultimate cult object, the artwork in its sacred setting, the museum. It was about experiencing a spiritual moment of pure solitary contemplation in the least obvious part of an institution, something that doesn't happen that often.

I hope that the future owner of *America* uses it for what it is, so fulfilling its significance as a work of art. I don't know if it's true, but I heard a story about Marcel Duchamp being pestered by a relative to give her one of his works. In the end Duchamp agreed and gave her a book to hang outside the window. The work was the book hanging outside the window. If the owner brought the book inside to show it off, then it wasn't a work of art anymore. I think much the same about *America*. If it hasn't been used, it regresses to a simple expensive toilet, not a work of art. Duchamp's urinal needed to be taken out of its context, but now that cycle is over, with its return to its original place, the toilet.

At the Guggenheim there was a line from morning till night outside the bathroom with *America* for the whole year it was shown. I never managed to use it. The toilet was always occupied, and before the opening I was traveling. I believe the first person to use it was the plumber, to test it. When I arrived it was already late, the line was too long. I hoped I would be luckier at Blenheim Palace, where *America* was installed in 2019 for my solo show. Churchill was born there. It was installed in his bathroom, a very humble place compared to the rest of the building. The morning after the opening dinner, Michael Frahm, the curator of the exhibition, called me to say that *America* had been stolen. At first I thought it was a joke. It took me a while, after some checks, to come to the conclusion that it was the truth, not some surreal film in which, instead of the crown jewels, the thieves left with a damn toilet. Many of my works had been vandalized or thrown in the trash by mistake, but I'd never experienced the "loss" of one of them before. Being in a movie was new to me.

There's another story about *America*. When the White House asked the Guggenheim for the loan of a Van Gogh in 2017, Nancy Spector rec-

300

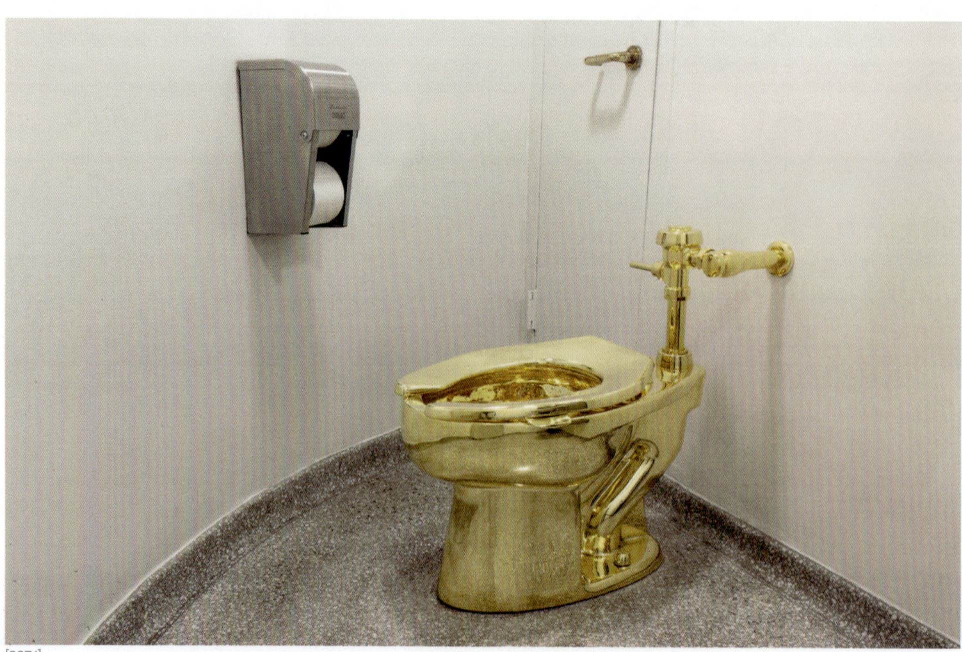

[207.1]

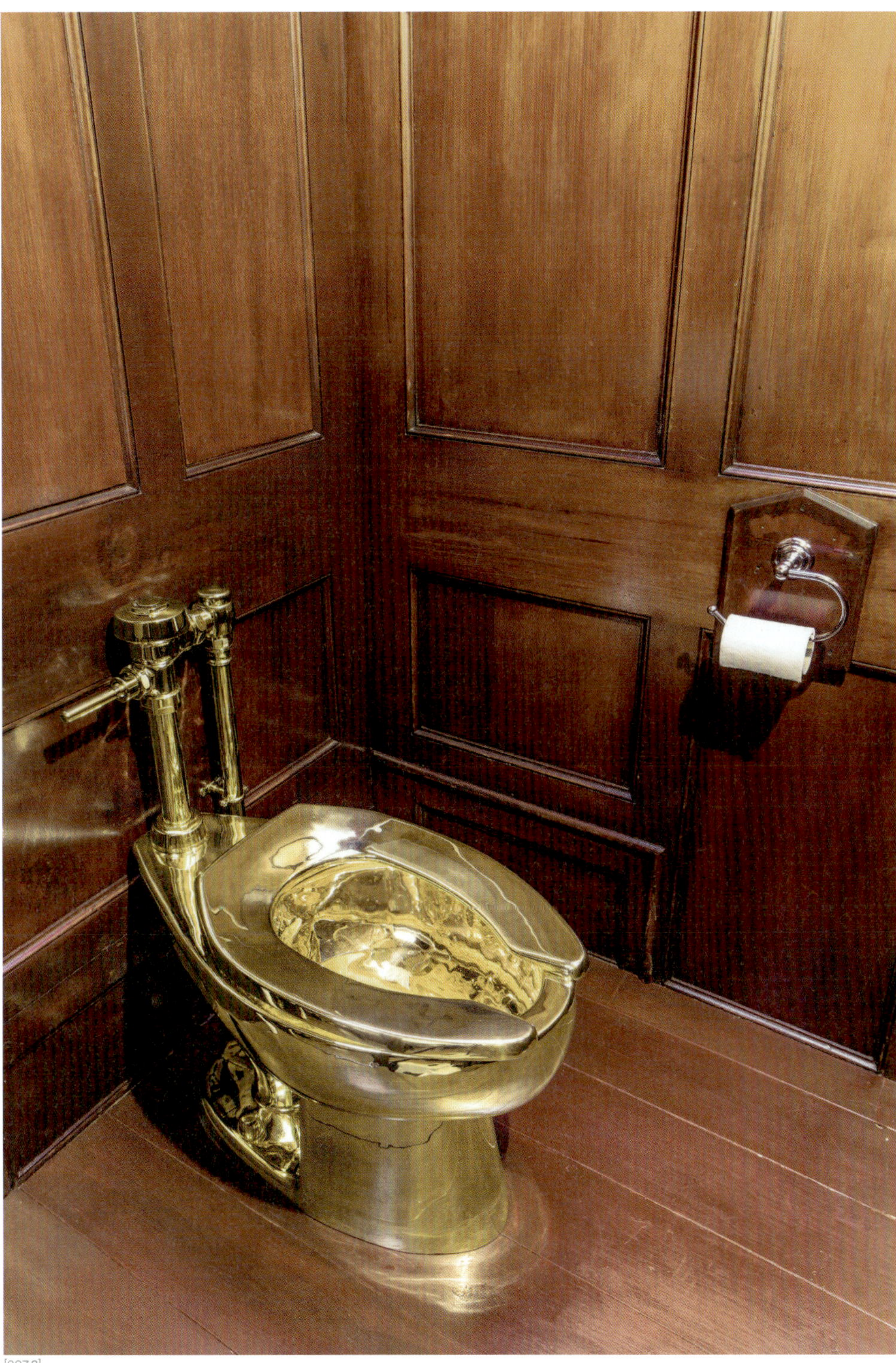

[207.2]



[207.1]    *America*, 2016
"Maurizio Cattelan. America," Solomon R. Guggenheim Museum, New York, September 15, 2016–September 15, 2017, installation in the museum's public bathrooms

[207.2]    *America*, 2016
"Victory Is Not An Option," curated by Michael Frahm, Blenheim Palace, Woodstock, United Kingdom, September 12–October 27, 2019 (solo show)

ommended *America* instead. Nancy is a great curator with a really sharp mind. She had the right to suggest any work from the collection, and I would have been honored to have my work exhibited in a prestigious place like the White House. But Trump refused. I'm sure Churchill would have had a better sense of humor.

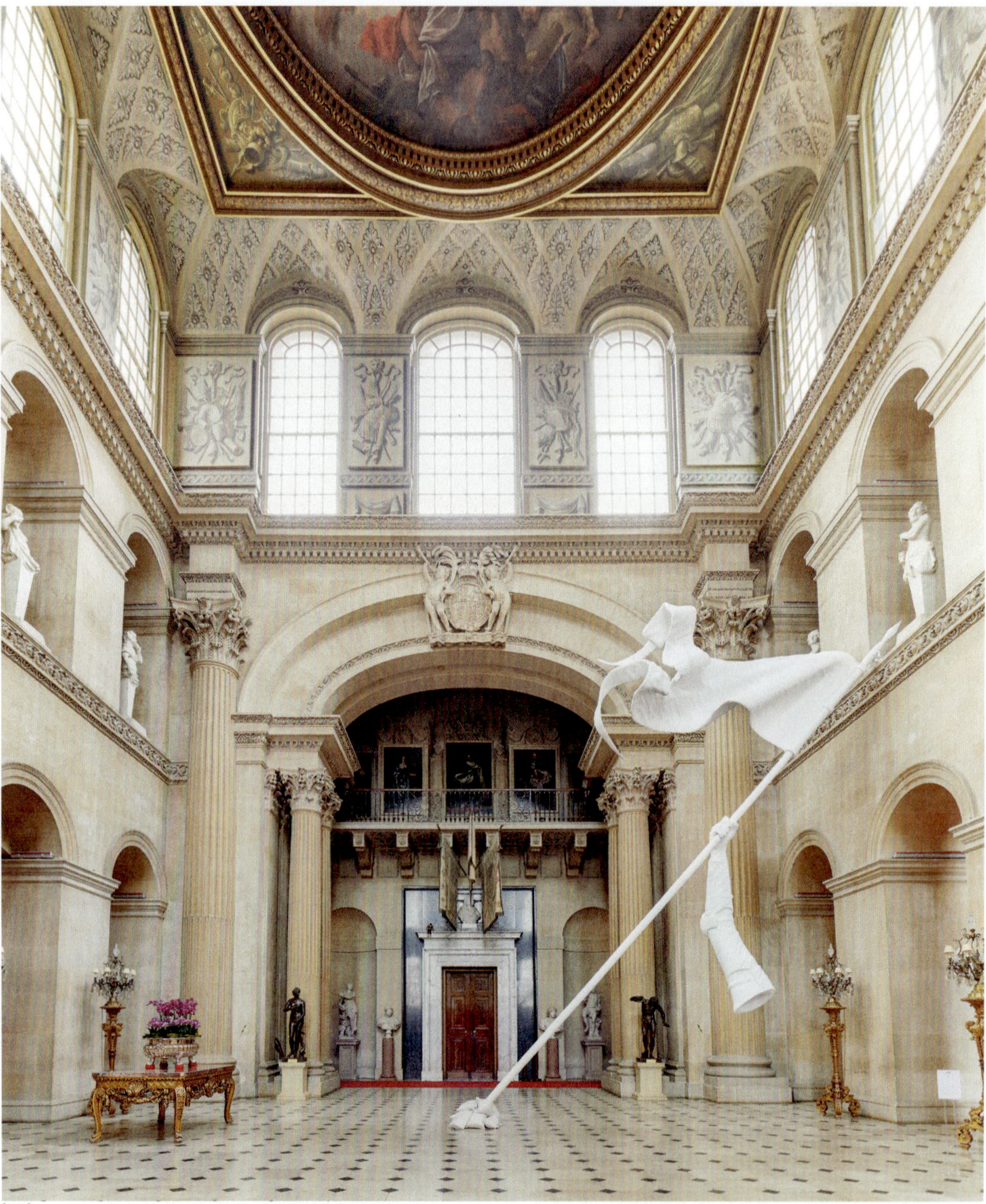



[208] **_We'll Never Die_, 2019**
Expanded polystyrene, aluminum,
polyurethane resin, metal structure,
paint
580 × 1240 × 310 cm

In the late 1990s I kept thinking about the idea
of monument, and I remembered the statue
of Joan of Arc in Paris near the Louvre, which
shows her on horseback holding her banner. For
French nationalists, this monument had a strong
symbolic value and it was a place where they
gathered. My idea was to cut the arm with the
banner off the statue using an electric saw and
take them somewhere in England. I didn't do

anything about it. All the same, the idea stayed
in my mind and many years later, for the exhibition at Blenheim Palace, I decided to make a
sculpture with the arm and the flag, which is
still a symbol.

[208] _We'll Never Die_, 2019
"Victory Is Not An Option," curated by Michael Frahm,
Blenheim Palace, Woodstock, United Kingdom,
September 12–October 27, 2019 (solo show)

[209] **_Tears_**, 2020
Steel, paint, bullets
70 × 140 × 4 cm

[210] **_Night_**, 2021
Steel, paint, bullets
148 × 281 × 6,6 cm

[211] **_Morning_**, 2021
Steel, paint, bullets
198 × 376 × 6.5 cm

[212] **_Meat_**, 2021
Steel, paint, bullets
150 × 300 × 6.6 cm

[213] **_Under_**, 2024
Panels of stainless steel, plated in 24
karat gold, shot with different calibre
weapons
100 × 190 × 4 cm

When I was a child, going to school meant defending the national flag. There was one flying above the facade of every school, every public sports facility and all official buildings. At some point, every child would receive an atlas at Christmas, in which they would be absorbed gazing at those hundreds of colored rectangular shapes.
Flags are like ideas: they look different but in the end they're all the same. The first time I really noticed one was when I saw it flying at half-mast. I kept asking myself: how can a symbol of power become so tragic? How can you turn something so venerated into something so frail with a simple gesture? Some people might think my dream is to design a flag, an icon that survives generations, that's looked at with respect as it flutters during sports events and official celebrations, and is replicated thousands of times. But artists are not made for flags.
Flags are conceived to be untouchable, so they bear enormous power, on the one hand, and they're very fragile on the other. It's probably for this reason that very few artists have challenged the image of a flag. Jasper Johns and David Hammons broke the high and solid wall of art visibility and gained access to a much wider public by humanizing the act of creating a flag and redefining the colors of the American identity, but they're exceptional cases. Most people can't even think of the flag as something truly modifiable. We take flags for granted, we never question them and we rarely understand the sometimes cruel symbolism that lies behind a color, the design or the pattern. Did you know that there is only one national flag that represents human beings as its main symbol (Belize), but four with images of guns (Mozambique, Bolivia, Haiti, Guatemala)?
Flags are a memory of our history and a projection into our future, so they should be looked at with equal amounts of respect and suspicion. And, as with anything else in life, I'm magnetically attracted to whatever I don't understand or I dislike. Through this contrast I've learned that the true power of images lies in friction, conflict and doubt. Flags don't accept mistakes: they simply shout their truth. But the truth is so hard to tell and sometimes it needs fiction to make it plausible.

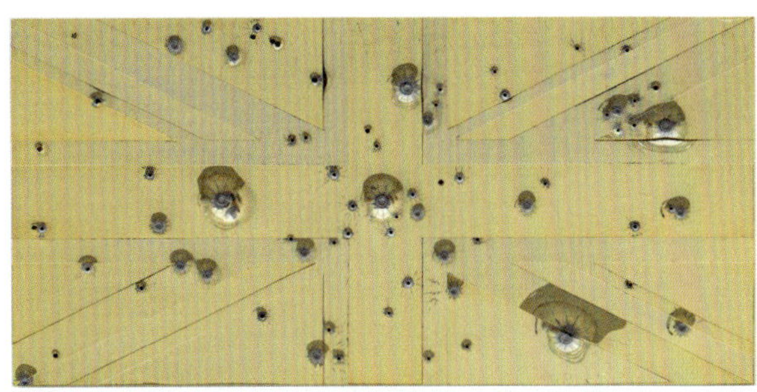

[209]

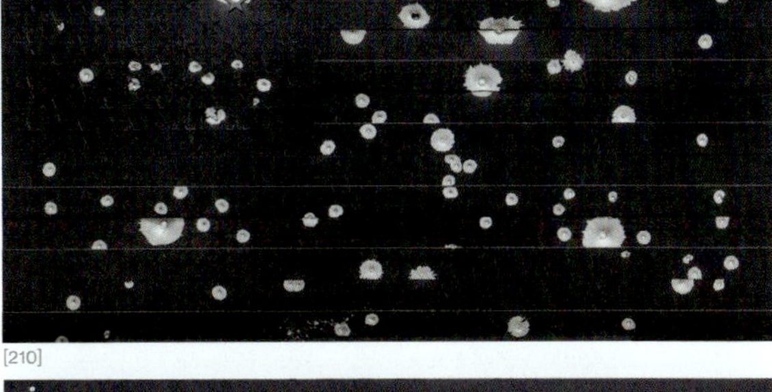

[210]

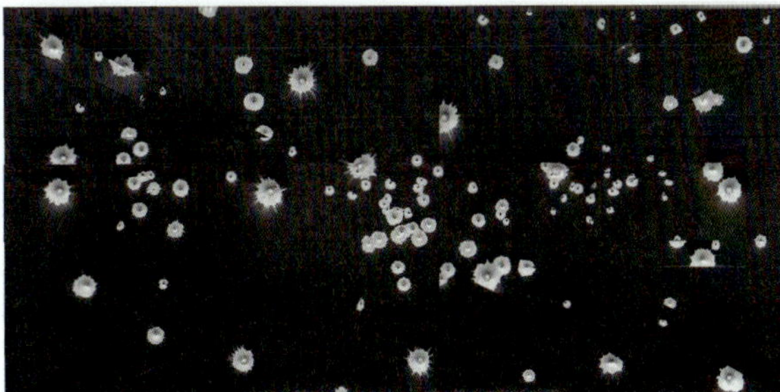

[211]

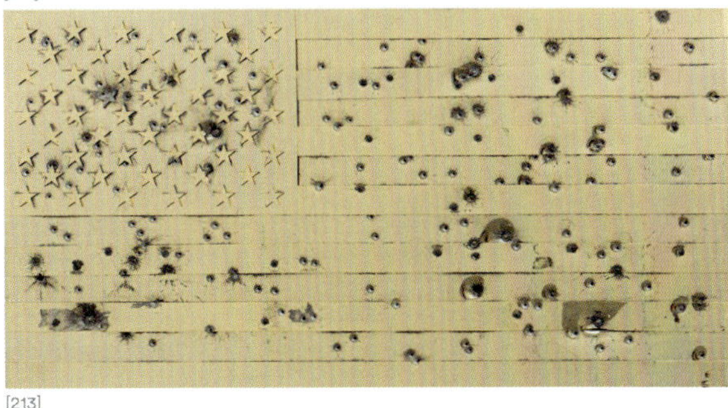

[212]

[213]

[209] _Tears_, 2020

[210] _Night_, 2021

[211] _Morning_, 2021

[212] _Meat_, 2021

[213] _Under_, 2024

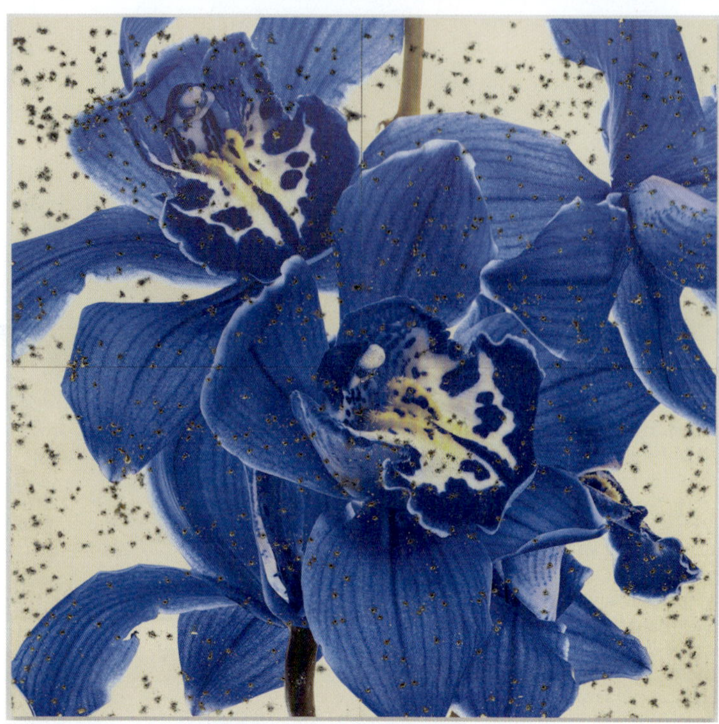

[214]

[214] *MEAT*, 2024
UV LED inkjet print
on wood
250 × 250 × 2 cm

[215] *Bees*, 2025
Watercolor on paper
Unframed: 50 × 70 cm;
framed: 76.7 × 57 × 3.7 cm

[216] *Window*, 2025
Watercolor on paper
Unframed: 50 × 70 cm;
framed: 76.7 × 57 × 3.7 cm

[217] *Back*, 2025
UV LED Inkjet print
on wood
Unframed: 124.7 × 124.7 ×
5.5 cm

304

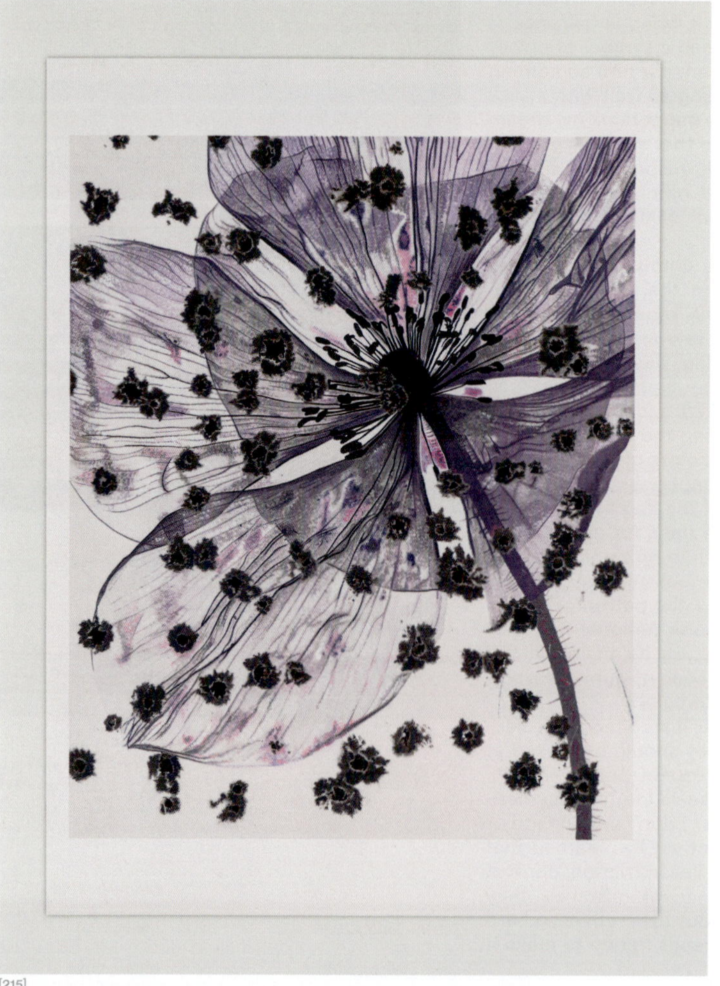

[215]

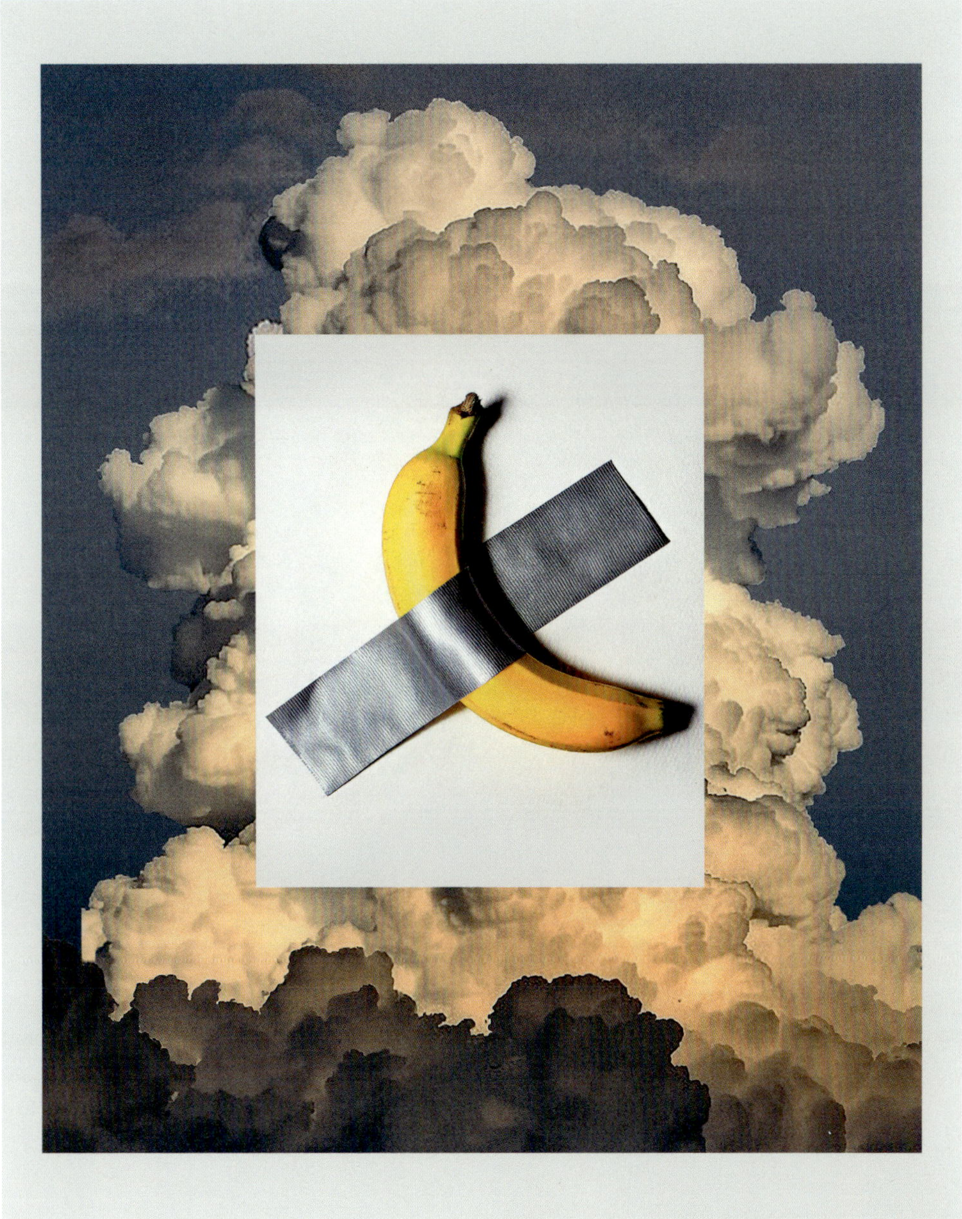

[216]



I started working on the flags of the United Kingdom (*Victory Is Not an Option*, 2019), but in our era the American flag remains unsurpassed. After working on the Stars and Stripes, I moved on to abstract variants, without retaining any trace of the original design, on reflective surfaces and then went so far as to spoil apparently bucolic images like that of flowers or landscapes (*Bees*, *MEAT*, *Window*). And finally even my own portrait (*Back*).

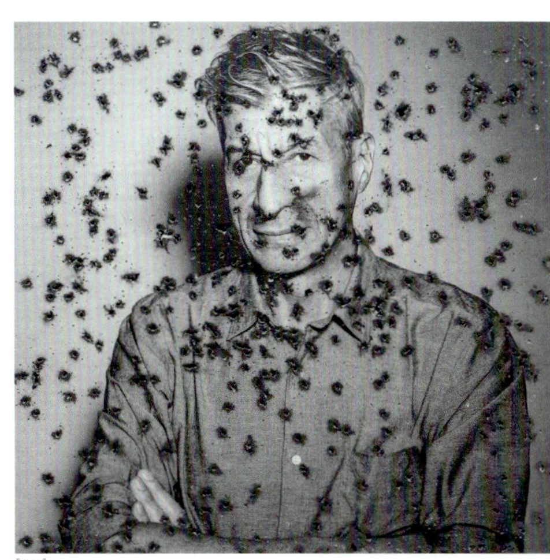

[217]

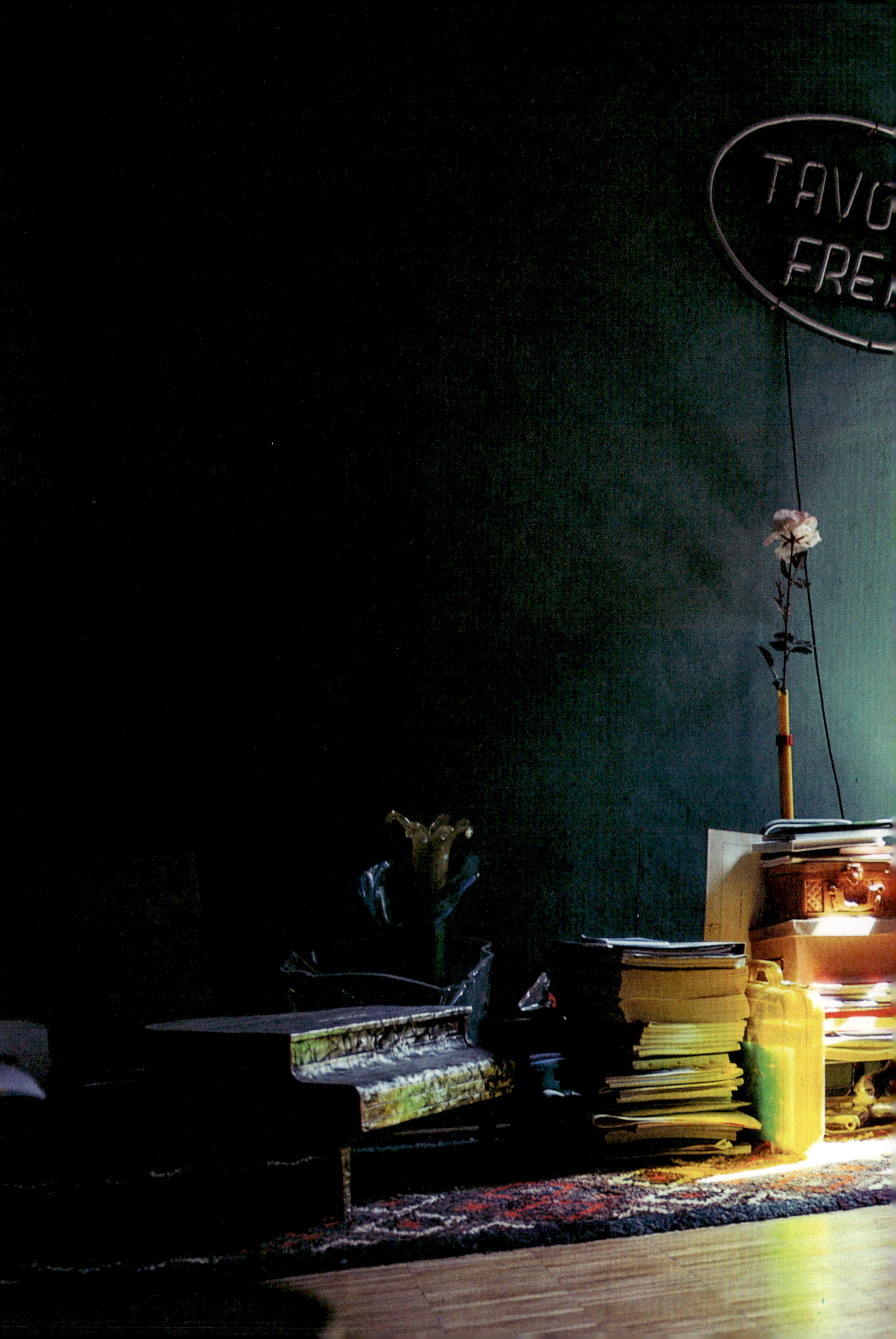
TAVO
FRE

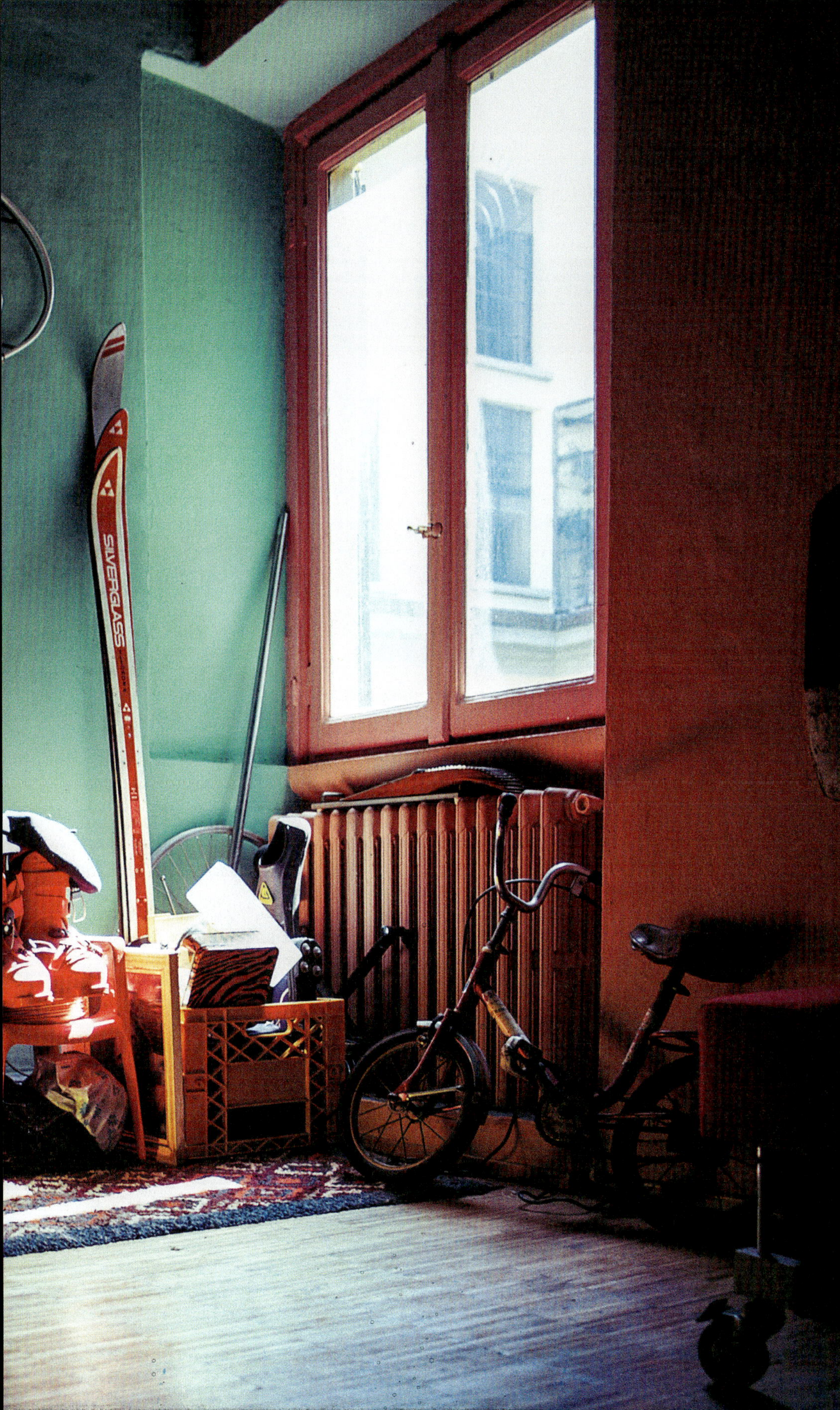

Before getting to Milan I spent five years in limbo. Determination brought me to Milan, the longing for a life different from the one I'd been living until then. I'd promised myself that I would never work for someone again, and Milan is the city where I first realized how to do this. It was a city open to the new and everybody was ready to encourage and support young artists, from the editorial staff of magazines to galleries and non-profit associations. It was a relatively small network but very receptive. I don't usually look back, but the few times I did I told myself that if I'd stayed where I was I would probably be in jail now. I would have applied my creativity to robberies. Sadly, to be recognized in Italy I then had to move to New York. Milan was a springboard, a phase of transition between being dry and plunging into the water.

I lived in Milan for a long time. I see cities as open-air offices. New York works around the clock, so it's perfect for work, for being constantly overstimulated and confused. Milan for some reason I associate with the fog and gray of the sky. It is a city that sometimes scares me. Some days the sky is so low that you feel you're stifling. But when I lack air, the best ideas come to me. Art is also this for me, a kind of escape from the boredom of everyday life.

Today I'm increasingly in Milan. It's become a pleasant city to live in, not just a spot to go to for a specific event. The small network of the past has expanded a lot, and Milan today is not only a city that goes beyond the temporal boundaries of the Salone del Mobile, the Fashion Week or miart. It also extends beyond its geographical boundaries and takes in Bergamo, Turin, even Bologna. The commercial factor was the motive for setting up the Salone, but the results achieved over the years go far beyond this. The energy released during that week is extremely vital and stimulating, comparable to that of cultural centers such as Paris or New York. The city is populated by creatives, ideas circulate, productive relationships develop. I find that in recent times this energy never completely abandons Milan. You feel it all the year round.

Milan has never been the cheeriest of cities. My first Milan, that of the late eighties, encapsulated its essence in Totò's question to the traffic policeman in Piazza Duomo: "To go where we have to go to, from where do we have to go?" The city had the charm of a mirage. In the 1980s it was described as a city you could drink like a cocktail. It was depicted as a fantasy world of partying, elegance and abundance, but when I moved there I didn't see anything like that. Even today, when I hear about that period, I'm baffled. Then over the years the city has changed a lot, like me, as everyone changes. It's better now, aware of its contradictions and that it has to come to terms with an ever-changing identity. It's a city that finally has a European flavor, not an overgrown province. Every city is made up above all of the people who live in it, and its social fabric is reflected in part by its architectural landscape. This contemporary Milan with ambitious architecture is also possible because it's inhabited by ambitious people.

On the other hand, the Porta Nuova district, which has now concentrated the economic part of Milan in one area, has changed its features, like a facelift or a boxing match, depending on your point of view. The risk of this type of operation is that the costs of living in the city rise to such exorbitant levels that people are forced out. We see this happening in many cities abroad, such as New York, an exemplary case. When this happens, the changing city is unfortunately no longer ours. Instead of fearing migrants arriving by sea, we should be frightened of the hedge fund managers coming and carving up our cities. That's the immigration we ought to be worried about.

As for my favorite part of the city, Milan has the most efficient and affordable system of swimming pools I've ever found, and I've seen quite a few cities over the years. Then there is *Toiletpaper*, which most of the time is conceived and produced in Milan, between Pierpaolo Ferrari's home and the studio where we take the photos. But my favorite place is definitely the Monumental Cemetery. It's an incredibly peaceful place, full of artworks by artists from Medardo Rosso to Fontana. The whole history of Milan's excellence passes through there. A kind of outdoor museum, but without curators, collectors or gallery owners. Only the dead.

[218]  *Lullaby*, 1994
Canvas industrial bag, rubble
135 × 85 × 85 cm

[219]  *Lullaby*, 1994
2 wooden pallet, rubble, plastic wrap
135 × 100 × 120 cm each

In 1993 there was a wave of Mafia attacks against cultural targets in Florence, Milan, and Rome. In Milan, the PAC – Padiglione d'Arte Contemporanea was shattered and five people were killed in the explosion. At that time I used to spend every evening riding my bicycle around Milan, and it was only by chance, because of a girl, that I didn't pass by the PAC on that fateful night. I immediately felt I had to do something. The result was *Lullaby*.

I'd been invited to do my first exhibition abroad, a solo show in London, at the Laure Genillard Gallery. I thought: "Why don't I bring something from my country as a snapshot?" What could it be? I decided to bring some rubble from the PAC. I packed it as if for an official shipment in a large blue industrial bag, like a huge laundry bag, and sent it off to London. It looked like the grave of some washing. It reminded me of the bags they use in hospitals for transporting dirty linen. I put some more rubble on two pallets wrapped in plastic and sent it to Paris, where I'd been invited to the collective exhibition "L'Hiver de l'amour" at the Musée d'Art Moderne de la Ville de Paris. In *Lullaby* my only feeling was of taking part in an event that I'd experienced firsthand and that concerned everyone. The reactions to the work were immediate and regrettably unpleasant. It

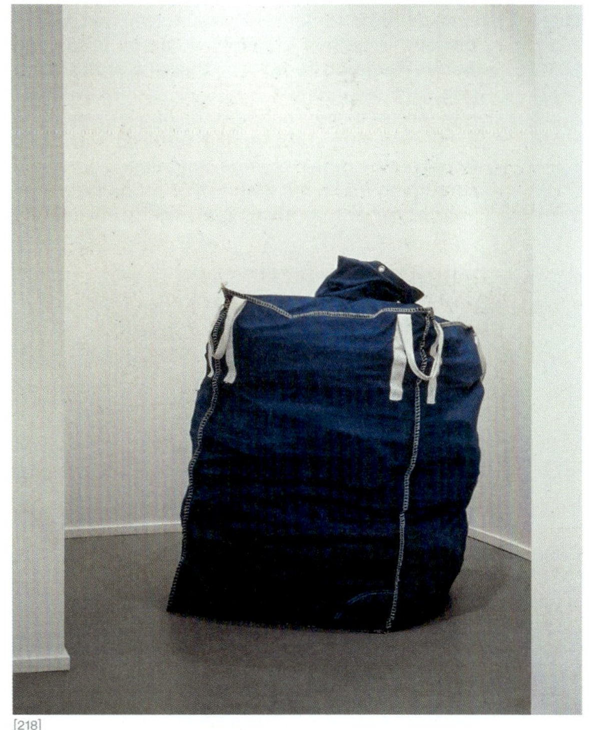

[218]

[218]  *Lullaby*, 1994
"Maurizio Cattelan," Laure Genillard Gallery, London,
January 28–March 5, 1994 (solo show)

was sharply attacked in the Italian press. They said I was rummaging through the garbage cans of our bad history, or something of the sort. The thing got out of control. I was particularly stung by an article by Emilio Tadini, not because it contained a criticism of me, but because it was written by an artist, someone you might expect to show a deeper sensibility on the subject. His views were as cheap and reductive as a tabloid columnist's. It seemed his main concern was the good name of contemporary art. I guess he saw art still as an ornament, a space carefully marked off around his armchair. Then I was led to reflect on information in the media. None of the people who wrote had picked up the phone to ask me about it, to discover one line more than whatever they read in the press release. And if that scoop was based on the press release and nothing more, goodness knows how the rest of the news gets written.

The problem of information interests me a lot. Often a work has no need of a description to function, but simply some external factor that prompts you to reflect on its meaning. The same goes for *Lullaby*. To a certain extent this is its limitation—needing information as a support. But not all my works are like this. I believe that others are more direct, and their meaning can be understood more easily. That rubble, to me, is not just itself, but a kind of polaroid of what was happening then, and that even affected someone like me, averse to almost everything. However, as with a lot of art produced in recent decades, if you don't know the story behind it and its author, it remains unintelligible.

And perhaps sometimes I'm unclear myself, especially if pathos is involved, as in this work. Before deciding to do it, I thought about it for two or three months. I had to decide whether my egoism or the feeling of having experienced something that all of us had suffered was more important. I didn't change anything, I just said something more, but I felt a little more deeply involved, rather than absent, as I nearly always am,

uninformed about the life around me. Whenever I venture into a new setting, I do in part to feel a bit more alive, to give my own interpretation of it, basically to express myself. I think it takes centuries to change things, but you can relate them a bit more closely to your own sphere and make them less distant.

The true history of this work was also, and again, of disquiet. I reasoned on the disquiet I felt in presenting myself in contexts where I was nobody (I wasn't an author), and of the need to immediately manage to involve people who were approaching my work for the first time. Then, for a moment, I saw myself almost as an emigrant, certainly as an outsider. I thought that the best thing then was to be one hundred percent an outsider, so I could assert my independence and my origins. In this way the situation could take on a dignity of its own, even if I was going to touch something that I had inside me and that might disturb the viewer, if only because people had died. Anyway, it wasn't the best image of us that I could have exported.

Looking back, I also thought of how I was introducing the remains of another museum into a museum or gallery. The image of the destroyed PAC has remained inside me. I had just arrived in Milan. From the security of the province, which is like a family, for the first time I felt vulnerable. The PAC was a significant place, and artists aspired to it. This increased my bewilderment. To make us feel exposed, defenseless: this was the aim of the people who planted the bomb. I felt that something was in danger. It was a time when two great forces were facing off, with one wanting renewal and the other resisting it. It seemed like the start of a grand design, a strategy: trying to put everyone in a state where they lost their bearings. The bomb at the PAC had really exploded, and there was a profound sense of menace. I felt that the event was an extremely representative image of the great opposites: life and death, hatred and love. It was a symbol.

The memory of a traumatic event often requires us to put a certain distance between ourselves and what happened. *Lullaby* has always belonged to Milan, in its physical substance and significance, but distance was necessary, in time and space, for it to return to the city and its citizens. In 2020 I learned that the work, in the version originally intended for Paris, was up for auction, and it struck me as absurd that it shouldn't return to Milan. I decided to buy it and make a monument of it in memory of the wound suffered by the city, by donating it to the municipality. There are many ways of remembering. In the summer of 2022, to commemorate the anniversary of the explosion, we organized a concert with *Mozart's Requiem* at the Monumental Cemetery in Milan, where *Lullaby* was temporarily installed.

310

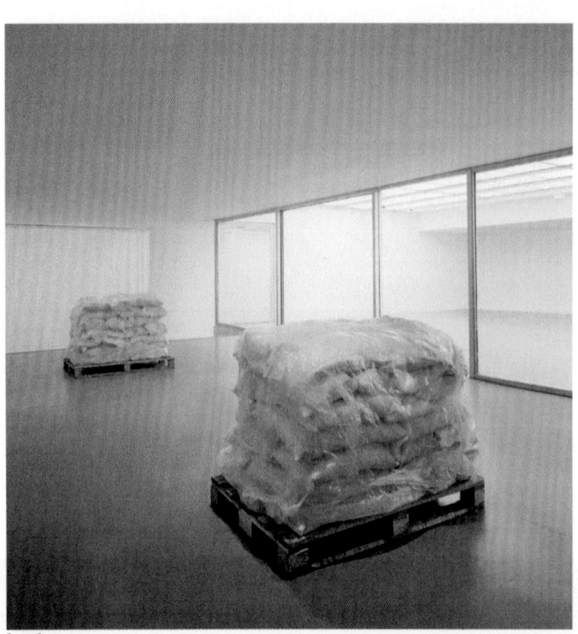

[219.1]

[219.1]    *Lullaby*, 1994
"L'Hiver de l'amour," curated by Olivier Zahm and Elein Fleiss, Musée d'Art Moderne de la Ville de Paris, February 10–March 13, 1994 (group show)

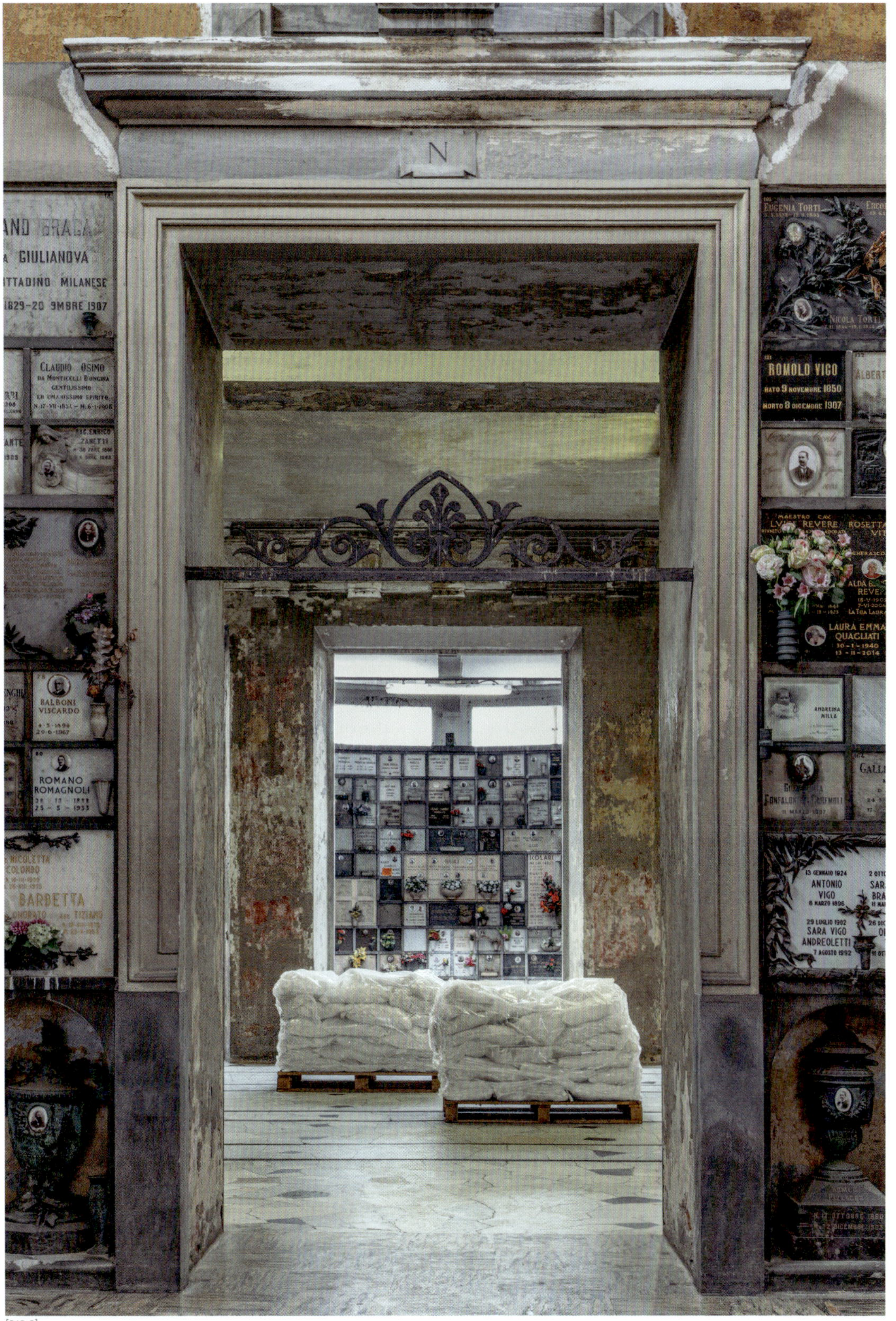



[219.2]

[219.2]  *Lullaby*, 1994
"NinnaNanna," Crematorium Temple, Monumental
Cemetery, Milan, March 30–November 6, 2022 (solo show)

**[220]** ***Souvenir di Milano*, 1994**
Plastic toy camera with preloaded
images
6.5 × 11 × 9.8 cm

**[221]** ***Untitled*, 1994**
25 knotted handkerchiefs knotted with
nylon thread, label with signature and
date, cardboard box
30 × 15 × 7 cm

In the small toy cameras of *Souvenir di Milano*,
I inserted some photos of the PAC, destroyed
in 1993 by a Mafia bomb. I may have taken the
photos, I don't remember. You can see them in
sequence by advancing the roll of film, as in all
these souvenir machines used in the past. I made
a dozen. It was my way of remembering Milan at
that moment, a souvenir of grief.
You could see an affinity in the work of the same
year in which I put together twenty-five handkerchiefs bought at a market and tied them with a
ribbon made of nylon, the kind used for stock-
ings. For me every interpretation is right, and

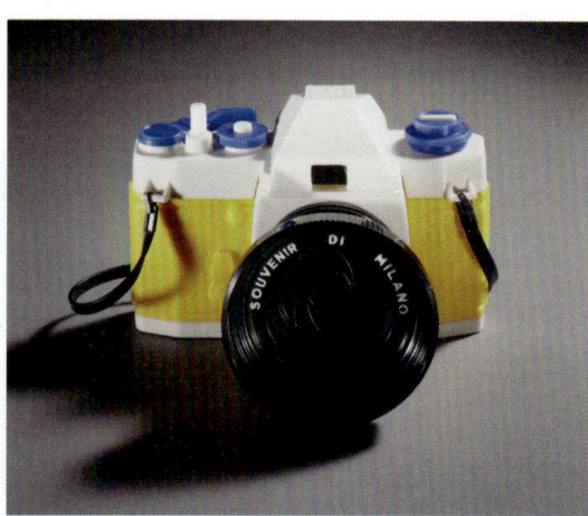

[220]

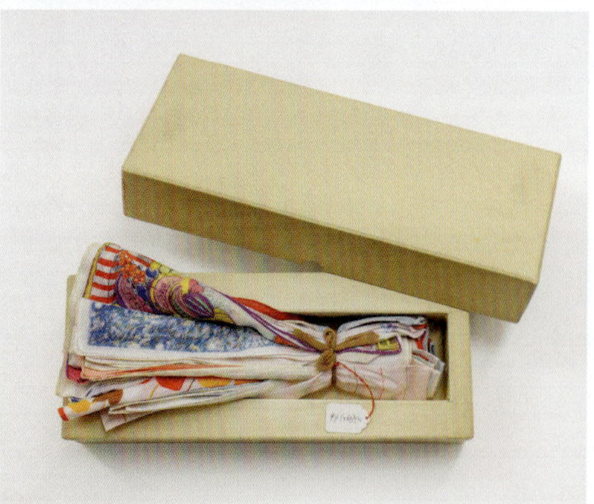

[221]

[220]    *Souvenir di Milano*, 1994

[221]    *Untitled*, 1994

[222.4]    "Maurizio Cattelan. Contro le ideologie,"
Palazzo Reale, Milan, 2010
Poster made for the exhibition but never displayed

sometimes others see more clearly than I do. It
was the period when I used to work on found objects, putting them together.

**[222]** **"Maurizio Cattelan. Contro
le ideologie," 2010**
Solo show curated by Francesco Bonami,
Sala delle Cariatidi, Palazzo Reale, Milan,
September 25–October 24, 2010

I didn't want to do the exhibition at the Palazzo
Reale in Milan, but I did want to do something in
the city itself. There wasn't even the budget for a
major retrospective, such as the one the Municipality of Milan planned to do at first, but I kept
on with it, because I strongly believed in the project of the statue outside the Stock Exchange. I
was interested in the strength of the piazza. So
"Contro le ideologie" and *L.O.V.E.* developed together. Besides, many of my best works are either the result of mistakes or situations in which,
as happened then, I'm forced to turn setbacks
into positives.
For Palazzo Reale, given the tight budget, I made
a selection, mainly guided by how disturbing the
works would be, until I got to the final group.
While preparing the show I realized the works
I'd chosen formed a perfect triptych. They made
up a dysfunctional family, like mine was: a mar-
tyred woman takes her son's place on the cross
(*Untitled*, 2007), a father whose authority is questioned (*La Nona Ora*, 1999), and an inscrutable
child who cannot communicate except by beat-
ing his drum (*Untitled*, 2003). If I'd tried to plan it
at the drawing board, I wouldn't have thought of
an exhibition like this.
The way I installed the child in the Sala delle Cariatidi was perfect: high up, on the sill of one of the
upper windows, alone and distant. It was there
and it wasn't, suspended in the point of view of
the external viewer, which I've always adopted

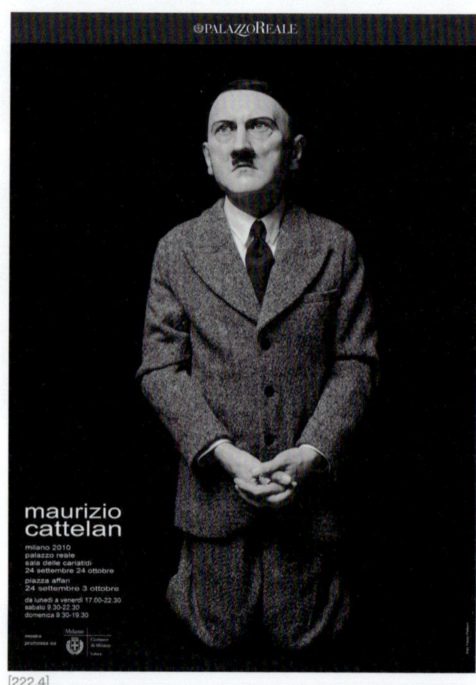


[222.4]

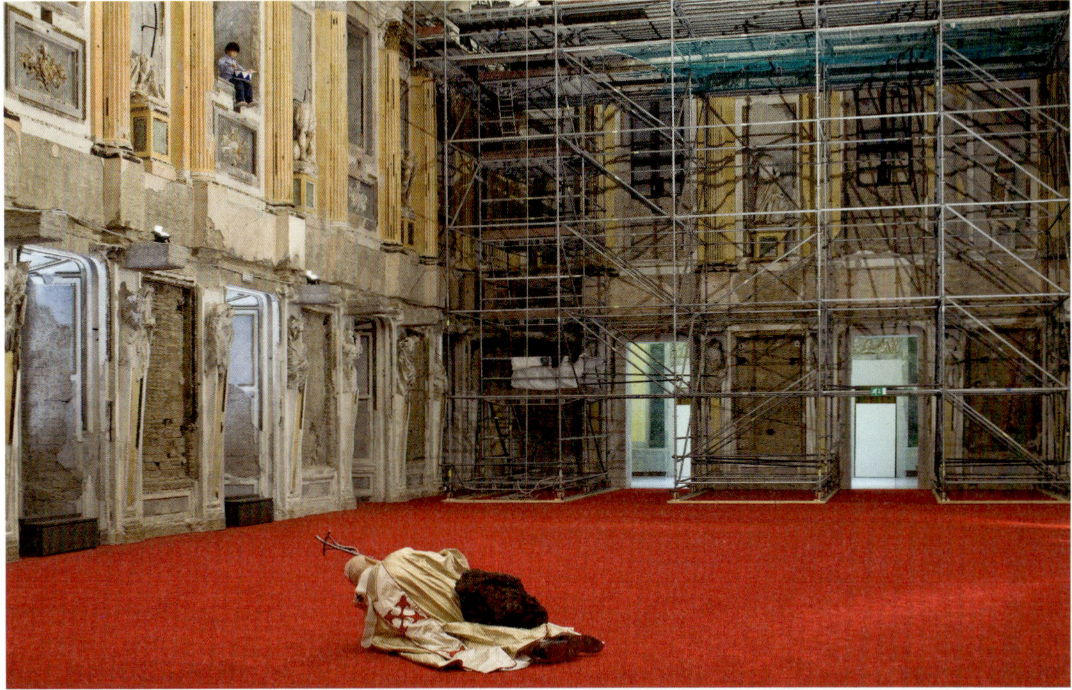

[222.1]

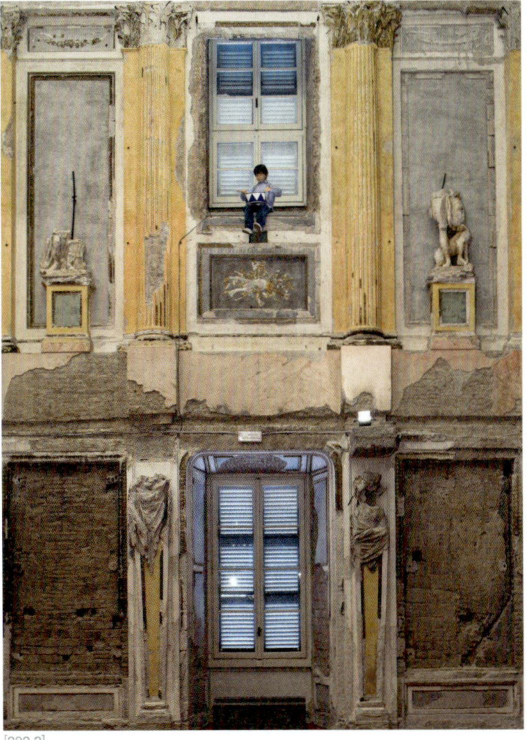

[222.2]

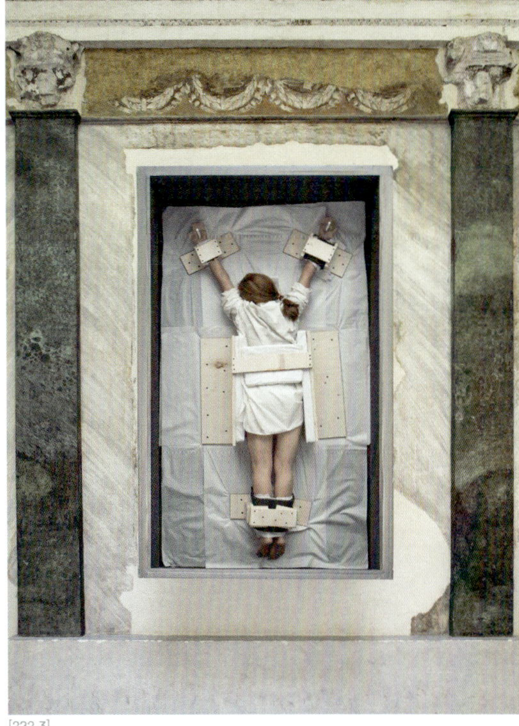

[222.3]

[222.1]   *La Nona Ora,* 1999 [56], and *Untitled*, 2003 [8]
"Maurizio Cattelan. Contro le ideologie," Palazzo Reale,
Milan, 2010

[222.2]   *Untitled*, 2003 [8]
"Maurizio Cattelan. Contro le ideologie," Palazzo Reale,
Milan, 2010

[222.3]   *Untitled*, 2007 [67.2-3]
"Maurizio Cattelan. Contro le ideologie," Palazzo Reale,
Milan, 2010

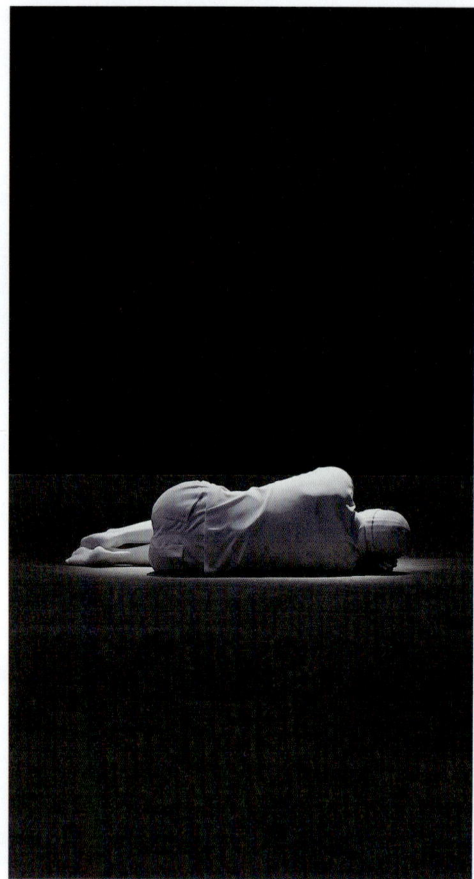

[223.1]

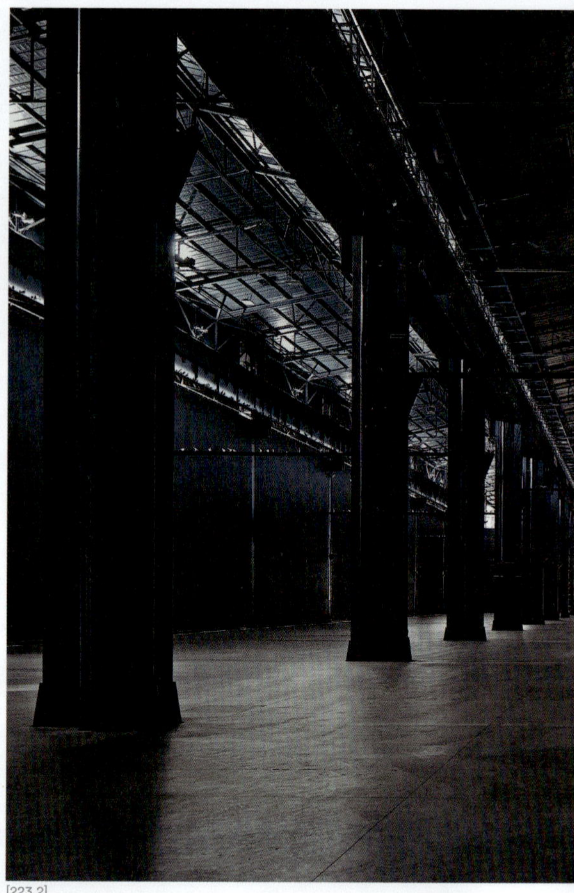

[223.2]

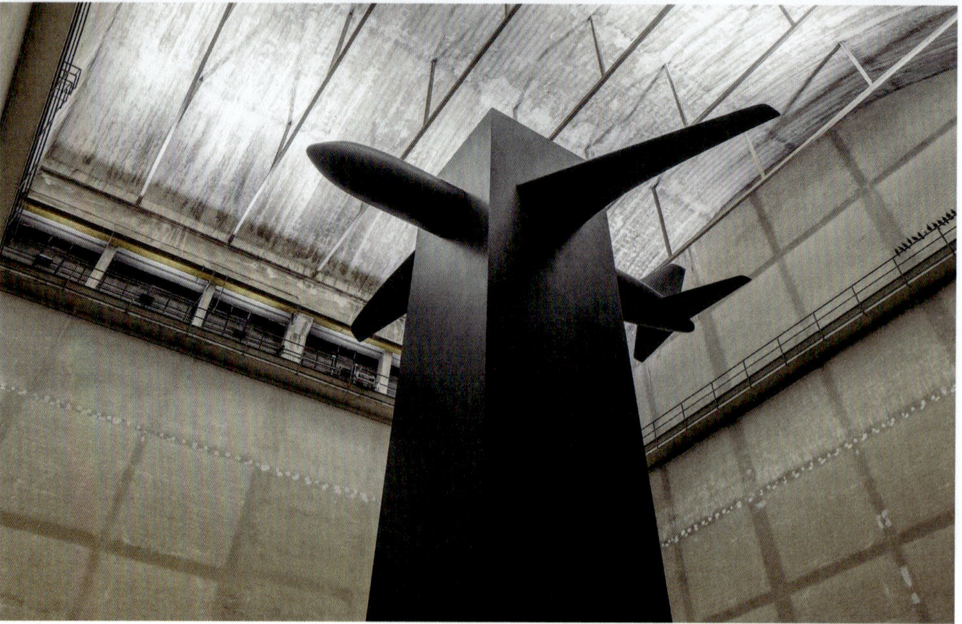

[223.3]



[223.1]  *Breath*, 2021 [129]
"Maurizio Cattelan. Breath Ghosts Blind,"
Pirelli HangarBicocca, Milan, 2021–22

[223.2]  *Ghosts*, 2021 [240]
"Maurizio Cattelan. Breath Ghosts Blind,"
Pirelli HangarBicocca, Milan, 2021–22

[223.3]  *Blind*, 2021 [224]
"Maurizio Cattelan. Breath Ghosts Blind,"
Pirelli HangarBicocca, Milan, 2021–22

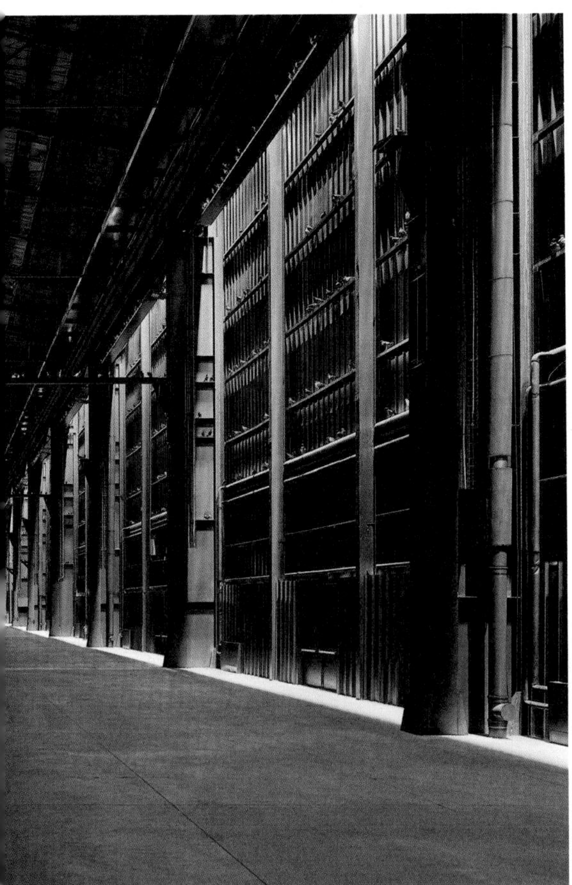

[The forty-nine loose pages of the artist's book *The Three Qattelan*, published by Three Star Books, Paris, in 2010, were also exhibited in the Sala del Trono of Palazzo Reale, adjoining the exhibition]

[223] **"Maurizio Cattelan. Breath Ghosts Blind," 2021–22**
Solo show curated by Roberta Tenconi and Vicente Todolí, Pirelli HangarBicocca, Milan, July 15, 2021–February 20, 2022

I had a very Catholic upbringing, and to me the Pirelli HangarBicocca space looks like a giant church. I think this interpretation isn't far from the truth, given that the first industrial architectures were modeled on churches. My feeling is it's a sacred space and I tried to treat it like that in "Breath Ghosts Blind."

I don't remember who said that exhibitions are made up of two elements, a beginning and an end. It's a very linear view, perhaps too much so, and I can't hide the fact that the first time I walked about that space I thought of this. The Hangar works differently, just like a church, because the path is circular. From the apse—where the highest spiritual expression is usually found—you retrace your steps, and with new eyes you go back over what the old you has already seen.

I was the intruder there, so all I could do was harness the sense of danger I felt. I started from the end with *Blind* (2021), with the rest of the works blended into the space, as if they'd always been there. The pigeons (*Ghosts*, 2021) colonized the place, just like in Hitchcock's film *The Birds*, while the dog beside the man on the ground (*Breath*, 2021) became the guardian of the exhibition. It was there to defend us. The three words of the exhibition represented the three phases of the exhibition. Originally it was chaos, or maybe just *Breath*. The second phase was *Ghosts*. Imagine you're observing an anthill. You understand the ants are very busy doing something important, industriously and diligently, but their vital reasons escape you. Every life is like this: if you look at it from the outside, it's very easy to question its meaning. From the outside, we can look like ghosts without souls. *Blind* is what we all become in the end. All together, the three works represented the cycle of life.

It wasn't the first time I'd presented an exhibition with only a few works. I'd already done it, for instance, at the Kunsthaus Bregenz in 2008, where there was only one work per floor. Or in Milan in 2010 in "Contro le ideologie" at Palazzo Reale. The truth is that the void fills the space and certain works expand given the right conditions. "Breath Ghosts Blind" was an expanded exhibition, I'd say it was full.

The leading image of the exhibition with a man sitting underwater documented the final moment of its gestation, when anything could happen. The moment of suspension before the finish line. I couldn't even imagine how I would come out of that exhibition. I rid myself of a great burden. It was a silent exhibition, with great pauses. Sometimes you think better in confusion, at others you need absolute silence. We're machines that work with emotions, and their echo resonates in what we do.



in life. At first the statue of Pope Wojtyła was standing up, but I felt it wasn't right. When I was going to show it for the first time at the Kunsthalle Basel, I thought about how to destroy it. In the end I came up with the idea of the meteorite. It was like an epiphany. I realized I had overthrown the father figure. It's what an important work can do. If I had an epiphany in creating it, then someone else could have one in viewing it. As for the third figure, in art history the woman is the Madonna and the representation of beauty, but in my family the woman was suffering. I've never seen that work as an inverted crucifixion, but in the triptych of Palazzo Reale I feel like justifying it as my vision of woman in the domestic sphere. The exhibition was talked about in the press even before it opened. But then, on visiting it, you wondered what all the fuss was about. To be honest, though, I think that without the press taking an interest in it, perhaps the show would never have opened. Even so, it was postponed three times, and the city council only authorized it just over a month before the official opening. The poster advertising the exhibition had similar problems. It was printed but never posted. To shake things up a bit, I put the pope/*La Nona Ora* on display and proposed showing Hitler/*Him* in the streets. Someone on the city council disliked the poster, so it wasn't approved but paradoxically it was published in a newspaper. The censorship was stupid, because if it had been posted no one would have seen it. A hundred posters pass unnoticed in a city.

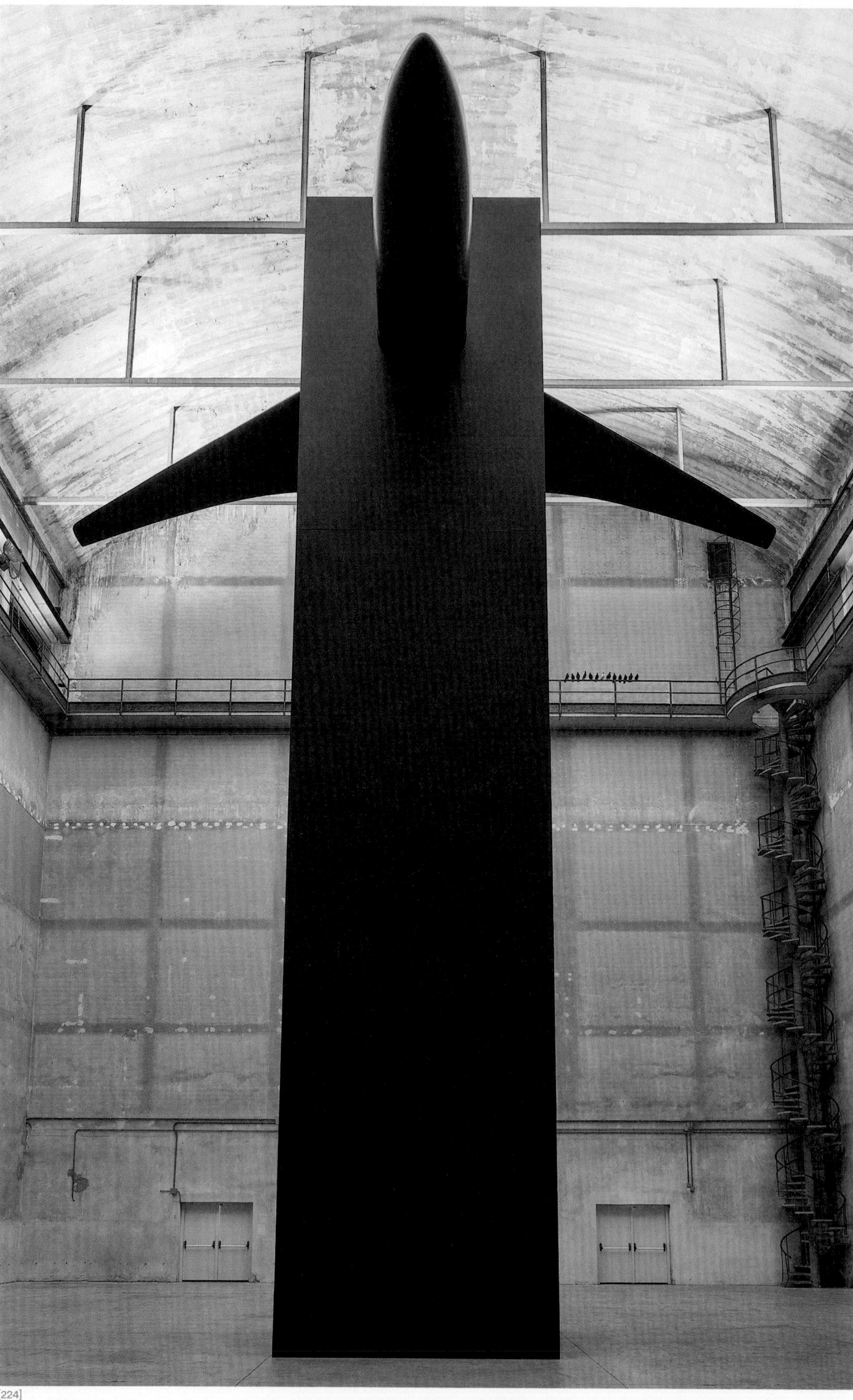

[224] *Blind*, **2021**
Resin, wood, steel, aluminum,
polystyrene, paint
1695 × 1300 × 1195 cm

An artwork always brings together rational and unconscious thoughts. Some things I've done because I felt at the time it was important to do them, but maybe I didn't consciously understand them—things that became clearer and more obvious to me over time. And so achieving a certain distance, not just in space but in time, becomes a necessary step to understand and remember.
*Blind* was something I'd been thinking about for years. Making it happen was in part the cure for a shock that left an indelible scar in the visual memory of anyone old enough to remember that moment. I was in New York on September 11, and getting ready to board a plane. They had canceled all the flights. I had to walk home from LaGuardia, which took hours, and the things I saw stayed with me. Those scenes were terrible, apocalyptic. That event revealed the full fragility of the human condition. I immediately had the awareness that it would be necessary to wait, so as not to risk appearing a simple illustrator of the times.
Originally, I wanted to show this work in New York, but it was rejected. Then Vicente Todolí, the Artistic Director of Pirelli HangarBicocca in Milan, supported me. In 2021 it may have still seemed too soon to show the work outside the United States, but I also thought that twenty years and 6,000 kilometers away was the right distance.
I feel like today's world is lacking in symbols, yet some ancestral images or metaphors do linger on and are capable of giving a foundation and meaning to our lives. Certain images and objects do have incredible power. They are so highly charged that they take on a broader meaning and become evocative of many things, not just the event they are most closely bound up with. *Blind* is not just a work about September 11, but a work about grief and its social dimension. It evokes the frailty of a society in which loneliness and selfishness are increasing. Some may see a crucifixion in its shape, and others may see a *2001: A Space Odyssey* monolith stabbed by a plane. I'd been thinking about this work for years, but I must say that when it was made the pandemic had made death visible in our lives again. It's something we're always trying to suppress and forget, we're all so focused on comfort and warding off any kind of pain, as if it were just a medical problem. But perhaps for the first time since our parents' generation that lived through the war, death was once again an everyday threat. in this work I wanted to show the complexity of opposites encountering each other, with all it entails: life and death, hatred and love. There are situations or places that can turn in a flash from heaven into hell, and that's true both for individuals and for a community as a whole. I'm interested in working with shared symbols and fears, so *Blind* became an emblem of that. The feeling is like being in a cemetery with no gravestones, a mixture of foreboding and empathy.



[224] *Blind*, 2021
"Maurizio Cattelan. Breath Ghosts Blind,"
Pirelli HangarBicocca, Milan, 2021–22

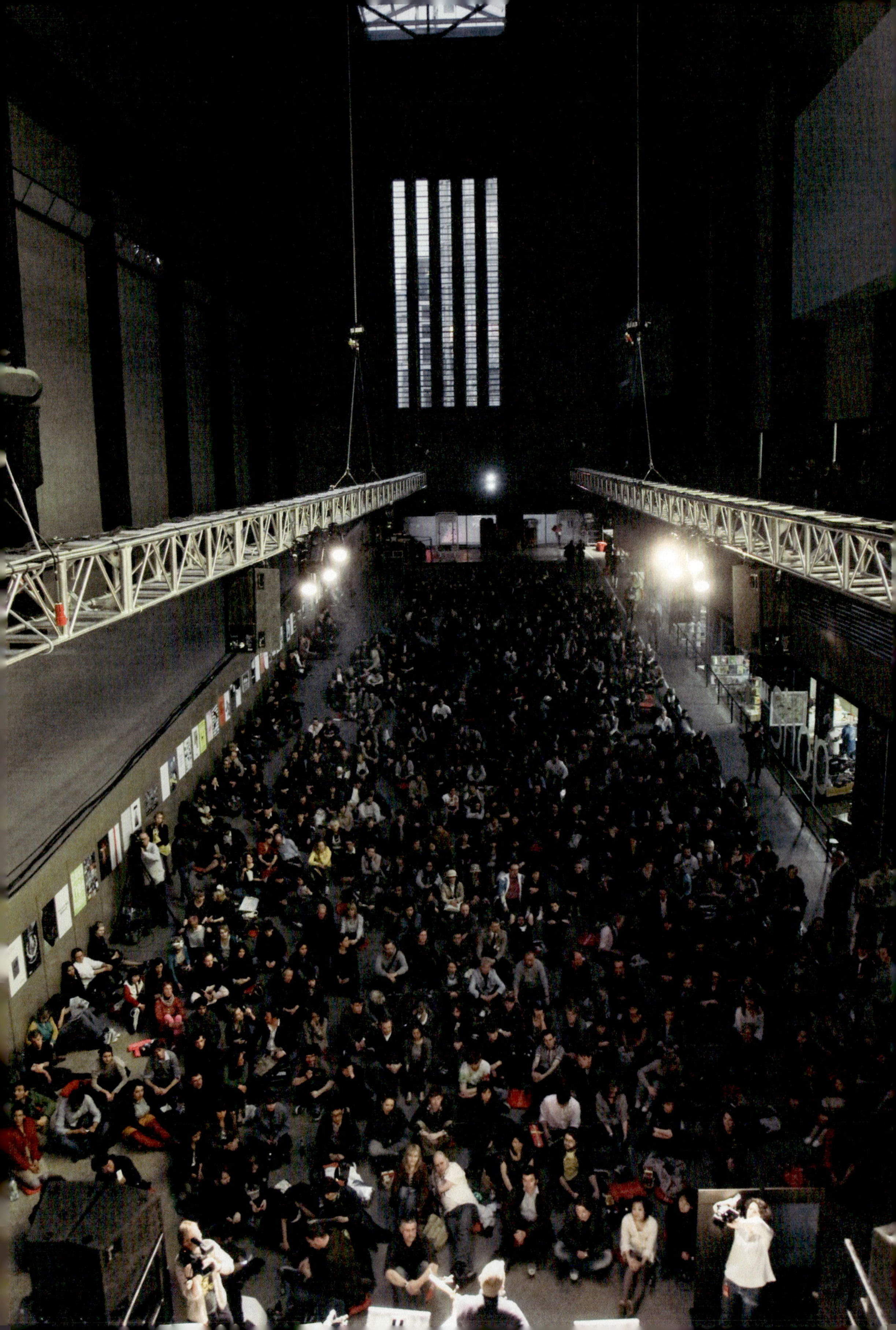

←    "No Soul For Sale – A Festival of Independents,"
curated by Cecilia Alemani, Maurizio Cattelan, and
Massimiliano Gioni, Turbine Hall, Tate Modern, London,
May 14–16, 2010. Photograph published in *Being Cattelan*,
ed. Paola Nicolin, monographic issue of *Abitare*, no. 517
(2011): 191

All art is social, even if you make it in a cellar, provided there are at least two people: one to invent the work and the other to look at it. If you don't have a viewer, the work is dead. On the other hand, I believe that every artist has in mind someone he's addressing when he creates an artwork. I've always worked mainly for myself and for two or three other people who are in my head, the most exacting. I say to myself: if I satisfy them, the public, the critics and everyone else will be satisfied, without having to think about it. Of course, the public can decide the success of a work, but I find the work's limits much more interesting, and these are never decided by the public. I've always been the harshest judge of my own work, and that's the only pressure I've ever been interested in. Still, I think that any authoritative criticism is useful and can never be threatening. If you're sure of what you're doing, and if the content you've produced is true, significant, even urgent, then no criticism can get at you. I don't mean presumption. I always assume that it's impossible to please everyone, and I don't think it's even desirable when it comes to art. The collective response helps me understand better what I've done; it reveals nuances that I myself didn't see so clearly just a moment before. It's a moment of growth, never of fear. On the other hand, I'm a bit old-school, and I think that when the artist has finished a work it no longer belongs to him. I limit myself to seeing what people make of it.

Someone wiser than me once said that art is not art about itself but about the attention we bring to it. No work exists until it's seen, and I think the same goes for exhibitions. Every type of art engages the observer. In a way, even the great medieval frescoes required the active involvement of the viewers. The point is not about being an insider or an outsider, but an artwork needs to be seen in order to exist. In fact art is in the service of others, and I don't say this in a negative sense. It's nurtured by others, it lives on the opinions of others. An artwork is not complete without the comments, words, and ideas of the people who happen engage with it. In reality, it's the viewers who make the works. I don't do anything: without different points of view and interpretations, art doesn't exist.

So it's pointless to try and get your idea across to the public. The secret is to show them life, and people will find their favorite meaning within themselves. The more powerful your images are, the more viewers will have nightmares and dreams to project into it. And when it comes to the morals of others, I have no filters or preconceptions, as well as no control once the work is out of my head. Trying to predict the public's reaction is a useless exercise. It's actually harmful to art itself. I just think that when art makes us feel something and conveys a sense of discomfort, then it has made an impact. The thing that pleases me most is that people start asking themselves questions when they're engaging with my work. If my questions are different from the visitors', it doesn't really matter.

I believe it's essential to recognize the independence of the artwork, which is made up of thousands of elements: some belong to the author, some to the context, others to the time when it was created, others to the time when it's looked at. Much of its meaning belongs to the public, in the eyes of the viewers. Art is universal because everyone can interpret it or see whatever they like, in terms of their own experience of life. We might come from the same part of the world, but if we have totally different backgrounds, we'll still see two different things. Everyone is free to complete and interpret a work, and for this reason the best art is immortal: it continues to live in the viewer's gaze.

So while a mirror reflects appearances, art is more like a Rorschach test with inkblots. What you see in it is your inner and unutterable self. It's alarming when the response is superficial and debate is absent. It's terrifying, because you realize that people may have died culturally and socially without knowing it. On the other hand, as my newsagent often says: "Some people feel the rain, others just get wet." Art is probably when everyone thinks they can feel the rain, even though they're actually just getting wet.



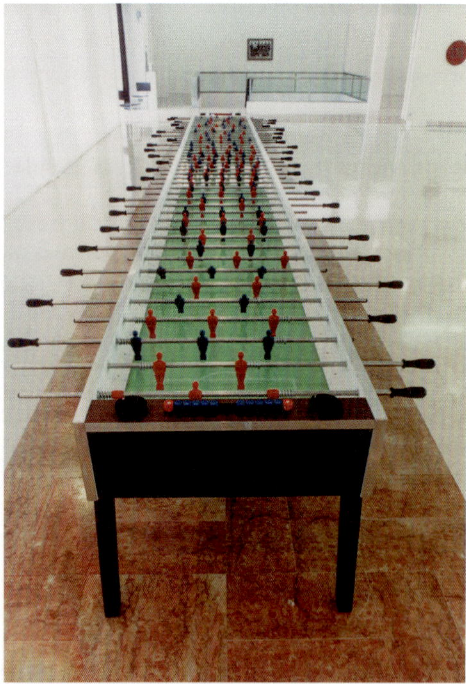

[225.1]

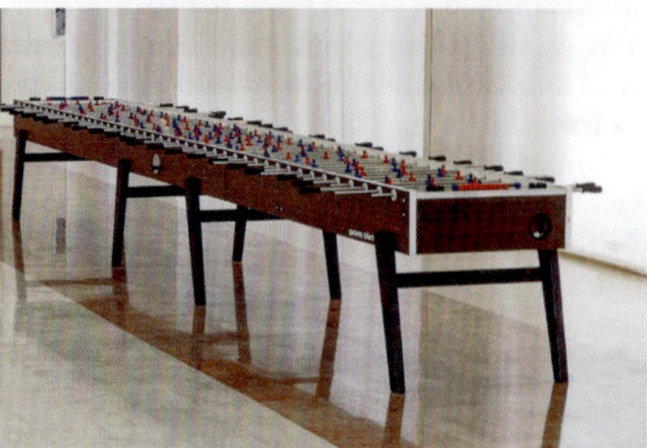

[225.2]

[225]  *Stadium*, 1991
Wood, acrylic, steel, paper, plastic
100.3 × 651 × 120 cm

In 1991 I created *A.C. Forniture Sud*, a soccer team made up of immigrants, then went and promoted it with an unauthorized stand at Arte Fiera in Bologna. Each morning I set up the table, the chair and, to look more professional, a telephone, and I displayed the folding pop-up figures with a photo of the team and its crest. I think the art critic Renato Barilli saw me on that occasion and so decided to invite me to the "AnniNovanta" exhibition at the GAM in Bologna. I would have liked to have the team play, but the museum lacked the space to improvise a soccer field, so I had the idea of transferring the games to a specially made foosball table, for eleven players against eleven, two complete soccer teams. Incredibly, I found a manufacturer, Garlando, who was ready to alter his model, as long as he first did a test in the company with his employees. So I had foosball table almost seven meters long at my disposal. I organized some matches between A.C. Forniture Sud and teams that played in the Italian soccer championship. My guys kept losing. It was bad. There's a romantic idea about losing, but the point with my team wasn't really that they would win or lose—just that they would be a team and play. I think it's the closest thing to a performance I've ever done.

[226]  *Tarzan & Jane*, 1993
Silver dye bleach print
140 × 70 cm
Performance with lion costumes during the solo exhibition "Tarzan & Jane" at the Galleria Raucci/Santamaria, Naples, April 27–May 15, 1993

This is the first experiment I did by putting my gallerists to the test. Two subsequent variants were *Errotin, le vrai lapin*, with Emmanuel Perrotin (1995), and the one with Massimo De Carlo (*Untitled*, 1999). The lions were guys at the Galleria Raucci/Santamaria in Naples, forced to dress up like that for the duration of my "Tarzan & Jane" exhibition in the gallery. There was nothing else to see or buy: they were the artwork.

[227]   ***Errotin, le vrai lapin*, 1995**
Silver dye bleach print, face-mounted to plexiglas, mounted on board
182.9 × 121.9 cm
Performance with costume during the solo show "Maurizio Cattelan. Errotin, le vrai lapin" at the Galerie Emmanuel Perrotin, Paris, January 26–March 11, 1995

I think this work was devoid of any provocation. I simply asked my gallerist to wear a rabbit costume for the duration of one of my exhibitions. The project had a degree of transgression equal to zero. It was only a comment on Emmanuel Perrotin's private life. A game played between

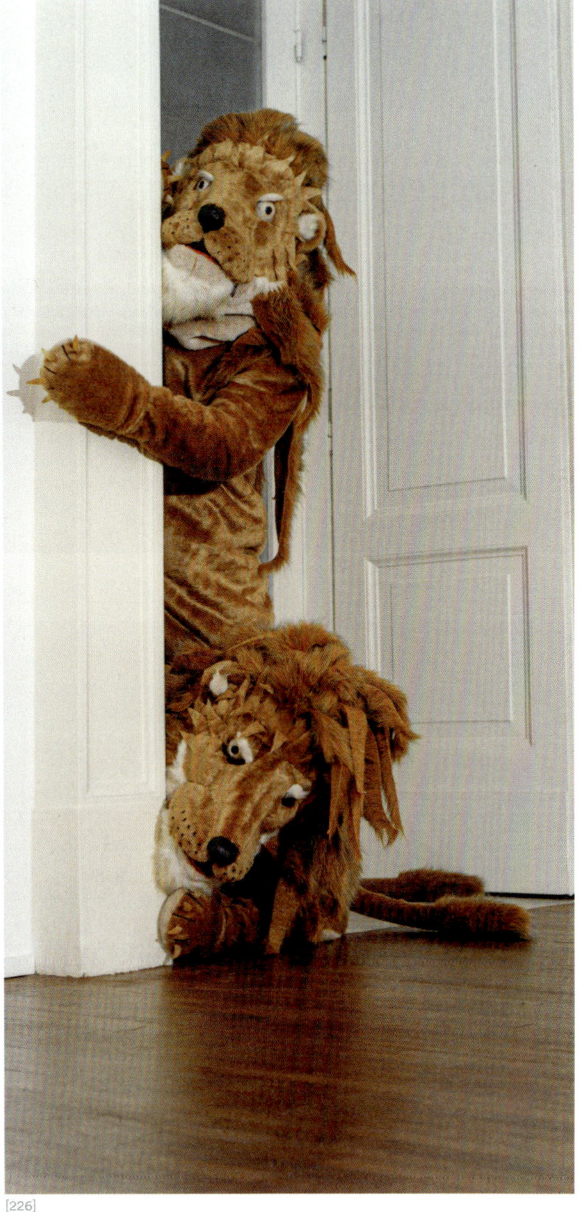

[226]

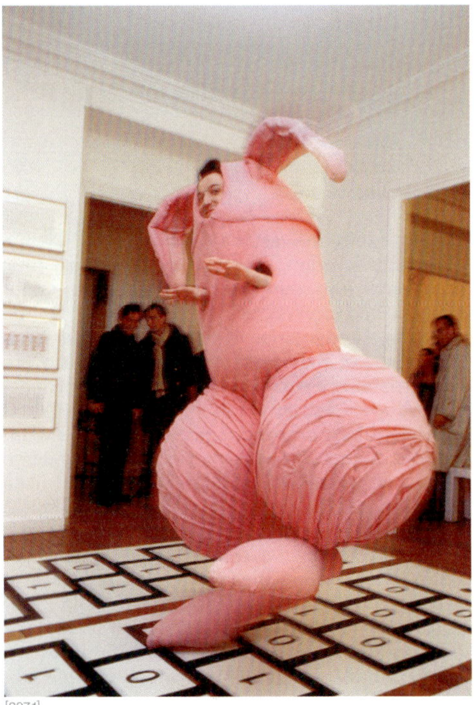

[227.1]

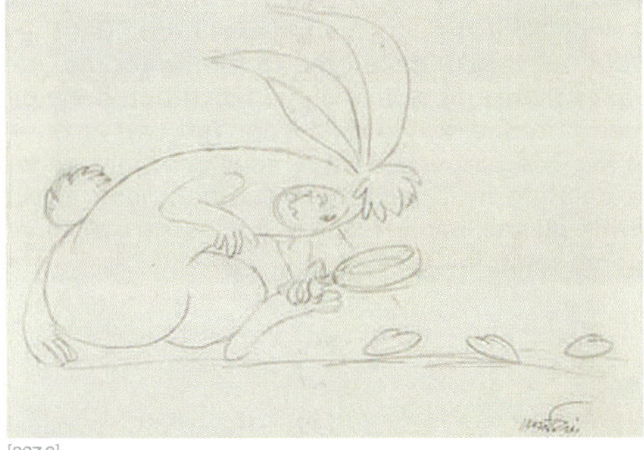

[227.2]

[225.1-2]   *Stadium*, 1991
"AnniNovanta," curated by Renato Barilli and Roberto Daolio, GAM – Galleria comunale d'arte moderna, Bologna, May 28–September 8, 1991 (group show)

[226]   *Tarzan & Jane*, 1993

[227.1]   *Errotin, le vrai lapin*, 1995

Maurizio Cattelan with Umberto Manfrin
[227.2]   *Comic Strip*, 1995
Pencil on paper
32 × 41 cm

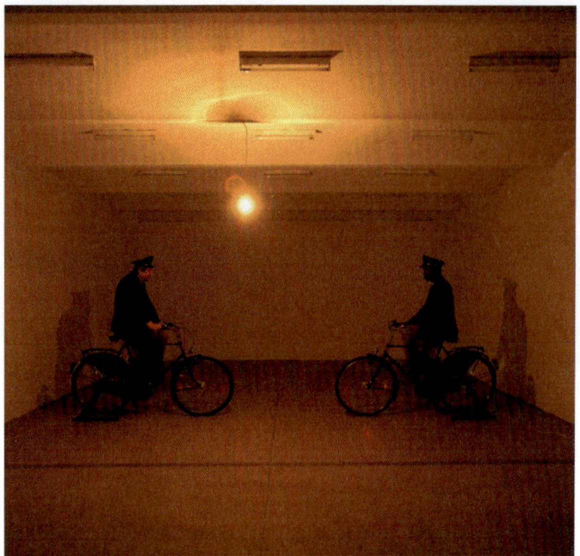

[228]

two people creating a new power dynamic between gallerist and artist, that's all. It was fantastic, because Emmanuel was perfectly ready to play along and laugh with me. It was good of him to be ready to be presented in that ironic way. All the same, I realize that, seen from outside, the performance could have seemed provocative. The viewer could feel he was being treated like an idiot or that some kind of bizarre theater was being performed in the gallery. There's always this tension in my work, between my intentions and the reality, between what I set out to do and what people end up thinking.

I wanted Emmanuel's appearance to reflect his deeper personality. I think we should all dress to express our personality, in a costume that conveys who we are. Certain colors would explain our character. I think it would make everyone's life a lot easier. If Emmanuel had worn that costume for just one day, it might have been described as a kind of punishment, but he did it for a month and a half, making the costume a more serious business.

The costume itself was quite professional. I'd worked with an illustrator to make it and I still have the preparatory drawings.

[228]  ***Dynamo Secession*, 1997**
2 bicycles, 2 museum guards, generator, lightbulbs
Environmental dimensions

[229]  ***Untitled*, 1997**
Bicycles
Lifesize

For an exhibition at the Secession in Vienna I left all the rooms empty, except the last one. You went in and found nothing there except light bulbs. I had connected the light bulbs in the rooms to the dynamos of two bicycles placed in the last room, in the basement. The bicycles were facing each other and two guards had to pedal to produce electricity and light the rooms—the little electricity needed, since they were incandescent bulbs. The guards only pedaled when some visitors arrived, though they should have kept going all the time.

Again in 1997, at the Venice Biennale, I set up some bicycles in the then Italian Pavilion, but without connecting them to anything. It was as if they served to give the idea of a work in progress, and then there was some scaffolding, the wooden kind used for exhibition designs. There are no photos recording my work as a whole, but only one detail. In the rooms assigned to me I had to exhibit with Enzo Cucchi, and at one point I said: "I'd just put some pigeons here." But they told me they'd invited me to fill the rooms, not leave them empty. In the end I distributed the pigeons in one or two rooms and left two or three bikes lying around. I remember one right under a painting by Cucchi, and another, hung about with plastic bags, leaning against a wall near some scaffolding.

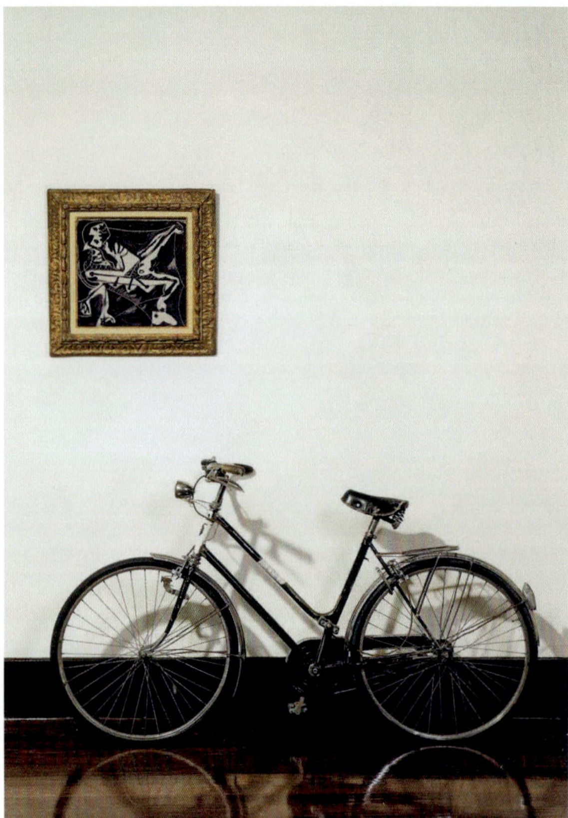

[229]

[228]  *Dynamo Secession*, 1997
"Maurizio Cattelan. Dynamo Secession," curated by Kathrin Rhomberg, Wiener Secession, Vienna, January 31–March 9, 1997 (solo show)

[229]  *Untitled*, 1997 (detail)
"Future Present Past," 47th Venice Biennale, curated by Germano Celant, June 15–November 9, 1997, Italian Pavilion (group show). On the wall, a work by Enzo Cucchi

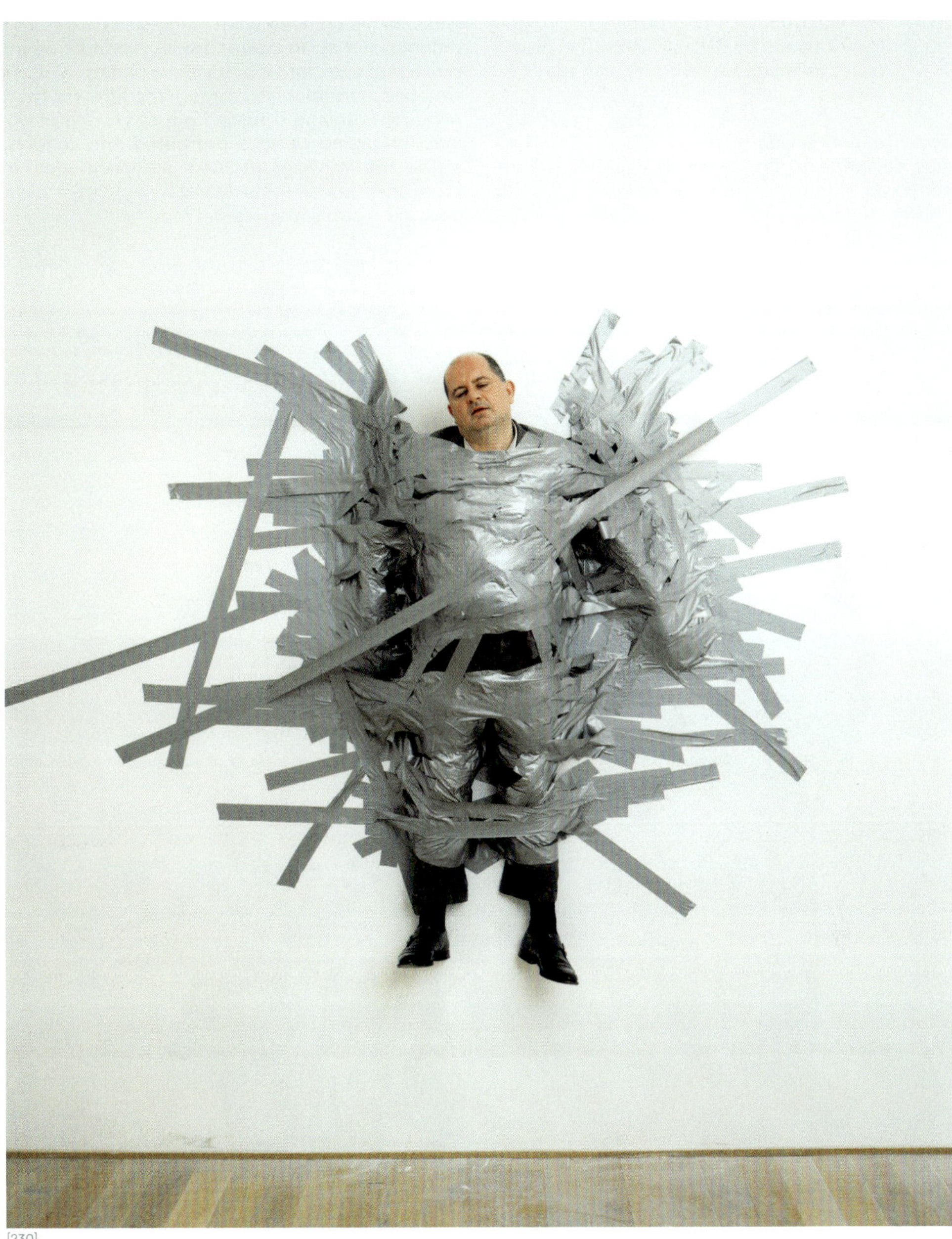

[230]



[230] ***Untitled*, 1999**
[Initially titled: *A Perfect Day*]
Offset print mounted on aluminum
258 × 192 cm
Performance during the solo exhibition
"Maurizio Cattelan" at the Galleria
Massimo De Carlo, Milan, September
27–October 1999

*Untitled* represented the commitment made by the gallery owner to the artist: his vow of loyalty, his proof of love. But Massimo De Carlo stuck on the wall was also a demonstration of mutual affection and esteem: a rite of passage to be able to continue working together.

To be honest, I'd hoped to get rid of him by stunning him with narcotics and letting him wake up only after it was all over, but he didn't report me and he still talks to me. He immediately and willingly accepted the test, showing I could trust him. But we had probably also reached the point where he had to do it, as a small punishment. A bit of mischief was justified.

Over the years I've often put my gallerists to the test, or I've simply thought about doing it. For instance, when Marian Goodman asked me for a work for a group show, I suggested the ceiling of the corridor between the two parts of her gallery be lowered to her height. It was like saying: you're our yardstick, we measure ourselves against you. But in the end nothing came of it.

[230] *Untitled*, 1999

[231] ***Punki*, 2005**
Performance by Bernard Wilson in his costume (height c. 100 cm), various venues

The intention wasn't to annoy people. The work was designed to create an anomalous, unconventional situation. Even the name I gave the character, Punki, with an I, was obviously an intentional mistake. But the costume and the person inside it existed: a busker, Bernard Wilson. I'd seen him somewhere in the Netherlands and then I went all the way to Spain looking for him, to persuade him to work with me. He was terrific at getting people involved and I gave him *carte blanche*. He decided what to say and do. I hadn't thought of it as an interactive work but being inside a museum, and maybe the very nature of the situation, turned it into something different from my intention, and it turned out to be one of my most engaging works. I presented it in London, at the Tate Modern, in 2005, and then again in other institutions—the MMK in Frankfurt even devoted a publication to it.

[231] *Punki*, 2005
"The Long Weekend," Tate Modern, London, May 25–28, 2007 (group show)

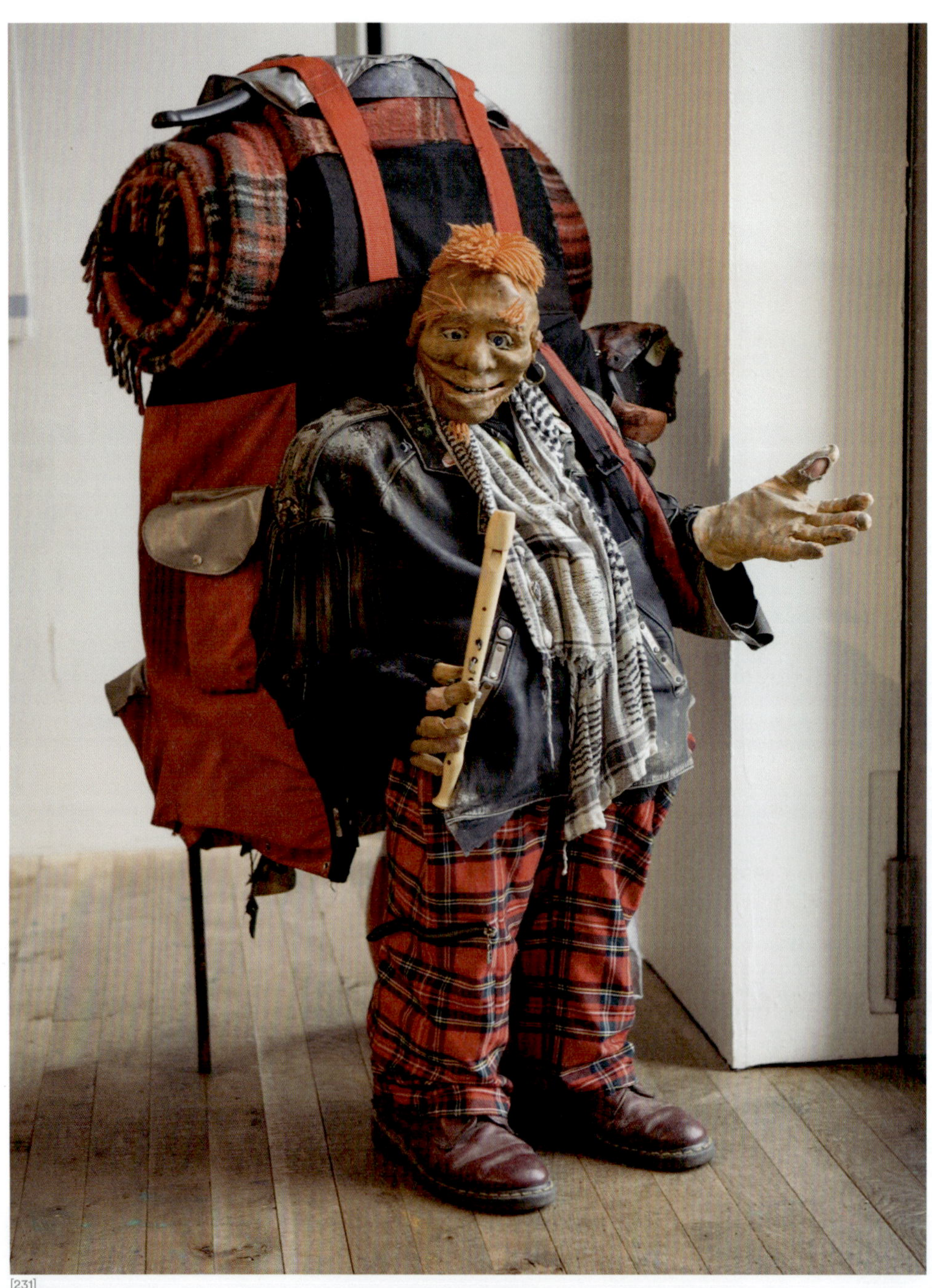



[231]

**[Speech at the Academy of Fine Arts in Carrara on His Appointment as Honorary Professor of Sculpture, April 23, 2018]**

This the first time I've ever spoken in public…
So, first of all, I would like to thank this academy, its teaching staff, and its director for this beautiful ceremony and for this honor.
Sorry, I'll try again…
My case is the demonstration that sometimes you learn more on the way to school than in school. I want to thank all the artists past and present for being my silent teachers. Each of them has shown me that borders do not exist, that our vocabulary can be reinvented every day, and that if something does not exist we can create it. They taught me that the rules have to be learned, but that so as not to miss out on all the fun, they have to be regularly broken. Some of them have shown me that making art is like possessing minds. By their practice, many artists have suggested to me that without discipline, silence, determination, sacrifice, passion, joy, madness, risk, and irrationality, the result of our work is purely an exercise in style.
Everyone agrees that an artist's mission is to discover symbols. Only with those can we transcend fashions, taste, and the right minded, and engage in a battle with history and dialogue with our darkest fears.
I'm almost done…
I would like to thank all the people who have been by my side over the years and with a lot of patience have helped, advised, and often usefully criticized me: without them my work would have been less precise and much more studded with mistakes.
Thanks to the friends who are here with me today and with whom I work on various projects for enabling me to explore the peripheries of the language of art and discover new languages.
A special thanks to Lucio Zotti, whom I could call my third eye. Together we set out on this adventure called art, and together we have seen the creation of many of my works.
Finally, I would like to thank Carrara, its marble, and the pride of those who work it, because here I have discovered a material with which history is written.
I would also like to thank all the students of this academy, who with their enthusiasm and creativity will be the artists of tomorrow.
I'm done.

[Transcript of *Maurizio Cattelan a Carrara, il video dell'intervento integrale*, in YouTube, by the channel *Finestre sull'Arte*, October 24, 2019; https://www.youtube.com/watch?v=dsOjjqcl8Os]

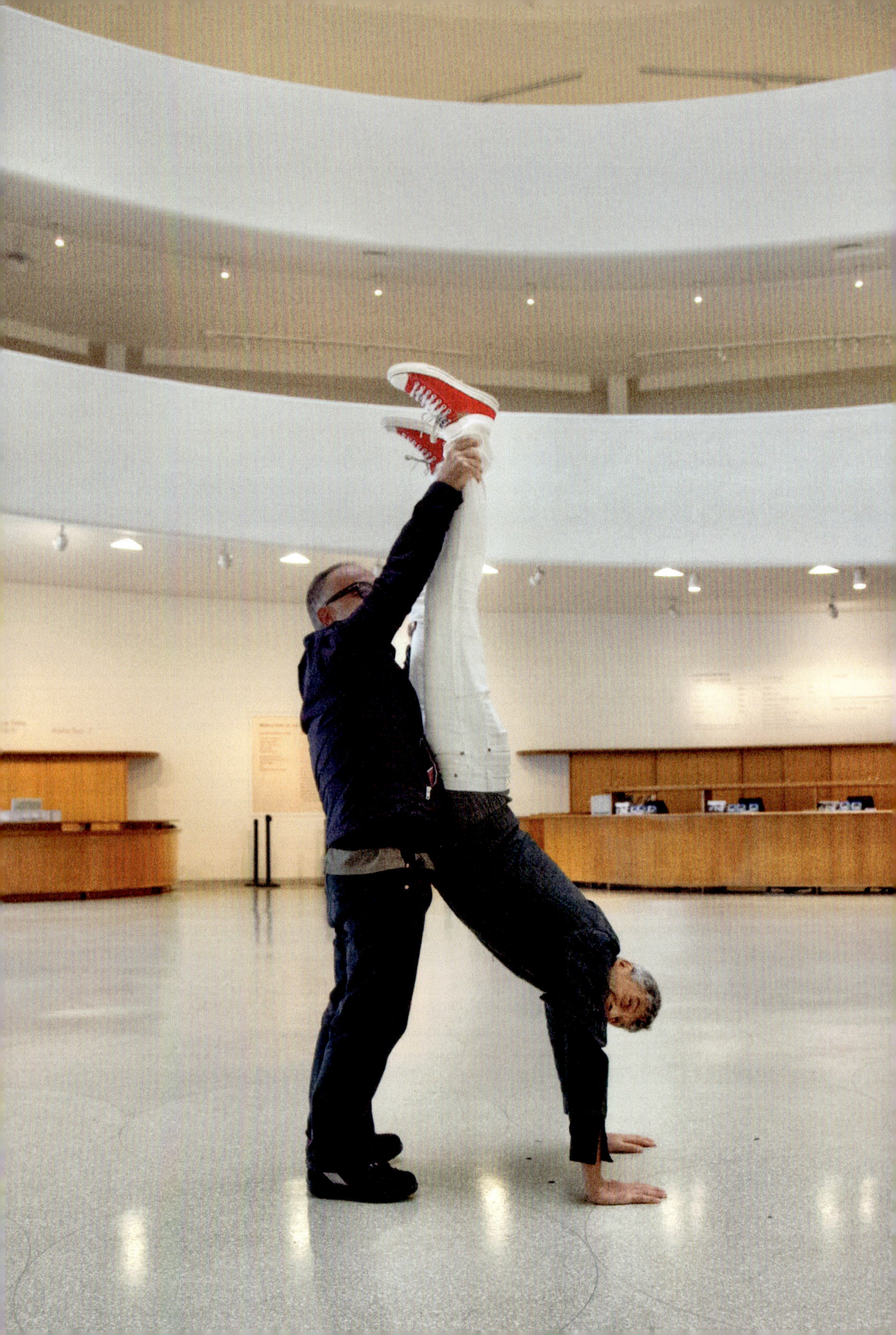

Art should change our lives. We shouldn't remain unaffected when we engage with art. Art should have the energy to transport us to the deepest areas of our consciousness, places we can't go when we're left to ourselves. An artwork should shake us and surprise us, leading to the discovery of a dimension that our limited awareness has never explored or experienced before, and so has never understood. There are all sorts of ways that art can take us into this dimension: by provoking us with violence, religiosity, curiosity, sympathy, annoyance, detachment, contradiction, irony, shame, faith. All these provocations are fair game, because art should not be a dispenser of moral lessons. It's a Trojan horse that enables you to make direct contact with the subconscious, affecting the imagination and triggering visceral reactions.

As an artist, nuances are your duty. As an artist you have to avoid simplifications. As an artist you should aim to suggest contradictions, not effacing or denying them, but admitting them and welcoming them. Otherwise you will be turning out propaganda and distributing a product, amounting to the death of art. Being a provocateur is not directly my goal in making art, but, when you avoid simplifications and focus on nuances, then you might say something people would rather not hear. Provocation can only be a means. When it becomes an end, it loses all interest as art. I believe that causing a scandal today means showing that we don't need anything, making everyone see that the king is naked.

Scandal is an accident, a side effect. I work with images, trying to reflect the schizophrenia of reality. The scandal is raised by others, when they try to impose their own interpretation as the only possible truth. I've never decided point-blank to cause a scandal or be provocative. Images sometimes manage to anticipate the future and perhaps this is what scandalizes the public, who still can't recognize themselves in what they see. I don't care much for provocations. The provocations that really interest me are those that transform a personal emergency into a public act. They're the only ones that have a reason for existing. Provocations as ends in themselves are sad and useless, like unexploded Molotov cocktails. The other kind can also be dangerous to the arm throwing them. It's the price to be paid. My three sculptures suspended from a tree in Milan (*Untitled*, 2004) were vandalized. What I like about the audience's reaction is its utter unpredictability. There's no way of foreseeing it.

The sense of desecration exists in the gaze of the spectators. I don't feel good in the role of the hero. I'm just a speaker, or maybe a sponge, a sensor of the world. I don't think I've ever done anything more provocative, cynical or ruthless than the things I see around me all the time. I think reality is much more provocative than my art. You should walk down a street and see the real beggars, not my fake ones. You should see a real skinhead rally. I just take what's out there. I borrow pieces—crumbs, in fact—of every-day reality. If you think my work is very provocative, it shows that reality is extremely provocative, but we simply don't react to it. Perhaps we no longer pay attention to how we live in the world. We're constantly surrounded by shocking events, yelled out in block capitals from every newsstand. Being shocked is our daily bread. We're getting used to it, becoming increasingly anesthetized. This has raised the threshold of what deeply touches people, leading to increasingly shocking events. It seems there's no end to the horror. Of course, it depends on the point of view. In 1955 it was shocking when Rosa Parks refused to give up her seat on the bus to a white passenger, while to-day she's the symbol of change for the better. The shocks I like are direct ones, which produce a debate. A provocation is nothing more than an uncomfortable truth spoken out loud. Art sometimes succeeds where words fail to reach.

328

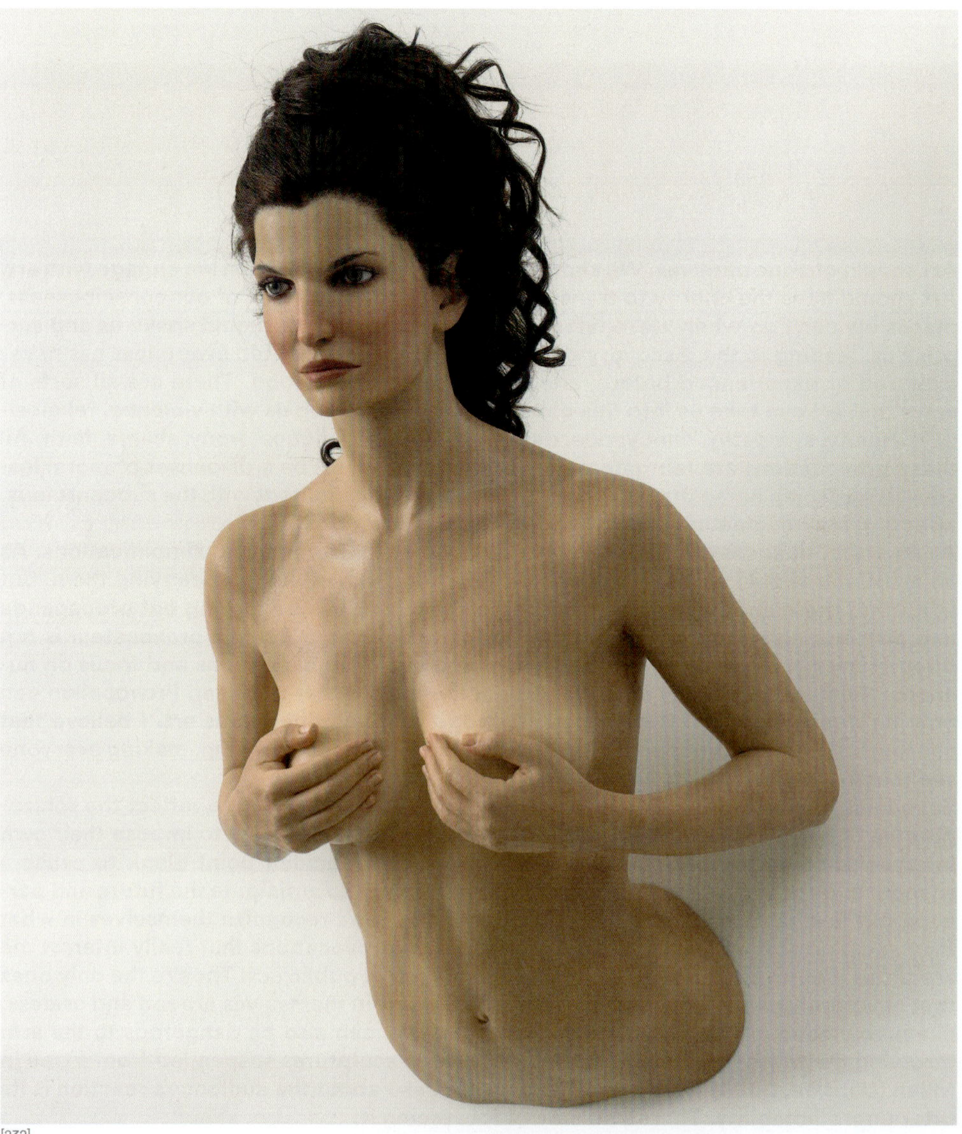

[232]

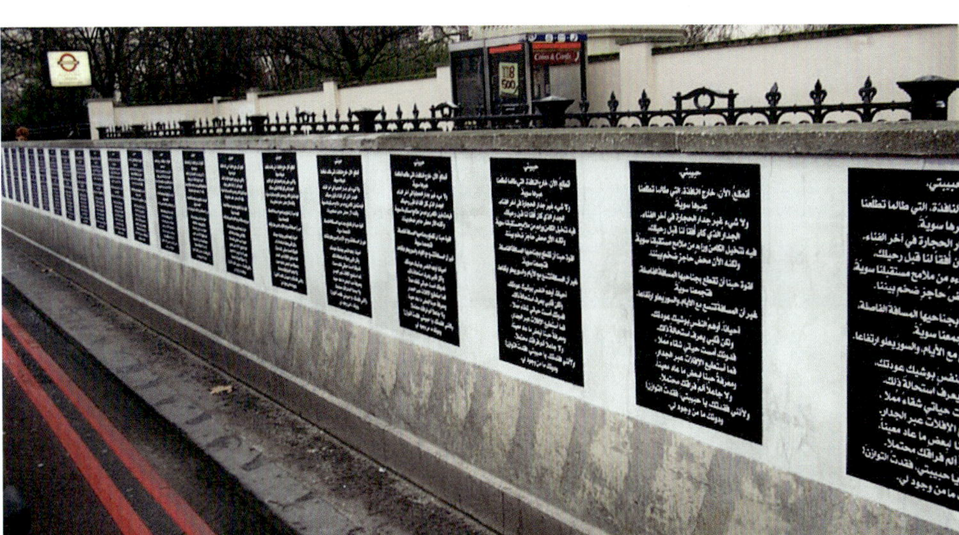

[233.1]

[232]  **Stephanie**, 2003
Wax, pigment, synthetic hair, metal
109.9 × 64.8 × 41.9 cm

I made this portrait of the model Stephanie Seymour because her husband, Peter Brant, was creating a collection of works by different artists about her. It's another fine story. I went to Brant's home because he wanted to commission a work from me. As I went inside the house I saw the walls covered with hunting trophies of all kinds of animals. I immediately knew what I was going to do. It was consequential to add one more, a portrait of his beautiful wife. He seemed happy. Rules are just hurdles to be jumped over, as in a horse race, higher and higher. Never give an artist like me *carte blanche*.

[233]  **Untitled**, 2004
Offset prints on paper
70 × 50 cm each

I was asked to exhibit at the group show "State of Play" at the Serpentine Gallery in London. It was the time of the attacks by Islamic fundamentalists and I decided to put up posters around London with a love letter in Arabic. It was a dedication to the confusion of messages, and in fact it sparked some unnecessary agitation. Printed in white on a black ground, they looked like declarations of war. Later I planned to make T-shirts with the words "Love New York," again in Arabic.

[233.2]

329

[The poster reads: "My love, / I look out now from the window through which / we often looked together, / and there is nothing but the stone wall at the beyond. / The wall that was our horizon before you left, / behind which we imagined our future together, / has turned into an insurmountable obstacle between us. / May the strength of our love on its two wings fly over the distance that separates us, / bringing us together again. / But with time the distance increases and the wall grows higher. / Sometimes I deceive myself into thinking that you will return soon, / but my heart knows that it is impossible. / Without you, my life has become wretchedly tedious. / I cannot escape through the wall. / Knowing of the love we feel for each other is no longer a comfort, / it does not ease the pain of your departure. / Since I have lost you, my love, I have also lost my harmony. / Without you I do not exist"]

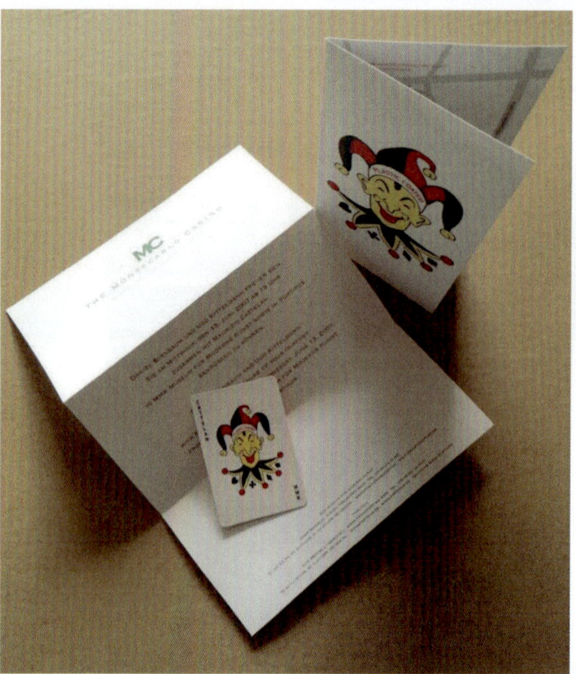



[234]



[234] **"Maurizio Cattelan," 2007**
Solo show curated by Andreas Bees and
Udo Kittelmann, MMK – Museum für
Moderne Kunst, Frankfurt, March 1–
September 23, 2007

[235] *Untitled*, 2007
Lacquered plywood, wood,
aluminum, metal, artificial cake
(polyurethane foam, plastic, wax)
Table: 74 × 350 × 80 cm;
cake: Ø 23.5 cm

One day Andreas Slominski was having a solo show at the Museum für Moderne Kunst in Frankfurt and he called me and asked: "Why don't you do a work for my show?" Without announcing it, we installed a table that went right through a wall of the museum, the first work I did after co-curating the fourth Berlin Biennale. I was returning to the other side of the barricade: a leap into the void.

An image from the film *Brazil* stuck in my mind, of a table that went from one side of a wall to the other and you could pull it this way and that. On the third floor of the museum they cut a slit in an outside wall. When the table was pulled out, it could be up to three meters long. The rest remained on the outside anyway and on top of that part there was a cake—just to put something on it.

From March 2007 I continued to infiltrate my new works into the museum's permanent collection, first the horse with its head embedded in the wall (*Untitled*, 2007), then *Ave Maria* (2007). In June, with the posters of the German flag (*Untitled*, 2007) and *Frau C.* (2007), installed above the trees in front of the entrance to the Portikus contemporary art center, near the MMK, the presence of my works perhaps became a little clearer, but for a time it was interesting to observe the public looking at works without an artist's name. Later I added *Punki* (2005), which spent two weeks going around the rooms in the museum. As an idealist, I didn't know where I was going, but I felt I was on the right track.

At one point an invitation to the exhibition also appeared, but not from the museum: the sender was The Montecarlo Casino. The letter, sent together with the revisitation of a playing card I had found somewhere, was in the name of Daniel Birnbaum, Udo Kittelmann and me, and gave the day of the opening as the day before the inauguration of Documenta in Kassel. But we decided to send the invitation late, so that no one would receive it before leaving for the so-called grand tour of art, which that year consisted of the Venice Biennale, Art Basel, Skulptur Projekte in Münster and Documenta. If you're part of the game you can't not be there, but after all everyone—like me—would have liked to be elsewhere. I would have liked to give others the opportunity to use me as a wild card and disappear. A lone voice that I really liked was raised by a priest of Frankfurt cathedral, Stefan Scholz, who published a text entitled *Concealing Walls*, focusing in particular on two of the works exhibited at the MMK. As for *Ave Maria*, he wrote: "Mass demonstrations and parades in the National Socialist period, filmed from above. Individuals disappear among the masses, and the masses disappear under the arms raised in a Nazi salute. What remains is a bulwark of lances made up of bones, flesh, hair and fabric, a collective gesture of clenched aggression and determination. Each arm covers the head of the man in front, and what remains is pure will for power. A creature with a thousand arms is shouting its spirit of conflict at the Führer. Cattelan dissects three limbs from this beast and fastens them to the wall. [...] One single extended arm would seem ridiculous, two would still be tolerable, a third already suggests a crowd and gives the installation a threatening aspect. It is the dark, cleanly placed male hairs on the back of the hand that symbolize the joys of fighting. Our imaginations have to shape the other parts of the body from the wall, the faces in particular. [...] The serious suit fabrics suggest contemporary faces and features. The cramped space increases the potential for danger by one more factor. Cattelan is not alluding to any figures from the past. The bogeymen the arms belong to remain anonymous. People you might least expect to do so will, even today, confidently raise their arms and whet their knives behind alleged promises of prosperity and protection. A horse with its head going through a wall is amusing. Three separate arms would be just as amusing, if the National Socialist period were merely history now, and people did not need to be afraid that dubious characters from earlier days have spawned numerous intellectual and spiritual heirs. If it were possible to laugh out loud at Cattelan's installation, it would be a good sign for our society." And then: "Half a table disappears into a wall that has been torn open, holding two of its four legs in the air. The cake on the outside part can be seen only from the inside, and could only be eaten on the outside, sitting down. It is hidden from the outside. People standing inside wonder how they can get at the cake; people standing outside wonder why a table is hanging half in the air

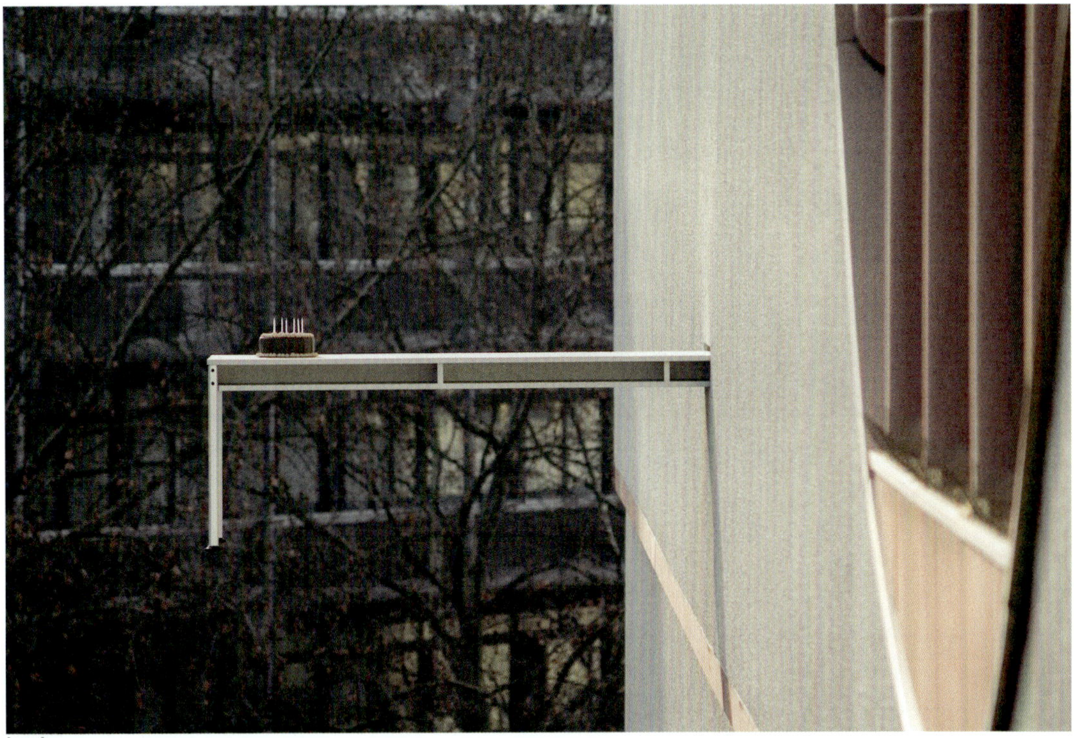

[235.1]

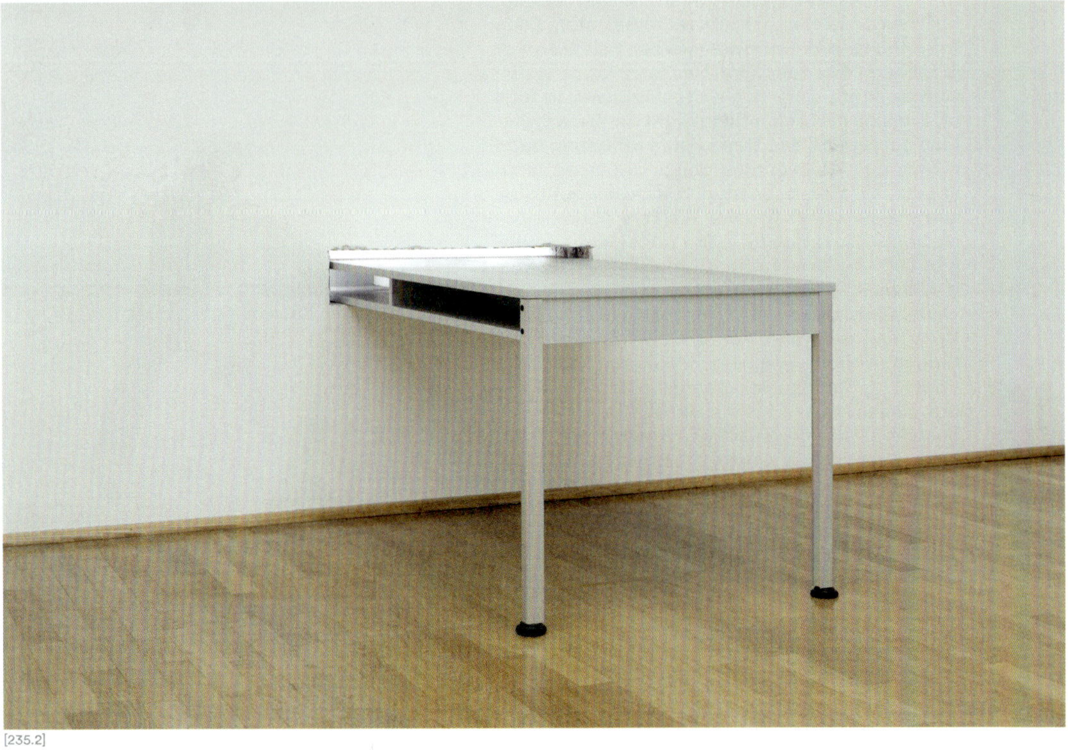

[235.2]

[234]  "Maurizio Cattelan," MMK – Museum für Moderne
Kunst, Frankfurt, 2007
Invitation for the exhibition sent from the Montecarlo Casino

[235.1-2]  *Untitled*, 2007
"Maurizio Cattelan," MMK – Museum für Moderne Kunst,
Frankfurt, 2007, installation inside and outside the museum

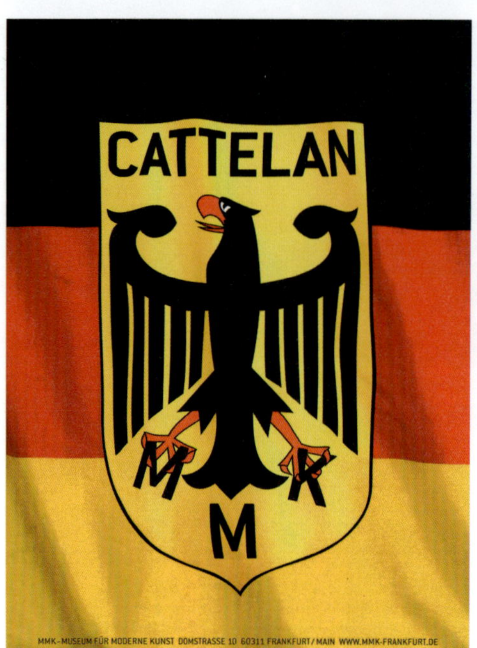



[236]

332

like that. Cattelan's table is a problem whichever way you look at it. Seen from the inside, because the table is inseparably connected with eating, but the edible element refuses to be eaten. Seen from the outside, a table you can't sit down at is robbed of its function. This installation is disturbing from every angle. It is amusing to look at, but also casts significant light on the way human perception and the insights reflecting upon it function. An everyday object is placed in an essentially absurd setting. It arouses curiosity, and makes something we scarcely notice—because it is so ordinary, just a table—into an object creating profound insights. The wit of this installation is not revealed by external scrutiny alone. Only those who take the trouble to look from the inside and the outside will see more, though without grasping its ultimate implications. [...] Cattelan makes the visitors run from the outside to the inside and the inside to the outside as if on a treadmill, without their ever being able to get a view of the object as a whole. Human beings are either driven mad by the urge to know, or learn to laugh at themselves, to stop being so grim and dogged about everything, to see life as a game and not take themselves too seriously, or if they want to be serious, they learn to become humble."

[236]   *Untitled*, 2007
Multicolor print on paper
119 × 84 cm

Traveling around Germany with Ali Subotnick and Massimiliano Gioni while preparing for the 2006 Berlin Biennale, I saw so many flags that I felt a new nationalism was in the air. Perhaps the Germans were also looking for a new flag. For every question there is only one possible answer, but infinite points of view. I gave mine.

[237]   *You*, 2021
Platinum silicone, epoxy fiberglass, natural hair, clothing, stainless steel, hemp rope, flowers
140 × 40 × 25 cm

At first this work was installed outside, on the facade of the Luxembourg + Co. gallery in London. But it only hung there for a day, due to protests from the neighbors, and we had to take it inside. When I saw it in its new location I realized I should have thought of moving it before, because it worked much better. So in its final form, it's installed in an interior.
*You* is a self-portrait. It's me, barefooted, with some flowers in my hand, hanging from the gallows. The more I reproduce myself, the more it becomes a way to disappear.

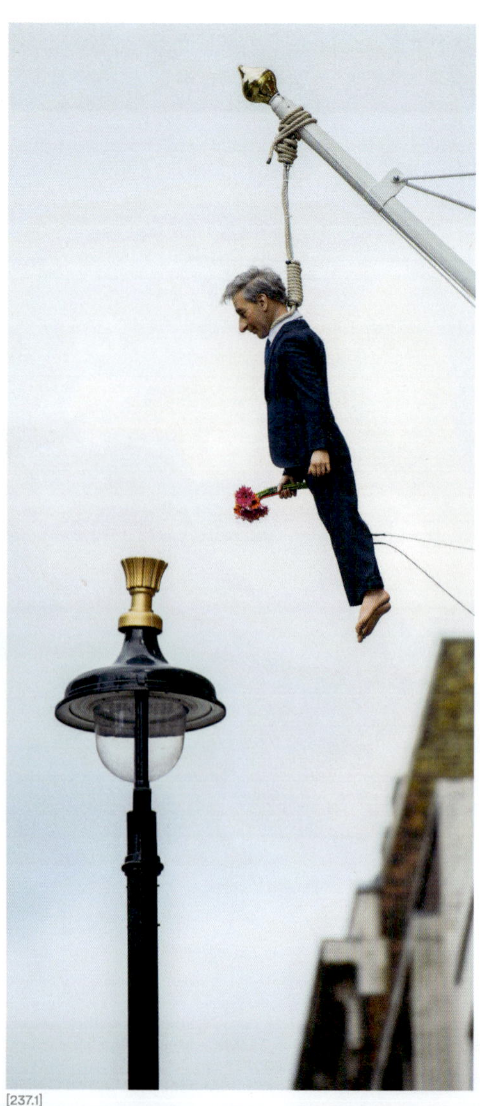

[237.1]

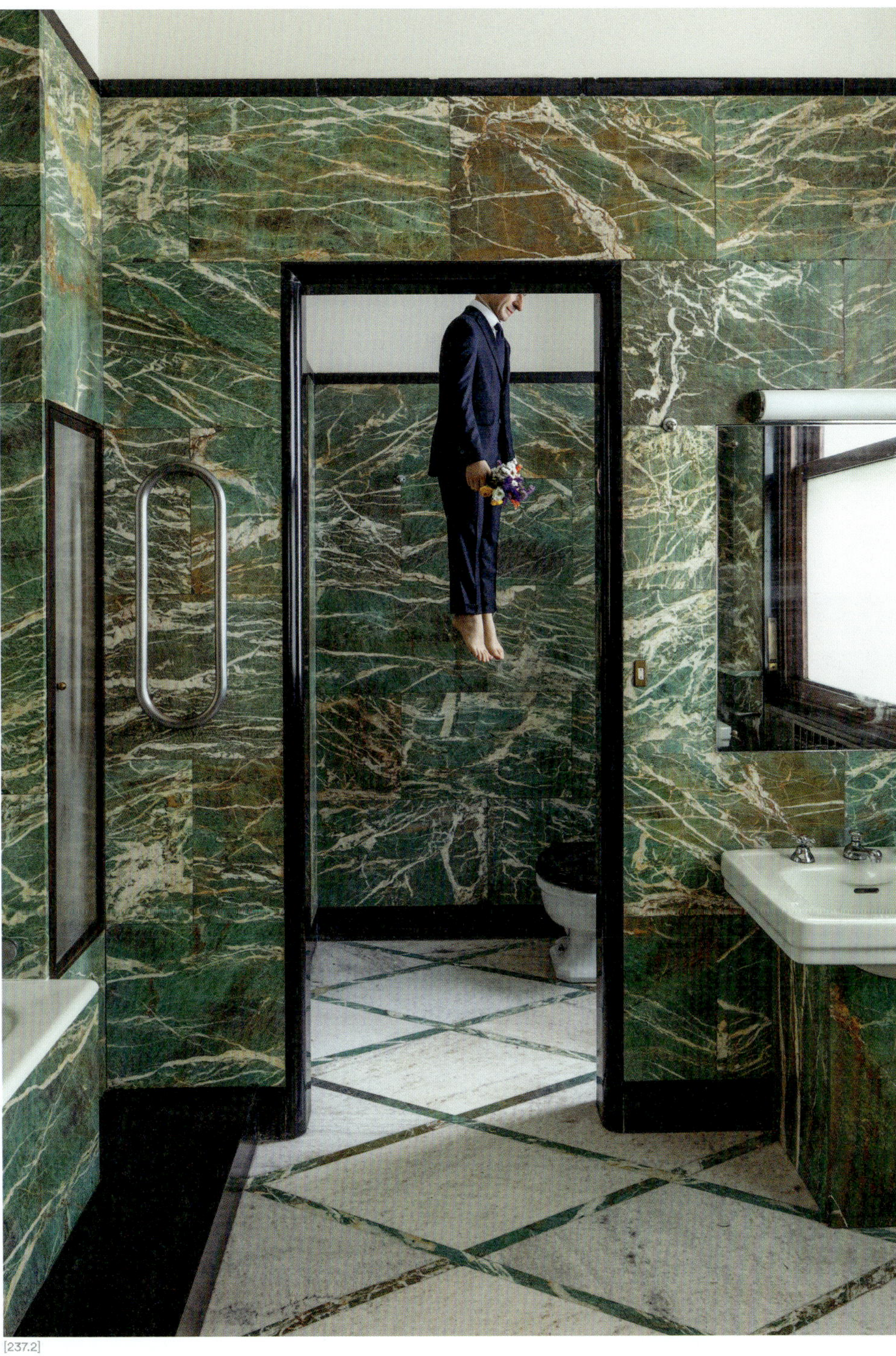

[237.2]



[236]   *Untitled*, 2007

[237.1]   *You*, 2021
"Lost in Italy," curated by Francesco Bonami, Luxembourg +
Co., London, May 6–July 24, 2021 (group show)

[237.2]   *You*, 2021
"You," Massimo De Carlo, Milan, March 28–June 25, 2022
(solo show)

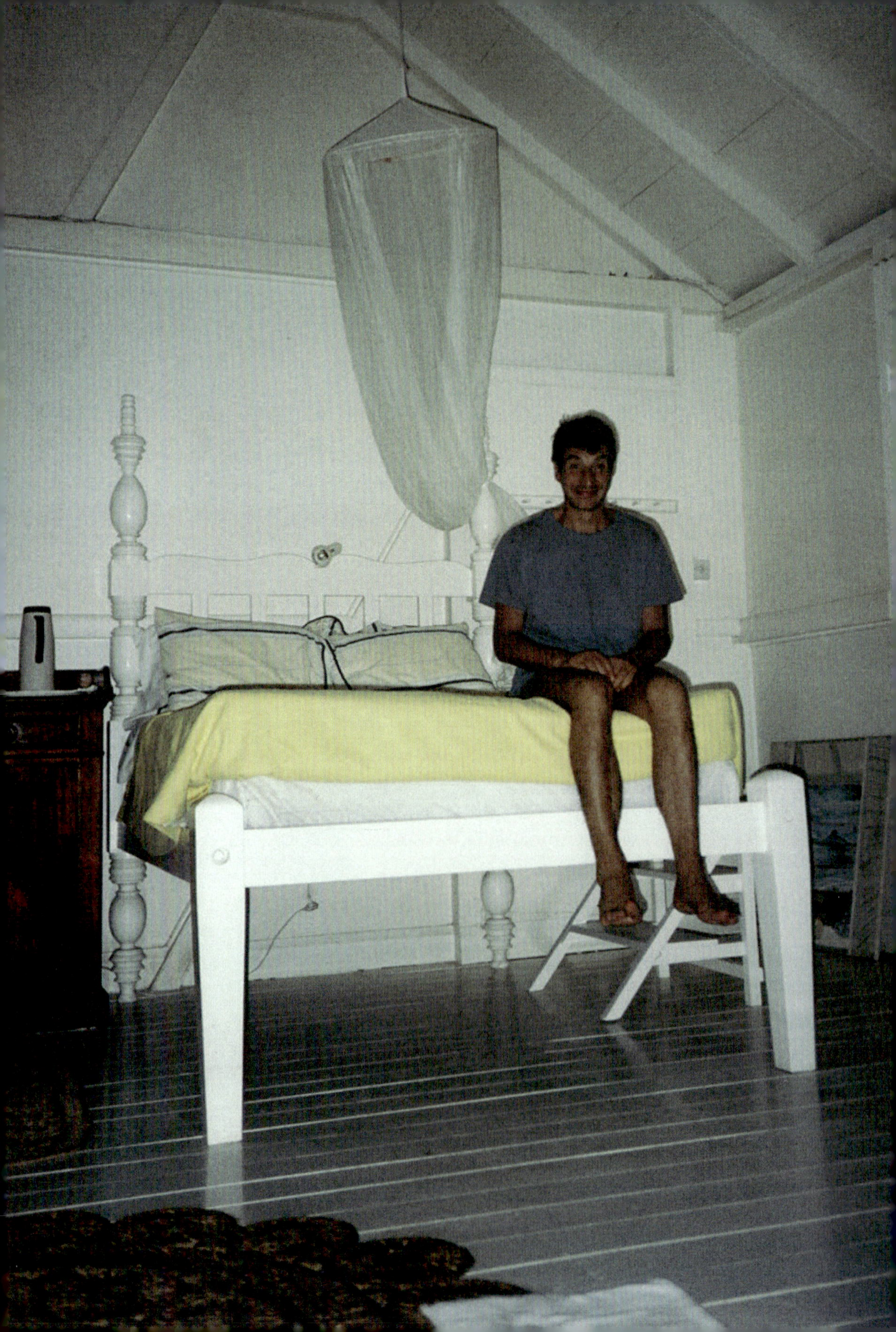

I remember clearly when I decided to stop working for others. I think it must have been with the time when I started trying to do art. At that time I started wondering when I'd start feeling like an artist, but now I've given up worrying it might never happen. I only know that I spend every day doing what I like, whether it's exhibitions, magazines or swimming lengths of the pool. I don't think that being an artist is an existential condition. Essentially it's a label like any other, and I've always been allergic to the labels that others apply to you. The real question is perhaps different. At school they tell you that if you don't study you'll become a dunce. Are you born or a dunce or do you become one? And can you stay that way your whole life? If you're lucky, you'll die an artist. Everything that comes before is a long journey towards understanding something.

It took me a long time to get to where I am and I'm still terrified of being kicked out. I have an intruder complex. I'm afraid that sooner or later they'll find out I wasn't invited and throw me out of the art world. But an impostor is someone who wants to be someone else, who passes himself off as someone he's not. You can say what you like about me, but not that I've ever tried or would try to be someone else. Actors play different roles for so long when they're working that when they're offstage I feel it's hard to see them as individuals. Artists don't have this problem—most of the time they're exactly how they appear. I don't think there's any separation between all my different selves; they're all sides of the same figure. I see myself in all the portraits made of me and my self-portraits and selfies and in all those to come. If they could be pieced together, perhaps they would convey some idea of who I am.

Essentially I'm the same person as always. I have many flaws, of course, but my flaws are not someone else's. I don't work on my flaws, because I've built my identity on them, and if I've ever managed to do a good work of art, I owe it to my flaws and those of the people I grew up with. You work on your flaws, if they no longer allow you to be what you want to be, or to be a success in what you do. I just tried to turn my weaknesses into strength, the way everyone does.

I think each of my works can be considered the image of a problem that I've understood and internalized. However, works of art, even the most mysterious ones, are never the product of a single person. They're the result of a negotiation between the artist and society. The problem is that you can never draw a precise boundary between yourself and the world. And I'm empty without others.

Being an artist was never a choice but a necessity. I couldn't have done anything else with my life. But as far as I'm concerned working as an artist means always living in contact with the ideas, views and perversions of others. This naturally leads you to take an interest in them, whoever they are, and in my case the others are often artists, so through them I've come to see visions rich in meaning.

I work for fun. This is the most exciting bit of not having anything to do. I came to art by trial and error after working at a lot of different jobs. When I started, art fascinated me because it seemed like a way out of wage labor, of rewriting the rules so that I wouldn't be someone's employee. Marcel Duchamp always used to say: "I like breathing better than working." In art, every minute of the day and every situation is work. Perhaps this is why there is no "where" as much as there is a "through" or a "thanks to." Producing an artwork is a diffuse process. It can take months and has no schedule. It's not like putting on a suit and tie and clocking in, or going home and putting on your pajamas. You never stop wearing these clothes, a bit like the costumes of religious people or doctors. The arrival of an idea is between the chemical and the alchemical. You take what seems like a good intuition and start testing it with different reagents. Then you keep mixing until it crystallizes. It doesn't happen all the time, but those two times a year that it does happen are the reason why you get up every morning.

Actually, I've never had any ideas. Artists don't have ideas. The image of the inspired creator hunting for new emotions is just a movie stereotype. The realm of ideas is within everyone's reach, and it's free. Artists grind, filter, connect and dismantle. Ideas, if they arrive, stem from continuous practice, from dealing directly with things. Ideas are dialectical short circuits. As for the way all this happens, I've always thought of the absence of quality as a stimulus for a personal research, and this is the starting point of every artist. I never know what project I'll work on next. I'm a researcher without theory and without method. My career is made up of accidents along the way that turned out to be interesting, in retrospect.



Someone once called me a concept worker. Maybe being an artist is just about looking at reality and reflecting it, trying to show the details that would otherwise go unnoticed. Artists are the antennae of the present, whatever present they find themselves in. I certainly feel more like an antenna installer than an artist. As an artist your duty is not to simplify. Even if you choose to express yourself in the simplest way, the duty remains to express the nuance, explain the complication, suggest the contradiction and see within the contradiction where the stricken human being stands. To make allowance for chaos, and let it in. You have to let it in. Otherwise you'll only produce propaganda. So I successfully play the role of the artist when I can go deeper, when my works have an impact that makes you feel uncomfortable, make you change your mind or lead you to see everyday life differently.

Artists should try to fulfil their dreams, otherwise it would be better to go and work in a bank. If you dare to dream, go out and achieve your dream. Yet, as I see it, the artist should never be present. On the contrary, the more elusive you are as an artist, the more room you leave for others to interpret your work. The more independent your works are of your life, the more they can take their place in history. I must admit that I'm rather traditionalist about it. I believe that when an artist hands over a work it no longer belongs to them.

I feel it's always true that everyone chooses a path of their own by interweaving three factors: skill, motivation and attitude. Skill is what you're capable of doing, motivation determines what you do, attitude how well you do it. My luck lies in having had the strength to weave together these elements so well that I was able to emancipate myself from my past. It's a very personal thing. In the art world, you create your own rules and you have to respect them. I did it and I think I could easily have given away my ass far more than I ever did. The temptation of money and the privileges it can bring is very, very strong. You can then find yourself producing things just to sell them. If this choice is consistent with your work, that's fine, but if the financial factor becomes overriding and weakens it, then it's a shame. From this point of view I can't say I'm immaculate, but I've managed to defend myself.

I've been an artist for thirty-five years, and when I think about it I'm amazed, because in the past I could never o keep a job for long. Art saved me. Not in the sense of giving

**me well-being and security but precisely by saving me from the street. Otherwise I'd have ended up in prison. Or dead.**

[238] *Tourists*, 1997
Taxidermied pigeons
Environmental dimensions

At the 1997 Venice Biennale, directed by Germano Celant, the struggle for me was ultimately that my project always seemed to have to fill another room. Everyone thought I was happy about it. Every day they said: "Here's another two hundred square meters for you." I thought: "Are you crazy?" What could I do with it? Instead of feeling empowered by the situation, all my energy was being drained out of me. It was as if they wanted me to buy the space this time. I'd got away with it in 1993 but in 1997 they really wanted me to sit down and do something.
I went to see the pavilion in Venice about a month before the exhibition opened. The inside was a shambles, filled, really filled with pigeons. To me, as an Italian, it was like seeing something you're not meant to see, like the pope's dressing room. But then again, that's the situation in Venice, so I thought I should just present it as it is, a normal situation. And of course, wherever there are pigeons there's pigeon droppings. In the end I thought the project almost did enough. I would have liked to fill the whole international exhibition with birds, but I had to limit myself to the rooms in the Italian Pavilion. I also had in mind Hitchcock's *The Birds*. As a kid, I used to see all these pigeons in the public squares in my hometown, and one day my mother took me to the cinema to see the movie. It terrified me. For years I wouldn't go anywhere near a square with pigeons swarming in it.
I think that, if there really was something provocative about the work, it was in its relationship with time. Time doesn't affect this place. Basically all the Biennales seem the same. If I could, I would love to set up the same work in two consecutive Biennales. I think no would notice. I was later able to bring it back to the Biennale in 2011 (*Others*). Meanwhile, I installed the birds and their poop to show that everything stands still there, that *Time Goes By So Slowly*—but that's another song.

[Curator Germano Celant invited Cattelan to exhibit in the Italian Pavilion together with two artists of different generations, Ettore Spalletti (1940–2019) and Enzo Cucchi (1949). Cattelan's intervention also involved scattering some bicycles around the spaces in the pavilion (*Untitled*, 1997)]



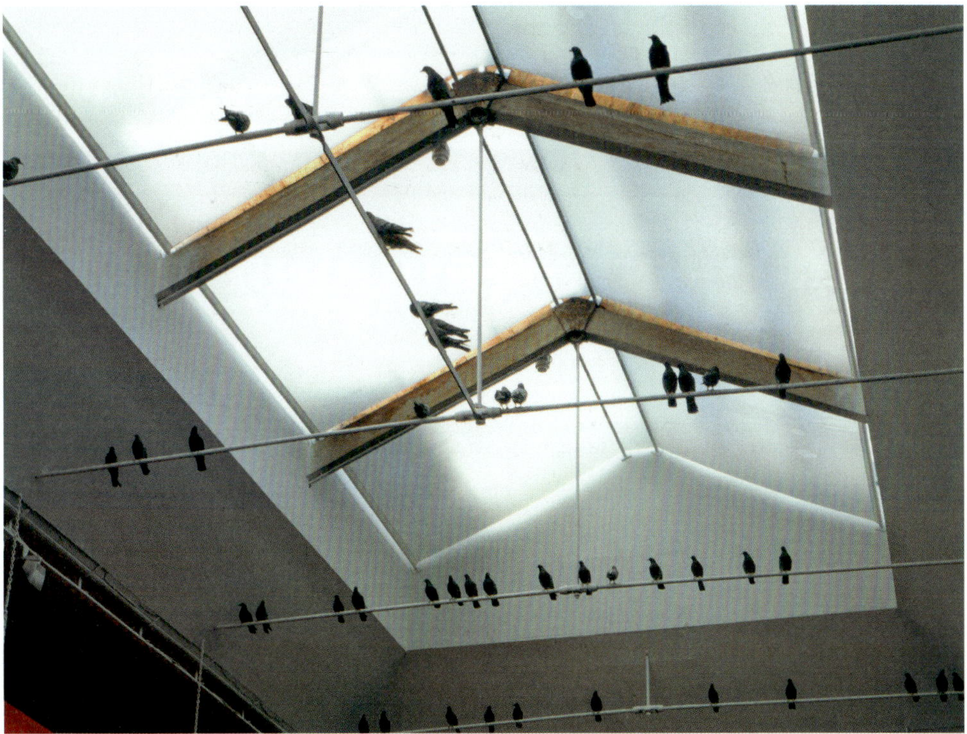

[238]

[238] *Tourists*, 1997
"Future Present Past," 47th Venice Biennale, curated by Germano Celant, June 15–November 9, 1997, Italian Pavilion (group show)

**[239]** ***Others*, 2011**
Taxidermied pigeons
Environmental dimensions

**[240]** ***Ghosts*, 2021**
Taxidermied pigeons
Environmental dimensions

When Bice Curiger invited me to take part in the 2011 Venice Biennale, I immediately thought of a long-standing wish: to exhibit the same work twice at the Biennale, because no one would notice anyway. So I presented the 1997 pigeons (*Tourists*) again. But this time there were thousands of them, inside and outside the Central Pavilion of the Giardini. I changed the title and called this nondescript crowd *Others*.

We live in a society where we're under constant surveillance, with someone or something always watching us. It's like being in *The Truman Show*. Up to the very end you don't know whether you're the subject or object of what's going on. Pigeons are extraordinary, with an incredible sense of orientation. If they're released in an unfamiliar place they always manage to find their way home. They're among the few animals that

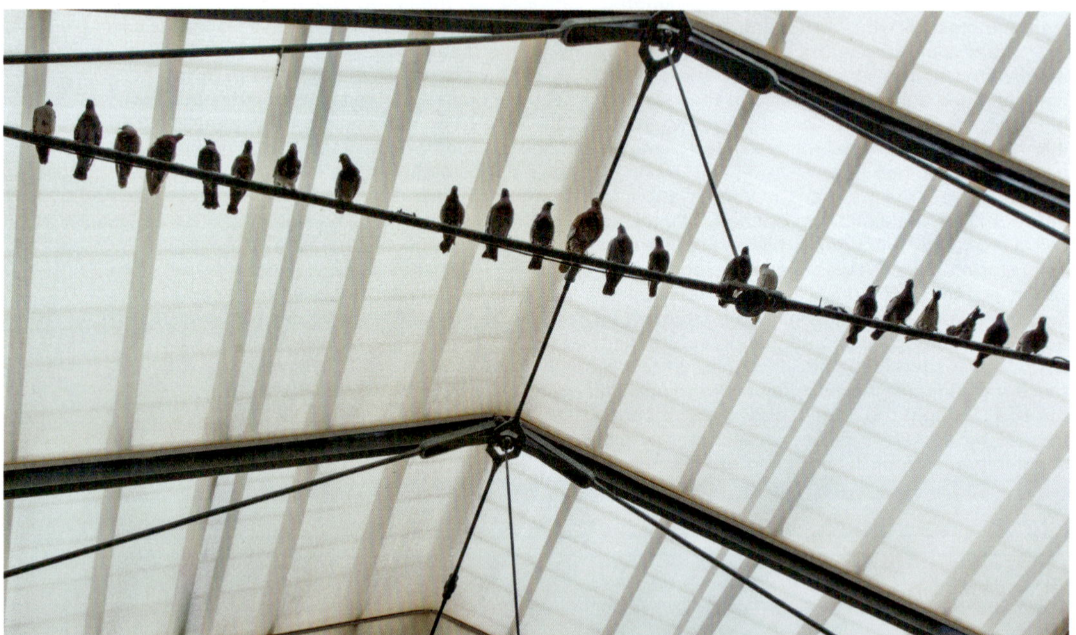

[239]

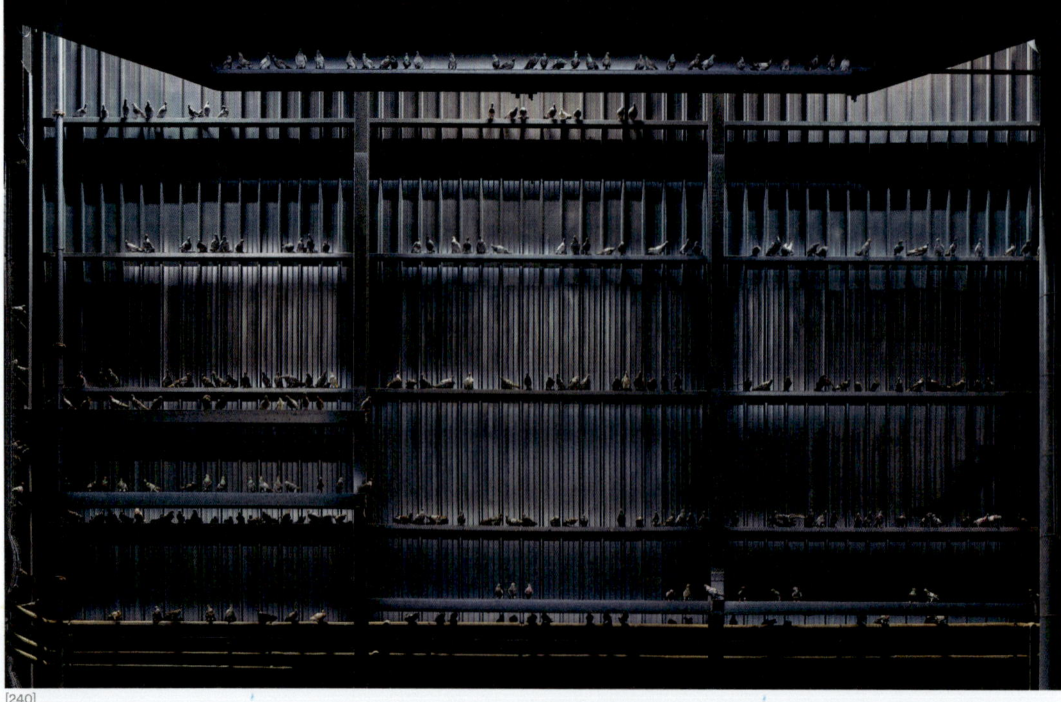

[240]

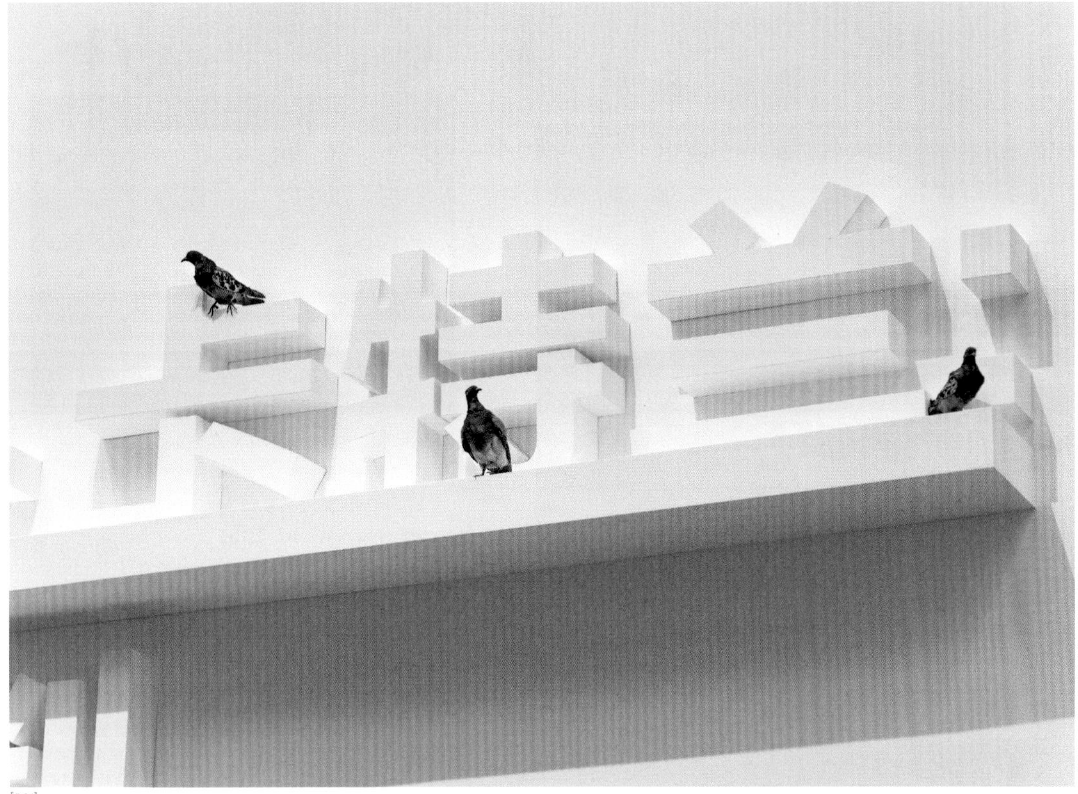



can recognize themselves in a mirror, and they've been used in all kinds of lab and field tests, in studies ranging from psychology to ornithology. My pigeons have evolved since the first time I exhibited them at the 1997 Venice Biennale. First they were called *Tourists*, then they became *Others*, and then again *Ghosts* and finally *Kids*. Not even I know the reason for this transformation, but maybe it's in their nature: they're good at adapting and they understand situations. They're very trustworthy creatures, but for better or for worse they carry with them a piece of everything they land on. In Venice in 2008 the municipality had to ban people feeding them in Piazza San Marco, because cleaning up their droppings was costing millions of euros, and from companion animals they'd become the bearers of contagion. And so it happened with *Ghosts*, with which I filled every corner of Pirelli HangarBicocca's Navate space. Their eyes, hundreds and thousands of them, were watching us, monitoring us, and we no longer knew whether to see them as friends or enemies.

[239]  *Others*, 2011 (detail)
"ILLUMInations," 54th Venice Biennale, curated by
Bice Curiger, June 4–November 27, 2011 (group show)

[240]  *Ghosts*, 2021 (detail)
"Maurizio Cattelan. Breath Ghosts Blind," curated by
Roberta Tenconi and Vicente Todolí, Pirelli HangarBicocca,
Milan, July 15, 2021–February 20, 2022 (solo show)

[241]  *Kids*, 2021 (detail)
"Maurizio Cattelan. The Last Judgment," curated by
Francesco Bonami, UCCA Center for Contemporary Art,
Beijing, November 20, 2021–February 20, 2022 (solo show)

[241]  **_Kids_, 2021**
Taxidermied pigeons
Environmental dimensions

In all the iterations of my work with pigeons, the titles usually refer to groups of individuals seen as a whole. To *Tourists*, in particular. In Italy we see tourists not as a group of people each with his or her own identity, but as a bunch of humans who all look the same and who are threatening our environment and peaceful daily life. With *Kids* is much the same. They move in a group; they're noisy and in some ways also a menace. Kids together can produce quite a bit of damage. They're a liability. *Ghosts*, I don't know but I feel they're the same: ghosts move in groups and gather together to divide up the houses to haunt among themselves. You think of pigeons as a mass, not as individual animals. Forget about pets.
I use them as decoration, in the same way that someone would use a floral pattern running high up around the walls of a room. But my decoration is disturbing. Actually I think decoration always is—I agree with Adolf Loos on this. Pigeons give any space or architecture an eerie feeling. The visitor feels watched, controlled in some way by an unknown entity. When people feel uncomfortable, they're more aware of what they're looking at. I believe that pigeons help my work to avoid being dismissed out of hand.

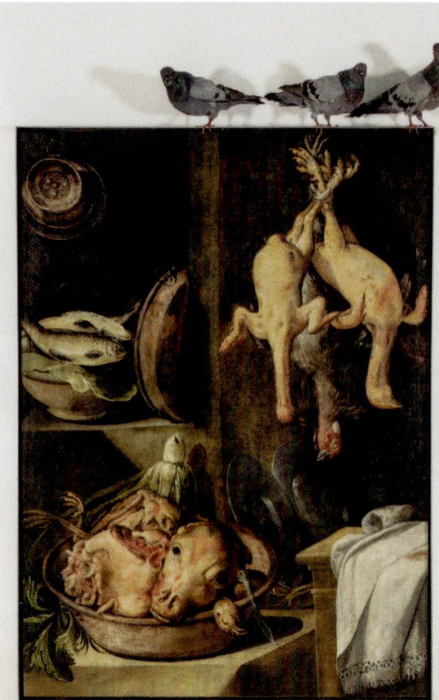

[242]

[243]



**[242]  *Raw*, 2021**
Painting, 3 taxidermied pigeons
Overall dimensions: 149 × 93 × 13 cm;
painting: 129 × 93 × 11 cm

**[243]  *Roma*, 2023**
Painting, 3 taxidermied pigeons
Overall dimensions: 98 × 109.5 ×
15.5 cm; painting: 70 × 105 × 12 cm

I've also used pigeons, not on their own but
by putting them together with objects from
the past. At an antiques fair I bought a seventeenth-century painting, then another from the
eighteenth century. This was the origin. I liked
the idea of creating combinations of different
ages and settings.

**[244.1-2]  *Hollywood*, 2001**
Scaffold, aluminum, halogen headlights
23.35 × 166.2 × 9 m

**[244.3]  *Hollywood*, 2001**
Color print face-mounted to acrylic
180 × 400 cm

For the 2001 Venice Biennale I wanted to shift the
center of attention, and above all I was fascinated by the idea of creating a short circuit between
California and Sicily.
On the day the work was inaugurated, a Sicilian
newspaper published on its front page a photo of
an old woman hanging out her washing with the
"Hollywood" sign looming up in the background.
It was installed on the hill of Bellolampo, above
Palermo, near a garbage dump. I don't know
what that lady or the other people of Palermo
thought about it. To me it was a way of shuffling
the cards and sharing the torments and plea-
sures of two attainable dreams, of celebrity and
normality.
Of course, in doing something like this you have
to go the whole hog. So with the Fondazione
Sandretto Re Rebaudengo we organized a flight
and transported the art world from Venice to the
landfill. Some of our guests had to defend themselves from the highly voracious seagulls. But I
think it went off happily for everyone, with grani-
tas and ice creams.
Building the sign was a huge job, like managing a
construction site. I couldn't find funding or support. Everyone said it was impossible and would
take longer. But there wasn't time, the opening
was two months away. In the end, I self-financed
the installation by buying back a work of mine
from one of my galleries and selling it on to a
collector for the sum I needed. It was an act of
stubbornness. Until the last, we weren't sure
we'd secure all the permits. Perhaps bureaucracy
is sometimes frightened of dreams.

[242]    *Raw*, 2021

[243]    *Roma*, 2023

[244.3]    *Hollywood*, 2001

[244.1-2] *Hollywood*, 2001
Special project for "Plateau of Humankind," 49th Venice
Biennale, curated by Harald Szeemann, June 10–November
4, 2001, installation on the hill of Bellolampo, Palermo

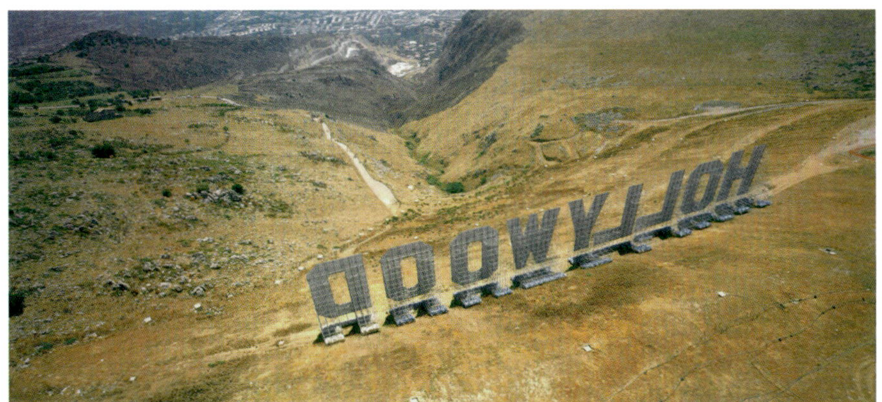

[244.3]

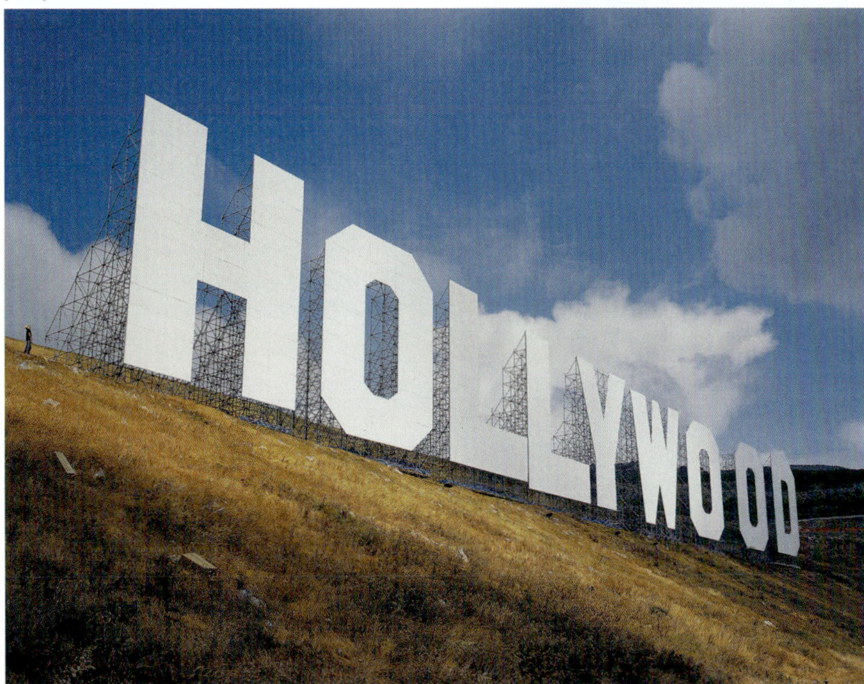

[244.1]



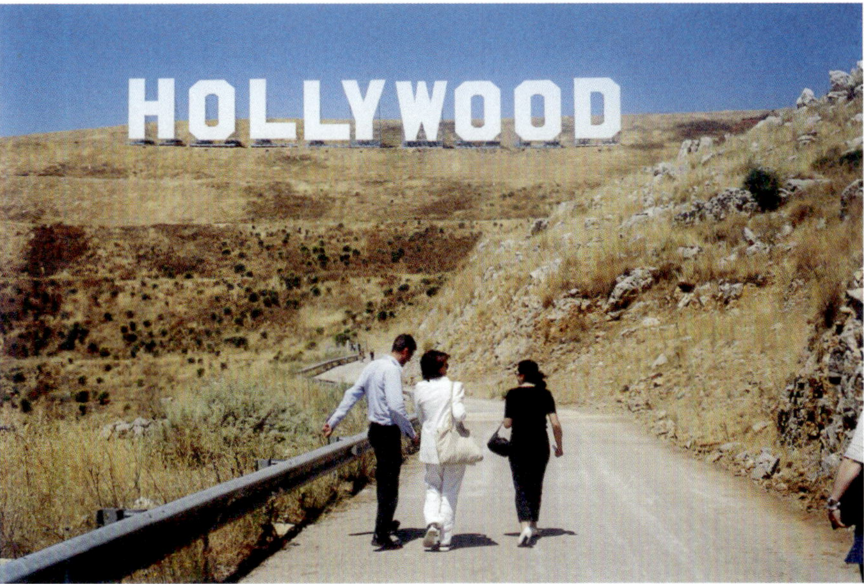

[244.2]

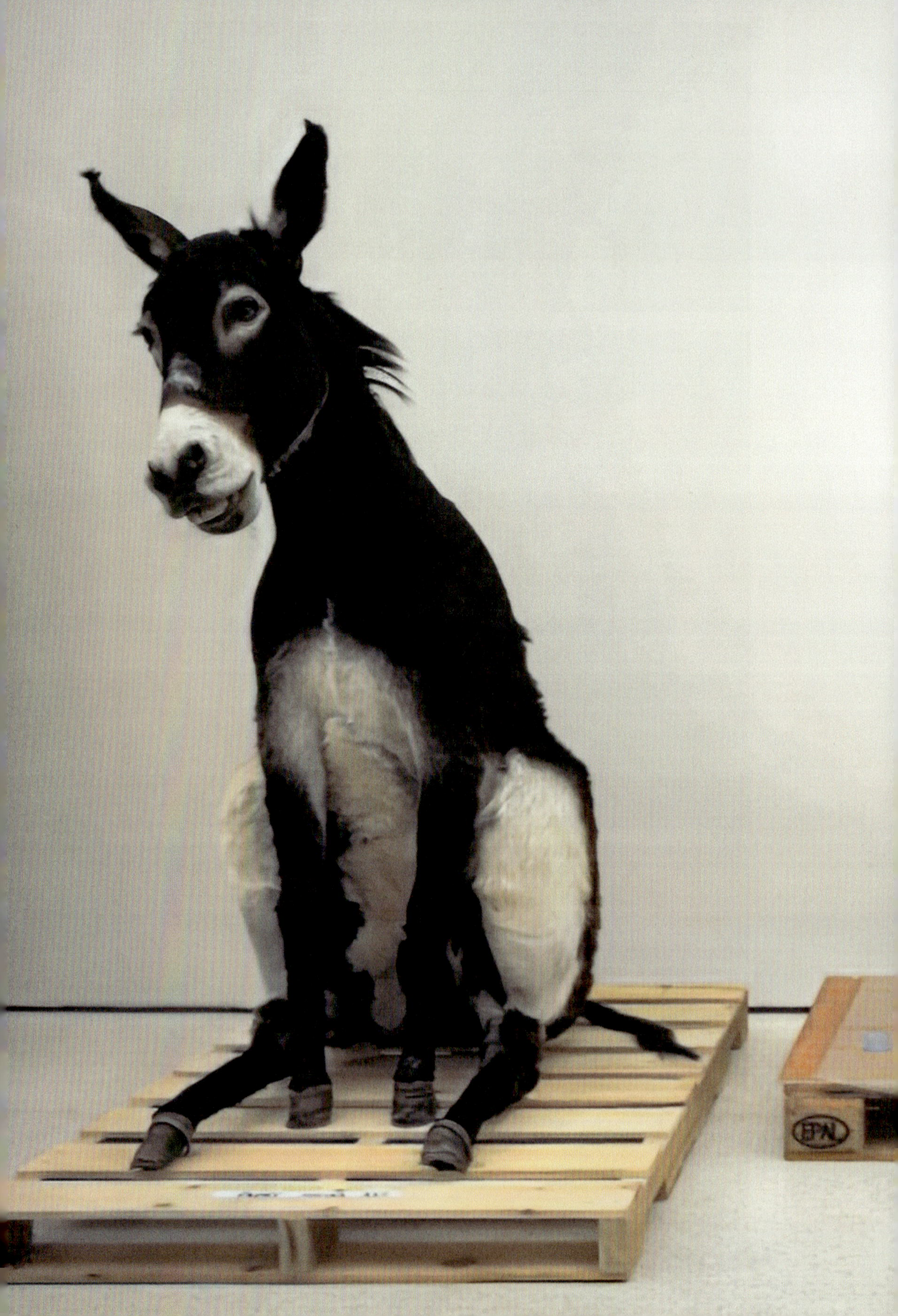

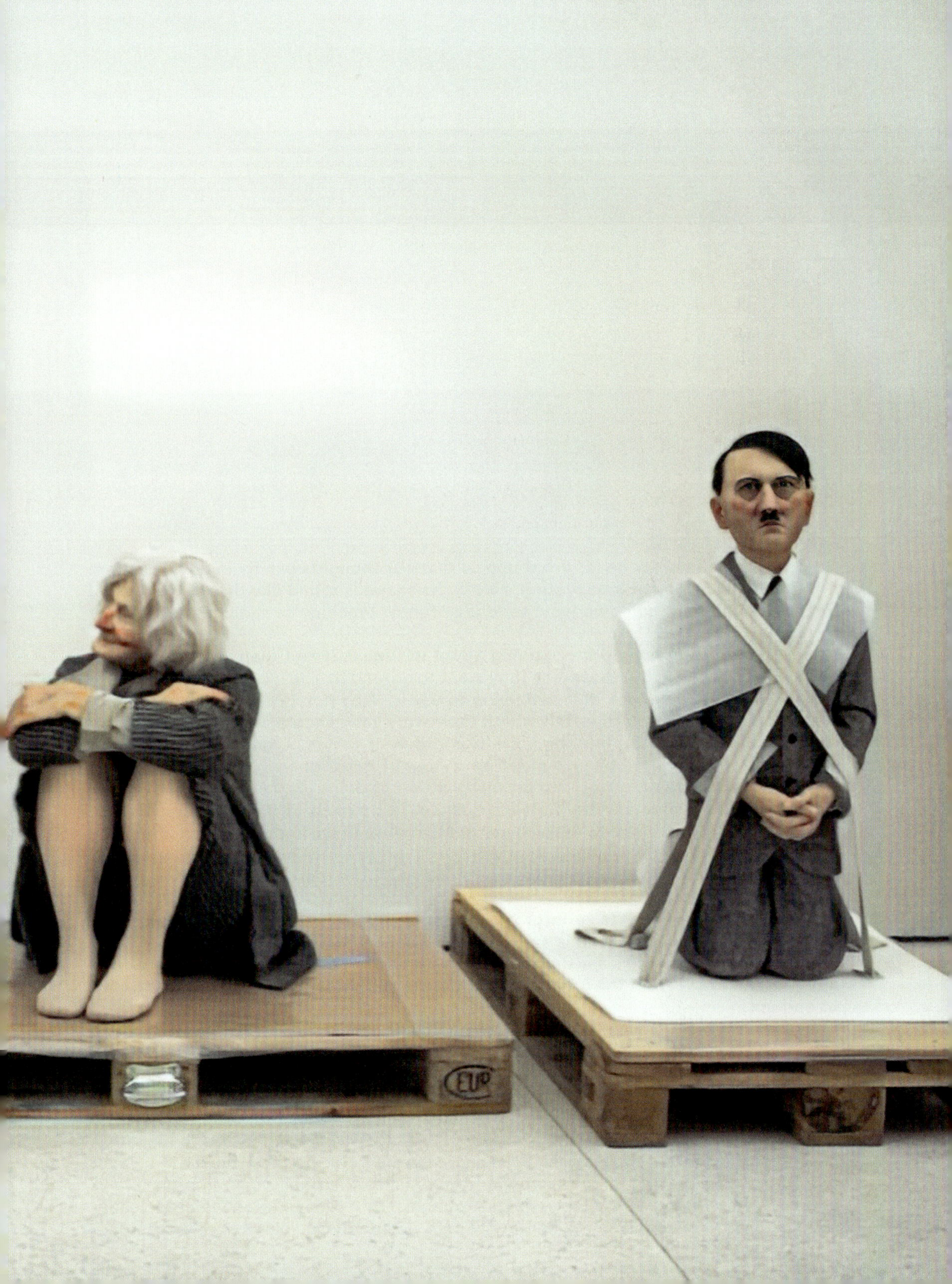

Someone once said our heads are round so that our thoughts can fly in any direction. There's no given way of interpreting a work: its shape is round like that of our heads. Each of us can find their own way: serious or funny, touching or shocking, every way is viable.

I don't like defining my work or talking about it. I make it and then it's out there for people to build whatever discourse they want to around it. The meaning of a work lies simply in how people look at it and mean to use it. Why don't I express my thoughts clearly? Because when artists talk about their work they should never be listened to. What you see and what they think are two different things. A good artwork has to appeal to the eyes and be surrounded by a host of questions which no one has the answer to. In my work I want to offer many different points of view and my aim is to be as open and as incomprehensible as possible. There must be a perfect balance between openness and closure. Art also has to be a cause of misunderstanding, precisely because people can do anything they want with it. I see misunderstanding or optical and mental deception as the real driving force of art. The more contradictions a work contains the better.

I don't think there's any false information about my works, because of the simple fact that every interpretation is valid. I myself am searching for the significance of what I do, even when it's finished and goes on show. I'm not sure I'd still produce anything if I knew from the beginning, in a clear and linear way, where I was going to end up.

I never thought of art as a way of spreading specific messages, which is more like a Miss Universe acceptance speech. At most, the purpose of my work could be to tell jokes that don't make you laugh, or that make you laugh because you would cry if you didn't. I hope to be believed when I say that I'm always desperately serious. Life is often tragic and comic at the same time, and my work deals with these two facets. I use playfulness to express myself or deal with sensitive topics, but not to make fun of someone or make people laugh. So I think that the ironic surface is just a first level of interpretation, a sort of cozy wrapping that makes the public feel comfortable in approaching a work, and then they get gut-punched by a second level, which is deadly serious. They've even given me and my work a decidedly sociological role, a bit like a value-obsessed Damien Hirst or a Banksy obsessed with street art and theme parks. Can I now claim the tradition of Boetti or de Dominicis?

Psychology and catharsis are of course possible ways of interpreting my works. I think that the perception of my work has sometimes been excessively influenced by media sensationalism, leading the public to read it superficially. The frightening thing about the way information circulates today is that the people doing the informing work on the assumption that people won't understand, they won't have the patience to think or pay sufficient attention to do it. This implies a degree of superficiality. On the contrary, the most necessary task of civilization is to teach people to think. This should be the primary purpose of every means of communication. The value comes from learning something new: in art, criticism and the market are the means by which new content can receive more attention and reach more people.

However, what really matters is time, seeing a work in perspective with the passing of time. Some works are needed at a specific time, others grow little by little, and if you're lucky they last longer. More than anything else, I like to see how the meanings of the works change based on what happens around them; it's as if they had many lives. We deceive ourselves by giving meanings to objects and images, as if, by doing so, we can control them. The only truth is that we're always conditioned by the culture we were born and raised in. We should all have a skeptical attitude towards our creative impulses.

[245]  *November*, 2024
Statuario Michelangelo marble,
water pump
88 × 70 × 200 cm

In New York, in 2024, Lucio was there looking at the exhibition, as he liked to do. For me Lucio Zotti was like a big brother, sometimes maybe even a father, for many years close to my work, ever since the early days in Milan. Why did I call the piece *November*? Because it's a sad month. It's not winter, it's not Christmas, it's fog. The figure is peeing because, before I decided to give it Lucio's face, I wanted to make fountains. So I don't think *November* is close to my series of sculptures of homeless people. Rather, it shows a man who's generous with his time. It's a fountain that instead of being celebratory or decorative is a monument to marginality, to what isn't visible. In the New York exhibition, *November* was put opposite *Sunday* but when you entered you could only see it from behind. It was a response to the other work, close to it in the opulence of the material but diametrically opposed in terms of meaning.

345

[245]  *November*, 2024
"Sunday," curated by Francesco Bonami, Gagosian, West 21st Street, New York, April 30–June 29, 2024 (solo show)

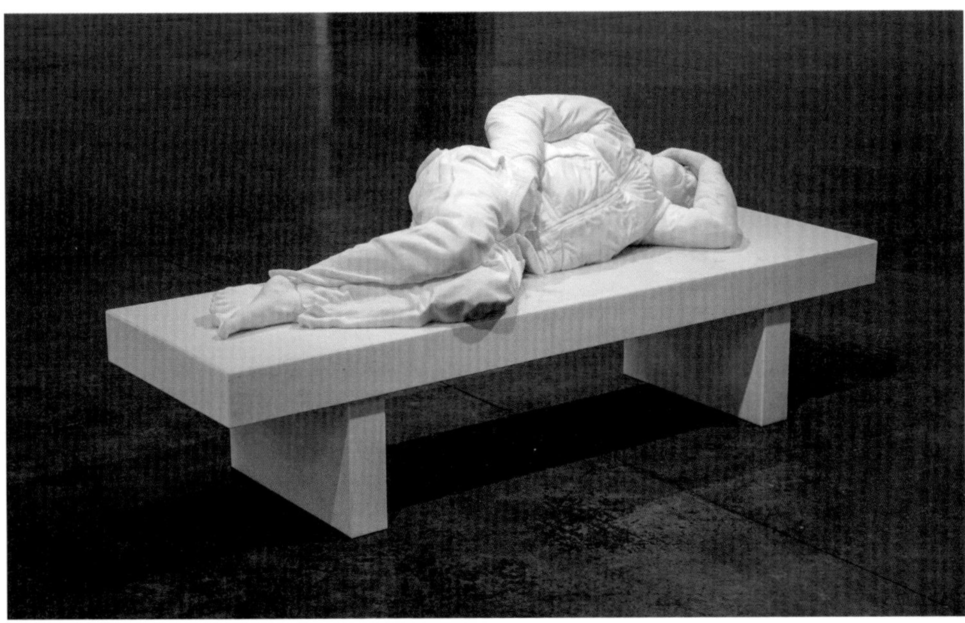

[245]

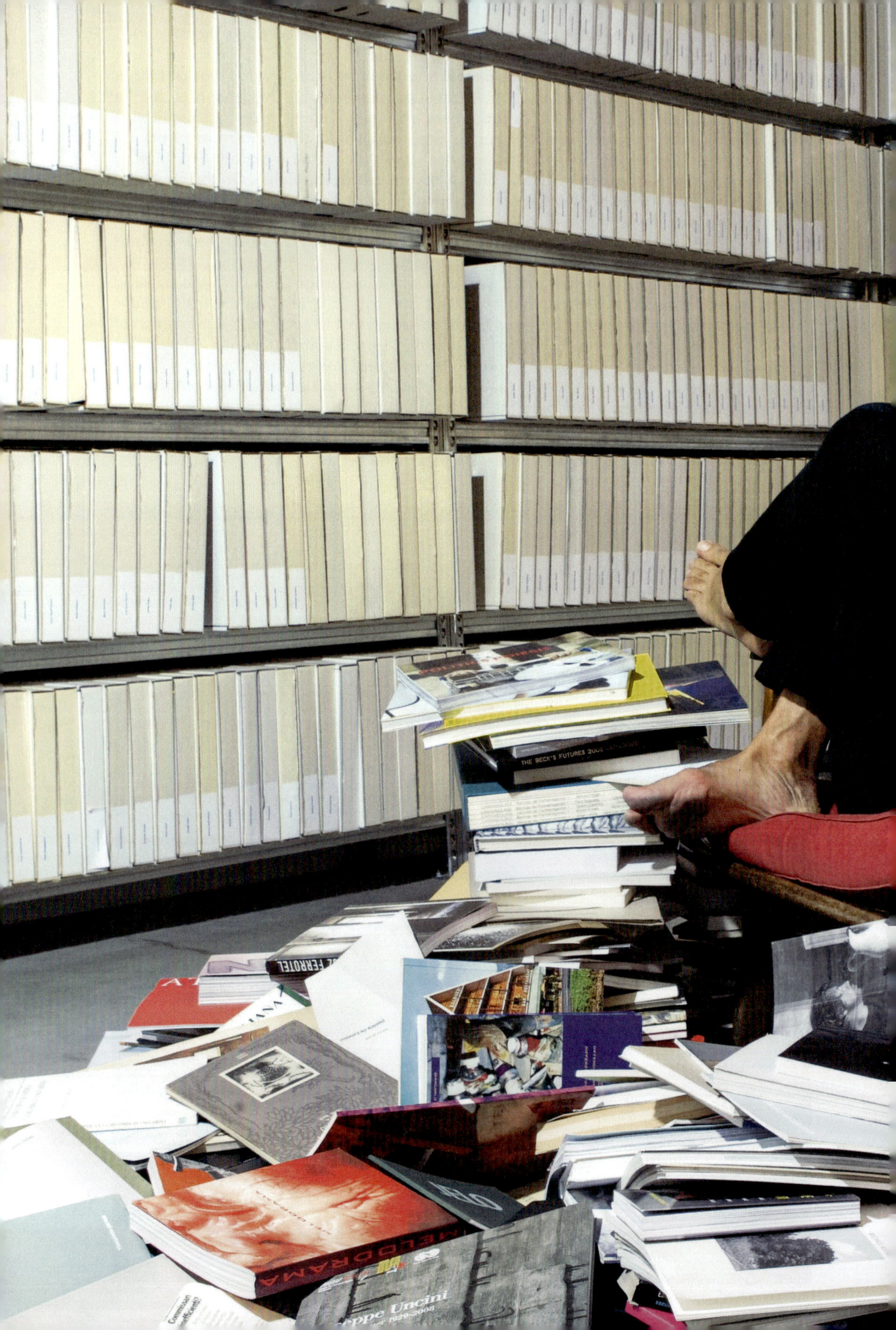

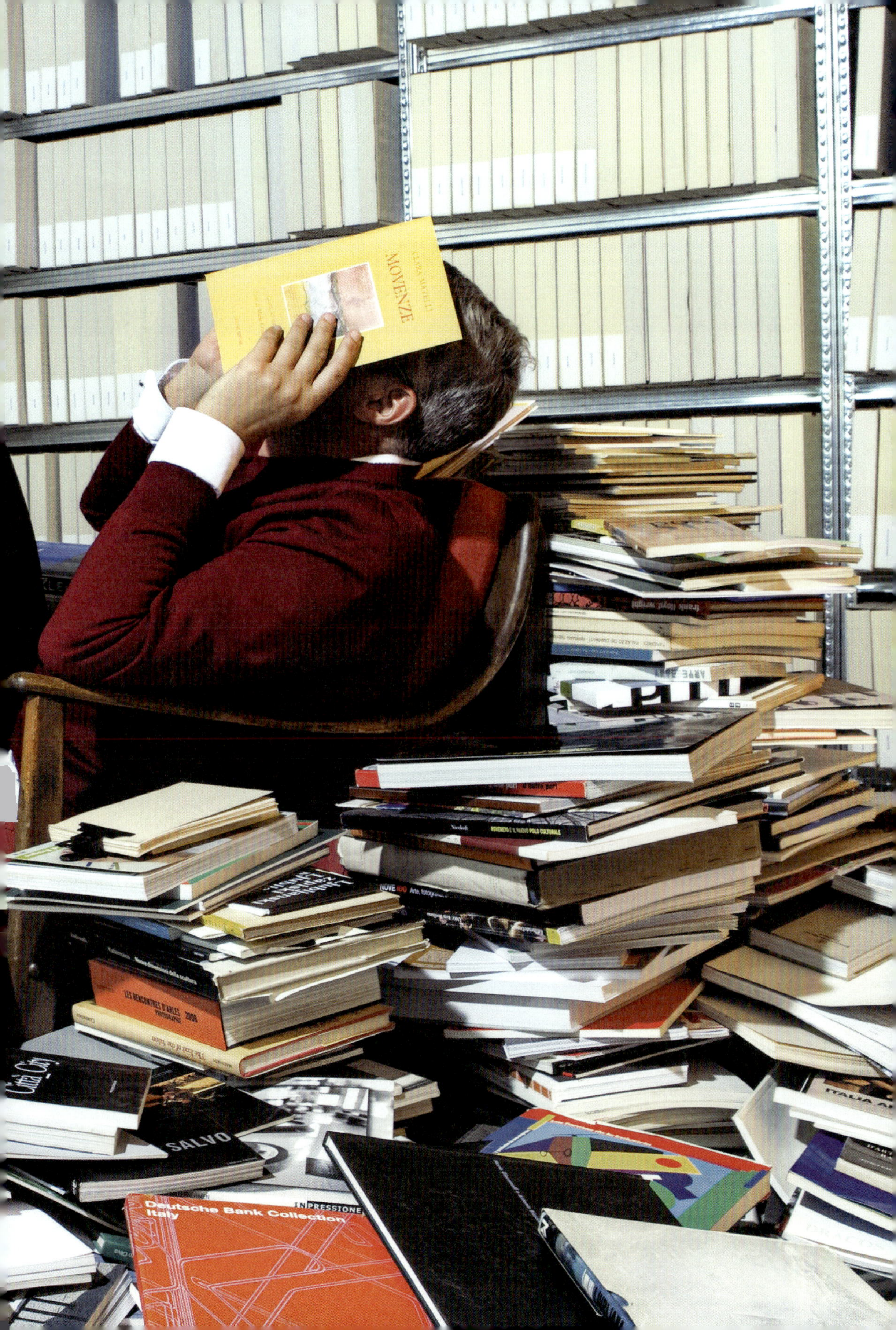
CLARA MATTELI
MOVENZE

↵ Maurizio Cattelan portrayed by Pierpaolo
Ferrari at Archivio Careof and Viafarini in Milan, 2011.
Photograph published in *Being Cattelan*, ed. Paola Nicolin,
monographic issue of *Abitare*, no. 517 (2011): 35



Titling a work is just as hard as making it, and it's always been my nightmare. It's the last step in leaving a moderately fuzzy zone around the work, the finishing touch that gives it the necessary dose of ambiguity, ensuring no one can interpret it literally. At the same time, a good title completes and protects the work like a bulletproof vest. To name something is to possess it. The title is as important as a surname is to people. It's part of the identity of the work. Then a title ought to be instantly comprehensible. Yet, even though I know all this, a lot of my works are untitled, and sometimes I feel like I've abandoned them. They're mutilated beings. I'm not good with titles, but it's also true that a bad title is worse than putting "untitled," and I've always chosen to take the lesser risk. Giving titles to exhibitions is also difficult, although in a very different way. But when an exhibition is almost complete, the title has to be able to support the scenario. When a title does emerge, its always at the end. I've never happened on a title and built the work around it. I'm always trying to figure out something about myself and the world I live in, which is why an image or a certain theme always comes first. If a title is apt, it becomes as important as the work itself. It's as if they resonate together. You're standing in front of a work, you look at it, you read the title, then you think about the meaning, then you go back to the work, to the title and again to what it represents… It's a triangulation, and if it sets off an interplay of ideas, that's great.
All the same, I have to admit that I don't feel comfortable with written words, which strike me as definitive as tombstones. This also explains why my works are often untitled. It's like writing a joke on my gravestone. Not only are my works born as images from the first moment I conceive them, but in that form they also continue to live in the media, arousing reactions. After all, as long as a sculpture is a powerful image at first glance, I don't worry about how it was made or what it's titled.

[246] ***Love Lasts Forever*, 1997**
Donkey, dog, cat and rooster skeletons
185.9 × 120 × 59.7 cm

[247] ***The first, they said, should be sweet like love; the second bitter, like life; and the third soft, like death*, 1998**
Taxidermied donkey, dog, cat and rooster, stone
165 × 120 × 40 cm

The second version of *Love Saves Life* (1995) came about almost three years after the first, when the curator Kasper König asked me to show the piece at Skulptur Projekte in Münster (1997). I didn't like the idea of exhibiting this piece again, so I just thought about how time would have redefined the work. It seemed to me that after three years, the animals would have been reduced to skeletons, so that's what I showed: the same stack of animals—a rooster, a cat, a dog and a donkey—but as bones.
It's more romantic than melancholic to me. It reminds me of the idea of bonding that survives beyond death. But I guess it depends on the point of view you're seeing it from. In love I personally feel I'm above all an idealist. In fact, a year later, I brought the animals back to life, this time as babies on a smaller scale. It might have been a suggestion from a dealer, but in a way it was an opportunity to think about the life of a work in a non-linear way. After all, evolution is not always in a straight line.

[246] *Love Lasts Forever*, 1997
"Skulptur. Projekte in Münster 1997," curated by Kasper König, Münster, June 22–September 28, 1997 (group show), installation at the Westfälisches Landesmuseum für Kunst und Kulturgeschichte

[247] *The first, they said, should be sweet like love; the second bitter, like life; and the third soft, like death,* 1998

349

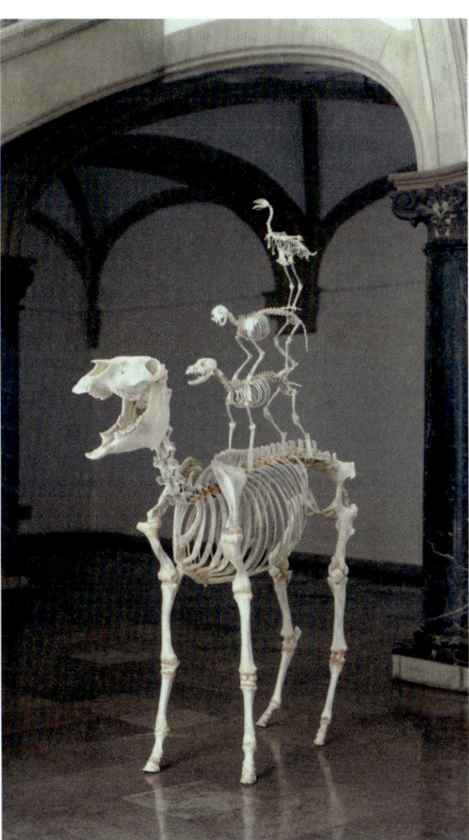

[246]

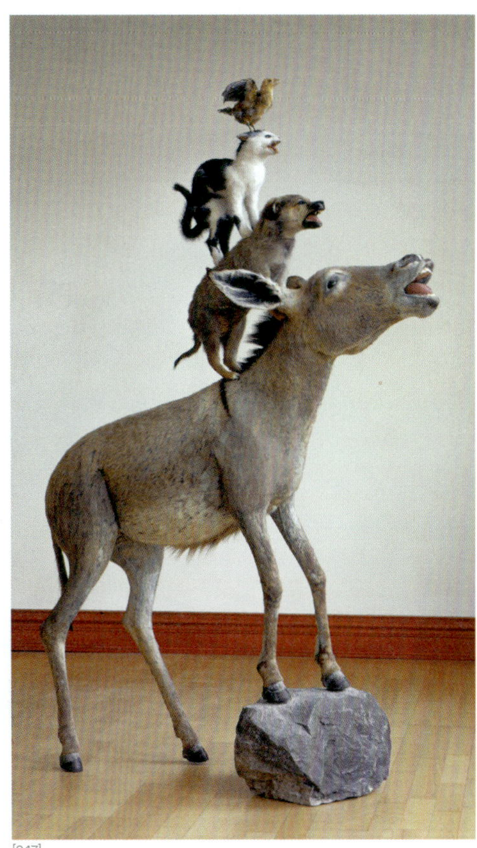

[247]

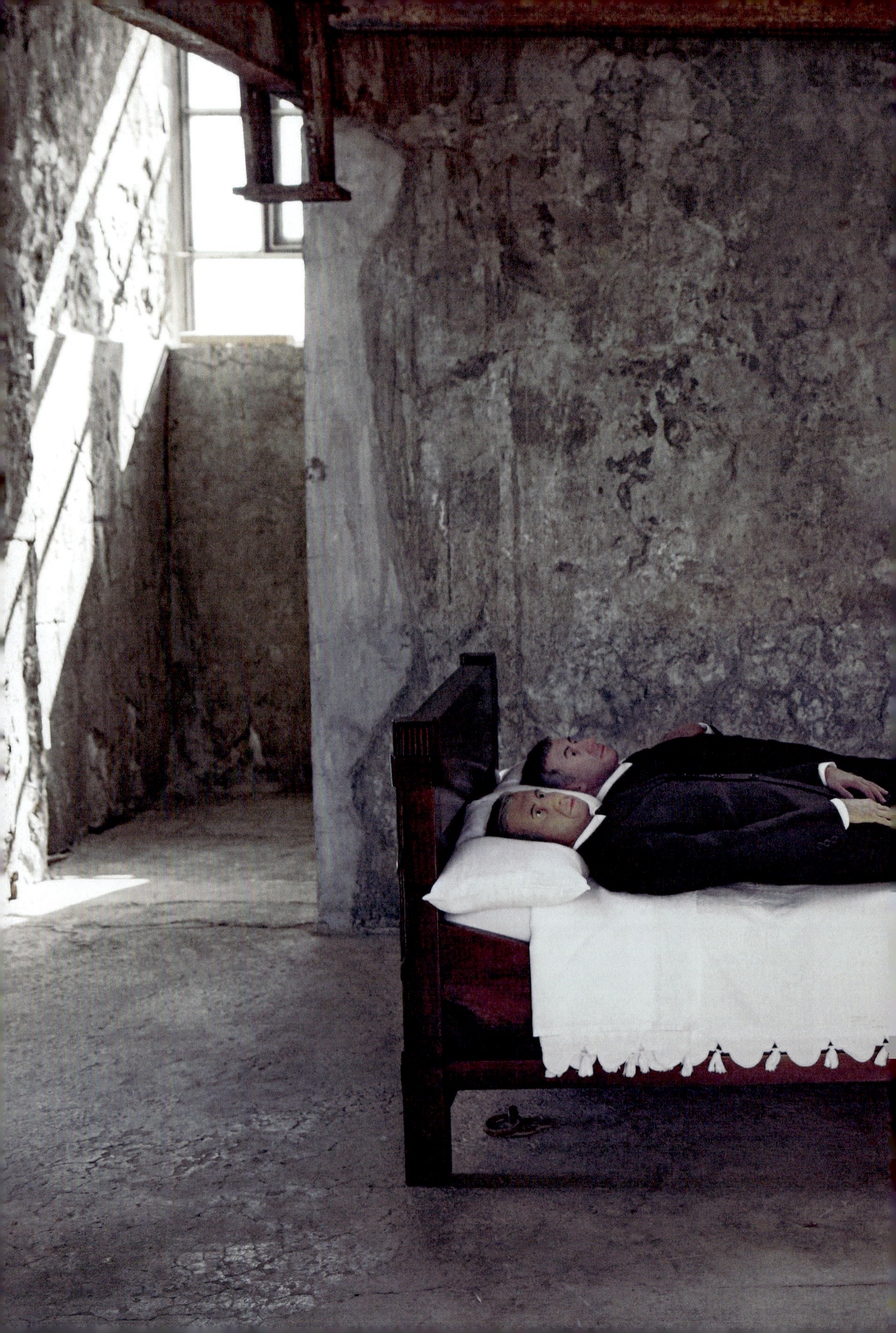

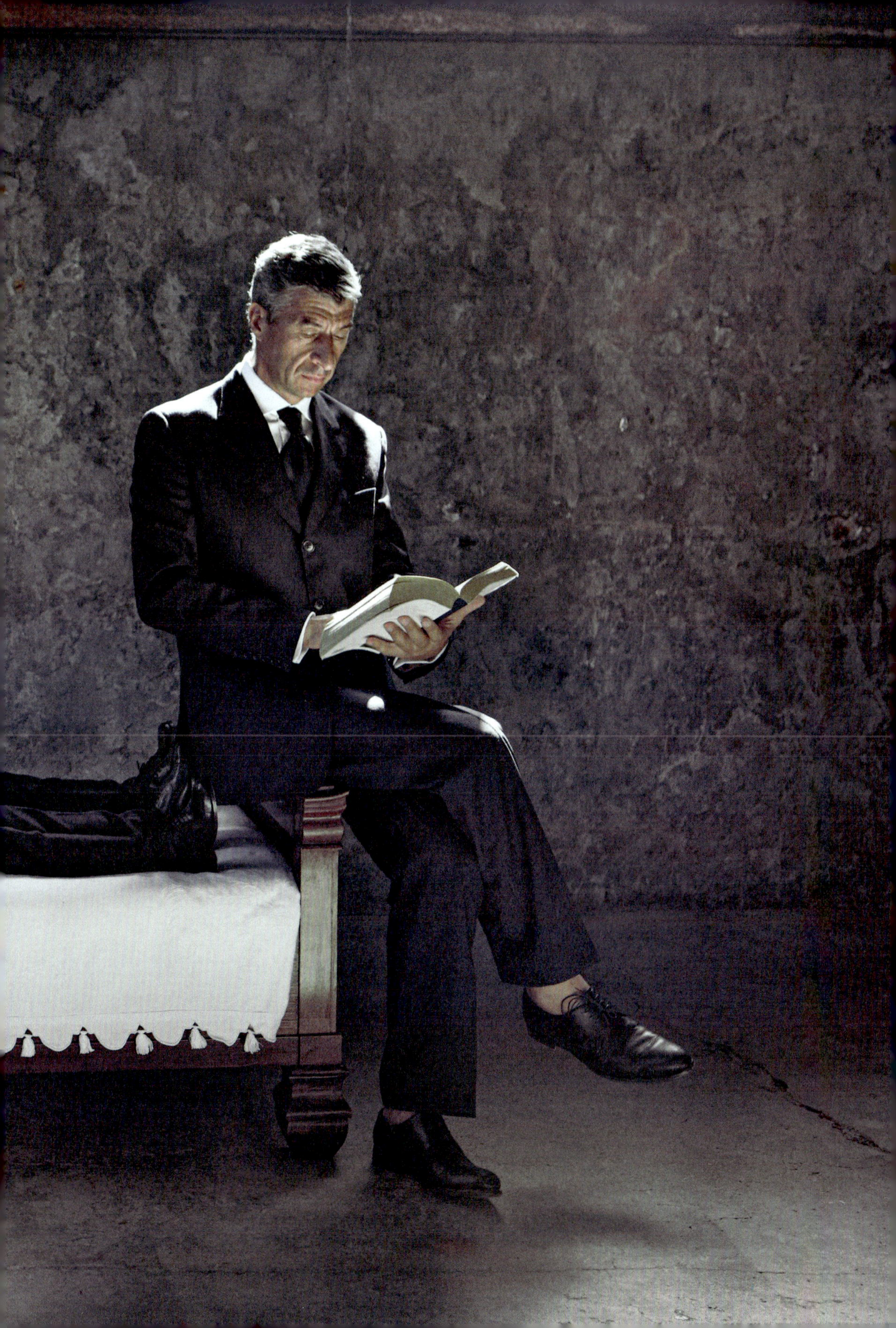

## The Problem That Has No Name

Maurizio Cattelan portrayed by Pierpaolo Ferrari
with *We* at the DESTE Foundation Project Space,
Slaughterhouse, Hydra, 2010

Can something logical not make sense?
Vegetables are more serious than men and more sensitive to frost.
Everything we experience is an answer.
If we're just going to grow old and die why are we here?
Do not mistake temptation for opportunity.
If the word doesn't exist, invent it; but first be sure it doesn't exist.
Looking or reading?
Strong and bitter words indicate a weak cause.
People will do anything, no matter how absurd, to avoid facing their own soul.
When I pronounce the word Silence I destroy it.
Why Kamikaze pilots wear helmets?
Can art produce reality?
Repetition is a form of change.
Where does the object begin and where does the author finish?
Facts do not cease to exist because they are ignored.
When I die, the world is in my room.
What are the boundaries of architecture?
The universe is made of stories, not atoms.
A conclusion is simply the place where you got tired of thinking.
Can you think about nothing?
Which is more useful, built or imagined architecture?
Where everything is bad it must be good to know the worst.
Don't be afraid of things because they're easy to do.
It takes more than good memory to have good memories.
Don't stress one thing more than another.
Look closely at the most embarrassing details and amplify them.
I'm part of the problem, not the solution.

[Text published in *Domus*, no. 945 (March 2011). Courtesy of Domus – © Editoriale Domus S.p.A.]

BEING AN ARTIST IS NOT A JOB, IT'S A MALFUNCTION

ART IS A WAY TO SURVIVE, NOT A WAY TO LIVE
IF I KNEW WHAT I WAS DOING, I WOULD HAVE STOPPED A LONG TIME AGO
SOMETIMES THE BEST IDEA IS THE ONE YOU'RE TOO ASHAMED TO SAY OUT LOUD
FAILURE IS MY FAVORITE COLOR
I DON'T MAKE ART TO COMMUNICATE, I MAKE IT TO ESCAPE
IF YOU WANT TO SAY SOMETHING SERIOUS, WEAR A CLOWN'S NOSE
I DON'T BELIEVE IN INSPIRATION, I BELIEVE IN GOOD TIMING AND BETTER EXCUSES
YOU DON'T MAKE A MASTERPIECE, YOU SURVIVE ONE
BEAUTY IS THE PERFECT ALIBI
MY GOAL IS TO VANISH COMPLETELY, LEAVING BEHIND JUST A QUESTION MARK
AS LONG AS YOU DON'T CHOOSE, EVERYTHING IS POSSIBLE
BEING ORIGINAL IS OVERRATED, BEING PRECISE IS TERRIFYING
GUILT IS ONE OF THE PUREST MATERIALS AN ARTIST CAN USE
SOMETIMES I WISH I COULD COPYRIGHT SILENCE
IF I BELIEVED IN MESSAGES, I'D WORK IN ADVERTISING
I DON'T CREATE MEANING, I OFFER TRAPS FOR IT
TRUTH IS NOT AN INGREDIENT, IT'S THE AFTERTASTE
EVERY ARTWORK IS A LOOPHOLE
YOU KNOW IT'S WORKING WHEN YOU START REGRETTING IT
IF I WANTED COMFORT, I'D BUY FURNITURE
THE BEST ARTWORKS ARE MISTAKES NO ONE DARED TO FIX
A GOOD WORK DOESN'T ASK FOR ATTENTION, IT STEALS IT
A BANANA ON A WALL IS STILL MORE HONEST THAN MOST PEOPLE I'VE MET
THE MORE YOU POLISH AN IDEA, THE LESS IT CUTS
IF YOU CAN LIVE WITHOUT IT, IT WASN'T ART
CONCEPTUAL ART? ALL ART IS CONCEPTUAL IF YOU THINK LONG ENOUGH
EVEN THE SILENCE IN A GALLERY SMELLS LIKE STRATEGY
I TREAT EXHIBITIONS LIKE FUNERALS: SILENT, AWKWARD, AND FULL OF FLOWERS
SUCCESS IS JUST FAILURE THAT FORGOT TO STOP
EVERY EXHIBITION SHOULD FEEL LIKE A CRIME SCENE
A GOOD ARTWORK SHOULD MAKE THE MUSEUM A LITTLE NERVOUS
EVERY OBJECT IS A HOSTAGE OF ITS OWN INTERPRETATION
WHEN IN DOUBT, CARVE IT IN MARBLE
I NEVER TRUSTED THINGS THAT COME WITH A LABEL
THE MOST RADICAL GESTURE IS TO DO NOTHING AND MAKE PEOPLE TALK ABOUT IT
THE LESS I EXPLAIN, THE MORE THEY WRITE

[Text published in *Maurizio Cattelan: Sussurro*, ed. Philippe Vergne, exhibition catalog (Porto, Museu de Arte Contemporánea and Parque de Serralves, Fundação de Serralves, July 4, 2025–January 11, 2026) (Porto: Fundação de Serralves, 2025), 39]

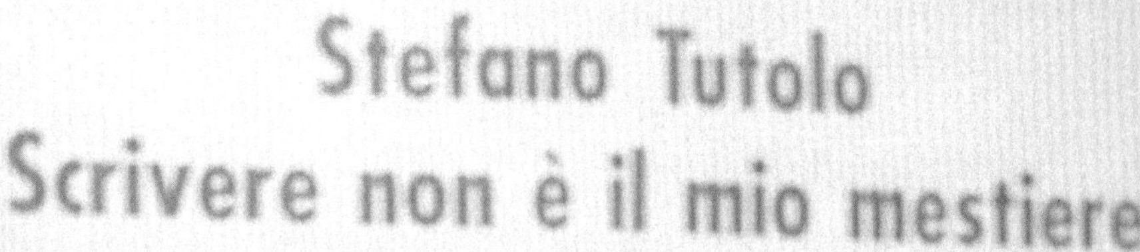

Stefano Tutolo
Scrivere non è il mio mestiere


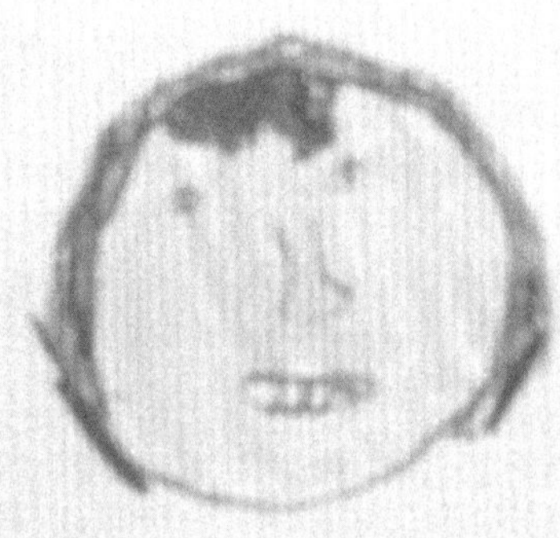


Edizioni dell'Obbligo

## The Title Should Go Here, but I Can't Do It

←  Maurizio Cattelan portrayed by Alberto Callari in front of the poster of the *Edizioni dell'Obbligo* at the publishing fair "Parole nel tempo," Castello di Belgioioso, May 4–5, 1991

Anyway, here's the editorial. Even a scoundrel like me at this point could hardly have walked away from it. Perhaps it would have been better to bury my head in the sand like an ostrich. But leaving a blank page would have made the printers suspicious, with a knock-on effect that would have ended by making the poor editorial staff of *Ventiquattro* seem culpablc. Actually, I'm invariably the culprit, unlike the big bosses, who hardly ever are. As far as I know, the man of power, the leader, is one of the commonest icons used in the history of art. In the past, the more powerful a man was, the more he surrounded himself with artists who were meant to celebrate his dedication and distinction. Princes, politicians, generals, and popes felt the urge to have themselves depicted and portrayed to affirm their prestige and power, and also to fill the grade school primers with images. Even God was once the main, and sometimes the only commissioner of portraits. Hee-hee-hee! Perhaps things are not so very different today, although you can finally choose who to represent and how to do it. And artists have learned to use portraiture not so much to celebrate the greatness and fame of leaders as to reduce them to their earthly nature, compelling them to descend to the realm of human beings. Today perhaps even God has a boss. For this very reason, the topic of leadership is interesting today. It's hard to be a leader. I'm told that in English the noun *lead*, meaning command, also means a leash. Perhaps it is proof that all leadership conceals bondage, just as defeat is always lying in wait for every success. It isn't easy to persuade, to be a role model, a guide, a leader. It's not easy to say interesting things, get other people to follow you, take command, and find new paths. It's not easy, because, whenever someone points a finger in the right direction, there's always the risk that the idiot will look at the finger.

355

["Qui dovrebbe esserci il titolo ma io non lo so fare," text published in *Ventiquattro*, supplement of *Il Sole 24 Ore*, no. 5 (May 6, 2006): 11]

[1960]    Maurizio Cattelan is born on September 21 in Padua.

[1972]    He dislikes school and fails the first year of middle school. The following summer, aged twelve, he works in the souvenir shop of the Basilica of Sant'Antonio in Padua, and as a gardener, a seasonal job that he also does in the following years.

[1975]    Enrolls in a technical high school in Padua.

[1977]    At the end of the second year of high school, he fails three subjects. He spends the summer in Venice, working as an aerial installer and repairs TV sets and other home appliances. In September he decides not to take the exams, drops out of school and starts working full time to become financially independent. He later resumes his studies by enrolling in evening classes.

[1978]    At eighteen he leaves his family to live on his own. He supports himself by doing various odd jobs (gardener, cook, postman, apprentice accountant, baker, and others), most of them lasting no more than three months.

[1980]    Completes the evening technical high school and enrolls in the Faculty of Architecture at the IUAV in Venice. He soon realizes that he does not want to spend any more years studying and drops out without attending any courses.

[1981]    Starts working with a regular contract at the hospital in Padua, where he also attends a nursing course. Due to a staff shortage he is immediately employed in the wards. He stays there for a few months, then asks to be given different tasks. He fills in for staff in various departments, works in the kitchens, the laundry, as a cleaner, in intensive care and, in the last six months, in the mortuary.
By chance, in June, on his way to work at the hospital, he comes across his first contemporary art exhibition, a solo show by Michelangelo Pistoletto at the Galleria Stevens in Padua.

[1982–83]    Together with two friends he founds the Attrazioni Magnetiche group in Padua. They manipulate images with video and computer equipment. In 1983 the group presents their works to the magazine *Frigidaire*, which includes them in some related publications, including *Tempi Supplementari*.

[1984]    Resigns from his hospital job in Padua to his family's dismay.

[1985]    Makes his first trip to New York. On the advice of an acquaintance who lives there and works at the Sonnabend Gallery, he arranges a meeting at the Postmasters Gallery to present the Attrazioni Magnetiche photos. The gallery suggests holding an exhibition, but the plan falls through, in part because of Cattelan's return to Italy. Shortly after, his collaboration with Attrazioni Magnetiche ends and Cattelan concentrates on producing individual projects and works.
He moves to Forlì, where he stays for five years. He lives in a seventeenth-century building in the town center nicknamed "Palazzo del Diavolo" (Palazzo Sassi Masini). There, as a self-taught artist, he starts making furniture and other designer objects out of recycled materials, turning his apartment into a workshop. He experiments and assembles objects, often starting from his own domestic needs.

[1987]    He presents his experiments in design at Palazzo Albertini in Forlì, at the solo exhibition "Peep Show," together with an image screen-printed on white canvas that evolved out of an earlier project (shoe boxes containing photos of naked friends viewed through slits). He tries to promote his work by sending letters of introduction to galleries in Italy and New York. The only one to display any interest is the Galleria Neon in Bologna. It invites him to exhibit in the group show "Emergenze," where between May and June of the same year he presents some experiments in digital animation.

[1988]    In January, again at the Galleria Neon, he exhibits some of the works created at Palazzo del Diavolo in the solo show "Natura Codarda," accompanied by the catalogue of the same name, the first publication on his work.

[1989–90]  Between late 1989 and early 1990 he leaves Forlì for Milan to be closer to the world of design and contemporary art and try to make art his work. He contacts the experimental design gallery Dilmos, which markets his lamp *Trifidi*, and lets him to sleep in the store when it closes at night.
He takes part in a series of group exhibitions and between May and June holds his second solo show, "Biologia delle passioni," again accompanied by a publication, in Bologna at the Galleria Neon.

[1993]  Using the money raised with his project *Oblomov Foundation* (1992), a fictitious scholarship awarded to an artist who agrees not to exhibit for a year, he returns to New York. For the first time he stays several months and frequents the art scene. In the following years he returns to the city regularly. This period also marks the beginning of his passion for swimming, which becomes a fundamental part of his daily routine.
He participates for the first time in the Venice Biennale, in the exhibition "Aperto '93," coordinated by Helena Kontova. In response to an invitation by Francesco Bonami, curator of one of the sections of the exhibition, he presents *Lavorare è un brutto mestiere*, renting the space intended for his work to an advertising agency. The work marks a breakthrough in his career.

[1994]  He holds his first solo shows abroad, starting with one at the Laure Genillard Gallery in London. From now on he exhibits continuously in both solo and group shows in public and private venues.

[1995]  With the curator Jade Dellinger he receives sponsorship for a stay in Florida from the University of South Florida Contemporary Art Museum in Tampa. The operation is titled *Choose Your Destination: How to Get a Museum-Paid Vacation*. It contains the embryo of the idea of the fictitious Caribbean Biennial (1999).
Together with Dominique Gonzalez-Foerster he founds the magazine *Permanent Food*, the start of a series of publishing and exhibition projects blurring the traditional outlines of the image of the artist, performing different roles such as curator, publisher, producer, designer. After the third issue, Dominique Gonzalez-Foerster leaves the project, and Cattelan continues it with Paola Manfrin until 2007.

[1999]  Moves permanently to New York, where he is welcomed as one of the most original and controversial figures in contemporary art. In November, with the curator Jens Hoffmann, he organizes the fictitious 6th Caribbean Biennial, "Blown Away," on the island of Saint Kitts.

[2001]  With the critic Ali Subotnick and curator Massimiliano Gioni he founds the magazine *Charley* in New York.

[2002]  Again with Ali Subotnick and Massimiliano Gioni he founds The Wrong Gallery, an independent gallery in New York.

[2004]  On March 30, the University of Trento awards him an honorary degree in Sociology.

[2005]  With Ali Subotnick and Massimiliano Gioni he is appointed curator of the fourth edition of the Berlin Biennale. In September, as part of the Biennale project and before it opens, the trio inaugurate the Gagosian Gallery, a small exhibition space at 50A Auguststraße in the heart of Mitte, using the brand of the international gallery of the same name.

[2006]  The fourth edition of the Berlin Biennale, "Of Mice and Men," is held in various exhibition venues all on the Auguststraße, including private apartments, artists' studios, a long-established Jewish girls' school and the historic premises of the KW Institute for Contemporary Art.

[2008]  Establishes the Maurizio Cattelan's Archive in Milan, returning regularly to the city, which, like New York, he considers his home.

[2010]  With the photographer Pierpaolo Ferrari he founds the magazine *Toiletpaper*, consisting only of images.

[2011]  With a statement reported in an article by Dario Pappalardo in *la Repubblica* on April 1, he announces his retirement as an artist: he will no longer produce new works.
In October *Un salto nel vuoto* is published, a book containing a long interview in which he openly dialogues with the curator Catherine Grenier. The book is considered his first autobiography.
In November he opens his first retrospective, "Maurizio Cattelan. All," at the Solomon R. Guggenheim Museum in New York, where all his works are hung in the museum's rotunda, presenting a unified, non-hierarchical view of his work.

[2012–15] Takes part in international exhibitions and holds solo shows presenting only works created down to 2011. At the same time he is busy with other projects, such as *Toiletpaper* and curating exhibitions.

[2016]  After a five-year interval, he starts producing artworks again. The first is *America*, a solid 18-karat gold toilet installed in September in a bathroom at the Solomon R. Guggenheim Museum in New York, freely usable by visitors.

[2018]  On April 23 the Academy of Fine Arts in Carrara names him an Honorary Professor of Sculpture.

[2019]  The work *America* (2016) is exhibited in a solo exhibition at Blenheim Palace, Winston Churchill's birthplace, in Oxfordshire. On the night before the inauguration, the work, installed in the bathroom that belonged to the prime minister, is torn out and stolen. (In 2024 a man pleads guilty to the theft; in March 2025 two others are sentenced by an English court.)
In December, he presents *Comedian*, a banana duct-taped to a wall, at Art Basel Miami Beach. The work sells for 120,000 dollars, and an edition of it is set to enter as a promised gift the collection of the Solomon R. Guggenheim Museum in New York.

[2024]  After more than twenty years he presents a new solo exhibition in a New York gallery, "Sunday" at Gagosian.

[2024–25]  While continuing to exhibit and act as curator, he receives commissions to work on the collections of international museums (the Moderna Museet in Stockholm and Centre Pompidou in Metz), creating exhibition projects that combine historical exhibits with works by other artists and his own.

357

358

Maurizio Cattelan's words and thoughts, published between 1987 and 2025 in conversations, interviews, and texts, have been revised to integrate them into the contents of this volume.
Over the years, many people have worked with Cattelan in various ways, actively participating in the writing of the texts: in particular, Massimiliano Gioni wrote almost every contribution from 1997 to 2006, Michele Robecchi from 2009 to 2011, and Marta Papini from 2013 onwards. Over the years, the following have also participated sporadically in their creation: Flavio Del Monte in 2007 and 2021, Annalisa Inzana in 2021, and Assunta Bruno in 2023–24. Recognition is also due to the fundamental role of the authors, curators, and interlocutors whose questions and observations have prompted and recorded the artist's thoughts and voice over the years.

## WRITINGS BY THE ARTIST

[1987]
— [Senza titolo / Untitled], in *Maurizio Cattelan: Personale* (n.p.: Palazzo del Diavolo Edizioni, 1987).

[1989]
— "Pensieri molesti," *Gran Bazaar Harper's Italia*, no. 68 (June–July 1989): 96.
— Maurizio Cattelan *et al.*, "Dedicato all'abitare: Progettare il processo," *GAP Casa*, no. 58 (June 1989): 105, collected in the context of the round table "Dedicato a… chi produce e a chi vende," curated by Clara Mantica and Luciana Cuomo, at the Dilmos showroom in Milan.

[1993]
— "Maurizio Cattelan," in *Sonsbeek 93*, eds. Jan Brand, Catelijne de Muynck, and Valerie Smith (Ghent: Snoeck-Ducaju & Zoon, 1993), 34–35 and 94–95.

[1997]
— "Maurizio Cattelan," in *Unbuilt Roads: 107 Unrealized Projects*, eds. Hans Ulrich Obrist, Guy Tortosa, and Jonas Mekas (Ostfildern-Ruit: Hatje, 1997), n.p.

[1998]
— "Maurizio Cattelan," in *Flash Art Italia* 31, no. 213 (December 1998–January 1999): 72–73.

[2000]
— "Things I'll Never Do Again: The Truth Is Not Out There" and "Influences," in "Statement 1999," in *Maurizio Cattelan*, eds. Francesco Bonami, Nancy Spector, and Barbara Vanderlinden (London: Phaidon, 2000), 124 and 125.

[2001]
— "A. All is Falling: Art—Artist—Attention," "B. Blown Away," and "C. Maurizio Cattelan," in *6th Caribbean Biennial: A Project by Maurizio Cattelan* (Dijon: Les Presses du réel, 2001), n.p.
— "Untitled," in "Surrealism, Sex and Desire," ed. David Hopkins, *Tate: The Art Magazine*, no. 26 (Fall 2001): 30.

— "New York Stories: Art & the Art World After the Attack in New York," *Flash Art International* 34, no. 221 (November–December 2001): 62.

**[2004]**
— Maurizio Cattelan and Philippe Daverio, "Ma è davvero arte mostrare tre bimbi impiccati?," *Gente* (May 10, 2004): 21.
— "Lectio magistralis all'Università di Trento," *Work: Art in Progress*, no. 9 (Summer 2004): 94. Reprinted as "Lectio magistralis all'Università di Trento," *Maurizio Cattelan*, eds. Elio Grazioli and Bianca Trevisan, monographic issue of *Riga*, no. 39 (2019).
— "My Warhol: Army of One," as told to Katy Siegel, *Artforum International* 43, no. 2 (October 2004): 148–49.
— "Maurizio Cattelan: Aux arts citoyen!," *Le Monde* (October 2, 2004): 34–39.

**[2005]**
— "The Fat Is on the Table: Maurizio Cattelan on Joseph Beuys," in "The Legacy of a Myth Maker: Joseph Beuys," ed. Francesco Bonami, *Tate Etc.*, no. 3 (Spring 2005): 80–81.

**[2006]**
— "Qui dovrebbe esserci il titolo ma io non lo so fare," *Ventiquattro*, supplement of *Il Sole 24 Ore*, no. 5 (May 6, 2006): 11.
— "Hindsight Foresight," *ArtReview*, no. 5 (May–June 2006): 130.

**[2007]**
— "Firmato Cattelan," ed. Alessandra Mammì, *L'Espresso* (September 2007): 128–29.

**[2009]**
— "Every Other Decade," *Kaleidoscope*, no. 3 (September–October 2009): 64–65.

**[2011]**
— "Double," in *Carsten Höller: Experience*, ed. Massimiliano Gioni, exhibition catalog (New York, New Museum, October 26, 2011–January 15, 2012) (New York: Skira Rizzoli, 2011), 79–80.
— "The Problem That Has No Name / Il problema che non ha nome," in "Domus Cattelan," "Diario," ed. Loredana Mascheroni, *Domus*, no. 945 (March 2011): II.

**[2018]**
— "What I've Learned About Copies: Artist Maurizio Cattelan on the Strange Saga of the Nine Lassies," *Artnet* (September 18, 2018).
— "What I've Learned About Copies: Artist Maurizio Cattelan on Barack Obama's Secret Pharaonic Past," *Artnet* (September 25, 2018).

**[2024]**
— "Battiti / Heartbeats," in *Con i miei occhi / With My Eyes*, eds. Bruno Racine and Chiara Parisi, exhibition catalog (Holy See Pavilion, 60th Venice Biennale, April 20–November 24, 2024) (Venice: Marsilio Arte, 2024), 26 (Italian) and 31 (English).

**[2025]**
— "abécédaire," in *Endless Sunday: Maurizio Cattelan and the Centre Pompidou Collection*, ed. Chiara Parisi *et al.*, exhibition catalog (Metz, Pompidou-Metz, May 8, 2025–February 2, 2027) (Metz: Éditions du Centre Pompidou-Metz, 2025), 18-355.
— "Being an Artist is Not a Job, It's a Malfunction," in *Maurizio Cattelan: Sussurro*, ed. Philippe Vergne, exhibition catalog (Porto, Museu de Arte Contemporánea and Parque de Serralves, Fundação de Serralves, July 4, 2025–January 11, 2026) (Porto: Fundação de Serralves, 2025), 39.


## INTERVIEWS AND CONVERSATION WITH MAURIZIO CATTELAN

### In Exhibition Catalogues and Other Volumes

**[2000]**
— *Maurizio Cattelan*, eds. Francesco Bonami, Nancy Spector, and Barbara Vanderlinden (London: Phaidon, 2000).
— "Nancy Spector in Conversation with Maurizio Cattelan," *Maurizio Cattelan*, eds. Francesco Bonami, Nancy Spector, and Barbara Vanderlinden (London: Phaidon, 2000), 8–36.

**[2003]**
— Hans Ulrich Obrist, "Cattelan, Maurizio," in *Hans Ulrich Obrist: Interviews, Volume I / Hans Ulrich Obrist: Interviste, volume I*, ed. Thomas Boutoux (Florence: Pitti Immagine; Milan: Charta, 2003), separate editions in English and Italian, 141–54 and 145–59. Shortened version reprinted as "We Are Too Many," *Work: Art in Progress*, no. 8 (January–March 2004). Reprinted in Italian as "Intervista a Maurizio Cattelan," in *Maurizio Cattelan*, eds. Elio Grazioli and Bianca Trevisan, monographic issue of *Riga*, no. 39 (2019): 18–32.
— "Free for All: Interview with Alma Ruiz 2002," in *Maurizio Cattelan*, eds. Francesco Bonami, Nancy Spector, and Barbara Vanderlinden (London: Phaidon, 2003): 148–57.
— "Sparizione," Maurizio Cattelan (alias Massimiliano Gioni) in conversation with Giorgio Verzotti on the occasion of "Incontri Contemporanei" (Venice, Fondazione Querini Stampalia, May 21, 1998), in *Incontri Contemporanei*, ed. Chiara Bertola (Venice: Fondazione Querini Stampalia, 2003), 124–45.
— Tom Morton, "The Wrong Questions: An Interview with the Wrong Gallery," *Perfect Magazine*, ed. Mathieu Copeland (Djion: Les Presses du réel, 2003): 87.

**[2006]**
— Paolo Vagheggi, "Maurizio Cattelan," in *Contemporanei: Conversazioni d'artista* (Milan: Skira, 2006), 61–63.

**[2011]**
— Maurizio Cattelan with Catherine Grenier, *Un salto nel vuoto: La mia vita fuori dalle cornici*, trans. Francesco Peri (Milan: Rizzoli, 2011); *Le saut dans le vide*, trans. Ségolène Dargnies (Paris: Éditions du Seuil, 2011).
— Michele Robecchi, "Cattelan Maurizio," in *Elogio del dubbio / In Praise of Doubt / Éloge du doute*, ed. Caroline Bourgeois, exhibition catalog (Venice, Punta della Dogana, April 10, 2011–March 17, 2013) (Milan: Electa, 2011), 54–56 (Italian), 56–58 (English), and 58–61 (French).

**[2016]**
— "Conversation entre Maurizio Cattelan & Chiara Parisi," in *Maurizio Cattelan: Not Afraid of Love*, ed. Chiara Parisi, exhibition catalog (Paris, Monnaie de Paris, October 21, 2016–January 8, 2017) (Paris: Monnaie de Paris, 2016), 11–65.

**[2018]**
— Oliviero Toscani, "È solo quando non penso che affiorano le immagini migliori," in *Il destino*, vol. 28 of *Oliviero Toscani: Lezioni di fotografia* (Milan: Corriere della Sera, 2018), 1–17.

**[2019]**
— Maurizio Cattelan and Michael Frahm, "In Conversation," in *Victory Is Not an Option: Maurizio Cattelan at Blenheim*, exhibition catalog (Woodstock, United Kingdom, Blenheim Palace, September 12–October 27, 2019) (Woodstock: Blenheim Art Foundation, 2019), 25–98.

**[2021]**
— Maurizio Cattelan, "Let's Go Bananas!," in *Face à Arcimboldo*, eds. Chiara Parisi and Anne Horvath, exhibition catalog (Metz, Centre Pompidou-Metz, May 29–November 22, 2021) (Paris: Beaux Arts éditions, 2021).
— Roberta Tenconi and Vicente Todolí, "Faits Divers, Faith Divers, Fatti Diversi," in *Maurizio Cattelan: Breath Ghosts Blind*, eds. Roberta Tenconi and Vicente Todolí, exhibition catalog (Milan, Pirelli HangarBicocca, July 15, 2021–February 20, 2022) (Venice: Marsilio Arte, 2021), 60–109.

[2022]

— "Running Away from Nothing: Francesco Bonami and Maurizio Cattelan in Conversation," in *Maurizio Cattelan: The Last Judgment*, ed. Francesco Bonami, exhibition catalog (Beijing, UCCA Center for Contemporary Art, November 20, 2021–February 20, 2022) (Beijing: UCCA Center for Contemporary Art, 2022), 11–25.

[2023]

— "Laure Genillard in Conversation with Maurizio Cattelan: 26 January 1994," in *Laure Genillard Gallery: 28 Years, 152 Exhibitions, 278 Artists* (London: Laure Genillard Gallery, 2023), 88–97.

[2025]

— Conversation with Chiara Parisi, in *Endless Sunday: Maurizio Cattelan and the Centre Pompidou Collection*, ed. Chiara Parisi *et al.*, exhibition catalog (Metz, Pompidou-Metz, Metz, May 8, 2025–February 2, 2027) (Metz: Éditions du Centre Pompidou-Metz, 2025), 400–12.

**In Magazines and Newspapers**

[1989]

— "Dedicato a… chi produce e a chi vende,"eds. Clara Mantica and Luciana Cuomo, with contributions by Laura Agnoletto, Michele Barro Savonuzzi, Clare Brass, Maurizio Cattelan, Dante Donegani, Daniela Galassi, Toni Larosa, Marco Mencacci, Marco Minoggio, Ivano Boscardini per Nautilus, Claudio Piccini, Shama Cinzia Tandoi, Antonio Villas, and Laura Polinoro, *GAP Casa*, no. 58 (June 1989): 90–104.

[1990]

— Serena Simoni, "Maurizio Cattelan," *Juliet*, no. 47 (April 1990): 41.

[1991]

— Roberto Pinto, "Un artista abusivo sempre presente," *Flash Art Italia* 24, no. 164 (October–November 1991): 82–83; https://flash---art.it/article/un-artista-abusivo-sempre-presente/. Reprinted in *All Cattelan*, monographic issue of *Flash Art Italia* 45, no. 299 (February 2012): 38–41.

[1993]

— Tommaso Corvi Mora, "In Italy There is No Sport as Popular as Football," *Purple Prose*, no. 3 (Summer 1993): 30–32.

— Emanuela De Cecco, "Maurizio Cattelan," *Flash Art Daily: Quotidiano della XLV Biennale di Venezia* (June 10, 1993).

[1994]

— Emanuela De Cecco and Roberto Pinto, "Incursioni," *Flash Art Italia* 27, no. 182 (March 1994): 25–27; https://flash---art.it/article/incursioni/. Reprinted in *All Cattelan*, monographic issue of *Flash Art Italia* 45, no. 299 (February 2012): 42–47. Shortened version published in English as "Incursions: Interview with Emanuela De Cecco and Roberto Pinto (Extract)," in *Maurizio Cattelan*, eds. Francesco Bonami, Nancy Spector, and Barbara Vanderlinden (London: Phaidon, 2000), 116–22.

[1997]

— Jean Budney and Uwe Schwarzer, "Cityscape: Milan," *Flash Art International* 30, no. 194 (May–June 1997): 61–63.

— Roberto Pinto, "Un linguaggio di confine: Maurizio Cattelan, l'architettura del pensiero," *Linea d'Ombra* 15, no. 126 (June 1997): 72–75.

[1998]

— Angelo Capasso, "Maurizio Cattelan: The Mouse that Roared," *Time* (Atlantic Edition) 152, no. 17 (October 26, 1998): 10–11.

[1999]

— Daniel Pinchbeck, "Maurizio Cattelan," *The Art Newspaper* 10, no. 88 (January 1, 1999).

— Barbara Casavecchia, "Voglio essere famoso," *Flash Art Italia* 32, no. 215, (April–May 1999): 80–81; https://flash---art.it/article/voglio-essere-famoso/. Reprinted in *All Cattelan*, monographic issue of *Flash Art Italia* 45, no. 299 (February 2012): 60–63. Published in English as "I Want to Be Famous: Strategies for Successful Living: Interview with Barbara Casavecchia," in *Maurizio Cattelan*, eds. Francesco Bonami, Nancy Spector, and Barbara Vanderlinden (London: Phaidon, 2000), 132–39.

— Robert Nickas, "Maurizio Cattelan," *Index Magazine*, no. 20 (September–October 1999). Shortened version reprinted in *Maurizio Cattelan*, eds. Francesco Bonami, Nancy Spector, and Barbara Vanderlinden (London: Phaidon, 2000), 128–29.

— "Blown Away – Blown to Pieces: Conversation with Massimiliano Gioni and Jens Hoffmann," *Material* (Migros Museum für Gegenwartskunst, Zurich), no. 2 (November 1999) . Reprinted in *Maurizio Cattelan*, eds. Francesco Bonami, Nancy Spector, and Barbara Vanderlinden (London: Phaidon, 2000), 140–42.

[2000]

— "Face to Face: Interview with Giacinto Di Pietrantonio (extract)," in *Maurizio Cattelan*, eds. Francesco Bonami, Nancy Spector, and Barbara Vanderlinden (London: Phaidon, 2000), 112–13. [This interview borrowed the conversation between Giacinto Di Pietrantonio and Ange Leccia in *Flash Art Italia* (1988).]

— Ivan Maria Vele, "La Nona Ora, an Interview to [*sic*] Maurizio Cattelan," *Boiler Magazine* (September 24, 2000) (originally published in *Boilermaga.it*). Published in Italian as "Mai far sapere alla tua mano destra quello che sta facendo la mano sinistra: Intervista di Ivan Maria Vele a Maurizio Cattelan," *KM*, no. 2 (July 2001).

[2001]

— Jean-Yves Jouannais and Christophe Kihm, "The Witz Kid," *Art Press*, no. 265 (February 2001): 18–23.

— Massimiliano Gioni, "Giù la maschera," *Flash Art Italia* 34, no. 227 (April–May 2001): 78–81; https://flash---art.it/2024/05/giu-la-maschera/. Reprinted in *All Cattelan*, monographic issue of *Flash Art Italia* 45, no. 299 (February 2012): 64–67. Published in English as "Maurizio Cattelan / Face Off," *Flash Art International* 34, no. 218 (May–June 2001): 114–17.

— Michele Robecchi, "Angry Art-Goers Fight Back!," *Flash Art International* 34, no. 217 (March–April 2001): 45.

— Paolo Vagheggi, "Cattelan, il sogno di Hollywood," *la Repubblica* (May 14, 2001): 44.

— Christian Rocca, "Chi è Maurizio Cattelan?," *Linkiesta* (September 1, 2001); https://www.linkiesta.it/blog/2001/09/maurizio-cattelan/.

[2002]

— Jan Estep, "I'll Be Right Back: An Interview with Maurizio Cattelan," *New Art Examiner*, no. 4 (March–April 2002): 38–45.

— Adriana Polveroni, "Ground Zero: Cai Guo-Qiang e Maurizio Cattelan rispondono all'11 settembre / Cai Guo-Qiang and Maurizio Cattelan Respond to the 11th September," *Work: Art in Progress*, no. 1 (April–June 2002): 8–17.

— Carol Vogel, "Don't Get Angry. He's Kidding. Seriously.," *The New York Times* (May 13, 2002): 1; https://www.nytimes.com/2002/05/13/arts/don-t-get-angry-he-s-kidding-seriously.html.

[2003]

— Roberta Smith, "Cattelan Uncovered," *ArtReview*, no. 54 (2003): 40–47.

— Helena Kontova, "The Wrong Gallery," *Flash Art International* 36, no. 228 (January–February 2003): 45. Published in Italian as "The Wrong Gallery: Intervista a Maurizio Cattelan," *Flash Art Italia* 36, no. 238 (February-March 2003), 72.

— Giovanni Cervi, "Ufficio dei concetti smarriti: Intervista a Maurizio Cattelan, artista di spaesamento," *PIG Mag* (February 3, 2003): 74–80.

— Marco Tomasini, "Senza scadenza: Intervista a Maurizio Cattelan su *Permanent Food* / No Expiry Date: Interview with Maurizio Cattelan on *Permanent Food*," *Work: Art in Progress* (October–December 2003): 44–45.

[2004]

— Massimiliano Gioni, "Lessico famigliare / Family Sayings," *Work: Art in Progress*, no. 8 (January–March 2004): 46–49.

— Hans Ulrich Obrist, "We Are Too Many," *Work: Art in Progress*, no. 8 (January–March 2004): 32–41. Extended version originally published as "Cattelan, Maurizio," in *Hans Ulrich Obrist: Interviews, Volume I / Hans Ulrich*

*Obrist: Interviste, volume I*, ed. Thomas Boutoux (Florence: Pitti Immagine; Milan: Charta, 2003), separate editions in English and Italian, 141–54 and 145–59. Reprinted in Italian as "Intervista a Maurizio Cattelan," *Maurizio Cattelan*, eds. Elio Grazioli and Bianca Trevisan, monographic issue of *Riga*, no. 39 (2019): 18–32.

— Leeji Choi, "Maurizio Cattelan Interview," *Designboom* (April 13, 2004); https://www.designboom.com/interviews/designboom-interview-maurizio-cattelan/.

— Valentina Agostinis, "Catte va in città," *Carnet* (May 2004): 42–48.

— Ivan Maria Vele, "Cattelan a Milano," *The Rodeo Magazine* (May 2004): 51.

— Deborah Ameri, "Nel mondo di Cattelan tra bluff e provocazioni," *Metro* (May 3, 2004): 9.

— Paolo Vagheggi, "Cattelan, l'artista da un milione di euro," *la Repubblica* (May 3, 2004): 28.

— Francesca Bonazzoli, "Cattelan, scandalo sotto la quercia," *Corriere della Sera* (May 5, 2004): 57.

— Anna Cirillo, "Quell'opera è un monito i nostri figli ci giudicano," *la Repubblica* (May 6, 2004): 25.

— "Maurizio Cattelan," *Kwart.kataweb.it* (May 7, 2004).

— Gian Marco Walch, "La violenza esiste, io la evoco soltanto," *Il Giorno* (May 7, 2004): 5.

— Alessandra Mammì, "Lei non sa chi sono io," interview with Maurizio Cattelan and Massimiliano Gioni, *L'Espresso*, no. 20 (May 20, 2004): 98–100.

— Anna Assumma, "Maurizio Cattelan," *Flair* (June 2004): 216–19.

— Chiara Canali, "Tre domande a Maurizio Cattelan," *Extrart* (June 2004): 4.

— Luca Campana, "'Sono soltanto un venditore ambulante,'" *Soprattutto* (June 4, 2004): 20–21.

— Sophie Arie, "'I Don't Do Anything: I Just Eat Images,'" *The Guardian* (June 23, 2004); https://www.theguardian.com/artanddesign/2004/jun/23/art.

— Giancarlo Politi and the readers of *Flash Art*, "Coraggio fatti ammazzare: Intervista a più voci con Maurizio Cattelan," *Flash Art Italia* 37, no. 247 (August–September 2004): 92–97; https://flash---art.it/article/coraggio-fatti-ammazzare/. Reprinted in *All Cattelan*, monographic issue of *Flash Art Italia* 45, no. 299 (February 2012): 76–83. Shortened version in English published as "Killing Me Softly: A Conversation with Maurizio Cattelan," *Flash Art International* 37, no. 237 (July–September 2004): 90–95. Reprinted in *Flash Art International* 41, no. 261 (July–September 2008): 220–23.

— Francesca Bonazzoli, "Cattelan: 'Provocazione è portare il profumo di Hollywood in discarica,'" *Corriere della Sera* (September 13, 2004): 3.

— Hans Ulrich Obrist, "Cattelan Meets Rondinone," *Vogue Hommes International*, no. 16 (Fall/Winter 2004–05): 152–58.

— Gianni Romano, "Maurizio Cattelan: 'No soy un profeta: Como mucho un ladrón,'" *EXIT Express*, no. 6 (October 2004): 6–7.

— Calvin Tomkins, "The Prankster," *The New Yorker* 80, no. 29 (October 4, 2004): 80–89. Reprinted in Calvin Tomkins, *Lives of the Artists* (London: Phaidon, 2019), vol. 5, 28–44.

— Francesca Cibrario, "Provocarte," *GQ* (December 2004): 68.

— Pino Corrias, "Mister tre milioni di dollari: 'Io creo al telefono,'" *la Repubblica* (December 5, 2004): 38.

— Diamante D'Alessio, "'Macché star, sono un operaio dell'arte,'" *Panorama* (December 10, 2004): 228–35.

[2005]

— Ken Miller, "Maurizio Cattelan," *High Low*, special issue of *Tokion*, no. 47 (March–April 2005): 50–54.

— Markus Zehentbauer and Sabine Zeller, "Die Stadt der kühnen Gesten," interview with Maurizio Cattelan and Massimiliano Gioni, *Süddeutsche Zeitung* (April 26, 2005).

— Silvia Bombino, "Caro Maurizio, ti scrive Vanessa Beecroft: Sempre che sia tu a rispondere," *Vanity Fair*, no. 32 (August 18, 2005): 134.

— Andrea Bellini, "An Interview with Maurizio Cattelan / Un'intervista con Maurizio Cattelan," *Sculpture* 34, no. 7 (September 1, 2005): 54–59. Reprinted in Italian in *Maurizio Cattelan*, eds. Elio Grazioli and Bianca Trevisan, monographic issue of *Riga*, no. 39 (2019): 39–43.

— Michele Robecchi, "Maurizio Cattelan and Massimiliano Gioni," *Contemporary* 21, n. 77 (Fall 2005): 42–45.

— Alberto Fiz, "Signor Cattelan: Impiegato di concetto," *Style* (October 14, 2005).

— Holger Liebs, "Von Menschenzungen und Mäusen: Das Kuratorentrio der 4. Berlin Biennale über Fratzen, Geld und Galeristen," interview with Maurizio Cattelan, Massimiliano Gioni, and Ali Subotnick, *Süddeutsche Zeitung* (November 28, 2005).

— [Editorial staff], "Die Dreierbande," interview with Maurizio Cattelan, Massimiliano Gioni and Ali Subotnick, *Berliner Morgenpost* (December 27, 2005).

— [Editorial staff], "Karneval in Mitte," interview with Maurizio Cattelan, Massimiliano Gioni, and Ali Subotnick, *Die Welt* (December 28, 2005).

— Silke Bender, "Zwei Italiener in Berlin," interview with Maurizio Cattelan and Massimiliano Gioni, *Max*, no. 1 (December 30, 2005).

[2006]

— Francesca Di Nardo, "Interview with Maurizio Cattelan," *Janus*, no. 20 (2006): 35.

— Jörg Heiser, "4th Berlin Biennial 2006," interview with Maurizio Cattelan, Massimiliano Gioni, and Ali Subotnick, *Frieze*, no. 96 (January–February 2006): 126–27.

— Marcus Woeller, "Die 3 Kuratöre: Instinkt Statt Struktur," interview with Maurizio Cattelan, Massimiliano Gioni, and Ali Subotnick, *Style & the Family Tunes*, no. 89 (January–February 2006): 52–55.

— Francesco Galdieri, "Cattelan: 'Provocare è arte,'" *Il Mattino* (January 12, 2006): 23.

— Nicole Büsing and Heiko Klass, "Das Abenteuer wartet an der Ecke," interview with Maurizio Cattelan, Massimiliano Gioni and Ali Subotnick, *Kieler Nachrichten* (January 19, 2006).

— [Editorial staff], "Hat man Vertrauen in das Logo oder in die Kunst?," interview with Maurizio Cattelan, Massimiliano Gioni and Ali Subotnick, *Kultur Kanal* (February 2006), 18–19.

— Daniela Zenone, "Siamo uomini o topi?," interview with Maurizio Cattelan, Massimiliano Gioni and Ali Subotnick, *Kult* (February 2006).

— Severin Dünser, Vivian Kea, and Florian Rehn, "Falling and Walking Ahead," interview with Maurizio Cattelan, Massimiliano Gioni, and Ali Subotnick, *Mono: Kultur*, no. 5 (February–March 2002): entire issue.

— [Editorial staff], "Berlin Biennale 04: 7 ½ Questions to Maurizio Cattelan, Massimiliano Gioni and Ali Subotnick," *Fucking Good Art*, no. 12 (March 2006), 6–10.

— Francesco Bonami, "The Wrong Way," interview with Maurizio Cattelan, Massimiliano Gioni, and Ali Subotnick, *Modern Painters*, no. 18 (March 2006): 86–91.

— Paolo Vagheggi, "Maurizio Cattelan: 'Così scandalizzerò Berlino,'" *la Repubblica* (March 13, 2006): 36.

— Lotte Møller, "bb4," interview with Maurizio Cattelan, Massimiliano Gioni, and Ali Subotnick, *Tema Celeste*, no. 114 (March–April 2006): 94–97.

— Aaron Moulton, "Taking the Wrong's Way to Berlin: Interview with the Curators of Berlin Biennale," interview with Maurizio Cattelan, Massimiliano Gioni and Ali Subotnick, *Flash Art International* 39, no. 247 (March–April 2006): 46–47. Published in Italian as "Di uomini e topi: Parlano i curatori della Biennale di Berlino," *Flash Art Italia* 39, no. 247 (April–May 2006): 61–62.

— Estelle Nabeyrat, "4e Biennale de Berlin," interview with Maurizio Cattelan, Massimiliano Gioni, and Ali Subotnick, *Standard*, no. 11 (March–May 2006): 169.

— Walter Rauhe, "Un villaggio globale di uomini e topi," interview with Maurizio Cattelan and Massimiliano Gioni, *Il Messaggero* (March 20, 2006).

— Nicole Büsing and Heiko Klaas, "Straßenkarneval der Kunst mit ernsten Themen," interview with Maurizio Cattelan, Massimiliano Gioni, and Ali Subotnick, *Nürnberger Nachrichten*, *Fränkischer Anzeiger*, *Erlanger Nachrichten*, and *Altmühlbote* (March 24, 2006).

— Ernesto L. Francalanci, "La macchina del tempo e dell'arte in Auguststrasse," interview with Maurizio Cattelan, Massimiliano Gioni, and Ali Subotnick, *l'Unità* (March 25, 2006): 25.

— Silke Bender, "Zwei Italiener und Eine Amerikanen," interview with Maurizio Cattelan, Massimiliano Gioni, and Ali Subotnick, *030*, no. 7 (March 30, 2006): 4–5.

— Maria Cristina Didero, "Some Days I Laugh, Some Days I Cry," *Sleek*, no. 10 (Spring 2006): 42–49.

— "Casa Cattelan," interview with Maurizio Cattelan and Massimiliano Gioni, *Rolling Stone Italia* (April 2006).

— Ulrich Clewing, "Der Künstler als Kurator," *Architectural Digest Germany*, no. 68 (April 2006): 212–14.

— Thibaut De Ruyter, "Des souris et des hommes: 4e Biennale d'art contemporain," interview with Maurizio


361

Cattelan, Massimiliano Gioni, and Ali Subotnick, *Art Press*, no. 322 (April 2006): 18–21.
— Kito Nedo, "Es gibt kein Konzept," interview with Maurizio Cattelan, Massimiliano Gioni, and Ali Subotnick, *Art: Das Kunstmagazin*, no. 4 (April 2006): 29.
— Augustine Zenakos, "We Are Three People Who Can Barely Make One Mind," interview with Maurizio Cattelan, Massimiliano Gioni and Ali Subotnick, *To Vima*, no. 26 (April 2, 2006).
— Alessandra Mammì, "Dietrofront d'artista," *L'Espresso* (April 6, 2006).
— Bruno LeMieux-Ruibal, "No disparen a la ardilla / Don't Shoot the Squirrel," *LAPIZ*, no. 223 (May 2006): 28–41.
— Nancy Spector, "De ratones y hombres," interview with Maurizio Cattelan, Massimiliano Gioni, and Ali Subotnick, *Fahrenheit*, no. 17 (June–July 2006): n.p.
— Alain Elkann, "Maurizio Cattelan," *Alain Elkann Interviews* (June 4, 2006); https://www.alainelkanninterviews.com/maurizio-cattelan/.
— Annamaria Sbisà, "Due giorni d'artista inventati sul web," *la Repubblica* (July 1, 2006): 12.

[2007]
— Paolo Vagheggi, "Il cavallo a metà di Cattelan," *la Repubblica* (June 25, 2007): 36.
— Paola Naldi, "Maurizio Cattelan: 'Vi seduco. No, scherzo!,'" *Riflessi*, no. 8 (September 2007): 43–47.
— Marco Gregoretti, "Maurizio Cattelan: 'Creare, che rottura,'" *Class*, no. 259 (November 2007): 56–70.
— Helena Kontova, "Maurizio Cattelan: No Cakes for Special Occasion," *Flash Art International* 40, no. 257 (November–December 2007): 74–76; https://flash---art.com/article/maurizio-cattelan-3/. Published in Italian as "Maurizio Cattelan. Qualsiasi cosa è interessante, se la guardi a lungo," *Flash Art Italia* 40, no. 267 (December 2007–January 2008): 66–68. Reprinted in *All Cattelan*, monographic issue of *Flash Art Italia* 47, no. 299: 84–87.

[2008]
— Caroline Corbetta, "Art is a Never Ending Project," *L'Uomo Vogue*, no. 394 (October 2008): 68.

[2009]
— Daniele Perra, "Maurizio Cattelan," *Kult Magazine* (May 2009): 106.
— Irene Maria Scalise, "Maurizio Cattelan," *la Repubblica* (May 3, 2009): 40.
— Michele Robecchi, "Maurizio Cattelan," *Interview* 39, no. 5 (June–July 2009): 63–65.
— Henri-François Debailleux, "L'œuvre n'est jamais une scandale," *Le mag*, supplement of *Libération* (September 12–13, 2009): XIV–XV.
— Michèle Gerber-Klein, "Maurizio Cattelan," *BOMB* (September 19, 2009); https://bombmagazine.org/articles/maurizio-cattelan/.
— Michele Robecchi, "Crisi come opportunità: L'Italia può giocarla a suo vantaggio," *Corriere d'Italia* (October 2, 2009): 11.

[2010]
— Daniele Perra, "Concentrate a Houston le visioni di Maurizio Cattelan," *Luxory* 24, online supplement of *Il Sole 24 Ore* (February 11, 2010).
— Caroline Corbetta, "Maurizio Cattelan," *Klat*, no. 2 (April 2010): 36–52.
— Alessandra Mammì, "Il mio Craxi incompreso," *L'Espresso* (May 24, 2010).
— Raffaele Panizza, "Maurizio Cattelan: 'Dopo il dito medio vorrei celebrare le battone,'" *Panorama* (July 20, 2010).
— Francesca Bonazzoli, "Cattelan: 'Così ho abbattuto mio padre,'" *Corriere della Sera* (September 13, 2010): 33.
— Massimo Arcidiacono, "Cattelan show: 'Mi prendo Milano e il cambio faccia,'" *La Gazzetta dello Sport* (September 25, 2010).
— Irene Hernández Velasco, "Jamás he buscado escandalizar," *El Mundo* (September 25, 2010): 47.
— Armando Stella, "Morbose le mie opere? Soltanto negli occhi di chi le guarda," *Corriere della Sera* (September 25, 2010).
— Alexi Worth, "A Fine Italian Hand," *The New York Times* (October 11, 2010).

[2011]
— Elisabeth Sobieski, "The Mysteries and Magic of Maurizio Cattelan," *The Art Economist* 1, no. 3 (March 1, 2011): 42–47.

— Dario Pappalardo, "Cattelan: 'Addio all'arte, basta pupazzi, mi ritiro,'" *la Repubblica* (April 1, 2011): 1.
— Philippe Dagen, "Maurizio Cattelan: L'agitateur," *Le Monde Magazine* (April 9, 2011): 46–49; https://static.perrotin.com/pdf/press_review/press_review_maurizio-cattelan_le-monde-magazine_2011-04-09_1290.pdf.
— Dario Pappalardo, "Il cielo sopra la Biennale con i piccioni di Cattelan," *la Repubblica* (May 30, 2011): 1.
— Francesco Bonami, "Lasciatemi sparire come Mina," *Vanity Fair* (June 1, 2011): 157–60.
— Donatien Grau, "Maurizio Cattelan," *AnOther Magazine* (June 28, 2011); https://www.anothermag.com/fashion-beauty/1185/maurizio-cattelan.
— Giancarlo Politi, "Zoo Cattelan," *Flash Art Italia* 44, no. 295 (July–September 2011): 96–97; https://flash---art.it/article/zoo-cattelan/.
— Dario Pappalardo, "Va bene, adesso che è tutto finito ci consoleremo solo con YouTube," *la Repubblica* (September 3, 2011): 37.
— Carole Sabas, "Adieu l'artiste?," *Vogue Hommes International* (Fall/Winter 2011–2012): 194–201.
— Randy Kennedy, "Hanging with Cattelan," with contributions by Nancy Spector, *The New York Times* (September 29, 2011): 1; https://www.nytimes.com/2011/10/02/arts/design/maurizio-cattelan-retrospective-at-guggenheim.html.
— "Il caso Cattelan: genio o sberleffo?," *Vernissage*, supplement of *Il Giornale dell'Arte*, no. 313 (October 2011).
— Camilla Baresani, "Ricomincio da pittore. Anche se non so dipingere," *Io Donna* (October 15, 2011): 64–70.
— Maike Cruse, "He's Finished," *Monopol* (November 2011): 18–35.
— Franco Fanelli, "Maurizio Cattelan: Genius or Joker?," *The Art Newspaper*, no. 16 (November 2011): 56.
— Paola Manfrin, "Maurizio Cattelan: What Motivates the Shocking Announcement of His Retirement," *L'Uomo Vogue*, no. 425 (November 2011): 48; https://www.vogue.it/en/uomo-vogue/people-stars/2011/11/cattelan.
— Charmaine Picard, "A Q&A with Maurizio Cattelan," *Modern Painters* (November 2011): 68–71.
— Michele Robecchi, "Maurizio Cattelan: All in One," *Art in America* (November 1, 2011); https://www.artnews.com/art-in-america/features/maurizio-cattelan-all-in-one-62911/.
— James Tarmy, "Suicide Squirrel, Struck Pope: Interview with Maurizio Cattelan," *Bloomberg Businessweek* (November 10, 2011).
— Natalia Aspesi, "Cattelan volteggia sul cielo di New York," *la Repubblica* (November 11, 2011): 1.
— Jarrett Earnest, "Charm Like a Drug: Maurizio Cattelan with Jarrett Earnest," *The Brooklyn Rail* (December 1, 2011).
— Aurélie Raya, "Maurizio Cattelan: artiste de haut vol," *Paris Match* (December 12, 2011); https://www.parismatch.com/Culture/Art/Maurizio-Cattelan-artiste-de-haut-vol-150964.

[2012]
— Anna Sansom, "Maurizio Cattelan," *Whitewall* (Winter 2012).
— Irene Gludowacz, "Greatest Gauner," *Art Investor* (January 2012): 62–71.
— *All Cattelan*, monographic issue of *Flash Art Italia*, no. 299 (February 2012).
— Irene Maria Scalise, "Maurizio Cattelan: 'Vivere trenta ore al giorno,'" *la Repubblica* (March 31, 2012): 39.
— Peifen Sung, "Maurizio Cattelan: Art Terminator," *Bazaar Art* (May 2012): 84–111; https://static.perrotin.com/pdf/press_review/press_review_maurizio-cattelan_bazaar-art_2012-05-01_1272.pdf.
— Heinz-Norbert Jocks, "Ich Bin Es Immer Selbst, Selbst Wenn Ich Es Nicht Bin!," *Kunstforum International* (April–June 2012): 220–35.
— Rozmawiała Dorota Jarecka, "Maurizio Cattelan o sztuce i religii," *Gazeta* (November 19, 2012).
— Dario Pappalardo, "Così ho chiuso con lo stress," *la Repubblica* (November 22, 2012): 45.
— Dario Pappalardo, "Quel blob d'immagini firmato da Cattelan," *la Repubblica* (December 4, 2012): 53.
— Riccardo Fano, "Toilet Paper: il libro. L'intervista esclusiva a Maurizio Cattelan e Pierpaolo Ferrari," *Panorama* (December 21, 2012); https://www.panorama.it/cultura/toilet-paper-libro-damiani.
— Dario Pappalardo, "Cattelan: perché ho portato Hitler nel ghetto di Varsavia. L'ultimo scandalo di Cattelan," *la Repubblica* (December 30, 2012): 1.

[2013]
— "Ein Paar Minuten im Leben eines Künstlers," *Das Magazin* (September 7, 2013).
— Holly Fraser, "Toiletpaper," *Hunger*, no. 5 (Fall/Winter 2013): 214–19.
— Barbara Tomasino, "Intervista a Maurizio Cattelan: 'Beppe Grillo come Silvio Berlusconi, un ottimo showman,'" *Huffington Post* (February 7, 2013); https://www.huffingtonpost.it/2013/02/02/intervista-a-maurizio-cattelan_n_2605089.html.
— [Editorial staff], "Toiletpaper," *Marfa* (March 2013): 282–87.
— Caroline Corbetta, "Padiglione Crepaccio," *Domus*, no. 969 (May 2013), 166–67; https://www.domusweb.it/it/arte/2013/05/14/padiglione_crepaccio.html.
— Pierluigi Panza, "Cattelan non c'è (ma un po' sì)," *Corriere della Sera* (May 26, 2013): 19.
— Boris Pofalla, "Die Kunst der Faulheit," *Monopol* (June 2013): 86–88.
— Rachel Spence, "Until the Laughter Gets Stuck in Our Throat…," *Financial Times* (June 7, 2013); https://www.ft.com/content/71ac2700-cd0e-11e2-9efe-00144feab7de.
— Hugo Vitrani, "Cattelan, l'artiste 'qui danse sur la frontière,'" *Mediapart* (June 10, 2013); https://www.mediapart.fr/journal/culture-idees/070713/cattelan-lartiste-qui-danse-sur-la-frontiere?onglet=full.
— Kerry Olsen, "Isn't It Ironic: Maurizio Cattelan on His New Capsule Sweatshirt Collection with MSGM," *Vogue* (June 14, 2013); https://www.vogue.com/article/isnt-it-ironic-maurizio-cattelan-on-his-new-capsule-sweatshirt-collection-with-msgm.
— Sylvian Bourmeau, "Notre declaration d'amour pour l'image pure," *Libération* (June 19, 2013): 30–31.
— Alex Moshakis, "Maurizio Cattelan's Shocking Window Displays at the Palais de Tokyo," *T Magazine* (June 21, 2013); https://archive.nytimes.com/tmagazine.blogs.nytimes.com/2013/06/21/on-view-maurizio-cattelans-shocking-window-displays-at-the-palais-de-tokyo/.
— Constance Breton, "Héritage tragi-comique," *Air France Magazine*, no. 195 (July 2013): 76–80.
— Christian Spies, "Ein idealer Nährboden für schwierige Projekte," *Basler Zeitung* (July 3, 2013).
— Catherine Delmas, "En privé avec Maurizio Cattelan," *Madame Figaro* (August 12, 2013); https://madame.lefigaro.fr/art-de-vivre/prive-avec-maurizio-cattelan-120813-442816.
— Christophe Ono-dit-Diot, "Cattelan crée le virus visuel," *Le Point* (August 15, 2013): 88–89.
— Enrico Dal Buono, "Catto Cattelan," *Marie Claire* (September 1, 2013), 193–96.
— Lisa Vignoli, "3 questions à Maurizio Cattelan," *M: Le magazine du Monde* (September 14, 2013).
— Oliver Prange, "Schauen Sie bitte nur auf meine Arbeiten, da liegen die Antworten," *Du* (October 1, 2013).
— Paola Naldi, "Cattelan: 'Amare l'arte senza riserve è la lezione che ha dato Bologna,'" *la Repubblica Bologna* (October 25, 2013); https://bologna.repubblica.it/cronaca/2013/10/25/news/bologna_arte_premio_alinovi_e_daolio_paola_naldi_intervista_maurizio_cattelan-69420555/.
— Henry Giardina, "The White Wipe," *Bullett*, no. 9 (Winter 2013).
— Kristine Dabbay, "Toilet Humor," *Status* (December 2013–January 2014): 72–79.

[2014]
— Mujde Metin, "Maurizio Cattelan: Bibbidi Bobbidi Boo," *XOXO: The Mag* (February 2014): 69–72.
— Woo Lee, "Toiletpaper," interview with Maurizio Cattelan and Pierpaolo Ferrari, *W Korea* (March 5, 2014).
— Francesco Bonami and Olivier Zahm, "Toiletpaper," *Purple Magazine*, no. 21 (Spring/Summer 2014), 202–09; https://purple.fr/magazine/ss-2014-issue-21/toiletpaper/.
— Valentina Raggi, "Maurizio Cattelan: Il maniaco dell'arte," *Grazia Casa* (April 2014): 80.
— Raffele Panizza, "Conversazione con Maurizio Cattelan: 'Ecco il mio souvenir per Milano,'" *Panorama* (April 7, 2014); https://www.panorama.it/cultura/maurizio-cattelan-epoca-monumento-che-si-merita.
— Kingston Trinder, "Provocation Is in the Eye of the Beholder," interview with Maurizio Cattelan and Pierpaolo Ferrari, *Dazed* (April 14, 2014); https://www.dazeddigital.com/photography/article/19565/1/provocation-is-in-the-eye-of-the-beholder.

— Francesco Bonami, "La bolla dell'arte? Forse sta già esplodendo ma non ce ne accorgiamo," *La Stampa* (April 15, 2014): 28–29.
— Francesca Pini, "La guerra l'amore e le brutture dell'arte. La crisi Renzo, Grillo anche Marzullo. La ricetta? Seguire l'esempio di Ratzinger," *Sette*, supplement of *Corriere della Sera* (October 17, 2014): 38–42.
— Paola Tognon, "Artista o curatore? Sempre meglio che lavorare," *Exibart*, no. 88 (November 2014): 34–35.
— [Editorial staff], "Le 3M e la sorpresa della forca!," interview with Maurizio Cattelan, Myriam Ben Salah, and Marta Papini, *ATPdiary* (November 11, 2014).
— Molly Gottschalk, "Retired Artist Maurizio Cattelan's New Position: 'Non-Curator,'" *Artsy* (November 14, 2014); https://www.artsy.net/article/editorial-retired-artist-maurizio-cattelans-new-position-non-curator.
— Elena Cué, "Maurizio Cattelan: 'El mundo necesita encontrar a un provocador de vez en cuando,'" *ABC* (November 17, 2014); https://www.abc.es/cultura/arte/20141116/abci-entrevista-maurizio-cattelan-201411152231.html. Reprinted in English as "Interview with Maurizio Cattelan," *Alejandra De Argos* (November 24, 2014); https://www.alejandradeargos.com/index.php/es/viajeslist/21-english/posts/guests-with-art/373-interview-maurizio-cattelan-by-elena-cue.
— Peter Aspden, "Maurizio Cattelan on Art and Curating His Punchy Turin Show," *Financial Times* (November 21, 2014); https://www.ft.com/content/9f484082-6fdc-11e4-90af-00144feabdc0.
— Elena Livieri, "La provocazione è in chi guarda," *Corriere delle Alpi* (November 26, 2014): 28.
— Clelia Patella, "Intervista a Maurizio Cattelan sulla sua mostra 'Shit And Die,'" *ArtsLife* (November 27, 2014); https://artslife.com/2014/11/27/intervista-a-cattelan-sulla-sua-mostra-shit-and-die/.
— "Maurizio Cattelan's L.A. Art Tour, with a Stop at Jim Carrey's Painting Studio," with Maurizio Cattelan and Ali Subotnick, *Vulture* (December 11, 2014).
— Alessia Carlino, "Risponde Cattelan," *Inside Art* (December 18, 2014).

[2015]
— Nadia Afragola, "Milano (quasi) meglio di New York," *Club Milano*, no. 24 (January–February 2015).
— Alicia Reuter, "Food Poisoning: An Interview with Maurizio Cattelan," *Sleek*, no. 44 (January 7, 2015); https://www.sleek-mag.com/article/maurizio-cattelan-interview/.
— Emma Allen, "Rest in Pieces," *The New Yorker* (May 4, 2015).
— [Editorial staff], "Maurizio Cattelan: 'Show Them Life,'" *The Talks* (May 27, 2015); https://the-talks.com/interview/maurizio-cattelan/.
— Fan Zhong, "Maurizio Cattelan on Retirement, Instagram and That Documentary," *W Magazine* (December 1, 2015); https://www.wmagazine.com/story/maurizio-cattelan-untitled-miami-beach.
— Lorena Muñoz-Alonso, "Artnet Asks: Artist, Prankster, and Designer Maurizio Cattelan," *Artnet* (December 3, 2015); https://news.artnet.com/art-world/artnet-asks-maurizio-cattelan-383957.

[2016]
— Dario Pappalardo, "Maurizio Cattelan: 'L'ansia non si addice all'arte di oggi,'" *la Repubblica* (January 31, 2016): 41; https://www.repubblica.it/cultura/2016/01/31/news/cattelan_l_ansia_non_si_addice_all_arte_di_oggi_-132428006/.
— Lily Silverton, "Artist Maurizio Cattelan on Mortality, the Internet and Identity," *Hunger*, no. 10 (Spring/Summer 2016), n.p.
— Marta Galli, "Sai di essere un genio Cattelan?," *i-D* (April 9, 2016); https://i-d.vice.com/it/article/xwxzea/maurizio-cattelan.
— Ilaria Iacoboni, "Cattelan: 'Un'opera è arte solo se dura nel tempo, altrimenti si chiama merchandising,'" *la Repubblica* (October 19, 2016): 35; https://www.repubblica.it/cultura/2016/10/19/news/cattelan_un_opera_e_arte_solo_se_dura_nel_tempo_altrimenti_si_chiama_merchandising_-150133934/.
— Benjamin Locoge and Elisabeth Couturier, "Maurizio Cattelan: 'Le diable fait toujours vendre!,'" *Paris Match* (October 23, 2016); https://www.parismatch.com/Culture/Art/Maurizio-Cattelan-Le-diable-fait-toujours-vendre-1101074.
— Ivo Bonacorsi, "Not Afraid of Love," *Domus* (November 7, 2016); https://www.domusweb.it/it/

interviste/2016/11/07/maurizio_cattelan_not_afraid_of_
love.html.
— Thibaut Wychowanok-Dumas, "We Met Maurizio
Cattelan: Is This Interview Our First Analysis Session?,"
*Numéro* (December 5, 2016).

[2017]
— Sara Waka and Elisa Da Rin, "Maurizio Cattelan,"
*Playboy* (April 2017): 60–67.
— Ludovico Pratesi, "La Parola all'Artista," *Art e
Dossier*, no. 345 (July–August 2017): 48–49.
— Rossella Farinotti, "Maurizio Cattelan: Instagram
secondo Cattelan," *Zero* (August 16, 2017); https://zero.eu/
en/persone/maurizio-cattelan/.
— Cristiano De Majo, "Il ritorno di Maurizio Cattelan,"
*Rivista Studio* (August 28, 2017); https://www.rivistastudio.
com/maurizio-cattelan/.
— Irene Maria Scalise, "Maurizio Cattelan: smetto
quando voglio," *la Repubblica* (September 9, 2017): 37;
https://www.repubblica.it/rclub/persone/2017/09/09/
news/maurizio_cattelan_smetto_quando_voglio-
174698183/?ref=search.
— Marta Galli, "Intervista a Maurizio Cattelan," *Vogue
Italia*, no. 807 (November 2017): 69; https://www.vogue.
it/news/vogue-arte/2017/11/09/intervista-a-maurizio-
cattelan-vogue-italia-novembre-2017.

[2018]
— Masoud Golsorkhi, "Original Copy," *Tank*, no. 77
(Winter 2018).
— Paloma Powers, "Interview: A Conversation with
Maurizio Cattelan," *Culture*[TM] (2018).
— Isaac Pérez Solano, "Brace Yourself, Maurizio
Cattelan's Art Feels Like a Big Slap in the Face," *Odda
Magazine*, no. 14 (Fall/Winter 2018–19).
— Nicolas Ballario, "Maurizio Cattelan: 'Io sono la fake
news,'" *Rolling Stone Italia* (February 28, 2018); https://
www.rollingstone.it/cultura/interviste-cultura/maurizio-
cattelan-io-sono-la-fake-news/402786/#Part1.
— Paolo Bricco, "L'arte? È come possedere le menti,"
*Il Sole 24 Ore* (April 15, 2018): 23; https://www.ilsole24ore.
com/art/maurizio-cattelan-fare-arte-e-come-possedere-
menti-AER1EeYE.
— Federico Giannini, "Maurizio Cattelan: 'Ho sempre
qualcosa da imparare,'" *Finestre sull'Arte* (April 19, 2018);
https://www.finestresullarte.info/interviste/intervista-a-
maurizio-cattelan-ho-sempre-qualcosa-da-imparare.
— Chiara Maffioletti, "Maurizio Cattelan: 'Da
infermiere a creativo. E ora vendo la mia fronte per
finanziare buone azioni,'" *Corriere della Sera* (April 22,
2018); https://www.corriere.it/cronache/18_aprile_22/
maurizio-cattelan-da-infermiere-creativo-ora-vendo-mia-
fronte-b6572cb2-4665-11e8-9661-d18d4bfcda1f.shtml.
— Alessandra Vivoli, "Cattelan è vivo e premiato (e si
'regala' una lapide," *Il Tirreno* (April 23, 2018): 37.
— Rita Vittorelli, "If I Tell You I Have to Kill You with My
Laser Vision," *Spike Art Magazine* (May 12, 2018).
— Ali Y. Khadra, "What Is Original?," *Canvas*
(September 2018): 54–55.
— Anna Daneri, "Maurizio Cattelan: I Copy Therefore I
Am," *L'Officiel Art International* (September–November 2018).
— "L'invité du mois Maurizio Cattelan: Buenos Aires,"
with Maurizio Cattelan and Myriam Ben Salah, *Numéro Art*,
no. 3 (September 2018–February 2019): 42–50.
— Mark Rappolt, "Maurizio Cattelan," *ArtReview Asia*
(Fall 2018): 60–63.
— Cloé Perrone, "Maurizio Cattelan: The Artist Is
Present," *Kaleidoscope* (Fall/Winter 2018): 60–61.
— Nilüfer Sasmazer, "Maurizio Cattelan: Imitation Is
Authentic," *212* (Fall/Winter 2018): 54–57.
— Alexandra English, "Copy That," *Harper's Bazaar
Australia* (October 2018): 157.
— Shruti Kapur Malhotra, "The Artist Is Present:
Maurizio Cattelan," *Platform India* (October 2018): 112–13.
— Jiseon Kim, "The Artist Is Present," *Bazaar Art Korea*
(October 2018).
— Eunkyoung Kwon, "The Artist Is Present," *W Korea*
(October 2018): 179.
— Lella Scalia, "Una copia è una copia è una copia,"
*Vogue Italia* (October 2018): 150.
— Febe Riri Siahaan, "Seniman & Orisinalitas," *Harper's
Bazaar Indonesia* (October 2018): 126–27.
— Sonia Xie, "The Artist Is Present," *The Art
Newspaper China* (October 2018).
— Barbara Pollack, "Gucci and Cattelan in Shanghai,"
*Modern Weekly* (October 6, 2018): 32–33.

— Michele Falcone, "La creatività nell'era digitale:
Intervista a Maurizio Cattelan," *Living Corriere* (October 8,
2018); https://living.corriere.it/design/lifestyle/intervista-
maurizio-cattelan/.
— Xueer Qian, "The Artist Is Present," *The Paper*
(October 9, 2018); https://www.thepaper.cn/newsDetail_
forward_2509020.
— Serena Tibaldi, "Il gioco delle copie: Quando
l'imitazione rafforza l'arte (e la moda)," interview with
Maurizio Cattelan and Alessandro Michele, *la Repubblica*
(October 13, 2018): 44–45.
— Ziren Lin, "The Artist Is Present," *Jiemian* (October
16, 2018); https://m.jiemian.com/article/2531339.html.
— Benoît Loiseau, "Maurizio Cattelan Discusses His
Joint Show with Gucci's Alessandro Michele at the Yuz
Museum," *Cultured* (October 16, 2018); https://www.
culturedmag.com/article/2018/10/15/maurizio-cattelan-
discusses-joint-show-with-guccis-alessandro-michele-at-
the-yuz-museum.
— Yoko Choy, "Gucci and Maurizio Cattelan Explore
the Power of Appropriation in Shanghai Show," *Wallpaper*
(October 19, 2018); https://www.wallpaper.com/fashion/
gucci-maurizio-cattelan-the-artist-is-present-shanghai.
— Fan Zhong, "Maurizio Cattelan Explains How to
Plagiarize Artfully," *W Magazine* (October 21, 2018); https://
www.wmagazine.com/story/maurizio-cattelan-interview-
yuz-museum-exhibit-gucci.
— Emily Farra, "Maurizio Cattelan on 'The Artist
Is Present,' His Mind-Bending New Exhibition with
Alessandro Michele in Shanghai," *Vogue* (October 22,
2018); https://www.vogue.com/article/the-artist-is-present-
maurizio-cattelan-gucci-alessandro-michele-shanghai.
— Rafa Rodriguez, "Maurizio Cattelan: 'Soy artista
porque no era bueno como falsificador,'" *El País* (October
22, 2018): 35.
— Jun Ishida, "The Age of the Appropriation,"
*T Magazine Japan* (October 31, 2018).
— Camila Garcia, "Nada se cria," *Vogue Brazil*
(November 2018).
— Keiko Niiyama, "The Magic of Appropriation,"
*Harper's Bazaar Japan* (November 2018): 387.
— Wenjia Sheng, "The Artist Is Present," *T Magazine
China* (November 2018).
— Matteo Persivale, "Copiate! Anche la Cappella
Sistina," *La Lettura*, supplement of *Corriere della Sera*
(November 11, 2018): 45.
— Tanya Tang, "The Artist Is Present," *Ideat China*
(December 2018): 110–15.
— Ali Y. Khadra, "Can the Real Maurizio Please Stand
Up," *Sorbet* (December 2018).
— Armelle Leturcq, "The Artist Is Present: Maurizio
Cattelan," *Crash* (December 2018): 70–75.
— Felipe Pando, "Original y Copia," *L'Officiel México*
(December 2018): 148–50.
— Joerg Koch, "Overcoming Originality: Maurizio
Cattelan and Gucci Steal Shanghai," *032c* (December 3,
2018); https://032c.com/magazine/overcoming-originality-
maurizio-cattelan-and-gucci-steal-shanghai.
— Xue Peng, "Is Copying Necessarily Bad?," *Life Week*
(December 3, 2018).
— Dario Pappalardo, "Siamo i geni del calendario,"
interview with Maurizio Cattelan and Martin Parr, *Robinson*,
supplement of *la Repubblica* (December 9, 2018): 20–28.

[2019]
— [Editorial staff], "My Confidences (2019): Maurizio
Cattelan," in *Conversations: Now. Just now. Then.*, no. 3
(London: Luxembourg & Dayan, 2019): 42–47.
— Marco Belpoliti, Elio Grazioli, and Bianca Trevisan,
"Intervista a Maurizio Cattelan," *Maurizio Cattelan*, eds.
Elio Grazioli and Bianca Trevisan, monographic issue of
*Riga*, no. 39 (2019): 44–51.
— Andrea Lazarov, "Fake/Off," *Buffalo Zine*, no. 9
(2019): 76–81.
— Aimée McLaughlin, "How We Met: Toiletpaper,"
interview with Maurizio Cattelan and Pierpaolo Ferrari,
*Creative Review* (January 30, 2019); https://www.
creativereview.co.uk/how-we-met-toiletpaper/.
— Giacomo Papi, "Maurizio Cattelan raccontato da
Giacomo Papi: L'oracolo dell'arte," *Wired*, no. 88 (Spring
2019): 38–49.
— Terry Marocco, "Cattelan, il ficcanaso del design,"
*Panorama* (April 11, 2019); https://www.panorama.it/
societa/maurizio-cattelan-intervista-del-design.
— [Editorial staff], "Toiletpaper's Photos Push the
Boundaries of Absurdist Photography," interview with

Maurizio Cattelan and Pierpaolo Ferrari, *Vice* (May 6, 2019); https://www.vice.com/en/article/pajgdz/toiletpapers-photos-push-the-boundaries-of-absurdist-photography-v26n2.
— Simone Sbarbati, "Toiletpaper × Nike Air Max 270 React: Intervista a Maurizio Cattelan," *Frizzifrizzi* (July 4, 2019); https://www.frizzifrizzi.it/2019/07/04/toiletpaper-x-nike-air-max270-react-intervista-a-maurizio-cattelan/.
— Annie Armstrong, "Maurizio Cattelan on His Show of Artists Named Smith, His Retirement Status, and Where His Golden Toilet is Headed Next," *ARTnews* (July 24, 2019); https://www.artnews.com/art-news/artists/maurizio-cattelan-the-smiths-retirement-golden-toilet-13024/.
— Louis Wise, "Flushed with Success," *The Sunday Times* (August 25, 2019): 18–19.
— Alex Needham, "Your Chance to Feel Very Flush: The 18-Carat Golden Toilet Hits Britain," *The Guardian* (September 3, 2019); https://www.theguardian.com/artanddesign/2019/sep/03/maurizio-cattelan-golden-toilet-blenheim-palace-america.
— Louisa Buck, "Nothing is Sacred: Artist Provocateur," *The Art Newspaper* (September 12, 2019).
— Miguel Figueroa, "Maurizio Cattelan Interview: 'Mad Scientist,'" *Twelv* (September 17, 2019); https://twelvny.com/art-culture/maurizio-cattelan-interview-mad-scientist.
— Malcolm Pagani, "Ma come Cattelan è successo?," *Vanity Fair*, no. 39 (October 3, 2019).
— [Editorial staff], "An Exclusive Interview with Maurizio Cattelan about the Blenheim Palace Heist," *Garage* (September 29, 2019).
— Tobias Haberl, "Meine Mutter Starb in dem Glauben, dass ich als Terrorist Ende," *Süddeutsche Zeitung Magazine*, no. 46 (November 15, 2019): 16–26.

[2020]
— Francesco Bonami, "La banana della Repubblica," *Vogue Italia*, no. 834 (February 2020): 107–08; https://www.vogue.it/news/article/la-banana-della-repubblica-una-conversazione-tra-maurizio-cattelan-e-francesco-bonami.
— [Redazione], "Unhinged! Kendall Jenner Embodies Iconic Artworks by Maurizio Cattelan," *Garage* (February 19, 2020).
— Valentina Raggi, "Abbiamo intervistato Maurizio Cattelan, per parlare di tutto… Da Milano al mondo," *Elle Decor* (March 21, 2020); https://www.elledecor.com/it/people/a31813239/maurizio-cattelan-intervista/.
— "A Conversation between Maurizio Cattelan and Sasha Grey," *Autre* (March 24, 2020); https://autre.love/interviewsmain/2020/3/24/a-conversation-between-maurizio-cattelan-and-sasha-grey.
— Julie Belcove, "Bananas, Duct Tape and Loads of Ambition: How Maurizio Cattelan Became the Art World's Merry Prankster," *Robb Report Singapore* (May 4, 2020); https://www.robbreport.com.sg/bananas-duct-tape-and-loads-of-ambition-how-maurizio-cattelan-became-the-art-worlds-merry-prankster/.
— Alessandra Mammì, "Maurizio Cattelan e il suo modo di prendersi sul serio: Una raffica di aforismi per rivelare un percorso unico," *GQ* (September 2020): 177–85.
— Candida Morvillo, "Maurizio Cattelan compie 60 anni: 'Il mio debutto? Quando falsificai la firma di papà,'" *Corriere della Sera* (September 21, 2020); https://www.corriere.it/cronache/20_settembre_21/maurizio-cattelan-compie-60-anni-il-mio-debutto-quando-falsificai-firma-papa-9dd6e7b4-fb7a-11ea-a2be-cc6f2f2b148b.shtml.
— Antonio Gnoli, "Maurizio Cattelan: 'La prima follia? Fuggire in Spagna con il motorino,'" *Robinson*, supplement of *la Repubblica* (December 19, 2020): 44–45; https://www.repubblica.it/robinson/2020/12/20/news/cattelan-279048384/.

[2021]
— "Maurzio Cattelan on VEXILLOLOGY," in "How to Spend It," *Financial Times* (February 6–7, 2021): 54.
— Philippe Pourhashemi, "Natural Provocateur," *Shadowplay* (June 2021): 188–97.
— Francesco Bonami, "Maurizio Cattelan: 'E ora silenzio,'" *Vanity Fair* (July 7, 2021): 28–30; https://www.vanityfair.it/show/agenda/2021/07/07/maurizio-cattelan-e-ora-silenzio.
— Marco Enrico Giacomelli, "Respiro, fantasmi, cecità: Maurizio Cattelan in mostra a Milano," *Artribune* (July 13, 2021); https://www.artribune.com/arti-visive/arte-contemporanea/2021/07/maurizio-cattelan-mostra-milano-intervista/.
— Luigi Mascheroni, "La 'trilogia' di Cattelan, fra vita, morte, dolore (e una torre di 18 metri)," *Il Giornale* (July 14, 2021): 21.
— Elena Bordignon, "L'arte incendiaria! Parola di Maurizio Cattelan," *ICON* (July 20, 2021); https://www.iconmagazine.it/eventi/larte-incendiaria-parola-di-maurizio-cattelan/.
— Juliana Neira, "In Conversation with Maurizio Cattelan on His 'Breath Ghosts Blind' Show," *Designboom* (July 23, 2021) https://www.designboom.com/art/maurizio-cattelan-interview-breath-ghosts-blind-07-23-2021/.
— Gabriele Micciché, "Maurizio Cattelan: 'Lavorare è una malattia,'" *Millennium* (August 2021): 116–23.
— Simone Intermite, "Intervista – Maurizio Cattelan: 'Siamo delle macchine alimentate da emozioni, mi tengo cara la mia irrequietezza, è il miglior antidoto che ho,'" *Domanipress* (August 12, 2021); https://www.domanipress.it/intervista-maurizio-cattelan-siamo-delle-macchine-alimentate-da-emozioni-mi-tengo-cara-la-mia-irrequietezza-e-il-miglior-antidoto-che-ho/.
— Nicola Ricciardi, "New Ancestral Images," *My Art Guides* (September 1, 2021); https://myartguides.com/interviews/new-ancestral-images-nicola-ricciardi-interviews-maurizio-cattelan/.
— [Editorial staff], "Respiro, Fantasmi, Cecità," *Milanovibra* (September 30, 2021): 26–30.
— [Editorial staff], "Maurizio Cattelan: Being an Artist," *Wallpaper China* (November 2021): 60–65.
— Emmanuelle Jardonnet, "Maurizio Cattelan: 'Être artiste, c'est comme être prêtreou médecin,'" *Le Monde* (November 10, 2021); https://www.lemonde.fr/culture/article/2021/11/10/maurizio-cattelan-etre-artiste-c-est-comme-etre-pretre-ou-medecin_6101565_3246.html.
— [Editorial staff], "Maurizio Cattelan: An Artist Who Doesn't Allow Himself to Be Happy," *Super Elle China* (December 2021): 68–81.
— Gareth Harris, "Maurizio Cattelan: 'Life Is often Tragic and Comedic at the Same Time,'" *The Art Newspaper* (December 1, 2021); https://www.theartnewspaper.com/2021/11/30/maurizio-cattelan-interview-miami-beach.
— Dario Pappalardo, "Il personaggio. Maurizio Cattelan: 'Vorrei essere Angela Merkel,'" *la Repubblica* (December 21, 2021): 42; https://www.repubblica.it/cultura/2021/12/20/news/il_personaggio_maurizio_cattelan_vorrei_essere_angela_merkel_-330984655/.
— Yang Fan, "Maurizio Cattelan," *The Art Newspaper China* (December 24, 2021).

[2022]
— Martina Tronconi, "Maurizio Cattelan, una vita per l'arte: Dagli esordi al successo," *Gilt* (March 6, 2022); https://www.giltmagazine.it/interview/maurizio-cattelan-una-vita-per-larte-dagli-esordi-al-successo/.
— Francesco Bonami, "Maurizio Cattelan: The Last Judgment," *Gagosian Quarterly* (Spring 2022): 50–56; https://gagosian.com/quarterly/2022/02/28/interview-maurizio-cattelan-the-last-judgment/.
— Fabio Pariante, "An Uncomfortable Truth Spoken Out Loud: Maurizio Cattelan," *Frontrunner* (June 13, 2022); https://frontrunnermagazine.com/posts/an-uncomfortable-truth-spoken-out-loud-maurizio-cattelan/.
— Cristiana Campanini, "Il mio concerto per via Palestro," *la Repubblica* (July 26, 2022): 29.
— Harvey Byworth-Morgan, "Maurizio Cattelan: The Tragical Ridiculousness of Modern Art," *Metal Magazine*, no. 47 (Fall/Winter 2022–23).

[2023]
— Eunkyoung Kwon, "Maurizio Cattelan, Comedian Who Has No Intention of Becoming a Comedian," *W Korea* (February 26, 2023).
— Narang Kim, "Intruder, Maurizio Cattelan," *Vogue Korea* (February 28, 2023).
— Hyejin Jeon, "Asked Maurizio Cattelan," *Elle Korea* (March 1, 2023); https://www.elle.co.kr/article/75421.
— Francesca Pini, "Maurizio Cattelan: Il coccodrillo & la banana," *Sette*, supplement of *Corriere della Sera* (June 16, 2023): 64–68.
— Maurizio Marsico, "Non solo il nome," *Linus* (September 2023): 88–94.
— Antonio Privitera, "Intervista a Maurizio Cattelan, che nelle sue opere inscena spettacoli paradossali, provocatori, impattanti," *Harper's Bazaar Italia*, no. 5 (September 7, 2023); https://www.harpersbazaar.com/it/cultura/costume/a45033044/intervista-a-maurizio-cattelan/.

— Darius Sanai, "An Interview with Maurizio Cattelan," *LUX* (Fall/Winter 2023–2024); https://www.lux-mag.com/an-interview-with-maurizio-cattelan/.
— Marco Bassan, "Intervista a Maurizio Cattelan sul futuro (con consigli per giovani artisti)," *Artribune* (October 18, 2023); https://www.artribune.com/arti-visive/arte-contemporanea/2023/10/maurizio-cattelan-intervista/.
— Joshua Glass, "Uncanny Art for the Post-Truth Era," *T Magazine* (October 20, 2023).
— Ivan Carozzi, "Cuore," *Frankenstein*, no. 9 (November 2023): 166–67.

[2024]
— Paola Naldi, "Maurizio Cattelan: 'Sono diventato un classico,'" *la Repubblica* (January 30, 2024): 30; https://bologna.repubblica.it/cronaca/2024/01/29/news/maurizio_cattelan_intervista_arte_fiera_bologna-422007139/.
— [Editorial staff], "Interview with Maurizio Cattelan," *Artlover*, no. 60 (April 2024).
— Alastair Sooke, "'I Am Not a Satanist!': Meet the Great Blasphemer of Contemporary Art," *The Telegraph* (April 18, 2024); https://www.telegraph.co.uk/art/artists/maurizio-cattelan-interview-venice-biennale-2024/.
— Laura Rysman, "Maurizio Cattelan Turned a Banana into Art. Next Up: Guns," *The New York Times* (April 25, 2024); https://www.nytimes.com/2024/04/25/arts/design/cattelan-guns-gagosian-art.html.
— Timothée Chaillou, interview with Maurizio Cattelan, *Connaissancedesarts.com* (May 3, 2024).
— Marta Papini, "Maurizio Cattelan, quale arte si merita di essere esposta?," *ICON* (May 15, 2024); https://www.iconmagazine.it/eventi/maurizio-cattelan-intervista-arte-mostra-stoccolma/.
— Oliver Kupper, "Everything is Beautiful When You Look at It with Love: Maurizio Cattelan," *Autre* (June 17, 2024); https://autre.love/the-levity-issue/2024/6/1/everything-is-beautiful-when-you-look-at-it-with-love-maurizio-cattelan?rq=cattelan%202024.
— [Editorial staff], "Vulnerabilità e innocenza: Questo mi interessa," *L'Osservatore Romano* (July 6, 2024); https://www.osservatoreromano.va/it/news/2024-07/ods-023/vulnerabilita-e-innocenza-questo-mi-interessa.html.
— Timothée Chaillou, "An Encounter with Maurizio Cattelan," *Profane*, no. 19 (Fall/Winter 2024–25): 20–33.
— Dario Pappalardo, "Cattelan: 'Il mercato è scivolato sulla mia banana,'" *la Repubblica* (November 22, 2024): 28.

[2025]
— Francesca Pini, "Intervista a Maurizio Cattelan: 'La povertà non ti lascia mai,'" *Sette*, supplement of *Corriere della Sera* (February 7, 2025): 60–63; https://www.corriere.it/sette/25_febbraio_09/maurizio-cattelan-la-poverta-non-ti-lascia-mai-il-carbone-in-cantina-da-piccolo-e-un-ricordo-e-non-un-dramma-00c8c6e6-8d2f-48ef-a25a-c402cdb4exlk.shtml.
— Gianluca Cantaro, "Interview with Maurizio Cattelan," *Sei un Mito*, issue of *Alla Carta*, no. 26 (Spring/Summer 2025):10–15.
— Marco Missiroli, "Nel mio mondo libero," *La casa degli artisti*, special issue of *Grazia* (April 2025): 40–52.
— Cristina D'Antonio, "Maurizio Cattelan a Bergamo, un gioco tra arte, tempo e invisibile," *Esquire Italia*, no. 40 (April 10, 2025): 130–41; https://www.esquire.com/it/cultura/arte-design/a64340104/intervista-maurizio-cattelan-gamec-bergamo/.
— Dario Pappalardo, "In Italia il fascismo non è mai finito," *la Repubblica* (June 1, 2025): 30–31.

**In videos and films**

[2016]
— *Maurizio Cattelan. Be Right Back*, documentary film directed by Maura Axelrod, with Francesco Bonami, Maurizio Cattelan, and Massimiliano Gioni, Maura Axelrod Productions, USA, 2016, 1h 35'. [In the movie Massimiliano Gioni is interviewed and plays as Maurizio Cattelan, reprising a project and a role he had actively carried out between 1997–98 and 2006, during which he regularly appeared in the artist's place at interviews, awards, or conferences, providing responses and statements both in person and in written form.]

[2018]
— *Maurizio Cattelan a Carrara, il video dell'intervento integrale*, in YouTube, by the channel *Finestre sull'Arte*, October 24, 2019; https://www.youtube.com/watch?v=dsOjjqcl8Os].

[1987]
— "Peep Show," Palazzo Albertini, Forlì, 1987.

[1988]
— "Natura Codarda," Galleria Neon, Bologna, January 16–February 13, 1988.

[1989]
— "Biologia delle passioni," Galleria Neon, Bologna, May 6–June 12, 1989. Subsequent venues: Galleria Fuxia, Verona; Loggetta Lombardesca, Ravenna, November 1989.

[1990]
— "Strategie," Galleria Neon, Bologna, May 11– June 12, 1990. Subsequent venues: Studio Oggetto, Milano, June 12–July 12, 1990, Leonardi V-Idea, Genova, June 20–July 20, 1990.

[1991]
— Unauthorized stand, Arte Fiera, Bologna, January 25–28, 1991.

[1992]
— "Edizioni dell'Obbligo," Spazio Juliet, Trieste, February 6–28, 1992.

[1993]
— "Maurizio Cattelan," Galleria Massimo De Carlo, Milan, January–February 14, 1993.
— "Tarzan & Jane," Galleria Raucci/Santamaria, Naples, April 27–May 15, 1993.

[1994]
— "Maurizio Cattelan," Galerie Analix-B & L Polla, Geneva, 1994.
— "Maurizio Cattelan," Laure Genillard Gallery, London, January 28–March 5, 1994.
— "Warning! Enter at your own risk. Do not touch, do not feed, no smoking, no photographs, no dogs, thank you," Daniel Newburg Gallery, New York, May 28–29, 1994.
— "Maurizio Cattelan," Galerie Daniel Buchholz, Cologne, December 15, 1994–January 22, 1995.



— "Errotin, le vrai lapin," Galerie Emmanuel Perrotin, Paris, January 26–March 11, 1995.

[1996]
— "Maurizio Cattelan," Laure Genillard Gallery, London, February 7–March 23, 1996.
— "Maurizio Cattelan," Galleria Massimo De Carlo, Milan, February 16–March 1996.
— "San Temple Sect," Ars Futura Galerie, Zurich, October 1996.

[1997]
— "Maurizio Cattelan," Le Consortium – Centre d'art contemporain, Dijon, January 24–March 22, 1997.
— "Maurizio Cattelan. Dynamo Secession," curated by Kathrin Rhomberg, Wiener Secession, Vienna, January 31–March 9, 1997.
— "Moi-Même-Soi-Même," Galerie Emmanuel Perrotin, Paris, May 24–July 19, 1997.
— "Maurizio Cattelan. Tre installazioni per il Castello," curated by Giorgio Verzotti, Castello di Rivoli Museo d'Arte Contemporanea, Rivoli-Turin, September 25, 1997–January 8, 1988. [141] p. 227
— "Maurizio Cattelan," Galleria Massimo Minini, Brescia, October 9–November 20, 1997.
— "Maurizio Cattelan," Centre d'art – Espace Jules Verne, Brétigny-sur-Orge, December 13, 1997–February 21, 1998.

[1998]
— "Projects 65. Maurizio Cattelan," curated by Laura Hoptman, MoMA – The Museum of Modern Art, New York, November 6–December 4, 1998.

[1999]
— "Maurizio Cattelan," Anthony d'Offay Gallery, London, April 30–June 16, 1999.
— "Maurizio Cattelan," Galleria Massimo De Carlo, Milano, September 27–October 1999.
— "Maurizio Cattelan," curated by Madeleine Schuppli, Kunsthalle Basel, October 16–November 21, 1999.

[2000]
— "Maurizio Cattelan. L'Arbre," Forum du Centre

Pompidou – Musée national d'art moderne, Paris, January 1–April 1, 2000.
— "Maurizio Cattelan," Marian Goodman Gallery, New York, February 22–March 25, 2000.
— "Maurizio Cattelan," Artpace, San Antonio, Texas, June 8–July 16, 2000.
— "Maurizio Cattelan. La rivoluzione siamo noi," Migros Museum für Gegenwartskunst, Zurich, June 17–August 13, 2000.
— "Maurizio Cattelan," CCA – Center for Contemporary Art, Kitakyūshū, November 27–December 15, 2000.

[2001]
— "Maurizio Cattelan. Him," Färgfabriken, Stockholm, February 10–April 4, 2001.
— *Hollywood*, special project for "Plateau of Humankind," 49th Venice Biennale, curated by Harald Szeemann, hill of Bellolampo, Palermo, June 10–November 4, 2001.

[2002]
— "Maurizio Cattelan," Marian Goodman Gallery, New York, April 30–June 15, 2002.
— "Maurizio Cattelan. Felix," curated by Francesco Bonami, MCA – Museum of Contemporary Art Chicago, November 28, 2002–April 4, 2003.

[2003]
— "Maurizio Cattelan," Museum Ludwig, Cologne, May 16–September 2003.
— "Maurizio Cattelan," MOCA – The Museum of Contemporary Art, Los Angeles, July 20–October 27, 2003.

[2004]
— "Maurizio Cattelan," project for the Galleria civica di arte contemporanea, University of Trento, Faculty of Sociology, March 31–September 26, 2004.
— "Maurizio Cattelan," curated by Massimiliano Gioni, Fondazione Nicola Trussardi, Piazza XXIV Maggio, Milan, May 5–June 6, 2004. Work destroyed one day after the opening.
— "Now," curated by Laurence Bossé, Hans Ulrich Obrist, and Angeline Scherf, Chapelle des Petits Augustins, École nationale supérieure des Beaux-Arts, Paris, exhibition held by the Musée d'Art Moderne de La Ville de Paris/ARC, October 1–31, 2004.

[2007]
— "Maurizio Cattelan. New Works," curated by Vicente Todolí, Tate Modern, London, 2007.
— "Maurizio Cattelan," curated by Andreas Bee and Udo Kittelmann, MMK – Museum für Moderne Kunst, Frankfurt, March 1–September 23, 2007. [234] p. 330
— "Maurizio Cattelan. A Miracle in Frankfurt," curated by Andreas Bee and Udo Kittelmann, Portikus, Frankfurt, June 3–September 23, 2007.

[2008]
— "Maurizio Cattelan," curated by Eckhard Schneider, Kunsthaus Bregenz, February 2–March 24, 2008. [147] p. 228
— "Maurizio Cattelan," Kunstprojekt Synagoge Stommeln, June 1–August 10, 2008. [69] p. 130

[2010]
— "Is There Life Before Death?," curated by Franklin Sirmans, The Menil Collection, Houston, February 12–August 15, 2010. [143] p. 227
— "Maurizio Cattelan," DESTE Foundation Project Space, Slaughterhouse, Hydra, June 16–September 30, 2010.
— "Maurizio Cattelan. Contro le ideologie," curated by Francesco Bonami, Sala delle Cariatidi, Palazzo Reale, Milan, September 25–October 24, 2010; in conjunction: *L.O.V.E.*, Piazza degli Affari, Milano. [222] p. 312

[2011]
— "Maurizio Cattelan. All," curated by Nancy Spector, Solomon R. Guggenheim Museum, New York, November 4, 2011–January 22, 2012. [140] p. 220

[2012]
— "Collezione Sandretto Re Rebaudengo. Maurizio Cattelan," curated by Achim Borchardt-Hume, Kirsty Ogg, and Francesco Bonami, Whitechapel Gallery, London, September 25–December 2, 2012.

— "Amen," curated by Justyna Wesołowska, Centre for Contemporary Art, Ujazdowski Castle, Warsaw, November 15, 2012–February 24, 2013. [146] p. 228

[2013]
— "Maurizio Cattelan. Kaputt," curated by Michiko Kono and Sam Keller, Fondation Beyeler, Basel, June 8–October 6, 2013.

[2016]
— "Not Afraid of Love," curated by Chiara Parisi, Monnaie de Paris, Octotber 21, 2016–January 8, 2017. [149] p. 230

[2019]
— "Victory Is Not An Option," curated by Michael Frahm, Blenheim Palace, Woodstock, United Kingdom, September 12–October 27, 2019. [150] p. 232

[2021]
— "Maurizio Cattelan. Breath Ghosts Blind," curated by Roberta Tenconi and Vicente Todolí, Pirelli HangarBicocca, Milan, July 15, 2021–February 20, 2022. [223] p. 315
— "Maurizio Cattelan. The Last Judgment," curated by Francesco Bonami, UCCA Center for Contemporary Art, Beijing, November 20, 2021–February 20, 2022.

[2022]
— "You," Massimo De Carlo, Milan, March 28–June 25, 2022.
— "NinnaNanna," Crematorium Temple, Monumental Cemetery, Milan, March 30–November 6, 2022.
— "Maurizio Cattelan. Wish You Were Here," curated by Francesco Bonami, Sea World Culture and Arts Center (SWCAC), Shenzhen, July 9–October 16, 2022.

[2023]
— "WE," curated by Sungwon Kim, Leeum Museum of Art, Seoul, January 31–July 16, 2023.

[2024]
— "Maurizio Cattelan. BECAUSE," project by Mutina for Art curated by Sarah Cosulich, with a display by Michael Anastassiades, Arte Fiera, Bologna, February 2–4, 2024.
— "The Third Hand. Maurizio Cattelan and the Moderna Museet Collection," curated by Gitte Ørskou, Moderna Museet, Stockholm, February 2024–January 12, 2025. [173] p. 255
— "Sunday," a cura di Francesco Bonami, Gagosian, West 21st Street, New York, April 30–June 29, 2024.

[2025]
— "Maurizio Cattelan. Bones," Gagosian, Davies Street, London, April 8–May 24, 2025.
— "Endless Sunday. Maurizio Cattelan and the Pompidou Collection," curated by Maurizio Cattelan and Chiara Parisi, with Sophie Bernal, Elia Biezunski, Anne Horvath, Laureen Picaut, Zoe Stillpass, and Marta Papini, Centre Pompidou-Metz, May 8, 2025–February 2, 2027. [175] p. 255
— "Maurizio Cattelan," Casa Malaparte, Capri, exhibition held by Gagosian, July 2025.
— "Maurizio Cattelan. Seasons," curated by Lorenzo Giusti, GAMeC – Galleria d'Arte Moderna e Contemporanea di Bergamo and other venues, June 7–October 26, 2025. [152] p. 235
— "Sussurro," curated by Philippe Vergne, Museu de Arte Contemporánea e Parque de Serralves, Fundação de Serralves, Porto, July 4, 2025–January 11, 2026.

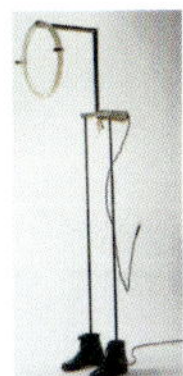

*Il ripetente*, 1987
Metal, electric wire, neon, shoes
Height 188 cm
[15.10] p. 49

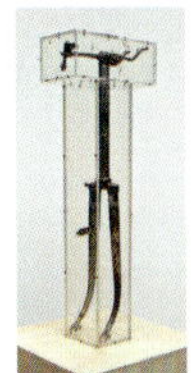

*Untitled*, 1987
Plexiglas, iron
74.5 × 25 × 14 cm
[15.8] p. 49

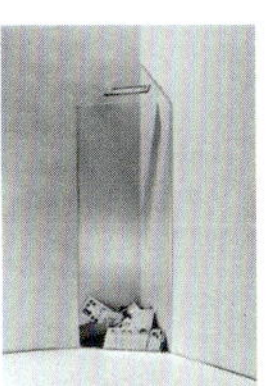

*Angolo dei Ricordi*, 1989
Plexiglas, brass, correspondence
145 × 45 × 37 cm
[15.14] p. 50

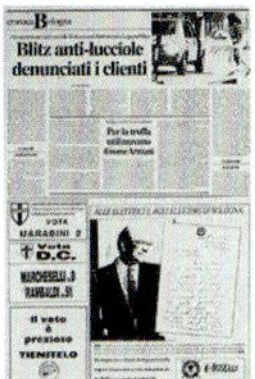

*Campagna elettorale*, 1989
Newspaper advertisement
[36] p. 92

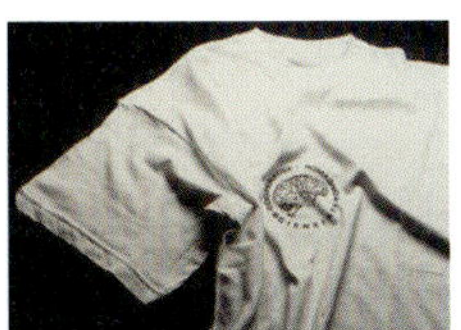

Cooperativa Scienziati Romagnoli, 1989
[37] p. 92

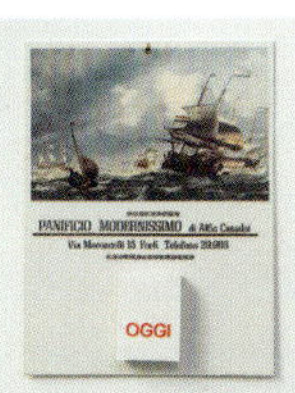

*Grammatica quotidiana*, 1989
Offset lithography on letterpress-printed board and paper
29.2 × 21 × 5.1 cm
[17] p. 60

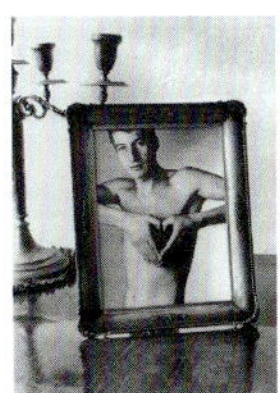

*Lessico familiare*, 1989
Black-and-white photography, silver frame
19.7 × 15.2 cm
[16] p. 59

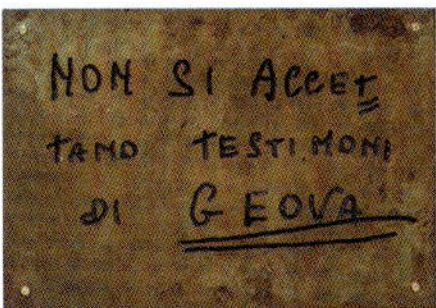

*Non si accettano testimoni di Geova*, 1989
6 plates in engraved brass
Variable dimensions
[15.17] p. 51

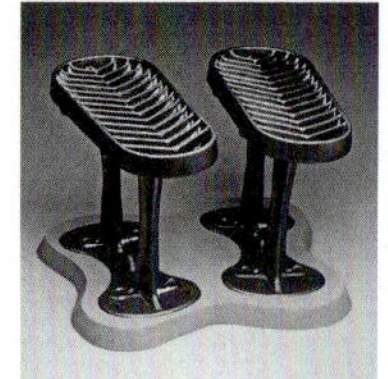

*Punto di vista mobile*, 1989
Cast iron, lacquered wood
40 × 33 × 30 cm
[15.4] p. 48

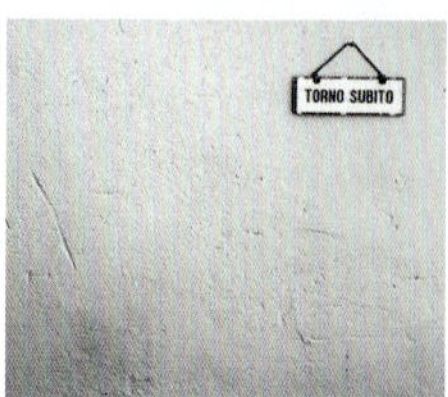

*Torno subito*, 1989
Engraved plexiglas
4 × 12 cm
[105] p. 178

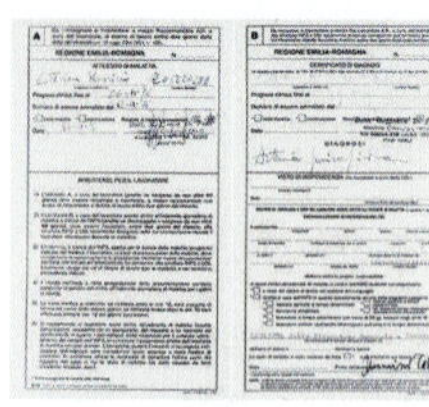

*Untitled*, 1989
Typewritten paper with
additions in ink
35 × 22 cm
[18] p. 60

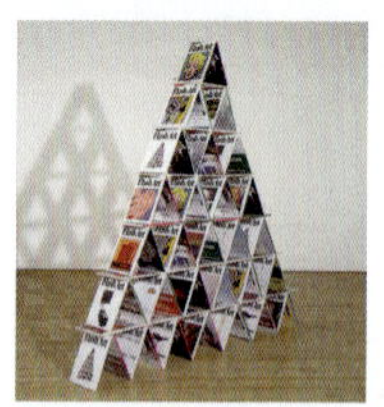

*Strategie*, 1990
77 copies of *Flash Art*,
stickers, aluminum
supports
173 × 161.3 × 20.3 cm
Castello di Rivoli Museo d'Arte
Contemporanea, Rivoli-Turin.
Long term loan. Private
collection, 2020
[20.1] p. 62

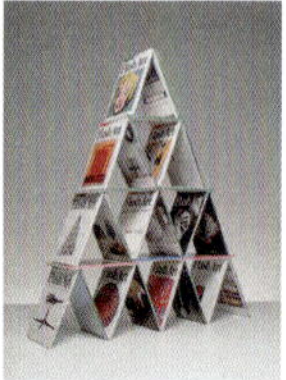

*Strategie*, 1990
26 copies of *Flash Art*,
stickers, aluminum
supports
[20.2] p. 62

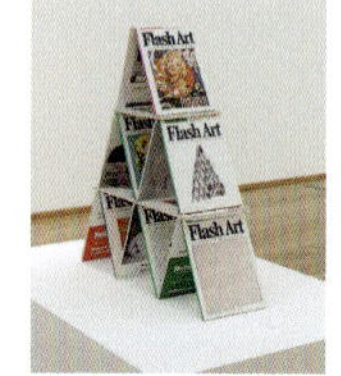

*Strategie*, 1990
15 copies of *Flash Art*,
stickers, aluminum
supports
76 × 71 × 20.5 cm
MAMbo – Museo d'Arte
Moderna di Bologna. Gift
of the artist, 1989
[20.3] p. 62

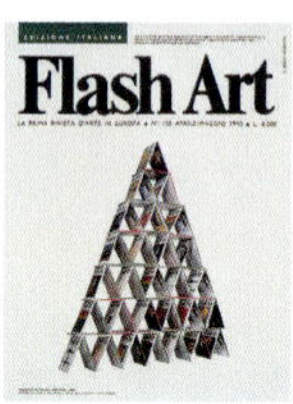

*Strategie*, 1990
Issue of *Flash Art Italia*
(no. 155, April–May 1990),
with modified cover
27 × 20.5 × 1 cm
[20.4] p. 62

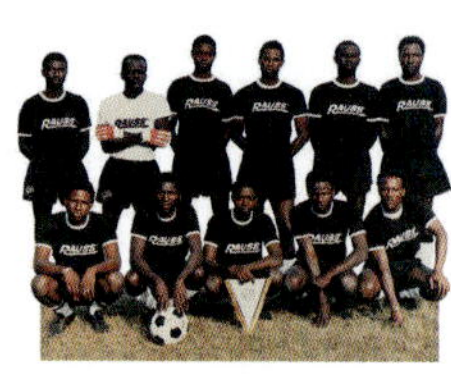

*A.C. Forniture Sud*, 1991
Photographic collage
77 × 100 cm
[33.3] p. 84

370

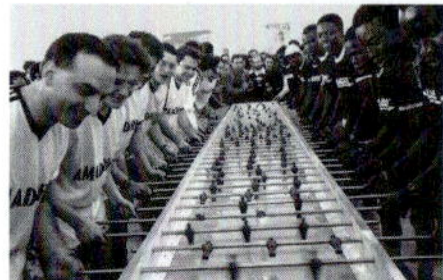

*Cesena 47 - A.C. Forniture
Sud 12*, 1991
Black and white
photographic print
120 × 190 cm
[33.1] p. 84

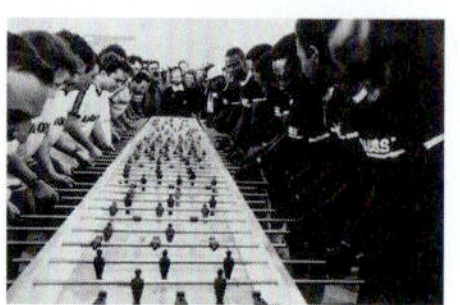

*Cesena 47 - A.C. Forniture
Sud 12 (2° tempo)*, 1991
Black and white
photographic print on
aluminum
125 × 195 cm
Fondazione Sandretto Re
Rebaudengo
[33.2] p. 84

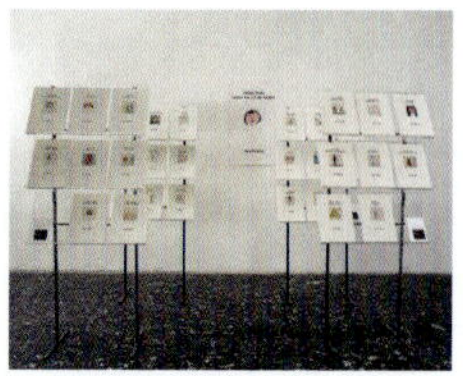

*Edizioni dell'Obbligo*, 1991
Notebooks, plexiglas, iron
Notebooks: 29.7 × 21 cm
each
[24] p. 73

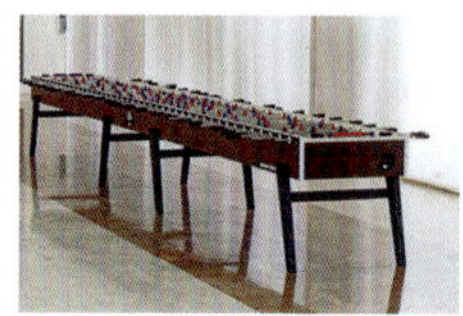

*Stadium*, 1991
Wood, acrylic, steel, paper,
plastic
100.3 × 651 × 120 cm
[225] p. 320

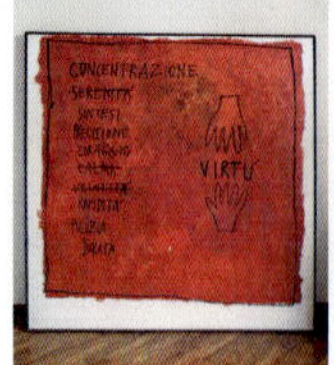

*Untitled*, 1991
Mixed media on canvas
200 × 200 × 4 cm
[15.19] p. 51

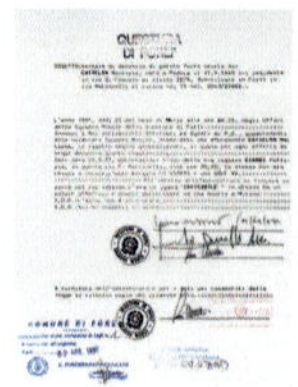

*Untitled*, 1991
Typewritten paper with
additions in ink
29.2 × 21 cm
[19] p. 60

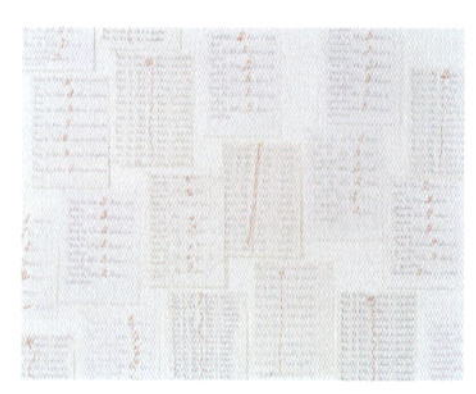

*Untitled*, 1991
[Initially titled:
*Repetita Iuvant*]
29 sheets, ballpoint pen ink
30 × 21 cm each
[25] p. 75

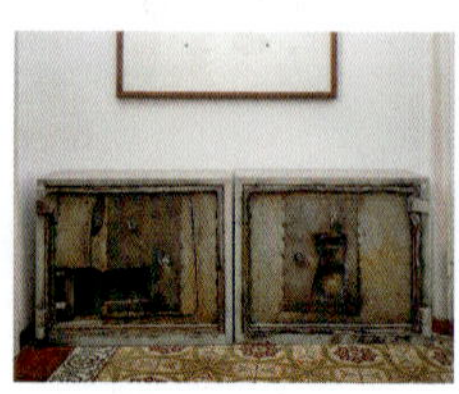

*- 43.500.000*, 1992
2 broken safes
73 × 85 × 32 cm each
[76] p. 141

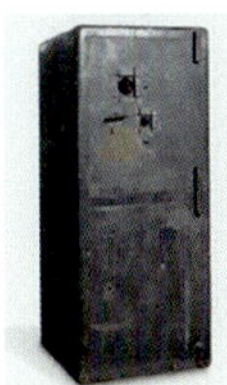

*- 76.000.000*, 1992
Broken safe
[77] p. 141

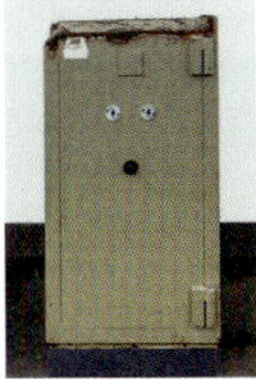

*- 157.000.000*, 1992
Broken safe
142 × 74 × 79 cm
GAMeC – Galleria d'Arte
Moderna e Contemporanea
di Bergamo
[78] p. 141

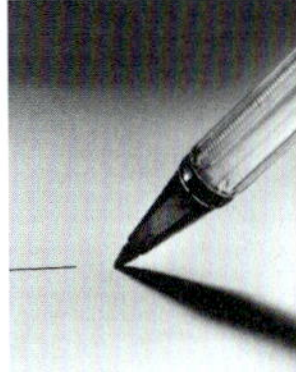

*Esaurita*, 1992
Black and white
photographic print
35.6 × 27.9 cm
[80] p. 143

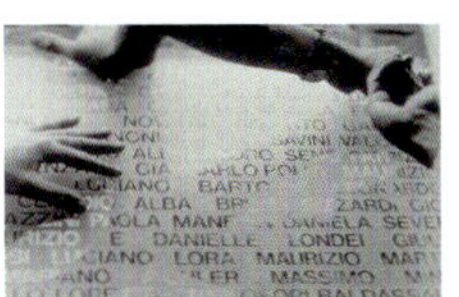

*Oblomov Foundation*, 1992
Engraved glass plate (100
x 100 cm) installed on the
exterior of the Accademia
di Belle Arti di Brera, Milan,
1992–93
[133] p. 217

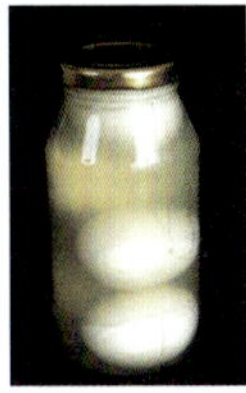

*Perita*, 1992
Glass jar, eggs
Height 20 cm, Ø 12 cm
[40] p. 94

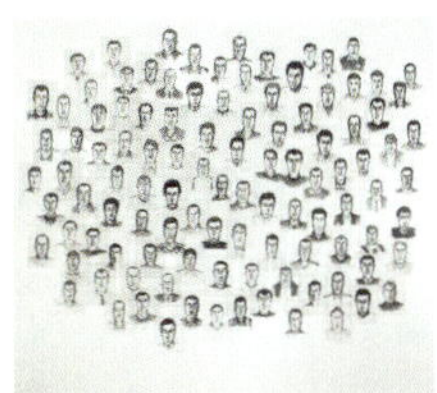

*Super Us*, 1992
50 acetate sheets
29.8 × 21 cm each
[45] p. 103

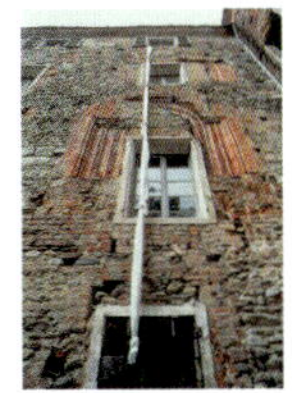

*Una Domenica a Rivara*,
1992
Knotted sheets
Length 12 m
[106] p. 178

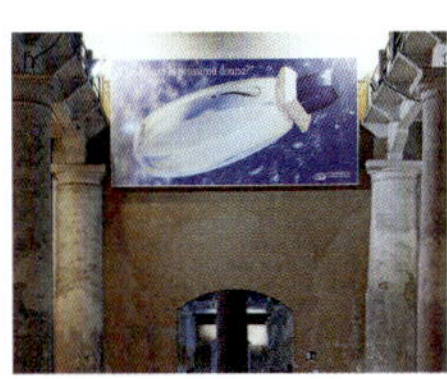

*Lavorare è un brutto
mestiere*, 1993
Inkjet print on plastic
280 × 580 cm
Rubell Museum, Miami
and Washington DC
[108] p. 179



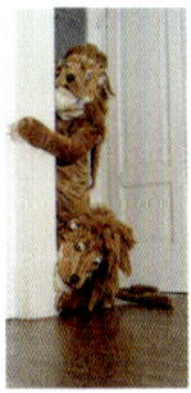

*Tarzan & Jane*, 1993
Silver dye bleach print
140 × 70 cm
Performance with lion
costumes during the solo
exhibition "Tarzan & Jane"
at the Galleria Raucci/
Santamaria, Naples, April
27–May 15, 1993
[226] p. 320

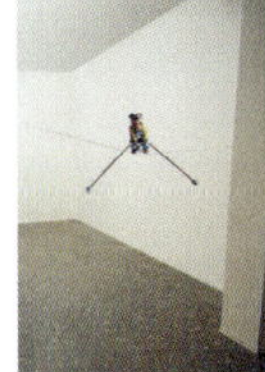

*Untitled*, 1993
Plastic, fabric, wood,
lead, strings
Environmental dimensions
[107] p. 179

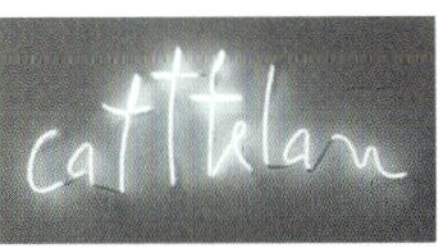

*Catttelan*, 1994
Neon
40 × 130 × 3 cm
Fondazione Sandretto
Re Rebaudengo
The Dakis Joannou Collection
Foundation
[60] p. 124

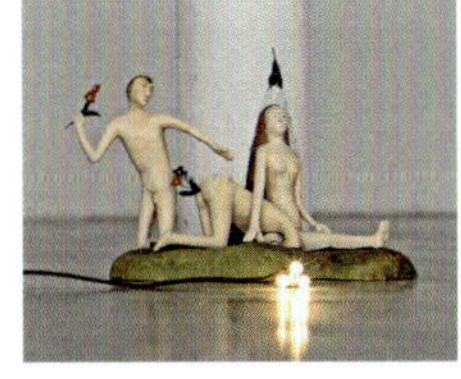

*Christmas '94*, 1994
[Initially titled: *Il giardino
delle delizie*]
Painted plaster,
incandescent lightbulbs
20 × 30 × 15 cm
[61] p. 125

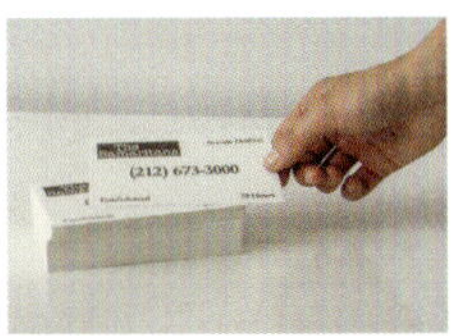

*Hotline*, 1994
Printed cards
C. 6 × 10 cm each
[81] p. 143

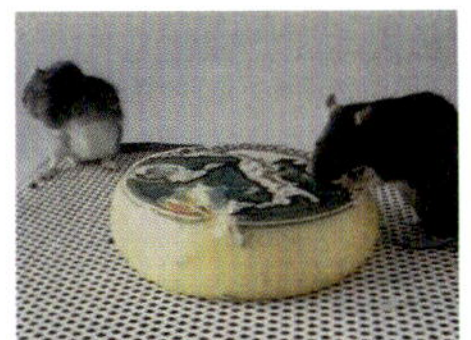

*I Found My Love in
Portofino*, 1994
Bel Paese cheese, rats,
plexiglas
160 × 150 × 60 cm
[39] p. 94

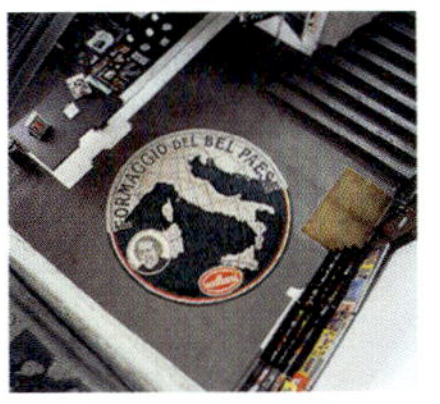

*Il Bel Paese*, 1994
Tufted wool carpet
Ø 300 cm
Castello di Rivoli Museo d'Arte
Contemporanea, Rivoli-Turin.
Purchased with funds contributed
by the artist, Massimo De Carlo,
and Pulsar Group Insurance
Brokers, 1994
[38] p. 94

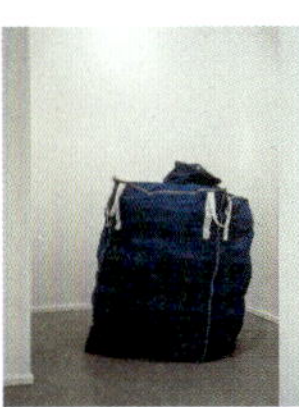

*Lullaby*, 1994
Canvas industrial bag,
rubble
135 × 85 × 85 × cm
Fondazione Sandretto
Re Rebaudengo
[218] p. 309

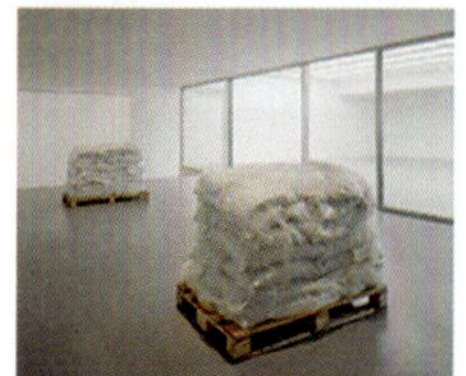

*Lullaby*, 1994
2 wooden pallet, rubble,
plastic wrap
135 × 100 × 120 cm each
Museo del Novecento, Milan.
Gift of the artist, December 2022
CAPC Musée d'art contemporain
de Bordeaux
[219] p. 309

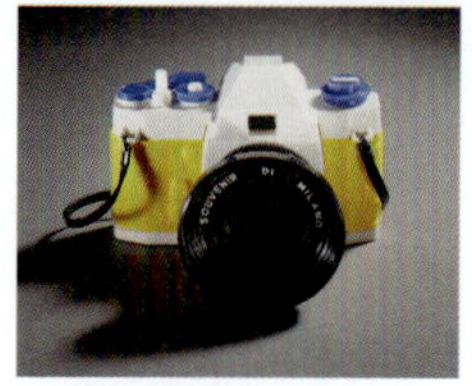

*Souvenir di Milano*, 1994
Plastic toy camera with
preloaded images
6.5 × 11 × 9.8 cm
[220] p. 312

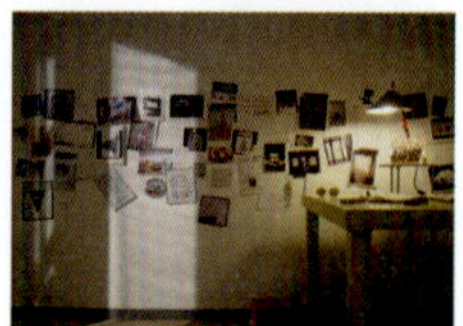

*Untitled*, 1994
Color photograph, face
mounted to acrylic
25 × 58 cm
[22] p. 66

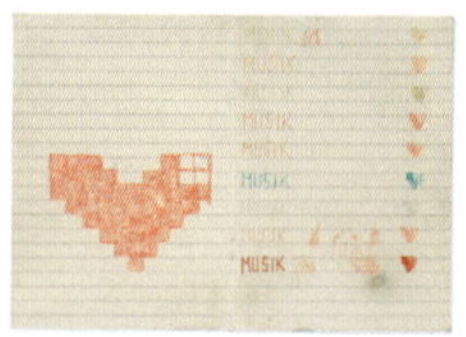

*Untitled*, 1994
3 used school notebooks,
sound
19.5 × 13.5 cm each (closed)
[26] p. 75

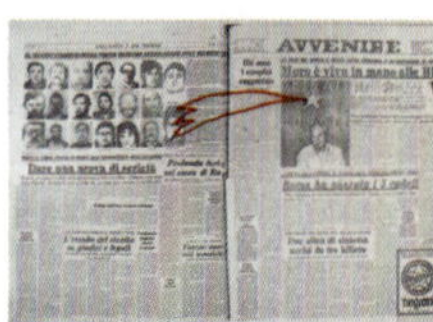

*Untitled*, 1994
Photocopy, spray paint
450 × 600 cm
[191] p. 291

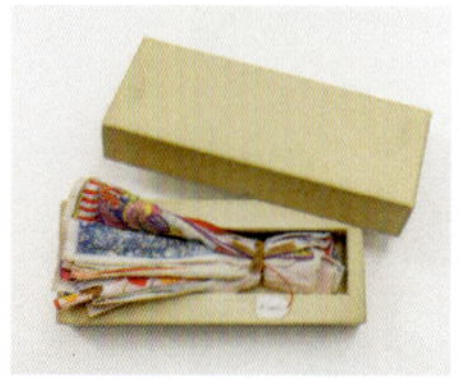

*Untitled*, 1994
25 knotted handkerchiefs
knotted with nylon thread,
label with signature and
date, cardboard box
30 × 15 × 7 cm
Isabel and Agustin Coppel
Collection, Mexico
[221] p. 312

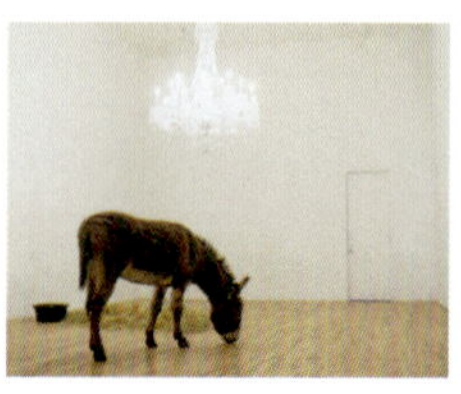

*Warning! Enter at your
own risk. Do not touch,
do not feed, no smoking,
no photographs, no dogs,
thank you*, 1994
Donkey, crystal chandelier
Environmental dimensions
[134] p. 218

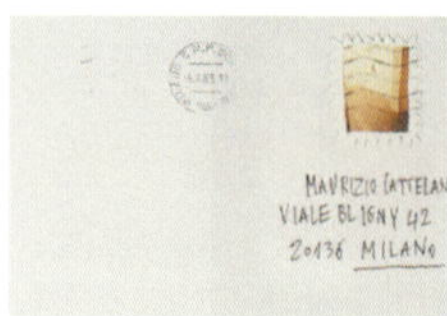

*Untitled*, 1994–95
Envelopes, fake postage
stamps, ink
10 × 15 cm each
Isabel and Agustin Coppel
Collection, Mexico
[23] p. 66

372

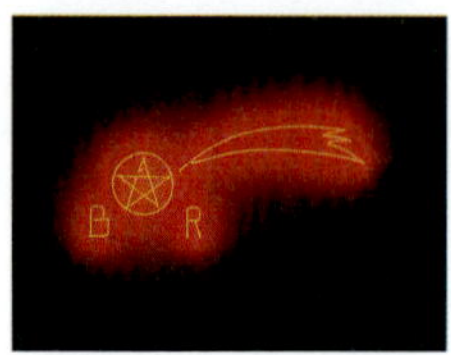

*Christmas '95*, 1995
Neon
38 × 82 × 4 cm
Fondazione Sandretto
Re Rebaudengo
[62] p. 125

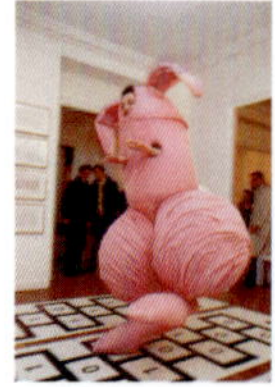

*Errotin, le vrai lapin*, 1995
Silver dye bleach
print, face-mounted to
plexiglas, mounted on
board
182.9 × 121.9 cm
Performance with
costume during the solo
show "Maurizio Cattelan.
Errotin, le vrai lapin" at
the Galerie Emmanuel
Perrotin, Paris, January
26–March 11, 1995
[227] p. 321

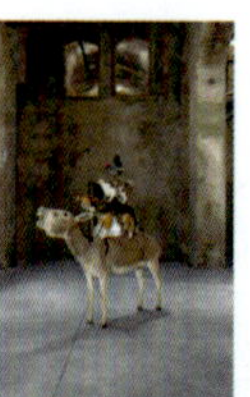

*Love Saves Life*, 1995
Taxidermied donkey, dog,
cat and rooster
190 × 120 × 60 cm
[1] p. 16

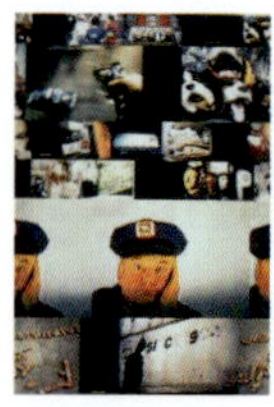

*Monday Nothing*, 1995
Collage for the
exhibition "Fuori Uso '95.
Caravanserraglio Arte
Contemporanea," curated
by Giacinto Di Pietrantonio,
Pescara, 1995
[136] p. 219

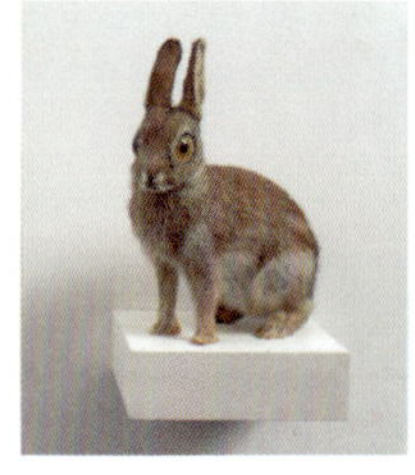

*Untitled*, 1995
[Initially titled: *Richard*]
Taxidermied rabbit, lion
glass eyes
23 × 9 × 22 cm
[47] p. 105

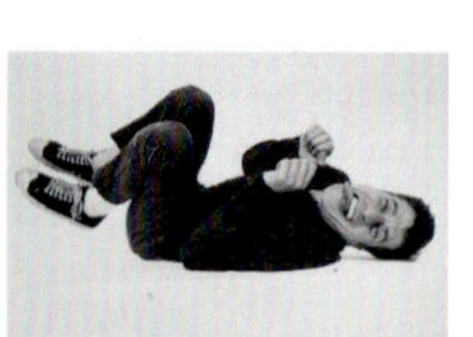

*Untitled*, 1995
Black and white
photographic print
mounted on aluminum
125 × 190 cm
MOCA – The Museum of
Contemporary Art, Los Angeles.
Gift of Alan Hergott and Curt
Shepard
[111] p. 192

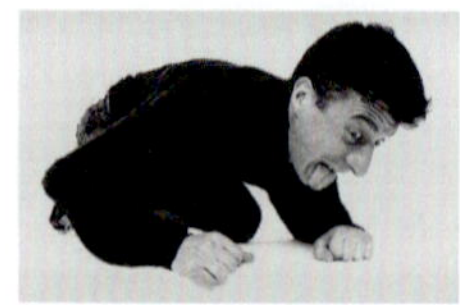

*Untitled*, 1995
Black and white
photographic print
mounted on aluminum
125 × 190 cm
[112] p. 192

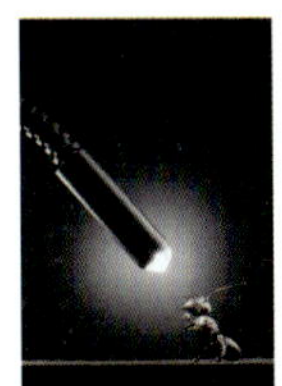

*Untitled*, 1995
Metal, paint, plastic,
lightbulb
Ant: 2.1 × 1.4 × 1 cm
[157] p. 243

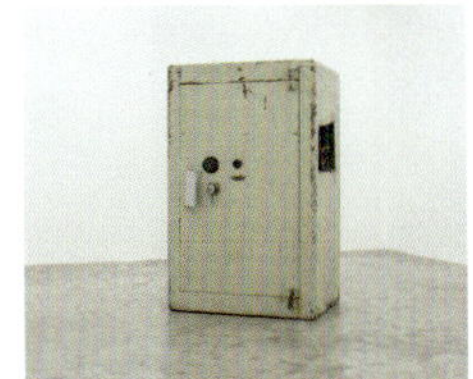

*- 74.400.000*, 1996
Broken safe
140 × 85 × 64 cm
[79] p. 141

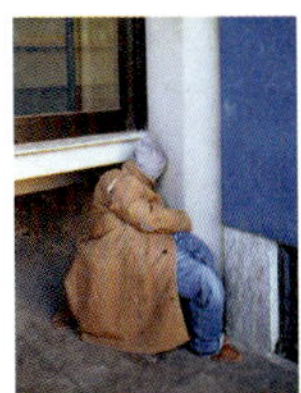

*Andreas e Mattia*, 1996
Stuffed cloth, clothing,
shoes
[192] p. 292

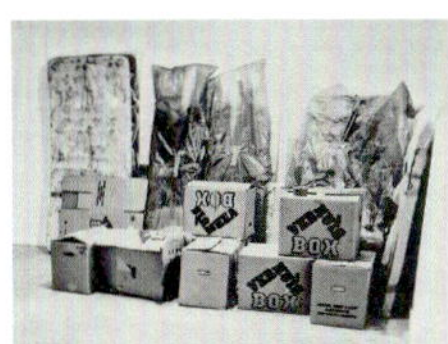

*Another Fucking
Readymade*, 1996
Crated and wrapped gallery
contents
Environmental dimension
[83] p. 144

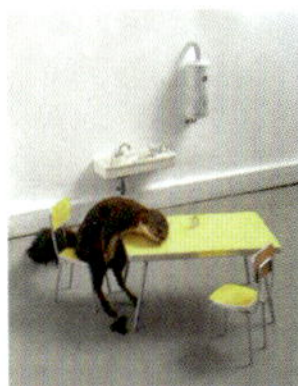

*Bidibidobidiboo*, 1996
Taxidermied squirrel,
ceramic, formica, wood,
steel, paint
45 × 60 × 58 cm
Fondazione Sandretto
Re Rebaudengo
[11] p. 39

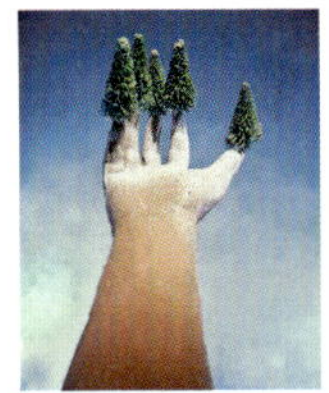

*Christmas '96*, 1996
Rubber, model trees,
artificial snow
35 × 16.5 × 17.5 cm
[63] p. 125

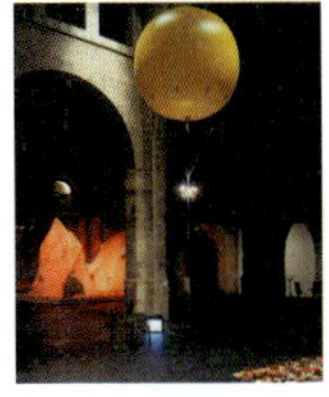

Maurizio Cattelan and
Philippe Parreno
*La Dolce Utopia*, 1996
Balloon filled with helium,
chandelier
1000 × Ø 400 cm
Frac Poitou-Charentes [blue
balloon version, Ø 250 cm]
[184] p. 269

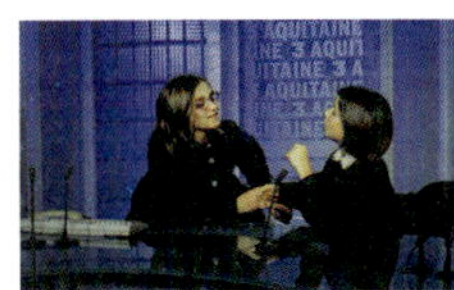

Maurizio Cattelan and
Philippe Parreno
*CPC Channel*, 1996
TV station
[185] p. 269



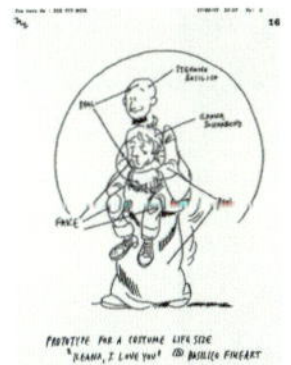

*Ileana, I Love You*, 1996
Ink on paper
29 × 21 cm
Project for lifesize costume
for Basilico Fine Art, New
York; pre-production
drawing done with Umberto
Manfrin; published
in *Unbuilt Roads: 107
Unrealized Projects*, eds.
Hans Ulrich Obrist and Guy
Tortosa (Ostfildern-Ruit:
Hatje, 1997), n.p.
[51] p. 106

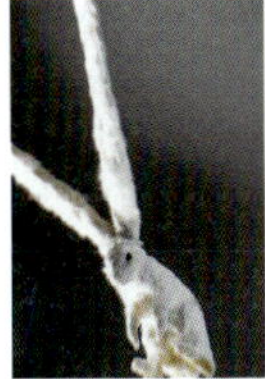

*Untitled*, 1996
[Initially titled: *Free Carrot*]
Taxidermied rabbit,
rabbit parts
250 × 10 × 20 cm
[48] p. 105

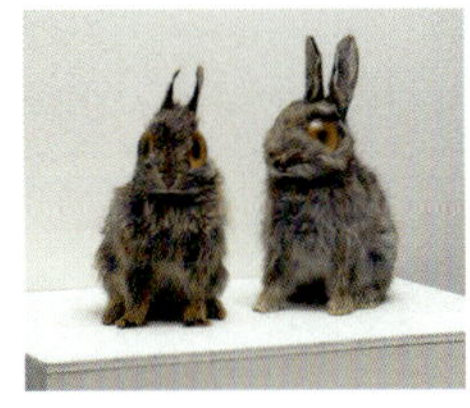

*Untitled*, 1996
2 taxidermied hares,
glass eyes
Overall dimensions:
20.3 × 29.8 × 20.3 cm
[49] p. 105

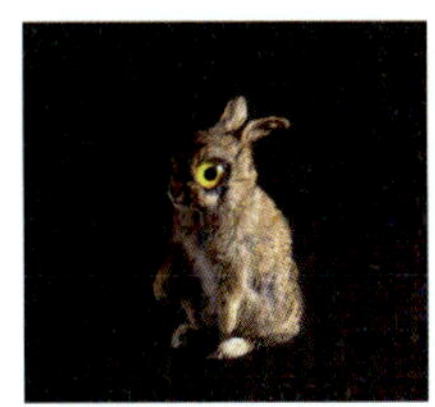

*Untitled*, 1996
[Initially titled: *Richard*]
Taxidermied rabbit,
lion glass eyes
18 × 9 × 8 cm
[50] p. 105

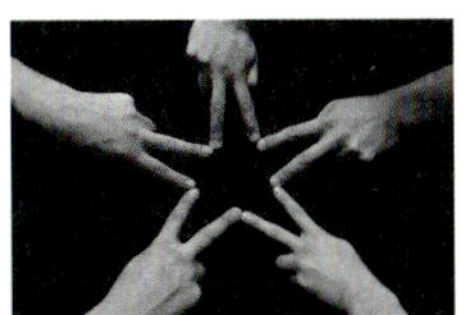

*Untitled*, 1996
Gelatin silver print
101.6 × 152.4 cm
[55] p. 110

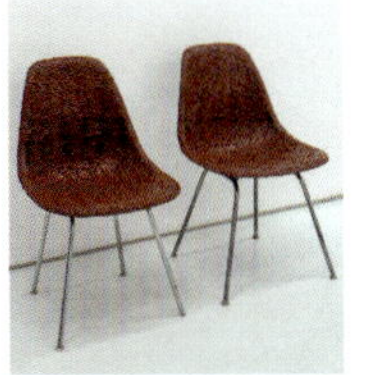

*Untitled*, 1996
2 chairs, Nutella
Lifesize
[82] p. 143

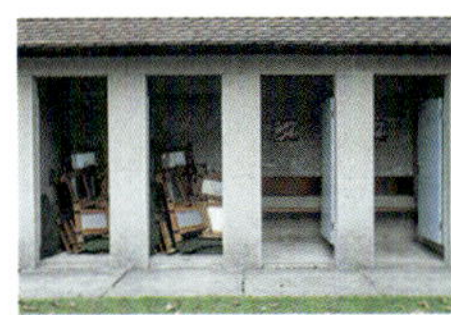

*Untitled*, 1996
Exact replicas of adjacent
works by John Armleder,
fabricated on instructions
of the artist for the
exhibition "Cabin de bain"
in Fribourg, 1996
[84] p. 144

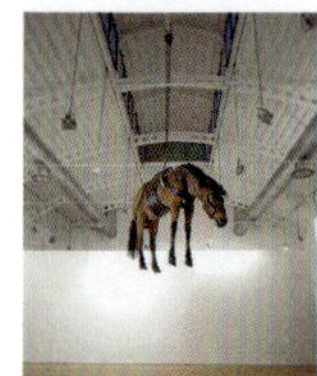

*Untitled*, 1996
[Initially titled: *La Ballata di Trotsky*]
Taxidermied horse, leather saddlery, rope, pulley
223 × 265 × 85 cm
Fondation Louis Vuitton
[200] p. 294

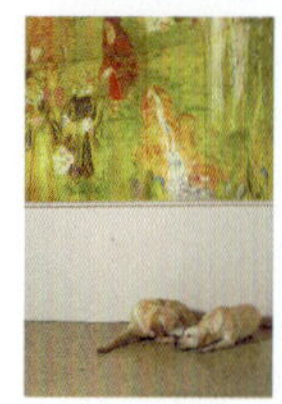

*13.3.81 My Last Kiss*, 1997
2 taxidermied dogs
Overall dimensions:
30.5 × 135.9 × 94 cm
[115] p. 192

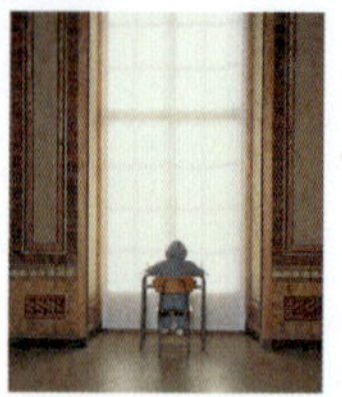

*Charlie Don't Surf*, 1997
Latex mannequin, clothing, shoes, pencils, school desk, chair
112 × 71 × 70 cm
Castello di Rivoli Museo d'Arte Contemporanea, Rivoli-Turin, 1998
Fondation Louis Vuitton
[27] p. 76

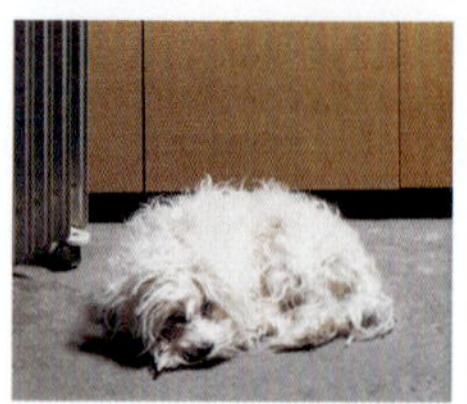

*Cheap to Feed*, 1997
Taxidermied dog
40.5 × 35.5 × 16.5 cm
[114] p. 192

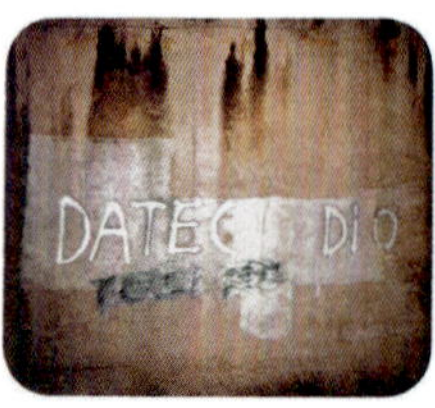

*Christmas '97*, 1997
Print on mouse pad
19.8 × 23.5 × 1 cm
[64] p. 125

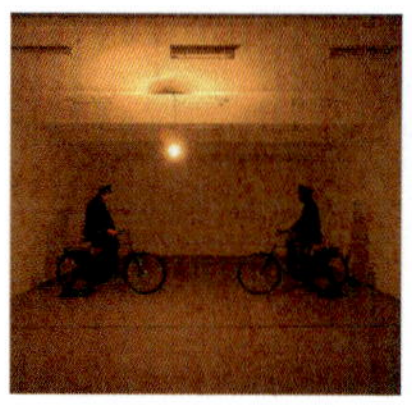

*Dynamo Secession*, 1997
2 bicycles, 2 museum guards, generator, lightbulbs
Environmental dimensions
[228] p. 322

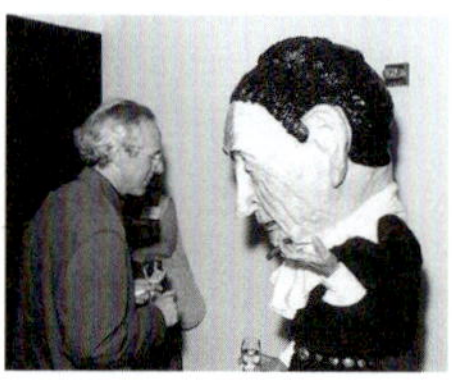

*Georgia on My Mind*, 1997
*Papier mâché*, paint, clothing, cigar
Performance with mask during the opening of "TRUCE. Echoes of Art in an Age of Endless Conclusions," curated by Francesco Bonami, SITE Santa Fe, July 18–October 12, 1997 (group show)
[12] p. 40

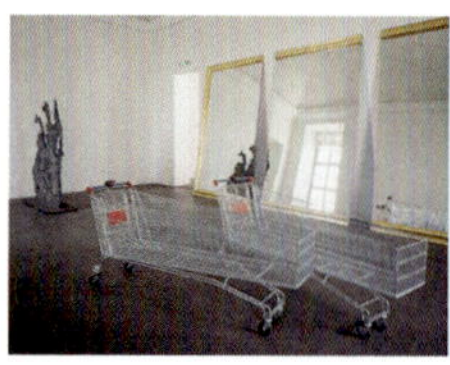

*Less than ten items*, 1997
Steel, rubber, plastic
120 × 220 × 60 cm
[142] p. 227

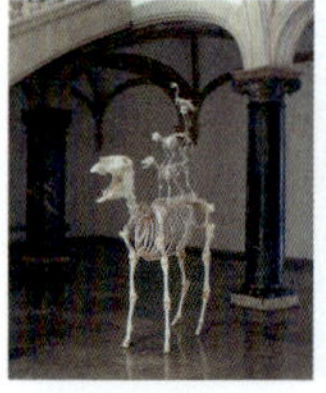

*Love Lasts Forever*, 1997
Donkey, dog, cat and rooster skeletons
185.9 × 120 × 59.7 cm
[246] p. 349

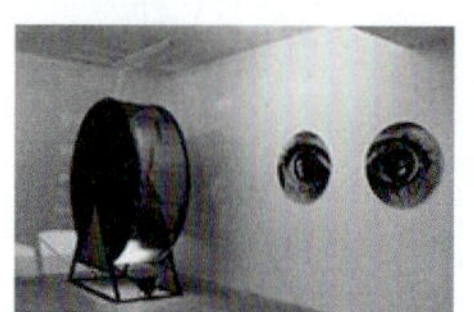

*Moi-Même-Soi-Même*, 1997
Exact replica of exhibition installation by Carsten Höller "Moi-Même-Soi-Même," Air de Paris, Paris, May 24–July 19, 1997, at the Galerie Emmanuel Perrotin, Paris, same dates
[87] p. 146

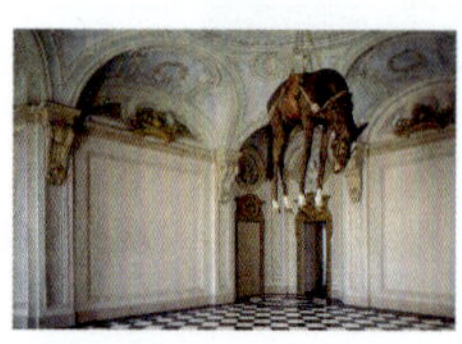

*Novecento*, 1997
Taxidermied horse, leather saddle, rope
200 × 270 × 70 cm
Castello di Rivoli Museo d'Arte Contemporanea, Rivoli-Turin. Gift of the Supporting Friends and Benefactors of the Castello di Rivoli, 1997
[201] p. 294

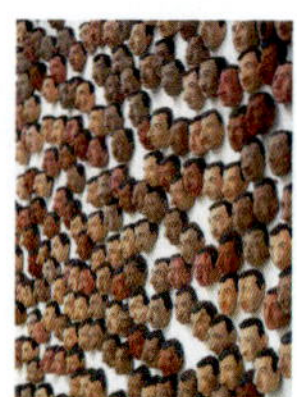

*Spermini*, 1997
Painted latex masks
C. 17.3 × 8.4 × 9.8 cm each
Fondation Louis Vuitton
The Dakis Joannou Collection Foundation
[2] p. 20

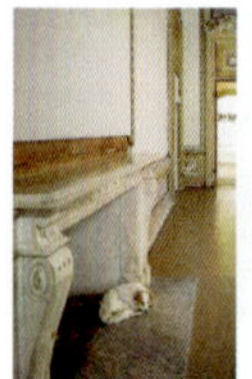

*Stone Dead*, 1997
Taxidermied dog
30 × 38 × 15 cm
[113] p. 192

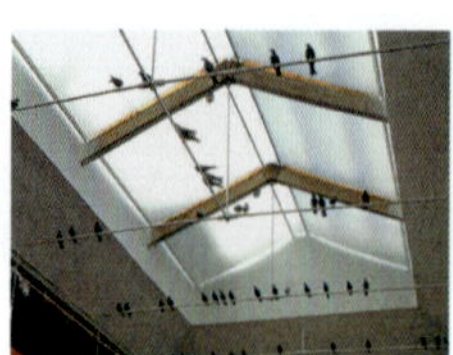

*Tourists*, 1997
Taxidermied pigeons
Environmental dimensions
Rubell Museum, Miami and Washington DC
[238] p. 337

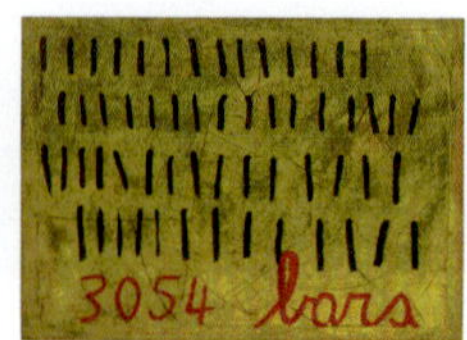


*Untitled*, 1997
Mixed media on canvas
78 × 103.5 × 3 cm
[15.20] p. 51

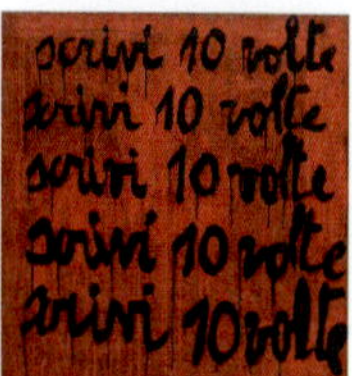


*Untitled*, 1997
Mixed media on canvas
120 × 110 × 3 cm
[15.21] p. 51

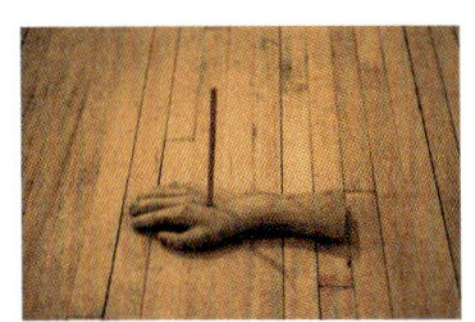

*Untitled*, 1997
Polyurethanic rubber,
pigment, pencil
18 × 27 × 10 cm
[28] p. 76

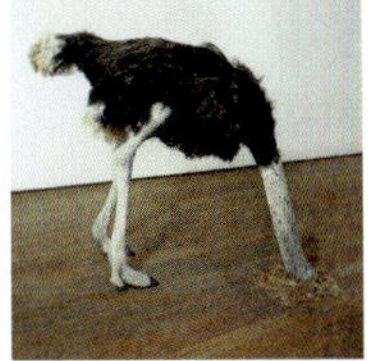

*Untitled*, 1997
Taxidermied ostrich, wood
chips
124.5 × 134.6 × 50.8 cm
[34.1] p. 89

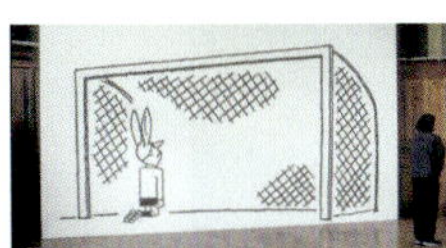

*Untitled*, 1997
Print, wall posting
Environmental dimensions
[42] p. 96

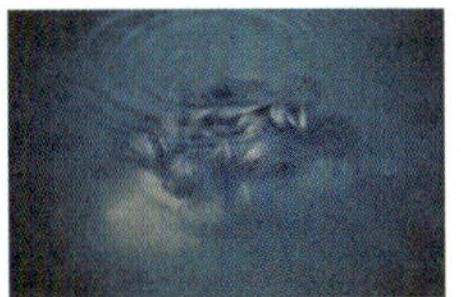

*Untitled*, 1997
[Initially titled:
*Out of the Blue*]
Latex, clothing
Height 170 cm
[52] p. 106

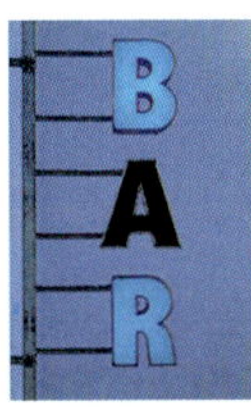

*Untitled*, 1997
Plexiglas, neon, stainless
steel
160.8 × 54 × 16 cm
[85.1] p. 145

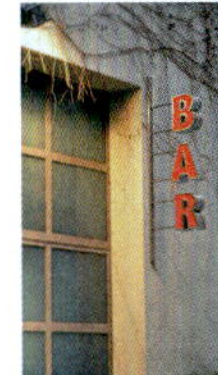

*Untitled*, 1997
[Titolo iniziale: *Bar Bocconi*]
Plexiglas, neon, stainless
steel
160.8 × 54 × 16 cm
[85.2] p. 145

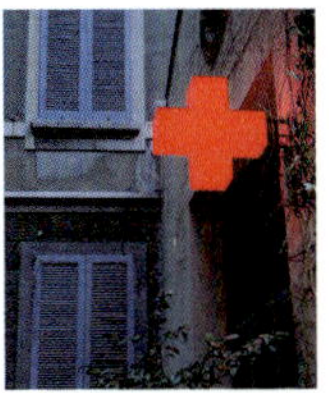

*Untitled*, 1997
Plexiglas, neon
60 × 60 × 18 cm
[86] p. 145

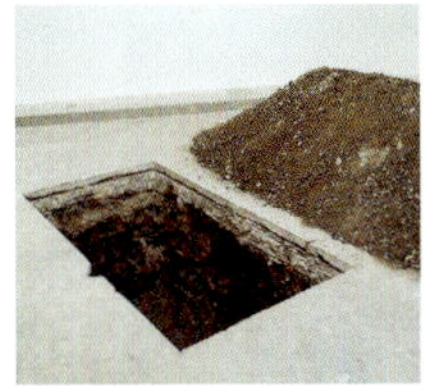

*Untitled*, 1997
Rectangular hole, pile
of removed soil
200 × 100 × 150 cm
[109] p. 191

375

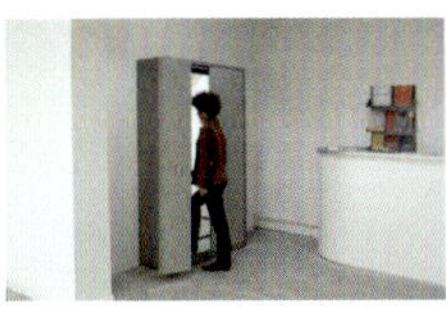

*Untitled*, 1997
Wardrobe door (wood,
paint, metal) installed in
museum doorway
C. 200 × 100 × 40 cm
[110] p. 191

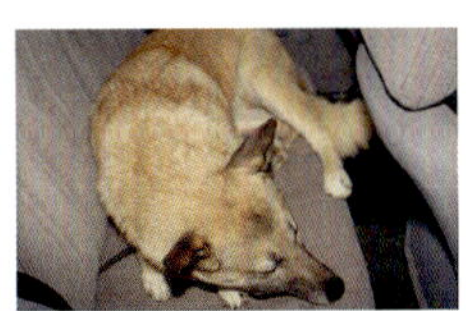

*Untitled*, 1997
Taxidermied dog
Lifesize
[116] p. 192

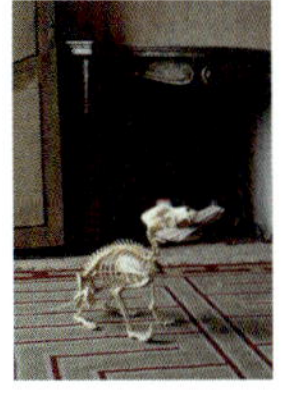

*Untitled*, 1997
[Initially titled: *Pluto*]
Dog skeleton, newspaper
50 × 80 × 40 cm
Pinault Collection
[119] p. 194

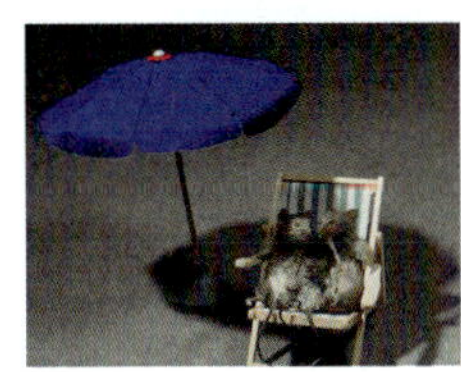

*Untitled*, 1997
Taxidermied mice, wood,
fabric
[158] p. 243

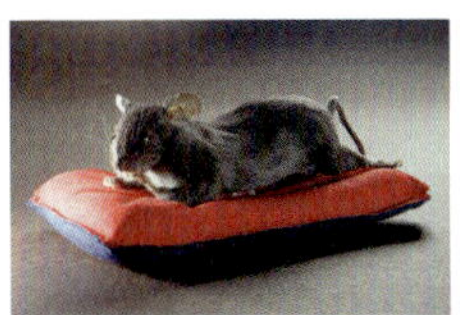

*Untitled*, 1997
Taxidermied mouse, fabric
4 × 13 × 6 cm
[159] p. 243

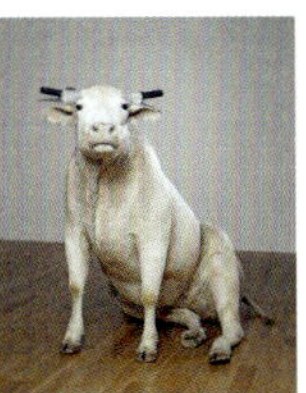

*Untitled*, 1997
Taxidermied cow, scooter
handles
231.6 × 140.3 × 160 cm
[161] p. 244

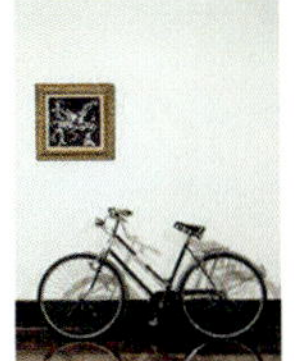

*Untitled*, 1997
Bicycles
Lifesize
[229] p. 322

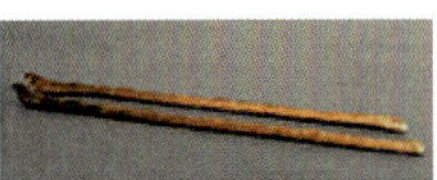

*13-11-1998: My Last Kiss*,
1998
Bread
Length c. 200 cm
[41] p. 94

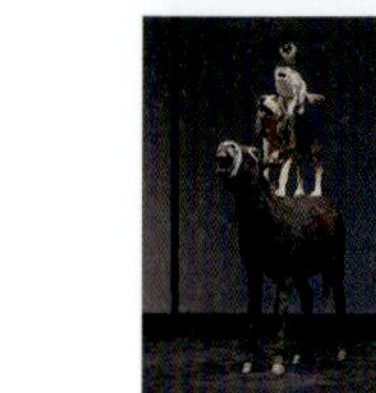

*Family*, 1998
Taxidermied donkey, dog,
cat and crow
227 × 197 × 55 cm
Leeum Museum of Art, Seoul
Ref. p. 16 [1]

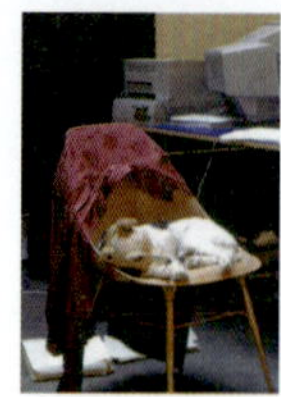

*Good Boy*, 1998
Taxidermied dog, chair
Dog: 12.7 × 40.6 × 27.9 cm;
chair: 81.3 × 45.7 × 50.8 cm
SAM – Seattle Art Museum. Gift
of the Virginia and Bagley Wright
Collection in honor of the 75th
Anniversary of the Seattle Art
Museum, 2020.15.5
[117] p. 192

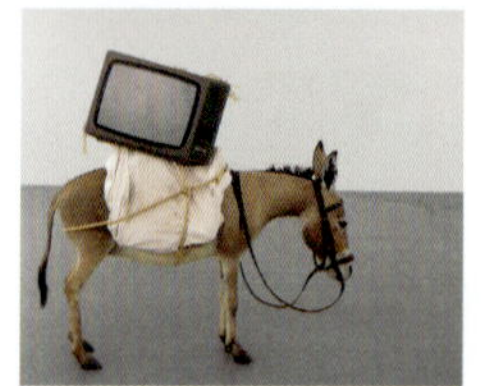

*If a Tree Falls in the Forest
and There Is No One Around
It, Does It Make a Sound?*,
1998
Taxidermied donkey,
television, rope, saddle,
blanket
150 × 154 × 46 cm
Migros Museum für
Gegenwartskunst, Zurich
[100] p. 167

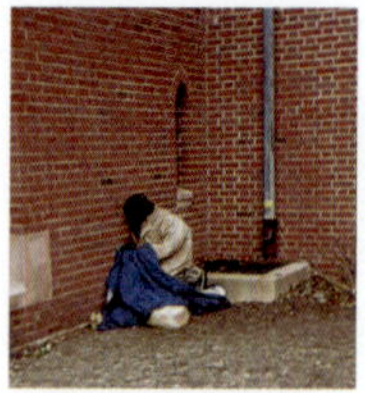

*Kenneth*, 1998
Plastic, clothing, shoes,
blanket
[193] p. 292

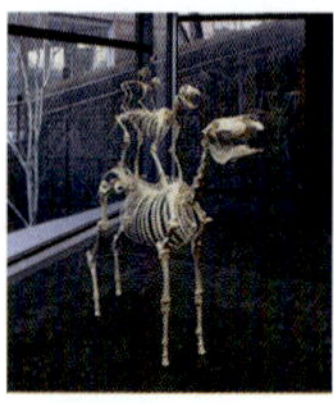

*Secrets*, 1998
Donkey, dog, cat and crow
skeletons
210 × 205 × 45 cm
Leeum Museum of Art, Seoul
Ref. p. 349 [246]

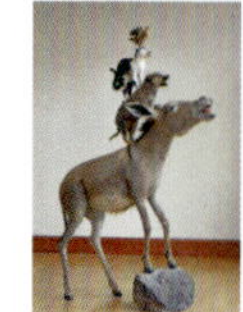

*The first, they said, should
be sweet like love; the
second bitter, like life; and
the third soft, like death*,
1998
Taxidermied donkey, dog,
cat and rooster, stone
165 × 120 × 40 cm
[247] p. 349

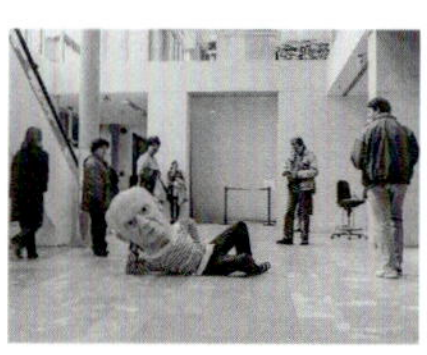

*Untitled*, 1998
Polystyrene, resin, cotton,
leather
217.2 × 139.7 × 59.7 cm
Performance with mask
during "Projects 65.
Maurizio Cattelan,"
curated by Laura
Hoptman, MoMA – The
Museum of Modern Art,
New York, November 6–
December 4, 1998 (solo
show)
Pinault Collection
[13.1] p. 40

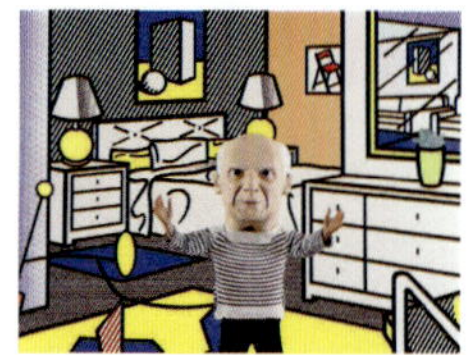

*Untitled*, 1998
Chromogenic print
182.9 × 228.6 cm
Performance with mask
during "Projects 65.
Maurizio Cattelan,"
curated by Laura
Hoptman, MoMA – The
Museum of Modern Art,
New York, November 6–
December 4, 1998
(solo show)
Fondation Carmignac
[13.2] p. 40

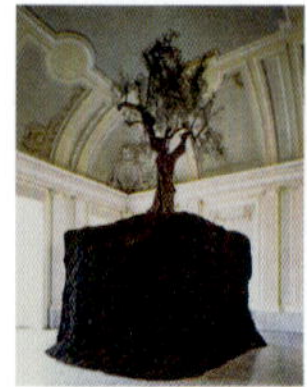

*Untitled*, 1998
Olive tree, soil, water, wood
and metal structure
800 × 500 × 500 cm
Castello di Rivoli Museo d'Arte
Contemporanea, Rivoli-Turin
[96] p. 156

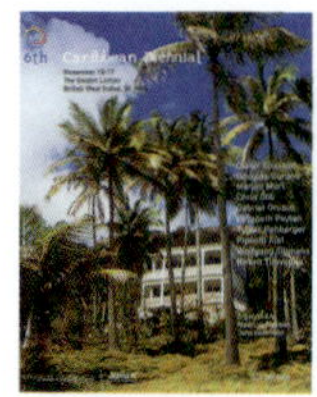

6th Caribbean Biennial,
1999
[186] p. 270



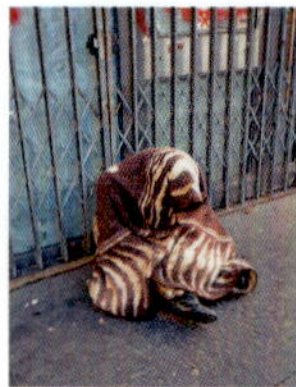

*Gérard*, 1999
Plastic, clothing, shoes,
blanket
82 × 66 × 87 cm
The Dakis Joannou Collection
Foundation
[194] p. 292

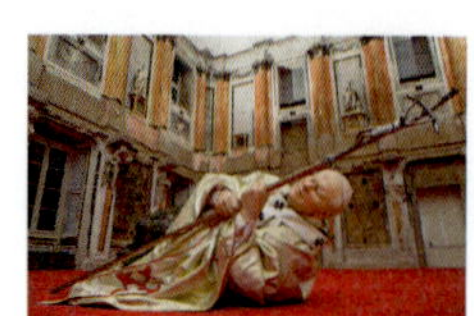
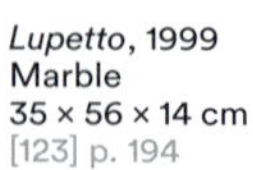

*La Nona Ora*, 1999
Polyester resin, wax,
pigment, natural
hair, fabric, clothing,
accessories, stone, carpet
Variable dimensions
Pinault Collection
[56] p. 110

*Lupetto*, 1999
Marble
35 × 56 × 14 cm
[123] p. 194

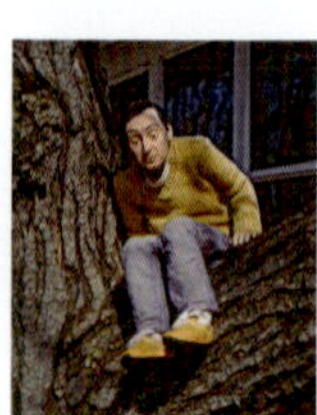

*Mini-me*, 1999
Resin, rubber, paint,
synthetic hair, clothing
45 × 20 × 23 cm
Glenstone Museum, Potomac
[3] p. 23

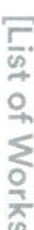

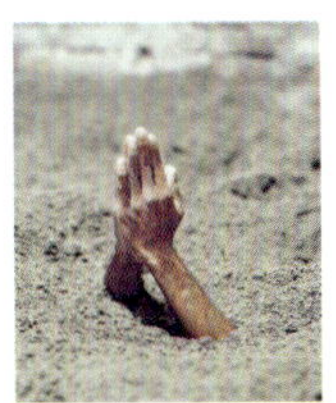

*Mother*, 1999
Cibachrome print
face mounted on
plexiglas
156.2 × 122 cm
Performance
with fakir during
"dAPERTutto," 48th
Venice Biennale,
curated by Harald
Szeemann, June
13–November 17,
1999 (group show)
Pinault Collection
Rubell Museum, Miami
and Washington DC
[65.1] p. 126

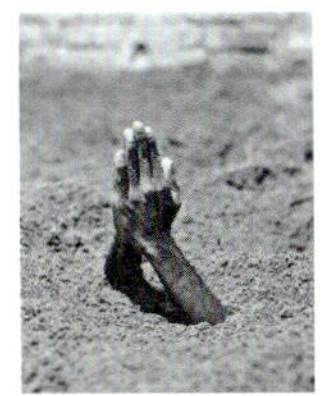

*Mother*, 1999
Black and white
photographic print
88.9 × 71.1 cm
Performance
with fakir during
"dAPERTutto," 48th
Venice Biennale,
curated by Harald
Szeemann, June 13–
November 17, 1999
(group show)
MAXXI – Museo delle
arti del XXI secolo,
Rome
The Dakis Joannou
Collection Foundation
[65.2] p. 126

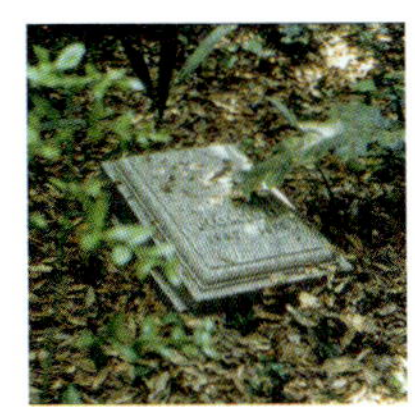

*Piumino*, 1999
Marble
56 × 35 × 14 cm
[120] p. 194

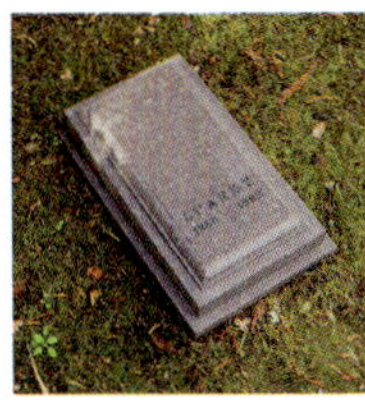

*Sparky*, 1999
Marble
14 × 34.9 × 55.9 cm
[121] p. 194

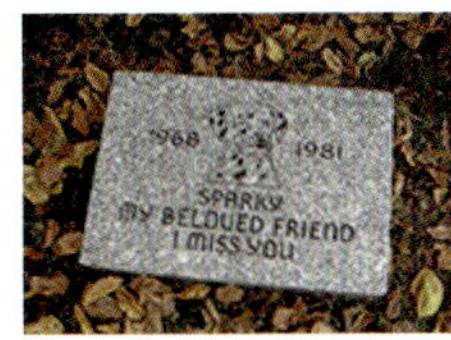

*Sparky*, 1999
Marble
[122] p. 194

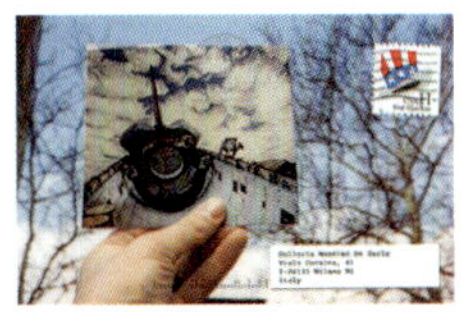

*Ten Part Story*, 1999
10 chromogenic prints,
postal stamps, labels
10.2 × 15.2 cm each
Isabel and Agustin Coppel
Collection, Mexico
[135] p. 219

377

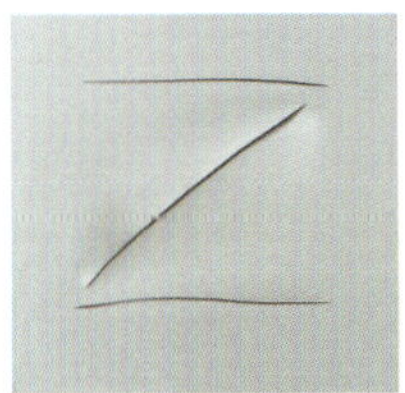

*Untitled*, 1999
Acrylic on canvas
71 × 71 cm
[21.1] p. 64

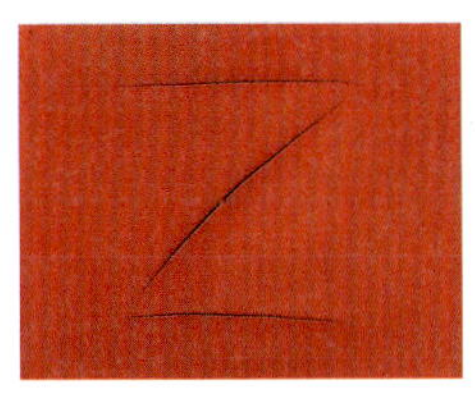

*Untitled*, 1999
Acrylic on canvas
100 × 120 cm
[21.2] p. 64

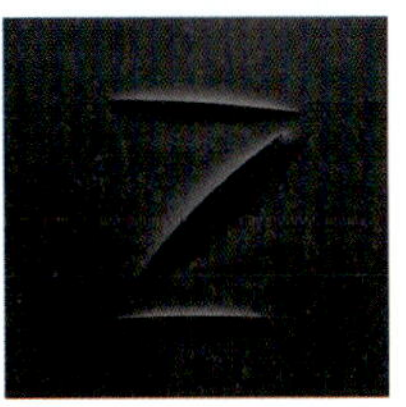

*Untitled*, 1999
Acrylic on canvas
110 × 110 cm
[21.3] p. 64

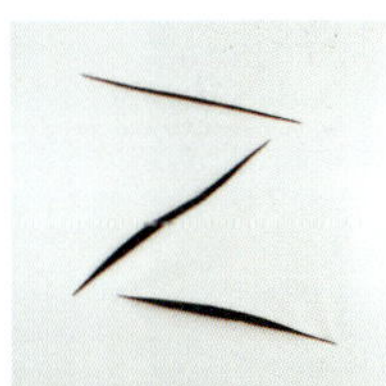

*Untitled*, 1999
Acrylic on canvas
110 × 110 cm
[21.4] p. 64

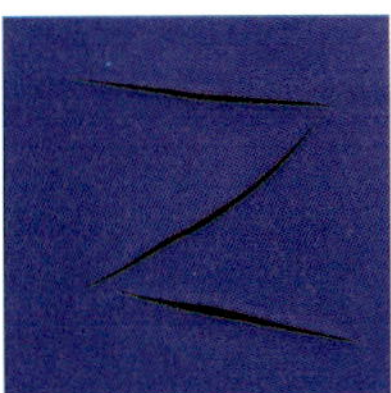

*Untitled*, 1999
Acrylic on canvas
110 × 110 cm
[21.5] p. 64

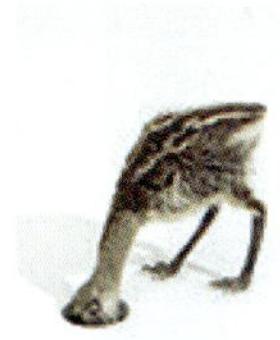

*Untitled*, 1999
Taxidermied baby ostrich
17.8 × 12.7 × 16.5 cm
[34.3] p. 89

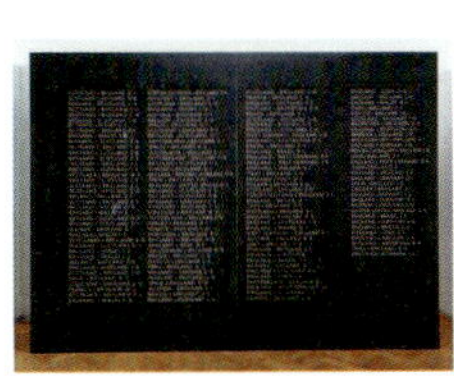

*Untitled*, 1999
Hand-carved granite,
medium-density fiberboard,
steel
219.4 × 277.3 × 33.8 cm
[35] p. 89

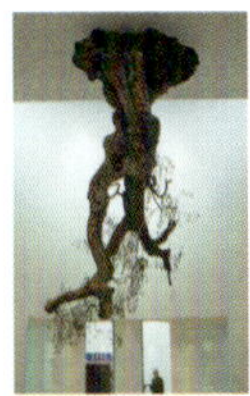

*Untitled*, 1999
Wood, soil
Height c. 500 cm
[97] p. 156

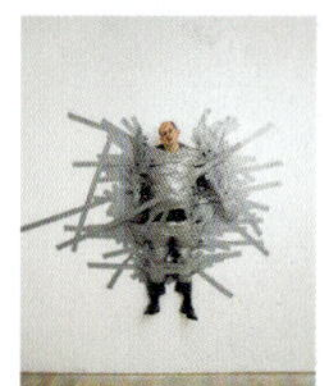

*Untitled*, 1999
[Initially titled:
*A Perfect Day*]
Offset print mounted
on aluminum
258 × 192 cm
Performance during
the solo exhibition
"Maurizio Cattelan"
at the Galleria
Massimo De Carlo,
Milan, September 27–
October 1999
Castello di Rivoli Museo
d'Arte Contemporanea,
Rivoli-Turin. Gift by
Associazione Artissima,
2001
[230] p. 323

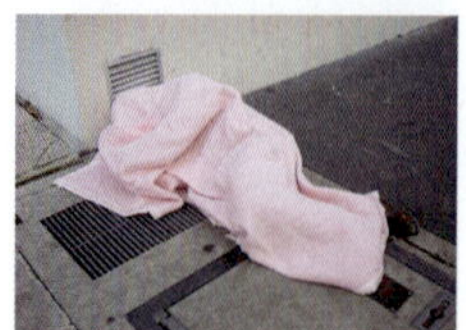

*Jean-Pierre*, 1999
Stuffed figure, clothing,
shoes, blanket
45.7 × 83.8 × 148 cm
[195] p. 292

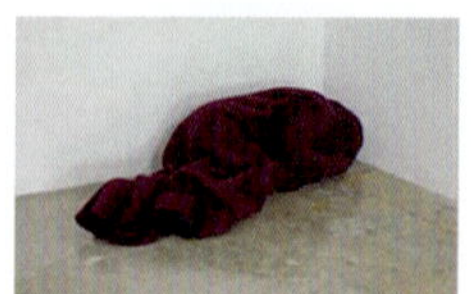

*Untitled (Philippe)*, 1999
Stuffed figure, plastic,
fabric
38 × 152.5 × 68.5 cm
Rubell Museum, Miami
and Washington DC
Rif. p. 292

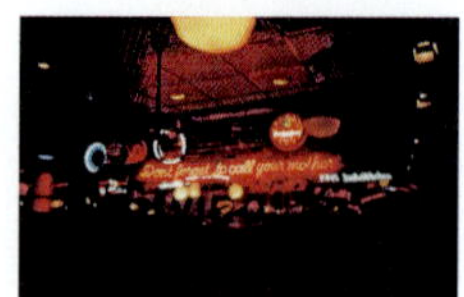

*Don't forget to call your
mother*, 2000
Silver dye bleach print
face-mounted to acrylic
66 × 101.6 cm
MET – The Metropolitan
Museum of Art
[137] p. 220

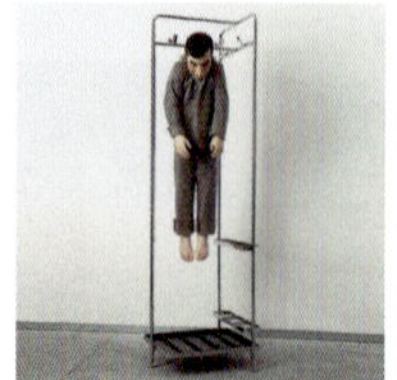

*La Rivoluzione siamo noi*,
2000
Polyester resin, wax,
pigment, hair, felt suit,
metal coat rack
Figure: 123.8 × 35.6 × 43.2 cm;
overall dimensions:
190 × 47 × 52 cm
Fondazione Sandretto Re
Rebaudengo
Migros Museum für
Gegenwartskunst, Zurich
Rubell Museum, Miami
and Washington DC
Solomon R. Guggenheim
Museum, New York. Purchased
with funds contributed by the
International Director's Council
and Executive Committee
Members: Ann Ames, Edythe
Broad, Henry Buhl, Elaine Terner
Cooper, Dimitris Daskalopoulos,
Harry David, Gail May Engelberg,
Linda Fischbach, Ronnie
Heyman, Dakis Joannou, Cindy
Johnson, Barbara Lane, Linda
Macklowe, Peter Norton,
Willem Peppler, Denise Rich,
Simonetta Seragnoli, David
Teiger, Ginny Williams,
and Elliot K. Wolk, 2000
[130] p. 205

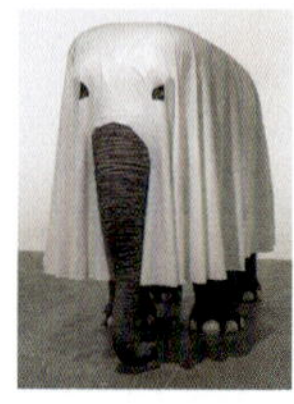

*Not Afraid of Love*, 2000
Styrene, polyester resin,
paint, hair, fabric
205.7 × 312.4 × 137.4 cm
Rubell Museum, Miami
and Washington DC
[4] p. 25

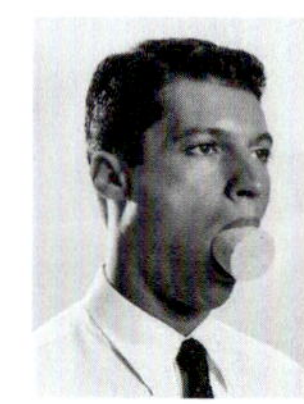

*Untitled*, 2000
Gelatin silver print
41.3 × 33 cm
Edition of 60 copies realized
for *Parkett* 59, 2000
MoMA – The Museum of
Modern Art, New York. Virginia
Cowles Schroth Fund
Rubell Museum, Miami
and Washington DC
[6] p. 26

378

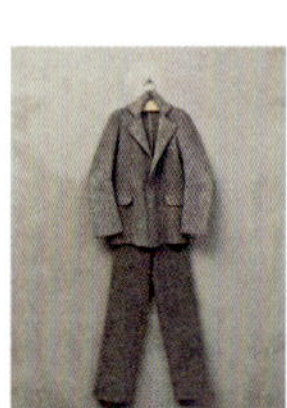

*Untitled*, 2000
Project for gravestone.
Unrealized
[53] p. 107

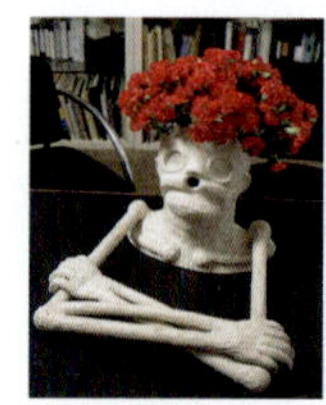

*Untitled*, 2000
Polyesther resin, paint,
synthetic flowers
30.5 × 43.2 × 43.2 cm
[124] p. 195

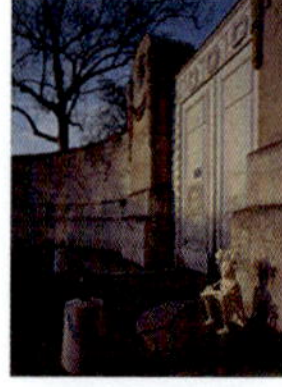

*Untitled*, 2000
Polyesther resin, paint,
synthetic flowers
[125] p. 195

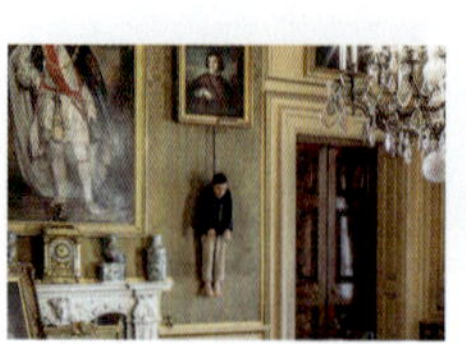

*Untitled*, 2000
Felt suit, wooden hanger
110.8 × 48.3 × 5.7 cm
Isabel and Agustin Coppel
Collection, Mexico
[131] p. 205

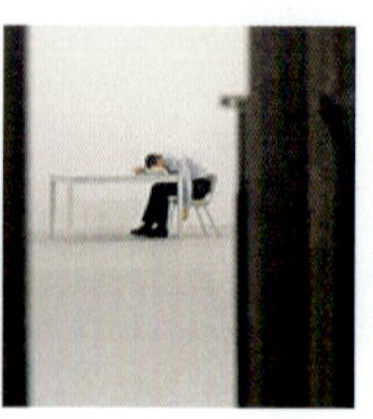

*Untitled*, 2000
Polyester resin, wax,
pigment, hair, clothes
Figure: 123.8 × 35.6 × 43.2 cm
[132] p. 205

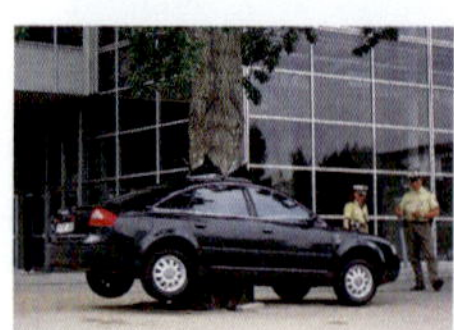

*Untitled*, 2000
Resin, clothes, table, chair
Environmental dimensions
[138] p. 220

*Untitled*, 2000
Audi car, tree
Environmental dimensions
[163] p. 244

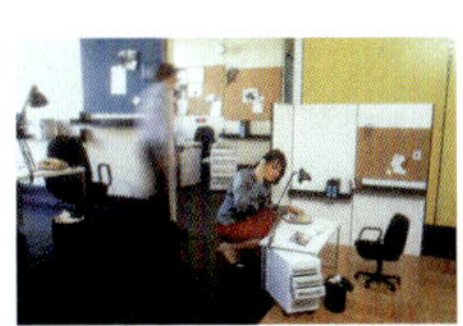

*Untitled*, 2000
Mixed media
Environmental dimensions
[179] p. 262

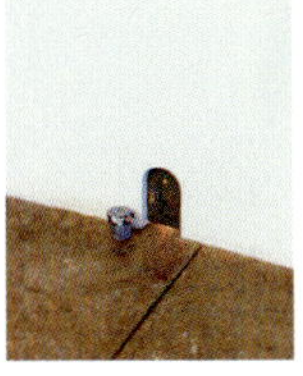

*Untitled*, 2000
Polyester resin, brass
fixture, digital audio
soundtrack, electric lights
Door: 13 × 4 cm; garbage
can: 6 × Ø 2.5 cm
Isabel and Agustin Coppel
Collection, Mexico
[160] p. 243

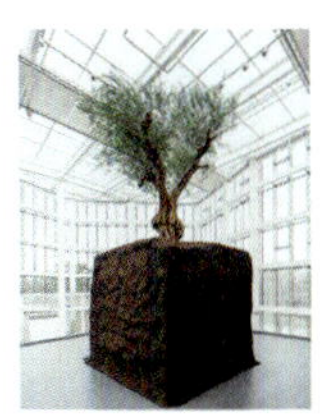

*Untitled*, 2000
Olive tree, soil, water,
wood, metal, plastic
800 × 400 × 400 cm
Collection of Yuz Foundation
p. 156 [96]

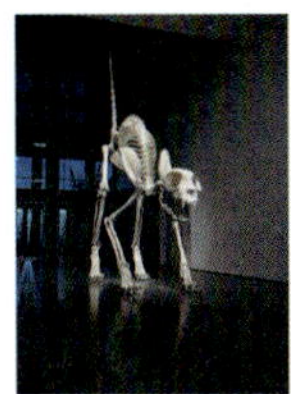

*Felix*, 2001
Oil on polyvinyl resin,
fiberglass
610 × 183 × 792 cm
Collection of Yuz Foundation
MCA – Museum of
Contemporary Art Chicago.
The Edlis/Neeson Art
Acquisition Fund
[164] p. 244

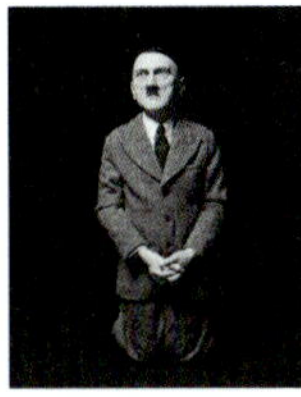

*Him*, 2001
Polyester resin, wax,
pigment, natural hair, suit,
boots
100 × 40 × 67 cm
Glenstone Museum, Potomac
Pinault Collection
[203] p. 296

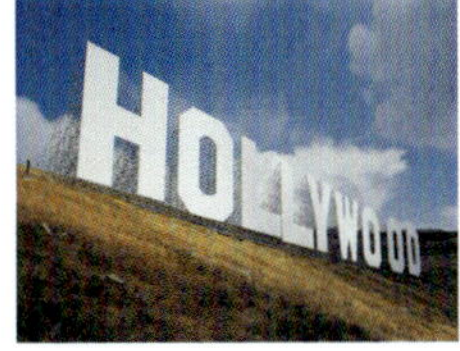

*Hollywood*, 2001
Scaffold, aluminum, halogen
headlights
23.35 × 166.2 × 9 m
[244.1-2] p. 340

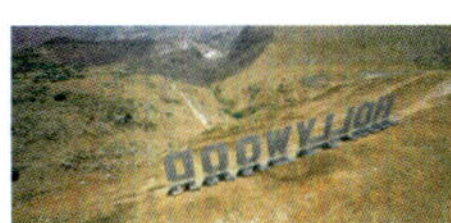

*Hollywood*, 2001
Color print face-mounted
to acrylic
180 × 400 cm
LACMA – Los Angeles County
Museum of Art. Gift of William
J. Bell
[244.3] p. 340

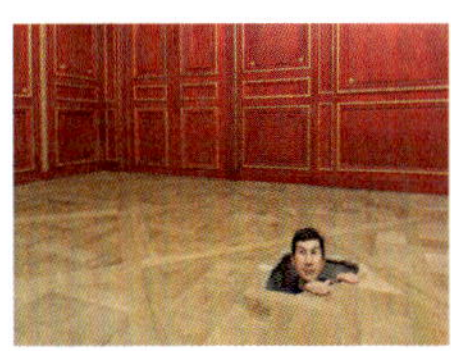

*Untitled*, 2001
Silicon rubber, epoxy
fiberglass, natural hair,
fabric
Figure: 150 × 60 × 40 cm
Museum Boijmans Van
Beuningen, Rotterdam. Long
term loan
The Dakis Joannou Collection
Foundation
[7] p. 26

379

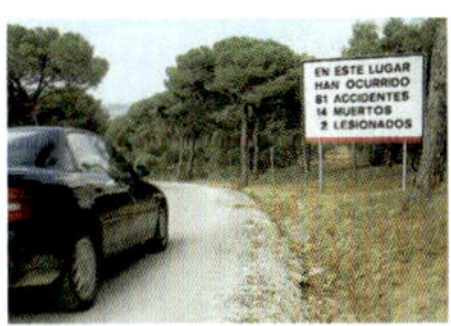

*Untitled*, 2001
Aluminum panel
200 × 300 cm
Fundación NMAC – Montenmedio
Contemporánea, Vejer de la
Frontera
[88] p. 147

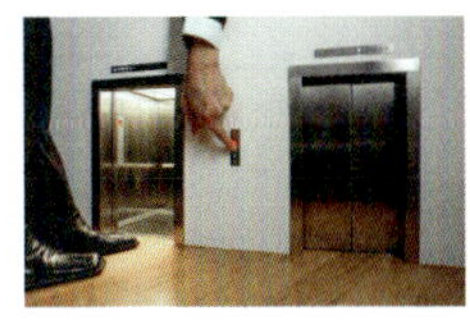

*Untitled*, 2001
Stainless steel, wood, electric
motor, light, bell, computer
59.7 × 85.4 × 47.3 cm
Collection of Yuz Foundation
LACMA – Los Angeles County
Museum of Art. Modern and
Contemporary Art Council Fund
Taguchi Art Collection
[89] p. 147

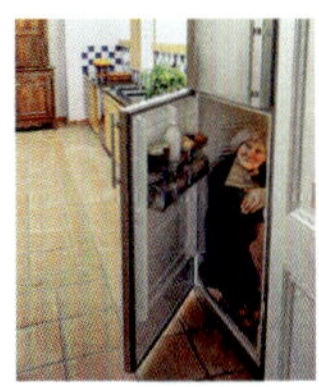

*Betsy*, 2002
Polyester resin, wax,
pigment, natural hair,
clothing, refrigerator
188 × 75 × 66 cm
[9] p. 30

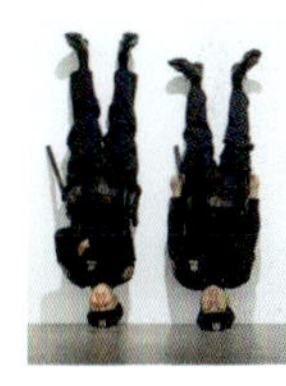

*Frank and Jamie*, 2002
Polyester resin, wax,
pigment, natural hair,
clothing, shoes, accessories
Frank: 191.8 × 63.5 × 50.8 cm;
Jamie: 182.3 × 62.9 × 45.7 cm
Nicola Erni Collection
[57] p. 114

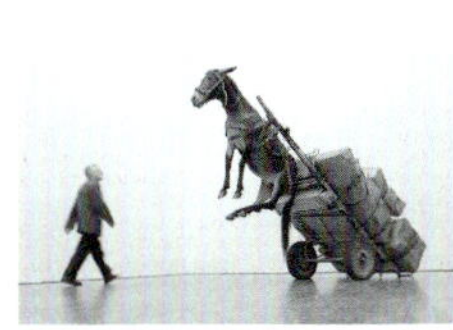

*Untitled*, 2002
Taxidermized donkey,
wood, metal, fabric, paper,
rope, rubber
250 × 400 × 165 cm
The Dakis Joannou Collection
Foundation
[101] p. 167

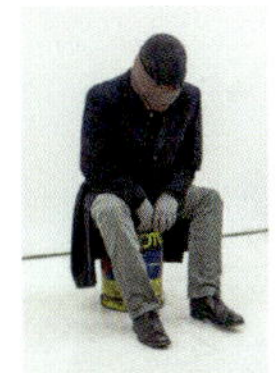

*Steve*, 2002
Silicone rubber, blanket,
clothes, shoes, steel
[196] p. 292

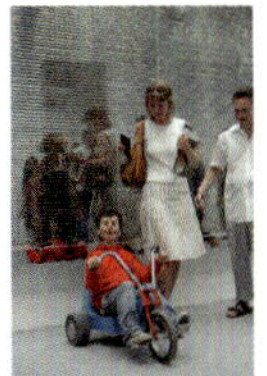

*Charlie*, 2003
Tricycle, steel, varnish,
rubber, resin, silicone, natural
hair, paint, clothing, shoes
82 × 92 × 56 cm
MOCA – The Museum of
Contemporary Art, Los Angeles.
Gift of Beth Swofford, in honor
of Klaus Biesenbach
Pinault Collection
[30] p. 78

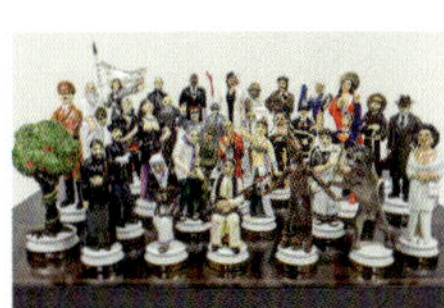

*Good Versus Evil*, 2003
32 hand-painted porcelain
figures, wood, chessboard,
travel case
Maja Hoffmann/LUMA
Foundation Collection
[204] p. 298

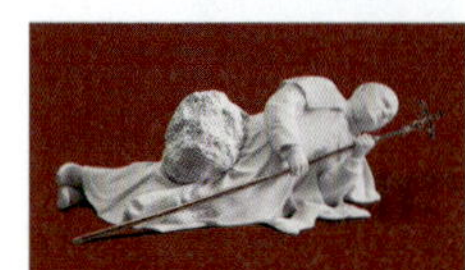

*La Nona Ora*, 2003
Marble, silver
17 × 63 × 22 cm
Ref. p. 110 [56]

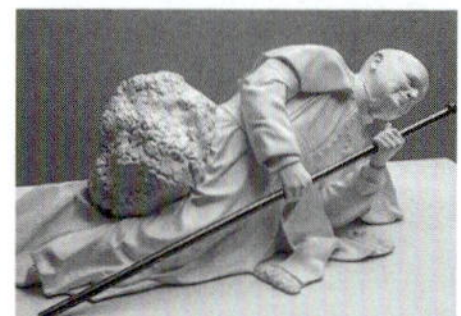

*La Nona Ora*, 2003
Plaster, silver
17 × 63 × 22 cm
MOCA – The Museum of
Contemporary Art, Los Angeles.
Gift of Beth Swofford
Ref. p. 110 [56]

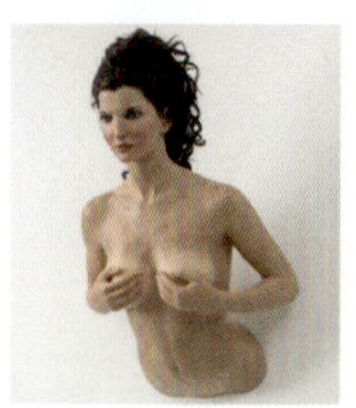

*Stephanie*, 2003
Wax, pigment, synthetic
hair, metal
109.9 × 64.8 × 41.9 cm
[232] p. 329

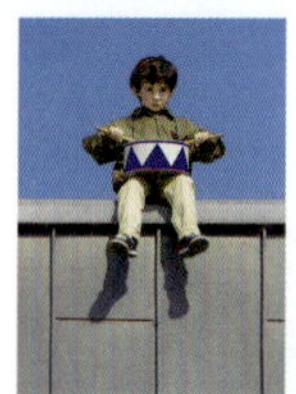

*Untitled*, 2003
Resin, paint, synthetic hair,
clothing, shoes, electronic
device, steel drum
80 × 85 × 55.9 cm
The Rachofsky Collection
[8] p. 29

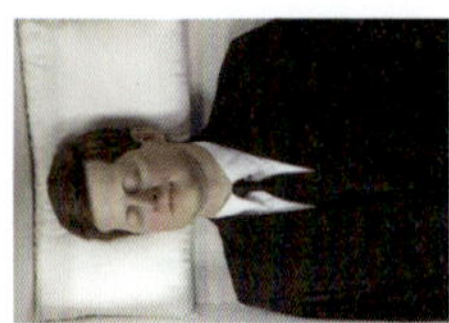

*Now*, 2004
Polyester resin, wax,
pigment, natural hair,
clothing, wood
85 × 225 × 78 cm
The Dakis Joannou Collection
Foundation
[103] p. 169

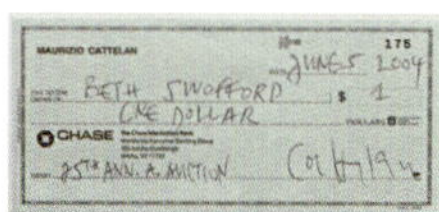

*Untitled*, 2004
Check with additions in ink
7 × 15.2 cm
[90] p. 148

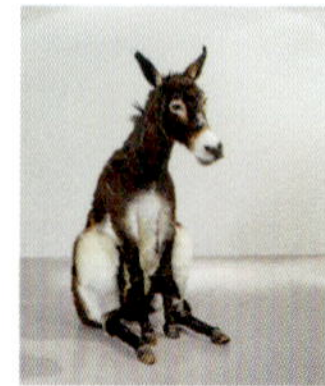

*Untitled*, 2004
Taxidermied donkey
160 × 80 × 175 cm
Isabel and Agustin Coppel
Collection, Mexico
[102] p. 167

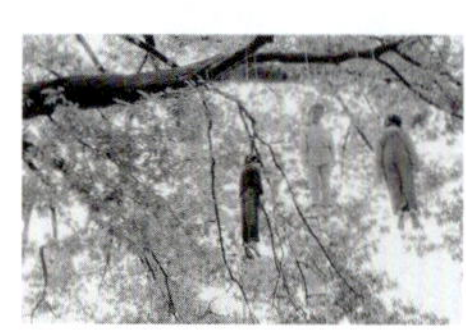

*Untitled*, 2004
Resin, fiberglass, synthetic
hair, clothing, rope
Variable dimensions;
130 × 50 × 55 cm each
of the 3 figures
[98] p. 158

380

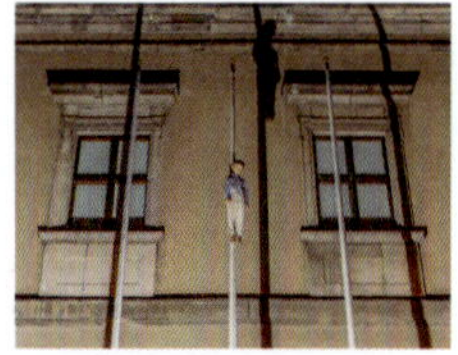

*Untiled*, 2004
3 flag poles, polyurethane,
polyester resin, paint,
synthetic hair, clothing, rope
Figure: 130 × 50 × 55 cm;
flag poles: 900 × 20 ×
20 cm each
[99] p. 160

*Untitled*, 2004
Concrete, fiberglass
39.4 × 48.3 × 37.5 cm
Whitney Museum of American
Art, New York. Gift of the artist
[139] p. 220

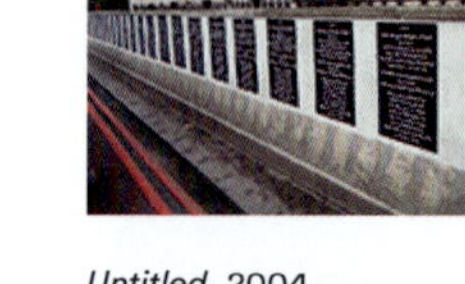

*Untitled*, 2004
Offset prints on paper
70 × 50 cm each
[233] p. 329

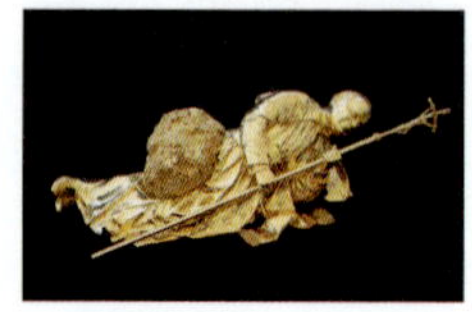

*La Nona Ora*, 2005
Gold 18 karat
17 × 63 × 22 cm
The Dakis Joannou Collection
Foundation
[56] p. 110

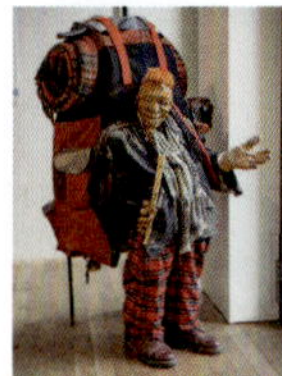

*Punki*, 2005
Performance by Bernard
Wilson in his costume
(height c. 100 cm), various
venues
[231] p. 324

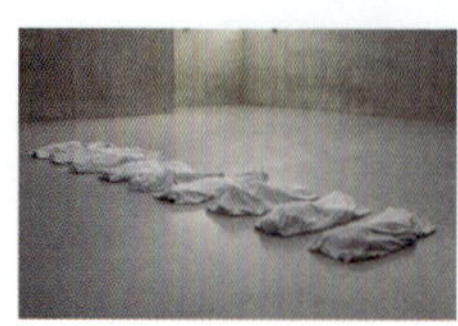

*All*, 2007
Carrara marble
C. 30 × 100 × 200 cm each
of the 9 elements
Pinault Collection
The Dakis Joannou Collection
Foundation
[127] p. 197

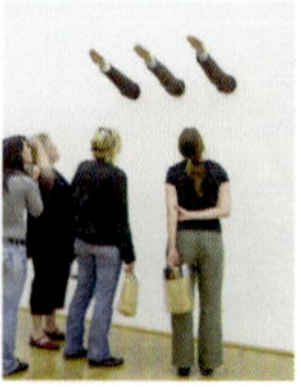

*Ave Maria*, 2007
Polyurethane, paint,
clothing, metal
Overall width: 65 cm;
74 × Ø 13 cm each of the
3 elements
The Dakis Joannou Collection
Foundation
[58] p. 115

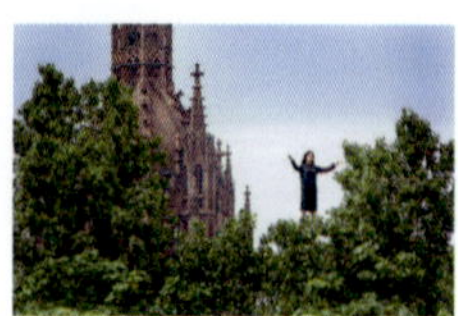

*Frau C.*, 2007
Polyester resin, paint,
natural hair, clothing, shoes
190 × 140 × 38 cm
[68] p. 129

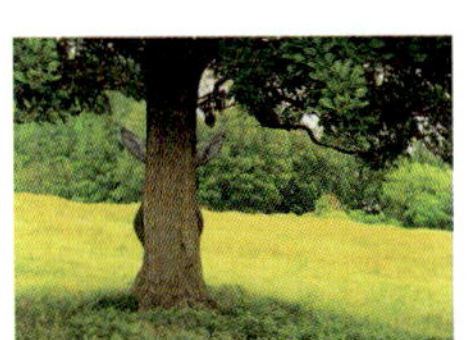

*Untitled*, 2007
Poster
70 × 100 cm
[5] p. 25

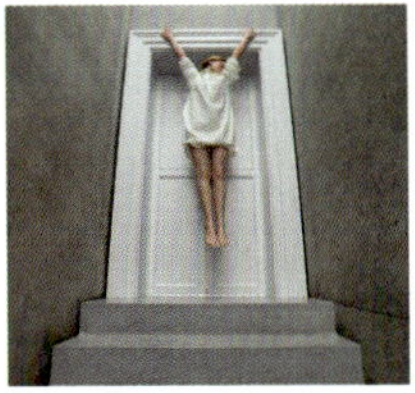

*Untitled*, 2007 (first version)
Resin, paint, natural hair,
clothes
Site-specific installation
at the Kunsthaus Bregenz
[67.1] p. 128

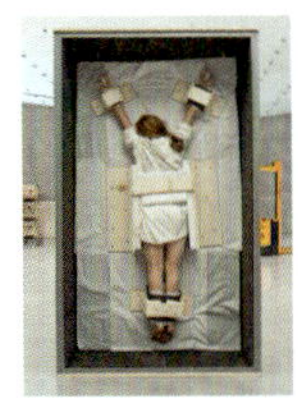

*Untitled*, 2007
Resin, paint, natural hair,
clothes, wrapping paper,
wood, screws
235.6 × 137.2 × 47 cm
[67.2-3] p. 128

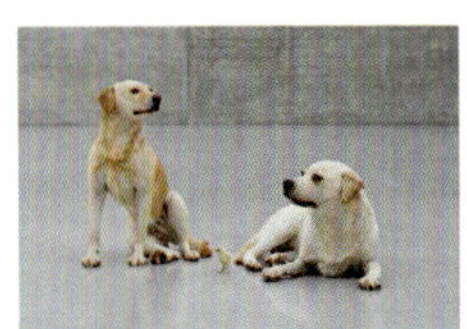

*Untitled*, 2007
2 taxidermied dogs,
taxidermied chick
Lifesize
[118] p. 192

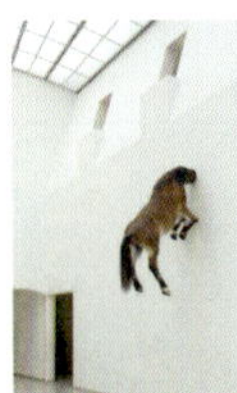

*Untitled*, 2007
Taxidermized horse
370 × 170 × 80 cm
Pinault Collection
The Dakis Joannou Collection
Foundation
[202] p. 294

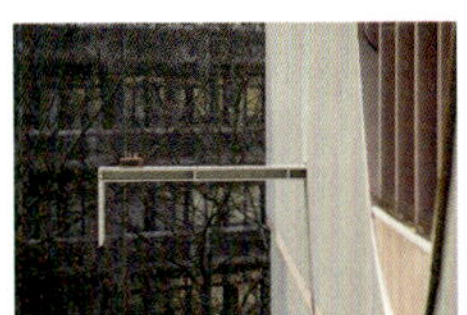
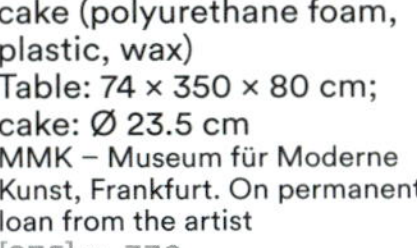

*Untitled*, 2007
Lacquered plywood, wood,
aluminium, metal, artificial
cake (polyurethane foam,
plastic, wax)
Table: 74 × 350 × 80 cm;
cake: Ø 23.5 cm
MMK – Museum für Moderne
Kunst, Frankfurt. On permanent
loan from the artist
[235] p. 330

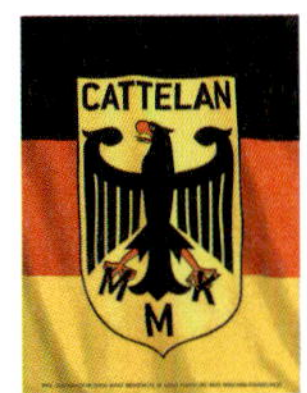



*Untitled*, 2007
Multicolor print on paper
119 × 84 cm
MMK – Museum für Moderne
Kunst, Frankfurt
[236] p. 332

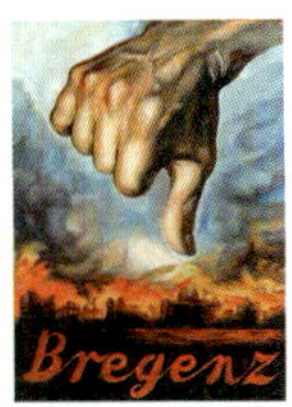



*Bregenz*, 2008
Digital pigment print
on Photo Rag paper,
67 × 50 cm
Edition of 45 copies
realized for the exhibition
at Kunsthaus Bregenz, 2008
p. 188

381

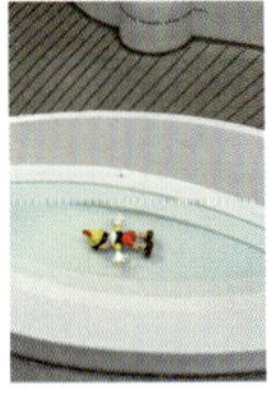

*Daddy, Daddy*, 2008
Polyurethane resin, steel,
epoxy paint
37.5 × 97.8 × 87.6 cm
Solomon R. Guggenheim
Museum, New York. Anonymous
gift, 2012
[14.1] p. 43

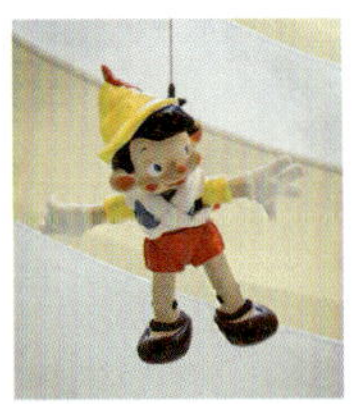

*Daddy, Daddy*, 2008
Polyurethane resin, steel,
epoxy paint
110 × 94 × 34 cm
Ref. p. 43 [14]

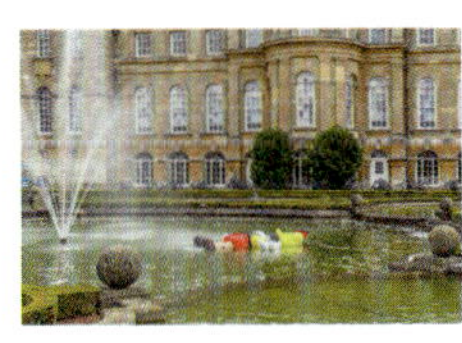

*Daddy, Daddy*, 2008
Polyurethane resin, steel,
epoxy paint
272 × 123 × 300 cm
[14.2] p. 43

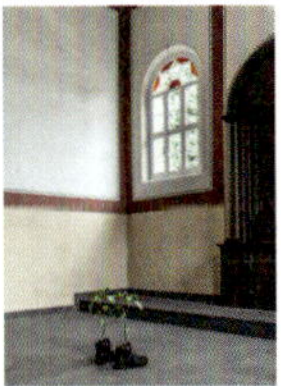

*Untitled*, 2008
Boots, plants, soil
Variable dimensions
[70] p. 130

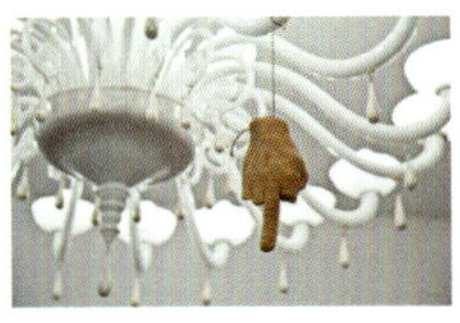

*Untitled*, 2009
Polyurethanic rubber,
pigment
20 × 10 × 7 cm
Edition of 80 copies
Museo del Novecento, Milan
Rubell Museum, Miami
and Washington DC
The Dakis Joannou Collection
Foundation
[29] p. 76

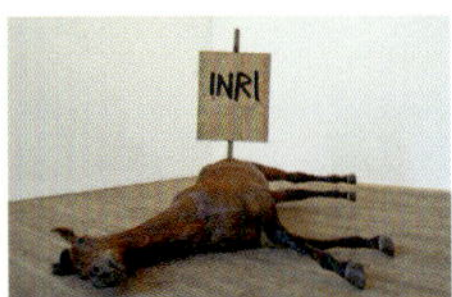



*Untitled*, 2009
Taxidermied horse, steel,
felt-tip pen on wood
Horse: 55.3 × 201.1 × 188.9 cm
[104] p. 169

*Untitled*, 2009
Canvas, broom
210 × 85 × 60 cm
Joint acquisition of The Menil
Collection, with funds provided
by Nina and Michael Zilkha;
Dallas Museum of Art, gift
of The Rachofsky Collection
and Deedie and Rusty Rose;
The Rachofsky Collection;
Deedie and Rusty Rose
[144] p. 227

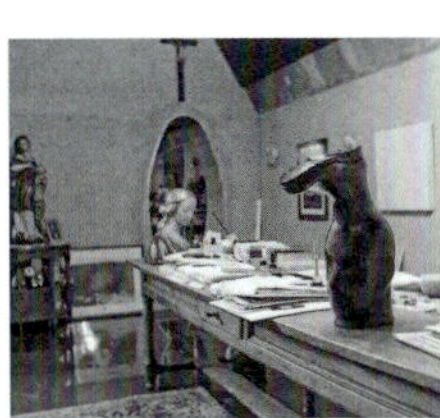

*Untitled*, 2009
Polyurethane rubber, steel
51 × 38 × 18 cm
[205] p. 299

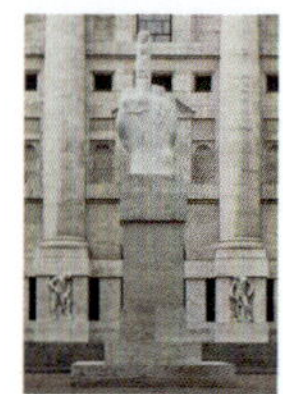

*L.O.V.E.*, 2010
Carrara marble, Roman
travertine
Hand: 470 × 220 × 72 cm;
base: 630 × 470 × 470 cm
Piazza degli Affari, Milan,
permanent installation
since September 25, 2010
Gift of the artist to the City
of Milan, September 27, 2012
[43] p. 96

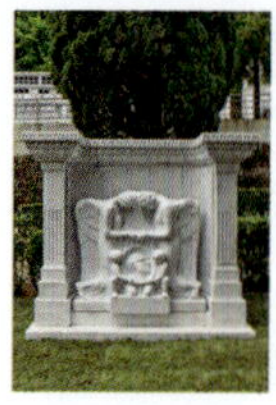

*Untitled*, 2010
Carrara marble
155 × 140 × 40 cm
[44] p. 99

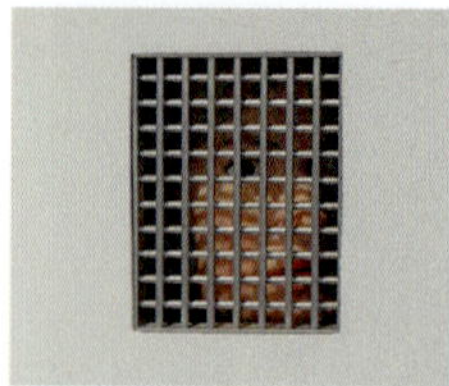

*Untitled*, 2010
Silicone, paint, natural hair,
metal grid
18 × 13 cm
[145] p. 227

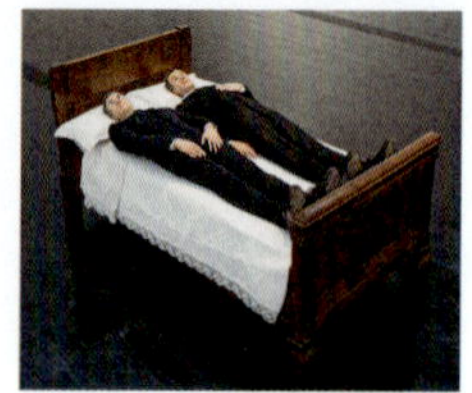

*We*, 2010
Polyester resin,
polyurethane, rubber,
paint, synthetic hair, fabric,
clothing, shoes, wood
68 × 148 × 79 cm
Pinault Collection
The Dakis Joannou Collection
Foundation
[10] p. 31

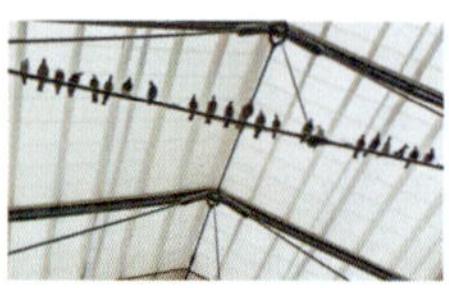

*Others*, 2011
Taxidermied pigeons
Environmental dimensions
Pinault Collection
The Dakis Joannou Collection
Foundation
[239] p. 338

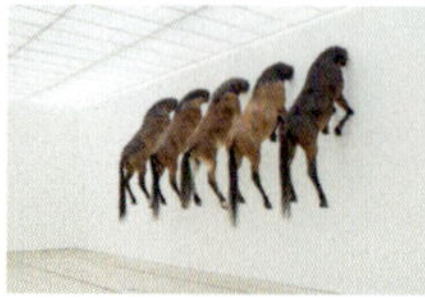

*Kaputt*, 2013
5 taxidermied horses
C. 300 × 170 × 80 cm each
[148] p. 229

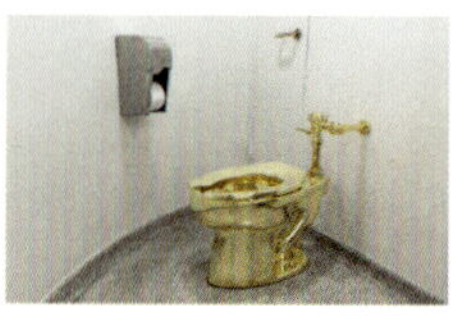

*America*, 2016
18 karat gold
48 × 35.6 × 65 cm
[207] p. 300

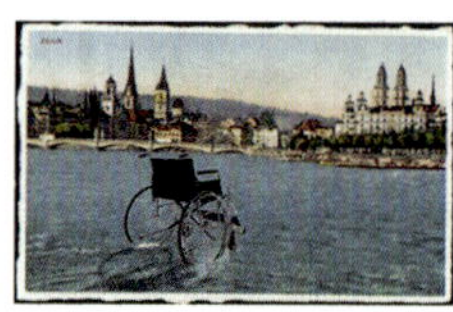

*Untitled*, 2016
Action during Manifesta
11, curated by Christian
Jankowski, Zurich, June
11–September 18, 2016
(group show)
[54] p. 107

382

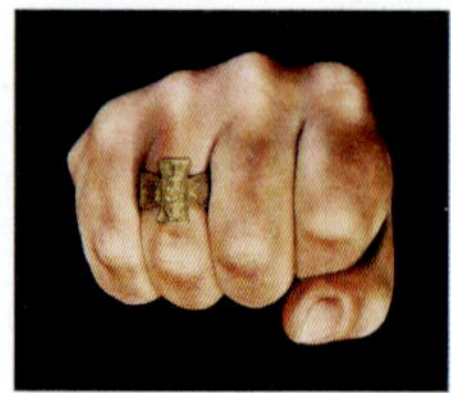

*Untitled*, 2017
Silkscreen print
50 × 50 cm
Edition of 35 copies realized
for *Parkett* 100/101, 2017
MoMA – The Museum
of Modern Art, New York.
Monroe Wheeler Fund
p. 90

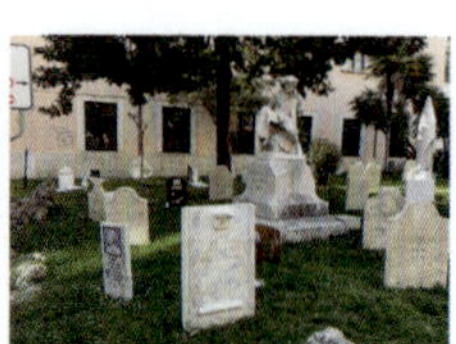

*Eternity*, 2018
Gravestones, mixed media
Environmental dimensions
[128] p. 197

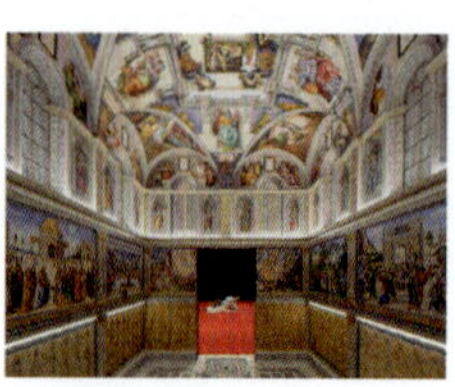

*Untitled*, 2018
Fresco painting, pine wood,
steel
Interior: 365 × 730 ×
243 cm; exterior: 376 ×
830 × 333 cm
Courtesy Perrotin
[71] p. 132

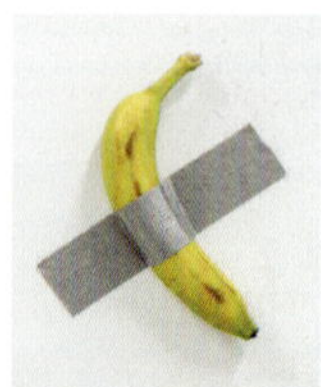

*Comedian*, 2019
Banana, duct tape
Variable dimensions
Promised gift to Solomon R.
Guggenheim Museum, New York
Courtesy Perrotin
[92] p. 150

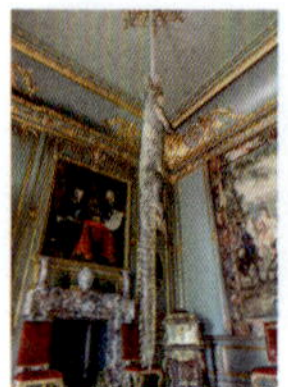

*Ego*, 2019
Taxidermied crocodile, rope
346 × 60 × 36 cm
[73.1] p. 134

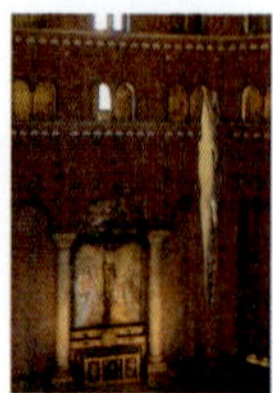

*Ego*, 2019
Taxidermied crocodile, rope
433 × 70 × 40 cm
[73.2] p. 134

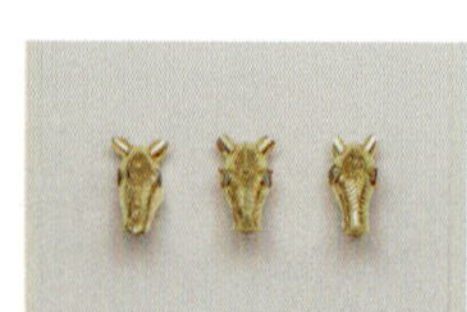

*Glory Glory Hallelujah*, 2019
Bone, 24 karat gold-plates
steel
66 × 25 × 35 cm each
element
[72] p. 134

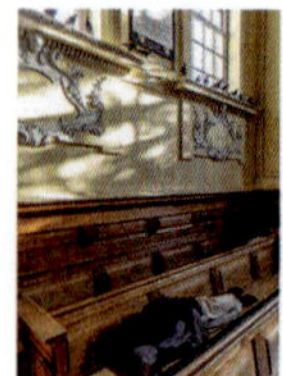

*Tom*, 2019
Clothes, shoes, fabric
[197] p. 292

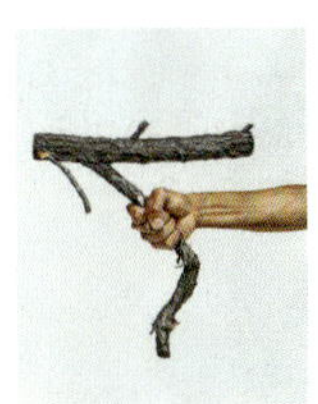

*Untitled*, 2019
Watercolor
43 × 32.5 cm
Image used as invitation
for the exhibition "Smoke"
[166] p. 246

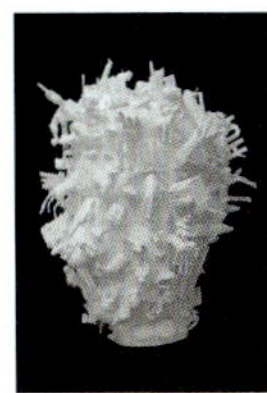

*Untitled*, 2019
Polystyrene, epoxy resin,
fiberglass, paint
150 × 135 × 110 cm
[183] p. 265

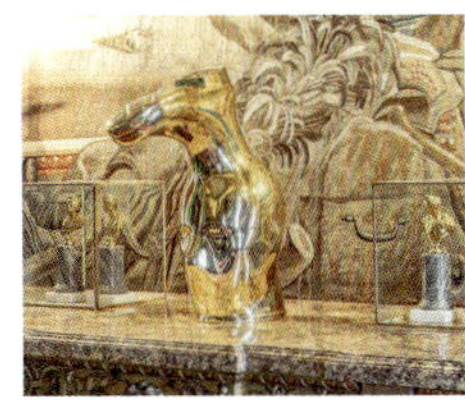

*Untitled*, 2019
24 karat gold-plated brass
49 × 40.5 × 18 cm
[206] p. 298

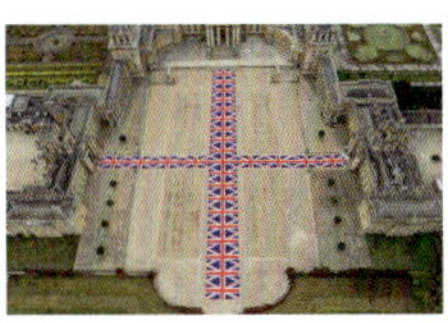

*Victory Is Not An Option*,
2019
Decotex 220 g/m²,
rubber matting, felt
2048 m²
[151] p. 232

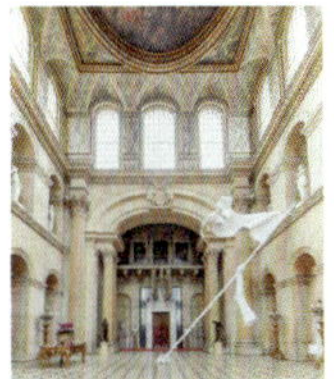

*We'll Never Die*, 2019
Expanded polystyrene,
aluminum, polyurethane
resin, metal structure, paint
580 × 1240 × 310 cm
[208] p. 302

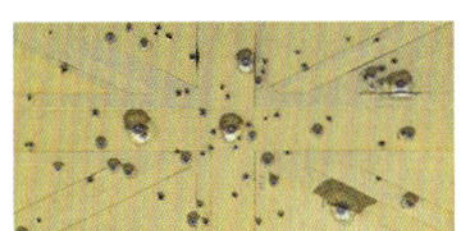

*Tears*, 2020
Steel, paint, bullets
70 × 140 × 4 cm
[209] p. 303

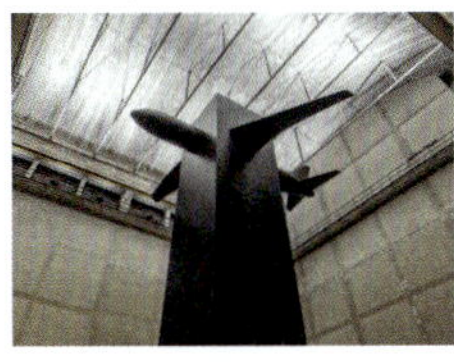

*Blind*, 2021
Resin, wood, steel,
aluminum, polystyrene,
paint
1695 × 1300 × 1195 cm
Work produced by Marian
Goodman Gallery, New York,
and Pirelli HangarBicocca, Milan
[224] p. 317

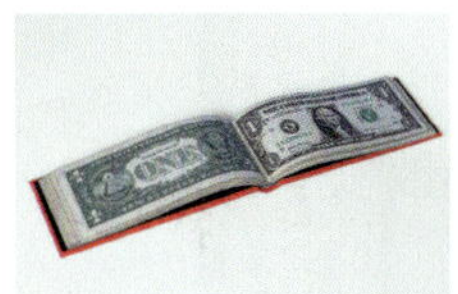

*BREAD*, 2021
Artist's book of one
hundred US one-dollar
bills bound in a fabric
hardcover volume
inserted in a slipcase set
in a box; published by
Three Star Books, Paris
Pages: 6.6 × 15.5 cm
each; closed book:
7.6 × 15.9 × 1.9 cm;
slipcase:
8.3 × 16.1 × 2.5 cm; box:
16.7 × 22,7 × 3.8 cm
MoMA – The Museum
of Modern Art, New York.
Monroe Wheeler Fund
[94] p. 152

383

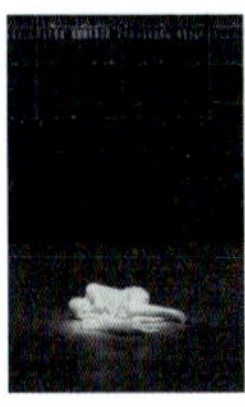

*Breath*, 2021
Carrara marble
Figure: 40 × 78 × 131 cm;
dog: 30 × 65 × 40 cm
[129] p. 199

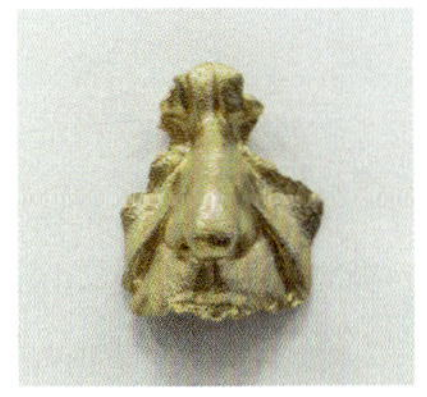

*Brother*, 2021
18 karat gold
12.5 × 10 × 6 cm
[167] p. 246

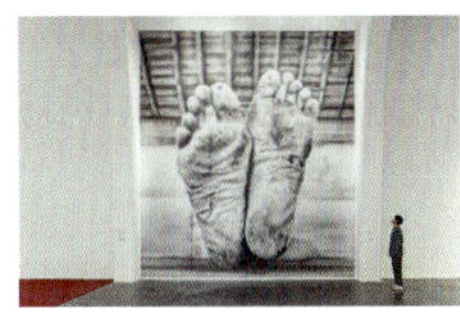

*Father*, 2021
Hand-painted mural
Environmental dimensions
Leeum Museum of Art, Seoul
[190] p. 286

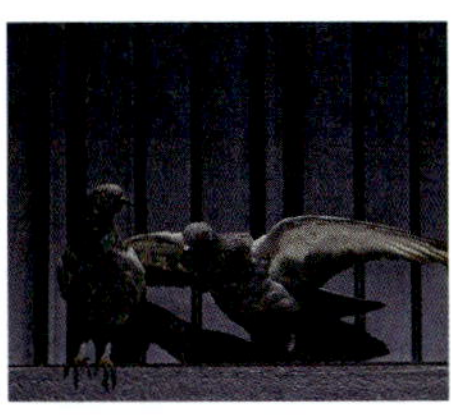

*Ghosts*, 2021
Taxidermied pigeons
Environmental dimensions
Leeum Museum of Art, Seoul
The Dakis Joannou Collection
Foundation
[240] p. 338

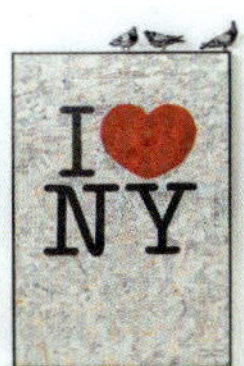

*Ghosts*, 2021 + found work
Taxidermied pigeons, found
work
Found work: 180 × 163 × 11 cm;
overall dimensions: 200 ×
163 × 11 cm
[168] p. 246

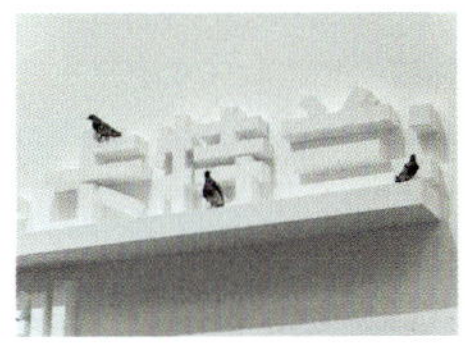

*Kids*, 2021
Taxidermied pigeons
Environmental dimensions
[241] p. 339

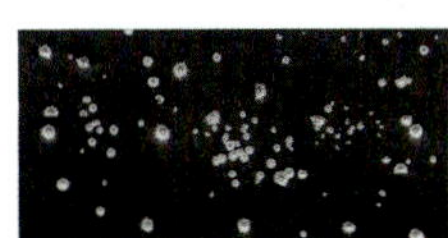

*Meat*, 2021
Steel, paint, bullets
150 × 300 × 6.6 cm
[212] p. 303

*Morning*, 2021
Steel, paint, bullets
198 × 376 × 6.5 cm
[211] p. 303

*Night*, 2021
Steel, paint, bullets
148 × 281 × 6,6 cm
[209] p. 303

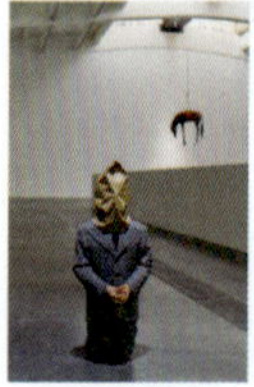

*No*, 2021
Platinum silicone, resin,
hair, clothing, boots,
paper bag
101 × 41 × 53 cm
[59] p. 116

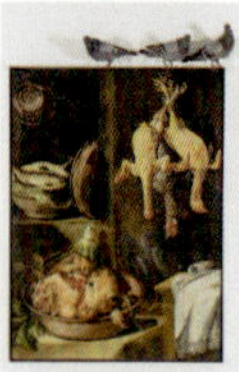

*Raw*, 2021
Painting, 3 taxidermied
pigeons
Overall dimensions:
149 × 93 × 13 cm;
painting: 129 × 93 × 11 cm
[242] p. 340

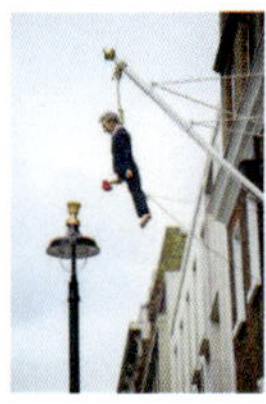

*You*, 2021
Platinum silicone, epoxy
fiberglass, natural hair,
clothing, stainless steel,
hemp rope, flowers
140 × 40 × 25 cm
[237] p. 332

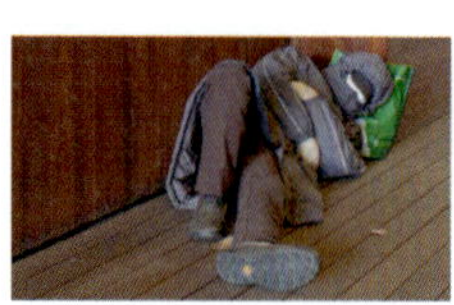

*Donghoon*, 2023
Clothes, shoes, fabric
[198] p. 292

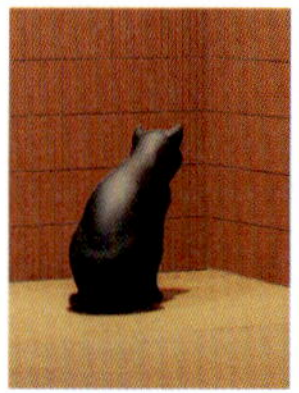

*IT*, 2023
Belgian black marble
37 × 19 × 41.5 cm
[32] p. 80

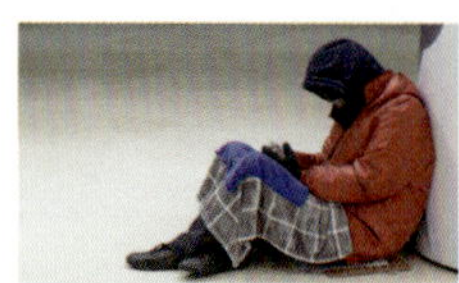

*Junho*, 2023
Wood, polystyrene,
stainless steel, clothing,
shoes, accessories
75 × 85 × 115 cm
Centre Pompidou. Gift of the
artist, 2024
[199] p. 292



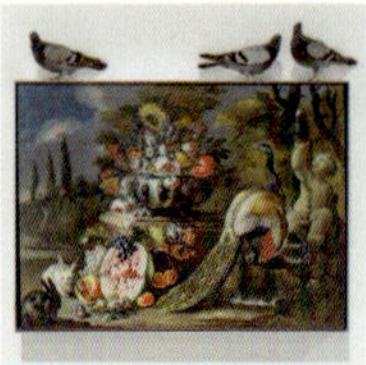

*Roma*, 2023
Painting, 3 taxidermied
pigeons
Overall dimensions:
98 × 109.5 × 15.5 cm;
painting: 70 × 105 × 12 cm
[243] p. 340

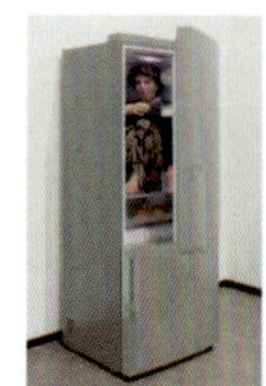

*Shadow*, 2023
Platinum silicone, glass
fiber, steel, hair, clothing,
refrigerator, food
180 × 75 × 50 cm
[66] p. 126

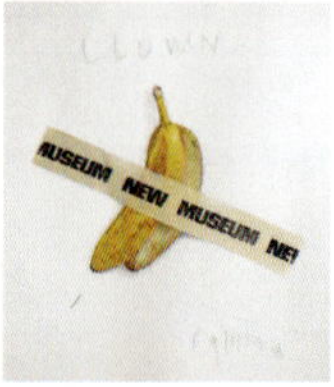

*Clown*, 2024
Watercolor on Fabriano
paper, collage of UV-printed
Japanese paper, rubber
stamped
41.9 × 47 cm
Edition
Series of 20 variants
[93] p. 150

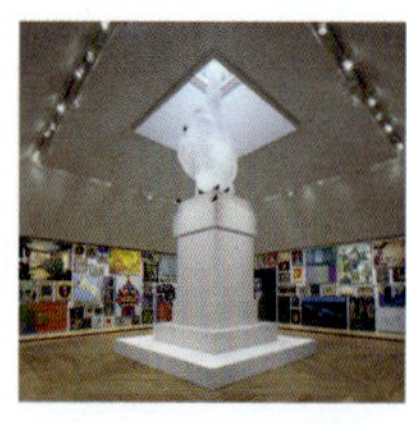

*L.O.V.E.*, 2024
Cellulose plastic, jesmonite,
fiberglass
Overall dimensions:
1000 × 470 × 470 cm
[174] p. 255

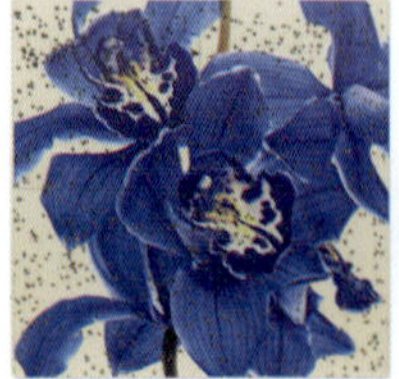

*MEAT*, 2024
UV LED inkjet print
on wood
250 × 250 × 25 cm
[214] p. 304

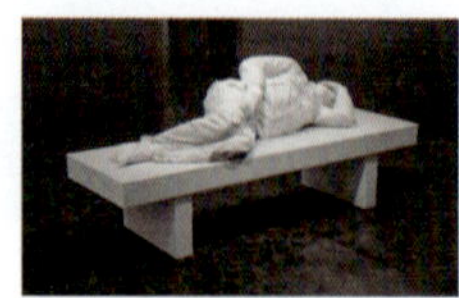

*November*, 2024
Statuario Michelangelo
marble, water pump
88 × 70 × 200 cm
[245] p. 345

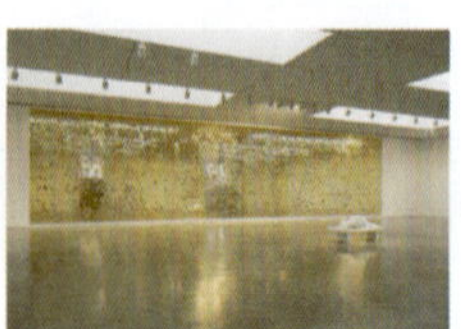

*Sunday*, 2024
64 Panels of stainless steel,
plated in 24 karat gold
136 × 136 × 4 cm each;
overall dimensions:
544 × 2176 × 4 cm
[72] p. 137

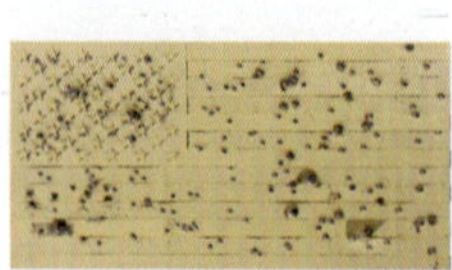

*Under*, 2024
Panels of stainless steel,
plated in 24 karat gold,
shot with different calibre
weapons
100 × 190 × 4 cm
[213] p. 303

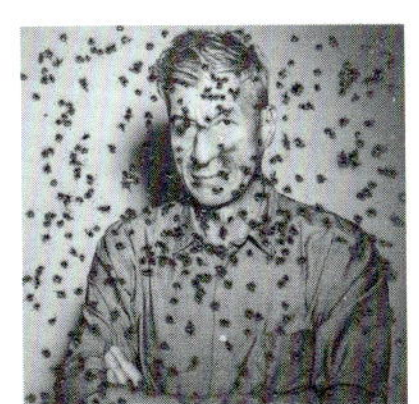

*Back*, 2025
UV LED Inkjet print
on wood
Unframed: 124.7 × 124.7 ×
5.5 cm
Art Jameel Collection, Dubai
Fondazione Sandretto Re
Rebaudengo
[217] p. 305

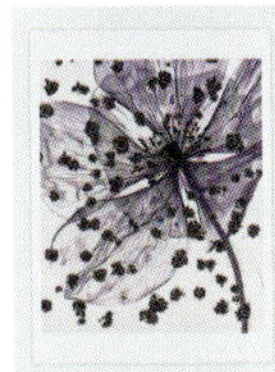

*Bees*, 2025
Watercolor on paper
Unframed: 50 × 70 cm;
framed: 76.7 × 57 × 3.7 cm
[215] p. 304

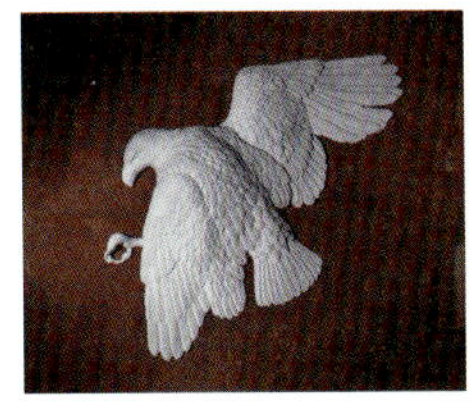

*Bones*, 2025
Statuario Michelangelo
statuary marble
35 × 270 × 174 cm
[154] p. 235

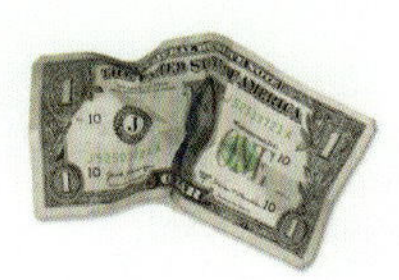

*Crumbs*, 2025
Acrylic on paper, wood
frame with gold finish
50 × 70 cm
[95] p. 152

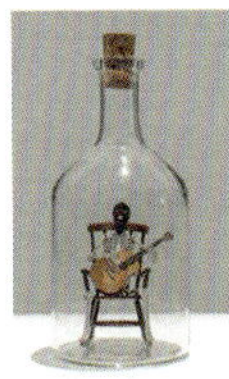

*Deaf*, 2025
Glass, bronze, wood, cork,
silver, fabric
27.5 × Ø 12 cm
[126] p. 195

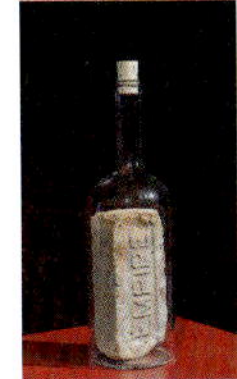

*Empire*, 2025
Glass, cork, brick
41 × Ø 12 cm
[153] p. 235

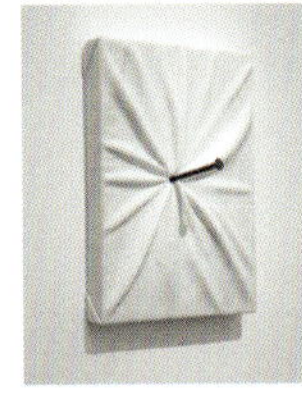

*Envy*, 2025
Michelangelo statuary
marble, nail
36 × 26 × 14 cm
[176] p. 255

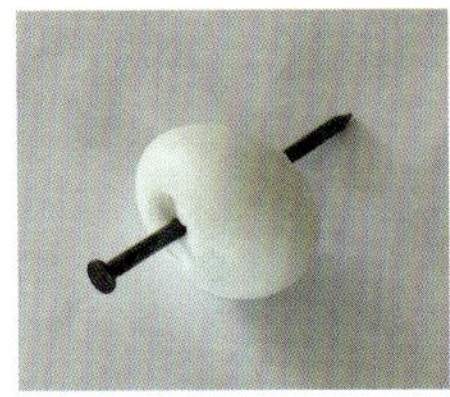

*First*, 2025
Michelangelo statuary
marble, nail
12 × 10 × 5 cm
[177] p. 255



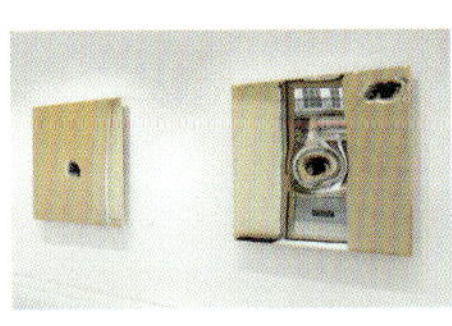

*Mouth*, 2025
24 karat gold-plated steel
panel shot with 12-gauge
weapon
136 × 136 × 4 cm each
[75] p. 137

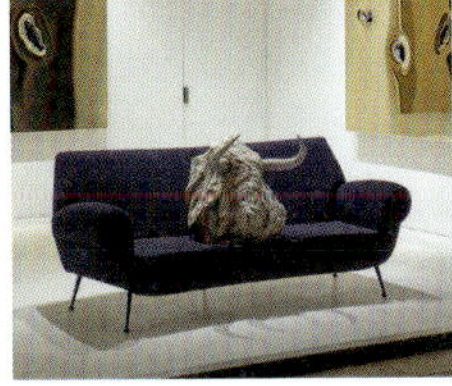

*Notre Dame*, 2025
Carrara marble, fabric sofa
100 × 197.4 × 81 cm
[162] p. 244

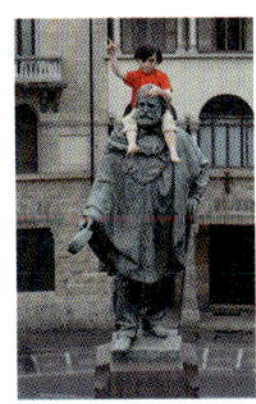

*One*, 2025
Silicone, resin, glue,steel,
synthetic hair, paint,
clothinges, wood
153 × 87 × 100 cm
[155] p. 235

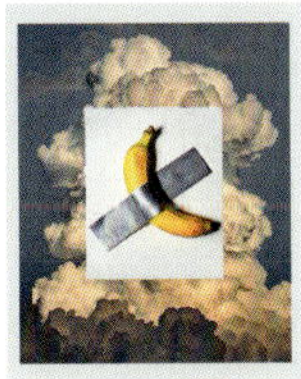

*Window*, 2025
Watercolor on paper
Unframed: 50 × 70 cm;
framed: 76.7 × 57 × 3.7 cm
[216] p. 305

For all works, if not otherwise stated:
Courtesy Maurizio Cattelan's Archive

**Pirelli HangarBicocca**


*Chairman*
Marco Tronchetti Provera
*Board of Directors*
Maurizio Abet,
Federica Barbaro,
Andrea Casaluci,
Ilaria Tronchetti Provera
*General Manager*
Alessandro Bianchi

*Artistic Director*
Vicente Todolí

*Chief Curator*
Roberta Tenconi
*Curator*
Lucia Aspesi
*Curator*
Fiammetta Griccioli
*Assistant Curator*
Tatiana Palenzona
*Research and Editorial Coordinator*
Teodora di Robilant
*Researcher*
Chiara Lupi
*Senior Exhibition Coordinator*
Marcella Ferrari

*Head of Public and Educational Programs*
Giovanna Amadasi
*Educational Projects*
Laura Zocco
*Public Program Organization*
Angela Della Porta

*Head of Communication and Press Office*
Angiola Maria Gili
*Communication*
Giorgia Giulia Campi
*Media Relations and Social Media*
Sofia Baronchelli

*Partnership Development*
Fabienne Binoche

*Head of Events and Bookshop*
Valentina Piccioni
*Event Organization*
Serena Jessica Boiocchi

*Services Marketing & Operations*
Erminia De Angelis

*Head of Production and Budgeting*
Valentina Fossati
*Installation*
Matteo De Vittor
*Installation*
Cesare Rossi
*Security and Facility*
Renato Bianconi

*Manager Assistant*
Alessandra Abbate

*Registrar*
Dario Leone

**Beware of Yourself**
**Maurizio Cattelan**

*Edited by*
Roberta Tenconi and Vicente Todolí
with Tatiana Palenzona

*Managing Editor*
Teodora di Robilant

*Design and Layout*
Carmen Malafronte

*Editing*
Riccardo Dirindin

*Copyediting*
Giulia Bilancetti

*Translations*
Richard Sadleir


© 2025 Maurizio Cattelan
© 2025 Pirelli HangarBicocca
© 2025 Marsilio Arte® s.r.l., Venice

*First Edition* October 2025
ISBN 979-12-5463-246-8

Available through
ARTBOOK | D.A.P.
75 Broad Street, Suite 630
New York, NY 10004
www.artbook.com


*Color Reproduction and Printing*
Grafiche Antiga S.p.A.,
Crocetta del Montello (TV)
*for* Marsilio Arte® s.r.l., Venice

www.marsilioarte.it

Pirelli HangarBicocca and Marsilio Arte would like to thank all those who have given their kind permission to reproduce the material for this book. Every effort has been made to achieve permission for the images in this catalogue. However, as in standard editorial policy for publications, Pirelli HangarBicocca and Marsilio Arte remain available in the case preliminary agreements were not able to be made with copyright holders.

All Rights Reserved. No part of this publication may be reproduced or transmitted in any form or by any means, electronic or mechanical, including photocopy, recording or any other information storage and retrieval system, without prior permission in writing from the publisher.

## [Acknowledgments]

Our heartfelt thanks go to Maurizio Cattelan for his commitment to this project and boundless generosity in sharing his thoughts, projects, and the many stories behind the works.
Organizing his show at Pirelli HangarBicocca in 2021 gave us the privilege of delving deeply into his practice and inspired us to further explore his universe. After the exhibition catalogue *Maurizio Cattelan: Breath Ghosts Blind* and *INDEX*, a volume encompassing all his interviews with other artists and thinkers, *Beware of Yourself* marks the third book we have produced together—a result of the closeness and ongoing relationship between Maurizio and our institution and team.
Over the past three years, we've seen him arriving with his bicycle in all weathers, ready to tell new stories about his works, select images together, and review layouts. We are deeply grateful for the trust and openness with which he has shared even his most intimate thoughts—now offered to readers through this book.

The Maurizio Cattelan's Archive, and in particular Zeno Zotti, Jacopo Zotti, and Giorgina Piovene Porto Godi, have been essential throughout every phase of the book's development. A special mention to Zeno and Jacopo, who patiently guided us through the archive, helping us gather images and details. A heartfelt thought goes to Lucio Zotti, who is no longer with us to see the final result, but who supported the idea of this book from the very beginning, even when we didn't yet know where it would lead.
We would also like to thank our partner, the publisher Marsilio Arte and its entire team, who so enthusiastically worked on the book. From the first conversation with CEO Luca De Michelis and the Editor in Chief Rossella Martignoni in December 2021, when the idea for this book slowly took shape, it has been a wonderful collaboration. We are especially grateful to Clara Pagnacco, who coordinated every editorial step with incredible precision—even when the flood of content had yet to find its form. Thanks to Carmen Malafronte, who translated the material into a coherent and yet enjoyable graphic design, giving each element—from short texts and thematic reflections to exhibition projects and captions—a place of its own. Our thanks go to the entire editorial team, especially Riccardo Dirindin, who skillfully and diligently edited the texts, harmonizing them and eliminating repetitions, becoming the book's first true reader. And to Richard Sadleir and Laura Guidetti for their outstanding English and Italian translations. We are also grateful to Giulia Bilancetti for her meticulous proofreading, encouraging precision down to the smallest details. Thanks also to Alessandra Crosato from the technical office and the photolithographer Enrico Cattelan, who oversaw the production and the final realization of the book. The volume would not exist without the essential work of communication, press office, and national and international distribution entrusted to Giovanna Ambrosano, Chiara Pellizzaro, Fabio Ferlin, Davide Quattrocchi, and Martina Mian.

Special thanks to the friends, authors, curators, and individuals who over the years wrote or revised interviews and texts, and who were instrumental in realizing this publication and tracing much of the material. In particular: Massimiliano Gioni, Marta Papini, and Michele Robecchi, who actively contributed in different situations and phases, along with other ghostwriters who helped over the years, such as Flavio Del Monte, Annalisa Inzana, and Assunta Bruno. This book would not exist without all the questions and the opportunities given to Maurizio by all the authors and editors who, through their interviews, made the space for the answers that followed, along with all the partners in crime in various projects that have found their way into this book, among them: Cecilia Alemani, Yuri Ancarani, Carlo Antonelli, Myriam Ben Salah, Stefania Biliato, Francesco Bonami, Christophe Boutin, Patrizia Brusarosco, Barbara Casavecchia, Fabio Cavallucci, Antonio Colomboni, Caroline Corbetta, Sarah Cosulich, Bice Curiger, Anna Daneri, Giacinto Di Pietrantonio, Ulla Dreyfus, Ilenia Durazzi, Rossella Farinotti, Pierpaolo Ferrari, Michael Frahm, Laure Genillard, Lorenzo Giusti, David Goldsmith, Catherine Grenier, Jens Hoffmann, Carsten Höller, Laura Hoptman, Anne Horvath, Dakis and Lietta Joannou, Dodie Kazanjian, Sam Keller, Udo Kittelmann, Michiko Kono, Helena Kontova, Alessandra Mammì, Paola Manfrin, Loredana Mascheroni, Luciano Massari, Sebastiano Mastroeni, Alessandro Michele, Paola Nicolin, Hans Ulrich Obrist, Gitte Ørskou, Dario Pappalardo, Chiara Parisi, Philippe Parreno, Roberto Pinto, Gea Politi, Giancarlo Politi, Bruno Racine, Federico Rahola, Kathrin Rhomberg, Patrizia Sandrello Re Rebaudengo, Mélanie Scarciglia, Eckhard Schneider, Madeleine Schuppli, Cristiano Seganfreddo, Stefano Seletti, Franklin Sirmans, Nancy Spector, Ali Subotnick, Sungwon Kim, Micol Talso, Calvin Tomkins, Beatrice Trussardi, Luisella Valtorta, Barbara Vanderlinden, Philippe Vergne, Giorgio Verzotti, Charley Vezza, Paride Vitale, and Justyna Wesołowska, together with: Nadia Afragola, Valentina Agostinis, Emma Allen, Deborah Ameri, Massimo Arcidiacono, Sophie Arie, Annie Armstrong, Peter Aspden, Natalia Aspesi, Anna Assumma, Nicolas Ballario, Silvano Banfi, Camilla Baresani, Marco Bassan, Julie Belcove, Andrea Bellini, Marco Belpoliti, Silke Bender, Chiara Bertola, Bertozzi & Casoni, Francesca Bonazzoli, Stefano Biochini, Silvia Bombino, Ivo Bonacorsi, Elena Bordignon, Sylvian Bourmeau, Jan Brand, Tommaso Bressan, Constance Breton, Paolo Bricco, Roberto Bruno, Jean Budney, Louisa Buck, Nicole Büsing, Harvey Byworth-Morgan, Luca Campana, Cristiana Campanini, Chiara Canali, Gianluca Cantaro, Angelo Capasso, Alessia Carlino, Ivan Carozzi, Francesca Cefis, Andrea Ceppi, Enrico Cerchioni, Giovanni Cervi, Timothée Chaillou, Leeji Choi, Yoko Choy, Francesca Cibrario, Anna Cirillo, Ulrich Clewing, Mathieu Copeland, Pino Corrias, Tommaso Corvi Mora, Elisabeth Couturier, Maike Cruse, Elena Cué, Luciana Cuomo,

Diamante D'Alessio, Cristina D'Antonio, Elisa Da Rin, Kristine Dabbay, Philippe Dagen, Enrico Dal Buono, Philippe Daverio, Emanuela De Cecco, Cristiano De Majo, Catelijne de Muynck, Thibaut De Ruyter, Henri-François Debailleux, Federico Delle Piane, Catherine Delmas, Francesca Di Nardo, Maria Cristina Didero, Maria Cristina Du Stasio, Fabrizio Donadoni, Matteo Doni, Severin Dünser, Myriam El Assil, Jarrett Earnest, Alain Elkann, Alexandra English, Jan Estep, Federico Faccioli, Michele Falcone, Yang Fan, Franco Fanelli, Riccardo Fano, Emily Farra, Miguel Figueroa, Alberto Fiz, Ernesto L. Francalanci, Holly Fraser, Francesco Galdieri, Marta Galli, Camila Garcia, Michèle Gerber-Klein, Marco Gerosa, Irene Ghillani, Marco Enrico Giacomelli, Federico Giannini, Henry Giardina, Joshua Glass, Irene Gludowacz, Antonio Gnoli, Masoud Golsorkhi, Molly Gottschalk, Elio Grazioli, James Greenwood, Marco Gregoretti, Sarah Grittini, Tobias Haberl, Gareth Harris, Jörg Heiser, Irene Hernández Velasco, David Hopkins, Ilaria Iacoboni, Simone Intermite, Jun Ishida, Emmanuelle Jardonnet, Rozmawiała Dorota Jarecka, Hyejin Jeon, Heinz-Norbert Jocks, Jean-Yves Jouannais, Shruti Kapur Malhotra, Vivian Kea, Randy Kennedy, Christophe Kihm, Ali Y. Khadra, Jiseon Kim, Narang Kim, Heiko Klass, Joerg Koch, Oliver Kupper, Eunkyoung Kwon, Andrea Lazarov, Ange Leccia, Woo Lee, Armelle Leturcq, Bruno LeMieux-Ruibal, Holger Liebs, Ziren Lin, Elena Livieri, Benjamin Locoge, Benoît Loiseau, Elsen Lupic, Chiara Maffioletti, Clara Mantica, Ilaria Marchetti, Mariano Martin, Terry Marocco, Maurizio Marsico, Luigi Mascheroni, Aimée McLaughlin, Mujde Metin, Jonas Mekas, Gabriele Micciché, Ken Miller, Marco Missiroli, Lotte Møller, Tom Morton, Candida Morvillo, Alex Moshakis, Aaron Moulton, Lorena Muñoz-Alonso, Michela Natella, Estelle Nabeyrat, Paola Naldi, Jim Nedd, Kito Nedo, Alex Needham, Juliana Neira, Robert Nickas, Keiko Niiyama, Kerry Olsen, Christophe Ono-dit-Biot, Malcolm Pagani, Felipe Pando, Raffaele Panizza, Giacomo Papi, Fabio Pariante, Clelia Patella, Pierluigi Panza, Giulia Pasqualetti, Xue Peng, Federico Pepe, Isaac Pérez Solano, Daniele Perra, Cloé Perrone, Matteo Persivale, Charmaine Picard, Daniel Pinchbeck, Francesca Pini, Antonio Privitera, Boris Pofalla, Barbara Pollack, Adriana Polveroni, Philippe Pourhashemi, Paloma Powers, Oliver Prange, Ludovico Pratesi, Chiara Quadri, Xueer Qian, Valentina Raggi, Antonio Rainone, Mark Rappolt, Walter Rauhe, Aurélie Raya, Florian Rehn, Alicia Reuter, Nicola Ricciardi, Christian Rocca, Rafa Rodriguez, Gianni Romano, Mariano Romanò, Laura Rysman, Carole Sabas, Darius Sanai, Anna Sansom, Nilüfer Sasmazer, Simone Sbarbati, Annamaria Sbisà, Lella Scalia, Irene Maria Scalise, Lily Silverton, Serena Simoni, Uwe Schwarzer, Wenjia Sheng, Febe Riri Siahaan, Katy Siegel, Roberta Smith, Valerie Smith, Elisabeth Sobieski, Alastair Sooke, Rachel Spence, Christian Spies, Armando Stella, Peifen Sung, Tanya Tang, James Tarmy, Emanuela Tediosi, Serena Tibaldi, Paola Tognon, Marco Tomasini, Barbara Tomasino, Guy Tortosa, Oliviero Toscani, Bianca Trevisan, Kingston Trinder, Claudio Troiano, Martina Tronconi, Ivan Maria Vele, Giulia Venturini, Caterina Viganò, Lisa Vignoli, Hugo Vitrani, Rita Vittorelli, Alessandra Vivoli, Carol Vogel, Sara Waka, Gian Marco Walch, Alexi Worth, Bernard Wilson, Louis Wise, Marcus Woeller, Thibaut Wychowanok-Dumas, Sonia Xie, Elisa Zaccanti, Alberto Zanetti, Lorenzo Zavatta, Markus Zehentbauer, Sabine Zeller, Augustine Zenakos, Daniela Zenone, Fan Zhong.

This publication would not have been possible without the invaluable help of many individuals, colleagues, and friends who have supported Maurizio Cattelan's work and have enthusiastically embraced this project and helped in finding, gathering and sharing information and material: Regina Alivisatos, Edgardo Altieri, Alessio Ascari, Enrico Astuni, Lorenzo Balbi, Lisa Barkley, Amina Berdin, Federico Bianchi, Agata Boetti, Caroline Bourgeois, Irma Boom, Hester Borrett-Lynch, Katherine Brinson, Arianna Campanelli, Sandra Cane, Chiara Ceccutti, Martino De Vincenti, Francesca di Giuda, Roberto Dipasquale, Dines Dorothess, Lara Facco, Bernardo Follini, Milly Fruen, Valentina Gervasoni, Raphaele Godin, Audrey Gregorczyk, Janne Hagge Ellhöft, Heyeon Kim, Krista Hollis, Daria Irincheeva, Philip Karjeker, Mariagiulia Leuzzi, Carla Mantovani, Gianfranco Maraniello, Pasquale Mari, Kirsty McIntosh, Margaret McKee, Francesca Minini, Massimo Minini, Cristina Molteni, Tommy Napier, Helen Neven, Camilla Nova, Natasha Polymeropoulos, Iolanda Ratti, Francesca Rebecchi, Julie Redon, Barbara Roncari, Elena Roseras, Mera Rubell, Simona Saraniti, Barbara Secci, Max Shackleton, Diego Sileo, Denise Solenghi, Rhiannon Stanford, Susan Thompson, Katya Tylevich, Katy Wan, Olivier Zahm.

Our deep gratitude goes to all the people, and especially the photographers, archives, galleries, institutions, and individuals involved in the iconographic research for this catalogue: Archivio Careof and Viafarini, Nick Ash, Lina Bertucci, Giulio Buono, Alberto Callari, Elisabetta Calligaro, Austin Kennedy, Kim Heyeon, Kim Kyoungtae, Armin Linke, Attilio Maranzano, Craig McDean, Jason Nocito, Agostino Osio, Lorenzo Palmieri, Nicholas Samartis, Anders Sune, and Dario Ballestri, Elena Capra, Gracey Connelly, Marco Dabbiaco, Paloma Gómez, Janelle Grace, Chiara Maranzana, Reina Nakagawa, Mai Nozoe, Alexandra Perez, Katalin Simon, Rhiannon Stanford, Anna Tallone, Juan Valadez, Simone Valentini, Constanza Valenzuela, Michael Van Horne, Siwei Zen.

We are especially thankful to all the collections and institutions—who, in preserving Maurizio Cattelan's legacy and works, have generously allowed the works to be made available and shared in this publication: Art Jameel Collection, Dubai; Castello di Rivoli Museo d'Arte Contemporanea, Rivoli-Turin; CAPC Musée d'art contemporain de Bordeaux; Centre Pompidou; Dallas Museum of Art; Fondation Carmignac; Fondation Louis Vuitton; Fondazione Sandretto Re Rebaudengo;

Frac Poitou-Charentes; Fundación NMAC – Montenmedio Arte Contemporánea, Vejer de la Frontera; GAMeC – Galleria d'Arte Moderna e Contemporanea di Bergamo; Glenstone Museum, Potomac; Isabel and Agustin Coppel Collection, Mexico; Leeum Museum of Art, Seoul; LACMA – Los Angeles County Museum of Art; MAMbo – Museo d'Arte Moderna di Bologna; MAXXI – Museo delle arti del XXI secolo, Rome; Maja Hoffmann/LUMA Foundation Collection; MCA – Museum of Contemporary Art Chicago; Migros Museum für Gegenwartskunst, Zurich; MMK – Museum für Moderne Kunst, Frankfurt; MOCA – The Museum of Contemporary Art, Los Angeles; MoMA – The Museum of Modern Art, New York; Museo del Novecento, Milan; Museum Boijmans Van Beuningen, Rotterdam; Nicola Erni Collection; Pinault Collection; Rubell Museum, Miami and Washington DC; SAM – Seattle Art Museum; Solomon R. Guggenheim Museum, New York; Taguchi Art Collection; The Menil Collection; The Dakis Joannou Collection Foundation; The Rachofsky Collection; Whitney Museum of American Art, New York; Yuz Foundation; as well as those who prefer to remain anonymous.

Finally, we would like to thank all Maurizio's galleries for their unwavering support and valuable insights throughout the making of this project: Andisheh Avini, Pepi Marchetti Franchi, and Serena Cattaneo Adorno at Gagosian; Junette Teng, Rose Lord, and Linda Pellegrini, along with Jonathan Safdie at Marian Goodman Gallery; Massimo De Carlo, Ludovica Barbieri, and Stella Gianotti at MASSIMODECARLO; Emmanuel Perrotin, Marine Moulin, Coralie David, and Emannuelle Orenga, along with Quentin Metayer at Perrotin.

I would like to thank Vicente Todolí for generously offering this opportunity and these energies—once again.
To Ilaria Tronchetti Provera, for the continuous complicity.
To Roberta Tenconi, for the unique ability to make the impossible possible with this book.
To Tatiana Palenzona and Teodora di Robilant, who worked side by side bringing this book to life with care, precision, and perseverance.
To Alessandro Bianchi, for all the support to the publications.
To the entire team at Pirelli HangarBicocca: your dedication has been truly commendable.
To the entire team at Marsilio Arte for holding everything together.

A very special thanks to the Zottis, who have been around forever, quietly making miracles happen.

Special thanks also to all the authors, and in particular to Massimiliano Gioni, who created a monster.
To Marta Papini, who helped me escape that monster and realize I could be something else too.
To Michele Robecchi, for the gift of speaking with the dead.
To myself, for doing this alone now.

*Maurizio*

[Photo Credits]

pp. 14, 29, 53 (15.25): Courtesy Maurizio Cattelan's Archive. Photo Lucio Zotti

pp. 16, 107 (52), 156, 244 (163): Courtesy Maurizio Cattelan's Archive. Photo Roman Mensing

pp. 17, 73 (24.2), 74, 142 (77), 179: Courtesy Maurizio Cattelan's Archive. Photo Roberto Marossi

pp. 18, 22 (3.1), 23, 36–37, 40, 47 (15.2–3), 48–53 (15.5–10, 15.12, 15.15–18, 15.22–.24, 15.26, 15.28, 15.29), 54, 60 (17.1), 61, 62, 63 (20.4), 64 (21.1), 67, 75, 85, 86–87 (33.4–7), 88–89, 93, 95 (40, 41), 96 (42), 106, 107 (53), 118, 124 (60.2), 125 (64), 132 (71.1), 133 (71.3), 141, 143, 144 (84), 145 (85.1), 148, 151 (93), 157 (97), 166 (101), 180, 193 (114, 116, 117), 194 (120–22), 195 (125), 217 (133.2), 219, 220 (137, 138), 246 (166), 262 (179), 264, 265 (182), 271, 284, 291 (191.1), 292 (192, 193), 306–07, 312, 320 (225.2), 322 (229), 330, 332 (236), 334, 349 (247): Courtesy Maurizio Cattelan's Archive

pp. 21, 24, 27 (7.1), 30, 111, 126, 127 (65.2), 147 (89), 167, 194 (119), 195 (124), 292 (194), 296, 324, 337, 341 (244.1): Courtesy Maurizio Cattelan's Archive. Photo Attilio Maranzano

pp. 22 (3.2), 27 (7.2), 28, 31 (10.1), 48–53 (15.19–21), 59, 64 (21.2), 65 (21.4, 21.5), 77 (27.3, 29), 78 (30.1), 82, 86 (33.3), 96 (43.1, 43.2), 97, 98, 103, 112, 113, 128, 129 (67.3), 130, 131 (69, 70.2), 134, 150, 151 (92.2), 160, 161, 169, 193 (118), 195 (126), 196 (127.2), 205 (131) 206–07, 220 (139), 224, 227 (145), 228 (146, 147), 229, 230, 231, 232 (151.2), 246 (167), 247, 252–53, 256, 257 (176, 177), 265 (183), 287, 291 (191.2), 293 (196, 197), 298–99, 301, 303 (210–12), 305, 311, 313, 326, 338 (239), 340, 345: Courtesy Maurizio Cattelan's Archive. Photo Zeno Zotti

p. 25 (5.1): Courtesy Maurizio Cattelan's Archive and AMACI

pp. 25 (5.2), 31 (10.2): Courtesy Maurizio Cattelan's Archive. Photo Pierpaolo Ferrari

pp. 26, 78 (30.2, 30.3), 110, 192 (111, 112), 323, 341 (244.3), cover: Courtesy Maurizio Cattelan's Archive. Photo Armin Linke

pp. 32, 138, 174–75, 200, 346–47, 350–51: Photo Pierpaolo Ferrari

p. 39: Courtesy Maurizio Cattelan's Archive and Laure Genillard Gallery

p. 41: Courtesy Maurizio Cattelan's Archive. Digital image © 2018 The Museum of Modern Art, New York. Photo Thomas Greisel (13.1); Courtesy Maurizio Cattelan's Archive. Photo Mauricio Guillen. © Estate of Roy Lichtenstein, by SIAE 2025 (13.2)

p. 42 (14.1): Courtesy Maurizio Cattelan's Archive. Photo David Heald © The Solomon R. Guggenheim Museum, New York

pp. 42–43, 232 (151.1): Courtesy Maurizio Cattelan's Archive and Blenheim Art Foundation. Photo Pete Seaword

p. 44: Courtesy GAMeC Bergamo. Photo Lorenzo Palmieri

pp. 47 (15.1), 48–53 (15.4, 15.11, 15.13, 15.27), 58, 60 (17.2), 63 (20.2), 92, 178 (105), 320 (225.1): Courtesy Maurizio Cattelan's Archive. Photo Fausto Fabbri

p. 50 (15.14): Courtesy Maurizio Cattelan's Archive. Photo Studio Blu

p. 63 (20.3): Courtesy Maurizio Cattelan's Archive and MAMbo - Museo d'Arte Moderna di Bologna. Photo Matteo Monti

pp. 65 (21.3), 80 (32.1), 127 (66), 133 (71.4), 293 (198, 199): Courtesy Maurizio Cattelan's Archive. Photo Kim Kyoungtae

p. 66: Courtesy Maurizio Cattelan's Archive. Photo Kristopher McKay © The Solomon R. Guggenheim Museum, New York

pp. 68, 288–89: Photo Craig McDean

pp. 73 (24.1), 354: Courtesy Maurizio Cattelan's Archive. Photo Alberto Callari

pp. 76, 227 (142): Courtesy Maurizio Cattelan's Archive and Castello di Rivoli Museo d'Arte Contemporanea, Rivoli-Turin. Photo Studio Blu – Giulio Buono

pp. 77 (27.2), 94, 157 (96.2), 192 (113), 294–95 (201): Courtesy Maurizio Cattelan's Archive and Castello di Rivoli Museo d'Arte Contemporanea, Rivoli-Turin. Photo Paolo Pellion di Persano

pp. 77 (28), 105 (48, 49), 125 (61–63), 178 (106), 243 (157, 159), 294 (200): Courtesy Maurizio Cattelan's Archive. Photo Studio Blu – Giulio Buono

pp. 79, 238, 239 (156.9, 156.10, 156.11, 156.12), 276: Courtesy Pirelli HangarBicocca. Photo Lorenzo Palmieri

pp. 80–81 (32.2): Courtesy Maurizio Cattelan's Archive, MASSIMODECARLO and Perrotin. Photo Piergiorgio Soggetti

p. 90: Courtesy Maurizio Cattelan's Archive and Parkett

p. 95: Courtesy Maurizio Cattelan's Archive. Photo Paola Manfrin (39.1); Courtesy Maurizio Cattelan's Archive and MoMA PS1 (39.2)

pp. 100–01, 258, 262 (180.1), 263: Courtesy Toiletpaper

p. 104: Courtesy Sonsbeek 93

p. 105 (47, 50): Courtesy Maurizio Cattelan's Archive and Laure Genillard. Photo Peter White FXP London

p. 107 (54): Courtesy Maurizio Cattelan's Archive and Manifesta

p. 108: Courtesy Ulla Dreyfus

p. 114: Courtesy Maurizio Cattelan's Archive and Marian Goodman Gallery. Photo Attilio Maranzano

p. 115: Courtesy Maurizio Cattelan's Archive. Photo Axel Schneider

pp. 116, 117, 131 (70.3–4), 286, 339: Courtesy Maurizio Cattelan's Archive and UCCA Center for Contemporary Art. Photo Sun Shi

p. 122: Courtesy Maurizio Cattelan's Archive. Photo Tagliapietra, Padua

pp. 124 (60.1), 309: Courtesy Maurizio Cattelan's Archive. Photo FXP, Ltd., London © Laure Genillard Gallery, London

p. 129 (68): Courtesy Maurizio Cattelan's Archive. Photo Wonge Bergmann

pp. 132 (71.2), 233, 234, 302: Courtesy Maurizio Cattelan's Archive and Blenheim Art Foundation. Photo Tom Lindboe

p. 135: Courtesy Maurizio Cattelan's Archive. Photo Andrea Rossetti

p. 136 (75): Courtesy Maurizio Cattelan's Archive and Gagosian. Photo Lucy Dawes

pp. 136–37 (74): Courtesy Maurizio Cattelan's Archive and Gagosian. Photo Maris Hutchinson

p. 142 (78): Courtesy Maurizio Cattelan's Archive and GAMeC Bergamo. Photo Antonio Maniscalco (78); Courtesy Maurizio Cattelan's Archive. Photo Guillaume Ziccarelli (79)

p. 144 (83): Courtesy Maurizio Cattelan's Archive. Photo Niels Den Haan

p. 145 (85.2, 86): Courtesy Maurizio Cattelan's Archive and MASSIMODECARLO. Photo Studio Blu – Giulio Buono

p. 146: Courtesy Maurizio Cattelan's Archive and Perrotin. Photo Peggy Leboeuf

p. 147 (88): Courtesy Maurizio Cattelan's Archive. Photo E. Hirsch © Fundación NMAC, Cádiz, Spain

p. 149: Courtesy Yuz Foundation

p. 152: Courtesy Maurizio Cattelan's Archive and Three Star Books

p. 153: Courtesy Maurizio Cattelan's Archive and Three Star Books. Photo Three Star Books, Paris

p. 154: Photo Paola Manfrin

pp. 158–59: Courtesy Maurizio Cattelan's Archive and Fondazione Nicola Trussardi. Photo Attilio Maranzano

pp. 162–63, 218: Courtesy Maurizio Cattelan's Archive. Photo Lina Bertucci

p. 166 (100): Courtesy Maurizio Cattelan's Archive. Photo Stefan Altenburger

p. 168: Courtesy Maurizio Cattelan's Archive. Photo André Morin

p. 170: Courtesy Maurizio Cattelan's Archive. Posted image by Andrew B. Myers

p. 178 (107): Courtesy Maurizio Cattelan's Archive and MASSIMODECARLO. Photo Santi Caleca

pp. 184–85, 210: Photo © Armin Linke, 1999

p. 188: Courtesy Maurizio Cattelan's Archive and Kunsthaus Bregenz

pp. 190, 191: Courtesy Maurizio Cattelan's Archive. Photo André Morin © Le Consortium, Dijon

p. 193 (115): Courtesy Maurizio Cattelan's Archive. Photo Marc Domage

pp. 196–97 (127.1), 228 (148): Courtesy Maurizio Cattelan's Archive and Kunsthaus Bregenz. Photo Markus Tretter

p. 197: Photo Luciano Massari © Accademia di Carrara (128.1); Photo Muriel Bruschi © Art Basel (128.2)

pp. 198, 314–16, 338 (240): Courtesy Maurizio Cattelan's Archive and Pirelli HangarBicocca. Photo Agostino Osio

p. 205 (130): Courtesy Fondazione Sandretto Re Rebaudengo

pp. 214–15: Courtesy of Friends of the High Line. Photo Austin Kennedy

p. 217 (133.1): Courtesy Maurizio Cattelan's Archive. Photo Santi Caleca

pp. 221–23: Courtesy Maurizio Cattelan's Archive. Photo Zeno Zotti © Solomon R. Guggenheim Museum, New York

pp. 235–37: Courtesy Maurizio Cattelan's Archive

and GAMeC Bergamo. Photo Lorenzo Palmieri
p. 239 (156.5–8): Courtesy Three Star Books, Paris.
Photo © Florian Kleinefenn, by SIAE 2025
p. 243: Courtesy Maurizio Cattelan's Archive and Marian
Goodman Gallery (158); Courtesy Maurizio Cattelan's
Archive. Photo Seales Studios (160)
p. 244: Courtesy Maurizio Cattelan's Archive. Photo
Sotheby's (161); Courtesy Maurizio Cattelan's Archive and
Gagosian. Photo Prudence Cuming Associates Ltd (162)
p. 245: Courtesy Maurizio Cattelan's Archive. Photo Nathan
Keay © MCA Chicago
p. 248: Photo © Francesca Pini
p. 250: Courtesy Berlin Biennale. Photo Uwe Walter
p. 251: Photo Jason Nocito
p. 254: Courtesy Marlborough Gallery. Photo Luke Walker
p. 255: Courtesy Maurizio Cattelan's Archive. Photo Zeno
Zotti. © Estate of Roy Lichtenstein, by SIAE 2025
p. 257 (175): Courtesy Centre Pompidou Metz
p. 261: Courtesy Maurizio Cattelan, Paola Manfrin,
Dominique Gonzalez-Foerster
pp. 266–67: Courtesy DESTE Foundation. Photo © Nicholas
Samartis
p. 269: Courtesy Maurizio Cattelan and Philippe Parreno.
Photo Frédéric Delpech
p. 273: Photo Jason Nocito, Courtesy the artists: Daniel
Squires (187.2); Paul McCarthy and Jason Rhoades (187.3);
Pawel Althamer (187.5, 187.6, 187.7); Cameron Jamie
(187.8); Keegan McHargue & Matt Leines (187.9); Keegan
McHargue (187.10); Mark Handforth (187.11); Michael
Wilkinson (187.12, 187.13); Piotr Janas (187.14); Tommy
White (187.15); Carol "Riot" Kane (187.16); Justin Lowe
(187.17); Dara Friedman (187.18). © Martin Creed, by SIAE
2025 (187.1); © Sam Durant, by SIAE 2025 (187.4)
p. 277: Courtesy Maurizio Cattelan and Massimiliano Gioni
p. 280: Courtesy Maurizio Cattelan's Archive and The Menil
Collection, Houston
p. 293 (195): Courtesy Maurizio Cattelan's Archive. Photo
Peggy Leboeuf
p. 295 (202): Courtesy Maurizio Cattelan's Archive. Photo
Axel Schneider MMK
p. 297: Courtesy Maurizio Cattelan's Archive. Photo Paolo
Pellion di Persano
p. 300: Courtesy Maurizio Cattelan's Archive. Photo Jacopo
Zotti © Solomon R. Guggenheim Museum, New York
p. 303 (209, 213): Courtesy Maurizio Cattelan's Archive.
Photo Alessandro Zambianchi
p. 304 (214, 215): Courtesy Maurizio Cattelan's Archive.
Photo Courtesy of Gagosian. Owen Conway
p. 310: Courtesy Maurizio Cattelan's Archive. Photo ©
Musée d'Art Moderne de la Ville de Paris/ARC. Tout
droits réservés.
p. 321: Photo © Galleria Raucci/Santamaria, Napoli (226);
Courtesy Maurizio Cattelan's Archive and Perrotin. Photo
Lionel Founeaux (227.1); Courtesy Maurizio Cattelan's
Archive and Umberto Manfrin. Photo Marc Domage
(227.2)
p. 322 (228): Courtesy Maurizio Cattelan's Archive. Photo
Matthias Herrmann
p. 328: Courtesy Maurizio Cattelan's Archive. Photo Achim
Hatzius
p. 329: Courtesy Maurizio Cattelan's Archive and Serpentine
Gallery, London
p. 331: Courtesy Maurizio Cattelan's Archive and MMK,
Museum für Moderne Kunst, Frankfurt. Photo Axel
Schneider
p. 332 (237.1): Courtesy Maurizio Cattelan's Archive
and Luxembourg + Co Gallery. Photo Joe Maher/Getty
Images
p. 333: Courtesy Maurizio Cattelan's Archive and
MASSIMODECARLO. Photo Zeno Zotti
p. 341 (244.2): Courtesy Maurizio Cattelan's Archive and
Fondazione Sandretto Re Rebaudengo. Photo R. Goffi
pp. 342–43: Video still Yuri Ancarani
p. 349 (246): Courtesy Maurizio Cattelan's Archive and
Westfälisches Landesmuseum, Münster. Photo Roman
Mensing

Cover
Maurizio Cattelan. *Untitled*, 1995
Black and white photographic print mounted on aluminum
125 × 190 cm
[111] p. 192

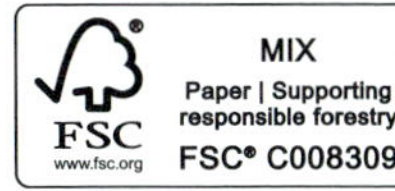